PEN(

THE PORTAI

ROXANE GAY's writing appears in *Best American Mystery Stories 2014*, *Best American Short Stories 2012*, *Best Sex Writing 2012*, *A Public Space*, *McSweeney's*, *Tin House*, *Oxford American*, *American Short Fiction*, *Virginia Quarterly Review*, and many others. She is a contributing opinion writer for *The New York Times*. She is the author of the books *Ayiti*, *An Untamed State*, the bestselling *Bad Feminist*, the nationally bestselling *Difficult Women* and the *New York Times* bestselling *Hunger*. She is also the author of *World of Wakanda* for Marvel. She has several books forthcoming and is at work on television and film projects. She also has a newsletter, *The Audacity*.

The Portable Feminist Reader

Edited with an Introduction by
ROXANE GAY

PENGUIN BOOKS

PENGUIN BOOKS
An imprint of Penguin Random House LLC
penguinrandomhouse.com

LIBRARY OF CONGRESS CATALOGING-IN-PUBLICATION DATA
Names: Gay, Roxane, editor.
Title: The portable feminist reader / edited with an introduction by Roxane Gay.
Description: New York : Penguin Books, [2025] | Includes bibliographical references.
Identifiers: LCCN 2024018835 (print) | LCCN 2024018836 (ebook) |
ISBN 9780143110392 (trade paperback) | ISBN 9781101992678 (ebook)
Subjects: LCSH: Feminism.
Classification: LCC HQ1150 .P556 2025 (print) |
LCC HQ1150 (ebook) | DDC 305.42—dc23/eng/20240815
LC record available at https://lccn.loc.gov/2024018835
LC ebook record available at https://lccn.loc.gov/2024018836

Printed in the United States of America
1st Printing

Set in Sabon LT Pro

Contents

THE PORTABLE FEMINIST READER

PART I:
LAYING A FOUNDATION

PART II:
EARLY FEMINIST TEXTS

PART III:
MULTICULTURAL PERSPECTIVES

PART IV:
FEMINIST LABORS

PART V:
GENDER CONSIDERATIONS

PART VI:
BLACK FEMINISM(S)

PART VII:
SEXUAL POLITICS

PART VIII:
FEMINIST PRAXIS

PART IX:
LOOKING BACK, LOOKING AHEAD

Introduction

At the beginning of the COVID-19 pandemic, when many of us were isolating in some form or fashion, my wife Debbie and I started to watch older television shows. For several months, we worked our way through all of the seasons of *Columbo*, soothing our anxieties about the pandemic and then president Donald Trump with the familiar rhythms of the show. We would watch Columbo perambulate a crime scene in his rumpled clothing, chewing on a cigar and studying seemingly innocuous things with great intent. When we were finished with that show, we turned our attention to *Murder, She Wrote* and marveled at how Jessica Fletcher always found herself in the thick of things, whether in Cabot Cove or New York or London.

More recently, we've taken to watching *L.A. Law*, a melodrama about a successful law firm in the 1980s. The show was a hybrid of soap opera and procedural with lots of palace intrigue, revolving bedrooms, and salacious litigation to keep viewers watching from one episode to the next. There has been something different about this viewing experience, perhaps because the show did not have the singular focus of a titular character and their misadventures. The palpable misogyny is most striking. In every episode, there are constant reminders of challenges women faced a mere forty years ago. As I've watched, I've found myself thinking, "Was it really that bad?"

In the early episodes of the first season, litigator Michael Kuzak relentlessly pursues Grace Van Owen, a Los Angeles district attorney. She is engaged and soon to be married when they first meet, but that is not at all a deterrent for Kuzak. He chases her, makes sexual advances, sets up a meeting with her unsuspecting fiancé under false pretenses to size up the competition, ignores Grace's entreaties for him to stop his pursuit, to stop seducing her, to stop all of it. And then he shows up at her wedding in a gorilla suit to declare his love, and finally, she surrenders to his persistence. This is all supposed to be romantic, but with the distance of nearly forty years, Kuzak seems more like a stalker than a paramour. A man ignoring a woman's lack of consent seems quotidian rather than aberrant.

Another attorney at the firm, Ann Kelsey, is the hardened, ambitious career woman who has put her personal life on hold to grind it out as an associate and then a partner in the firm. She is always treated as a woman first and a lawyer second. She has to contend with the bigotry of low expectations, sexual advances by clients, and the condescension of her male peers. Another woman at the firm, Abby Perkins, has an abusive estranged husband and a child with whom the husband has absconded. Her travails as she tries to regain custody of her son and then as a single mother are treated as inconveniences to the firm, more than anything else, even by other women.

Shows like *L.A. Law* are a product of their time, but we cannot help but watch them with contemporary sensibilities, and it is through popular culture like this that I am reminded that no matter how it feels, even though we haven't made enough progress, we actually have made significant progress as feminists. Things are largely better today than they were forty years ago, and we can only hope they will be better in forty years than they are now. To be clear, I did not need a television show to illustrate this progress. Instead, it served as a welcome reminder.

———

More than a decade ago, I wrote an essay called "Bad Feminist," where I grappled with my relationship to feminism through cultural criticism. The title was a bit tongue-in-cheek—catchy and provocative. I believed in feminism then as I do now, understood its importance, but I also worried that I fell woefully short of what a "good" or ideal feminist should be. I worried because I am human and, at times, inconsistent despite my best intentions.

How, for example, could I believe in and fight for women's liberation while enjoying deeply misogynistic hip-hop lyrics? Calling myself a bad feminist and using that phrase as the essay's title felt like the best way to encapsulate my relationship to feminism.

In that essay, I did not arrive at definitive conclusions, but I allowed myself space to think through how I define feminism, how I do or don't live up to my feminist ideals, and how my feminism influences my opinions, the culture I consume, my relationships with friends, family, and partners, and my work. I was also thinking about being a bad feminist as a repudiation of any feminism that overlooks the intersections of identities we inhabit. As a Black queer woman, I understood that I could not separate my race and ethnicity from my gender or my sexuality or any other aspect of who I am. If good feminism dictates we are women first to the detriment of acknowledging the other parts of our lived experiences, I was and am unequivocally a bad feminist.

It has been interesting to see how people have engaged with the essay and ensuing essay collection *Bad Feminist* for going on a decade now. Many people enjoyed the provocation of the title and, when they read them, the essays in the book. The idea that we could be both imperfect and feminists with good intentions resonated with a lot of people. The book, I think, created space for people to engage with feminism on pragmatic terms. But then, there were people who decided that if they called themselves bad feminists, they were also granted carte blanche to make decidedly anti-feminist choices and claim feminism, nonetheless. This was a convenient fiction to justify bad decisions, but once you put ideas into the world, you cannot control what people do with them.

Over the past decade, I have often been asked what I would change about my thinking in *Bad Feminist*. The truth is that I wouldn't change anything, not because I got everything right but because the book is a reflection of who I was in the years I wrote those essays. Fortunately, my thinking is not static and my relationship to feminism continues to evolve. I would like to believe I am a better feminist today and am still evolving, even if I am not and, frankly, never hope to be the kind of *good* feminist that flattens women's experiences into something more easily digested.

As I consider what I would write about feminism if I were to write "Bad Feminist" today, I would focus more on holding ourselves accountable for our choices more than the choices themselves. Nothing we do happens in a vacuum. I still believe, for example, that we can make flawed choices, but I understand, with far more moral clarity, that our choices have consequences. The better our choices, the more our choices arc toward the greater good, the better the outcomes. At least, that's the hope. What I do know is that if we keep accepting and sometimes celebrating an unacceptable status quo where women are demeaned, dismissed, or diminished, the status quo will never change. Sometimes, we have to recognize and call out certain choices as anti-feminist and actively detrimental to the feminist project.

And so here we are, in 2025. Feminism has made a great deal of progress, but we have also lost critical ground. Many people remain reluctant to identify as feminists. They treat the label as a slur. They worry how they will be perceived for daring to believe in ideals as simple as gender equity and liberation for all of us. Many people are still asking for elementary definitions of feminism, though rarely are they doing so in good faith, because they already know the answers to the questions they're asking. We're seeing strange cultural regressions like the tradwife movement and bimbo feminism even as trends like #GirlBoss flame out because they lack substance. Most of us will tell ourselves anything to justify our choices. That's human. But as "good" feminists, we're supposed to embrace women's choices no matter what those choices are. That feels nearly impossible when certain choices are detrimental to us all and when the women making those choices refuse to recognize that it is, in fact, feminism that allows them to make regressive choices.

Then, of course, there is the political ground we have lost. In June 2022, the Supreme Court overturned *Roe v. Wade* in the *Dobbs v. Jackson Women's Health Organization* decision, upending fifty years of legal precedent. Reproductive freedom activists warned us that this day would come, and we fought hard to prevent it, but it happened nonetheless. In the immediate aftermath, millions of women across the United States lost access to abortion care. At least twenty-four states have enacted Draconian legislation either banning abortion outright or implementing six- or twelve-week bans, which may as well be total bans. Some of these states have moved to restrict women's ability to travel across state lines, threatening the prosecution of women who seek abortion care in other states as well as anyone who provides assistance in doing so. Next on the extremist conservative agenda is no-fault divorce, a practice that has allowed countless women to leave bad marriages without protracted legal proceedings. It is all quite dystopic. These setbacks are a stark reminder that women's bodies, movements, and choices are contingent on the whims of men in power. We have made progress but we are not yet free.

We are not yet free and we do not all envision freedom in the same ways. All too often, we frame feminist progress as finally being able to enjoy the privileges that have long benefitted men. This is flawed thinking. If more women were CEOs, we would not magically address all the woes of late-stage capitalism. If a woman were to become president of the United States, that would not guarantee a more perfect union. The desire to make up for lost time, to have a taste of all we have been denied, is understandable. Power is seductive. Moving through the world freely, taking up space without apology, speaking and being heard without condition, wielding authority, commanding respect, these are privileges everyone should have. But we should not strive to emulate the worst of men by hoarding power, taking up so much space that we leave little for everyone else. That is neither good nor bad feminism; that is unacceptable feminism.

———

Intellectuals are often very attached to the idea of canon, the notion that there is a definitive set of works for any given field that is incontrovertibly exemplary and foundational. It's comforting, I suppose, to believe we can identify a canon and trust that these works will stand the test of time, the test of change. Canon serves as a touchstone, as if we are saying the world is often unknowable, but *we know these things to be true.*

It is important, though, to resist or at the very least complicate our understanding of canon, not because we shouldn't have foundational texts in a given field but because canon is, generally, static. The excellence of the texts elevated to canon is subjective and, in many instances, represents a narrow ideal curated by people who are, implicitly or explicitly, invested in upholding patriarchy and white supremacy. Literary critic Harold Bloom was an ardent supporter of canon, going so far as to compile a collection of what he deemed the canonical works of Western literature in the volume *The Western Canon: The Books and School of the Ages.* He was particularly invested in prioritizing "aesthetic quality" and felt that attempts at diversifying the canon merely diluted it by including works that did not possess the necessary aesthetic merits. In his "Elegy for the Canon," Bloom wrote, "We are destroying all intellectual and aesthetic standards in the humanities and social sciences, in the name of social justice." This treatise was quite the provocation. It was biased at best, this valorization of flagrant exclusion. And it was a sad reminder that texts written by marginalized writers are assumed to be lesser, to not possess the aesthetic excellence of those written mostly by white men and a few white women.

For Bloom, the canon is not an ever-evolving body of work representing the best of literature. Instead, he understands canon as an impenetrable fortress protecting a singular set of works. There is only one way into the canon and no way out. "One breaks into the canon only by aesthetic strength," he says without acknowledging that historically, only one group of people was allowed to define aesthetic strength and determine which writers possessed it.

The written record of feminist ideas is centuries long. As we engage with feminist works across time, we examine the state of feminism, what feminism looks like in practice, and its successes and failures. And over the years, feminists have criticized the idea of the canon—they highlight the ways women have been excluded from canons, how men's experiences are considered universal and objective while women's experiences are considered niche and subjective. American art historian Linda Nochlin offered one such intervention in her 1971 essay, "Why Have There Been No Great Women Artists?" She challenged feminists to question the ideological foundations of intellectual disciplines. Nochlin noted that "in the field of art history, the white Western male viewpoint, unconsciously accepted as *the* viewpoint of the art historian, may—and does—prove to be inadequate not merely on moral and ethical grounds, or because it is elitist, but on purely intellectual ones." She questions the uncritical acceptance of "white male sub-jectivity" and suggests that feminists should not engage in canon-ical debates on those terms. For example, in art and in many other disciplines, people will ask where all the historical women greats are. And feminists often try to answer that question, explaining why that question is disingenuous, why women have been ob-scured from much of history, and so on.

Nochlin says we don't need to answer that question because in doing so, we "tacitly reinforce its negative implications." We al-low the people who created the status quo to dictate the rules of engagement. Feminist scholar Dale Spender also interrogates canon in "Women and Literary History," when she notes that in the eighteenth century, women were as prolific and successful as men if not more, and despite those contributions, they were elided from the contemporary canon. She discusses how male critics have overlooked women's contributions and says, "Whether the men of letters have overlooked women's writing, or whether they have exploited it, what can be stated unequivocally is that they have in effect suppressed the traditions of women's writing." Like many feminists challenging canon, Spender argues that any canon that ignores history and women's contributions is illegitimate.

Feminist skepticism of canon is healthy, but I believe there is a feminist canon, one that is subjective and always evolving but also representative of a long, rich tradition of feminist scholar-ship. Dynamism was the guiding principle as I assembled *The Portable Feminist Reader*. I wanted to contribute to the feminist canon by choosing works that reflect compelling, fiercely intelli-gent, and diverse in every sense of the word, feminist thought. To our detriment, we try to be definitive about what feminism is or isn't, and how it should be represented. It serves us better to be more expansive. This text recognizes that no one collection could or should cover every aspect of a sociopolitical movement. In these pages you will find traditional scholarship alongside poetry and personal essays. There are ancient texts, pieces published within the past five years, and everything in between. I've in-cluded work from established feminists like bell hooks, Gloria Anzaldúa, and Hélène Cixous alongside more recent feminist thinkers like Jessica Valenti, Brittney Cooper, and Sara Ahmed.

More than anything, this feminist reader is not a fortress; it is not an end point. It is the beginning of what I hope will be a vibrant and vigorous conversation about historical and contemporary feminist thought. This is a text that embraces contradiction and complexity. You could, I suppose, think of this as a Bad Feminist Reader.

ROXANE GAY

A Note on the Text

Original sources of excerpts in this anthology are referenced in the headnotes. Spelling and punctuation are Americanized. Footnotes and parenthetical citations have been eliminated from the texts without marking. The figures referenced in "Thinking Sex" by Gayle S. Rubin may be found in the original work. Small edits for singular and plural consistency have been made to the excerpts from "Derailing for Dummies." Aside from edits outlined here, text selections retain their original language. "Women and the Myth of Consumerism" includes a term used in its historical period that is a racialized slur.

The Portable
Feminist Reader

PART I

LAYING A FOUNDATION

Demarginalizing the Intersection of Race and Sex

BY KIMBERLÉ CRENSHAW

Although the term *intersectionality* is now nearly ubiquitous in feminist discourse, it was unknown before Crenshaw coined the term in this 1989 article. Kimberlé Crenshaw is a lawyer, a philosopher, a professor at both Columbia Law School and the UCLA School of Law, and a leading Black feminist scholar. The law has historically been framed as neutral, which is a convenient fiction that serves the status quo, but Crenshaw's work reveals its profound structural inequalities and the unique ways these systems oppress Black women. Crenshaw analyzes how the courts, as well as feminist and civil rights thinkers, have often considered race and sex discrimination separately rather than in conjunction. This approach, she argues, is insufficient at meeting the needs or recognizing the challenges facing Black women, who experience race and sex discrimination simultaneously and thus are "theoretically erased." She describes this "multiply-burdened" and "compounded" identity experience using the term *intersectionality*. Crenshaw's term later became the foundation for "intersectional feminism," an important evolution of feminist theory providing a framework that illustrates how people with intersecting social identities (ethnicity, sexuality, gender, race, class, and other identity markers) are often oppressed by systems and institutions that do not understand or recognize the unique challenges facing those identities.

II. FEMINISM AND BLACK WOMEN:
"AIN'T WE WOMEN?"

Oddly, despite the relative inability of feminist politics and theory to address Black women substantively, feminist theory and tradition borrow considerably from Black women's history. For example, "Ain't I a Woman" has come to represent a standard refrain in feminist discourse. Yet the lesson of this powerful oratory is not fully appreciated because the context of the delivery is seldom examined. I would like to tell part of the story because it establishes some themes that have characterized feminist treatment of race and illustrates the importance of including Black women's experiences as a rich source for the critique of patriarchy.

In 1851, Sojourner Truth declared "Ain't I a Woman?" and challenged the sexist imagery used by male critics to justify the disenfranchisement of women. The scene was a Women's Rights Conference in Akron, Ohio; white male hecklers, invoking stereotypical images of "womanhood," argued that women were too frail and delicate to take on the responsibilities of political activity. When Sojourner Truth rose to speak, many white women urged that she be silenced, fearing that she would divert attention from women's suffrage to emancipation. Truth, once permitted to speak, recounted the horrors of slavery, and its particular impact on Black women:

> Look at my arm! I have ploughed and planted and gathered into barns, and no man could head me—and ain't I a woman? I could work as much and eat as much as a man—when I could get it—and bear the lash as well! And ain't I a woman? I have born thirteen children, and seen most of 'em sold into slavery, and when I cried out with my mother's grief, none but Jesus heard me—and ain't I a woman?

By using her own life to reveal the contradiction between the ideological myths of womanhood and the reality of Black women's experience, Truth's oratory provided a powerful rebuttal to the claim that women were categorically weaker than men. Yet Truth's personal challenge to the coherence of the cult of true womanhood was useful only to the extent that white women were willing to reject the racist attempts to rationalize the contradiction—that because Black women were something less than real women, their experiences had no bearing on true womanhood. Thus, this 19th-century Black feminist challenged not only patriarchy, but she also challenged white feminists wishing to embrace Black women's history to relinquish their vestedness in whiteness.

Contemporary white feminists inherit not the legacy of Truth's challenge to patriarchy but, instead, Truth's challenge to their forebearers. Even today, the difficulty that white women have traditionally experienced in sacrificing racial privilege to strengthen feminism renders them susceptible to Truth's critical question. When feminist theory and politics that claim to reflect *women's* experience and *women's* aspirations do not include or speak to Black women, Black women must ask: "Ain't *We* Women?" If this is so, how can the claims that "women are," "women believe" and "women need" be made when such claims are inapplicable or unresponsive to the needs, interests and experiences of Black women?

The value of feminist theory to Black women is diminished because it evolves from a white racial context that is seldom acknowledged. Not only are women of color in fact overlooked, but their exclusion is reinforced when *white* women speak for and as *women*. The authoritative universal voice—usually white male subjectivity masquerading as non-racial, non-gendered objectivity—is merely transferred to those who, but for gender, share many of the same cultural, economic and social characteristics. When feminist theory attempts to describe women's experiences through analyzing patriarchy, sexuality, or separate spheres ideology, it often overlooks the role of race. Feminists thus ignore how their own race functions to mitigate some aspects of sexism and, moreover, how it often privileges them over and contributes to the domination of other women. Consequently, feminist theory remains *white*, and its potential to broaden and deepen its analysis by addressing non-privileged women remains unrealized.

An example of how some feminist theories are narrowly constructed around white women's experiences is found in the separate spheres literature. The critique of how separate spheres ideology shapes and limits women's roles in the home and in public life is a central theme in feminist legal thought. Feminists have attempted to expose and dismantle separate spheres ideology by identifying and criticizing the stereotypes that traditionally have justified the disparate societal roles assigned to men and women. Yet this attempt to debunk ideological justifications for *women's* subordination offers little insight into the domination of *Black* women. Because the experiential base upon which many feminist insights are grounded is white, theoretical statements drawn from them are overgeneralized at best, and often wrong. Statements such as "men and women are taught to see men as independent, capable, powerful; men and women are taught to see women as dependent, limited in abilities, and passive," are common within this literature. But this "observation" overlooks the anomalies created by crosscurrents of racism and sexism. Black men and women live in a society that creates sex-based norms and expectations which racism operates simultaneously to deny; Black men are not viewed as powerful, nor are Black women seen as passive. An effort to develop an ideological explanation of gender domination in the Black community should proceed from an understanding of how crosscutting forces establish gender norms and how the conditions of Black subordination wholly frustrate access to these norms. Given this understanding, perhaps we can begin to see why Black women have been dogged by the stereotype of the pathological matriarch or why there have been those in the Black liberation movement who aspire to create institutions and to build traditions that are intentionally patriarchal.

Because ideological and descriptive definitions of patriarchy are usually premised upon white female experiences, feminists and others informed by feminist literature may make the mistake of assuming that since the role of Black women in the family and in other Black institutions does not always resemble the familiar manifestations of patriarchy in the white community, Black women are somehow exempt from patriarchal norms. For example, Black women have traditionally worked outside the home in numbers far exceeding the labor participation rate of white women. An analysis of patriarchy that highlights the history of white women's exclusion from the workplace might permit the inference that Black women have not been burdened by this particular gender-based expectation. Yet the very fact that Black women must work conflicts with norms that women should not, often creating personal, emotional and relationship problems in Black women's lives. Thus, Black women are burdened not only because they often have to take on responsibilities that are not traditionally feminine but, moreover, their assumption of these roles is sometimes interpreted within the Black community as either Black women's failure to live up to such norms or as another manifestation of racism's scourge upon the Black community. This is one of the many aspects of intersectionality that cannot be understood through an analysis of patriarchy rooted in white experience.

Another example of how theory emanating from a white context obscures the multidimensionality of Black women's lives is found in feminist discourse on rape. A central political issue on the feminist agenda has been the pervasive problem of rape. Part of the intellectual and political effort to mobilize around this issue has involved the development of a historical critique of the role that law has played in establishing the bounds of normative sexuality and in regulating female sexual behavior. Early carnal knowledge statutes and rape laws are understood within this discourse to illustrate that the objective of rape statutes traditionally has not been to protect women from coercive intimacy but to protect and maintain a property-like interest in female chastity. Although feminists quite rightly criticize these objectives, to characterize rape law as reflecting male control over female sexuality is for Black women an oversimplified account and an ultimately inadequate account.

Rape statutes generally do not reflect male control over *female* sexuality, but *white* male regulation of *white* female sexuality. Historically, there has been absolutely no institutional effort to regulate Black female chastity. Courts in some states had gone so far as to instruct juries that, unlike white women, Black women were not presumed to be chaste. Also, while it was true that the attempt to regulate the sexuality of white women placed unchaste women outside the law's protection, racism restored a fallen white woman's chastity where the alleged assailant was a Black man. No such restoration was available to Black women.

The singular focus on rape as a manifestation of male power over female sexuality tends to eclipse the use of rape as a weapon of racial terror. When Black women were raped by white males, they were being raped not as women generally, but as Black women specifically: Their femaleness made them sexually vulnerable to racist domination, while their Blackness effectively denied them any protection. This white male power was reinforced by a judicial system in which the successful conviction of a white man for raping a Black woman was virtually unthinkable.

In sum, sexist expectations of chastity and racist assumptions of sexual promiscuity combined to create a distinct set of issues confronting Black women. These issues have seldom been explored in feminist literature nor are they prominent in antiracist politics. The lynching of Black males, the institutional practice that was legitimized by the regulation of white women's sexuality, has historically and contemporaneously occupied the Black agenda on sexuality and violence. Consequently, Black women are caught between a Black community that, perhaps understandably, views with suspicion attempts to litigate questions of sexual violence, and a feminist community that reinforces those suspicions by focusing on white female sexuality. The suspicion is compounded by the historical fact that the protection of white female sexuality was often the pretext for terrorizing the Black community. Even today some fear that antirape agendas may undermine antiracist objectives. This is the paradigmatic political and theoretical dilemma created by the intersection of race and gender: Black women are caught between ideological and political currents that combine first to create and then to bury Black women's experiences. [. . .]

According to William Julius Wilson, author of *The Truly Disadvantaged*, the decline in Black marriages is not attributable to poor motivation, bad work habits or irresponsibility but instead is caused by structural economics which have forced Black unskilled labor out of the workforce. Wilson's approach represents a significant move away from that of Moynihan/Moyers in that he rejects their attempt to center the analysis on the morals of the Black community. Yet, he too considers the proliferation of female-headed households as dysfunctional *per se* and fails to explain fully why such households are so much in peril. Because he incorporates no analysis of the way the structure of the economy and the workforce subordinates the interests of women, especially childbearing Black women, Wilson's suggested reform begins with finding ways to put Black men back in the family. In Wilson's view, we must change the economic structure with an eye toward providing more Black jobs for Black men. Because he offers no critique of sexism, Wilson fails to consider economic or social reorganization that directly empowers and supports these single Black mothers.

IV. EXPANDING FEMINIST THEORY AND ANTIRACIST POLITICS BY EMBRACING THE INTERSECTION

If any real efforts are to be made to free Black people of the constraints and conditions that characterize racial subordination, then theories and strategies purporting to reflect the Black community's needs must include an analysis of sexism and patriarchy. Similarly, feminism must include an analysis of race if it hopes to express the aspirations of non-white women. Neither Black liberationist politics nor feminist theory can ignore the intersectional experiences of those whom the movements claim as their respective constituents. In order to include Black women, both movements must distance themselves from earlier approaches in which experiences are relevant only when they are related to certain clearly identifiable causes (for example, the oppression of Blacks is significant when based on race, of women when based on gender). The praxis of both should be centered on the life chances and life situations of people who should be cared about without regard to the source of their difficulties.

I have stated earlier that the failure to embrace the complexities of compoundedness is not simply a matter of political will, but is also due to the influence of a way of thinking about discrimination which structures politics so that struggles are categorized as singular issues. Moreover, this structure imports a descriptive and normative view of society that reinforces the status quo.

It is somewhat ironic that those concerned with alleviating the ills of racism and sexism should adopt such a top-down approach to discrimination. If their efforts instead began with addressing the needs and problems of those who are most disadvantaged and with restructuring and remaking the world where necessary, then others who are singularly disadvantaged would also benefit. In addition, it seems that placing those who currently are marginalized in the center is the most effective way to resist efforts to compartmentalize experiences and undermine potential collective action.

It is not necessary to believe that a political consensus to focus on the lives of the most disadvantaged will happen tomorrow in order to recenter discrimination discourse at the intersection. It is enough, for now, that such an effort would encourage us to look beneath the prevailing conceptions of discrimination and to challenge the complacency that accompanies belief in the effectiveness of this framework. By so doing, we may develop language which is critical of the dominant view and which provides some basis for unifying activity. The goal of this activity should be to facilitate the inclusion of marginalized groups for whom it can be said: "When they enter, we all enter."

White Privilege: Unpacking the Invisible Knapsack

BY PEGGY MCINTOSH

Published in 1989, "White Privilege: Unpacking the Invisible Knapsack" was a groundbreaking essay and tool for analyzing white privilege and how such privilege contributes to systemic racism. McIntosh—an American feminist, anti-racism activist, scholar, speaker, and senior research scientist at the Wellesley Centers for Women—listed her own "unearned advantages" and white privilege and revolutionized the way we examine overlapping systems of power and manifestations of systemic racism. Studying women led McIntosh to see both unearned male privilege and then unearned white privilege: "being born white in a culture that favors whites." The origins of this piece are in McIntosh's 1988 paper "White Privilege and Male Privilege: A Personal Account of Coming to See Correspondences Through Work in Women's Studies."

Through work to bring materials from Women's Studies into the rest of the curriculum, I have often noticed men's unwillingness to grant that they are overprivileged, even though they may grant that women are disadvantaged. They may say they will work to improve women's status, in the society, the university, or the curriculum, but they can't or won't support the idea of lessening men's. Denials which amount to taboos surround the subject of advantages which men gain from women's disadvantages. These denials protect male privilege from being fully acknowledged, lessened or ended.

Thinking through unacknowledged male privilege as a phenomenon, I realized that, since hierarchies in our society are interlocking, there was most likely a phenomenon of white privilege that was similarly denied and protected. As a white person, I realized I had been taught about racism as something that puts others at a disadvantage, but had been taught not to see one of its corollary aspects, white privilege, which puts me at an advantage.

I think whites are carefully taught not to recognize white privilege, as males are taught not to recognize male privilege. So I have begun in an untutored way to ask what it is like to have white privilege. I have come to see white privilege as an invisible package of unearned assets that I can count on cashing in each day, but about which I was "meant" to remain oblivious. White privilege is like an invisible weightless knapsack of special provisions, maps, passports, codebooks, visas, clothes, tools and blank checks.

Describing white privilege makes one newly accountable. As we in Women's Studies work to reveal male privilege and ask men to give up some of their power, so one who writes about white privilege must ask, "Having described it, what will I do to lessen or end it?"

After I realized the extent to which men work from a base of unacknowledged privilege, I understood that much of their oppressiveness was unconscious. Then I remembered the frequent charges from women of color that white women whom they encounter are oppressive.

I began to understand why we are justly seen as oppressive, even when we don't see ourselves that way. I began to count the ways in which I enjoy unearned skin privilege and have been conditioned into oblivion about its existence.

My schooling gave me no training in seeing myself as an oppressor, as an unfairly advantaged person, or as a participant in a damaged culture. I was taught to see myself as an individual whose moral state depended on her individual moral will. My schooling followed the pattern my colleague Elizabeth Minnich has pointed out: whites are taught to think of their lives as morally neutral, normative, and average, and also ideal, so that when we work to benefit others, this is seen as work which will allow "them" to be more like "us."

I decided to try to work on myself at least by identifying some of the daily effects of white privilege in my life. I have chosen those conditions which I think in my case *attach somewhat more to skin-color privilege* than to class, religion, ethnic status, or geographic location, though of course all these other factors are intricately intertwined. As far as I can see, my African American coworkers, friends, and acquaintances with whom I come into daily or frequent contact in this particular time, place and line of work cannot count on most of these conditions.

1. I can if I wish arrange to be in the company of people of my race most of the time.

2. If I should need to move, I can be pretty sure of renting or purchasing housing in an area which I can afford and in which I would want to live.

3. I can be pretty sure that my neighbors in such a location will be neutral or pleasant to me.

4. I can go shopping alone most of the time, pretty well assured that I will not be followed or harassed.

5. I can turn on the television or open to the front page of the paper and see people of my race widely represented.

6. When I am told about our national heritage or about "civilization," I am shown that people of my color made it what it is.

7. I can be sure that my children will be given curricular materials that testify to the existence of their race.

8. If I want to, I can be pretty sure of finding a publisher for this piece on white privilege.

9. I can go into a music shop and count on finding the music of my race represented, into a supermarket and find the staple foods that fit with my cultural traditions, into a hairdresser's shop and find someone who can cut my hair.

10. Whether I use checks, credit cards or cash, I can count on my skin color not to work against the appearance of financial reliability.

11. I can arrange to protect my children most of the time from people who might not like them.

12. I can swear, or dress in secondhand clothes, or not answer letters, without having people attribute these choices to the bad morals, the poverty, or the illiteracy of my race.

13. I can speak in public to a powerful male group without putting my race on trial.

14. I can do well in a challenging situation without being called a credit to my race.

15. I am never asked to speak for all the people of my racial group.

16. I can remain oblivious of the language and customs of persons of color who constitute the world's majority without feeling in my culture any penalty for such oblivion.

17. I can criticize our government and talk about how much I fear its policies and behavior without being seen as a cultural outsider.

18. I can be pretty sure that if I ask to talk to "the person in charge," I will be facing a person of my race.

19. If a traffic cop pulls me over or if the IRS audits my tax return, I can be sure I haven't been singled out because of my race.

20. I can easily buy posters, postcards, picture books, greeting cards, dolls, toys, and children's magazines featuring people of my race.

21. I can go home from most meetings of organizations I belong to feeling somewhat tied in, rather than isolated, out of place, outnumbered, unheard, held at a distance, or feared.

22. I can take a job with an affirmative action employer without having coworkers on the job suspect that I got it because of race.

23. I can choose public accommodations without fearing that people of my race cannot get in or will be mistreated in the places I have chosen.

24. I can be sure that if I need legal or medical help, my race will not work against me.

25. If my day, week, or year is going badly, I need not ask of each negative episode or situation whether it has racial overtones.

26. I can choose blemish cover or bandages in "flesh" color and have them more or less match my skin.

I repeatedly forgot each of the realizations on this list until I wrote it down. For me, white privilege has turned out to be an elusive and fugitive subject. The pressure to avoid it is great, for in facing it I must give up the myth of meritocracy. If these things are true, this is not such a free country; one's life is not what one makes it; many doors open for certain people through no virtues of their own.

In unpacking this invisible knapsack of white privilege, I have listed conditions of daily experience that I once took for granted. Nor did I think of any of these perquisites as bad for the holder. I now think that we need a more finely differentiated taxonomy of privilege, for some of these varieties are only what one would want for everyone in a just society, and others give license to be ignorant, oblivious, arrogant and destructive.

I see a pattern running through the matrix of white privilege, a pattern of assumptions that were passed on to me as a white person. There was one main piece of cultural turf; it was my own turf, and I was among those who could control the turf. *My skin color was an asset for any move I was educated to want to make.* I could think of myself as belonging in major ways and of making social systems work for me. I could freely disparage, fear, neglect, or be oblivious to anything outside of the dominant cultural forms. Being of the main culture, I could also criticize it fairly freely.

In proportion as my racial group was being made confident, comfortable, and oblivious, other groups were likely being made unconfident, uncomfortable, and alienated. Whiteness protected me from many kinds of hostility, distress and violence, which I was being subtly trained to visit, in turn, upon people of color.

For this reason, the word "privilege" now seems to me misleading. We usually think of privilege as being a favored state, whether earned or conferred by birth or luck. Yet some of the conditions I have described here work systematically to overempower certain groups. Such privilege simply *confers dominance* because of one's race or sex.

I want, then, to distinguish between earned strength and unearned power conferred systemically. Power from unearned privilege can look like strength when it is in fact permission to escape or to dominate. But not all of the privileges on my list are inevitably damaging. Some, like the expectation that neighbors will be decent to you, or that your race will not count against you in court, should be the norm in a just society. Others, like the privilege to ignore less powerful people, distort the humanity of the holders as well as the ignored groups.

We might at least start by distinguishing between positive advantages, which we can work to spread, and negative types of advantage, which unless rejected will always reinforce our present hierarchies. For example, the feeling that one belongs within the human circle, as Native Americans say, should not be seen as privilege for a few. Ideally it is an *unearned entitlement.* At present, since only a few have it, it is an *unearned advantage* for them. This paper results from a process of coming to see that some of the power that I originally saw as attendant on being a human being in the United States consisted in unearned advantage and conferred dominance.

I have met very few men who are truly distressed about systemic, unearned male advantage and conferred dominance. And so one question for me and others like me is whether we will be like them, or whether we will get truly distressed, even outraged, about unearned race advantage and conferred dominance, and, if so, what will we do to lessen them. In any case, we need to do more work in identifying how they actually affect our daily lives. Many, perhaps most, of our white students in the U.S. think that racism doesn't affect them because they are not people of color; they do not see "whiteness" as a racial identity. In addition, since race and sex are not the only advantaging systems at work, we need similarly to examine the daily experience of having age advantage, or ethnic advantage, or physical ability, or advantage related to nationality, religion, or sexual orientation.

Difficulties and dangers surrounding the task of finding parallels are many. Since racism, sexism, and heterosexism are not the same, the advantages associated with them should not be seen as the same. In addition, it is hard to disentangle aspects of unearned advantage which rest more on social class, economic class, race, religion, sex, and ethnic identity than on other factors. Still, all of the oppressions are interlocking, as the Combahee River Collective Statement of 1977 continues to remind us eloquently.

One factor seems clear about all of the interlocking oppressions. They take both active forms, which we can see, and embedded forms, which as a member of the dominant group one is taught not to see. In my class and place, I did not see myself as a racist because I was taught to recognize racism only in individual acts of meanness by members of my group, never in invisible systems conferring unsought racial dominance on my group from birth.

Disapproving of the systems won't be enough to change them. I was taught to think that racism could end if white individuals changed their attitudes. But a "white" skin in the United States opens many doors for whites whether or not we approve of the way dominance has been conferred on us. Individual acts can palliate, but cannot end, these problems.

To redesign social systems, we need first to acknowledge their colossal unseen dimensions. The silences and denials surrounding privilege are the key political tool here. They keep the thinking about equality or equity incomplete, protecting unearned advantage and conferred dominance by making these taboo subjects. Most talk by whites about equal opportunity seems to me now to be about equal opportunity to try to get into a position of dominance while denying that *systems* of dominance exist.

It seems to me that obliviousness about white advantage, like obliviousness about male advantage, is kept strongly inculturated in the United States so as to maintain the myth of meritocracy, the myth that democratic choice is equally available to all. Keeping most people unaware that freedom of confident action is there for just a small number of people props up those in power and serves to keep power in the hands of the same groups that have most of it already.

Although systemic change takes many decades, there are pressing questions for me and I imagine for some others like me if we raise our daily consciousness on the perquisites of being light-skinned. What will we do with such knowledge? As we know from watching men, it is an open question whether we will choose to use unearned advantage to weaken hidden systems of advantage, and whether we will use any of our arbitrarily awarded power to try to reconstruct power systems on a broader base.

"Derailing for Dummies"

BY UNKNOWN

As more women moved to online spaces including social media, and blogs, racist, sexist, and anti-LGBTQIA+ harassment escalated into threats and violence. This harassment earned its own name, *trolling*, and harassers used online spaces like Reddit to organize GamerGate, a coordinated harassment campaign that rose out of misogynist frustrations about diversity and inclusion in the gaming community. "Derailing for Dummies," first established online in 2009, is both satirical and offers useful tools to understand and combat bigoted harassment in the form of "derailing," or the ways in which much of the harassment is intended to divert discussions of race, gender, or sexualized oppression. The authors remain anonymous to protect themselves from the very harassers they hope to disempower. "Derailing for Dummies" remains a useful primer on how to keep necessary conversations about social justice focused on what matters most.

DERAIL USING EDUCATION

If You Won't Educate Me How Can I Learn?

While seemingly simple on the surface, there is some intertwining subtext embedded within this one. First of all, you're placing responsibility for your education back onto the marginalized person. As they are obviously engaged with these issues, and care about them, they are hopeful that privileged people may one day start listening and taking on board what they have to say.

By placing responsibility to educate in their hands, you tug at this yearning. You may even successfully make many question themselves and their selfish expectations that you utilize the hundreds upon hundreds of resources on the subject available to you as a privileged person! After all, anyone who expects you to be able to research a topic by yourself also clearly expects you to be far more of a functioning adult than you're acting! By insisting you can only learn if they right then and there sacrifice further hours of time going over the same ground they have so often in the past, you may also make them give up and go away altogether, enabling you to win by default. But further, you give the impression that you really want to learn, but they're holding you back! That's right, using this tactic you can suggest that full understanding is what you crave—you want to be a better, more connected and compassionate person—but it's not your fault! Nobody ever gave you the education! And now that someone is here who is so obviously qualified and benefited from using a smart writing service, they're denying you your privilege given right to have everything you want handed to you on a platter! Which brings us to another key component of this argument—it is very important, in conversations with marginalized people to constantly remind them that you are, indeed, privileged.

By demonstrating your belief that marginalized people should immediately gratify your every whim, you remind them of their place in society. After all, they're not there to live lives free of discrimination and in happy, independent and fulfilling ways! Please! marginalized people exist for your curiosity and to make you generally feel better about your place in society and don't let them forget it! Point one to you!

If You Cared About These Matters
You'd Be Willing to Educate Me

This is the natural follow-up to the above argument, although it can also be used independently. You see, often in these discussions a marginalized person will tell you it's not their responsibility to educate you. This is because marginalized people believe that they have other priorities in life, like working and studying and being with their families for example. Clearly, they are laboring under a misconception—as a privileged person you have far more right to their time than they do, and besides, don't they want to make the world a better place? Isn't that why they alerted you to the fact you were being offensive in the first place? Well, now clearly your education is their responsibility!

By placing this burden of responsibility onto them you remind them of just how daunting a task that is and how their lives are constantly being monopolized by the privileged, even in something that should be empowering to them, like deconstructing discrimination. You trivialize their lives, needs, interests and obligations by suggesting they should be spending all of their time and energy in engaging with clueless privileged people, putting in hours and hours of effort in repeating the exact same thing they've already said three thousand times to three thousand other privileged people in their past. And furthermore, you remind them that, if they really cared about their own issues, they'd willingly take that task on! Surely it's a small price to pay to change people's minds? Well, you want them to think that, but of course it isn't. After all, most of the conversations they have with privileged people often feel to them like beating their heads repeatedly against a brick wall embedded with rusty spikes. Which is entirely the point. Keep them worn out and exhausted and maybe they'll just go away.

DERAIL USING ANGER

You're Being Hostile

This is a great one to pop out if it seems like they're going to push the matter. After all, nobody wants to be "hostile," do they? In a culture rigidly defined by social protocol, invariably designed to favor the privileged, people are very concerned about "getting along with others." Especially marginalized people! Know why? Well, since they're marginalized they experience a variety of discrimination usually in many aspects of their daily lives. It is not at all unusual, therefore, for marginalized people to have to be accustomed to being very, very cautious about the way they engage with the privileged. This is because discrimination may mean they routinely encounter violence, silencing, oppression or just good old-fashioned outright ridicule and diminished [sic]. That can make life stressful and exhausting, so many marginalized people develop complex strategies to avoid hostile engagements with privileged people. Further to this, marginalized people are forced into a certain sort of social behavior by privileged people—"appropriate" behavior. After all, there are different rules for them than there are for the privileged.

This training in "appropriate" behavior usually begins when they are very young, so it is well-ingrained. By accusing them of hostility, you will successfully enliven their sense of caution and anxiety around this matter. You may also provoke a feeling of guilt that they are not "behaving" the way they have been trained to. But even better—by accusing them of hostility, you pass the blame back to them, rather than consider what you might have said that was so offensive and hurtful it caused the "hostility"! This will definitely work in your favor, because it will further insult and enrage them. You are making progress . . .

You've Lost Your Temper So I Don't Have to Listen to You Anymore

This one is particularly effective because it really pushes home a sense of futility and hopelessness to the marginalized people. Remember they should never get the impression they can win one of these arguments, because you should be consistently implying that there was never anything to argue over to begin with.

If you've been following the steps correctly so far, by this point any reasonable person is going to be feeling pretty angry. This anger could lead to them being more aggressive and abrasive. The marginalized people have possibly even decided that you're simply too obnoxious to waste patience on and are venting their sense of frustration. This is when you whip this step out! You can use it to disregard everything they've said to you and just not deal with the issue, in particular ignoring your prior behavior that led to the anger.

Conventions of social conduct hold civil discourse as the ideal at all times. When people get angry, it gives you a convenient "out" without having to concede to any of their objections or acknowledge their pain. Furthermore, with this one you can make it seem as though you were ready and willing to listen, but then they ruined it. This way you can leave them with the sense that if only they'd been a good little marginalized people and toed the line, then they may have won someone over to the cause! It just adds a particular distaste to the whole affair that no derailing should be without!

You Are Damaging Your Cause by Being Angry

By now their feelings are probably deeply hurt and they're very angry. Don't forget they encounter this kind of discrimination in subtle ways every single day of their life, so they're bound to be emotional about it, even resentful. You can take advantage of this weakness to emerge the victor! After all, everyone knows the marginalized have an obligation to conduct themselves with quiet dignity in the face of infuriating tribulation and if your quarry begins to get angry and "aggressive" then you have won! Why? Well, it's very simple—just hold them as representative of their entire group! You could try saying something like "you realize you're making all X look bad?," or "well, congratulations for backing up the stereotype of X as being angry, irrational and oversensitive!"

Maybe you can even say "well, I was about to say I was willing to listen to you, but then you got insulting so now I don't have to!" Don't worry about silly things like their feelings—c'mon, they're grownups, aren't they! The only thing that matters is defending your discrimination as completely fair and to avoid examining your prejudiced arguments in ways that may challenge them. You could even drop this little bomb: "You are damaging your cause by being angry, real understanding can only happen if all sides are respectful and patient."

Not only do you come across as a smug, self-righteous asshat (though you may prefer the term "bigger person") you can also manage to subtly make them feel guilty about their anger, as though it's undeserved! Everybody wins! Well, except them of course.

DERAIL USING EMOTION

You're Being Overemotional

It is very likely that the whole reason the marginalized person in question is debating with you is because they've made a conscious decision to speak out about these issues, despite the pain and heartache it can often cause them. Therefore, the "you're being hostile" bomb can often lead to an increase of anger and/or hurt. Sometimes it just leads to greater emphasis and exasperation in the argument. It really doesn't matter, because you can still use it against them by accusing them of being overemotional. You may wish to use the word "hysterical" instead. "Hysterical" is also a word laden with negative connotations, so it's particularly effective. Using this one in discussions with women is highly advisable, as the opinions and feelings of women have historically been denied as mere "hysteria," but it works against almost anyone. A great one to use with women as well is to ask them if they're "PMSing." Yes, it's an oldie but a classic.

If you need more variety, some more handy argument winners involving speculating as to people's neurotypical status: ask them if they're "neurotic" or "schizo" for example. Implying people have mental health issues is a great way to dismiss their concerns; it's also insensitive to people with actual mental health issues!

After all, proper "intellectual" discussions always involve detachment and rationality. What is "rationality"? It's a way of approaching emotional matters devoid of sentiment, particularly prized by Privileged People® as it enables a continuing inequity of power that favors them: after all, if they aren't emotionally attached to the topic by way of lived experience, it is easier for them to be "rational."

You're Just Oversensitive

Once again, though very similar to You're Being Overemotional, this one has a slightly different nuance. What you're implying is that the marginalized person is looking for offense where none exists. Once again, you're disowning your own responsibility, and this is absolutely the crux of any derailment—you just can't repeat or reinforce it often enough. No matter what, none of this is your fault—nothing you said that was hurtful, offensive, bigoted or discriminatory is really to blame here, because you said it in all innocence! After all, what reason have you ever had to examine your ingrained prejudices? Why should you start now? So you want the marginalized person to know this is how you feel and that you really believe the responsibility is all theirs—if they weren't looking so hard for offense, everything would be a lot more pleasant!

You're Taking Things Too Personally

Similar to You're Being Overemotional and yet with particular uses of its own. You see, when you say "you're taking things too personally" you demonstrate your ignorance that these issues ARE personal for them! That's highly insulting and is sure to rub anyone up the wrong way. That you're already refusing to consider their reality is giving them a pretty good indication of how the conversation is going to digress yet the natural human need for understanding will probably compel them to try and reason with you, or at least to point you in the direction of some educational resources that will help you gain insight into their experiences. This can enable you to once again make a demand for them to personally educate you instead.

By denying the conversation is personal for them, you also reveal your own detachment: there's really nothing at stake for you in getting into this argument, you're just doing it for kicks. They will be all too aware of this, and it will begin to work on their emotions, preparing them nicely for the next steps you will take them through.

DERAIL USING ENTITLEMENT

But That Happens to Me Too!

In attempting to communicate with you, the marginalized person may bring up examples of the sorts of daily manifestations of discrimination they face. Many of these examples seem trivial to privileged people but clearly reflect the way the marginalized person has been "othered" by society. "Othering" is a system of social markers that defines "Us" and "them," neatly and conveniently categorizing people into their appropriate places within society. It's a way of defining a secured and positive position in the world by stigmatizing "others." In other words, it's the process of dehumanizing anyone different to the Chosen Privileged. The marginalized person you're dealing with has been subjected to this "othering." This means that their body is viewed as public property and the personal, intricate details of their lives and being are perceived as free information. You must nod patiently as the marginalized person tries to gain your understanding of the many complicated and subtle ways this othering impacts their lives until they come across a point that seems particularly grating for them. Then you must say "oh, but I experience that too!" For example, people of African descent often express outrage and irritation at the fact many white people believe they can freely touch their hair. This invasion of their personal space is dressed up as flattery—"oh, what beautiful hair you have!" and permission is not sought or granted before the action is taken. "That happens to everyone!" you must exclaim. "My child has beautiful white-blonde hair and people are always touching it!"

Sex workers, as another example, often endure highly intimate questions regarding all aspects of their lives, sexual habits and client interactions. When they gripe about how invasive this is, you must equate it to your own work: "Oh, I know, I'm a lawyer and people always want to know what goes on in court!" "Totally, I'm a doctor and people are always asking about gross conditions I see!"

With a trans person, many people expect all the details of the transition process should be made available to them, including details of how they "transform." When they talk about how frustrating this is, you must commiserate: "Yeah, don't you hate the way men always want you to explain the mysteries of make-up and skin care!" you should blithely exclaim.

If you are speaking to a fat person who is complaining about the lack of fashion-forward and beautiful clothing made in their size, try something like: "The fashion industry sucks! They just do not make clothes for real bodies—I mean, just because I am a size four doesn't mean I'm short! Jeans are always too short on me!"

Without a doubt, one of the most powerful tactics to use here is comparing male circumcision to female genital mutilation. In any discussion around FGM, make sure you quickly leap in and say: "But why is it OK for little boys to be mutilated? Why isn't anyone talking about that?" Because the removal of a tiny flap of skin is entirely comparable to the crippling mutilation many young girls are subjected to.

What this demonstrates is your total lack of understanding of what "othering" means in a practical sense. You're ignoring the way your life is otherwise entirely immersed in a state of absolute privilege and revealing the fact you fail to comprehend the process of objectification and marginalizing they go through all the time. When you are privileged, "similar" experiences simply do not happen on an equal footing because they do not otherwise reflect marginalization. This obliviousness is highly insensitive and trivializing and will definitely cause them to grind their teeth!

But it's also an important step in affirming your privilege: privileged people are accustomed, after all, to it being "all about them." Not used to simply sitting back and listening to othered people's issues, privileged people like to be the center of attention at all times. It reminds them that they are important. By doing this, you will feel good about yourself and send a crucial message to the marginalized person (yes you really can diminish their experience by making it all about you, all the time!).

But If It's Okay for Marginalized People to Use Those Words, Why Can't I?

As a privileged person, it is natural that you would feel excluded and frustrated by the recent spate of marginalized person "reclaiming" historically negative words to refer to themselves. Not only do these marginalized people kick up a great big ole stink by making it "politically incorrect" for privileged people to use these words—even going so far as to have some of them defined under "hate crime" legislation!—they take the insult one step further and use them freely among themselves! This is very perplexing and annoying for privileged people, who can only stand on the outside, gazing wistfully in, wishing it were a simpler time when it was totally okay for everyone to call women whores, Mexicans spics, Trans folk trannies, gay men faggots and people of African descent the n-word. After all, who do those marginalized people think they are, taking ownership of language traditionally used to oppress them! That just isn't playing fair! But take heart, because there is a way you can worm around this one—where there's privilege, there's always a way!

First of all, you must feign utter cluelessness about the ins & outs of reclamation and behave as though you were under the impression that in these "post race/sex/sexuality/gender/etc times" that we had all evolved into a new era where "words don't mean anything" and it's totally okay for everyone to use offensive slurs and then . . . well: use them.

When a marginalized person calls you out on it, become indignant. Express confusion. Demand an explanation. Say that you just don't understand—if you people use those words to refer to each other, why can't I?!

You see, you're implying that they're being hypocritical. That if they are going to use abusive & oppressionist language among each other, they simply have to accept that they're employing a "double standard" by preventing the privileged from using them.

What this enables you to ignore is the reality of the power dynamic involved. Language reclamation is a means by which marginalized people gain back some power they are traditionally denied by taking control of words used to demean and discriminate against them. When these words come from privileged people, there is a long and very serious negative history behind them that cannot be divorced from the words themselves. Thus, when privileged people employ these words, they are perpetuating that history and the psychology behind the word. They are exercising oppressive power that have become inherent to those words—a power marginalized people seek to subvert and dismantle when they use them.

Pretend not to understand this. Just continue to imply hypocrisy and pout that it isn't fair. It also ignores the fact that, from within marginalized groups, discourses around abusive language are actually not simple and there are many divided and varied opinions on the subject. Treating marginalized people like a hive

mind is always a great way to further subtly insult them and
since the point of this entire debacle is to come out with as many
notches on your belt as possible, you want to make sure you slip
in as many knocks below their belt as you can manage.

"It's a Conspiracy!"

Rather than deal with the actual issues on the table or stop and
listen and take into consideration what the marginalized person is
saying, just whip this out instead! Essentially, what you are doing
is claiming that any endeavor by marginalized people to improve
their standing within society and the treatment they experience is
a "conspiracy" "against" the privileged and that the ultimate objective of this fearsome "conspiracy" is to ultimately oppress the
Privileged. It is a common misconception of the Privileged to believe that any effort by the marginalized to gain equity undermines the privileged and their lives.

It is a very unique and special trait to personalize something
like Black History Month, for example, as being an effort to make
the history and accomplishments of white people invisible. Although this is obviously ridiculous when white history is so prominently covered in every aspect of culture from film, books,
monuments and education, it is a great way to once again make
the dialogue about the privileged and the privileged's perceived ill-
treatment, imaginary though this may be. This way you manage
to keep the focus off the topic at hand and on your own sense of
wounded comfort—a lovely way to remind the marginalized their
issues are thoroughly devalued. Naturally, it is of extreme frustration to marginalized people, when all they are attempting to do is
draw attention to the extreme discrimination they are obliged to
face, to have it characterized as a calculated attack on the rights
of the privileged. You can further underscore and intensify this
frustration by accusing them of a conspiracy, the ultimate objective of which is to make your life as a Privileged Person a living
hell! Go so far as to suggest they intend to turn the tables—that if
given an inch they will simply take a mile and if the Privileged
budge or relent, in the blink of an eye the marginalized will over-
throw and oppress the oppressors! After all, how dare they think

they are entitled to the same human rights you enjoy automatically by virtue of your privilege!

Anything You Can Do

If a marginalized person should remark that many marginalized people report overwhelmingly similar experiences of discrimination and silencing from the Privileged, do not despair: this is a unique opportunity to turn one of their own arguments back on them! Tell them they are making "generalizations." Salt with "unwarranted" as necessary and if you can work "stereotyping" in there too (playing on that guilt that THEY may be doing what they accuse others of), and you're golden. You have still managed to entirely undermine their voice as well as insinuate they're hypocrites—all the while presenting yourself as being blissfully unaware that stereotypes of the privileged rarely, if ever, actively work to disadvantage them in life. They'll inevitably retreat to a YMMV, IMHO multi-disclaimered "Lived Experience" (don't forget, as discussed in You're Arguing With Opinions, Not Fact, this is worthless) at which point you can tell them that's "anecdotal" and proves nothing. Slam dunk. BOOYAH!

But I'm Not Like That—Stop Stereotyping!

Personalizing anything the marginalized person may say is a great way of distracting attention from the issue at hand, forcing the marginalized person to soothe your wounded feelings or sense of indignation rather than concentrating on the argument they were making. Rather than simply listening to criticism of a group of Privileged People with respect and consideration for the marginalized person, you must immediately take offense and leap in to defend yourself. For example, when queer people are criticizing the tendencies of some straight people, jump in and say something like: "Not all of us are like that—you're prejudiced against straight people! You're judging straight people the same way that they judge you, and it's hateful! We need to not categorize people and make assumptions about them based on their identity! I resent feeling like I'm part of a group that oppresses you!"—even though the criticism was very explicitly leveled at a specified behavior. (i.e., "I don't like straight people who do_____.")

But of course, this can work in many different situations where Privileged behavior is being deconstructed or criticized. Its resonance is in its lack of acknowledgment of the balance of power by suggesting that reasonable criticism of oppressive or discriminatory behavior is equivalent to the oppressive and discriminatory behavior itself. Remember that while the marginalized person's criticism can never adversely affect your life in significant ways, you must rank the discrimination they face—which does significantly affect them—as equal to the discomfort of your wounded feelings, to demonstrate how highly you rank yourself and how lowly you rank them.

Who Wins Gold in the Oppression Olympics?

Following on from this, if you are a member of another marginalized group, you can also exploit it to indicate to the marginalized person how absolutely disdainful you are of their concerns and issues by making out that yours are far more important and imperative. You can even suggest that your issues are more valuable than theirs, implying a hierarchy of oppression in which you always win. You see, as a marginalized person yourself, it is all the more infuriating to another marginalized person that you're exercising the exact same prejudices and discrimination that privileged people exercise against you! The marginalized person will be tearing their hair out at your obliviousness and lack of perception and this will weaken their defenses.

No More Miss America

BY VARIOUS

In 1968, a group called New York Radical Women staged a protest of the Miss America contest that brought the women's liberation movement into public consciousness. The myth of the "bra burning" feminist began here as the radicals tossed "instruments of female torture" such as girdles, high heels, bras, and *Playboy* magazines into a Freedom Trash Can (although they didn't burn them). Radical feminist activist Carol Hanisch came up with the idea for the action, and writer, poet, and activist Robin Morgan wrote the press release "No More Miss America," which demonstrated the direct connection between the pageant and its objectification of women to racism, consumerism, patriarchal oppression, and war. Several members of the group managed to hang a banner over the balcony at that year's ceremony and shouted, "Women's liberation," during the crowning of Miss America. The action made national headlines and was an introduction for many to the growing feminist movement. The piece remains a strident manifesto and call to action for dismantling the patriarchy.

NO MORE MISS AMERICA

On September 7th in Atlantic City, the Annual Miss America Pageant will again crown "your ideal." But this year, reality will liberate the contest auction-block in the guise of "genyooine" deplasticized, breathing women. Women's Liberation Groups, black women, high school and college women, women's peace groups, women's welfare and social-work groups, women's job-equality groups, pro-birth control and pro-abortion groups—women of every political persuasion—all are invited to join us in a day-long boardwalk-theater event, starting at 1:00 P.M. on the Boardwalk in front of Atlantic City's Convention Hall. We will protest the image of Miss America, an image that oppresses women in every area in which it purports to represent us. There will be: Picket Lines; Guerrilla Theater; Leafleting; Lobbying Visits to the contestants urging our sisters to reject the Pageant Farce and join us; a huge Freedom Trash Can (into which we will throw bras, girdles, curlers, false eyelashes, wigs, and representative issues of *Cosmopolitan*, *Ladies' Home Journal*, *Family Circle*, etc.—bring any such woman-garbage you have around the house); we will also announce a Boycott of all those commercial products related to the Pageant, and the day will end with a Women's Liberation rally at midnight when Miss America is crowned on live television. Lots of other surprises are being planned (come and add your own!) but we do not plan heavy disruptive tactics and so do not expect a bad police scene. It should be a groovy day on the Boardwalk in the sun with our sisters. In case of arrests, however, we plan to reject all male authority and demand to be busted by policewomen only. (In Atlantic City, women cops are not permitted to make arrests—dig that!)

Male chauvinist-reactionaries on this issue had best stay away, nor are male liberals welcome in the demonstrations. But sympathetic men can donate money as well as cars and drivers.

Male reporters will be refused interviews. We reject patronizing reportage. *Only newswomen will be recognized.*

THE TEN POINTS

We Protest:

1. *The Degrading Mindless-Boob-Girlie Symbol.* The Pageant contestants epitomize the roles we are all forced to play as women. The parade down the runway blares the metaphor of the 4-H Club county fair, where the nervous animals are judged for teeth, fleece, etc., and where the best "specimen" gets the blue ribbon. So are women in our society forced daily to compete for male

approval, enslaved by ludicrous "beauty" standards we ourselves are conditioned to take seriously.

2. *Racism with Roses.* Since its inception in 1921, the Pageant has not had one Black finalist, and this has not been for a lack of test-case contestants. There has never been a Puerto Rican, Alaskan, Hawaiian, or Mexican-American winner. Nor has there ever been a *true* Miss America—an American Indian.

3. *Miss America as Military Death Mascot.* The highlight of her reign each year is a cheerleader-tour of American troops abroad—last year she went to Vietnam to pep-talk our husbands, fathers, sons and boyfriends into dying and killing with a better spirit. She personifies the "unstained patriotic American womanhood our boys are fighting for." The Living Bra and the Dead Soldier. We refuse to be used as Mascots for Murder.

4. *The Consumer Con-Game.* Miss America is a walking commercial for the Pageant's sponsors. Wind her up and she plugs your product on promotion tours and TV—all in an "honest, objective" endorsement. What a shill.

5. *Competition Rigged and Unrigged.* We deplore the encouragement of an American myth that oppresses men as well as women: the win-or-you're-worthless competitive disease. The "beauty contest" creates only one winner to be "used" and forty-nine losers who are "useless."

6. *The Woman as Pop Culture Obsolescent Theme.* Spindle, mutilate, and then discard tomorrow. What is so ignored as last year's Miss America? This only reflects the gospel of our society, according to Saint Male: women must be young, juicy, malleable—hence age discrimination and the cult of youth. And we women are brainwashed into believing this ourselves!

7. *The Unbeatable Madonna-Whore Combination.* Miss America and Playboy's centerfold are sisters over the skin. To win approval, we must be both sexy and wholesome, delicate but able to cope, demure yet titillatingly bitchy. Deviation of any sort brings, we are told, disaster; "You won't get a man!!"

8. *The Irrelevant Crown on the Throne of Mediocrity.* Miss
America represents what women are supposed to be: unoffensive,
bland, apolitical. If you are tall, short, over or under what weight
The Man prescribes you should be, forget it. Personality, articu-
lateness, intelligence, commitment—unwise. Conformity is the
key to the crown—and, by extension, to success in our society.

9. *Miss America as Dream Equivalent To—?* In this reputedly
democratic society, where every little boy supposedly can grow up
to be President, what can every little girl hope to grow to be? Miss
America. That's where it's at. Real power to control our own lives
is restricted to men, while women get patronizing pseudo-power,
an ermine cloak and a bunch of flowers; men are judged by their
actions, women by their appearance.

10. *Miss America as Big Sister Watching You.* The Pageant exercises Thought Control, attempts to scar the Image onto our
minds, to further make women oppressed and men oppressors; to
enslave us all the more in high-heeled, low-status roles; to incul-
cate false values in young girls; to use women as beasts of buying;
to seduce us to prostitute ourselves before our own oppression.

NO MORE MISS AMERICA

PRINCIPLES

New York Radical Women

*This brief position statement sketches out a radical feminist per-
spective of the late sixties.*

We take the woman's side in everything.
　　We ask not if something is "reformist," "radical," "revolution-
ary," or "moral." We ask: is it good for women or bad for women?
　　We ask not if something is "political." We ask: is it effective?
Does it get us closest to what we really want in the fastest way?
　　We define the best interests of women as the best interests of the

poorest, most insulted, most despised, most abused woman on earth. Her lot, her suffering and abuse is the threat that men use against all of us to keep us in line. She is what all women fear being called, fear being treated as and yet what we all really are in the eyes of men. She is Everywoman: ugly, dumb (dumb broad, dumb cunt), bitch, nag, hag, whore, fucking and breeding machine, mother of us all. Until Everywoman is free, no woman will be free. When her beauty and knowledge is revealed and seen, the new day will be at hand.

We are critical of all past ideology, literature and philosophy, products as they are of male supremacist culture. We are re-examining even our words, language itself.

We take as our source the hitherto unrecognized culture of women, a culture which from long experience of oppression developed an intense appreciation for life, a sensitivity to unspoken thoughts and the complexity of simple things, a powerful knowledge of human needs and feelings.

We regard our feelings as our most important source of political understanding.

We see the key to our liberation in our collective wisdom and our collective strength.

Feminism Is So Last Week

BY JESSICA VALENTI

At a time when mainstream media was describing American culture as "postfeminist," Jessica Valenti co-founded the award-winning blog *Feministing*, which interrogated patriarchal norms, inequality, and rape culture and inspired the creation of a new generation of feminist blogs. She was a columnist for *The Guardian* from 2014 to 2018 and is the author of several books, most recently *Sex Object: A Memoir*, which was a *New York Times* bestseller. Throughout her career, Valenti has been targeted by misogynists online with rape and death threats. She has called attention to the ways this harassment is used to silence women and marginalized people while refusing to be silenced herself. In "Feminism Is So Last Week," an excerpt from the first chapter of her 2007 book, *Full Frontal Feminism*, Valenti addresses feminism as a necessary tool to empower young women facing structural sexism and oppression.

Every once in a while, there's some big article about feminism being dead—the most famous of which is the aforementioned *Time* piece. And if feminism isn't dead, it's equally often accused of being outdated. Or a failure. Or unnecessary.

But if feminism is dead, then why do people have to keep on trying to kill it? Whether it's in the media, politics, or conservative organizations, there's a big trend of trying to convince the world that feminism is long gone.

The argument is either that women don't need feminism anymore, or that those crazy radical feminists don't speak for most women. Never mind that recent polls show that most women support feminist goals, like equal pay for equal work, ending violence against women, childcare, women's healthcare, and getting more women in political office. Here comes that "I'm not a feminist, but . . ." stuff again!

The obsession with feminism's demise is laughable. And if the powers that be can't convince you that it's dead, that's when the blame game starts. Feminism is the media's favorite punching bag.

The horrors that feminism is supposedly responsible for range from silly contradictions to plainly ludicrous examples. In recent articles, feminism has been blamed for promoting promiscuity; promoting man-hating; the torture at Abu Ghraib; ruining "the family"; the feminization of men; the "failures" of Amnesty International; and even unfairness to Michael Jackson. I'm not kidding. You name it, feminism is the cause.

My all-time favorite accusation: Feminism is responsible for an increase in the number of women criminals. You're going to love this. Wendy Wright of Concerned Women for America—a conservative anti-feminist organization—is quoted in a 2005 article, "Rising Crime Among Women Linked to Feminist Agenda," as saying it's pesky feminists who are to blame for the increase of women in prison.

Wright claims that women are committing crimes because feminism has taught them that "women should not be dependent on others" and that "they don't need to be dependent on a husband," which inevitably forces them to "fend for themselves."

Got that, girls? Without a husband to depend on, you'll be a murderer in no time!

For something that is so tired and outdated, feminism certainly seems to be doing a lot of damage, huh?

Obviously there's an awful lot of effort being put into discrediting the f-word—but why all the fuss? If folks didn't see feminism as a threat—and a powerful one—they wouldn't spend so much time putting it down, which is part of what attracted me to feminism in the first place. I wanted to know what all the brouhaha was about.

It's important to remember that all of these stereotypes and scare tactics serve a specific purpose—to keep you away from feminism.

'Cause don't forget—there are a lot of people benefiting from your feeling like shit about yourself. Think about it: If you don't feel fat, you won't buy firming lotions and diet pills and the like.

If you don't feel stupid, you might speak out against all the screwy laws that adversely affect women. It pays—literally—to keep women half there. And god forbid you get involved in anything that would make you wonder why in the world women are having surgery to make their vaginas "prettier." (Sorry, I couldn't help but mention it; it's too freaky not to.)

The solution? Don't fall for it. If feminism isn't for you, fine. But find that out for yourself. I'm betting that you're more likely to be into something that encourages you to recognize that you're already pretty badass than something that insists you're a fat, dumb chick.

FEMI-WHA?

There are so many stereotypes about feminism, and so many different definitions of it, that what feminism actually is gets insanely confusing—even for women who have been working on women's issues for years. But I always was a fan of the dictionary definition. And I promise this is the only time I'll be quoting the frigging dictionary:

fem·i·nism

1 Belief in the social, political, and economic equality of the sexes.

2 The movement organized around this belief.

Hmm . . . don't see anything about man-hating in there. Or hairy legs. Obviously, there are tons of different kinds of feminism and schools of thought, but I'd say the above is enough to get you started. Besides, at the end of the day, feminism is really something you define for yourself.

SISTERHOOD, MY ASS

No matter how clear-cut (or how complex) feminism can be, not all women are feminists by virtue of having ovaries. And that's just fine by me. I realized this in a big way recently. I was quoted in Rebecca Traister's 2005 Salon.com article entitled "The

F-Word," airing my feelings about the word "feminist"—and I got a little pissy. "Part of me gets so angry at younger women who are nervous about feminism because they're afraid that boys won't like them. . . . Part of me wants to say, 'Yeah, someone's going to call you a lesbian. Someone's going to say you're a fat, ugly dyke. Suck it up.'" My attempt to strongly defend the word "feminism" didn't go over well with a lot of people. One woman actually posted a homophobic rant of a response to Salon.com:

> I'll call myself a feminist when the fat, mannish dykes who do run around calling themselves "Feminist" very loudly and constantly concede that my decision to groom and dress myself as a twenty-first-century professional woman is every bit as valid a choice as their decision to become stereotypical jailhouse bulldaggers. Ovaries only make you female, they do not make you woman, and I am a woman. In other words, I will call myself a feminist when those mannabees are as proud of and joyful in their womanhood as I am in mine . . . Until then, fuck off and take your hairy legs with you.

Ok then! I didn't need much more than this to realize that feminism isn't for everybody. I never really bought the "We're all sisters" thing anyway. I've met enough racist, classist, homophobic women to know better. Feminism's power isn't in how many women identify with the cause. I'll take quality over quantity any day.

QUALITY WOMEN

So who are these elusive feminists? Like I've said—you are, even if you don't know it yet. Though I'm hoping by now you're at least slightly convinced. The smartest, coolest women I know are feminists. And they're everywhere. You don't need to be burning bras (actually, this never happened—total myth) or standing on a picket line to be a feminist. Chances are, you've already done stuff that makes you a feminist. You don't have to be a full-time activist to be an awesome feminist.

The work that young women are doing across the country is

pretty goddamn impressive. Do they all consider themselves feminists? Probably not. But a lot of the work they're doing is grounded in feminist values. Just a few examples:

A group of high school girls in Allegheny County, Pennsylvania, organized a "girlcott" of Abercrombie & Fitch when the clothing company came out with a girls' shirt that read: WHO NEEDS BRAINS WHEN YOU HAVE THESE? After the group caused quite a ruckus in the media, A&F pulled the shirt.

Two young women in Brooklyn, Consuelo Ruybal and Oraia Reid, used their own money to start an organization called Right-Rides after a number of young women were raped in their neighborhood. Women can call the service anytime from midnight to 4 AM on the weekends and get a free ride home. Simple, but damn effective. Their motto is: "Because getting home safe should not be a luxury."

The documentary film *The Education of Shelby Knox* was inspired by a high school student in Lubbock, Texas, who took on her town's school board to fight for comprehensive sex education. Shockingly, the abstinence-only brand they were receiving wasn't quite cutting it.

A group of queer women, tired of seeing the art world bypass great women artists, started *riffRAG* magazine. The magazine features work that slips under the mainstream's radar.

Misty McElroy decided to start Rock 'n' Roll Camp for Girls as part of a class project at Portland State University. She expected about twenty girls to sign up—she ended up getting three hundred. Rock 'n' Roll Camp for Girls teaches young girls to play instruments, deejay, sing, and write songs and ends with a live performance. The camp was so popular in Oregon that there are now rock camps in New York City, Washington, D.C., Nashville, Tennessee, Tucson, Arizona, and various California locations.

This is just a small sampling of the amazing work young women are already doing (and they say we're apathetic!), and it doesn't even touch on all the women's blogs, online and print zines, and community programs that are out there. These women and their work prove that feminism is not only alive and well, but also energized and diverse. Not to mention fun.

You can be a feminist without making it your life's work. It's about finding the cause that works for you, and makes you happy, and doing something about it. (Trust me, getting off your ass can be more fun than you think.) For some women, that means working in women's organizations, fighting against sexist laws. For others, it means volunteering time to teach young girls how to deejay. It doesn't matter what you're doing, so long as you're doing something. Even if it's as simple as speaking up when someone tells a nasty-ass sexist joke.

There's a popular feminist shirt these days that reads: THIS IS WHAT A FEMINIST LOOKS LIKE. Ashley Judd wore one at the 2004 pro-choice March for Women's Lives in Washington, D.C. Margaret Cho wore one on the Spring 2003 cover of *Ms.* magazine. I wear one, too; I love this shirt. Because you never really do know what a feminist looks like. And believe me, we're everywhere.

Women's March Guiding Vision and Definition of Principles

BY VARIOUS

On January 12, 2017—eight days before Donald Trump's inauguration—the organizers of the Women's March released a policy platform to counter Trump's misogynist, racist, ableist, anti-immigrant rhetoric and proposed policies. This new policy platform addressed reproductive rights, immigration reform, healthcare reform, religious discrimination (primarily against Muslim Americans), LGBTQIA+ rights, gender and racial inequities (primarily those that favor men and non-Hispanic whites, respectively), workers' rights, and other issues. The four co-chairs were Linda Sarsour, the executive director of the Arab American Association of New York; Tamika Mallory, a political organizer and former executive director of the National Action Network; Carmen Perez, an executive director of the political action group the Gathering for Justice; and Bob Bland, a fashion designer who focuses on ethical manufacturing. Gloria Steinem, Harry Belafonte, LaDonna Harris, Angela Davis, and Dolores Huerta served as honorary co-chairs. The Women's March, a worldwide protest against Trump, took place on January 21, the day after Trump's inauguration. The main protest was the Women's March on Washington; many other marches took place in cities and countries around the world. The Washington march was streamed live on YouTube, Facebook, and Twitter. Four hundred seventy thousand people marched in Washington, and an estimated 5.2 million people participated in the marches across the US. Worldwide participation was estimated at over seven million.

OVERVIEW AND PURPOSE

The Women's March on Washington is a women-led movement bringing together people of all genders, ages, races, cultures, political affiliations, disabilities and backgrounds in our nation's capital on January 19, 2019, to affirm our shared humanity and pronounce our bold message of resistance and self-determination.

Recognizing that women have intersecting identities and are therefore impacted by a multitude of social justice and human rights issues, we have outlined a representative vision for a government that is based on the principles of liberty and justice for all. *As Dr. King said, "We cannot walk alone. And as we walk, we must make the pledge that we shall always march ahead. We cannot turn back."*

Our liberation is bound in each other's. The Women's March on Washington includes leaders of organizations and communities that have been building the foundation for social progress for generations. We welcome vibrant collaboration and honor the legacy of the movements before us—the suffragists and abolitionists, the Civil Rights Movement, the feminist movement, the American Indian Movement, Occupy Wall Street, Marriage Equality, Black Lives Matter, and more—by employing a decentralized, leaderfull structure and focusing on an ambitious, fundamental and comprehensive agenda.

#WHYWEMARCH

We are empowered by the legions of revolutionary leaders who paved the way for us to march, and acknowledge those around the globe who fight for our freedoms. We honor these women and so many more. They are #WhyWeMarch.

- Bella Abzug
- Corazon Aquino
- Ella Baker
- Grace Lee Boggs
- Berta Cáceres
- Rachel Carson
- Shirley Chisholm
- Angela Davis
- Miss Major Griffin-Gracy
- LaDonna Harris
- Dorothy I. Height
- bell hooks
- Judith Heumann
- Dolores Huerta

- Marsha P. Johnson
- Barbara Jordan
- Yuri Kochiyama
- Winona LaDuke
- Audre Lorde
- Wilma Mankiller
- Diane Nash

- Sylvia Rivera
- Barbara Smith
- Gloria Steinem
- Hannah G. Solomon
- Harriet Tubman
- Edith Windsor
- Malala Yousafzai

VALUES AND PRINCIPLES

- We believe that Women's Rights are Human Rights and Human Rights are Women's Rights. This is the basic and original tenet for which we unite to March on Washington.
- We believe Gender Justice is Racial Justice is Economic Justice. We must create a society in which all women—including Black women, Indigenous women, poor women, immigrant women, disabled women, Jewish women, Muslim women, Latinx women, Asian and Pacific Islander women, lesbian, bi, queer and trans women—are free and able to care for and nurture themselves and their families, however they are formed, in safe and healthy environments free from structural impediments.
- Women have the right to live full and healthy lives, free of all forms of violence against our bodies. One in three women have been victims of some form of physical violence by an intimate partner within their lifetime; and one in five women have been raped. Further, each year, thousands of women and girls, particularly Black, Indigenous and transgender women and girls, are kidnapped, trafficked, or murdered. We honor the lives of those women who were taken before their time and we affirm that we work for a day when all forms of violence against women are eliminated. We believe that gun violence is a women's issue and that guns are not how we keep our communities free from violence.
- We believe in accountability and justice for police brutality and ending racial profiling and targeting of communities of color and Indigenous peoples. Women of color and Indigenous women are killed in police custody at greater rates, and are more likely to be sexually assaulted by police, and women with

disabilities are disproportionately likely to experience use of force at the hands of police, and sexual assault in general. We also call for an immediate end to arming police with the military grade weapons and military tactics that are wreaking havoc on communities of color and sovereign tribal lands. No woman or mother should have to fear that she or her loved ones will be harmed at the hands of those sworn to protect.

- We believe it is our moral imperative to dismantle the gender and racial inequities within the criminal justice system. The rate of imprisonment has grown faster for women than men, increasing by 700% since 1980, and the majority of women in prison have a child under the age of 18. Incarcerated women also face a high rate of violence and sexual assault. We are committed to ensuring access to gender-responsive programming and dedicated healthcare including substance abuse treatment, mental and maternal health services for women in prison. We believe in the promise of restorative justice and alternatives to incarceration. We are also committed to disrupting the school-to-prison pipeline that prioritizes incarceration over education by systematically funneling our children—particularly children of color, queer and trans youth, foster care children, and girls—into the justice system.

- We believe in Reproductive Freedom. We do not accept any federal, state or local rollbacks, cuts or restrictions on our ability to access quality reproductive healthcare services, birth control, HIV/AIDS care and prevention, or medically accurate sexuality education. This means open access to safe, legal, affordable abortion and birth control for all people, regardless of income, location or education. We understand that we can only have reproductive justice when reproductive health care is accessible to all people regardless of income, location or education.

- We believe in Gender Justice. We must have the power to control our bodies and be free from gender norms, expectations and stereotypes. We must free ourselves and our society from the institution of awarding power, agency and resources disproportionately to masculinity to the exclusion of others.

- We firmly declare that LGBTQIA+ Rights are Human Rights and that it is our obligation to uplift, expand and protect the rights of our gay, lesbian, bi, queer, trans, two-spirit or gender non-conforming brothers, sisters and siblings. This includes access to non-judgmental, comprehensive healthcare with no exceptions or limitations; access to name and gender changes on identity documents; full antidiscrimination protections; access to education, employment, housing and benefits; and an end to police and state violence.

- We believe in an economy powered by transparency, accountability, security and equity. We believe that creating workforce opportunities that reduce discrimination against women and mothers allow economies to thrive. Nations and industries that support and invest in caregiving and basic workplace protections—including benefits like paid family leave, access to affordable childcare, sick days, healthcare, fair pay, vacation time, and healthy work environments—have shown growth and increased capacity.

- We believe in equal pay for equal work and the right of all women to be paid equitably. We must end the pay and hiring discrimination that women, particularly mothers, women of color, Indigenous women, lesbian, queer and trans women still face each day in our nation, as well as discrimination against workers with disabilities, who can currently legally be paid less than federal minimum wage. Many mothers have always worked and in our modern labor force; and women are now 50% of all family breadwinners. We stand for the 82% of women who become moms, particularly moms of color, being paid, judged, and treated fairly. Equal pay for equal work will lift families out of poverty and boost our nation's economy.

- We recognize that women of color and Indigenous women carry the heaviest burden in the global and domestic economic landscape, particularly in the care economy. We further affirm that all care work—caring for the elderly, caring for the chronically ill, caring for children and supporting independence for people with disabilities—is work, and that the burden of care falls disproportionately on the shoulders of women, particularly women of color. We stand for the rights, dignity, and fair treatment of all unpaid and paid caregivers. We must repair and replace the systemic disparities that permeate caregiving at every level of society.

- We believe that all workers—including domestic and farm workers—must have the right to organize and fight for a living minimum wage, and that unions and other labor associations are critical to a healthy and thriving economy for all. Undocumented and migrant workers must be included in our labor protections, and we stand in full solidarity with the sex workers' rights movement. We recognize that exploitation for sex and labor in all forms is a violation of human rights.

- We believe Civil Rights are our birthright. Our Constitutional government establishes a framework to provide and expand rights and freedoms—not restrict them. To this end, we must protect and restore all the Constitutionally-mandated rights to all our citizens, including voting rights, freedom to worship without fear of intimidation or harassment, freedom of speech, and protections for all citizens regardless of race, gender, age or disability. We honor and respect tribal laws and jurisdictions.

- We support Indigenous women's right to access, own, develop and control land and its resources. We affirm that now is the time for the U.S. implementation of the UN Declaration on the Rights of Indigenous Peoples and to honor existing treaty rights and fulfill promises made.

- We believe that all women's issues are issues faced by women with disabilities and Deaf women. As mothers, sisters, daughters, and contributing members of this great nation, we seek to break barriers to access, inclusion, independence, and the full enjoyment of citizenship at home and around the world. We strive to be fully included in and contribute to all aspects of American life, economy, and culture.

- We believe it is time for an all-inclusive Equal Rights Amendment to the U.S. Constitution. Most Americans believe the Constitution guarantees equal rights, but it does not. The 14th Amendment has been undermined by courts and cannot produce real equity on the basis of race and/or sex. And in a true democracy, each citizen's vote should count equally. All Americans deserve equality guarantees in the Constitution that cannot be taken away or disregarded, recognizing the reality that inequalities intersect, interconnect and overlap.

- Rooted in the promise of America's call for huddled masses yearning to breathe free, we believe in immigrant and refugee rights regardless of status or country of origin. It is our moral duty to keep families together and empower all aspiring Americans to fully participate in, and contribute to, our economy and society. We reject mass deportation, family detention, violations of due process and violence against queer and trans migrants. Immigration reform must establish a roadmap to citizenship, and provide equal opportunities and workplace protections for all. We recognize that the call to action to love our neighbor is not limited to the United States, because there is a global migration crisis. We believe migration is a human right and that no human being is illegal.

- We believe that every person, every community and Indigenous peoples in our nation have the right to clean water, clean air, and access to and enjoyment of public lands. We believe that our environment and our climate must be protected, and that our land and natural resources cannot be exploited for corporate gain or greed—especially at the risk of public safety and health.

- We recognize that to achieve any of the goals outlined within this statement, we must work together to end war and live in peace with our sisters and brothers around the world. Ending war means a cessation to the direct and indirect aggression caused by the war economy and the concentration of power in the hands of a wealthy elite who use political, social, and economic systems to safeguard and expand their power.

PART II

EARLY
FEMINIST TEXTS

Declamation on the Nobility and Preeminence of the Female Sex

BY HENRICUS CORNELIUS AGRIPPA

At a time when the Catholic Church and medieval states in western Europe were violently enforcing patriarchal authority using the doctrine of original sin to exclude women from power and public life, Henricus Cornelius Agrippa—a German physician, soldier, legal scholar, and occult writer—argued that women are more than equal to men. His contention in the 1500s that the exclusion of women was based not on their gender, but upon social conditioning, education, and prejudices of the men in power still resounds today. The title is also excellent and, some might say, accurate.

So let me begin my subject at the beginning. Woman was created as much superior to man as the name she has received is superior to his. For Adam means earth, but Eve is translated as life. And as far as life is to be ranked above earth, so far is woman to be ranked above man.

Again after all this he created two human beings in his image, man first, then woman, in whom the heavens and the earth, and every embellishment of both, are brought to perfection. For when the Creator came to the creation of woman, he rested himself in this creation, thinking that he had nothing more honorable to create; in her were completed and consummated all the wisdom and power of the Creator; after her no creation could be found or imagined. Since, therefore, woman is the ultimate end of creation, the most perfect accomplishment of all the works of God and the perfection of the universe itself, who will deny that she possesses honor surpassing every other creature? Without her the world itself, already perfect to a fault and complete at every level, would have been imperfect; it could only be perfected in the creature of all others by far the most perfect. For it is unreasonable and absurd to think that God would have finished so great a work with something imperfect.

Since the world itself has been created by God as a circle of absolute perfection, it is fitting that the circle be perfected by this particle capable of being the link that unites perfectly the beginning of the circle with its end. That is how, at the time of creation, woman was the last in time of all things created; in the conception of the divine mind, however, she was first of all, as much in prestige as in honor, as was written about her by the prophet: "Before the heavens were created, God chose her and chose her first." Indeed, it is a commonplace among philosophers to say: "The end is always the first in intention and the last in execution." For a woman was the last work of God, who introduced her into our world as the queen of a kingdom already prepared for her, adorned and prefect in everything. It is therefore right that every creature love, honor, and respect her; right also that every creature submit to and obey her, for she is the queen of all creatures and their end, perfection, and glory, absolute perfection.

Thus, man is the work of nature, woman the creation of God. Therefore, woman is generally more capable than man of receiving the divine light with which she is often filled, something one can see even today in her refinement and extraordinary beauty.

So then the blessing has been given because of woman, but the law because of man, and this was a law of wrath and curse; for it was to the man that the fruit of the tree had been prohibited, and not to the woman who had not yet been created. God wished her to be free from the beginning, it was therefore the man who committed the sin in eating, not the woman, the man who brought death, not the woman. And all of us have sinned in Adam, not in Eve, and we are infected with original sin not from our mother, who is a woman, but from our father, a man. Moreover, the ancient law ordained the circumcision of all males but left women uncircumcised, deciding without doubt to punish original sin in the sex that had sinned. And besides, God did not punish woman for having eaten, but for having given to the man the occasion of evil, which she did through ignorance, tempted as she was by the devil. The man sinned in all knowledge, the woman fell into error through ignorance and because she was deceived. For she was also the first whom the devil tempted, knowing that she was the most excellent of creatures, and, as Bernard says: "The devil, seeing her admirable beauty and knowing that this beauty was the same that he had known in the divine light when he possessed it, that he enjoyed beyond all the other angels in conversation with God, directed his envy against the woman alone, by reason of her excellence."

Christ, born into our world in the greatest humility, took the more humble male sex and not the more elevated and noble female sex, in order to expiate by this humility the arrogant sin of the first father. In addition, because we have been condemned on account of the sin of the man and not of the woman, God wished that this sin be expiated by the sex that had sinned and that atonement come through the same sex that had been deceived in ignorance. This is why God said to the serpent that the woman, or rather, according to a better reading, the seed of the woman, would crush his head, and not the man or the seed of the man. Perhaps also this explains why the priesthood was conferred by the church on man rather than on woman, because every priest represents Christ, and Christ represents the first person who sinned, that is, Adam himself.

Moreover, when Christ rose from the dead, he appeared first to women, not to men. And it is well known that after the death of Christ some men abjured their faith, although no text attests that women abandoned the faith and the Christian religion. Still further, no persecution, no heresy, no aberration in faith ever occurred because of the deeds of women; one knows that it was otherwise with men. Christ was betrayed, sold, bought, accused, condemned, suffered the passion, was put on a cross, and finally delivered to death only by men. Even more, he was denied by Peter who loved him and abandoned by all the other disciples; only some women accompanied him to the cross and the tomb. Even a pagan, the wife of Pilate, made greater efforts to save Jesus than any of the men who had believed in him. Add to this the fact that theologians almost unanimously agree that the church at that time dwelled only in a single woman, the Virgin Mary, which makes it fitting to call the female sex religious and holy.

The excellence, goodness, and innocence of women can be amply enough proved by the fact that men, not women, are the origin of all evils. In fact, the first human creature, Adam, because he dared to transgress the law of the Lord, closed the doors of heaven and made us all subject to sin and death. For we have all sinned and we die in Adam, not in Eve. Moreover, his eldest son [Cain] opened the doors of Hell: he was the first envious person, the first homicide, the first fratricide, the first who despaired of the mercy of God. The first bigamist was Lamech. The first to get drunk was Noah; the first to bare the shamefulness of his father was Ham, the son of Noah. The first to be at once tyrant and idolater was Nimrod. The first adulterer was a man; the first incestuous person was a man.

Even in the time of Joshua and of King David men engaged in plunder, operating in gangs so numerous that they set up "princes" of their bands; even today there is an infinite number of them. Hence, all the prisons are filled with men and all gallows everywhere are laden with corpses of men.

Women, to the contrary, have invented all the liberal arts, every virtue and benefit, which the very names of the arts and virtues—being feminine in gender—show better than anything.

But since the excessive tyranny of men prevails over divine right and natural law, the freedom that was once accorded to women is in our day obstructed by unjust laws, suppressed by custom and usage, reduced to nothing by education. For as soon as she is born a woman is confined in idleness at home from her earliest years, and, as if incapable of functions more important, she has no other prospect than needle and thread. Further, when she has reached the age of puberty, she is delivered over to the jealous power of a husband, or she is enclosed forever in a workhouse for religious. She is forbidden by law to hold public office; even the most shrewd among them are not permitted to bring a suit in court.

A Serious Proposal to the Ladies

BY MARY ASTELL

Mary Astell wrote and advocated for educational opportunities for women at a time when their education was not prioritized and they were not allowed to own property. Astell was supported by patrons like Lady Anne Coventry, Lady Elizabeth Hastings, and John Norris. Along with her feminist writings, Astell was involved in contemporary political, religious, and philosophical debates and authored several books critical of the work of John Norris and John Locke. Often called "the first English feminist," she argued that the main reason for women's reputation for so-called frivolity and lack of intellect was that they were denied access to the same education as men rather than their inferior ability. She anonymously authored several groundbreaking pamphlets and books, including 1694's *A Serious Proposal to the Ladies*, which called for equal education for women and urged women to take up a life of the mind.

Now as to the Proposal it is to erect a *Monastery*, or if you will (to avoid giving offense to the scrupulous and injudicious, by names which tho' innocent in themselves, have been abus'd by superstitious Practices,) we will call it a *Religious Retirement*, and such as shall have a double aspect, being not only a Retreat from the World for those who desire that advantage, but likewise, an institution and previous discipline, to fit us to do the greatest good in it; such an institution as this (if I do not mightily deceive my self,) would be the most probable method to amend the present and improve the future Age. . . .

You are therefore Ladies, invited into a place, where you shall suffer no other confinement, but to be kept out of the road Of Sin: You shall not be depriv'd of your Grandeur, but only exchange the vain Pomps and Pageantry of the world, empty Titles and Forms of State, for the true and solid Greatness of being able to despise *them*. You will only quit the Chat of insignificant people for an ingenious Conversation; the froth of flashy Wit for real Wisdom; idle tales for instructive discourses. The deceitful Flatteries of those who under pretense of loving and admiring you, really served their *own* base ends, for the seasonable Reproofs and wholsom Counsels of your hearty well-wishers and affectionate Friends, which will procure you those perfections your feigned lovers pretended you had, and kept you from obtaining. . . .

[Y]our Retreat shall be so manag'd as not to exclude the good Works of an *Active*, from the pleasure and serenity of a *contemplative* Life, but by a due mixture of both retain all the advantages and avoid the inconveniences that attend either. It shall not so cut you off from the world as to hinder you from bettering and improving it, but rather qualify you to do it the greatest Good, and be a Seminary to stock the Kingdom with pious and prudent Ladies; whose good Example it is to be hop'd, will so influence the rest of their Sex, that Women may no longer pass for those little useless and impertinent Animals, which the ill conduct of too many has caus'd them to be mistaken for.

We have hitherto consider'd our Retirement only in relation to Religion, which is indeed its *main*, I may say its *only* design; nor can this be thought too contracting a word, since Religion is the adequate business of our lives, and largely consider'd, takes in all we have to do. . . . But because, as we have all along observ'd, Religion never appears in its true Beauty, but when it is accompanied with Wisdom and Discretion; and that without a good Understanding, we can scarce be *truly*, but never *eminently* Good; being liable to a thousand seductions and mistakes; for even the men themselves, if they have not a competent degree of Knowledge, they are carried about with every wind of Doctrine. Therefore, one great end of this institution, shall be to expel that cloud of Ignorance, which Custom has involv'd us in, to furnish our minds with a stock of solid and useful Knowledge, that the Souls of Women may no longer be the only unadorn'd and neglected things. . . .

For since GOD has given Women as well as Men intelligent Souls, why should they be forbidden to improve them? Since he has not denied us the faculty of Thinking, why shou'd we not (at least in gratitude to him) employ our Thoughts on himself their noblest Object, and not unworthily bestow them on Trifles and Gaities and secular Affairs? Being the Soul was created for the contemplation of Truth as well as for the fruition of Good, is it not as cruel and unjust to preclude Women from the knowledge of the one, as well as from the enjoyment of the other? . . .

We pretend not that Women shou'd teach in the Church, or usurp Authority where it is not allow'd them; permit us only to understand our *own* duty, and not be forc'd to take it upon trust from others; to be at least so far learned, as to be able to form in our minds a true Idea of Christianity. . . .

But since such Seminaries are thought proper for the Men, since they enjoy the fruits of those Noble Ladies' Bounty who were the foundresses of several of their Colleges, why shou'd we not think that such ways of Education wou'd be as advantageous to the Ladies? or why shou'd we despair of finding some among them who will be as kind to their own Sex as their Ancestors have been to the other? . . .

The Men therefore may still enjoy their Prerogatives for us, we mean not to intrench on any of their Lawful Privileges, our only Contention shall be that they may not out-do us in promoting his Glory who is Lord both of them and us; And by all that appears the generality will not oppose us in this matter, we shall not provoke them by striving to be better Christians. They may busy their Heads with Affairs of State, and spend their Time and Strength in recommending themselves to an uncertain Master, or a more giddy Multitude, our only endeavor shall be to be absolute Monarchs in our own Bosoms. They shall still if they please dispute about Religion, let 'em only give us leave to Understand and Practice it . . .

A Brief Summary, in Plain Language, of the Most Important Laws concerning Women;

Together with a Few Observations Thereon

BY BARBARA LEIGH SMITH BODICHON

In 1854, Barbara Leigh Smith Bodichon—an English educationist, artist, and a leading mid-nineteenth-century feminist and women's rights activist—published *A Brief Summary in Plain Language of the Most Important Laws concerning Women*, which was crucial in the passage of the Married Women's Property Act. In the tract, she outlined the restrictive laws women were forced to live with and also, in accessible language, articulated the few reasonable rights afforded to women. Not only did she write an influential legal text without any formal legal training but that text managed to pass muster with the "men of law." Bodichon, who co-founded the *English Woman's Journal* in 1858, also organized and led a highly effective campaign that served as a model for future forms of legal activism.

LAWS CONCERNING WOMEN.

Legal Condition of Unmarried Women or Spinsters.

A single woman has the same rights to property, to protection from the law, and has to pay the same taxes to the State, as a man.

Yet a woman of the age of twenty-one, having the requisite property qualifications, cannot vote in elections for members of Parliament.

A woman duly qualified can vote upon parish questions, and for parish officers, overseers, surveyors, vestry clerks, &c.

If her father or mother die *intestate* (*i.e.*, without a will) she takes an equal share with her brothers and sisters of the personal property (*i.e.*, goods, chattels, moveables), but her eldest brother, if she have one, and his children, even daughters, will take the *real* property (*i.e.*, not personal property, but all other, as land, &c.), as the heir-at-law; males and their issue being preferred to females; if, however, she have sisters only, then all the sisters take the real property equally. If she be an only child, she is entitled to all the intestate real and personal property.

The church and nearly all offices under government are closed to women. The Post-office affords some little employment to them; but there is no important office which they can hold, with the single exception of that of Sovereign.

The professions of law and medicine, whether or not closed by law, are closed in fact. They may engage in trade, and may occupy inferior situations, such as matron of a charity, sextoness of a church, and a few parochial offices are open to them. Women are occasionally governors of prisons for women, overseers of the poor, and parish clerks. A woman may be ranger of a park; a woman can take part in the government of a great empire by buying East India Stock.

A servant and a master or mistress are bound by a verbal or written agreement. If no special agreement is made, a servant is held by the common custom of the realm to be hired from year to year, and the engagement cannot be put an end to without a month's notice on either side.

If a woman is seduced, she has no remedy against the seducer; nor has her father, excepting as he is considered in law as being her master and she his servant, and the seducer as having deprived him of her services. Very slight service is deemed sufficient in law, but evidence of some service is absolutely necessary, whether the daughter be of full age or under age.

These are the only special laws concerning single women: the law speaks of men only, but women are affected by all the laws and incur the same responsibilities in all their contracts and doings as men.

Laws Concerning Married Women.

Matrimony is a civil and indissoluble contract between a consenting man and woman of competent capacity.

These marriages are prohibited:—A widower with his deceased wife's sister; a widow with the brother of her deceased husband; a widower with his deceased wife's sister's daughter, for she is by affinity in the same degree as a niece to her uncle by consanguinity; a widower with a daughter of his deceased wife by a former husband; and a widower with his deceased wife's mother's sister. Consanguinity or affinity, where the children are illegitimate, is equally an impediment.

A lunatic or idiot cannot lawfully contract a marriage, but insanity after marriage does not make the marriage null and void.

A lunatic may contract a marriage during a lucid interval. Deaf and dumb people may marry by signs.

The consent of the father or guardians is necessary to the marriage of an *infant* (*i.e.*, a person under twenty-one), unless the marriage takes place by banns. The consent of the mother is not necessary if there be a father or a guardian appointed by him.

A second marriage while a husband or wife is living is felony, and punishable by transportation.

An agreement to marry made by a man and woman who do not come under any of these disabilities is a contract of betrothment, and either party can bring an action upon a refusal to complete the contract in a superior court of Common Law.

Marriages may be celebrated as a religious ceremony after the requisite public proclamations or banns, or as a secular form.

The object of the Act for authorizing civil marriages was to relieve Dissenters and those who could not conscientiously join in the formulary of the Church. Due provision is made for necessary publicity, and the marriage can be legally contracted in a Register Office. Marriages in the Church of England (without banns or license), marriages of Quakers, Jews, Dissenters, and Roman Catholics, and marriages according to the civil or secular form, must be preceded by a given notice from one of the parties to the Superintendent-Registrar of the district.

The marriage law of Scotland is founded upon the *Canon* Law (*i.e.*, rules drawn from Scriptures and the writings of the Church).

In Scotland there are regular and irregular marriages. Irregular marriages are legal without any ceremony, and are of three sorts.

1. By a promise of marriage given in writing or proved by a reference to the oath of the party, followed by consummation.

2. By the solemn mutual declaration of a man and woman, either verbally or in writing, expressing that the parties consent to take each other for husband and wife.

3. By notorious cohabitation as man and wife.

Persons living in England and having illegitimate children, cannot by going to Scotland, there marrying, and then returning, legitimatize their children in England. A domicile (or abiding home) in Scotland, and a marriage of the father and mother, legitimatizes the children in Scotland whenever born.

Lawful marriages in foreign countries are valid in England unless they are directly contrary to our laws.

Marriage with a deceased wife's sister is valid in England, if it has been celebrated in a country where such marriage is legal, provided the parties were at the time of the marriage domiciled in such country.

A man and wife are one person in law; the wife loses all her rights as a single woman, and her existence is entirely absorbed in that of her husband. He is civilly responsible for her acts; she lives under his protection or cover, and her condition is called coverture.

A woman's body belongs to her husband; she is in his custody, and he can enforce his right by a writ of *habeas corpus.*

What was her personal property before marriage, such as money in hand, money at the bank, jewels, household goods, clothes, &c., becomes absolutely her husband's, and he may assign or dispose of them at his pleasure whether he and his wife live together or not.

A wife's *chattels real* (*i.e.*, estates held during a term of years, or the next presentation to a church living, &c.) become her husband's by his doing some act to appropriate them; but, if the wife survives, she resumes her property.

Equity is defined to be a correction or qualification of the law, generally made in the part wherein it faileth, or is too severe. In other words, the correction of that wherein the law, by reason of its universality, is deficient. While the Common Law gives the whole of a wife's personal property to her husband, the Courts of Equity, when he proceeds therein to recover property in right of his wife, oblige him to make a settlement of some portion of it upon her, if she be unprovided for and virtuous.

If her property be under 200*l.*, or 10*l.* a-year, a Court of Equity will not interpose.

Neither the Courts of Common Law nor Equity have any direct power to oblige a man to support his wife,—the Ecclesiastical Courts (*i.e.*, Courts held by the Queen's authority as governor of the Church, for matters which chiefly concern religion) and a Magistrate's court at the instance of her parish alone can do this.

A husband has a freehold estate in his wife's lands during the joint existence of himself and his wife, that is to say, he has absolute possession of them as long as they both live. If the wife dies without children, the property goes to her heir, but if she has borne a child, her husband holds possession until his death.

Money earned by a married woman belongs absolutely to her husband; that and all sources of income, excepting those mentioned above, are included in the term personal property.

By the particular permission of her husband she can make a will of her personal property, for by such a permission he gives up his right. But he may revoke his permission at any time before *probate* (*i.e.*, the exhibiting and proving a will before the Ecclesiastical Judge having jurisdiction over the place where the party died).

The legal custody of children belongs to the father. During the life-time of a sane father, the mother has no rights over her children, except a limited power over infants, and the father may take them from her and dispose of them as he thinks fit.

If there be a legal separation of the parents, and there be neither agreement nor order of Court, giving the custody of the children to either parent, then the *right to the custody of the children* (except for the nutriment of infants) belongs legally to the father.

A married woman cannot sue or be sued for contracts—nor can she enter into contracts except as the agent of her husband; that is to say, her word alone is not binding in law, and persons giving a wife credit have no remedy against her. There are some exceptions, as where she contracts debts upon estates settled to her separate use, or where a wife carries on trade separately, according to the custom of London, &c.

A husband is liable for his wife's debts contracted before marriage, and also for her breaches of trust committed before marriage.

Neither a husband nor a wife can be witnesses against one another in criminal cases, not even after the death or divorce of either.

A wife cannot bring actions unless the husband's name is joined.

As the wife acts under the command and control of her husband, she is excused from punishment for certain offenses, such as theft, burglary, housebreaking, &c., if committed in his presence and under his influence. A wife cannot be found guilty of concealing her felon husband or of concealing a felon jointly with her husband. She cannot be found guilty of stealing from her husband or of setting his house on fire, as they are one person in law. A husband and wife cannot be found guilty of conspiracy, as that offense cannot be committed unless there are two persons.

Usual Precautions Against the Laws Concerning the Property of Married Women.

When a woman has consented to a proposal of marriage, she cannot dispose or give away her property without the knowledge of her betrothed; if she make any such disposition without his knowledge, even if he be ignorant of the existence of her property, the disposition will not be legal.

It is usual, before marriage, in order to secure a wife and her children against the power of the husband, to make with his consent a settlement of some property on the wife, or to make an agreement before marriage that a settlement shall be made after marriage. It is in the power of the Court of Chancery to enforce the performance of such agreements.

Although the Common Law does not allow a married woman to possess any property, yet in respect of property settled for her separate use, Equity endeavors to treat her as a single woman.

She can acquire such property by contract before marriage with her husband, or by gift from him or other persons.

There are great difficulties and complexities in making settlements, and they should always be made by a competent lawyer.

When a wife's property is stolen, the property (legally belonging to the husband) must be laid as his in the indictment.

Separation and Divorce.

A husband and wife can separate upon a deed containing terms for their immediate separation, but they cannot legally agree to separate at a *future* time. The trustees of the wife must be parties to the deed, and agree with the husband as to what property the wife is to take, for a husband and wife cannot covenant together. Divorce is of two kinds:—

1st. Divorce à mensâ et thoro, being only a separation from bed and board.

2nd. Divorce à vinculo matrimonii, being an entire dissolution of the bonds of matrimony.

The grounds for the first kind of divorce are, 1st. Adultery, 2nd. Intolerable Cruelty, and 3rd. Unnatural Practices. The Ecclesiastical Courts can do no more than pronounce for this first kind of divorce, or rather separation, as the matrimonial tie is not severed, and there is always a possibility of reconciliation.

The law cannot dissolve a lawful marriage; it is only in the Legislature that this power is vested. It requires an act of Parliament to constitute a divorce à vinculo matrimonii, but the investigation rests by usage with the Lords alone, the House of Commons acting upon the faith that the House of Lords came to a just conclusion.

This divorce is pronounced on account of adultery in the wife, and in some cases of aggravated adultery on the part of the husband.

The expenses of only a common divorce bill are between six hundred and seven hundred pounds, which makes the possibility of release from the matrimonial bond a privilege of the rich.

A wife cannot be plaintiff, defendant, or witness in an important part of the proceeding for a divorce, which evidently must lead to much injustice.

Laws Concerning a Widow.

A widow recovers her real property, but if there be a settlement she is restricted by its provisions. She recovers her chattels real if her husband has not disposed of them by will or otherwise.

A wife's paraphernalia (*i.e.*, her clothes and ornaments) which her husband owns during his lifetime, and which his creditors can seize for his debts, becomes her property on his death.

A widow is liable for any debts which she contracted before marriage, and which have been left unpaid during her marriage.

A widow is not bound to bury her dead husband, it being the duty of his legal representative.

If a man die intestate, the widow, if there are children, is entitled to one-third of the personalty; if there are no children, to one-half: the other is distributed among the next of kin, among whom the widow is not counted. If there is no next of kin the moiety goes to the crown.

A husband can, of course, by will deprive a wife of all right in the personalty.

A right is granted in Magna Charta to a widow to remain forty days in her husband's house after his death, provided she do not marry during that time.

A widow has a right to a third of her husband's lands and tenements for her life. Right of dower is generally superseded by settlements giving the wife a jointure. If she accept a jointure she has no claim to dower.

Laws Concerning Women in Other Relationships.

A woman can act as agent for another, and, as an attorney, legally execute her authority. A wife can so act if her husband do not dissent.

An unmarried woman can be vested with a trust, but if she marry, the complexities and difficulties are great, from her inability to enter alone into deeds and assurances.

A single woman can act as executrix under a will, but a wife cannot accept an executorship without her husband's consent.

A woman is capable of holding the office of administratrix to an intestate personalty, and administration will be granted to her if she be next of kin to the intestate. But a wife cannot act without the consent of her husband.

If a man place a woman in his house, and treat her as his wife, he is responsible for her debts.

Laws Concerning Illegitimate Children and Their Mothers.

A single woman having a child may throw the maintenance upon the putative father, so called to distinguish him from a husband, until the age of thirteen.

The law only enforces the parents to maintain such child, and the sum the father is obliged to pay, after an order of affiliation is proved against him, never exceeds two shillings and sixpence a week.

The mother, as long as she is unmarried or a widow, is bound to maintain such child as a part of her family until such child attain the age of sixteen.

A man marrying a woman having a child or children at the time of such marriage is bound to support them, whether legitimate or not, until the age of sixteen.

The rights of an illegitimate child are only such as he can acquire; he can inherit nothing, being in law looked upon as nobody's son, but he may acquire property by devise or bequest. He may acquire a surname by reputation, but does not inherit one.

The only incapacity under which he labors is that he cannot be heir-at-law nor next of kin to any person, nor can he have collateral heirs, but only lineal descendants; if he acquire property and die without a will, such property will go to the crown unless he have lineal descendants.

REMARKS.

These are the principal laws concerning women.

It is not now as it once was, when all existing institutions were considered sacred and unalterable; and the spirit which made Blackstone an admirer of, rather than a critic on, every law because it was *law*, is exchanged for a bolder and more discriminating spirit, which seeks to judge calmly what is good and to amend what is bad.

Philosophical thinkers have generally come to the conclusion that the tendency of progress is gradually to dispense with law,—that is to say, as each individual man becomes unto himself a law, less external restraint is necessary. And certainly the most urgently needed reforms are simple erasures from the statute book. Women, more than any other members of the community, suffer from over-legislation.

A woman of twenty-one becomes an independent human creature, capable of holding and administering property to any amount; or, if she can earn money, she may appropriate her earnings freely to any purpose she thinks good. Her father has no power over her or her property. But if she unites herself to a man, the law immediately steps in, and she finds herself legislated for, and her condition of life suddenly and entirely changed. Whatever age she may be of, she is again considered as an infant,—she is again under "*reasonable restraint*,"—she loses her separate existence, and is merged in that of her husband.

"In short," says Judge Hurlbut, "a woman is courted and wedded as an angel, and yet denied the dignity of a rational and moral being ever after."

"The next thing that I will show you is this particularitie of law; in this consolidation which we call wedlock is a locking together; it is true that man and wife are one person, but understand in what manner. When a small brooke or little river incorporateth with Rhodanus, Humber, or the Thames, the poore rivulet loseth her name, it is carried and recarried with the new associate, it beareth no sway, it possesseth nothing during coverture. A woman as soone as she is married is called covert, in Latine nupta, that is vailed, as it were clouded and overshadowed she hath lost her streame. I may more truly farre away say to a married woman, her new selfe is her superior, her companion, her master. The mastership shee is fallen into may be called in a terme which civilians borrow from Esop's Fables, Leonina societate."

Truly "she hath lost her streame," she is absorbed, and can hold nothing of herself, she has no legal right to any property; not even her clothes, books, and household goods are her own, and any money which she earns can be robbed from her legally by her husband, nay, even after the commencement of a treaty of marriage she cannot dispose of her own property without the knowledge of her betrothed. If she should do so, it is deemed a fraud in law and can be set aside after marriage as an injury to her husband.

It is always said, even by those who support the existing law, that it is in fact never acted upon by men of good feeling. That is true; but the very admission condemns the law, and it is not right that the good feeling of men should be all that a woman can look to for simple justice.

There is now a large and increasing class of women who gain their own livelihood, and the abolition of the laws which give husbands this unjust power is most urgently needed.

Rich men and fathers might still make what settlements they pleased, and appoint trustees for the protection of minors and such women as needed protection; but we imagine it well proved that the principle of protection is wrong, and that the education of freedom and responsibility will enable women to take better care of themselves and others too than can be insured to them by any legal precautions.

Upon women of the laboring classes the difficulty of keeping and using their own earnings presses most hardly. In that rank of life where the support of the family depends often on the joint earnings of husband and wife, it is indeed cruel that the earnings of both should be in the hands of one, and not even in the hands of that one who has naturally the strongest desire to promote the welfare of the children.

All who are familiar with the working classes know how much suffering and privation is caused by the exercise of this *right* by drunken and bad men. It is true that men are legally bound to support their wives and children, but this does not compensate women for the loss of their moral right to their own property and earnings, nor for the loss of the mental development and independence of character gained by the possession and thoughtful appropriation of money; nor, it must be remembered, can the claim to support be enforced on the part of the wife unless she appeals to a court of law. Alas, how much will not a woman endure before she will publicly plead for a maintenance!

Why, we ask, should there be this difference between the married and unmarried condition of women? And why does marriage make so little legal difference to men, and such a mighty legal difference to women? In France it is somewhat more equal; married women have a right, if they marry without a marriage contract, to claim at the death of a husband half of whatever he possessed at the time of marriage, or may have gained afterward. If a woman have property of her own, she may if she please marry under the "régime de séparation de corps et de biens," in which case she has the entire control of her own fortune, and has no need of trustees. But usually marriages in France are of another description, or under the "régime dotal," in which case a portion of the property of the wife is left at the disposal of the husband, and the rest placed in the hands of trustees, much as it is with us in England. The choice which the French law allows is however a great improvement on our law.

In Turkey, daughters succeed equally with sons in houses and landed property, and always take one-third of the personal property. A widow receives one-eighth of the personal property, and must be provided for during her life by the heirs. Women control their own inheritance when married; the husband has no power over the inherited portion of his wife or wives.

In Hungary, the common law, before 1849 (the German law is now introduced), made a broad distinction between *inherited* and *acquired* property, whether landed or personal. Whatever was inherited went to the heirs; it could not be subject to a will.

As to *acquired* property, the law only interfered to give half to the wife; it was her absolute property, of which she might dispose in any way during life or by will. Among the nobility this law did not obtain. In cases where inherited property had been so left by the will of the first *acquisitor* as to exclude the female sex, the brothers were oblige to give a handsome sum if they married to their sisters, and provide for them in a becoming way if they remained single.

The rights of a widow were great; she was guardian of children, administrator of property, and, as long as she bore the name of her husband, she could exercise all the political rights of a man;

she could vote in elections of county officers, and in those of the Deputies to the Diet.

Single females, according to the Hungarian law, were considered as minors, who became of age upon marriage, and by marriage came into full control of all their estates. They were not liable for the debts of their husbands; they were not even bound to provide for the domestic expenses, the care of providing for the house and the education of the children being incumbent on the husband. Wives could make wills and sign deeds without the consent of the husbands. If a wife died intestate, her property went to her children or collaterals.

In fact a wife was not regarded in Hungary as a minor, her husband was not her guardian, nor were there trustees appointed for her property. "None of my countrywomen would ever have submitted to such a marriage settlement as is usual in England," said a Hungarian lady, well known for her genius and reputation. With the one exception of considering all unmarried women as minors, the Hungarian law is very much in advance of ours.

The laws in the United States are generally much the same as ours. As a general rule married women cannot make a devise of real estate. In some of the States there are more reasonable laws, and a married woman may make a will and devise lands in the same manner as men. These States are Ohio, Illinois, Connecticut, Mississippi, and Louisiana. In Ohio the laws are remarkably liberal to women. The first section of the statute of wills in Ohio declares that any person of full age and sound mind and memory may make a will. By the statute of Ohio it is expressly provided that the will of an unmarried woman shall *not* be revoked by her subsequent marriage.

What changes we find in the American laws are improvements upon ours. Is there not evidence in our English laws of old opinions relating to women which are passing away with the old state of things which engendered them? In the early times, when women were obliged by the violent state of society to be always under the guardianship of father, brother, or husband, these laws might be necessary; but in our peaceful times, such guardianship is proved to be superfluous by the fact of the secure, honorable, and independent position of single women who are sufficiently protected by the sanctuary of civilization.

Since all the unmarried women in England are supported either by their own exertions or by the exertions or bequests of their fathers and relations, there is no reason why upon marriage they should be thrown upon the pecuniary resources of their husbands, except in so far as the claims of a third party—children—may lessen the wife's power of earning money, at the same time that it increases her expenses. Of course a woman may, and often does, by acting as housekeeper and manager of her husband's concerns, earn a maintenance and a right to share in his property, independent of any children which may come of the marriage. But it is evident that daughters ought to have some sure provision—either a means of gaining their own bread, or property—as it is most undesirable that they should look upon marriage as a means of livelihood.

Fathers seldom feel inclined to trust their daughters' fortunes in the power of a husband, and, in the appointment of trustees, partially elude the law by a legal device. Also, the much abused Court of Chancery tries to palliate the Common Law, and recognizes a separate interest between husband and wife, and allows the wife alone to file a bill to recover and protect her property, and trustees are not necessary if there has been an agreement.

Why should not these legal devices be done away with, by the simple abolition of a law which we have outgrown?

We do not say that these laws of property are the only unjust laws concerning women to be found in the short summary which we have given, but they form a simple, tangible, and not offensive point of attack.

THE END.

Are Women a Class?

BY LILLIE DEVEREUX BLAKE

Blake was already a published writer when the 1859 death of her husband made writing her main source of income. During an era when women couldn't vote or own property, Blake became an impassioned advocate and public speaker, a Civil War correspondent and activist. She led successful campaigns to establish pensions for Civil War nurses (1892), open civil service positions to women, give women joint custody of their children, enable women to serve on school boards, and allow women to work in institutions where women were incarcerated. Blake was active in the suffrage movement, but she later broke with Susan B. Anthony over their differing views on women's roles in the movement. Anthony and her followers emphasized the "separate spheres" ideology and women's innate moral authority as justification for their right to suffrage. Blake argued that gender roles are learned behaviors and socially constructed and therefore women should have the same rights as men—a theory that was radical for her time. Many of her writings were lost to purges, and her contributions to the suffrage movement were elided because of her rift with Anthony. Fortunately, this brief tract has survived. In it, Blake grapples with the question of whether women are a distinct class of people. This question has a far more definitive answer in this day and age, but in the nineteenth century, Blake's query was radical.

Are the women of this country to be regarded as a distinct class of people? If that is the case, then Miss Anthony—(we like better her plain Quaker name of Susan, which some of our brethren are doing their worst to trail in the mire)—if that is the case, we say, then Susan holds a logical position.

If, however, the opposite doctrine is true, then all that distinctive phase of the Woman Suffrage movement which is represented by Susan B. Anthony, must be regarded as pure moonshine, and entirely destitute of fructifying promise.

As a new comer into the ranks of the advocates of suffrage, one having only enjoyed the honor of Miss Anthony's acquaintance a short time, and not familiar with all her public utterances, I propose to confine my observations to this especial part of the article. To me it seems as if Miss Anthony had very much of reason in claiming that women so far as laws and representation are concerned, are a different class from men.

The opponents of Woman Suffrage frame their argument something like this. "Women are not a distinct class of the community, their interests are identical with those of the men among whom they live, and as they are feebler than men, their proper pursuits evidently within doors, therefore men ought to vote for them." Now let us see how men would like a similar course of reasoning as applied to themselves. Everyone knows that the number of men who vote at every election greatly complicate the difficulties of carrying it on, and increase the opportunities for fraud. Suppose, to remedy this, a law should be passed making physical strength the requisite for the ballot. This would exactly suit the opponents of Woman Suffrage, who think that women ought not to vote because they cannot do military duty—suppose then a law was to be framed declaring that only men who are six feet tall and can lift five hundred pounds shall vote, this would be fair, would it not? The interests of these men would be identical with that of the others, among whom they lived, and as the pursuits of many of these public men are within doors, therefore they ought to be content to let the strong men vote for them.

Lengthy comment is unnecessary. This proposition is as fair as the other, and yet what a storm of indignation it would raise to propose it! Those smaller men would declare that no one person can vote for another, that property and intellect, and not brute force ought to be the requisite for the ballot, and so one with most of the arguments now advanced for Woman Suffrage. Well, now it is as fair to claim that women are a class requiring the ballot as much as small men or even foreign men, or colored men; indeed I may say it would be fairer to let the native born American dry-goods man vote for the Irish and negro dry-goods man, than to allow the dry-goods husband to vote for the school teaching wife, the political interests here of the two being perchance at variance.

Every argument advanced to prove that women and men have different "spheres" in life and diverse places in the world, goes to prove that their interests must differ, and that women and men do form distinct classes. For to illustrate, if all women were to remain at home, merely caring for their households and children, while all men were to go out as workers, a radical difference of interests in political questions would spring up at once, the women as consumers might find free trade to their benefit, while the men as producers might desire various kinds of protection. It is this sort of difference of interests, coupled with the fact that while perhaps one half the women of the country have husbands able to provide for them, the other half either have no husbands at all, or must work for their living because the husband cannot earn it, which causes Miss Anthony and others to urge that this great class of the community require the ballot to give them direct representation.

The Yellow Wall-Paper

BY CHARLOTTE PERKINS GILMAN

Charlotte Perkins Gilman wrote poetry, articles, and novels, and advocated for social reform for women. In 1903 she wrote one of her most critically acclaimed books, *The Home: Its Work and Influence*, which expanded upon her earlier *Women and Economics,* exploring the ways women were oppressed in the home and how their environments should be modified to facilitate better mental health. From 1909 to 1916, Gilman single-handedly wrote and edited her own magazine, *The Forerunner,* in which much of her fiction appeared, including the feminist utopian novel *Herland.* Perkins wrote her canonical 1892 short story "The Yellow Wall-Paper" about her experience with a three-month confinement or "rest cure" prescribed by her physician and enforced by her husband in response to her postpartum depression. The haunting story revealed the many ways medicine and patriarchal rules of marriage limited women's bodily autonomy in ways that were profoundly detrimental to their mental, emotional, and physical health.

It is very seldom that mere ordinary people like John and myself secure ancestral halls for the summer.

A colonial mansion, a hereditary estate, I would say a haunted house, and reach the height of romantic felicity—but that would be asking too much of fate!

Still I will proudly declare that there is something queer about it.

Else, why should it be let so cheaply? And why have stood so long untenanted?

John laughs at me, of course, but one expects that in marriage.

John is practical in the extreme. He has no patience with faith, an intense horror of superstition, and he scoffs openly at any talk of things not to be felt and seen and put down in figures.

John is a physician, and *perhaps*—(I would not say it to a living soul, of course, but this is dead paper and a great relief to my mind—) *perhaps* that is one reason I do not get well faster.

You see he does not believe I am sick!

And what can one do?

If a physician of high standing, and one's own husband, assures friends and relatives that there is really nothing the matter with one but temporary nervous depression—a slight hysterical tendency—what is one to do?

My brother is also a physician, and also of high standing, and he says the same thing.

So I take phosphates or phosphites—whichever it is, and tonics, and journeys, and air, and exercise, and am absolutely forbidden to "work" until I am well again.

Personally, I disagree with their ideas.

Personally, I believe that congenial work, with excitement and change, would do me good.

But what is one to do?

I did write for a while in spite of them; but it *does* exhaust me a good deal—having to be so sly about it, or else meet with heavy opposition.

I sometimes fancy that in my condition if I had less opposition and more society and stimulus—but John says the very worst thing I can do is to think about my condition, and I confess it always makes me feel bad.

So I will let it alone and talk about the house.

The most beautiful place! It is quite alone, standing well back from the road, quite three miles from the village. It makes me think of English places that you read about, for there are hedges and walls and gates that lock, and lots of separate little houses for the gardeners and people.

There is a *delicious* garden! I never saw such a garden—large and shady, full of box-ordered paths, and lined with long grape-covered arbors with seats under them.

There were greenhouses, too, but they are all broken now.

There was some legal trouble, I believe, something about the heirs and co-heirs; anyhow, the place has been empty for years.

That spoils my ghostliness, I am afraid, but I don't care—there is something strange about the house—I can feel it.

I even said so to John one moonlight evening, but he said what I felt was a *draught*, and shut the window.

I get unreasonably angry with John sometimes. I'm sure I never used to be so sensitive. I think it is due to this nervous condition.

But John says if I feel so, I shall neglect proper self-control; so I take pains to control myself—before him, at least, and that makes me very tired.

I don't like our room a bit. I wanted one downstairs that opened on the piazza and had roses all over the window, and such pretty old-fashioned chintz hangings! but John would not hear of it.

He said there was only one window and not room for two beds, and no near room for him if he took another.

He is very careful and loving, and hardly lets me stir without special direction.

I have a schedule prescription for each hour in the day; he takes all care from me, and so I feel basely ungrateful not to value it more.

He said we came here solely on my account, that I was to have perfect rest and all the air I could get. "Your exercise depends on your strength, my dear," said he, "and your food somewhat on your appetite; but air you can absorb all the time." So we took the nursery at the top of the house.

It is a big, airy room, the whole floor nearly, with windows that look all ways, and air and sunshine galore. It was nursery first and then playroom and gymnasium, I should judge; for the windows are barred for little children, and there are rings and things in the walls.

The paint and paper look as if a boys' school had used it. It is stripped off—the paper—in great patches all around the head of my bed, about as far as I can reach, and in a great place on the other side of the room low down. I never saw a worse paper in my life.

One of those sprawling flamboyant patterns committing every artistic sin.

It is dull enough to confuse the eye in following, pronounced enough to constantly irritate and provoke study, and when you follow the lame uncertain curves for a little distance they suddenly commit suicide—plunge off at outrageous angles, destroy themselves in unheard of contradictions.

The color is repellant, almost revolting; a smouldering unclean yellow, strangely faded by the slow-turning sunlight.

It is a dull yet lurid orange in some places, a sickly sulphur tint in others.

No wonder the children hated it! I should hate it myself if I had to live in this room long.

There comes John, and I must put this away,—he hates to have me write a word.

———

We have been here two weeks, and I haven't felt like writing before, since that first day.

I am sitting by the window now, up in this atrocious nursery, and there is nothing to hinder my writing as much as I please, save lack of strength.

John is away all day, and even some nights when his cases are serious.

I am glad my case is not serious!

But these nervous troubles are dreadfully depressing.

John does not know how much I really suffer. He knows there is no *reason* to suffer, and that satisfies him.

Of course it is only nervousness. It does weigh on me so not to do my duty in any way!

I meant to be such a help to John, such a real rest and comfort, and here I am a comparative burden already!

Nobody would believe what an effort it is to do what little I am able,—to dress and entertain, and order things.

It is fortunate Mary is so good with the baby. Such a dear baby!

And yet I *cannot* be with him, it makes me so nervous.

I suppose John never was nervous in his life. He laughs at me so about this wall-paper!

At first he meant to repaper the room, but afterwards he said that I was letting it get the better of me, and that nothing was worse for a nervous patient than to give way to such fancies.

He said that after the wall-paper was changed it would be the heavy bedstead, and then the barred windows, and then that gate at the head of the stairs, and so on.

"You know the place is doing you good," he said, "and really, dear, I don't care to renovate the house just for a three months' rental."

"Then do let us go downstairs," I said, "there are such pretty rooms there."

Then he took me in his arms and called me a blessed little goose, and said he would go down cellar, if I wished, and have it whitewashed into the bargain.

But he is right enough about the beds and windows and things.

It is an airy and comfortable room as any one need wish, and, of course, I would not be so silly as to make him uncomfortable just for a whim.

I'm really getting quite fond of the big room, all but that horrid paper.

Out of one window I can see the garden, those mysterious deep-shaded arbors, the riotous old-fashioned flowers, and bushes and gnarly trees.

Out of another I get a lovely view of the bay and a little private wharf belonging to the estate. There is a beautiful shaded lane that runs down there from the house. I always fancy I see people walking in these numerous paths and arbors, but John has cautioned me not to give way to fancy in the least. He says that with my imaginative power and habit of story-making, a nervous weakness like mine is sure to lead to all manner of excited fancies, and that I ought to use my will and good sense to check the tendency. So I try.

I think sometimes that if I were only well enough to write a little it would relieve the press of ideas and rest me.

But I find I get pretty tired when I try.

It is so discouraging not to have any advice and companionship about my work. When I get really well, John says we will ask Cousin Henry and Julia down for a long visit; but he says he would as soon put fireworks in my pillow-case as to let me have those stimulating people about now.

I wish I could get well faster.

But I must not think about that. This paper looks to me as if it *knew* what a vicious influence it had!

There is a recurrent spot where the pattern lolls like a broken neck and two bulbous eyes stare at you upside down.

I get positively angry with the impertinence of it and the everlastingness. Up and down and sideways they crawl, and those absurd, unblinking eyes are everywhere. There is one place where two breadths didn't match, and the eyes go all up and down the line, one a little higher than the other.

I never saw so much expression in an inanimate thing before, and we all know how much expression they have! I used to lie awake as a child and get more entertainment and terror out of blank walls and plain furniture than most children could find in a toystore.

I remember what a kindly wink the knobs of our big, old bureau used to have, and there was one chair that always seemed like a strong friend.

I used to feel that if any of the other things looked too fierce I could always hop into that chair and be safe.

The furniture in this room is no worse than inharmonious, however, for we had to bring it all from downstairs. I suppose when this was used as a playroom they had to take the nursery things out, and no wonder! I never saw such ravages as the children have made here.

The wall-paper, as I said before, is torn off in spots, and it sticketh closer than a brother—they must have had perseverance as well as hatred.

Then the floor is scratched and gouged and splintered, the plaster itself is dug out here and there, and this great heavy bed which is all we found in the room, looks as if it had been through the wars.

But I don't mind it a bit—only the paper.

There comes John's sister. Such a dear girl as she is, and so careful of me! I must not let her find me writing.

She is a perfect and enthusiastic housekeeper, and hopes for no better profession. I verily believe she thinks it is the writing which made me sick!

But I can write when she is out, and see her a long way off from these windows.

There is one that commands the road, a lovely shaded winding road, and one that just looks off over the country. A lovely country, too, full of great elms and velvet meadows.

This wall-paper has a kind of sub-pattern in a different shade, a particularly irritating one, for you can only see it in certain lights, and not clearly then.

But in the places where it isn't faded and where the sun is just so—I can see a strange, provoking, formless sort of figure, that seems to skulk about behind that silly and conspicuous front design.

There's sister on the stairs!

———

Well, the Fourth of July is over! The people are all gone and I am tired out. John thought it might do me good to see a little company, so we just had mother and Nellie and the children down for a week.

Of course I didn't do a thing. Jennie sees to everything now.

But it tired me all the same.

John says if I don't pick up faster he shall send me to Weir Mitchell in the fall.

But I don't want to go there at all. I had a friend who was in his hands once, and she says he is just like John and my brother, only more so!

Besides, it is such an undertaking to go so far.

I don't feel as if it was worth while to turn my hand over for anything, and I'm getting dreadfully fretful and querulous.

I cry at nothing, and cry most of the time.

Of course I don't when John is here, or anybody else, but when I am alone.

And I am alone a good deal just now. John is kept in town very often by serious cases, and Jennie is good and lets me alone when I want her to.

So I walk a little in the garden or down that lovely lane, sit on the porch under the roses, and lie down up here a good deal.

I'm getting really fond of the room in spite of the wall-paper. Perhaps *because* of the wall-paper.

It dwells in my mind so!

I lie here on this great immovable bed—it is nailed down, I believe—and follow that pattern about by the hour. It is as good as gymnastics, I assure you. I start, we'll say, at the bottom, down in the corner over there where it has not been touched, and I determine for the thousandth time that I *will* follow that pointless pattern to some sort of a conclusion.

I know a little of the principle of design, and I know this thing was not arranged on any laws of radiation, or alternation, or repetition, or symmetry, or anything else that I ever heard of.

It is repeated, of course, by the breadths, but not otherwise.

Looked at in one way each breadth stands alone, the bloated curves and flourishes—a kind of "debased Romanesque" with *delirium tremens*—go waddling up and down in isolated columns of fatuity.

But, on the other hand, they connect diagonally, and the sprawling outlines run off in great slanting waves of optic horror, like a lot of wallowing seaweeds in full chase.

The whole thing goes horizontally, too, at least it seems so, and I exhaust myself in trying to distinguish the order of its going in that direction.

They have used a horizontal breadth for a frieze, and that adds wonderfully to the confusion.

There is one end of the room where it is almost intact, and there, when the crosslights fade and the low sun shines directly upon it, I can almost fancy radiation after all,—the interminable grotesques seem to form around a common centre and rush off in headlong plunges of equal distraction.

It makes me tired to follow it. I will take a nap I guess.

———

I don't know why I should write this.

I don't want to.

I don't feel able.

And I know John would think it absurd. But I *must* say what I feel and think in some way—it is such a relief!

But the effort is getting to be greater than the relief.

Half the time now I am awfully lazy, and lie down ever so much.

John says I mustn't lose my strength, and has me take cod liver oil and lots of tonics and things, to say nothing of ale and wine and rare meat.

Dear John! He loves me very dearly, and hates to have me sick. I tried to have a real earnest reasonable talk with him the other day, and tell him how I wish he would let me go and make a visit to Cousin Henry and Julia.

But he said I wasn't able to go, nor able to stand it after I got there; and I did not make out a very good case for myself, for I was crying before I had finished.

It is getting to be a great effort for me to think straight. Just this nervous weakness I suppose.

And dear John gathered me up in his arms, and just carried me upstairs and laid me on the bed, and sat by me and read to me till it tired my head.

He said I was his darling and his comfort and all he had, and that I must take care of myself for his sake, and keep well.

He says no one but myself can help me out of it, that I must use my will and self-control and not let any silly fancies run away with me.

There's one comfort, the baby is well and happy, and does not have to occupy this nursery with the horrid wall-paper.

If we had not used it, that blessed child would have! What a fortunate escape! Why, I wouldn't have a child of mine, an impressionable little thing, live in such a room for worlds.

I never thought of it before, but it is lucky that John kept me here after all, I can stand it so much easier than a baby, you see.

Of course I never mention it to them any more—I am too wise,—but I keep watch of it all the same.

There are things in that paper that nobody knows but me, or ever will.

Behind that outside pattern the dim shapes get clearer every day.

It is always the same shape, only very numerous.

And it is like a woman stooping down and creeping about behind that pattern. I don't like it a bit. I wonder—I begin to think— I wish John would take me away from here!

It is so hard to talk with John about my case, because he is so wise, and because he loves me so.

But I tried it last night.

It was moonlight. The moon shines in all around just as the sun does.

I hate to see it sometimes, it creeps so slowly, and always comes in by one window or another.

John was asleep and I hated to waken him, so I kept still and watched the moonlight on that undulating wall-paper till I felt creepy.

The faint figure behind seemed to shake the pattern, just as if she wanted to get out.

I got up softly and went to feel and see if the paper *did* move, and when I came back John was awake.

"What is it, little girl?" he said. "Don't go walking about like that—you'll get cold."

I thought it was a good time to talk, so I told him that I really was not gaining here, and that I wished he would take me away.

"Why, darling!" said he, "our lease will be up in three weeks, and I can't see how to leave before.

"The repairs are not done at home, and I cannot possibly leave town just now. Of course if you were in any danger, I could and would, but you really are better, dear, whether you can see it or not. I am a doctor, dear, and I know. You are gaining flesh and color, your appetite is better, I feel really much easier about you."

"I don't weigh a bit more," said I, "nor as much; and my appetite may be better in the evening when you are here, but it is worse in the morning when you are away!"

"Bless her little heart!" said he with a big hug, "she shall be as sick as she pleases! But now let's improve the shining hours by going to sleep, and talk about it in the morning!"

"And you won't go away?" I asked gloomily.

"Why, how can I, dear? It is only three weeks more and then we will take a nice little trip of a few days while Jennie is getting the house ready. Really dear you are better!"

"Better in body perhaps—" I began, and stopped short, for he sat up straight and looked at me with such a stern, reproachful look that I could not say another word.

"My darling," said he, "I beg of you, for my sake and for our child's sake, as well as for your own, that you will never for one instant let that idea enter your mind! There is nothing so dangerous, so fascinating, to a temperament like yours. It is a false and foolish fancy. Can you not trust me as a physician when I tell you so?"

So of course I said no more on that score, and we went to sleep before long. He thought I was asleep first, but I wasn't, and lay there for hours trying to decide whether that front pattern and the back pattern really did move together or separately.

———

On a pattern like this, by daylight, there is a lack of sequence, a defiance of law, that is a constant irritant to a normal mind.

The color is hideous enough, and unreliable enough, and infuriating enough, but the pattern is torturing.

You think you have mastered it, but just as you get well underway in following, it turns a back-somersault and there you are. It slaps you in the face, knocks you down, and tramples upon you. It is like a bad dream.

The outside pattern is a florid arabesque, reminding one of a fungus. If you can imagine a toadstool in joints, an interminable string of toadstools, budding and sprouting in endless convolutions—why, that is something like it.

That is, sometimes!

There is one marked peculiarity about this paper, a thing nobody seems to notice but myself, and that is that it changes as the light changes.

When the sun shoots in through the east window—I always watch for that first long, straight ray—it changes so quickly that I never can quite believe it.

That is why I watch it always.

By moonlight—the moon shines in all night when there is a moon—I wouldn't know it was the same paper.

At night in any kind of light, in twilight, candlelight, lamplight, and worst of all by moonlight, it becomes bars! The outside pattern I mean, and the woman behind it is as plain as can be.

I didn't realize for a long time what the thing was that showed behind, that dim sub-pattern, but now I am quite sure it is a woman.

By daylight she is subdued, quiet. I fancy it is the pattern that keeps her so still. It is so puzzling. It keeps me quiet by the hour.

I lie down ever so much now. John says it is good for me, and to sleep all I can.

Indeed he started the habit by making me lie down for an hour after each meal.

It is a very bad habit I am convinced, for you see I don't sleep.

And that cultivates deceit, for I don't tell them I'm awake—O no!

The fact is I am getting a little afraid of John.

He seems very queer sometimes, and even Jennie has an inexplicable look.

It strikes me occasionally, just as a scientific hypothesis,—that perhaps it is the paper!

I have watched John when he did not know I was looking, and come into the room suddenly on the most innocent excuses, and I've caught him several times *looking at the paper!* And Jennie too. I caught Jennie with her hand on it once.

She didn't know I was in the room, and when I asked her in a quiet, a very quiet voice, with the most restrained manner possible, what she was doing with the paper—she turned around as if she had been caught stealing, and looked quite angry—asked me why I should frighten her so!

Then she said that the paper stained everything it touched, that she had found yellow smooches on all my clothes and John's, and she wished we would be more careful!

Did not that sound innocent? But I know she was studying that pattern, and I am determined that nobody shall find it out but myself!

———

Life is very much more exciting now than it used to be. You see I have something more to expect, to look forward to, to watch. I really do eat better, and am more quiet than I was.

John is so pleased to see me improve! He laughed a little the other day, and said I seemed to be flourishing in spite of my wall-paper.

I turned it off with a laugh. I had no intention of telling him it was *because* of the wall-paper—he would make fun of me. He might even want to take me away.

I don't want to leave now until I have found it out. There is a week more, and I think that will be enough.

I'm feeling ever so much better! I don't sleep much at night, for it is so interesting to watch developments; but I sleep a good deal in the daytime.

In the daytime it is tiresome and perplexing.

There are always new shoots on the fungus, and new shades of yellow all over it. I cannot keep count of them, though I have tried conscientiously.

It is the strangest yellow, that wall-paper! It makes me think of all the yellow things I ever saw—not beautiful ones like butter-cups, but old foul, bad yellow things.

But there is something else about that paper—the smell! I noticed it the moment we came into the room, but with so much air and sun it was not bad. Now we have had a week of fog and rain, and whether the windows are open or not, the smell is here.

It creeps all over the house.

I find it hovering in the dining-room, skulking in the parlor, hiding in the hall, lying in wait for me on the stairs.

It gets into my hair.

Even when I go to ride, if I turn my head suddenly and surprise it—there is that smell!

Such a peculiar odor, too! I have spent hours in trying to analyze it, to find what it smelled like.

It is not bad—at first, and very gentle, but quite the subtlest, most enduring odor I ever met.

In this damp weather it is awful, I wake up in the night and find it hanging over me.

It used to disturb me at first. I thought seriously of burning the house—to reach the smell.

But now I am used to it. The only thing I can think of that it is like is the *color* of the paper! A yellow smell.

There is a very funny mark on this wall, low down, near the mopboard. A streak that runs round the room. It goes behind every piece of furniture, except the bed, a long, straight, even *smooch*, as if it had been rubbed over and over.

I wonder how it was done and who did it, and what they did it for. Round and round and round—round and round and round—it makes me dizzy!

———

I really have discovered something at last.

Through watching so much at night, when it changes so, I have finally found out.

The front pattern *does* move—and no wonder! The woman behind shakes it!

Sometimes I think there are a great many women behind, and sometimes only one, and she crawls around fast, and her crawling shakes it all over.

Then in the very bright spots she keeps still, and in the very shady spots she just takes hold of the bars and shakes them hard.

And she is all the time trying to climb through. But nobody could climb through that pattern—it strangles so; I think that is why it has so many heads.

They get through, and then the pattern strangles them off and turns them upside down, and makes their eyes white!

If those heads were covered or taken off it would not be half so bad.

———

I think that woman gets out in the daytime!

And I'll tell you why—privately—I've seen her!

I can see her out of every one of my windows!

It is the same woman, I know, for she is always creeping, and most women do not creep by daylight.

I see her in that long shaded lane, creeping up and down. I see her in those dark grape arbors, creeping all around the garden.

I see her on that long road under the trees, creeping along, and when a carriage comes she hides under the blackberry vines.

I don't blame her a bit. It must be very humiliating to be caught creeping by daylight!

I always lock the door when I creep by daylight. I can't do it at night, for I know John would suspect something at once.

And John is so queer now, that I don't want to irritate him. I wish he would take another room! Besides, I don't want anybody to get that woman out at night but myself.

I often wonder if I could see her out of all the windows at once.

But, turn as fast as I can, I can only see out of one at one time.

And though I always see her, she *may* be able to creep faster than I can turn!

I have watched her sometimes away off in the open country, creeping as fast as a cloud shadow in a high wind.

If only that top pattern could be gotten off from the under one! I mean to try it, little by little.

I have found out another funny thing, but I shan't tell it this time! It does not do to trust people too much.

There are only two more days to get this paper off, and I believe John is beginning to notice. I don't like the look in his eyes.

And I heard him ask Jennie a lot of professional questions about me. She had a very good report to give.

She said I slept a good deal in the daytime.

John knows I don't sleep very well at night, for all I'm so quiet!

He asked me all sorts of questions, too, and pretended to be very loving and kind.

As if I couldn't see through him!

Still, I don't wonder he acts so, sleeping under this paper for three months.

It only interests me, but I feel sure John and Jennie are secretly affected by it.

Hurrah! This is the last day, but it is enough. John to stay in town over night, and won't be out until this evening.

Jennie wanted to sleep with me—the sly thing! but I told her I should undoubtedly rest better for a night all alone.

That was clever, for really I wasn't alone a bit! As soon as it was moonlight and that poor thing began to crawl and shake the pattern, I got up and ran to help her.

I pulled and she shook, I shook and she pulled, and before morning we had peeled off yards of that paper.

A strip about as high as my head and half around the room.

And then when the sun came and that awful pattern began to laugh at me, I declared I would finish it to-day!

We go away to-morrow, and they are moving all my furniture down again to leave things as they were before.

Jennie looked at the wall in amazement, but I told her merrily that I did it out of pure spite at the vicious thing.

She laughed and said she wouldn't mind doing it herself, but I must not get tired.

How she betrayed herself that time!

But I am here, and no person touches this paper but me,—not *alive!*

She tried to get me out of the room—it was too patent! But I said it was so quiet and empty and clean now that I believed I would lie down again and sleep all I could; and not to wake me even for dinner—I would call when I woke.

So now she is gone, and the servants are gone, and the things are gone, and there is nothing left but that great bedstead nailed down, with the canvas mattress we found on it.

We shall sleep downstairs to-night, and take the boat home to-morrow.

I quite enjoy the room, now it is bare again.

How those children did tear about here!

This bedstead is fairly gnawed!

But I must get to work.

I have locked the door and thrown the key down into the front path.

I don't want to go out, and I don't want to have anybody come in, till John comes.

I want to astonish him.

I've got a rope up here that even Jennie did not find. If that woman does get out, and tries to get away, I can tie her!

But I forgot I could not reach far without anything to stand on!

This bed will *not* move!

I tried to lift and push it until I was lame, and then I got so angry I bit off a little piece at one corner—but it hurt my teeth.

Then I peeled off all the paper I could reach standing on the floor. It sticks horribly and the pattern just enjoys it! All those strangled heads and bulbous eyes and waddling fungus growths just shriek with derision!

I am getting angry enough to do something desperate. To jump out of the window would be admirable exercise, but the bars are too strong even to try.

Besides I wouldn't do it. Of course not. I know well enough that a step like that is improper and might be misconstrued.

I don't like to *look* out of the windows even—there are so many of those creeping women, and they creep so fast.

I wonder if they all come out of that wall-paper as I did?

But I am securely fastened now by my well-hidden rope—you don't get *me* out in the road there!

I suppose I shall have to get back behind the pattern when it comes night, and that is hard!

It is so pleasant to be out in this great room and creep around as I please!

I don't want to go outside. I won't, even if Jennie asks me to.

For outside you have to creep on the ground, and everything is green instead of yellow.

But here I can creep smoothly on the floor, and my shoulder just fits in that long smooch around the wall, so I cannot lose my way.

Why there's John at the door!

It is no use, young man, you can't open it!

How he does call and pound!

Now he's crying for an axe.

It would be a shame to break down that beautiful door!

"John dear!" said I in the gentlest voice, "the key is down by the front steps, under a plantain leaf!"

That silenced him for a few moments.

Then he said—very quietly indeed, "Open the door, my darling!"

"I can't," said I. "The key is down by the front door under a plantain leaf!"

And then I said it again, several times, very gently and slowly, and said it so often that he had to go and see, and he got it of course, and came in. He stopped short by the door.

"What is the matter?" he cried. "For God's sake, what are you doing!"

I kept on creeping just the same, but I looked at him over my shoulder.

"I've got out at last," said I, "in spite of you and Jane! And I've pulled off most of the paper, so you can't put me back!"

Now why should that man have fainted? But he did, and right across my path by the wall, so that I had to creep over him every time!

The Higher Education of Women

BY ANNA JULIA COOPER

Born enslaved in 1859, Anna Julia Cooper lived a remarkable life as a feminist activist, scholar, and teacher. In 1925, she became the fourth African American woman to ever receive a PhD when she graduated from the Sorbonne in France. Cooper was very community oriented in everything she did and engaged in many efforts to enrich the Black community. In the 1890–1891 essay "The Higher Education of Women," Cooper argued for the importance of educating all women but particularly Black women so women could have agency, more ably contribute to society, and use their voices to be heard. Her call was meant to be both motivational and aspirational. "Let our girls feel that we expect something more of them than that they merely look pretty and appear well in society," Cooper wrote.

In the very first year of our century, the year 1801, there appeared in Paris a book by Sylvain Maréchal, entitled "Shall Woman Learn the Alphabet." The book proposes a law prohibiting the alphabet to women, and quotes authorities weighty and various, to prove that the woman who knows the alphabet has already lost part of her womanliness. The author declares that woman can use the alphabet only as Moliére predicted they would, in spelling out the verb *amo*; that they have no occasion to peruse Ovid's *Ars Amoris*, since that is already the ground and limit of their intuitive furnishing; that Madame Guyon would have been far more adorable had she remained a beautiful ignoramus as nature made her; that Ruth, Naomi, the Spartan woman, the Amazons, Penelope, Andromache, Lucretia, Joan of Arc, Petrarch's Laura, the daughters of Charlemagne, could not spell their names; while Sappho, Aspasia, Madame de Maintenon, and Madame de Staël could read altogether too well for their good; finally, that if women were once permitted to read Sophocles and work with logarithms, or to nibble at any side of the apple of knowledge, there would be an end forever to their sewing on buttons and embroidering slippers.

Please remember this book was published at the *beginning* of the Nineteenth Century. At the end of its first third, (in the year 1833) one solitary college in America decided to admit women within its sacred precincts, and organized what was called a "Ladies' Course" as well as the regular B. A. or Gentlemen's course.

It was felt to be an experiment—a rather dangerous experiment—and was adopted with fear and trembling by the good fathers, who looked as if they had been caught secretly mixing explosive compounds and were guiltily expecting every moment to see the foundations under them shaken and rent and their fair superstructure shattered into fragments.

But the girls came, and there was no upheaval. They performed their tasks modestly and intelligently. Once in a while one or two were found choosing the gentlemen's course. Still no collapse; and the dear, careful, scrupulous, frightened old professors were just getting their hearts out of their throats and preparing to draw one good free breath, when they found they would have to change the names of those courses; for there were as many ladies in the gentlemen's course as in the ladies', and a distinctively Ladies' Course, inferior in scope and aim to the regular classical course, did not and could not exist.

Other colleges gradually fell into line, and to-day there are one hundred and ninety-eight colleges for women, and two hundred and seven coeducational colleges and universities in the United States alone offering the degree of B. A. to women, and sending out yearly into the arteries of this nation a warm, rich flood of strong, brave, active, energetic, well-equipped, thoughtful women—women quick to see and eager to help the needs of this needy world—women who can think as well as feel, and who feel none the less because they think—women who are none the less tender and true for the parchment scroll they bear in their hands—women who have given a deeper, richer, nobler and grander meaning to the word "womanly" than any one-sided masculine definition could ever have suggested or inspired—women whom the world has long waited for in pain and anguish till there should be at last added to its forces and allowed to permeate its thought the complement of that masculine influence which has dominated it for fourteen centuries.

Since the idea of order and subordination succumbed to barbarian brawn and brutality in the fifth century, the civilized world has been like a child brought up by his father. It has needed the great mother heart to teach it to be pitiful, to love mercy, to succor the weak and care for the lowly.

Whence came this apotheosis of greed and cruelty? Whence this sneaking admiration we all have for bullies and prize-fighters? Whence the self-congratulation of "dominant" races, as if "dominant" meant "righteous" and carried with it a title to inherit the earth? Whence the scorn of so-called weak or unwarlike races and individuals, and the very comfortable assurance that it is their manifest destiny to be wiped out as vermin before this advancing civilization? As if the possession of the Christian graces of meekness, non-resistance and forgiveness, were incompatible with a civilization professedly based on Christianity, the religion of love! Just listen to this little bit of Barbarian brag:

> "As for Far Orientals, they are not of those who will survive. Artistic attractive people that they are, their civilization is like their own tree flowers, beautiful blossoms destined never to bear fruit. If these people continue in their old course, their earthly career is closed. Just as surely as morning passes into afternoon, so surely are these races of the Far East, if unchanged, destined to disappear before the advancing nations of the West. Vanish, they will, off the face of the earth, and leave our planet the eventual possession of the dwellers where the day declines. Unless their newly imported ideas really take root, it is from this whole world that Japanese and Koreans, as well as Chinese, will inevitably be excluded. Their Nirvana is already being realized; already, it has wrapped Far Eastern Asia in its winding sheet."
>
> —*Soul of the Far East*—*P. Lowell.*

Delightful reflection for "the dwellers where day declines." A spectacle to make the gods laugh, truly, to see the scion of an upstart race by one sweep of his generalizing pen consigning to annihilation one-third the inhabitants of the globe—a people whose

civilization was hoary headed before the parent elements that be-
got his race had advanced beyond nebulosity.

How like Longfellow's Iagoo, we Westerners are, to be sure! In
the few hundred years, we have had to strut across our allotted
territory and bask in the afternoon sun, we imagine we have exhausted the possibilities of humanity. Verily, we are the people,
and after us there is none other. Our God is power; strength, our
standard of excellence, inherited from barbarian ancestors
through a long line of male progenitors, the Law Salic permitting
no feminine modifications.

Says one, "The Chinaman is not popular with us, and we do
not like the Negro. It is not that the eyes of the one are set bias,
and the other is dark-skinned; but the Chinaman, the Negro is
weak—*and Anglo Saxons don't like weakness.*"

The world of thought under the predominant man-influence,
unmollified and unrestrained by its complementary force, would
become like Daniel's fourth beast: "dreadful and terrible, and *strong*
exceedingly;" "it had great iron teeth; it devoured and brake in
pieces, and stamped the residue with the feet of it;" and the most
independent of us find ourselves ready at times to fall down and
worship this incarnation of power.

Mrs. Mary A. Livermore, a woman whom I can mention only
to admire, came near shaking my faith a few weeks ago in my theory of the thinking woman's mission to put in the tender and sympathetic chord in nature's grand symphony, and counteract, or
better, harmonize the diapason of mere strength and might.

She was dwelling on the Anglo-Saxon genius for power and his
contempt for weakness, and described a scene in San Francisco
which she had witnessed.

The incorrigible animal known as the American small-boy, had
pounced upon a simple, unoffending Chinaman, who was taking
home his work, and had emptied the beautifully laundried contents of his basket into the ditch. "And," said she, "when that
great man stood there and blubbered before that crowd of lawless
urchins, to any one of whom he might have taught a lesson with
his two fists, *I didn't much care.*

This is said like a man! It grates harshly. It smacks of the worship of the beast. It is contempt for weakness, and taken out of its
setting it seems to contradict my theory. It either shows that one

of the highest exponents of the Higher Education can be at times untrue to the instincts I have ascribed to the thinking woman and to the contribution she is to add to the civilized world, or else the influence she wields upon our civilization may be potent without being necessarily and always direct and conscious. The latter is the case. Her voice may strike a false note, but her whole being is musical with the vibrations of human suffering. Her tongue may parrot over the cold conceits that some man has taught her, but her heart is aglow with sympathy and loving kindness, and she cannot be true to her real self without giving out these elements into the forces of the world.

No one is in any danger of imagining Mark Antony "a plain blunt man," nor Cassius a sincere one—whatever the speeches they may make.

As individuals, we are constantly and inevitably, whether we are conscious of it or not, giving out our real selves into our several little worlds, inexorably adding our own true ray to the flood of starlight, quite independently of our professions and our masquerading; and so in the world of thought, the influence of thinking woman far transcends her feeble declamation and may seem at times even opposed to it.

A visitor in Oberlin once said to the lady principal, "Have you no rabble in Oberlin? How is it I see no police here, and yet the streets are as quiet and orderly as if there were an officer of the law standing on every corner."

Mrs. Johnston replied, "Oh, yes; there are vicious persons in Oberlin just as in other towns—*but our girls are our police.*"

With from five to ten hundred pure-minded young women threading the streets of the village every evening unattended, vice must slink away, like frost before the rising sun: and yet I venture to say there was not one in a hundred of those girls who would not have run from a street brawl as she would from a mouse, and who would not have declared she could never stand the sight of blood and pistols.

There is, then, a real and special influence of woman. An influence subtle and often involuntary, an influence so intimately interwoven in, so intricately interpenetrated by the masculine influence of the time that it is often difficult to extricate the delicate meshes and analyze and identify the closely clinging fibers. And yet, without this influence—so long as woman sat with bandaged eyes and manacled hands, fast bound in the clamps of ignorance and inaction, the world of thought moved in its orbit like the revolutions of the moon; with one face (the man's face) always out, so that the spectator could not distinguish whether it was disc or sphere.

Now I claim that it is the prevalence of the Higher Education among women, the making it a common everyday affair for women to reason and think and express their thought, the training and stimulus which enable and encourage women to administer to the world the bread it needs as well as the sugar it cries for; in short it is the transmitting the potential forces of her soul into dynamic factors that has given symmetry and completeness to the world's agencies. So only could it be consummated that Mercy, the lesson she teaches, and Truth, the task man has set himself, should meet together: that *righteousness*, or rightness, man's ideal,—and *peace*, its necessary "other half," should kiss each other.

We must thank the general enlightenment and independence of woman (which we may now regard as a *fait accompli*) that both these forces are now at work in the world, and it is fair to demand from them for the twentieth century a higher type of civilization than any attained in the nineteenth. Religion, science, art, economics, have all needed the feminine flavor; and literature, the expression of what is permanent and best in all of these, may be gauged at any time to measure the strength of the feminine ingredient. You will not find theology consigning infants to lakes of unquenchable fire long after women have had a chance to grasp, master, and wield its dogmas. You will not find science annihilating personality from the government of the Universe and making of God an ungovernable, unintelligible, blind, often destructive physical force; you will not find jurisprudence formulating as an axiom the absurdity that man and wife are one, and that one the man—that the married woman may not hold or bequeath her own property save as subject to her husband's direction; you will not find political economists declaring that the only possible adjustment between laborers and capitalists is that of selfishness and rapacity—that each must get all he can and keep all that he gets, while the world cries *laissez faire* and the lawyers explain, "it is the beautiful working of the law of supply and demand;" in fine, you will not find the law of love shut out from the affairs of men after the feminine half of the world's truth is completed.

Nay, put your ear now close to the pulse of the time. What is the key-note of the literature of these days? What is the banner cry of all the activities of the last half decade? What is the dominant seventh which is to add richness and tone to the final cadences of this century and lead by a grand modulation into the triumphant harmonies of the next? Is it not compassion for the poor and unfortunate, and, as Bellamy has expressed it, "indignant outcry against the failure of the social machinery as it is, to ameliorate the miseries of men!" Even Christianity is being brought to the bar of humanity and tried by the standard of its ability to alleviate the world's suffering and lighten and brighten its woe. What else can be the meaning of Matthew Arnold's saddening protest, "We cannot do without Christianity," cried he, "and we cannot endure it as it is."

When went there by an age, when so much time and thought, so much money and labor were given to God's poor and God's invalids, the lowly and unlovely, the sinning as well as the suffering— homes for inebriates and homes for lunatics, shelter for the aged and shelter for babes, hospitals for the sick, props and braces for the falling, reformatory prisons and prison reformatories, all show that a "mothering" influence from some source is leavening the nation.

Now please understand me. I do not ask you to admit that these benefactions and virtues are the exclusive possession of women, or even that women are their chief and only advocates. It may be a man who formulates and makes them vocal. It may be, and often is, a man who weeps over the wrongs and struggles for the amelioration: but that man has imbibed those impulses from a mother rather than from a father and is simply materializing and giving back to the world in tangible form the ideal love and tenderness, devotion and care that have cherished and nourished the helpless period of his own existence.

All I claim is that there is a feminine as well as a masculine side to truth; that these are related not as inferior and superior, not as better and worse, not as weaker and stronger, but as complements—complements in one necessary and symmetric whole. That as the man is more noble in reason, so the woman is more quick in sympathy. That as he is indefatigable in pursuit of abstract truth, so is she in caring for the interests by the way—striving tenderly and lovingly that not one of the least of these "little ones" should perish. That while we not unfrequently see women who reason, we say, with the coolness and precision of a man, and men as considerate of helplessness as a woman, still there is a general consensus of mankind that the one trait is essentially masculine and the other as peculiarly feminine. That both are needed to be worked into the training of children, in order that our boys may supplement their virility by tenderness and sensibility, and our girls may round out their gentleness by strength and self-reliance. That, as both are alike necessary in giving symmetry to the individual, so a nation or a race will degenerate into mere emotionalism on the one hand, or bullyism on the other, if dominated by either exclusively; lastly, and most emphatically, that the feminine factor can have its proper effect only through woman's development and education so that she may fitly and intelligently stamp her force on the forces of her day, and add her modicum to the riches of the world's thought.

> "For woman's cause is man's: they rise or sink
> Together, dwarfed or godlike, bond or free:
> For she that out of Lethe scales with man
> The shining steps of nature, shares with man
> His nights, his days, moves with him to one goal.
> If she be small, slight-natured, miserable,
> How shall men grow?
> *   *   *   Let her make herself her own
> To give or keep, to live and learn and be
> All that not harms distinctive womanhood.
> For woman is not undeveloped man
> But diverse: could we make her as the man
> Sweet love were slain; his dearest bond is this,
> Not like to like, but like in difference.
> Yet in the long years liker must they grow;
> The man be more of woman, she of man;
> He gain in sweetness and in moral height,
> Nor lose the wrestling thews that throw the world;

> She mental breadth, nor fail in childward care,
> Nor lose the childlike in the larger mind;
> Till at the last she set herself to man,
> Like perfect music unto noble words."

Now you will argue, perhaps, and rightly, that higher education for women is not a modern idea, and that, if that is the means of setting free and invigorating the long desired feminine force in the world, it has already had a trial and should, in the past, have produced some of these glowing effects. Sappho, the bright, sweet singer of Lesbos, "the violet-crowned, pure, sweetly smiling Sappho" as Alcaeus calls her, chanted her lyrics and poured forth her soul nearly six centuries before Christ, in notes as full and free, as passionate and eloquent as did ever Archilochus or Anacreon.

Aspasia, that earliest queen of the drawing-room, a century later ministered to the intellectual entertainment of Socrates and the leading wits and philosophers of her time. Indeed, to her is attributed, by the best critics, the authorship of one of the most noted speeches ever delivered by Pericles.

Later on, during the Renaissance period, women were professors in mathematics, physics, metaphysics, and the classic languages in Bologna, Pavia, Padua, and Brescia. Olympia Fulvia Morata, of Ferrara, a most interesting character, whose magnificent library was destroyed in 1553 in the invasion of Schweinfurt by Albert of Brandenburg, had acquired a most extensive education. It is said that this wonderful girl gave lectures on classical subjects in her sixteenth year, and had even before that written several very remarkable Greek and Latin poems, and what is also to the point, she married a professor at Heidelberg, and became a *help-meet for him.*

It is true then that the higher education for women—in fact, the highest that the world has ever witnessed—belongs to the past; but we must remember that it was possible, down to the middle of our own century, only to a select few; and that the fashions and traditions of the times were before that all against it. There were not only no stimuli to encourage women to make the most of their powers and to welcome their development as a helpful agency in the progress of civilization, but their little aspirations, when they had any, were chilled and snubbed in embryo, and any attempt at thought was received as a monstrous usurpation of man's prerogative.

Lessing declared that "the woman who thinks is like the man who puts on rouge—ridiculous;" and Voltaire in his coarse, flippant way used to say, "Ideas are like beards—women and boys have none." Dr. Maginn remarked, "We like to hear a few words of sense from a woman sometimes, as we do from a parrot—they are so unexpected!" and even the pious Fénelon taught that virgin delicacy is almost as incompatible with learning as with vice.

That the average woman retired before these shafts of wit and ridicule and even gloried in her ignorance is not surprising. The abbé de Choisy, it is said, praised the Duchesse de Fontanges as being pretty as an angel and silly as a goose, and all the young ladies of the court strove to make up in folly what they lacked in charms. The ideal of the day was that "women must be pretty, dress prettily, flirt prettily, and not be too well informed;" that it was the *summum bonum* of her earthly hopes to have, as Thackeray puts it, "all the fellows battling to dance with her that she had no God-given destiny, no soul with unquenchable longings and inexhaustible possibilities—no work of her own to do and give to the world—no absolute and inherent value, no duty to self, transcending all pleasure-giving that may be demanded of a mere toy; but that her value was purely a relative one and to be estimated as are the fine arts—by the pleasure they give." "Woman, wine and song," as "the world's best gifts to man," were linked together in praise with as little thought of the first saying, "What doest thou," as that the wine and the song should declare, "We must be about our Father's business."

Men believed, or pretended to believe, that the great law of self development was obligatory on their half of the human family only; that while it was the chief end of man to glorify God and put his five talents to the exchangers, gaining thereby other five, it was, or ought to be, the sole end of woman to glorify man and wrap her one decently away in a napkin, retiring into "Hezekiah Smith's lady during her natural life and Hezekiah Smith's relict on her tombstone;" that higher education was incompatible with the shape of the female cerebrum, and that even if it could be acquired it must inevitably unsex woman destroying the lisping, clinging, tenderly helpless, and beautifully dependent creatures whom men would so heroically think for and so gallantly fight for, and giving in their stead a formidable race of blue stockings with corkscrew ringlets and other spinster propensities.

But these are eighteenth century ideas.

We have seen how the pendulum has swung across our present century. The men of our time have asked with Emerson, "that woman only show us how she can best be served;" and woman has replied: the chance of the seedling and of the animalcule is all I ask—the chance for growth and self development, the permission to be true to the aspirations of my soul without incurring the blight of your censure and ridicule.

"Audetque viris concurrere virgo."

In soul-culture woman at last dares to contend with men, and we may cite Grant Allen (who certainly cannot be suspected of advocating the unsexing of woman) as an example of the broadening effect of this contest on the ideas at least of the men of the day. He says in his *Plain Words on the Woman Question*, recently published:

"The position of women was not a position which could bear the test of nineteenth-century scrutiny. Their education was inadequate, their social status was humiliating, their political power was nil, their practical and personal grievances were innumerable; above all, their relations to the family—to their husbands, their children, their friends, their property—was simply insupportable."

And again: "As a body we 'Advanced men' are, I think, prepared to reconsider, and to reconsider fundamentally, without prejudice or misconception, the entire question of the relation between the sexes. We are ready to make any modifications in those relations which will satisfy the woman's just aspiration for personal independence, for intellectual and moral development, for physical culture, for political activity, and for a voice in the arrangement of her own affairs, both domestic and national."

Now this is magnanimous enough, surely; and quite a step from eighteenth century preaching, is it not? The higher education of Woman has certainly developed the men;—let us see what it has done for the women.

Matthew Arnold during his last visit to America in '82 or '83, lectured before a certain co-educational college in the West. After the lecture he remarked, with some surprise, to a lady professor, that the young women in his audience, he noticed, paid as close attention as the men, *all the way through.* This led, of course, to a spirited discussion of the higher education for women, during which he said to his enthusiastic interlocutor, eyeing her philosophically through his English eyeglass: "But—eh—don't you think it—eh—spoils their *chawnces,* you know!"

Now, as to the result to women, this is the most serious argument ever used against the higher education. If it interferes with marriage, classical training has a grave objection to weigh and answer.

For I agree with Mr. Allen at least on this one point, that there must be marrying and giving in marriage even till the end of time.

I grant you that intellectual development, with the self-reliance and capacity for earning a livelihood which it gives, renders woman less dependent on the marriage relation for physical support (which, by the way, does not always accompany it). Neither is she compelled to look to sexual love as the one sensation capable of giving tone and relish, movement and vim to the life she leads. Her horizon is extended. Her sympathies are broadened and deepened and multiplied. She is in closer touch with nature. Not a bud that opens, not a dew drop, not a ray of light, not a cloud-burst or a thunderbolt, but adds to the expansiveness and zest of her soul. And if the sun of an absorbing passion be gone down, still 'tis night that brings the stars. She has remaining the mellow, less obtrusive, but none the less enchanting and inspiring light of friendship, and into its charmed circle she may gather the best the world has known. She can commune with Socrates about the *daimon* he knew and to which she too can bear witness; she can revel in the majesty of Dante, the sweetness of Virgil, the simplicity of Homer, the strength of Milton. She can listen to the pulsing heart throbs of passionate Sappho's encaged soul, as she beats her bruised wings against her prison bars and struggles to flutter out into Heaven's ether, and the fires of her own soul cry back as she listens. "Yes; Sappho, I know it all; I know it all." Here, at last, can be communion without suspicion; friendship without misunderstanding; love without jealousy.

We must admit then that Byron's picture, whether a thing of beauty or not, has faded from the canvas of to-day.

"Man's love," he wrote, "is of man's life a thing apart,
'Tis woman's whole existence.
Man may range the court, camp, church, the vessel and
   the mart,
Sword, gown, gain, glory offer in exchange.
Pride, fame, ambition, to fill up his heart—
And few there are whom these cannot estrange.
Men have all these resources, we *but one*—
To love again and be again undone."

This may have been true when written. *It is not true to-day.* The old, subjective, stagnant, indolent and wretched life for woman has gone. She has as many resources as men, as many activities beckon her on. As large possibilities swell and inspire her heart.

Now, then, does it destroy or diminish her capacity for loving?

Her standards have undoubtedly gone up. The necessity of speculating in "chawnces" has probably shifted. The question is not now with the woman "How shall I so cramp, stunt, simplify and nullify myself as to make me eligible to the honor of being swallowed up into some little man?" but the problem, I trow, now rests with the man as to how he can so develop his God-given powers as to reach the ideal of a generation of women who demand the noblest, grandest and best achievements of which he is capable; and this surely is the only fair and natural adjustment of the chances. Nature never meant that the ideals and standards of the world should be dwarfing and minimizing ones, and the men should thank us for requiring of them the richest fruits which they can grow. If it makes them work, all the better for them.

As to the adaptability of the educated woman to the marriage relation, I shall simply quote from that excellent symposium of learned women that appeared recently under Mrs. Armstrong's signature in answer to the "Plain Words" of Mr. Allen, already referred to. "Admitting no longer any question as to their intellectual equality with the men whom they meet, with the simplicity of conscious strength, they take their place beside the men who challenge them, and fearlessly face the result of their actions. They deny that their education in any way unfits them for the duty of wifehood and maternity or primarily renders these conditions any less attractive to them than to the domestic type of woman. On the contrary, they hold that their knowledge of physiology makes them better mothers and housekeepers; their knowledge of chemistry makes them better cooks; while from their training in other natural sciences and in mathematics, they obtain an accuracy and fair-mindedness which is of great value to them in dealing with their children or employees."

So much for their willingness. Now the apple may be good for food and pleasant to the eyes, and a fruit to be desired to make one wise. Nay, it may even assure you that it has no aversion whatever to being tasted. Still, if you do not like the flavor all these recommendations are nothing. Is the intellectual woman *desirable* in the matrimonial market?

This I cannot answer. I confess my ignorance. I am no judge of such things. I have been told that strong-minded women could be, when they thought it worth their while, quite endurable, and, judging from the number of female names I find in college catalogues among the alumnae with double patronymics, I surmise that quite a number of men are willing to put up with them.

Now I would that my task ended here. Having shown that a great want of the world in the past has been a feminine force; that that force can have its full effect only through the untrammeled development of woman; that such development, while it gives her to the world and to civilization, does not necessarily remove her from the home and fireside; finally, that while past centuries have witnessed sporadic instances of this higher growth, still it was reserved for the latter half of the nineteenth century to render it common and general enough to be effective; I might close with a glowing prediction of what the twentieth century may expect from this heritage of twin forces—the masculine battered and toil-worn as a grim veteran after centuries of warfare, but still strong, active, and vigorous, ready to help with his hard-won experience the young recruit rejoicing in her newly found freedom, who so confidently places her hand in his with mutual pledges to redeem the ages.

> "And so the twain upon the skirts of Time,
> Sit side by side, full-summed in all their powers,
> Dispensing harvest, sowing the To-be,
> Self-reverent each and reverencing each."

Fain would I follow them, but duty is nearer home. The high ground of generalities is alluring but my pen is devoted to a special cause: and with a view to further enlightenment on the achievements of the century for THE HIGHER EDUCATION OF COLORED WOMEN, I wrote a few days ago to the colleges which admit women and asked how many colored women had completed the B. A. course in each during its entire history. These are the figures returned: Fisk leads the way with twelve; Oberlin next with five; Wilberforce, four; Ann Arbor and Wellesley three each, Livingstone two, Atlanta one, Howard, as yet, none.

I then asked the principal of the Washington High School how many out of a large number of female graduates from his school had chosen to go forward and take a collegiate course. He replied that but one had ever done so, and she was then in Cornell.

Others ask questions too, sometimes, and I was asked a few years ago by a white friend, "How is it that the men of your race seem to outstrip the women in mental attainment?" "Oh," I said, "so far as it is true, the men, I suppose, from the life they lead, gain more by contact; and so far as it is only apparent, I think the women are more quiet. They don't feel called to mount a barrel and harangue by the hour every time they imagine they have produced an idea."

But I am sure there is another reason which I did not at that time see fit to give. The atmosphere, the standards, the requirements of our little world do not afford any special stimulus to female development.

It seems hardly a gracious thing to say, but it strikes me as true, that while our men seem thoroughly abreast of the times on almost every other subject, when they strike the woman question they drop back into sixteenth century logic. They leave nothing to be desired generally in regard to gallantry and chivalry, but they actually do not seem sometimes to have outgrown that old contemporary of chivalry—the idea that women may stand on pedestals or live in doll houses, (if they happen to have them) but they must not furrow their brows with thought or attempt to help men tug at the great questions of the world. I fear the majority of colored men do not yet think it worth while that women aspire to higher education. Not many will subscribe to the "advanced" ideas of Grant Allen already quoted. The three R's, a little music and a good deal of dancing, a first rate dress-maker and a bottle of magnolia balm, are quite enough generally to render charming any woman possessed of tact and the capacity for worshipping masculinity.

My readers will pardon my illustrating my point and also giving a reason for the fear that is in me, by a little bit of personal experience. When a child I was put into a school near home that professed to be normal and collegiate, i.e., to prepare teachers for colored youth, furnish candidates for the ministry, and offer collegiate training for those who should be ready for it. Well, I found after a while that I had a good deal of time on my hands. I had devoured what was put before me, and, like Oliver Twist, was looking around to ask for more. I constantly felt (as I suppose many an ambitious girl has felt) a thumping from within unanswered by any beckoning from without. Class after class was organized for these ministerial candidates (many of them men who had been preaching before I was born). Into every one of these classes I was expected to go, with the sole intent, I thought at the time, of enabling the dear old principal, as he looked from the vacant countenances of his sleepy old class over to where I sat, to get off his solitary pun—his never-failing pleasantry, especially in hot weather—which was, as he called out "Any one!" to the effect that "*any* one" then meant "*Annie* one."

Finally a Greek class was to be formed. My inspiring preceptor informed me that Greek had never been taught in the school, but that he was going to form a class *for the candidates for the ministry*, and if I liked I might join it. I replied—humbly I hope, as became a female of the human species—that I would like very much to study Greek, and that I was thankful for the opportunity, and so it went on. A boy, however meager his equipment and shallow his pretentions, had only to declare a floating intention to study theology and he could get all the support, encouragement and stimulus he needed, be absolved from work and invested beforehand with all the dignity of his far away office. While a self-supporting girl had to struggle on by teaching in the summer and working after school hours to keep up with her board bills, and actually to fight her way against positive discouragements to the higher education; till one such girl one day flared out and told the principal "the only mission opening before a girl in his school was to marry one of those candidates." He said he didn't know but it was. And when at last that same girl announced her desire and intention to go to college it was received with about the same incredulity and dismay as if a brass button on one of those candidate's coats had propounded a new method for squaring the circle or trisecting the arc.

Now this is not fancy. It is a simple unvarnished photograph, and what I believe was not in those days exceptional in colored schools, and I ask the men and women who are teachers and co-workers for the highest interests of the race, that they give the girls a chance! We might as well expect to grow trees from leaves as hope to build up a civilization or a manhood without taking into consideration our women and the home life made by them, which must be the root and ground of the whole matter. Let us insist then on special encouragement for the education of our women and special care in their training. Let our girls feel that we expect something more of them than that they merely look pretty and appear well in society. Teach them that there is a race with special needs which they and only they can help; that the world needs and is already asking for their trained, efficient forces. Finally, if there is an ambitious girl with pluck and brain to take the higher education, encourage her to make the most of it. Let there be the same flourish of trumpets and clapping of hands as when a boy announces his determination to enter the lists; and then, as you know that she is physically the weaker of the two, don't stand from under and leave her to buffet the waves alone. Let her know that your heart is following her, that your hand, though she sees it not, is ready to support her. To be plain, I mean let money be raised and scholarships be founded in our colleges and universities for self-supporting, worthy young women, to offset and balance the aid that can always be found for boys who will take theology.

The earnest well trained Christian young woman, as a teacher, as a home-maker, as wife, mother, or silent influence even, is as potent a missionary agency among our people as is the theologian; and I claim that at the present stage of our development in the South she is even more important and necessary.

Let us then, here and now, recognize this force and resolve to make the most of it—not the boys less, but the girls more.

On Women's Right to Vote

BY SUSAN B. ANTHONY

Susan B. Anthony was an American social reformer, abolitionist, and women's rights activist who played a pivotal role in the women's suffrage movement. She traveled the country giving speeches, gathering thousands of signatures on petitions, and lobbying Congress for women to have the right to vote. In November 1872, Anthony voted in the presidential election, even though women were still denied suffrage. Two weeks later, she was arrested. After her indictment, Anthony gave her famous "On Women's Right to Vote" speech, where she invoked the preamble to the US Constitution, pointing out that it addresses we, the people, and not we, the male citizens. At the end, she challenged her detractors to answer this question: "Are women persons?" Sadly, feminists are still asking that question today. Her speech and her continued advocacy for women's rights paved the way for Congress to eventually ratify the Nineteenth Amendment in 1920, which finally gave women the right to vote. Though Anthony was a critical figure in the suffrage movement, her legacy has been complicated by racist attitudes that imbued some of her work.

Friends and fellow citizens: I stand before you tonight under indictment for the alleged crime of having voted at the last presidential election, without having a lawful right to vote. It shall be my work this evening to prove to you that in thus voting, I not only committed no crime, but, instead, simply exercised my citizen's rights, guaranteed to me and all United States citizens by the National Constitution, beyond the power of any state to deny.

The preamble of the Federal Constitution says:

"We, the people of the United States, in order to form a more perfect union, establish justice, insure domestic tranquility, provide for the common defense, promote the general welfare, and secure the blessings of liberty to ourselves and our posterity, do ordain and establish this Constitution for the United States of America."

It was we, the people; not we, the white male citizens; nor yet we, the male citizens; but we, the whole people, who formed the Union. And we formed it, not to give the blessings of liberty, but to secure them; not to the half of ourselves and the half of our posterity, but to the whole people—women as well as men. And it is a downright mockery to talk to women of their enjoyment of the blessings of liberty while they are denied the use of the only means of securing them provided by this democratic-republican government—the ballot.

For any state to make sex a qualification that must ever result in the disfranchisement of one entire half of the people, is to pass a bill of attainder, or, an ex post facto law, and is therefore a violation of the supreme law of the land. By it the blessings of liberty are forever withheld from women and their female posterity.

To them this government has no just powers derived from the consent of the governed. To them this government is not a democracy. It is not a republic. It is an odious aristocracy; a hateful oligarchy of sex; the most hateful aristocracy ever established on the face of the globe; an oligarchy of wealth, where the rich govern the poor. An oligarchy of learning, where the educated govern the ignorant, or even an oligarchy of race, where the Saxon rules the African, might be endured; but this oligarchy of sex, which makes father, brothers, husband, sons, the oligarchs over the mother and sisters, the wife and daughters, of every household—which ordains all men sovereigns, all women subjects, carries dissension, discord, and rebellion into every home of the nation.

Webster, Worcester, and Bouvier all define a citizen to be a person in the United States, entitled to vote and hold office.

The only question left to be settled now is: Are women persons? And I hardly believe any of our opponents will have the hardihood to say they are not. Being persons, then, women are citizens; and no state has a right to make any law, or to enforce any old law, that shall abridge their privileges or immunities. Hence, every discrimination against women in the constitutions and laws of the several states is today null and void, precisely as is every one against Negroes.

The Black and White of It

BY IDA B. WELLS

Born enslaved in Mississippi in 1862, Ida B. Wells was a teacher, activist, and journalist whose investigative reporting on lynching in the South exposed it as a tool used by white supremacists to intimidate and murder Black people, especially those who created competition for whites. In response, the Memphis newspaper Wells co-owned was destroyed by a white mob. Wells left Memphis but continued her reporting, which brought her national attention. She was one of the founders of the NAACP and traveled nationally and internationally as a speaker and activist in the women's suffrage movement. Wells received a posthumous Pulitzer special citation in 2020 "for her outstanding and courageous reporting on the horrific and vicious violence against African Americans during the era of lynching." Her 1892 pamphlet *Southern Horrors: Lynch Laws in All Its Phases* includes "The Black and White of It," an essay that indicts the ways white people and particularly white women weaponized racism to secure social standing, hide infidelity, and otherwise wield power in the ways available to them, despite the grave consequences. It was not only reportage, it was condemnation, and it demanded white women's accountability for their complicities in the ills of racism.

THE BLACK AND WHITE OF IT

The *Cleveland Gazette* of January 16, 1892, publishes a case in point. Mrs. J. S. Underwood, the wife of a minister of Elyria, Ohio, accused an Afro-American of rape. She told her husband that during his absence in 1888, stumping the State for the

Prohibition Party, the man came to the kitchen door, forced his way in the house and insulted her. She tried to drive him out with a heavy poker, but he overpowered and chloroformed her, and when she revived her clothing was torn and she was in a horrible condition. She did not know the man but could identify him. She pointed out William Offett, a married man, who was arrested and, being in Ohio, was granted a trial.

The prisoner vehemently denied the charge of rape, but confessed he went to Mrs. Underwood's residence at her invitation and was criminally intimate with her at her request. This availed him nothing against the sworn testimony of a ministers wife, a lady of the highest respectability. He was found guilty, and entered the penitentiary, December 14, 1888, for fifteen years. Some time afterward the woman's remorse led her to confess to her husband that the man was innocent.

These are her words:

I met Offett at the Post Office. It was raining. He was polite to me, and as I had several bundles in my arms he offered to carry them home for me, which he did. He had a strange fascination for me, and I invited him to call on me. He called, bringing chestnuts and candy for the children. By this means we got them to leave us alone in the room. Then I sat on his lap. He made a proposal to me and I readily consented. Why I did so, I do not know, but that I did is true. He visited me several times after that and each time I was indiscreet. I did not care after the first time. In fact I could not have resisted, and had no desire to resist.

When asked by her husband why she told him she had been outraged, she said: "I had several reasons for telling you. One was the neighbors saw the fellows here, another was, I was afraid I had contracted a loathsome disease, and still another was that I feared I might give birth to a Negro baby. I hoped to save my reputation by telling you a deliberate lie." Her husband horrified by the confession had Offett, who had already served four years, released and secured a divorce.

There are thousands of such cases throughout the South, with the difference that the Southern white men in insatiate fury wreak their vengeance without intervention of law upon the Afro-Americans who consort with their women. A few instances to substantiate the assertion that some white women love the company of the Afro-American will not be out of place. Most of these cases were reported by the daily papers of the South.

In the winter of 1885–86 the wife of a practicing physician in Memphis, in good social standing whose name has escaped me, left home, husband and children, and ran away with her black coachman. She was with him a month before her husband found and brought her home. The coachman could not be found. The doctor moved his family away from Memphis, and is living in another city under an assumed name.

In the same city last year a white girl in the dusk of evening screamed at the approach of some parties that a Negro had assaulted her on the street. He was captured, tried by a white judge and jury, that acquitted him of the charge. It is needless to add if there had been a scrap of evidence on which to convict him of so grave a charge he would have been convicted.

Sarah Clark of Memphis loved a black man and lived openly with him. When she was indicted last spring for miscegenation, she swore in court that she was *not* a white woman. This she did to escape the penitentiary and continued her illicit relation undisturbed. That she is of the lower class of whites, does not disturb the fact that she is a white woman. "The leading citizens" of Memphis are defending the "honor" of *all* white women, *demimonde* included.

Since the manager of the *Free Speech* has been run away from Memphis by the guardians of the honor of Southern white women, a young girl living on Poplar St., who was discovered in intimate relations with a handsome mulatto young colored man, Will Morgan by name, stole her father's money to send the young fellow away from that father's wrath. She has since joined him in Chicago.

The *Memphis Ledger* for June 8 has the following:

If Lillie Bailey, a rather pretty white girl seventeen years of age, who is now at the City Hospital, would be somewhat less reserved about her disgrace there would be some very nauseating details in the story of her life. She is the mother of a little coon. The truth might reveal fearful depravity or it might reveal the evidence of a rank outrage. She will not divulge the name of the man who has left such black evidence of her disgrace, and, in fact, says it is a matter in which there can be no interest to the outside world. She came to Memphis nearly three months ago and was taken in at the Woman's Refuge in the southern part of the city. She remained there until a few weeks ago, when the child was born. The ladies in charge of the Refuge were horrified. The girl was at once sent to the City Hospital, where she has been since May 30. She is a country girl. She came to Memphis from her fathers farm, a short distance from Hernando, Miss. Just when she left there she would not say. In fact she says she came to Memphis from Arkansas, and says her home is in that State. She is rather good looking, has blue eyes, a low forehead and dark red hair. The ladies at the Woman's Refuge do not know anything about the girl further than what they learned when she was an inmate of the institution; and she would not tell much. When the child was born an attempt was made to get the girl to reveal the name of the Negro who had disgraced her, she obstinately refused and it was impossible to elicit any information from her on the subject.

Note the wording. "The truth might reveal fearful depravity or rank outrage." If it had been a white child or Lillie Bailey had told a pitiful story of Negro outrage, it would have been a case of woman's weakness or assault and she could have remained at the Woman's Refuge. But a Negro child and to withhold its father's name and thus prevent the killing of another Negro "rapist." A case of "fearful depravity."

The very week the "leading citizens" of Memphis were making a spectacle of themselves in defense of all white women of every kind, an Afro-American, M. Stricklin, was found in a white woman's room in that city. Although she made no outcry of rape, he was jailed and would have been lynched, but the woman stated she bought curtains of him (he was a furniture dealer) and his business in her room that night was to put them up. A white woman's word was taken as absolutely in this case as when the cry of rape is made, and he was freed.

What is true of Memphis is true of the entire South. The daily papers last year reported a farmer's wife in Alabama had given birth to a Negro child. When the Negro farm hand who was plowing in the field heard it he took the mule from the plow and fled. The dispatches also told of a woman in South Carolina who gave birth to a Negro child and charged three men with being its father, *every one of whom has since disappeared*. In Tuscumbia, Ala., the colored boy who was lynched there last year for assaulting a white girl told her before his accusers that he had met her there in the woods often before.

Frank Weems of Chattanooga who was not lynched in May only because the prominent citizens became his body guard until the doors of the penitentiary closed on him, had letters in his pocket from the white woman in the case, making the appointment with him. Edward Coy who was burned alive in Texarkana, January 1, 1892, died protesting his innocence. Investigation since as given by the Bystander in the *Chicago Inter Ocean*, October 1, proves:

1. The woman who was paraded as a victim of violence was of bad character; her husband was a drunkard and a gambler.

2. She was publicly reported and generally known to have been criminally intimate with Coy for more than a year previous.

3. She was compelled by threats, if not by violence, to make the charge against the victim.

4. When she came to apply the match Coy asked her if she would burn him after they had "been sweethearting" so long.

5. A large majority of the "superior" white men prominent in the affair are the reputed fathers of mulatto children.

These are not pleasant facts, but they are illustrative of the vital phase of the so-called race question, which should properly be designated an earnest inquiry as to the best methods by which religion, science, law and political power may be employed to excuse injustice, barbarity and crime done to a people because of race and color. There can be no possible belief that these people were inspired by any consuming zeal to vindicate God's law against miscegnationists of the most practical sort. The woman was a willing partner in the victim's guilt, and being of the "superior" race must naturally have been more guilty.

In Natchez, Miss., Mrs. Marshall, one of the *creme de la creme* of the city, created a tremendous sensation several years ago. She has a black coachman who was married, and had been in her employ several years. During this time she gave birth to a child whose color was remarked, but traced to some brunette ancestor, and one of the fashionable dames of the city was its godmother. Mrs. Marshall's social position was unquestioned, and wealth showered every dainty on this child which was idolized with its brothers and sisters by its white papa. In course of time another child appeared on the scene, but it was unmistakably dark. All were alarmed, and "rush of blood, strangulation" were the conjectures, but the doctor, when asked the cause, grimly told them it was a Negro child. There was a family conclave, the coachman heard of it and leaving his own family went West, and has never returned. As soon as Mrs. Marshall was able to travel she was sent away in deep disgrace. Her husband died within the year of a broken heart.

Ebenzer Fowler, the wealthiest colored man in Issaquena County, Miss., was shot down on the street in Mayersville, January 30, 1885, just before dark by an armed body of white men who filled his body with bullets. They charged him with writing a note to a white woman of the place, which they intercepted and which proved there was an intimacy existing between them.

Hundreds of such cases might be cited, but enough have been given to prove the assertion that there are white women in the South who love the Afro-American's company even as there are white men notorious for their preference for Afro-American women.

There is hardly a town in the South which has not an instance of the kind which is well known, and hence the assertion is reiterated that "nobody in the South believes the old thread bare lie that negro men rape white women." Hence there is a growing demand among Afro-Americans that the guilt or innocence of parties accused of rape be fully established. They know the men of the section of the country who refuse this are not so desirous of punishing rapists as they pretend. The utterances of the leading white men show that with them it is not the crime but the *class*.

Bishop Fitzgerald has become apologist for lynchers of the rapists of *white* women only. Governor Tillman, of South Carolina, in the month of June, standing under the tree in Barnwell, S.C., on which eight Afro-Americans were hung last year, declared that he would lead a mob to lynch a *negro* who raped a *white* woman. So say the pulpits, officials and newspapers of the South. But when the victim is a colored woman it is different.

Last winter in Baltimore, Md., three white ruffians assaulted a Miss Camphor, a young Afro-American girl, while out walking with a young man of her own race. They held her escort and outraged the girl. It was a deed dastardly enough to arouse Southern blood, which gives its horror of rape as excuse for lawlessness, but she was an Afro-American. The case went to the courts, an Afro-American lawyer defended the men and they were acquitted.

In Nashville, Tenn., there is a white man, Pat Hanifan, who outraged a little Afro-American girl, and, from the physical injuries received, she has been ruined for life. He was jailed for six months, discharged, and is now a detective in that city. In the same city, last May, a white man outraged an Afro-American girl in a drug store. He was arrested, and released on bail at the trial. It was rumored that five hundred Afro-Americans had organized to lynch him. Two hundred and fifty white citizens armed themselves with Winchesters and guarded him. A cannon was placed in front of his home, and the Buchanan Rifles (State Militia) ordered to the scene for his protection. The Afro-American mob did not materialize. Only two weeks before Eph. Grizzard, who had only been *charged* with rape upon a white woman, had been taken from the jail, with Governor Buchanan and the police and militia standing by, dragged through the streets in broad daylight, knives plunged into him at every step, and with every fiendish cruelty a frenzied mob could devise, he was at last swung out on the bridge with hands cut to pieces as he tried to climb up the stanchions. A naked, bloody example of the blood-thirstiness of the nineteenth-century civilization of the Athens of the South! No cannon or military was called out in his defense. He dared to visit a white woman.

At the very moment these civilized whites were announcing their determination "to protect their wives and daughters," by murdering Grizzard, a white man was in the same jail for raping eight-year-old Maggie Reese, an Afro-American girl. He was not harmed. The "honor" of grown women who were glad enough to be supported by the Grizzard boys and Ed Coy, as long as the liaison was not known, needed protection; they were white. The outrage upon helpless childhood needed no avenging in this case; she was black.

A white man in Guthrie, Oklahoma Territory, two months ago inflicted such injuries upon another Afro-American child that she died. He was not punished, but an attempt was made in the same town in the month of June to lynch an Afro-American who visited a white woman.

In Memphis, Tenn., in the month of June, Ellerton L. Dorr, who is the husband of Russell Hancock's widow, was arrested for attempted rape on Mattie Cole, a neighbor's cook; he was only prevented from accomplishing his purpose, by the appearance of Mattie's employer. Dorr's friends say he was drunk and not responsible for his actions. The grand jury refused to indict him and he was discharged.

PART III

MULTICULTURAL
PERSPECTIVES

Under Western Eyes

BY CHANDRA TALPADE MOHANTY

Dr. Chandra Mohanty is the Distinguished Professor of Women's and Gender Studies, Sociology, and the Cultural Foundations of Education and the Director of Graduate Studies at Syracuse University. Central to Mohanty's mission is the project of building a "noncolonizing feminist solidarity across the borders" through the intersectional analysis of race, nation, colonialism, sexuality, class, and gender. Mohanty critiques Western feminism and its category of the "Third World Woman" as a generic, homogenous, victimized stereotype that Western feminists must save. In "Under Western Eyes," first published in 1988, Mohanty demonstrated that Western feminism has created a homogenized ideal of women from the southern hemisphere who, in reality, experience oppression in myriad ways contingent on ethnicity, culture, language, race, geography, and class. "Under Western Eyes" was a groundbreaking work highlighting the problems feminists in developing countries faced in being heard within the broader feminist movement and was key to redefining power relationships between feminists worldwide.

It ought to be of some political significance at least that the term "colonization" has come to denote a variety of phenomena in recent feminist and left writings in general. From its analytic value as a category of exploitative economic exchange in both traditional and contemporary marxisms (particularly contemporary theorists such as Baran, Amin and Gunder-Frank) to its use by feminist women of color in the U.S. to describe the appropriation of their experiences and struggles by hegemonic white women's movements, colonization has been used to characterize everything from the most evident economic and political hierarchies to the production of a particular cultural discourse about what is called the "Third World." However sophisticated or problematical its use as an explanatory construct, colonization almost invariably implies a relation of structural domination, and a suppression—often violent—of the heterogeneity of the subject(s) in question. What I wish to analyze is specifically the production of the "Third World Woman" as a singular monolithic subject in some recent (Western) feminist texts. The definition of colonization I wish to invoke here is a predominantly *discursive* one, focusing on a certain mode of appropriation and codification of "scholarship" and "knowledge" about women in the third world by particular analytic categories employed in specific writings on the subject which take as their referent feminist interests as they have been articulated in the U.S. and Western Europe.

My concern about such writings derives from my own implication and investment in contemporary debates in feminist theory, and the urgent political necessity (especially in the age of Reagan) of forming strategic coalitions across class, race, and national boundaries. Clearly Western feminist discourse and political practice is neither singular nor homogeneous in its goals, interests or analyses. However, it is possible to trace a coherence of *effects* resulting from the implicit assumption of "the West" (in all its complexities and contradictions) as the primary referent in theory and praxis. My reference to "Western feminism" is by no means intended to imply that it is a monolith. Rather, I am attempting to draw attention to the similar effects of various textual strategies used by particular writers that codify Others as non-Western and hence themselves as (implicitly) Western. It is in this sense that I use the term "Western feminist." The analytic principles discussed below serve to distort Western feminist political practices, and limit the possibility of coalitions among (usually White) Western feminists and working class and feminists of color around the world. These limitations are evident in the construction of the (implicitly consensual) priority of issues around which apparently *all* women are expected to organize. The necessary and integral connection between feminist scholarship and feminist political practice and organizing determines the significance and status of Western feminist writings on women in the third world, for feminist scholarship, like most other kinds of scholarship, is not the mere production of knowledge about a certain subject. It is a directly political and discursive *practice* in that it is purposeful and ideological. It is best seen as a mode of intervention into particular hegemonic discourses (for example, traditional anthropology, sociology, literary criticism, etc.); it is a political praxis which counters and resists the totalizing imperative of age-old "legitimate" and "scientific" bodies of knowledge. Thus, feminist scholarly practices (whether reading, writing, critical or textual) are inscribed in relations of power—relations which they counter, resist, or even perhaps implicitly support. There can, of course, be no apolitical scholarship.

The relationship between "Woman"—a cultural and ideological composite Other constructed through diverse representational discourses (scientific, literary, juridical, linguistic, cinematic, etc.)—and "women"—real, material subjects of their collective histories—is one of the central questions the practice of feminist scholarship seeks to address. This connection between women as historical subjects and the re-presentation of Woman produced by hegemonic discourses is not a relation of direct identity, or a relation of correspondence or simple implication. It is an arbitrary relation set up by particular cultures. I would like to suggest that the feminist writings I analyze here discursively colonize the material and historical heterogeneities of the lives of women in the third world, thereby producing/re-presenting a composite, singular "Third World Woman"—an image which appears arbitrarily constructed, but nevertheless carries with it the authorizing signature of Western humanist discourse. I argue that assumptions of privilege and ethnocentric universality on the one hand, and inadequate self-consciousness about the effect of Western scholarship on the "third world" in the context of a world system dominated by the West on the other, characterize a sizable extent of Western feminist work on women in the third world. An analysis of "sexual difference" in the form of a cross-culturally singular, monolithic notion of patriarchy or male dominance leads to the construction of a similarly reductive and homogeneous notion of what I call the "Third World Difference"—that stable, ahistorical something that apparently oppresses most if not all the women in these countries. And it is in the production of this "Third World

Difference" that Western feminisms appropriate and "colonize" the fundamental complexities and conflicts which characterize the lives of women of different classes, religions, cultures, races and castes in these countries. It is in this process of homogenization and systematization of the oppression of women in the third world that power is exercised in much of recent Western feminist discourse, and this power needs to be defined and named.

In the context of the West's hegemonic position today, of what Anouar Abdel-Malek calls a struggle for "control over the orientation, regulation and decision of the process of world development on the basis of the advanced sector's monopoly of scientific knowledge and ideal creativity," Western feminist scholarship on the third world must be seen and examined precisely in terms of its inscription in these particular relations of power and struggle. There is, I shall argue, no universal patriarchal framework which this scholarship attempts to counter and resist—unless one posits an international male conspiracy or a monolithic, ahistorical power hierarchy. There is, however, a particular world balance of power within which any analysis of culture, ideology, and socioeconomic conditions has to be necessarily situated. Abdel-Malek is useful here, again, in reminding us about the inherence of politics in the discourses of "culture":

> Contemporary imperialism is, in a real sense, a hegemonic imperialism, exercising to a maximum degree a rationalized violence taken to a higher level than ever before—through fire and sword, but also through the attempt to control hearts and minds. For its content is defined by the combined action of the military-industrial complex and the hegemonic cultural centers of the West, all of them founded on the advanced levels of development attained by monopoly and finance capital, and supported by the benefits of both the scientific and technological revolution and the second industrial revolution itself.

Western feminist scholarship cannot avoid the challenge of situating itself and examining its role in such a global economic and political framework. To do any less would be to ignore the complex interconnections between first and third world economies and the profound effect of this on the lives of women in these countries. I do not question the descriptive and informative value of most Western feminist writings on women in the third world. I also do not question the existence of excellent work which does not fall into the analytic traps I am concerned with. In fact I deal with an example of such work later on. In the context of an overwhelming silence about the experiences of women in these countries, as well as the need to forge international links between women's political struggles, such work is both pathbreaking and absolutely essential. However, it is both to the *explanatory potential* of particular analytic strategies employed by such writing, and to their *political effect* in the context of the hegemony of Western scholarship, that I want to draw attention here. While feminist writing in the U.S. is still marginalized (except from the point of view of women of color addressing privileged White women), Western feminist writing on women in the third world must be considered in the context of the global hegemony of Western scholarship—i.e., the production, publication, distribution and consumption of information and ideas. Marginal or not, this writing has political effects and implications beyond the immediate feminist or disciplinary audience. One such significant effect of the dominant "representations" of Western feminism is its conflation with imperialism in the eyes of particular third world women. Hence the urgent need to examine the *political* implications of *analytic* strategies and principles.

My critique is directed at three basic analytic principles which are present in (Western) feminist discourse on women in the third world. Since I focus primarily on the Zed Press "Women in the Third World" series, my comments on Western feminist discourse are circumscribed by my analysis of the texts in this series. This is a way of limiting and focusing my critique. However, even though I am dealing with feminists who identify themselves as culturally or geographically from the "West," what I say about these analytic strategies or implicit principles holds for anyone who uses these methods, whether third world women in the West, or third world women in the third world writing on these issues and publishing in the West. (I am not making a culturalist argument about ethnocentrism; rather, I am trying to uncover how ethnocentric universalism is produced in certain analyses, and in the context of a hegemonic First/Third World connection, it is not very surprising to discover where the ethnocentrism derives from.) As a matter of fact, my argument holds for any discourse that sets up its own authorial subjects as the implicit referent, i.e., the yardstick by which to encode and represent cultural Others. It is in this move that power is exercised in discourse.

The first principle I focus on concerns the strategic location or situation of the category "women" vis-a-vis the context of analysis. The assumption of women as an already constituted, coherent group with identical interests and desires, regardless of class, ethnic or racial location or contradictions, implies a notion of gender or sexual difference or even patriarchy (as male dominance—men as a correspondingly coherent group) which can be applied universally and cross-culturally. The context of analysis can be anything from kinship structures and the organization of labor to media representations. The second principle consists in the uncritical use of particular methodologies in providing "proof" of universality and cross-cultural validity. The third is a more specifically political principle underlying the methodologies and the analytic strategies, i.e., the model of power and struggle they imply and suggest. I argue that as a result of the two modes—or, rather, frames—of analysis described above, a homogeneous notion of the oppression of women as a group is assumed, which, in turn, produces the image of an "average third world woman." This average third world woman leads an essentially truncated life based on her feminine gender (read: sexually constrained) and being "third world" (read: ignorant, poor, uneducated, tradition-bound, domestic, family-oriented, victimized, etc.). This, I suggest, is in contrast to the (implicit) self-representation of Western women as educated, modern, as having control over their own bodies and sexualities, and the freedom to make their own decisions. The distinction between Western feminist re-presentation of women in the third world, and Western feminist *self*-presentation is a distinction of the same order as that made by some marxists between the "maintenance" function of the housewife and the real "productive" role of wage labor, or the characterization by developmentalists of the third world as being engaged in the lesser production of "raw materials" in contrast to the "real" productive activity of the First World. These distinctions are made on the basis of the privileging of a particular group as the norm or referent. Men involved in wage labor, first world producers, and, I suggest, Western feminists who sometimes cast Third World women in terms of "ourselves undressed," all construct themselves as the referent in such a binary analytic.

"WOMEN" AS CATEGORY OF ANALYSIS, OR: WE ARE ALL SISTERS IN STRUGGLE

By women as a category of analysis, I am referring to the critical assumption that all of us of the same gender, across classes and cultures, are somehow socially constituted as a homogeneous group identified prior to the process of analysis. This is an assumption which characterizes much feminist discourse. The homogeneity of women as a group is produced not on the basis of biological essentials, but rather on the basis of secondary sociological and anthropological universals. Thus, for instance, in any given piece of feminist analysis, women are characterized as a singular group on the basis of a shared oppression. What binds women together is a sociological notion of the "sameness" of their oppression. It is at this point that an elision takes place between "women" as a discursively constructed group and "women" as material subjects of their own history. Thus, the discursively consensual homogeneity of "women" as a group is mistaken for the historically specific material reality of groups of women. This results in an assumption of women as an always-already constituted group, one which has been labeled "powerless," "exploited," "sexually harassed," etc., by feminist scientific, economic, legal and sociological discourses. (Notice that this is quite similar to sexist discourse labeling women weak, emotional, having math anxiety, etc.) The focus is not on uncovering the material and ideological specificities that constitute a particular group of women as "powerless" in a particular context. It is rather on finding a variety of cases of "powerless" groups of women to prove the general point that women as a group are powerless.

In this section I focus on five specific ways in which "women" as a category of analysis is used in Western feminist discourse on women in the third world. Each of these examples illustrates the construction of "Third World Women" as a homogeneous "powerless" group often located as implicit *victims* of particular socio-economic systems. I have chosen to deal with a variety of writers—from Fran Hosken who writes primarily about female genital mutilation, to writers from the Women in International Development school who write about the effect of development policies on third world women for both western and third world audiences. The similarity of assumptions about "third world women" in all these texts forms the basis of my discussion. This is not to equate all the texts that I analyze, nor is it to equalize their strengths and weaknesses. The authors I deal with write with varying degrees of care and complexity. However, the *effect* of the representation of third world women in these texts is a coherent one, due to the use of "women" as a homogeneous category of analysis, and it is this effect I focus on. In these texts women are defined as victims of male violence; victims of the colonial; victims of the Arab familial system; victims of the economic development process; and finally, victims of the Islamic code. This mode of defining women primarily in terms of their *object status* (the way in which they are affected or not affected by certain institutions and systems) is what characterizes this particular form of the use of "women" as a category of analysis. In the context of Western women writing/studying women in the third world, such objectification (however benevolently motivated) needs to be both named and challenged. As Valerie Amos and Pratibha Parmar argue quite eloquently in a recent essay, "Feminist theories which examine our cultural practices as 'feudal residues' or label us 'traditional,' also portray us as politically immature women who need to be versed and schooled in the ethos of Western Feminism. They need to be continually challenged . . ."

Women as Victims of Male Violence:

Fran Hosken, in writing about the relationship between human rights and female genital mutilation in Africa and the Middle East, bases her whole discussion/condemnation of genital mutilation on one privileged premise: the goal of genital mutilation is "to mutilate the sexual pleasure and satisfaction of woman." This, in turn, leads her to claim that women's sexuality is controlled, as is their reproductive potential. According to Hosken, "male sexual politics" in Africa and around the world "share the same political goal: to assure female dependence and subservience by any and all means." Physical violence against women (rape, sexual assault, excision, infibulation, etc.) is thus carried out "with an astonishing consensus among men in the world." Here, women are defined consistently as the *victims* of male control— the "sexually oppressed." Although it is true that the potential of male violence against women circumscribes and elucidates their social position to a certain extent, defining women as archetypal victims freezes them into "objects-who-defend-themselves," men into "subjects-who-perpetrate-violence," and (every) society into powerless (read: women) and powerful (read: men) groups of people. Male violence must be theorized and interpreted *within* specific societies, both in order to understand it better, as well as in order to effectively organize to change it. Sisterhood cannot be assumed on the basis of gender; it must be forged in concrete, historical and political practice and analysis.

Women as Universal Dependents:

Beverly Lindsay's conclusion to the book *Comparative Perspectives of Third World Women: The Impact of Race, Sex and Class* states: ". . . dependency relationships, based upon race, sex and class, are being perpetrated through social, educational, and economic institutions. These are the linkages among Third World Women." Here, as in other places, Lindsay implies that third world women constitute an identifiable group purely on the basis of shared dependencies. If shared dependencies were all that was needed to bind us together as a group, third world women would always be seen as an apolitical group with no subject status! Instead, if anything, it is the common context of political struggle against class, race, gender and imperialist hierarchies that may constitute third world women as a strategic group at this historical juncture. Lindsay also states that linguistic and cultural differences exist between Vietnamese and Black American women, but "both groups are victims of race, sex and class." Again Black and Vietnamese women are characterized by their victim status. Similarly, examine statements like: "My analysis will start by stating that all African women are politically and economically dependent." Or: "Nevertheless, either overtly or covertly, prostitution is still the main if not the only source of work for African women." All African women are dependent. Prostitution is the only work option for African women as a group. Both statements are illustrative of generalizations sprinkled liberally through a recent Zed Press publication, *Women of Africa: Roots of Oppression*, by Maria Rosa Cutrufelli, who is described on the cover as an Italian Writer, Sociologist, Marxist and Feminist. I wonder if, in 1984, anyone would write a book entitled "Women of Europe: Roots of Oppression"? What is it about cultural Others that make it so easy to analytically formulate them into homogeneous groupings with little regard for historical specificities? Again, I am not objecting to the use of universal groupings for descriptive purposes. Women from the continent of Africa can be descriptively characterized as "Women of Africa." It is when "women of Africa" becomes a homogeneous sociological grouping characterized by common dependencies or powerlessness (or even strengths) that problems arise.

Descriptive gender differences are transformed into the division between men and women. Women are constituted as a group via dependency relationships vis-a-vis men, who are implicitly held responsible for these relationships. When "women of Africa" as a group (versus "men of Africa" as a group?) are seen as a group precisely because they are generally dependent and oppressed, the analysis of specific historical differences becomes impossible, because reality is always apparently structured by divisions—two mutually exclusive and jointly exhaustive groups, the victims and the oppressors. Here the sociological is substituted for the biological in order, however, to create the same—a unity of women. Thus, it is not the descriptive potential of gender difference, but the privileged positioning and explanatory potential of gender difference as the *origin* of oppression that I question. In using "women of Africa" (as an already constituted group of oppressed peoples) as a category of analysis, Cutrufelli denies any historical specificity to the location of women as subordinate, powerful, marginal, central, or otherwise, vis-a-vis particular social and power networks. Women are taken as a unified "Powerless" group prior to the analysis in question. Thus, it is then merely a matter of specifying the context *after the fact*. "Women" are now placed in the context of the family, or in the workplace, or within religious networks, almost as if these systems existed outside the relations of women with other women, and women with men. The problem with this analytic strategy is that it assumes men and women are already constituted as sexual-political subjects *prior* to their entry into the arena of social relations. Only if we subscribe to this assumption is it possible to undertake analysis which looks at the "effects" of kinship structures, colonialism, organization of labor, etc., on women, who are already defined as a group apparently because of shared dependencies, but ultimately because of their gender. But women are *produced through these very relations* as well as being implicated in forming these relations. As Michelle Rosaldo states: ". . . woman's place in human social life is not in any direct sense a product of the things she does (or even less, a function of what, biologically, she is) but the meaning her activities acquire through concrete social interactions." That women mother in a variety of societies is not as significant as the *value* attached to mothering in these societies. The distinction between the act of mothering and the status attached to it is a very important one—one that needs to be made and analyzed contextually.

Married Women as Victims of the Colonial Process:

In Lévi-Strauss's theory of kinship structures as a system of the exchange of women, what is significant is that exchange itself is not constitutive of the subordination of women; women are not subordinate because of the *fact* of exchange, but because of the *modes* of exchange instituted, and the values attached to these modes. However, in discussing the marriage ritual of the Bemba, a Zambian matrilocal, matrilineal people, Cutrufelli in *Women of Africa* focuses on the *fact* of the marital exchange of women before and after Western colonization, rather than the *value* attached to the exchange in this particular context. This leads to her definition of Bemba women as a coherent group affected in a particular way by colonization. Here again, Bemba women are constituted as victims of the effects of Western colonization. Cutrufelli cites the marriage ritual of the Bemba as a multistage event "whereby a young man becomes incorporated into his wife's family group as he takes up residence with them and gives his services in return for food and maintenance." This ritual extends over many years, and the sexual relationship varies according to the degree of the girl's physical maturity. It is only after the girl undergoes an initiation ceremony at puberty that intercourse is sanctioned, and the man acquires legal rights over the woman. This initiation ceremony is the most important act of the consecration of women's reproductive power, so that the abduction of an uninitiated girl is of no consequence, while heavy penalty is levied for the seduction of an initiated girl. Cutrufelli asserts that *the effect of European colonization has changed this whole marriage system*. Now the young man is entitled to take his wife away from her people in return for money. The implication is that Bemba women have now lost the protection of tribal laws. However, while it is possible to see how the *structure* of the traditional marriage contract (versus the postcolonial marriage contract) offered women a certain amount of control over their marital relations, only an analysis of the political significance of the actual practice which privileges an initiated girl over an uninitiated one, indicating a shift in female power relations as a result of this ceremony, can provide an accurate account of whether Bemba women were indeed protected by tribal laws *at all times*. However, it is not possible to talk about Bemba women as a homogeneous group within the traditional marriage structure. Bemba women *before* the initiation are constituted within a different set of social relations compared to Bemba women *after* the initiation. To treat them as a unified group characterized by the fact of their "exchange" between male kin, is to deny the socio-historical and cultural specificities of their existence, and the differential *value* attached to their exchange before and after their initiation. It is to treat the initiation ceremony as a ritual with no political implications or effects. It is also to assume that in merely describing the *structure* of the marriage contract, the situation of women is exposed. Women as a group are positioned within a given structure, but there is no attempt made to trace the effect of the marriage practice in constituting women within an obviously changing network of power relations. Thus, women are assumed to be sexual-political subjects prior to entry into kinship structures.

Women and Familial Systems:

Elizabeth Cowie, in another context, points out the implications of this sort of analysis when she emphasizes the specifically political nature of kinship structures which must be analyzed as ideological practices which designate men and women as father, husband, wife, mother, sister, etc. Thus, Cowie suggests, women as women are not located within the family. Rather, it is *in* the family, as an effect of kinship structures, that women as women are constructed, defined within and by the group. Thus, for instance, when Juliette Minces cites *the* patriarchal family as the basis for "an almost identical vision of women" that *Arab* and *Muslim* societies have, she falls into this very trap. Not only is it problematical to speak of a vision of women shared by Arab and Muslim societies without addressing the particular historical, material and ideological power structures that construct such images, but to speak of *the* patriarchal family or *the* tribal kinship structure as the *origin* of the socio-economic status of women is to again assume that women are sexual-political subjects prior to their entry into the family. So while on the one hand women attain value or status *within* the family, the assumption of a singular patriarchal kinship system (common to all Arab and Muslim societies) is what apparently structures women as an oppressed group in these societies! This singular, coherent kinship system presumably influences another separate and given entity, "women." Thus, all women, regardless of class and cultural differences, are affected by this system. Not only are *all* Arab and Muslim women seen to constitute a homogeneous oppressed group, but there is no discussion of the specific practices within the family which constitute women as mothers, wives, sisters, etc. Arabs and Muslims it appears, don't change at all. Their patriarchal family is carried over from the times of the prophet Mohammed. They exist, as it were, "outside history."

Women and Religious Ideologies:

A further example of the use of "women" as a category of analysis is found in cross-cultural analyses which subscribe to a certain economic reductionism in describing the relationship between the economy and factors such as politics and ideology. Here, in reducing the level of comparison to the economic relations between "developed and developing" countries, any specificity to the question of women is denied. Mina Modares, in a careful analysis of women and Shi'ism in Iran, focuses on this very problem when she criticizes feminist writings which treat Islam as an ideology separate from and outside social relations and practices, rather than a discourse which *includes* rules for economic, social and power relations within society. Patricia Jeffery's otherwise excellent work on Pirzada women in purdah, considers Islamic ideology as a partial explanation for the status of women in that it provides a justification for the purdah. Here, Islamic ideology is reduced to a set of ideas whose internalization by Pirzada women contributes to the stability of the system. However, the primary explanation for purdah is located in the control that Pirzada men have over economic resources, and the personal security purdah gives to Pirzada women. By taking a specific version of Islam as *the* Islam, Jeffrey attributes a singularity and coherence to it. Modares notes, "'Islamic Theology' then becomes imposed on a separate and given entity called 'women.' A further unification is reached: Women (meaning *all women*), regardless of their differing positions within societies, come to be affected or not affected by Islam. These conceptions provide the right ingredients for an unproblematic possibility of a cross-cultural study of women." A number of cross-cultural studies of women's position which subscribe to this kind of economic reductionism do so by collapsing all ideological specificities into economic relations, and universalizing on the basis of this comparison.

Women and the Development Process:

The best examples of universalization on the basis of economic reductionism can be found in the liberal "Women in Development" literature. Proponents of this school seek to examine the effect of development on third world women, sometimes from feminist perspectives. At the very least, there is an evident interest in and commitment to improving the lives of women in "developing" countries. Scholars like Irene Tinker, Ester Boserup, and

Perdita Huston have all written about the effect of development policies on women in the third world. All three women assume "development" is synonymous with "economic development" or "economic progress." As in the case of Minces's patriarchal family, Hosken's male sexual control, and Cutrufelli's Western colonization, *Development* here becomes the all time equalizer. Women are affected positively or negatively by economic development policies. Cross-cultural comparison between women in different "developing" countries is made both possible and unproblematical by this assumption of women as a group affected (or not affected) by economic policies. For instance, Perdita Huston states that the purpose of her study is to describe the effect of the development process on the "family unit and its individual members" in Egypt, Kenya, Sudan, Tunisia, Sri Lanka and Mexico. She states that the "problems" and "needs" expressed by rural and urban women in these countries all center around education and training, work and wages, access to health and other services, political participation and legal rights. Huston relates all these "needs" to the lack of sensitive development policies which exclude women as a group or category. For her, the solution is simple: improved development policies which emphasize training for *women* field workers, use *women* trainees, *women* rural development officers, encourage *women's* cooperatives, etc. Here, again, women are assumed to be a coherent group or category prior to their entry into "the development process." Huston assumes that all third world women have similar problems and needs. Thus, they must have similar interests and goals. However, the interests of urban, middleclass, educated Egyptian housewives, to take only one instance, could surely not be seen as being the same as those of their uneducated, poor maids. Development policies do not affect both groups of women in the same way. Practices which characterize women's status and roles vary according to class. Women are constituted as women through the complex interaction between class, culture, religion and other ideological institutions and frameworks. They are not "women"—a coherent group—solely on the basis of a particular economic system or policy. Such reductive cross-cultural comparisons result in the colonization of the conflicts and contradictions which characterize women of different social classes and cultures.

Thus, according to Perdita Huston, women in the third world countries she writes about have "needs" and "problems," but few if any have "choices" or the freedom to act. This is an interesting representation of women in the third world, one which is significant in suggesting a latent self-presentation of Western women which bears looking at. She writes, "What surprised and moved me most as I listened to women in such very different cultural settings was the striking commonality—whether they were educated or illiterate, urban or rural—of their most basic values: the importance they assign to family, dignity, and service to others." I wonder if Huston would consider such values unusual for women in the West?

What is problematical, then, about this kind of use of "women" as a group, as a stable category of analysis, is that it assumes an ahistorical, universal unity between women based on a generalized notion of their subordination. Instead of analytically demonstrating the production of women as socio-economic political groups *within* particular local contexts, this move limits the definition of the female subject to gender identity, completely bypassing social class and ethnic identities. What characterizes women as a group is their gender (sociologically not necessarily biologically defined) over and above everything else, indicating a monolithic notion of sexual difference. Because women are thus constituted as a coherent group, sexual difference becomes coterminous with female subordination, and power is automatically defined in binary terms: people who have it (read: men), and people who do not (read: women). Men exploit, women are exploited. As suggested above, such simplistic formulations are both reductive and ineffectual in designing strategies to combat oppressions. All they do is reinforce binary divisions between men and women.

What would an analysis which did not do this look like? Maria Mies's work is one such example. It is an example which illustrates the strength of Western feminist work on women in the third world and which does not fall into the traps discussed above. Maria Mies's study of the lace makers of Narsapur, India (Zed Press, 1982) attempts to carefully analyze a substantial household industry in which "housewives" produce lace doilies for consumption in the world market. Through a detailed analysis of the structure of the lace industry, production and reproduction relations, the sexual division of labor, profits and exploitation, and the overall consequences of defining women as "non-working housewives" and their work as "leisure-time activity," Mies demonstrates the levels of exploitation in this industry and the impact of this production system on the work and living conditions of the women involved in it. In addition, she is able to analyze the "ideology of the housewife," the notion of a woman sitting in the house, as providing the necessary subjective and socio-cultural element for the creation and maintenance of a production system that contributes to the increasing pauperization of women, and keeps them totally atomized and disorganized as workers. Mies's analyses show the effect of a certain historically and culturally specific mode of patriarchal organization, an organization constructed on the basis of the definition of the lace makers as "non-working housewives" at familial, local, regional, state-wide and international levels. The intricacies and the effects of particular power networks are not only emphasized, but they form the basis of Mies's analysis of how this particular group of women is situated at the center of a hegemonic, exploitative world market. This is a good example of what careful, politically focused, local analyses can accomplish. It illustrates how the category of women is constructed in a variety of political contexts that often exist simultaneously and overlaid on the top of one another. There is no easy generalization in the direction of "women" in India, or "women in the third world"; nor is there a reduction of the political construction of the exploitation of the lace makers to cultural explanations about the passivity or obedience that might characterize these women and their situation. Finally, this mode of local, political analysis which generates theoretical categories from *within* the situation and context being analyzed, also suggests corresponding effective strategies for organizing against the exploitations faced by the lace makers. These Narsapur women are not mere victims of the production process, because they resist, challenge and subvert the process at various junctures. Here is one instance of how Mies delineates the connections between the housewife ideology, the self-consciousness of the lace makers and their inter-relationships as contributing to the latent resistances she perceives among the women:

The persistence of the housewife ideology, the self-perception of the lace makers as petty commodity producers rather than as workers, is not only upheld by the structure of the industry as such but also by the deliberate propagation and reinforcement of reactionary patriarchal norms and institutions. Thus, most of the lace makers voiced the same opinion about the rules of *purdah* and seclusion in their communities which were also propagated by the lace exporters. In particular, the *Kapu* women said that they had never gone out of their houses, that women of their community could not do any other work than housework and lace work etc. But in spite of the fact that most of them still subscribed fully to the patriarchal norms of the *gosha* women, there were also contradictory elements in their consciousness. Thus, although they looked down with contempt upon women who were able to work outside the house—like the untouchable *Mala* and *Madiga* women or women of other lower castes, they could not ignore the fact that these women were earning more money precisely because they were *not* respectable housewives but workers. At one discussion, they even admitted that it would be better if they could also go out and do coolie work. And when they were asked whether they would be ready to come out of their houses and work in one place in some sort of a factory, they said they would do that. This shows that the *purdah* and housewife ideology, although still fully internalized, already had some cracks, because it has been confronted with several contradictory realities.

It is only by understanding the *contradictions* inherent in women's location within various structures that effective political action and challenges can be devised. Mies's study goes a long way toward offering such analysis. While there are now an increasing number of Western feminist writings in this tradition there is also unfortunately a large block of writing which succumbs to the cultural reductionism discussed earlier.

Do Muslim Women
Really Need Saving?

Anthropological Reflections on
Cultural Relativism and Its Others

BY LILA ABU-LUGHOD

Lila Abu-Lughod is a Palestinian American anthropologist and the Joseph L. Buttenweiser Professor of Social Science in the Department of Anthropology at Columbia University. Her work focuses on ethnographic research in the Arab world and the intersections of culture and power, as well as gender and women's rights in the Middle East. This essay, originally published in 2002 in *American Anthropologist*, became the basis for her 2013 book of the same name, which criticized the United States' post-9/11 use of the narrative of the Muslim woman in need of saving as a rationalization for imperialist military aggression in Muslim countries such as Afghanistan and Iraq. Abu-Lughod deftly and specifically interrogates the motives of feminists who use this savior narrative while supporting systemic injustices in their own countries.

POLITICS OF THE VEIL

I want now to look more closely at those Afghan women Laura Bush claimed were "rejoicing" at their liberation by the Americans. This necessitates a discussion of the veil, or the burqa, because it is so central to contemporary concerns about Muslim women. This will set the stage for a discussion of how anthropologists, feminist anthropologists in particular, contend with the problem of difference in a global world. In the conclusion, I will return to the rhetoric of saving Muslim women and offer an alternative.

It is common popular knowledge that the ultimate sign of the oppression of Afghan women under the Taliban-and-the-terrorists is that they were forced to wear the burqa. Liberals sometimes confess their surprise that even though Afghanistan has been liberated from the Taliban, women do not seem to be throwing off their burqas. Someone who has worked in Muslim regions must ask why this is so surprising. Did we expect that once "free" from the Taliban they would go "back" to belly shirts and blue jeans, or dust off their Chanel suits? We need to be more sensible about the clothing of "women of cover," and so there is perhaps a need to make some basic points about veiling.

First, it should be recalled that the Taliban did not invent the burqa. It was the local form of covering that Pashtun women in one region wore when they went out. The Pashtun are one of several ethnic groups in Afghanistan and the burqa was one of many forms of covering in the subcontinent and Southwest Asia that has developed as a convention for symbolizing women's modesty or respectability. The burqa, like some other forms of "cover" has, in many settings, marked the symbolic separation of men's and women's spheres, as part of the general association of women with family and home, not with public space where strangers mingled.

Twenty years ago the anthropologist Hanna Papanek, who worked in Pakistan, described the burqa as "portable seclusion." She noted that many saw it as a liberating invention because it enabled women to move out of segregated living spaces while still observing the basic moral requirements of separating and protecting women from unrelated men. Ever since I came across her phrase "portable seclusion," I have thought of these enveloping robes as "mobile homes." Everywhere, such veiling signifies belonging to a particular community and participating in a moral way of life in which families are paramount in the organization of communities and the home is associated with the sanctity of women.

The obvious question that follows is this: If this were the case, why would women suddenly become immodest? Why would they suddenly throw off the markers of their respectability, markers, whether burqas or other forms of cover, which were supposed to assure their protection in the public sphere from the harassment of strange men by symbolically signaling to all that they were still in the inviolable space of their homes, even though moving in the public realm? Especially when these are forms of dress that had become so conventional that most women gave little thought to their meaning.

To draw some analogies, none of them perfect, why are we surprised that Afghan women do not throw off their burqas when we know perfectly well that it would not be appropriate to wear shorts to the opera? At the time these discussions of Afghan women's burqas were raging, a friend of mine was chided by her husband for suggesting she wanted to wear a pantsuit to a fancy wedding; "You know you don't wear pants to a WASP wedding," he reminded her. New Yorkers know that the beautifully coiffed Hasidic women, who look so fashionable next to their dour husbands in black coats and hats, are wearing wigs. This is because religious belief and community standards of propriety require the covering of the hair. They also alter boutique fashions to include high necks and long sleeves. As anthropologists know perfectly well, people wear the appropriate form of dress for their social communities and are guided by socially shared standards, religious beliefs, and moral ideals, unless they deliberately transgress to make a point or are unable to afford proper cover. If we think that U.S. women live in a world of choice regarding clothing, all we need to do is remind ourselves of the expression, "the tyranny of fashion."

What had happened in Afghanistan under the Taliban is that one regional style of covering or veiling, associated with a certain respectable but not elite class, was imposed on everyone as "religiously" appropriate, even though previously there had been many different styles, popular or traditional with different groups and classes—different ways to mark women's propriety, or, in more recent times, religious piety. Although I am not an expert on Afghanistan, I imagine that the majority of women left in Afghanistan by the time the Taliban took control were the rural or less educated, from nonelite families, since they were the only ones who could not emigrate to escape the hardship and violence that has marked Afghanistan's recent history. If liberated from the enforced wearing of burqas, most of these women would choose some other form of modest headcovering, like all those living nearby who were not under the Taliban—their rural Hindu counterparts in the North of India (who cover their heads and veil their faces from affines) or their Muslim sisters in Pakistan.

Even *The New York Times* carried an article about Afghan women refugees in Pakistan that attempted to educate readers about this local variety. The article describes and pictures everything from the now-iconic burqa with the embroidered eyeholes, which a Pashtun woman explains is the proper dress for her community, to large scarves they call chadors, to the new Islamic modest dress that wearers refer to as *hijab*. Those in the new Islamic dress are characteristically students heading for professional careers, especially in medicine, just like their counterparts from Egypt to Malaysia. One wearing the large scarf was a school principal; the other was a poor street vendor. The telling quote from the young street vendor is, "If I did [wear the burqa] the refugees would tease me because the burqa is for 'good women' who stay inside the home." Here you can see the local status associated with the burqa—it is for good respectable women from strong families who are not forced to make a living selling on the street.

The British newspaper *The Guardian* published an interview in January 2002 with Dr. Suhaila Siddiqi, a respected surgeon in Afghanistan who holds the rank of lieutenant general in the Afghan medical corps. A woman in her sixties, she comes from an elite family and, like her sisters, was educated. Unlike most women of her class, she chose not to go into exile. She is presented in the article as "the woman who stood up to the Taliban" because she refused to wear the burqa. She had made it a condition of returning to her post as head of a major hospital when the Taliban came begging in 1996, just eight months after firing her along with other women. Siddiqi is described as thin, glamorous, and confident. But further into the article it is noted that her graying bouffant hair is covered in a gauzy veil. This is a reminder that though she refused the burqa, she had no question about wearing the chador or scarf.

Finally, I need to make a crucial point about veiling. Not only are there many forms of covering, which themselves have different meanings in the communities in which they are used, but also veiling itself must not be confused with, or made to stand for, lack of agency. As I have argued in my ethnography of a Bedouin community in Egypt in the late 1970s and 1980s, pulling the black head cloth over the face in front of older respected men is considered a voluntary act by women who are deeply committed to being moral and have a sense of honor tied to family. One of the ways they show their standing is by covering their faces in certain contexts. They decide for whom they feel it is appropriate to veil.

To take a very different case, the modern Islamic modest dress that many educated women across the Muslim world have taken on since the mid-1970s now both publicly marks piety and can be read as a sign of educated urban sophistication, a sort of modernity. As Saba Mahmood has so brilliantly shown in her ethnography of women in the mosque movement in Egypt, this new form of dress is also perceived by many of the women who adopt it as part of a bodily means to cultivate virtue, the outcome of their professed desire to be close to God.

Two points emerge from this fairly basic discussion of the meanings of veiling in the contemporary Muslim world. First, we need to work against the reductive interpretation of veiling as the quintessential sign of women's unfreedom, even if we object to state imposition of this form, as in Iran or with the Taliban. (It must be recalled that the modernizing states of Turkey and Iran had earlier in the century banned veiling and required men, except religious clerics, to adopt Western dress.) What does freedom mean if we accept the fundamental premise that humans are social beings, always raised in certain social and historical contexts and belonging to particular communities that shape their desires and understandings of the world? Is it not a gross violation of women's own understandings of what they are doing to simply denounce the burqa as a medieval imposition? Second, we must take care not to reduce the diverse situations and attitudes of millions of Muslim women to a single item of clothing. Perhaps it is time to give up the Western obsession with the veil and focus on some serious issues with which feminists and others should indeed be concerned.

Ultimately, the significant political-ethical problem the burqa raises is how to deal with cultural "others." How are we to deal with difference without accepting the passivity implied by the cultural relativism for which anthropologists are justly famous—a relativism that says it's their culture and it's not my business to judge or interfere, only to try to understand. Cultural relativism is certainly an improvement on ethnocentrism and the racism, cultural imperialism, and imperiousness that underlie it; the problem is that it is too late not to interfere. The forms of lives we find around the world are already products of long histories of interactions.

I want to explore the issues of women, cultural relativism, and the problems of "difference" from three angles. First, I want to consider what feminist anthropologists (those stuck in that awkward relationship, as Strathern has claimed) are to do with strange political bedfellows. I used to feel torn when I received the e-mail petitions circulating for the last few years in defense of Afghan women under the Taliban. I was not sympathetic to the dogmatism of the Taliban; I do not support the oppression of women. But the provenance of the campaign worried me. I do not usually find myself in political company with the likes of Hollywood celebrities. I had never received a petition from such women defending the right of Palestinian women to safety from Israeli bombing or daily harassment at checkpoints, asking the United States to reconsider its support for a government that had dispossessed them, closed them out from work and citizenship rights, refused them the most basic freedoms. Maybe some of these same people might be signing petitions to save African women from genital cutting, or Indian women from dowry deaths. However, I do not think that it would be as easy to mobilize so many of these American and European women if it were not a case of Muslim men oppressing Muslim women—women of cover for whom they can feel sorry and in relation to whom they can feel smugly superior. Would television diva Oprah Winfrey host the Women in Black, the women's peace group from Israel, as she did RAWA, the Revolutionary Association of Women of Afghanistan, who were also granted the *Glamour Magazine* Women of the Year Award? What are we to make of post-Taliban "Reality Tours" such as the one advertised on the internet by Global Exchange for March 2002 under the title "Courage and Tenacity: A Women's Delegation to Afghanistan"? The rationale for the $1,400 tour is that "with the removal of the Taliban government, Afghan women, for the first time in the past decade, have the opportunity to reclaim their basic human rights and establish their role as equal citizens by participating in the rebuilding of their nation." The tour's objective, to celebrate International Women's Week, is "to develop awareness of the concerns and issues the Afghan women are facing as well as to witness the changing political, economic, and social conditions which have created new opportunities for the women of Afghanistan."

To be critical of this celebration of women's rights in Afghanistan is not to pass judgment on any local women's organizations, such as RAWA, whose members have courageously worked since 1977 for a democratic secular Afghanistan in which women's human rights are respected, against Soviet-backed regimes or U.S.-, Saudi-, and Pakistani-supported conservatives. Their documentation of abuse and their work through clinics and schools have been enormously important.

It is also not to fault the campaigns that exposed the dreadful conditions under which the Taliban placed women. The Feminist Majority campaign helped put a stop to a secret oil pipeline deal between the Taliban and the U.S. multinational Unocal that was going forward with U.S. administration support. Western feminist campaigns must not be confused with the hypocrisies of the new colonial feminism of a Republican president who was not elected for his progressive stance on feminist issues or of administrations that played down the terrible record of violations of women by the United States' allies in the Northern Alliance, as documented by Human Rights Watch and Amnesty International, among others. Rapes and assaults were widespread in the period of infighting that devastated Afghanistan before the Taliban came in to restore order.

It is, however, to suggest that we need to look closely at what we are supporting (and what we are not) and to think carefully about why. How should we manage the complicated politics and ethics of finding ourselves in agreement with those with whom we normally disagree? I do not know how many feminists who felt good about saving Afghan women from the Taliban are also asking for a global redistribution of wealth or contemplating sacrificing their own consumption radically so that African or Afghan women could have some chance of having what I do believe should be a universal human right—the right to freedom from the structural violence of global inequality and from the ravages of war, the everyday rights of having enough to eat, having homes for their families in which to live and thrive, having ways to make decent livings so their children can grow, and having the strength and security to work out, within their communities and with whatever alliances they want, how to live a good life, which might very well include changing the ways those communities are organized.

Suspicion about bedfellows is only a first step; it will not give us a way to think more positively about what to do or where to stand. For that, we need to confront two more big issues. First is the acceptance of the possibility of difference. Can we only free Afghan women to be like us or might we have to recognize that even after "liberation" from the Taliban, they might want different things than we would want for them? What do we do about that? Second, we need to be vigilant about the rhetoric of saving people because of what it implies about our attitudes.

Again, when I talk about accepting difference, I am not implying that we should resign ourselves to being cultural relativists who respect whatever goes on elsewhere as "just their culture." I have already discussed the dangers of "cultural" explanations; "their" cultures are just as much part of history and an interconnected world as ours are. What I am advocating is the hard work involved in recognizing and respecting differences—precisely as products of different histories, as expressions of different circumstances, and as manifestations of differently structured desires. We may want justice for women, but can we accept that there might be different ideas about justice and that different women might want, or choose, different futures from what we envision as best? We must consider that they might be called to personhood, so to speak, in a different language.

Reports from the Bonn peace conference held in late November to discuss the rebuilding of Afghanistan revealed significant differences among the few Afghan women feminists and activists present. RAWA's position was to reject any conciliatory approach to Islamic governance. According to one report I read, most women activists, especially those based in Afghanistan who are aware of the realities on the ground, agreed that Islam had to be the starting point for reform. Fatima Gailani, a U.S.-based advisor to one of the delegations, is quoted as saying, "If I go to Afghanistan today and ask women for votes on the promise to bring them secularism, they are going to tell me to go to hell." Instead, according to one report, most of these women looked for inspiration on how to fight for equality to a place that might seem surprising. They looked to Iran as a country in which they saw women making significant gains within an Islamic framework—in part through an Islamically oriented feminist movement that is challenging injustices and reinterpreting the religious tradition.

The situation in Iran is itself the subject of heated debate within feminist circles, especially among Iranian feminists in the West. It is not clear whether and in what ways women have made gains and whether the great increases in literacy, decreases in birthrates, presence of women in the professions and government, and a feminist flourishing in cultural fields like writing and film-making are because of or despite the establishment of a so-called Islamic Republic. The concept of an Islamic feminism itself is also controversial. Is it an oxymoron or does it refer to a viable movement forged by brave women who want a third way?

One of the things we have to be most careful about in thinking about Third World feminisms, and feminism in different parts of the Muslim world, is how not to fall into polarizations that place feminism on the side of the West. I have written about the dilemmas faced by Arab feminists when Western feminists initiate campaigns that make them vulnerable to local denunciations by conservatives of various sorts, whether Islamist or nationalist, of being traitors. As some like Afsaneh Najmabadi are now arguing, not only is it wrong to see history simplistically in terms of a putative opposition between Islam and the West (as is happening in the United States now and has happened in parallel in the Muslim world), but it is also strategically dangerous to accept this cultural opposition between Islam and the West, between fundamentalism and feminism, because those many people within Muslim countries who are trying to find alternatives to present injustices, those who might want to refuse the divide and take from different histories and cultures, who do not accept that being feminist means being Western, will be under pressure to choose, just as we are: Are you with us or against us?

My point is to remind us to be aware of differences, respectful of other paths toward social change that might give women better lives. Can there be a liberation that is Islamic? And, beyond this, is liberation even a goal for which all women or people strive? Are emancipation, equality, and rights part of a universal language we must use? To quote Saba Mahmood, writing about the women in Egypt who are seeking to become pious Muslims, "The desire for freedom and liberation is a historically situated desire whose motivational force cannot be assumed a priori, but needs to be reconsidered in light of other desires, aspirations, and capacities that inhere in a culturally and historically located subject." In other words, might other desires be more meaningful for different groups of people? Living in close families? Living in a godly way? Living without war? I have done fieldwork in Egypt over more than 20 years and I cannot think of a single woman I know, from the poorest rural to the most educated cosmopolitan, who has ever expressed envy of U.S. women, women they tend to perceive as bereft of community, vulnerable to sexual violence and social anomie, driven by individual success rather than morality, or strangely disrespectful of God.

Mahmood has pointed out a disturbing thing that happens when one argues for a respect for other traditions. She notes that there seems to be a difference in the political demands made on those who work on or are trying to understand Muslims and Islamists and those who work on secular-humanist projects. She, who studies the piety movement in Egypt, is consistently pressed to denounce all the harm done by Islamic movements around the world—otherwise she is accused of being an apologist. But there never seems to be a parallel demand for those who study secular humanism and its projects, despite the terrible violences that have been associated with it over the last couple of centuries, from world wars to colonialism, from genocides to slavery. We need to have as little dogmatic faith in secular humanism as in Islamism, and as open a mind to the complex possibilities of human projects undertaken in one tradition as the other.

Why Do They Hate Us?

(from *Headscarves and Hymens*)

BY MONA ELTAHAWY

Mona Eltahawy is an award-winning columnist, journalist, essayist, activist, and public speaker whose work
centers on global feminism, particularly its intersection
with Arab and Muslim issues. In 2011, she was beaten
and sexually assaulted by Egyptian riot police while covering the "Arab Spring" revolution in Egypt. Her provocative essay "Why Do They Hate Us?" published in
Foreign Policy in 2012, examines how sexual violence is
used to oppress women in Arab countries and the United
States' complicity in that oppression. The essay is striking for many reasons. Eltahawy is blunt in her assessment that Arab men hate Arab women. "Yes: They hate
us. It must be said," she writes. The entire essay is similarly clear-eyed and straightforward in the ways it identifies the hatred of women as the source of the oppression
of Arab women in myriad ways. As you might imagine,
people had a range of reactions to this essay. Some critics
suggested that Eltahawy narrowly portrayed Arab women
as victims while others suggested that Eltahawy was solely
interested in defaming Arab men.

In "Distant View of a Minaret," the late and much-neglected
Egyptian writer Alifa Rifaat begins her short story with a woman
so unmoved by sex with her husband that as he focuses solely on
his pleasure, she notices a spider web she must sweep off the ceiling and has time to ruminate on her husband's repeated refusal to
prolong intercourse until she too climaxes, "as though purposely
to deprive her." Just as her husband denies her an orgasm, the call
to prayer interrupts his, and the man leaves. After washing up, she

loses herself in prayer—so much more satisfying that she can't wait until the next prayer—and looks out onto the street from her balcony. She interrupts her reverie to make coffee dutifully for her husband to drink after his nap. Taking it to their bedroom to pour it in front of him as he prefers, she notices he is dead. She instructs their son to go and get a doctor. "She returned to the living room and poured out the coffee for herself. She was surprised at how calm she was," Rifaat writes.

In a crisp three-and-a-half pages, Rifaat lays out a trifecta of sex, death, and religion, a bulldozer that crushes denial and defensiveness to get at the pulsating heart of misogyny in the Middle East. There is no sugarcoating it. They don't hate us because of our freedoms, as the tired, post-9/11 American cliché had it. We have no freedoms because they hate us, as this Arab woman so powerfully says.

Yes: They hate us. It must be said.

Some may ask why I'm bringing this up now, at a time when the region has risen up, fueled not by the usual hatred of America and Israel but by a common demand for freedom. After all, shouldn't everyone get basic rights first, before women demand special treatment? And what does gender, or for that matter, sex, have to do with the Arab Spring? But I'm not talking about sex hidden away in dark corners and closed bedrooms. An entire political and economic system—one that treats half of humanity like animals—must be destroyed along with the other more obvious tyrannies choking off the region from its future. Until the rage shifts from the oppressors in our presidential palaces to the oppressors on our streets and in our homes, our revolution has not even begun.

So: Yes, women all over the world have problems; yes, the United States has yet to elect a female president; and yes, women continue to be objectified in many "Western" countries (I live in one of them). That's where the conversation usually ends when you try to discuss why Arab societies hate women.

But let's put aside what the United States does or doesn't do to women. Name me an Arab country, and I'll recite a litany of abuses fueled by a toxic mix of culture and religion that few seem willing or able to disentangle lest they blaspheme or offend. When more than 90 percent of ever-married women in Egypt—including my mother and all but one of her six sisters—have had their genitals cut in the name of modesty, then surely we must all blaspheme. When Egyptian women are subjected to humiliating "virginity tests" merely for speaking out, it's no time for silence. When an article in the Egyptian criminal code says that if a woman has been beaten by her husband "with good intentions" no punitive damages can be obtained, then to hell with political correctness. And what, pray tell, are "good intentions"? They are legally deemed to include any beating that is "not severe" or "directed at the face." What all this means is that when it comes to the status of women in the Middle East, it's not better than you think. It's much, much worse. Even after these "revolutions," all is more or less considered well with the world as long as women are covered up, anchored to the home, denied the simple mobility of getting into their own cars, forced to get permission from men to travel, and unable to marry without a male guardian's blessing—or divorce either.

Not a single Arab country ranks in the top 100 in the World Economic Forum's Global Gender Gap Report, putting the region as a whole solidly at the planet's rock bottom. Poor or rich, we all hate our women. Neighbors Saudi Arabia and Yemen, for instance, might be eons apart when it comes to GDP, but only four places separate them on the index, with the kingdom at 131 and Yemen coming in at 135 out of 135 countries. Morocco, often touted for its "progressive" family law (a 2005 report by Western "experts" called it "an example for Muslim countries aiming to integrate into modern society"), ranks 129; according to Morocco's Ministry of Justice, 41,098 girls under age 18 were married there in 2010.

It's easy to see why the lowest-ranked country is Yemen, where 55 percent of women are illiterate, 79 percent do not participate in the labor force, and just one woman serves in the 301-person parliament. Horrific news reports about 12-year-old girls dying in childbirth do little to stem the tide of child marriage there. Instead, demonstrations in support of child marriage outstrip those against it, fueled by clerical declarations that opponents of state-sanctioned pedophilia are apostates because the Prophet Mohammed, according to them, married his second wife, Aisha, when she was a child.

But at least Yemeni women can drive. It surely hasn't ended their litany of problems, but it symbolizes freedom—and nowhere does such symbolism resonate more than in Saudi Arabia, where child marriage is also practiced and women are perpetually minors regardless of their age or education. Saudi women far outnumber their male counterparts on university campuses but are reduced to watching men far less qualified control every aspect of their lives.

Yes, Saudi Arabia, the country where a gang-rape survivor was sentenced to jail for agreeing to get into a car with an unrelated male and needed a royal pardon; Saudi Arabia, where a woman who broke the ban on driving was sentenced to 10 lashes and again needed a royal pardon; Saudi Arabia, where women still can't vote or run in elections, yet it's considered "progress" that a royal decree promised to enfranchise them for almost completely symbolic local elections in—wait for it—2015. So bad is it for women in Saudi Arabia that those tiny paternalistic pats on their backs are greeted with delight as the monarch behind them, King Abdullah, is hailed as a "reformer"—even by those who ought to know better, such as *Newsweek*, which in 2010 named the king one of the top 11 most respected world leaders. You want to know how bad it is? The "reformer's" answer to the revolutions popping up across the region was to numb his people with still more government handouts—especially for the Salafi zealots from whom the Saudi royal family inhales legitimacy. King Abdullah is 87. Just wait until you see the next in line, Prince Nayef, a man straight out of the Middle Ages. His misogyny and zealotry make King Abdullah look like Susan B. Anthony.

SO WHY DO THEY HATE US?

Sex, or more precisely hymens, explains much.

"Why extremists always focus on women remains a mystery to me," U.S. Secretary of State Hillary Clinton said recently. "But they all seem to. It doesn't matter what country they're in or what religion they claim. They want to control women." (And yet Clinton represents an administration that openly supports many of those misogynistic despots.) Attempts to control by such regimes often stem from the suspicion that without it, a woman is just a few degrees short of sexual insatiability. Observe Yusuf al-Qaradawi, the popular cleric and longtime conservative TV host on Al Jazeera who developed a stunning penchant for the Arab Spring revolutions—once they were under way, that is—undoubtedly understanding that they would eliminate the tyrants who long tormented and oppressed both him and the Muslim Brotherhood movement from which he springs.

I could find you a host of crackpots sounding off on Woman the Insatiable Temptress, but I'm staying mainstream with Qaradawi, who commands a huge audience on and off the satellite channels. Although he says female genital mutilation (which he calls "circumcision," a common euphemism that tries to put the practice on a par with male circumcision) is not "obligatory," you will also find this priceless observation in one of his books: "I personally support this under the current circumstances in the modern world. Anyone who thinks that circumcision is the best way to protect his daughters should do it," he wrote, adding, "The moderate opinion is in favor of practicing circumcision to reduce temptation." So even among "moderates," girls' genitals are cut to ensure their desire is nipped in the bud—pun fully intended. Qaradawi has since issued a fatwa against female genital mutilation, but it comes as no surprise that when Egypt banned the practice in 2008, some Muslim Brotherhood legislators opposed the law. And some still do—including a prominent female parliamentarian, Azza al-Garf.

Yet it's the men who can't control themselves on the streets, where from Morocco to Yemen, sexual harassment is endemic and it's for the men's sake that so many women are encouraged to cover up. Cairo has a women-only subway car to protect us from wandering hands and worse; countless Saudi malls are for families only, barring single men from entry unless they produce a requisite female to accompany them.

We often hear how the Middle East's failing economies have left many men unable to marry, and some even use that to explain rising levels of sexual harassment on the streets. In a 2008 survey by the Egyptian Center for Women's Rights, more than 80 percent of Egyptian women said they'd experienced sexual harassment and more than 60 percent of men admitted to harassing women.

Yet we never hear how a later marriage age affects women. Do women have sex drives or not? Apparently, the Arab jury is still out on the basics of human biology.

Enter that call to prayer and the sublimation through religion that Rifaat so brilliantly introduces in her story. Just as regime-appointed clerics lull the poor across the region with promises of justice—and nubile virgins—in the next world rather than a reckoning with the corruption and nepotism of the dictator in this life, so women are silenced by a deadly combination of men who hate them while also claiming to have God firmly on their side.

I turn again to Saudi Arabia, and not just because when I encountered the country at age 15 I was traumatized into feminism—there's no other way to describe it—but because the kingdom is unabashed in its worship of a misogynistic God and never suffers any consequences for it, thanks to its double-whammy advantage of having oil and being home to Islam's two holiest places, Mecca and Medina.

Then—the 1980s and 1990s—as now, clerics on Saudi TV were obsessed with women and their orifices, especially what came out of them. I'll never forget hearing that if a baby boy urinated on you, you could go ahead and pray in the same clothes, yet if a baby girl peed on you, you had to change. What on Earth in the girl's urine made you impure? I wondered.

Hatred of women.

How much does Saudi Arabia hate women? So much so that 15 girls died in a school fire in Mecca in 2002, after "morality police" barred them from fleeing the burning building—and kept firefighters from rescuing them—because the girls were not wearing headscarves and cloaks required in public. And nothing happened. No one was put on trial. Parents were silenced. The only concession to the horror was that girls' education was quietly taken away by then-Crown Prince Abdullah from the Salafi zealots, who have nonetheless managed to retain their vise-like grip on the kingdom's education system writ large.

This, however, is no mere Saudi phenomenon, no hateful curiosity in the rich, isolated desert. The Islamist hatred of women burns brightly across the region—now more than ever.

In Kuwait, where for years Islamists fought women's

enfranchisement, they hounded the four women who finally made it into parliament, demanding that the two who didn't cover their hair wear hijabs. When the Kuwaiti parliament was dissolved this past December, an Islamist parliamentarian demanded the new house—devoid of a single female legislator—discuss his proposed "decent attire" law.

In Tunisia, long considered the closest thing to a beacon of tolerance in the region, women took a deep breath last fall after the Islamist Ennahda party won the largest share of votes in the country's Constituent Assembly. Party leaders vowed to respect Tunisia's 1956 Personal Status Code, which declared "the principle of equality between men and women" as citizens and banned polygamy. But female university professors and students have complained since then of assaults and intimidation by Islamists for not wearing hijabs, while many women's rights activists wonder how talk of Islamic law will affect the actual law they will live under in post-revolution Tunisia.

In Libya, the first thing the head of the interim government, Mustafa Abdel Jalil, promised to do was to lift the late Libyan tyrant's restrictions on polygamy. Lest you think of Muammar al-Qaddafi as a feminist of any kind, remember that under his rule girls and women who survived sexual assaults or were suspected of "moral crimes" were dumped into "social rehabilitation centers," effective prisons from which they could not leave unless a man agreed to marry them or their families took them back.

Then there's Egypt, where less than a month after President Hosni Mubarak stepped down, the military junta that replaced him, ostensibly to "protect the revolution," inadvertently reminded us of the two revolutions we women need. After it cleared Tahrir Square of protesters, the military detained dozens of male and female activists. Tyrants oppress, beat, and torture all. We know. But these officers reserved "virginity tests" for female activists: rape disguised as a medical doctor inserting his fingers into their vaginal opening in search of hymens. (The doctor was sued and eventually acquitted in March.)

What hope can there be for women in the new Egyptian parliament, dominated as it is by men stuck in the seventh century? A quarter of those parliamentary seats are now held by Salafis, who believe that mimicking the original ways of the Prophet Mohammed is an appropriate prescription for modern life. Last fall, when fielding female candidates, Egypt's Salafi Nour Party ran a flower in place of each woman's face.

Women are not to be seen or heard—even their voices are a temptation—so there they are in the Egyptian parliament, covered from head to toe in black and never uttering a word.

And we're in the middle of a revolution in Egypt! It's a revolution in which women have died, been beaten, shot at, and sexually assaulted fighting alongside men to rid our country of that uppercase Patriarch—Mubarak—yet so many lowercase patriarchs still oppress us. The Muslim Brotherhood, with almost half the total seats in our new revolutionary parliament, does not believe women (or Christians for that matter) can be president. The woman who heads the "women's committee" of the Brotherhood's political party said recently that women should not march or protest because it's more "dignified" to let their husbands and brothers demonstrate for them.

The hatred of women goes deep in Egyptian society. Those of us who have marched and protested have had to navigate a minefield of sexual assaults by both the regime and its lackeys, and, sadly, at times by our fellow revolutionaries. On the November day I was sexually assaulted on Mohamed Mahmoud Street near Tahrir Square, by at least four Egyptian riot police, I was first groped by a man in the square itself. While we are eager to expose assaults by the regime, when we're violated by our fellow civilians we immediately assume they're agents of the regime or thugs because we don't want to taint the revolution.

SO WHAT IS TO BE DONE?

First we stop pretending. Call out the hate for what it is. Resist cultural relativism and know that even in countries undergoing revolutions and uprisings, women will remain the cheapest bargaining chips. You—the outside world—will be told that it's our "culture" and "religion" to do X, Y, or Z to women. Understand that whoever deemed it as such was never a woman. The Arab uprisings may have been sparked by an Arab man—Mohamed Bouazizi, the Tunisian street vendor who set himself on fire in desperation—but they will be finished by Arab women.

Amina Filali—the 16-year-old Moroccan girl who drank poison after she was forced to marry, and beaten by, her rapist—is our Bouazizi. Salwa el-Husseini, the first Egyptian woman to speak out against the "virginity tests"; Samira Ibrahim, the first one to sue; and Rasha Abdel Rahman, who testified alongside her—they are our Bouazizis. We must not wait for them to die to become so. Manal al-Sharif, who spent nine days in jail for breaking her country's ban on women driving, is Saudi Arabia's Bouazizi. She is a one-woman revolutionary force who pushes against an ocean of misogyny.

Our political revolutions will not succeed unless they are accompanied by revolutions of thought—social, sexual, and cultural revolutions that topple the Mubaraks in our minds as well as our bedrooms.

"Do you know why they subjected us to virginity tests?" Ibrahim asked me soon after we'd spent hours marching together to mark International Women's Day in Cairo on March 8. "They want to silence us; they want to chase women back home. But we're not going anywhere."

We are more than our headscarves and our hymens. Listen to those of us fighting. Amplify the voices of the region and poke the hatred in its eye. There was a time when being an Islamist was the most vulnerable political position in Egypt and Tunisia. Understand that now it very well might be Woman. As it always has been.

La Guera

BY CHERRÍE MORAGA

Cherríe Moraga is a Chicana writer, feminist, activist, poet, essayist, and playwright. In 1983, Moraga, Barbara Smith, and Audre Lorde started Kitchen Table: Women of Color Press, which has been credited as the first publisher dedicated to the writing of women of color in the United States. Moraga has published numerous books and plays including *A Xicana Codex of Changing Consciousness: Writings, 2000–2010*, *The Last Generation* (1993), and *Waiting in the Wings: Portrait of a Queer Motherhood* (1997). At a time when second wave feminist discourse was dominated by heterosexual white and upper-middle-class women, Moraga co-edited *This Bridge Called My Back: Writings by Radical Women of Color* with Gloria Anzaldúa, to publish the works and words of women of color and lesbians. This 1981 anthology would become a foundational third wave and intersectional feminist text. In "La Guera," published in the anthology, an impassioned Moraga writes of her experience as a Chicana lesbian and the multiple ways women can be oppressed, complicating Western feminism's essentialist conception of sexism.

It requires something more than personal experience to gain a philosophy or point of view from any specific event. It is the quality of our response to the event and our capacity to enter into the lives of others that help us to make their lives and experiences our own.

—EMMA GOLDMAN

I am the very well-educated daughter of a woman who, by the standards in this country, would be considered largely illiterate. My mother was born in Santa Paula, Southern California, at a time when much of the central valley there was still farmland. Nearly thirty-five years later, in 1948, she was the only daughter of six to marry an anglo, my father.

I remember all of my mother's stories, probably much better than she realizes. She is a fine story-teller, recalling every event of her life with the vividness of the present, noting each detail right down to the cut and color of her dress. I remember stories of her being pulled out of school at the ages of five, seven, nine, and eleven to work in the fields, along with her brothers and sisters; stories of her father drinking away whatever small profit she was able to make for the family; of her going the long way home to avoid meeting him on the street, staggering toward the same destination. I remember stories of my mother lying about her age in order to get a job as a hat-check girl at Agua Caliente Racetrack in Tijuana. At fourteen, she was the main support of the family. I can still see her walking home alone at 3 a.m., only to turn all of her salary and tips over to her mother, who was pregnant again.

The stories continue through the war years and on: walnut-cracking factories, the Voit Rubber factory, and then the computer boom. I remember my mother doing piecework for the electronics plant in our neighborhood. In the late evening, she would sit in front of the TV set, wrapping copper wires into the backs of circuit boards, talking about "keeping up with the younger girls." By that time, she was already in her mid-fifties.

Meanwhile, I was college-prep in school. After classes, I would go with my mother to fill out job applications for her, or write checks for her at the supermarket. We would have the scenario all worked out ahead of time. My mother would sign the check before we'd get to the store. Then, as we'd approach the checkstand, she would say—within earshot of the cashier—"oh honey, you go 'head and make out the check," as if she couldn't be bothered with such an insignificant detail. No one asked any questions.

I was educated, and wore it with a keen sense of pride and satisfaction, my head propped up with the knowledge, from my mother, that my life would be easier than hers. I was educated; but more than this, I was "la guera": fair-skinned. Born with the features of my Chicana mother, but the skin of my Anglo father, I had it made.

No one ever quite told me this (that light was right), but I knew that being light was something valued in my family (who were all Chicano, with the exception of my father). In fact, everything about my upbringing (at least what occurred on a conscious level) attempted to bleach me of what color I did have. Although my mother was fluent in it, I was never taught much Spanish at home. I picked up what I did learn from school and from over-heard snatches of conversation among my relatives and mother. She often called other lower-income Mexicans "braceros," or "wetbacks," referring to herself and her family as "a different class of people." And yet, the real story was that my family, too, had been poor (some still are) and farmworkers. My mother can remember this in her blood as if it were yesterday. But this is something she would like to forget (and rightfully), for to her, on a basic economic level, being Chicana meant being "less." It was through my mother's desire to protect her children from poverty and illiteracy that we became "anglocized"; the more effectively we could pass in the white world, the better guaranteed our future.

From all of this, I experience, daily, a huge disparity between what I was born into and what I was to grow up to become. Because, (as Goldman suggests) these stories my mother told me crept under my "guera" skin. I had no choice but to enter into the life of my mother. *I had no choice.* I took her life into my heart, but managed to keep a lid on it as long as I feigned being the happy, upwardly mobile heterosexual.

When I finally lifted the lid to my lesbianism, a profound connection with my mother reawakened in me. It wasn't until I acknowledged and confronted my own lesbianism in the flesh, that my heartfelt identification with and empathy for my mother's oppression—due to being poor, uneducated, and Chicana—was realized. My lesbianism is the avenue through which I have learned the most about silence and oppression, and it continues to be the most tactile reminder to me that we are not free human beings.

You see, one follows the other. I had known for years that I was a lesbian, had felt it in my bones, had ached with the knowledge, gone crazed with the knowledge, wallowed in the silence of it. Silence *is* like starvation. Don't be fooled. It's nothing short of that, and felt most sharply when one has had a full belly most of her life. When we are not physically starving, we have the luxury to realize psychic and emotional starvation. It is from this starvation that other starvations can be recognized—if one is willing to take the risk of making the connection—if one is willing to be responsible to the result of the connection. For me, the connection is an inevitable one.

What I am saying is that the joys of looking like a white girl ain't so great since I realized I could be beaten on the street for being a dyke. If my sister's being beaten because she's Black, it's pretty much the same principle. We're both getting beaten any way you look at it. The connection is blatant; and in the case of my own family, the difference in the privileges attached to looking white instead of brown are merely a generation apart.

In this country, lesbianism is a poverty—as is being brown, as is being a woman, as is being just plain poor. The danger lies in ranking the oppressions. *The danger lies in failing to acknowledge the specificity of the oppression.* The danger lies in attempting to deal with oppression purely from a theoretical base. Without an emotional, heartfelt grappling with the source of our own oppression, without naming the enemy within ourselves and outside of us, no authentic, non-hierarchical connection among oppressed groups can take place.

When the going gets rough, will we abandon our so-called comrades in a flurry of racist/heterosexist/what-have-you panic? To whose camp, then, should the lesbian of color retreat? Her very presence violates the ranking and abstraction of oppression. Do we merely live hand to mouth? Do we merely struggle with the "ism" that's sitting on top of our own heads?

The answer is: yes, I think first we do; and we must do so thoroughly and deeply. But to fail to move out from there will only isolate us in our own oppression—will only insulate, rather than radicalize us.

To illustrate: a gay male friend of mine once confided to me that he continued to feel that, on some level, I didn't trust him because he was male; that he felt, really, if it ever came down to a "battle of the sexes," I might kill him. I admitted that I might very well. He wanted to understand the source of my distrust. I responded, "You're not a woman. Be a woman for a day. Imagine being a woman." He confessed that the thought terrified him because, to him, being a woman meant being raped by men. He *had* felt raped by men; he wanted to forget what that meant. What grew from that discussion was the realization that in order for him to create an authentic alliance with me, he must deal with the primary source of his own sense of oppression. He must, first, emotionally come to terms with what it feels like to be a victim. If he—or anyone—were to truly do this, it would be impossible to discount the oppression of others, except by again forgetting how we have been hurt.

And yet, oppressed groups are forgetting all the time. There are instances of this in the rising Black middle class, and certainly an obvious trend of such "unconsciousness" among white gay men. Because to remember may mean giving up whatever privileges we have managed to squeeze out of this society by virtue of our gender, race, class, or sexuality.

Within the women's movement, the connections among women of different backgrounds and sexual orientations have been fragile, at best. I think this phenomenon is indicative of our failure to seriously address ourselves to some very frightening questions: How have I internalized my own oppression? How have I oppressed? Instead, we have let rhetoric do the job of poetry. Even the word "oppression" has lost its power. We need a new language, better words that can more closely describe women's fear of and resistance to one another; words that will not always come out sounding like dogma.

What prompted me in the first place to work on an anthology by radical women of color was a deep sense that I had a valuable insight to contribute, by virtue of my birthright and background.

And yet, I don't really understand first-hand what it feels like being shitted on for being brown. I understand much more about the joys of it—being Chicana and having family are synonymous for me. What I know about loving, singing, crying, telling stories, speaking with my heart and hands, even having a sense of my own soul comes from the love of my mother, aunts, cousins . . .

But at the age of twenty-seven, it is frightening to acknowledge that I have internalized a racism and classism, where the object of oppression is not only someone outside of my skin, but the someone inside my skin. In fact, to a large degree, the real battle with such oppression, for all of us, begins under the skin. I have had to confront the fact that much of what I value about being Chicana, about my family, has been subverted by anglo culture and my own cooperation with it. This realization did not occur to me overnight. For example, it wasn't until long after my graduation from the private college I'd attended in Los Angeles, that I realized the major reason for my total alienation from and fear of my classmates was rooted in class and culture. CLICK.

Three years after graduation, in an apple-orchard in Sonoma, a friend of mine (who comes from an Italian Irish working-class family) says to me, "Cherrie, no wonder you felt like such a nut in school. Most of the people there were white and rich." It was true. All along I had felt the difference, but not until I had put the words "class" and "color" to the experience, did my feelings make any sense. For years, I had berated myself for not being as "free" as my classmates. I completely bought that they simply had more guts than I did—to rebel against their parents and run around the country hitch-hiking, reading books and studying "art." They had enough privilege to be atheists, for chrissake. There was no one around filling in the disparity for me between their parents, who were Hollywood filmmakers, and my parents, who wouldn't know the name of a filmmaker if their lives depended on it (and precisely because their lives didn't depend on it, they couldn't be bothered). But I knew nothing about "privilege" then. White was right. Period. I could pass. If I got educated enough, there would never be any telling.

Three years after that, another CLICK. In a letter to Barbara Smith, I wrote:

I went to a concert where Ntozake Shange was reading. There, everything exploded for me. She was speaking a language that I knew—in the deepest parts of me—existed, and that I had ignored in my own feminist studies and even in my own writing. What Ntozake caught in me is the realization that in my development as a poet, I have, in many ways, denied the voice of my brown mother—the brown in me. I have acclimated to the sound of a white language which, as my father represents it, does not speak to the emotions in my poems—emotions which stem from the love of my mother.

The reading was agitating. Made me uncomfortable. Threw me into a week-long terror of how deeply I was affected. I felt that I had to start all over again. That I turned only to the perceptions of white middle-class women to speak for me and all women. I am shocked by my own ignorance.

Sitting in that auditorium chair was the first time I had realized to the core of me that for years I had disowned the language I knew best—ignored the words and rhythms that were the closest to me. The sounds of my mother and aunts gossiping—half in English, half in Spanish—while drinking cerveza in the kitchen. And the hands—I had cut off the hands in my poems. But not in conversation; still the hands could not be kept down. Still they insisted on moving.

The reading had forced me to remember that I knew things from my roots. But to remember puts me up against what I don't know. Shange's reading agitated me because she spoke with power about a world that is both alien and common to me: "the capacity to enter into the lives of others." But you can't just take the goods and run. I knew that then, sitting in the Oakland auditorium (as I know in my poetry), that the only thing worth *writing* about is what seems to be unknown and, therefore, fearful.

The "unknown" is often depicted in racist literature as the "darkness" within a person. Similarly, sexist writers will refer to fear in the form of the vagina, calling it "the orifice of death." In contrast, it is a pleasure to read works such as Maxine Hong Kingston's *The Woman Warrior*, where fear and alienation are described as "the white ghosts." And yet, the bulk of literature in this country reinforces the myth that what is dark and female is evil. Consequently, each of us—whether dark, female, or both—has in some way *internalized* this oppressive imagery. What the oppressor often succeeds in doing is simply *externalizing* his fears, projecting them into the bodies of women, Asians, gays, disabled folks, whoever seems most "other."

> call me
> roach and presumptuous
> nightmare on your white pillow
> your itch to destroy
> > the indestructible
> > part of yourself
> > —Audre Lorde

But it is not really difference the oppressor fears so much as similarity. He fears he will discover in himself the same aches, the same longings as those of the people he has shitted on. He fears the immobilization threatened by his own incipient guilt. He fears he will have to change his life once he has seen himself in the bodies of the people he has called different. He fears the hatred, anger, and vengeance of those he has hurt.

This is the oppressor's nightmare, but it is not exclusive to him. We women have a similar nightmare, for each of us in some way has been both oppressed and the oppressor. We are afraid to look at how we have failed each other. We are afraid to see how we have taken the values of our oppressor into our hearts and turned them against ourselves and one another. We are afraid to admit how deeply "the man's" words have been ingrained in us.

To assess the damage is a dangerous act. I think of how, even as a feminist lesbian, I have so wanted to ignore my own homophobia, my own hatred of myself for being queer. I have not wanted to admit that my deepest personal sense of myself has not quite "caught up" with my "woman-identified" politics. I have been afraid to criticize lesbian writers who choose to "skip over" these issues in the name of feminism. In 1979, we talk of "old gay" and "butch and femme" roles as if they were ancient history. We toss them aside as merely patriarchal notions. And yet, the truth of the matter is that I have sometimes taken society's fear and hatred of lesbians to bed with me. I have sometimes hated my lover for loving me. I have sometimes felt "not woman enough" for her. I have sometimes felt "not man enough." For a lesbian trying to survive in a heterosexist society, there is no easy way around these emotions. Similarly, in a white-dominated world, there is little getting around racism and our own internalization of it. It's always there, embodied in someone we least expect to rub up against.

When we do rub up against this person, *there* then is the challenge. *There* then is the opportunity to look at the nightmare within us. But we usually shrink from such a challenge.

Time and time again, I have observed that the usual response among white women's groups when the "racism issue" comes up is to deny the difference. I have heard comments like, "Well, we're open to *all* women; why don't they (women of color) come? You can only do so much . . ." But there is seldom any analysis of how the very nature and structure of the group itself may be founded on racist or classist assumptions. More importantly, so often the women seem to feel no loss, no lack, no absence when women of color are not involved; therefore, there is little desire to change the situation. This has hurt me deeply. I have come to believe that the only reason women of a privileged class will dare to look at *how* it is that *they* oppress, is when they've come to know the meaning of their own oppression. And understand that the oppression of others hurts them personally.

The other side of the story is that women of color and working-class women often shrink from challenging white middle-class women. It is much easier to rank oppressions and set up a hierarchy, rather than take responsibility for changing our own lives. We have failed to demand that white women, particularly those who claim to be speaking for all women, be accountable for their racism.

The dialogue has simply not gone deep enough.

I have many times questioned my right to even work on an anthology which is to be written "exclusively by Third World women." I have had to look critically at my claim to color, at a time when, among white feminist ranks, it is a "politically correct" (and sometimes peripherally advantageous) assertion to make. I must acknowledge the fact that, physically, I have had a *choice* about making that claim, in contrast to women who have not had such a choice, and have been abused for their color. I must reckon with the fact that for most of my life, by virtue of the very fact that I am white-looking, I identified with and aspired toward white values, and that I rode the wave of that Southern Californian privilege as far as conscience would let me.

Well, now I feel both bleached and beached. I feel angry about this—the years when I refused to recognize privilege, both when it worked against me, and when I worked it, ignorantly, at the expense of others. These are not settled issues. That is why this work feels so risky to me. It continues to be discovery. It has brought me into contact with women who invariably know a hell of a lot more than I do about racism, as experienced in the flesh, as revealed in the flesh of their writing.

I think: what is my responsibility to my roots—both white and brown, Spanish-speaking and English? I am a woman with a foot in both worlds; and I refuse the split. I feel the necessity for dialogue. Sometimes I feel it urgently.

But one voice is not enough, nor two, although this is where dialogue begins. It is essential that radical feminists confront their fear of and resistance to each other, because without this, there *will* be no bread on the table. Simply, we will not survive. If we could make this connection in our heart of hearts, that if we are serious about a revolution—better—if we seriously believe there should be joy in our lives (real joy, not just "good times"), then we need one another. We women need each other. Because my/your solitary, self-asserting "go-for-the-throat-of-fear" power is not enough. There real power, as you and I well know, is collective. I can't afford to be afraid of you, nor you of me. If it takes head-on collisions, let's do it: this polite timidity is killing us.

As Lorde suggests in the passage I cited earlier, it is in looking to the nightmare that the dream is found. There, the survivor emerges to insist on a future, a vision, yes, born out of what is dark and female. The feminist movement must be a movement of such survivors, a movement with a future.

SEPTEMBER, 1979.

La Prieta

BY GLORIA E. ANZALDÚA

Gloria Anzaldúa, a lesbian Tejana poet, writer, and feminist theorist, has been awarded the Lambda Lesbian Small Book Press Award, a Sappho Award of Distinction, and an NEA creative nonfiction fellowship among others. She also co-edited the landmark anthology *This Bridge Called My Back: Writings by Radical Women of Color* (1981)—where "La Prieta" was first published—with Cherríe Moraga. In her semi-autobiographical work, *Borderlands/La Frontera: The New Mestiza* (1987), Anzaldúa called for a new consciousness, a hybrid identity to heal the wounds and fragmentation of culture and language wrought by colonization. Anzaldúa seamlessly slips from English to Spanish and Chicana to create new worlds and new identities for those marginalized by white supremacy, patriarchy, and heteronormativity. "La Prieta" became a foundational work for intersectional feminism, queer theory, and Chicana studies. It is lyrical and frank, and draws on personal narrative while looking well beyond the self. Anzaldúa recounts the challenges she faced as a dark-skinned woman who faced colorism not only from her community but her own family. It is interesting, then, that Anzaldúa has been criticized for appropriating Indigenous identities and eliding Afro-Latinos from much of her work.

IMAGES THAT HAUNT ME

When I was three months old tiny pink spots began appearing on my diaper. "She's a throwback to the Eskimo," the doctor told my mother. "Eskimo girl children get their periods early." At seven I had budding breasts. My mother would wrap them in tight cotton girdles so the kids at school would not think them strange beside their own flat brown mole nipples. My mother would pin onto my panties a folded piece of rag. "Keep your legs shut, Prieta." This, the deep dark secret between us, her punishment for having fucked before the wedding ceremony, my punishment for being born. And when she got mad at me she would yell, "He batallado más contigo que con todos los demas y no lo agradeces!" (I've taken more care with you than I have with all the others and you're not even grateful.) My sister started suspecting our secret—that there was something "wrong" with me. How much can you hide from a sister you've slept with in the same bed since infancy?

What my mother wanted in return for having birthed me and for nurturing me was that I submit to her without rebellion. Was this a survival skill she was trying to teach me? She objected not so much to my disobedience but to my questioning her right to demand obedience from me. Mixed with this power struggle was her guilt at having borne a child who was marked "con la seña," thinking she had made me a victim of her sin. In her eyes and in the eyes of others I saw myself reflected as "strange," "abnormal," "QUEER." I saw no other reflection. Helpless to change that image, I retreated into books and solitude and kept away from others.

The whole time growing up I felt that I was not of this earth. An alien from another planet—I'd been dropped on my mother's lap. But for what purpose?

One day when I was about seven or eight, my father dropped on my lap a 25¢ pocket western, the only type of book he could pick up at a drugstore. The act of reading forever changed me. In the westerns I read, the house servants, the villains and the cantineras (prostitutes) were all Mexicans. But I knew that the first cowboys (vaqueros) were Mexicans, that in Texas we outnumbered the Anglos, that my grandmother's ranch lands had been ripped off by the greedy Anglo. Yet in the pages of these books, the Mexican and Indian were vermin. The racism I would later recognize in my school teachers and never be able to ignore again I found in that first western I read.

My father dying, his aorta bursting while he was driving, the

truck turning over, his body thrown out, the truck falling on his
face. Blood on the pavement. His death occurred just as I entered
puberty. It irrevocably shattered the myth that there existed a
male figure to look after me. How could my strong, good, beautiful godlike father be killed? How stupid and careless of God.
What if chance and circumstance and accident ruled? I lost my father, God, and my innocence all in one bloody blow.

Every 24 days, raging fevers cooked my brain. Full flowing periods accompanied cramps, tonsillitis and 105° fevers. Every
month a trip to the doctors. "It's all in your head," they would
say. "When you get older and get married and have children the
pain will stop." A monotonous litany from the men in white all
through my teens.

The bloodshed on the highway had robbed my adolescence
from me like the blood on my diaper had robbed childhood from
me. And into my hands unknowingly I took the transformation of
my own being.

> Nobody's going to save you.
> No one's going to cut you down
> cut the thorns around you.
> No one's going to storm
> the castle walls nor
> kiss awake your birth,
> climb down your hair,
> nor mount you
> onto the white steed.
>
> There is no one who
> will feed the yearning.
> Face it. You will have
> to do, do it yourself.

My father dead, my mother and I turned to each other. Hadn't
we grown together? We were like sisters—she was 16 when she
gave birth to me.

Though she loved me she would only show it covertly—in the
tone of her voice, in a look. Not so with my brothers—there it was
visible for all the world to see. They were male and surrogate

husbands, legitimate receivers of her power. Her allegiance was and is to her male children, not to the female.

Seeing my mother turn to my brothers for protection, for guidance—a mock act. She and I both knew she wouldn't be getting any from them. Like most men they didn't have it to give, instead needed to get it from women. I resented the fact that it was OK for my brothers to touch and kiss and flirt with her, but not for my sister and me. Resenting the fact that physical intimacy between women was taboo, dirty.

Yet she could not discount me. "Machona—india ladina" (masculine—wild Indian), she would call me because I did not act like a nice little Chicanita is supposed to act: later, in the same breath she would praise and blame me, often for the same thing— being a tomboy and wearing boots, being unafraid of snakes or knives, showing my contempt for women's roles, leaving home to go to college, not settling down and getting married, being a politica, siding with the Farmworkers. Yet, while she would try to correct my more aggressive moods, my mother was secretly proud of my "waywardness." (Something she will never admit.) Proud that I'd worked myself through school. Secretly proud of my paintings, of my writing, though all the while complaining because I made no money out of it.

VERGUENZA (SHAME)

. . . being afraid that my friends would see my momma, would know that she was loud—her voice penetrated every corner. Always when we came into a room everyone looked up. I didn't want my friends to hear her brag about her children. I was afraid she would blurt out some secret, would criticize me in public. She always embarrassed me by telling everyone that I liked to lie in bed reading and wouldn't help her with the housework.

. . . eating at school out of sacks, hiding our "lonches" *papas con chorizo* behind cupped hands and bowed heads, gobbling them up before the other kids could see. Guilt lay folded in the tortilla. The Anglo kids laughing—calling us "tortilleros," the Mexican kids taking up the word and using it as a club with which to hit each other. My brothers, sister and I started bringing white bread sandwiches to school. After a while we stopped taking our lunch altogether.

There is no beauty in poverty, in my mother being able to give only one of her children lunch money. (We all agreed it should go to Nune, he was growing fast and was always hungry.) It was not very romantic for my sister and me to wear the dresses and panties my mother made us out of flour sacks because she couldn't afford store-bought ones like the other mothers.

> Well, I'm not ashamed of you anymore, Momma.
> My heart, once bent and cracked, once
> ashamed of your China ways.
> Ma, hear me now, tell me your story
> again and again.
>
> —Nellie Wong, "From a
> Heart of Rice Straw,"
> *Dreams of Harrison
> Railroad Park*

It was not my mother's fault that we were poor and yet so much of my pain and shame has been with our both betraying each other. But my mother has always been there for me in spite of our differences and emotional gulfs. She has never stopped fighting; she is a survivor. Even now I can hear her arguing with my father over how to raise us, insisting that all decisions be made by both of them. I can hear her crying over the body of my dead father. She was 28, had had little schooling, was unskilled, yet her strength was greater than most men's, raising us single-handed.

After my father died, I worked in the fields every weekend and every summer, even when I was a student in college. (We only migrated once when I was seven, journeyed in the back of my father's red truck with two other families to the cotton fields of west Texas. When I missed a few weeks of school, my father decided this should not happen again.)

. . . the planes swooping down on us, the fifty or a hundred of us falling onto the ground, the cloud of insecticide lacerating our eyes, clogging our nostrils. Nor did the corporate farm owners care that there were no toilets in the wide open fields, no bushes to hide behind.

Over the years, the confines of farm and ranch life began to chafe. The traditional role of la mujer was a saddle I did not want to wear. The concepts "passive" and "dutiful" raked my skin like spurs and "marriage" and "children" set me to bucking faster than rattlesnakes or coyotes. I took to wearing boots and men's jeans and walking about with my head full of visions, hungry for more words and more words. Slowly I unbowed my head, refused my estate and began to challenge the way things were. But it's taken over thirty years to unlearn the belief instilled in me that white is better than brown—something that some people of color *never* will unlearn. And it is only now that the hatred of myself, which I spent the greater part of my adolescence cultivating, is turning to love.

LA MUERTE, THE FROZEN SNOW QUEEN

I dig a grave, bury my first love, a German Shepherd. Bury the second, third, and fourth dog. The last one retching in the backyard, going into convulsions from insecticide poisoning. I buried him beside the others, five mounds in a row crowned with crosses I'd fashioned from twigs.

No more pets, no more loves—I court death now.

. . . Two years ago on a fine November day in Yosemite Park, I fall on the floor with cramps, severe chills and shaking that go into spasms and near convulsions, then fevers so high my eyes feel like eggs frying. Twelve hours of this. I tell everyone, "It's nothing, don't worry, I'm alright." The first four gynecologists advise a hysterectomy. The fifth, a woman, says wait.

. . . Last March my fibroids conspired with an intestinal tract infection and spawned watermelons in my uterus. The doctor played with his knife. La Chingada ripped open, raped with the white man's wand. My soul in one corner of the hospital ceiling, getting thinner and thinner telling me to clean up my shit, to release the fears and garbage from the past that are hanging me up. So I take La Muerte's scythe and cut away my arrogance and pride, the emotional depressions I indulge in, the head trips I do on myself and other people. With her scythe I cut the umbilical cord shackling me to the past and to friends and attitudes that drag me down. Strip away—all the way to the bone. Make myself utterly vulnerable.

. . . I can't sleep nights. The mugger said he would come and get me. There was a break in the county jail and I *just* know he is broken out and is coming to get me because I picked up a big rock and chased him, because I got help and caught him. How *dare* he drag me over rocks and twigs, the skin on my knees peeling, how *dare* he lay his hands on my throat, how *dare* he try to choke me to death, how dare he try to push me off the bridge to splatter my blood and bones on the rocks 20 feet below. His breath on my face, our eyes only inches apart, our bodies rolling on the ground in an embrace so intimate we could have been mistaken for lovers.

That night terror found me curled up in my bed. I couldn't stop trembling. For months terror came to me at night and never left me. And even now, seven years later, when I'm out in the street after dark and I hear running footsteps behind me, terror finds me again and again.

No more pets, no more loves.

. . . one of my lovers saying I was frigid when he couldn't bring me to orgasm.

. . . bringing home my Peruvian boyfriend and my mother saying she did not want her "Prieta" to have a "mojado" (wetback) for a lover.

. . . my mother and brothers calling me puta when I told them I had lost my virginity and that I'd done it on purpose. My mother and brothers calling me jota (queer) when I told them my friends were gay men and lesbians.

. . . Randy saying, "It's time you stopped being a nun, an ice queen afraid of living." But I did not want to be a snow queen regal with icy smiles and fingernails that ripped her prey ruthlessly. And yet, I knew my being distant, remote, a mountain sleeping under the snow, is what attracted him.

> A woman lies buried under me,
> interred for centuries, presumed dead.

> A woman lies buried under me.
> I hear her soft whisper
> the rasp of her parchment skin

fighting the folds of her shroud.
Her eyes are pierced by needles
her eyelids, two fluttering moths.

I am always surprised by the image that my white and non-Chicano friends have of me, surprised at how much they *do not* know me, at how I do not allow them to know me. They have substituted the negative picture the white culture has painted of my race with a highly romanticized, idealized image. "You're strong," my friends said, "a mountain of strength."

Though the power may be real, the mythic qualities attached to it keep others from dealing with me as a person and rob me of my being able to act out my other selves. Having this "power" doesn't exempt me from being prey in the streets nor does it make my scrambling to survive, to feed myself, easier. To cope with hurt and control my fears, I grew a thick skin. Oh, the many names of power—pride, arrogance, control. I am not the frozen snow queen but a flesh and blood woman with perhaps too loving a heart, one easily hurt.

I'm not invincible, I tell you. My skin's as fragile as a baby's. I'm brittle bones and human, I tell you. I'm a broken arm.

You're a razor's edge, you tell me. Shock them shitless. Be the holocaust. Be the black Kali. Spit in their eye and never cry. Oh broken angel, throw away your cast, mend your wing. Be not a rock but a razor's edge and burn with falling. —Journal Entry, Summer Solstice, 1978.

WHO ARE MY PEOPLE

I am a wind-swayed bridge, a crossroads inhabited by whirlwinds. Gloria, the facilitator, Gloria the mediator, straddling the walls between abysses. "Your allegiance is to La Raza, the Chicano movement," say the members of my race. "Your allegiance is to the Third World," say my Black and Asian friends. "Your allegiance is to your gender, to women," say the feminists. Then there's my allegiance to the Gay movement, to the socialist revolution, to the New Age, to magic and the occult. And there's my affinity to literature, to the world of the artist. What am I? *A third world lesbian feminist with Marxist and mystic leanings*. They would chop me up into little fragments and tag each piece with a label.

You say my name is ambivalence? Think of me as Shiva, a many-armed and legged body with one foot on brown soil, one on white, one in straight society, one in the gay world, the man's world, the women's, one limb in the literary world, another in the working class, the socialist, and the occult worlds. A sort of spider woman hanging by one thin strand of web.

Who, me confused? Ambivalent? Not so. Only your labels split me.

Years ago, a roommate of mine fighting for gay rights told MAYO, a Chicano organization, that she and the president were gay. They were ostracized. When they left, MAYO fell apart. They too, being forced to choose between the priorities of race, sexual preference, or gender.

In the streets of this gay mecca, San Francisco, a Black man at a bus stop yells, "Hey Faggots, come suck my cock." Randy yells back, "You goddamn nigger, I worked in the Civil Rights movement ten years so you could call me names." Guilt gagging in his throat with the word, nigger. . . . a white woman waiting for the J-Church streetcar sees Randy and David kissing and says, "You should be ashamed of yourselves. Two grown men—disgusting."

. . . Randy and David running into the house. The hair on the back of my neck rises, something in their voices triggers fear in me. Three Latino men in a car had chased them as they were walking home from work. "Gay boys, faggots," they yelled throwing a beer bottle. Getting out of their car, knife blades reflect the full moon. . . . Randy and David hitting each other in the hall. Thuds on the wall—the heavy animal sounds.

. . . Randy pounding on my door one corner of his mouth bleeding, his glasses broken, blind without them, he crying "I'm going to kill him, I'm going to kill the son of a bitch."

The violence against us, the violence within us, aroused like a rabid dog. Adrenaline-filled bodies, we bring home the anger and the violence we meet on the street and turn it against each other. We sic the rabid dog on each other and on ourselves. The black moods of alienation descend, the bridges we've extended out to each other crumble. We put the walls back up between us.

Once again it's faggot-hunting and queer-baiting time in the city. "And on your first anniversary of loving each other," I say to Randy, "and they had to be Latinos," feeling guilt when I look at David. Who is my brother's keeper, I wonder—knowing I have to be, we all have to be. We are all responsible. But who exactly are my people?

I identify as a woman. Whatever insults women insults me.
I identify as gay. Whoever insults gays insults me.
I identify as feminist. Whoever slurs feminism slurs me.

That which is insulted I take as part of me, but there is something too simple about this kind of thinking. Part of the dialectic is missing. What about what I do not identify as?

I have been terrified of writing this essay because I will have to own up to the fact that I do not exclude whites from the list of people I love, two of them happen to be gay males. For the politically correct stance we let color, class, and gender separate us from those who would be kindred spirits. So the walls grow higher, the gulfs between us wider, the silences more profound. There is an enormous contradiction in being a bridge.

DANCE TO THE BEAT OF
RADICAL COLORED CHIC

This task—to be a bridge, to be a fucking crossroads for goddess' sake.

During my stint in the Feminist Writers' Guild many white members would ask me why Third World women do not come to FWG meetings and readings. I should have answered, "Because their skins are not as thick as mine, because their fear of encountering racism is greater than mine. They don't enjoy being put down, ignored, not engaged in equal dialogue, being tokens. And, neither do I." Oh, I know, women of color are hot right now and hip. Our afro-rhythms and latin salsas, the beat of our drums is in. White women flock to our parties, dance to the beat of radical colored chic. They come to our readings, take up our cause. I have no objections to this. What I mind is the pseudo-liberal ones who suffer from the white women's burden. Like the monkey in the Sufi story, who upon seeing a fish in the water rushes to rescue it from drowning by carrying it up into the branches of a tree. She takes a missionary role. She attempts to talk *for* us—what a presumption! This act is a rape of our tongue and our acquiescence is a complicity to that rape. We women of color have to stop being modem medusas—throats cut, silenced into a mere hissing.

Growing Up as a Brown Girl

My *Chonga Manifesto*

BY PRISCA DORCAS MOJICA RODRÍGUEZ

In 2013 Prisca Dorcas Mojica Rodríguez founded the online activism platform Latina Rebels. Rodríguez is a Latina feminist writer born in Nicaragua but calls Nashville home. She has published over two hundred articles and essays online and has been featured in Telemundo, *HuffPost*'s Latino Voices, and *Cosmopolitan*. The bulk of Rodríguez's work is grounded in making theory and scholarly work accessible. In 2016, she wrote "Dear Woke Brown Girl" for *HuffPost*, in which she wrote about the stresses and pressures of living in a culture dominated by white men and the necessity of listening to internal voices. Her "Chonga Manifesto" was originally presented at the Fourth Biennial Meeting of the BABEL Working Group conference in Toronto in 2015 and sought to reappropriate and reimagine the identity "chonga." In the manifesto, Rodríguez writes, "The world is our sharpener and we have been chiseled into a weapon of self defense, because we have known people like you since we arrived into the land of the free and we will continue to run across people like you so long as white supremacy reigns." The "Chonga Manifesto" is a defiant celebration of Latina women who revel, unapologetically, in their contradictions.

I struggled with how I was supposed to write this. I struggled with how I was supposed to speak to a group of people who were unfamiliar with chongas, ABOUT chongas. You see, chongas have been vastly misunderstood within our cultures for various respectability/proximity to whiteness reasons. And outsiders misunderstand chongas, mainly because many are unfamiliar with the various subcultures of Latinx immigrants.

Yet one thing rings true all across the board, and that's that according to everyone (excluding chongas), chongas are:

Nasty
Disgusting
Have bad attitudes
Cheap
Too sexy
Our clothes are always tew tight
Speak with accented English
Speak "improper" Spanish
Wear too much make up

What is a chonga? A chonga is a Latina, usually first generation immigrant, from a working-poor context, who has adapted a tough exterior with an aesthetic to match. Also, chongas are primarily from South Florida. It is important to note that many chongas don't regularly refer to themselves as chongas, because the term has become a bit of a slur, an insult.

And before I start, let's get one thing straight: I have a decolonized perspective on chongas, which means that I reclaim this racialized slur into what it really is when we take the layers of self-hatred and oppression away from this subculture. Chongas are beautiful, strong, assertive. Chingonas who will love as passionately as we will hate those who try to harm us or those around us.

I decided that trying to explain a chonga to someone unfamiliar with our subculture is hard. So instead I decided to speak power to the truth that is our reality. I decided to write a manifesto, for this occasion. I wanted to speak in affirmatives about our boldness, power, and resilience. Because this is not a disembodied document; this document is reflexive of real women, real chingonas, who on a daily basis embody their praxis of resisting assimilation and white-washing. We put our brown bodies on display to disrupt narratives of respectability. Our bodies are very much attached this document, my body is in this manifesto.

Chongas have this agility to maneuver violent situations. We are raised in working poor neighborhoods aka barrios. Mine was pequeña Nicaragua. And we learn quickly that the police are quick to show up to our neighborhoods to arrest us, but slow to come and protect us. We learn that our families are the only people who have our best interests in mind. Because while Latinxs are generally family-oriented, nobody ever talks about why. It is because we have dealt with corruption in our motherlands and erasure in the land of the free that we have come to know that everyone around us is trying to get a handle on their poverty through some sort of income redistribution that can look like what the system calls illegal, but we call justice. When we get the torn up or nonexistent textbooks in our schools, food deserts in our neighborhoods, and dangerously unregulated housing situations—you learn that the system is not meant to protect you so you protect yourself. Chongas know how to fight and, hell, do we know how to redistribute that income of yours that you so closely clutch onto as you ride in our public transportations.

Chongas have sharp tongues. When your TFA teachers and counselors all tell you to stop dreaming because someone like you could never get into college, or dream of a different trajectory than the one that they have placed on your adolescent body, you learn to stick up for yourself. You learn to not let people tell you who you are, but demand that they see you as you say you are. And if you doubt us, if you think you can make us feel inferior because the accents in our immigrant mouths are too easy of a target for you, we will show you otherwise. We know how to tear you up, piece by piece, with our quick words and sharp responses. We had to learn to be this sharp. The world is our sharpener and we have been chiseled into a weapon of self defense, because we have known people like you since we arrived into the land of the free and we will continue to run across people like you so long as white supremacy reigns.

Chongas dress like goddesses. We see our femininity as a tool for our survival that was used by our mothers, grandmothers, and great grandmothers. And in this land of the free, we intend on utilizing those tools to maneuver spaces that seem uninviting to us. My grandmother did her nails, hair, and put on her Sunday's best to go to the grocery store—she did so because she did not want people to think she was there to steal. And because of that, I understand that growing up poor meant that people distrusted me because of my aesthetics, so I learned a particular kind of femininity, which bubbles to the surface as my class mobility. So when I wing my eyeliner, outline my lips, put on my mini skirt and crop top, I am adorning myself with my war paint and armor. Because to you, I am not human—but it's okay because to me and to those who understand: I am a goddess.

Chongas oscillate between Spanish and English—Spanglish—with an ease that can only be described as brilliant. We are primarily immigrants, and success here usually means assimilating into white upper middle class embodiment and comportment, and accents are viewed as inferior. So when we ignore the insistent requests to get rid of any signs of our migration, we are pushed aside. But you see, this entire side of the world belonged to our ancestors before yours even arrived, so when we can speak your forced languages, we will speak it however we please. You're on conquered land anyways. So we may accent it, spit it out, speak it quickly, and speak it loudly—it is our resistance to your extended visit.

Chongas are everywhere. When a chonga is around, you know it. We will make ourselves known. We are hypervisible, so you will remember our names, what we wore, what we said, and how we said it. And in a land that tries to ignore our existence and push us into living as the least of these, our visibility is power because you cannot erase what you have no control over and you cannot control those who have never bowed down to your notions of a hegemonic America. We are loud, we are proud, and we do not back down. Ask anyone who has gone up against a chonga about their experience. They will teach you to see us as we are: DIVINAS.

And to any chongas who may be in highly inaccessible space, you matter and you do not have to shed your toughness to exist in any space. Spaces are only elevated by your existence.

I Am Woman

BY LEE MARACLE

Lee Maracle is an award-winning poet, novelist, story-teller, scriptwriter, actor, activist, and keeper/myth-maker of the Stó:lō Nation. Maracle was one of the founders of the En'owkin International School of Writing in Penticton, British Columbia; she is also the cultural director of the Centre for Indigenous Theatre in Toronto and teaches at the University of Toronto First Nations House. Her primary focus was Indigenous women in the context of Western feminism, an approach she has described as "decolonizing in the feminine." Her work, including this 1988 autobiographical piece, addresses the colonization of Indigenous culture and bodies and explores the artificially constructed boundaries between colonized/colonizer, white/Indigenous, and man/woman. This writing builds on a rich tradition of women of color asserting their right to claim womanhood that they are so often denied. In this piece, Maracle is particularly incisive in addressing the ways Indigenous women have been marginalized, maligned, and mistreated.

I used to consider myself a liberated woman. I woke up at the bottom of the mine shaft one morning, darkness above me, screaming, "I'm not like the rest . . . I'm not an alcoholic . . . a skid row bum . . . a stupid Native," ad nauseam. Each time I confronted white colonial society I had to convince them of my validity as a human being. It was the attempt to convince them that made me realize that I was still a slave.

It was this enslavement which moved me to retrace my own desertion. In these pages I recount the color of traitorousness and my decision to reconnect myself to all of us struggling to remove the burden of a recent colonial history.

Striving

I drank heartily of the settlers wine
  learned his language well;
  gazed with awe at his success

no pretty woman was I, nor
  clever wit did possess

My striving went to naught
  it was the trying
  that shames me now.

Until March 1982, feminism, indeed womanhood itself, was meaningless to me. Racist ideology had defined womanhood for the Native woman as nonexistent, therefore neither the woman question nor the European rebel's response held any meaning for me. Ignorance is no crime. But when you trot your ignorance before the world as though it were part of some profound truth, that is a crime.

I apologize to Robert Mendoza's wife and all the Native women who watched the video that I made in San Francisco for International Women's Day in 1978. You must have been personally offended by my denial of my own womanhood. I will forever remember Robert's sensitive reply to my remark that it was irrelevant that I was a woman. In a phone call in which he praised my understanding of the colonial process, he added: "Couldn't you see that perhaps it was because you were Native and a woman that your insight was so powerful?"

His modest indignation sharpens the deep remorse I now feel for those women who had to watch, red-faced, while this traitor blurted into a microphone, in front of a multitude of non-Native women, that it mattered not that I was a Native woman. "It was such a great video, a great presentation . . . Don't you think that you could have taken responsibility for being a woman and inspired our sisters, just a little, with the fact that this incisive understanding that you have acquired was due, at least in part, to the fact that you were a Native woman?" Robert Mendoza pleaded into the phone from Pasmaquoddy, Maine. And the words of my granny echoed in my ears . . . "You will remember what you need to know when the time comes."

(Ah, Robert, don't you see, I could not have done that, not then.)

Before 1961, we were "wards of the government," children in the eyes of the law. We objected and became, henceforth, people. Born of this objection was the Native question—the forerunner of Native self-government, the Native land question, etc. The woman question still did not exist for us. Not then.

I responded, like so many other women, as a person without sexuality. Native women do not even like the words "women's liberation" and even now it burns my back. How could I resist the reduction of women to sex objects when I had not been considered sexually desirable, even as an object? We have been the object of sexual release for white males whose appetites are too gross for their own delicate women.

Fishwife

I am unclean,
daughter of an unwashed,
    fisherwoman
    loud, lean and raw.

I have no manners
no finesse
    Iron will
    and loyalty
are all that I possess.

I am not a docile forest creature
a quaint curio
    I am a burning flame
    not yet uhuru
    not yet woman
but very much alive.

I woke up. I AM WOMAN! Not the woman on the billboard for whom physical work is damning, for whom nothingness, physical oblivion is idyllic. But a woman for whom mobility, muscular movement, physical prowess are equal to the sensuous pleasure of being alive. The dead alone do nothing. Paraplegics move. I want to move.

I want to look across the table in my own kitchen and see, in the brown eyes of the man who shares my life, the beauty of my own reflection. More. I want to look across my kitchen table at the women of color who share my life and see the genius of their minds, uncluttered by white opinion. I want to sit with my grown daughters and experience the wonderment of our mutual affection. I want us to set the standard for judging our brilliance, our beauty and our passions.

Whereas Native men have been victims of the age-old racist remark "lazy drunken Indian," about Native women white folks ask, "Do they have feelings?" How many times do you hear from our own brothers, "Indian women don't whine and cry around, nag or complain." At least not "real" or "true" Indian women. Embodied in that kind of language is the negation of our femininity—the denial of our womanhood. And, let us admit it, beneath such a remark isn't there just a little coercion to behave and take without complaint whatever our brothers think "we have comin'"?

I used to believe such attempts at enforcing docility in women. Worse, I was convinced that love, passion/compassion were inventions of white folks. I believed that we never loved, wept, laughed or fought with each other. Divorce was unheard of. Did we then merely accept our wifely obligations to men the way a horse or an ox accepts yoke and bridle? I think not.

The denial of Native womanhood is the reduction of the whole people to a sub-human level. Animals beget animals. The dictates of patriarchy demand that beneath the Native male comes the Native female. The dictates of racism are that Native men are beneath white women and Native females are not fit to be referred to as women.

No one makes the mistake of referring to us as ordinary women. White women invite us to speak if the issue is racism or Native people. We are there to teach, to sensitize them or to serve them in some way. We are expected to retain our position well below them, as their servants. We are not, as a matter of course, invited as an integral part of "their movement"—the women's movement.

I am not now, nor am I likely to be, considered an authority on women in general by the white women's movement in this country. If I am asked to write, my topic is Native whatever, and like as not, the request comes replete with an outline and the do's and don'ts of what I may or may not say. Should I venture out on my own and deal with women as a whole and not in segregated Native fashion, the invitations stop coming.

I am not interested in gaining entry to the doors of the "white women's movement." I would look just a little ridiculous sitting in their living rooms saying "we this and we that." Besides, it is such a small movement. I say this for those Native women who think that they may find equal relations among white women and who think that there may be some solace to be found in those relations.

We are slaves with our own consent. As women, we do not support each other. We look at males when they speak and stare off into space when a woman steps assertively into the breach of leadership. Men who stand up and passionately articulate our aspirations about sovereignty are revered as powerful leaders; women who do so are "intimidating." We mock the liberation of women. I too am guilty of acceding to the erasure of our womanhood. I actually wrote articles with just the kind of strictures that today sicken me. No more.

I used to be uncomfortable being with women. I can remember saying to a close friend of mine that I had more men friends than women. She nodded, yes, unoffended, but neither of us could think of a single male to whom we could say the converse without offending his manhood. We both had become complicit in the erasure of ourselves as women, as Natives.

We have done enough to help Europeans wipe us off the face of the earth. Every day we trade our treasured women friends for the men in our lives. We even trade our sisters. Let Wounded Knee be the last time that they erased us from the world of the living. Let us all blossom beautiful and productive.

Sovereignty of the Soul

Exploring the Intersection of Rape Law Reform and Federal Indian Law

BY SARAH DEER

Sarah Deer is a legal scholar, University Distinguished Professor at the University of Kansas, chief justice for the Prairie Island Indian Community Court of Appeals, a citizen of the Muscogee Nation of Oklahoma, and a 2014 MacArthur Fellow. Deer's work—such as this chapter from 2015's *The Beginning and End of Rape: Confronting Sexual Violence in Native America*—examines the high rates of violence against Native women and the ways in which the United States justice system prevents Native courts and communities from punishing the mostly white male perpetrators who harm Native women. Deer uses Native women's personal testimony and detailed examinations of tribal and US legal systems to examine how sexual violence is used as a tool by colonizers to oppress Native communities. Her work was crucial to the reauthorization of the Violence Against Women Act (VAWA) in 2013, and she continues to advocate for cultural and legal reforms to protect Native women from endemic sexual violence and abuse.

This Article is about tribal issues and sexual assault, and it is directed not so much at "beyond prosecution" as it is "beyond jurisdiction." It focuses on an invisible legal challenge in addressing sexual violence. The focus is not on the federal or state system, but rather the "third sovereign" in this nation, the tribal justice system. There are over 550 federally-recognized tribal governments in the United States, each with a separate and distinct judicial system. Tribal justice systems can have a tremendous impact on the survivors of sexual violence, particularly Native American survivors who reside in tribal communities.

This Article is designed with two audiences in mind. On one hand, it is to enlighten sexual assault scholars and practitioners about the importance of sovereignty in the analysis of rape law and reform. On the other hand, to persuade Indian law scholars and practitioners that the development of sexual assault jurisprudence is central to the struggle for sovereignty. Ultimately, this Article argues that it is impossible to separate theories of indigenous self-determination from theories on sexual assault jurisprudence. It is critical that a dual analysis be employed in both disciplines because sexual violence is so deeply imbedded in colonizing and genocidal policies.

Sexual assault law and legal reform is incomplete without a discussion about Federal Indian Law. There are three main reasons for this: Native American women suffer the highest rate of sexual assault in the United States, rape and sexual violence were historically used as weapons of war against indigenous peoples, and contemporary tribal governments have been deprived of the ability to prosecute many sex offenders. These three facts provide justification for an in-depth analysis of the intersection between sexual violence and Federal Indian Law. In explaining my perspective, this Article begins with some basic information about rape and sexual assault against Native American women. Next, I will provide a historical context for the information. Finally, I will explain the numerous legal challenges faced by tribal governments in addressing the problem.

Notably, the statistics published by the Department of Justice in the last five to six years indicate that Native American women, per capita, experienced more rape and sexual assault than any other racial group in the United States. In fact, American Indian and Alaskan Native women experience a higher rate of violence than any other group, including African-American men and other marginalized groups. One Justice Department report concluded that over one in three American Indian and Alaskan Native women will be raped during their lives.

When I travel to Indian country, however, advocates tell me that the Justice Department statistics provide a very low estimate, and rates of sexual assault against Native American women are actually much higher. Many of the elders that I have spoken with in Indian country tell me that they do not know any women in their community who have not experienced sexual violence.

I want to briefly discuss the nature of rape against indigenous women in this country because the experience of Native American women, as captured in these national surveys, is significantly different than the experience of the mainstream population. Dr. Ronet Bachman, a statistician at the University of Delaware, recently reviewed the raw data from the National Crime Victimization Survey (NCVS) and presented new calculations. I am going to cover just a few of her findings, which were based on ten years of surveys spanning 1992–2002. First, in accordance with the Justice Department reports, Dr. Bachman found that Native American women suffer the highest rate of sexual victimization when compared to other races.

Additionally, the physical nature of the violence shows a significant difference with respect to rape involving Native Americans and other races. In discussing these differences, I do not mean to suggest that rape itself is not always violent. American Indian women, however, more often experience sexual assault accompanied by other overt forms of violence. For example, when asked whether aggressors physically hit them during the assault, over 90% of female Native American victims responded affirmatively as compared to 74% of the general population. Dr. Bachman also examined the number of women who reported suffering physical injuries. When asked if they suffered physical injuries in addition to the rape, 50% of female Native American victims reported such injuries, as compared to 30% of the general population, indicating a different level of violence. Although reluctant to compare traumas and declare that one person's rape was worse than another person's rape, when you see these numbers materialize consistently over a ten year period, you have to wonder why this is happening.

In general, very few rapes across the nation involve weapons. The NCVS results indicate that 11% of all reported rapes involve the use of a weapon. The numbers, however, are over three times as high, 34%, for female Native American victims. What is going on here? Why are Native American women victimized in such a brutal way, and what is happening on the reservations that can explain these horrifying statistics?

This final statistic is perhaps the most startling of all, and will become even more so when discussing the jurisdiction issues. Criminologists who study rape have determined that the vast majority of rapes are intra-racial. For example, a white man tends to rape a white woman and a black man tends to rape a black woman. When examining rape involving American Indian women, however, we see that over 70% of the assailants are white. The 1999 Department of Justice Bureau of Justice Statistics concluded that about nine in ten American Indian victims of rape or sexual assault had white or black assailants. This discrepancy will factor into the later discussion about colonization.

One major weakness in these statistics is that none of the surveys identify whether the crime happened on land subject to tribal jurisdiction. Until 1999, the NCVS did not include particularized questions about jurisdiction, except to distinguish between urban and rural areas. Knowing where these crimes occur is critical because, due to a complicated legal history, the jurisdiction of tribal governments is much more limited than the jurisdiction of the state and federal system.

In order to analyze the legal response to sexual violence in Indian country, it is important to examine the 500 year history of rape of Native American women by Europeans. One of the historical angles from which to begin this analysis is the arrival of Christopher Columbus. Columbus is one of the major symbols of colonization in the Western hemisphere. Columbus' arrival not only represents the destruction of indigenous cultures, but also the beginning of rape of Native American women by European men. A passage from the diary of one of Columbus' aristocratic friends who accompanied him on the second voyage describes one such encounter:

> When I was in the boat, I captured a very beautiful Carib woman . . . having brought her into my cabin, and she being naked as is their custom, I conceived desire to take my pleasure. I wanted to put my desire to execution, but she was unwilling for me to do so, and treated me with her nails in such wise that I would have preferred never to have begun. But seeing this . . . I took a rope-end and

thrashed her well, following which she produced such screaming and wailing as would cause you not to believe your ears. Finally we reached an agreement such that, I can tell you, she seemed to have been raised in a veritable school of harlots. . . .

So right away, upon contact, we are seeing immediate rape. We continue to see rape used as a tool of colonization and a tool of war against Native peoples for the next several hundred years, until the present day. Historian Susan Armitage writes, "It is well documented that Spanish-Mexican soldiers in Spanish California and New Mexico used rape as a weapon of conquest." The legal community recognizes that rape is used as a weapon in war and international tribunals have address the issue. This legal analysis, however, is rarely applied to historical events. There are instances throughout history of using rape and sexual violence as a means of destroying a people, of rendering them unable to protect their lives and their resources, especially as a means to remove them from land that was desired. Another historian, Albert L. Hurtado, notes of the California gold rush, "part of the invading population was imbued with a conquest mentality, fear and hatred of Indians that in their minds justified the rape of Indian women."

Much change has been attempted in the Anglo-American approach to sexual assault in the last thirty years, but things have not really changed for Native American women in about 500 years. Those in the anti-rape movement often talk about rape as an "equal opportunity" crime. Such sentiment, however, is a little short-sighted in that those in the anti-rape movement need to look at the specific impact of sexual violence on marginalized populations and indigenous populations. We also need to acknowledge that the United States was founded, in part, through the use of sexual violence as a tool, that were it not for the widespread rape of Native American women, many of our towns, counties, and states might not exist. This kind of analysis informs not only indigenous scholars, but also anti-rape scholars. Thus, critical to contemporary anti-rape dialogues is the inclusion of a historical analysis of colonization.

Language of the early European explorers and invaders makes numerous references to the land of this continent as "virgin land" or a "woman" available for seizure and invasion. The terminol-

ogy used to describe so-called explorations and settlements sometimes has violent sexual connotations. In fact, the language used
in illustrating colonization often parallels the language of sexual
violence. For example, words like "seize," "conquer," and "possess" are used to describe both rape and colonization. In fact,
when speaking with Native American women who have survived
rape, it is often difficult for them to separate the more immediate
experience of their assault from the larger experience that their
people have experienced through forced removal, displacement,
and destruction. Both experiences are attacks on the human soul;
both the destruction of indigenous culture and the rape of a
woman connote a kind of spiritual death that is difficult to describe to those who have not experienced it.

Given the history of colonization and the statistics showing significantly high rates of sexual assault for Native American women,
what are the contemporary sexual violence issues in the lives of
indigenous nations in the United States today? Two of the most
significant issues are jurisdiction and resources; in essence, two
integral facets of sovereignty that are integral to self-governance.

Substantial erosion of tribal jurisdiction over sexual assault has
occurred over the last 120 years. Contrary to popular myth, tribal
governments have always had justice systems, but recognition of
these systems by Europeans has not always occurred because of
ignorance and prejudice. Our histories and oral teachings reveal
the effectiveness of these justice systems. As sovereign nations, we
exercised full jurisdiction over our land and our people as well as
people entering our land against our wishes or with our consent.
Due to a series of federal laws, tribal governments have lost jurisdiction over the vast majority of sexual violence that happens to
Native American women. Although these laws are numerous, this
Article focuses on four: the Major Crimes Act, Public Law 280
(P.L. 280), the Indian Civil Rights Act (ICRA), and the case law
of *Oliphant v. Suquamish*.

The Major Crimes Act was one of the first major intrusions of
federal law into Indian country. Passed by Congress in 1885, the
Major Crimes Act served as the first suggestions that the federal
government would exercise authority over crimes that happened
in Indian country. Rape was included in the initial list of crimes
over which Congress authorized federal jurisdiction. At best, this

Act can be interpreted as a benevolent, yet paternalistic act. More likely, Congress intended to infiltrate and control the indigenous populations through increased legal authority. Interestingly, the Major Crimes Act itself never explicitly stripped the tribe of jurisdiction over the list of crimes. Although debate over the question of divestment has occurred over the years, most case law concludes that tribal governments retain concurrent jurisdiction over crimes enumerated in the Major Crimes Act. The practical impact of the Major Crimes Act, however, is that fewer tribes pursue prosecution of crimes such as murder and rape. Instead of a rape case being handled within the community using the laws, beliefs, and traditions of indigenous people, rape cases have become the domain of the federal government.

Passed in 1953, P.L. 280 served to transfer criminal jurisdiction in certain states from the federal government to the state government. Neither the states nor the tribes, however, consented to this arrangement and states were not provided with any additional resources with which to enforce crimes in Indian country. Instead, this national legislation resulted in what Carole Goldberg at UCLA has called a sense of "lawlessness" in some local communities. This occurs because the state government is supposed to assume responsibility for law enforcement, while at the same time, tribal governments develop their own justice systems, both lacking sufficient additional resources to do so effectively. Like the Major Crimes Act, the wording of P.L. 280 does not contain an explicit divestiture of concurrent tribal jurisdiction. For all practical purposes, though, the tribal governments in P.L. 280 states have historically been at a distinct disadvantage when it comes to crime control.

The third law creating barriers for tribal governments to address sexual assault is the ICRA. The title of ICRA, passed in 1968, suggests that this legislation would serve to enhance and protect the rights of Indian people. ICRA actually served as yet another imperial effort to assimilate tribal governments, by imposing the United States Bill of Rights onto tribal governments. All tribal governments were required to protect Constitutional rights developed by the United States government, a foreign sovereign. Tribal governments were not hostile to civil rights; in fact tribal governments understood and honored individual autonomy in very sophisticated ways. It was the imposition and lack of choice, however, in ICRA that implicitly continued to chip away at tribal sovereignty.

More central to the discussion of felony jurisdiction, ICRA imposes a limit on the punishment that a tribe may impose on any particular criminal defendant. When the law first passed in 1968, the law limited the ability of a tribal court to sentence offenders. Incarceration was limited to six months and fines were limited to $500. Again, the message and implication is that tribal governments do not have jurisdiction over felony crimes. As with the Major Crimes Act and P.L. 280, however, there was no explicit divestiture of jurisdiction. Therefore, tribes could conceivably prosecute a murder or a rape—but could not imprison the defendant for more than six months. This resulted in an implied divestment of that felony jurisdiction, and today we find that very few tribes are prosecuting sexual violence. Later, as part of drug control legislation, ICRA was amended to allow tribes to sentence offenders to one year of incarceration, a $5000 fine, or both. Also important to note is that ICRA did not limit other forms of sanctions, such as restitution, probation, and banishment.

The fourth and final jurisdiction barrier is the 1978 Supreme Court decision in *Oliphant v. Suquamish*, which eliminated tribal criminal jurisdiction over anyone who is not a member of a federally recognized tribe. If a non-Indian comes into a reservation and rapes a Native American woman, the tribe has absolutely no jurisdiction to punish the offender. Tribal police may be able to arrest a suspect if they are cross-deputized with a local or state government, but the tribal government cannot criminally prosecute that offender.

Since the *Oliphant* decision, tribal law enforcement and victim advocates report a large increase in the number of non-Indian criminals attracted to Indian country because of this gap in jurisdiction. This is not limited to sexual predators. For example, there are wide reports of methamphetamine labs, drug trafficking, and other crimes happening at a large rate in Indian country. Now, ideally the federal or state governments can step in and prosecute the non-Indian perpetrator, but the practical reality is that this intervention is not happening to the extent necessary in sexual assault cases. Tribal leaders and others have vocalized their concern about the low rates of prosecution of rape and other violent crimes by the federal government.

Certainly there have been prosecutions of non-Indian rapists, particularly in some areas where the federal or state government has developed strong relationships with the tribal governments. But when compared to the numbers of Native American women who are experiencing rape with the number of prosecutions, there is a significant imbalance. In some cases, it is difficult to even gain access to prosecution statistics that specify Native victims, because American Indians and Alaskan Natives are often classified in the "other" racial category. In the case of the federal government, different bureaucracies located in various departments have completely separate ways of counting and classifying sexual violence against adults.

In addition to the multitude of legal barriers restricting tribal governments from taking action against sexual violence, tribal nations are notoriously under-resourced. The United States Civil Rights Commission issued a report in February 2003 that strongly critiques the lack of resources allocated to tribal governments. A widely-quoted portion of this report notes that the federal government spends more per capita for health care in federal prisons than for health care on reservations. The report, however, covers many different kinds of resource limitations, including law enforcement and tribal justice systems.

> Despite the prevalence of crime, law enforcement in Native communities remains inadequate, with understaffed police departments and overcrowded correctional facilities. There are fewer law enforcement officers in Indian Country than in other rural areas and significantly fewer per capita than nationwide. In addition, per capita spending on law enforcement in Native American communities is roughly 60 percent of the national average.

These resource limitations have resulted in inferior systems of justice at the tribal level. Even a reported rape may not result in a comprehensive investigation, because staffing shortages and low morale at the tribal level can interfere with their respective counterparts at the federal or state level. Despite these limitations, some tribal governments have successfully prosecuted sexual assault.

Tribal governments face numerous barriers in adopting strong anti-rape laws and procedures. As a result, we have a situation in which all Native American people, namely women and children, are particularly vulnerable to sexual violence. A strong argument can be made that the high rates of violence are directly related to the lack of resources and the jurisdictional problems faced by tribal governments, as well as a continuation of the colonization process.

Due to these numerous barriers, I have attempted to determine how rape was dealt with by tribal nations prior to colonization, to see if there are some creative ways that contemporary tribal nations can address sexual violence even within the aforementioned limitations. The most important sources for this study are the oral traditions, the stories, the traditional belief systems, as well as statutes and contemporary tribal appellate case law that sometimes encompasses the traditional belief system. History and anthropology can be helpful in a limited sense, but these disciplines have historically distorted the perception of tribal justice systems, so I refer to those kinds of materials with caution.

In many tribal oral traditions, there are some interesting stories and dialogues describing the strength of women, the autonomy of women, and the right of women to sexual choice. These stories and traditions can be incorporated into contemporary tribal court systems. In fact, some tribal courts have requested elders to come in and testify as to traditional beliefs. Therefore, even if the tribe does not have a codified rape law, it may be possible to address illegal behavior through the introduction of these traditional laws.

Many of these traditional laws contain beliefs about individual autonomy and describe sexuality as being something very prized and very respected. Historically, many Europeans were horrified that the Native people actually allowed women to make autonomous sexual choices. Reviewing some historical letters and documents reveals that many tribal cultures allowed women to be leaders, to have multiple sex partners if they so chose and their sexuality was respected. If women did report a rape, they were believed. Moreover, there were significant punishments for rape and sexual assault including banishment and death.

As the federal government began to impose its laws and values upon Native peoples, many of the Anglo notions of rape assimilated into the tribal court systems. For the most part, there are very few references to Native American customs and beliefs in today's anti-rape scholarship. Non-Indian academics may also mistakenly believe that Native American cultures have nothing valuable to contribute to the legal scholarship. In fact, evidence exists that Native American people have always had well-developed theories of safety, trauma, and victims' rights.

A few years ago, I researched the evolution of my own tribe's laws. The Muscogee (Creek) Nation first started writing down laws in English in 1824 and this is the rape law contained in that original codification: "And be it farther enacted if any person or persons should undertake to force a woman and did it by force, *it shall be left to woman* what punishment she should satisfied with to whip or pay *what she say it be law.*"

Noting the awkwardness of the writing and realizing that it was written by someone whose first language was not English, the last clause is particularly interesting, in its mention of, "What she say, it be law." Language acknowledging the perspective of the victim is noticeably absent from American or European laws that existed in 1824, when this Creek Nation law was drafted. Instead, it is interesting to conceive of a justice system in which indigenous women were the central focus of adjudication of sexual violence.

For tribal governments, defining and adjudicating crimes such as sexual assault can be the purest exercise of sovereignty. What crime, other than murder, strikes at the hearts of its citizens more deeply than rape? Sexual violence impinges on our spiritual selves, creating emotional wounds that can feed into community trauma. Some scholars have theorized that the historical trauma of sexual abuse compounds the negative experiences of Native American women who are raped today. For sovereign tribal nations, the question is not just about protecting and responding to individual women who are sexually assaulted but also addressing the foundational wellness of the community where it occurs. Even without criminal jurisdiction over non-Indians, there may be ways in which to empower Native American survivors through a series of civil laws, including protection orders. The strength of the anti-rape sentiment in the community will ultimately illuminate the strength and resolve of the entire community to preserve and live healthy and happy lives.

This Article ends with the suggestion that we enlarge the mainstream dialogue about sexual violence to include the issues of tribal sovereignty and self-determination, not only because sexual assault is very common in the lives of Native American women, but also because the very system on which the United States bases its claim to this land has a long history of rape and sexual violence behind it. It is important that we not disregard the intersection between the rape of indigenous women and the destruction of indigenous legal systems. Anti-sexual assault work and decolonization work have a common philosophy and a common framework in which to develop appropriate legal responses.

Most importantly, if we cannot provide justice and accountability for the sex crimes that happen to the indigenous women, then we will continue to face a tremendous challenge in achieving justice for all women. It is so important that even those who do not work near Indian country become familiar with Federal Indian law and its impact on women because there were indigenous women in your area one time, and part of the reason that they are gone is because of forced removal and sexual violence. It is critical for anti-rape scholars to remember and honor the survivors of colonization in our work to hold perpetrators accountable. Likewise, it is critical that Federal Indian law scholars begin to engage in a dialogue concerning gendered violence and women's experiences in a more substantive way.

PART IV

FEMINIST LABORS

The Laugh of the Medusa

BY HÉLÈNE CIXOUS

Hélène Cixous is a Jewish Algerian French philosopher, professor, and writer for whom identity has always been complicated. She has won numerous awards for her work, and she consistently pushes the boundaries of methodology and genre with novel writing methods such as self-ethnography, in which she recorded her childhood stories of growing up in French-controlled Algeria. Her body of work consistently interrogates the ways in which language itself oppresses and must be reimagined in order to deconstruct sexist, racist categories. In her canonical "Laugh of the Medusa"—first translated into English and published in 1976—Cixous outlines her *écriture féminine*, a form of writing that deconstructs patriarchal forms of communication that exclude and other and creates new realities for the oppressed. For Cixous, language is a site of struggles over sexuality, identity, and difference. Conversely, language also carries potential for the empowerment of the marginalized. Instead of valorizing masculine approaches to writing, Cixous posits that there is something distinct and inherently valuable about women's writing, particularly when women afford themselves the space to write explicitly about their lived and embodied experiences.

Men have committed the greatest crime against women. Insidiously, violently, they have led them to hate women, to be their own enemies, to mobilize their immense strength against themselves, to be the executants of their virile needs. They have made for women an antinarcissism! A narcissism which loves itself only to be loved for what women haven't got! They have constructed the infamous logic of antilove.

We the precocious, we the repressed of culture, our lovely mouths gagged with pollen, our wind knocked out of us, we the labyrinths, the ladders, the trampled spaces, the bevies—we are black and we are beautiful.

We're stormy, and that which is ours breaks loose from us without our fearing any debilitation. Our glances, our smiles, are spent; laughs exude from all our mouths; our blood flows and we extend ourselves without ever reaching an end; we never hold back our thoughts, our signs, our writing; and we're not afraid of lacking.

What happiness for us who are omitted, brushed aside at the scene of inheritances; we inspire ourselves and we expire without running out of breath, we are everywhere!

From now on, who, if we say so, can say no to us? We've come back from always.

It is time to liberate the New Woman from the Old by coming to know her—by loving her for getting by, for getting beyond the Old without delay, by going out ahead of what the New Woman will be, as an arrow quits the bow with a movement that gathers and separates the vibrations musically, in order to be more than her self.

I say that we must, for, with a few rare exceptions, there has not yet been any writing that inscribes femininity; exceptions so rare, in fact, that, after plowing through literature across languages, cultures, and ages, one can only be startled at this vain scouting mission. It is well known that the number of women writers (while having increased very slightly from the nineteenth century on) has always been ridiculously small. This is a useless and deceptive fact unless from their species of female writers we do not first deduct the immense majority whose workmanship is in no way different from male writing, and which either obscures women or reproduces the classic representations of women (as sensitive—intuitive—dreamy, etc.).

———————

Nearly the entire history of writing is confounded with the history of reason, of which it is at once the effect, the support, and one of the privileged alibis. It has been one with the phallocentric tradition. It is indeed that same self-admiring, self-stimulating, self-congratulatory phallocentrism.

With some exceptions, for there have been failures—and if it weren't for them, I wouldn't be writing (I-woman, escapee)—in that enormous machine that has been operating and turning out its "truth" for centuries. There have been poets who would go to any lengths to slip something by at odds with tradition—men capable of loving love and hence capable of loving others and of wanting them, of imagining the woman who would hold out against oppression and constitute herself as a superb, equal, hence "impossible" subject, untenable in a real social framework. Such a woman the poet could desire only by breaking the codes that negate her. Her appearance would necessarily bring on, if not revolution—for the bastion was supposed to be immutable—at least harrowing explosions. At times it is in the fissure caused by an earthquake, through that radical mutation of things brought on by a material upheaval when every structure is for a moment thrown off balance and an ephemeral wildness sweeps order away, that the poet slips something by, for a brief span, of woman. Thus did Kleist expend himself in his yearning for the existence of sister-lovers, maternal daughters, mother-sisters, who never hung their heads in shame. Once the palace of magistrates is restored, it's time to pay: immediate bloody death to the uncontrollable elements.

But only the poets—not the novelists, allies of representationalism. Because poetry involves gaining strength through the unconscious and because the unconscious, that other limitless country, is the place where the repressed manage to survive: women, or as Hoffmann would say, fairies.

She must write her self, because this is the invention of a *new insurgent* writing which, when the moment of her liberation has come, will allow her to carry out the indispensable ruptures and transformations in her history, first at two levels that cannot be separated.

a) Individually. By writing her self, woman will return to the body which has been more than confiscated from her, which has been turned into the uncanny stranger on display—the ailing or dead figure, which so often turns out to be the nasty companion, the cause and location of inhibitions. Censor the body and you censor breath and speech at the same time.

Write your self. Your body must be heard. Only then will the immense resources of the unconscious spring forth. Our naphtha will spread, throughout the world, without dollars—black or gold—nonassessed values that will change the rules of the old game.

To write. An act which will not only "realize" the decensored relation of woman to her sexuality, to her womanly being, giving her access to her native strength; it will give her back her goods, her pleasures, her organs, her immense bodily territories which have been kept under seal; it will tear her away from the superegoized structure in which she has always occupied the place reserved for the guilty (guilty of everything, guilty at every turn: for having desires, for not having any; for being frigid, for being "too hot"; for not being both at once; for being too motherly and not enough; for having children and for not having any; for nursing and for not nursing . . .)—tear her away by means of this research, this job of analysis and illumination, this emancipation of the marvelous text of her self that she must urgently learn to speak. A woman without a body, dumb, blind, can't possibly be a good fighter. She is reduced to being the servant of the militant male, his shadow. We must kill the false woman who is preventing the live one from breathing. Inscribe the breath of the whole woman.

b) An act that will also be marked by woman's *seizing* the occasion to *speak*, hence her shattering entry into history, which has always been based *on her suppression*. To write and thus to forge for herself the antilogos weapon. To become *at will* the taker and initiator, for her own right, in every symbolic system, in every political process.

It is time for women to start scoring their feats in written and oral language.

Every woman has known the torment of getting up to speak. Her heart racing, at times entirely lost for words, ground and language slipping away—that's how daring a feat, how great a transgression it is for a woman to speak—even just open her mouth—in public. A double distress, for even if she transgresses, her words fall almost always upon the deaf male ear, which hears in language only that which speaks in the masculine.

It is by writing, from and toward women, and by taking up the challenge of speech which has been governed by the phallus, that women will confirm women in a place other than that which is reserved in and by the symbolic, that is, in a place other than silence. Women should break out of the snare of silence. They shouldn't be conned into accepting a domain which is the margin or the harem.

Listen to a woman speak at a public gathering (if she hasn't painfully lost her wind). She doesn't "speak," she throws her trembling body forward; she lets go of herself, she flies; all of her passes into her voice, and it's with her body that she vitally supports the "logic" of her speech. Her flesh speaks true. She lays herself bare. In fact, she physically materializes what she's thinking; she signifies it with her body. In a certain way she *inscribes* what she's saying, because she doesn't deny her drives the intractable and impassioned part they have in speaking. Her speech, even when "theoretical" or political, is never simple or linear or "objectified," generalized: she draws her story into history.

There is not that scission, that division made by the common man between the logic of oral speech and the logic of the text, bound as he is by his antiquated relation—servile, calculating—to mastery. From which proceeds the niggardly lip service which engages only the tiniest part of the body, plus the mask.

In women's speech, as in their writing, that element which never stops resonating, which, once we've been permeated by it, profoundly and imperceptibly touched by it, retains the power of moving us—that element is the song: first music from the first voice of love which is alive in every woman. Why this privileged relationship with the voice? Because no woman stockpiles as many defenses for countering the drives as does a man. You don't build walls around yourself, you don't forego pleasure as "wisely" as he. Even if phallic mystification has generally contaminated good relationships, a woman is never far from "mother" (I mean outside her role functions: the "mother" as nonname and as source of goods). There is always within her at least a little of that good mother's milk. She writes in white ink.

Woman for women.—There always remains in woman that force which produces/is produced by the other—in particular, the other woman. In her, matrix, cradler; herself giver as her mother and child; she is her own sister-daughter. You might object, "What about she who is the hysterical offspring of a bad mother?"

Everything will be changed once woman gives woman to the other woman. There is hidden and always ready in woman the source; the locus for the other. The mother, too, is a metaphor. It is necessary and sufficient that the best of herself be given to woman by another woman for her to be able to love herself and return in love the body that was "born" to her. Touch me, caress me, you the living no-name, give me my self as myself. The relation to the "mother," in terms of intense pleasure and violence, is curtailed no more than the relation to childhood (the child that she was, that she is, that she makes, remakes, undoes, there at the point where, the same, she others herself). Text: my body—shot through with streams of song; I don't mean the overbearing, clutchy "mother" but, rather, what touches you, the equivoice that affects you, fills your breast with an urge to come to language and launches your force; the rhythm that laughs you; the intimate recipient who makes all metaphors possible and desirable; body (body? bodies?), no more describable than god, the soul, or the Other; that part of you that leaves a space between yourself and urges you to inscribe in language your woman's style. In women there is always more or less of the mother who makes everything all right, who nourishes, and who stands up against separation; a force that will not be cut off but will knock the wind out of the codes. We will rethink womankind beginning with every form and every period of her body. The Americans remind us, "We are all Lesbians"; that is, don't denigrate woman, don't make of her what men have made of you.

Because the "economy" of her drives is prodigious, she cannot fail, in seizing the occasion to speak, to transform directly and indirectly *all* systems of exchange based on masculine thrift. Her libido will produce far more radical effects of political and social change than some might like to think.

The Politics of Housework

BY PAT MAINARDI

From 1986 until her retirement, Pat Mainardi was professor on the doctoral faculty in art history and women's studies at the Graduate Center of the City University of New York. She has also been a visiting professor at Princeton, the College of William & Mary, Williams College, and the University of Amsterdam, among other institutions. As a member of the radical feminist collective Redstockings, Mainardi was invested in women being liberated not only in society but at home, where domestic responsibilities were considered the sole purview of women. This essay was first published by Redstockings and later anthologized. The essay was a call to action and interrogated the ways in which housework was devalued as "real work" and yet was still expected of women. "Participatory democracy begins at home," Mainardi wrote before offering concrete ideas about what it will take to create an equitable domestic life and why doing so will be challenging. That she manages to do so with great wit is a credit to her talent. As we continue to strive for liberation and equity, Mainardi's work remains painfully relevant.

Though women do not complain of the power of husbands, each complains of her own husband, or of the husbands of her friends. It is the same in all other cases of servitude; at least in the commencement of the emancipatory movement. The serfs did not at first complain of the power of the lords, but only of their tyranny.

—JOHN STUART MILL, *THE SUBJECTION OF WOMEN*

Liberated women—very different from women's liberation! The first signals all kinds of goodies, to warm the hearts (not to mention other parts) of the most radical men. The other signals—*housework*. The first brings sex without marriage, sex before marriage, cozy housekeeping arrangements ("You see, I'm living with this chick") and the self-content of knowing that you're not the kind of man who wants a doormat instead of a woman. That will come later. After all, who wants that old commodity anymore, the Standard American Housewife, all husband, home and kids. The New Commodity, the Liberated Woman, has sex a lot and has a Career, preferably something that can be fitted in with the household chores—like dancing, pottery, or painting.

On the other hand is women's liberation—and housework. What? You say this is all trivial? Wonderful! That's what I thought. It seemed perfectly reasonable. We both had careers, both had to work a couple of days a week to earn enough to live on, so why shouldn't we share the housework? So I suggested it to my mate and he agreed—most men are too hip to turn you down flat. "You're right," he said. "It's only fair."

Then an interesting thing happened. I can only explain it by stating that we women have been brainwashed more than even we can imagine. Probably too many years of seeing television women in ecstasy over their shiny waxed floors or breaking down over their dirty shirt collars. Men have no such conditioning. They recognize the essential fact of housework right from the very beginning. Which is that it stinks. Here's my list of dirty chores: buying groceries, carting them home and putting them away; cooking meals and washing dishes and pots; doing the laundry, digging out the place when things get out of control; washing floors. The list could go on but the sheer necessities are bad enough. All of us have to do these things, or get someone else to do them for us. The longer my husband contemplated these chores, the more repulsed he became, and so proceeded the change from the normally sweet considerate Dr. Jekyll into the Mr. Hyde who would stop at nothing to avoid the horrors of—*housework*. As he felt himself backed into a corner laden with dirty dishes, brooms, mops, and reeking garbage, his front teeth grew longer and pointier, his fingernails haggled and his eyes grew wild. Housework trivial? Not on your life! Just try to share the burden.

So ensued a dialogue that's been going on for several years. Here are some of the high points:

"I don't mind sharing the housework, but I don't do it very well. We should each do the things we're best at."

Meaning: Unfortunately I'm no good at things like washing dishes or cooking. What I do best is a little light carpentry, changing light bulbs, moving furniture (*how often do you move furniture?*).

Also Meaning: Historically the lower classes (black men and us) have had hundreds of years experience doing menial jobs. It would be a waste of manpower to train someone else to do them now.

Also Meaning: I don't like the dull stupid boring jobs, so you should do them.

"I don't mind sharing the work, but you'll have to show me how to do it."

Meaning: I ask a lot of questions and you'll have to show me everything every time I do it because I don't remember so good. Also don't try to sit down and read while I'm doing my jobs because I'm going to annoy hell out of you until it's easier to do them yourself.

"We used to be so happy!" (Said whenever it was his turn to do something.)

Meaning: I used to be so happy.

Meaning: Life without housework is bliss. (*No quarrel here. Perfect agreement.*)

"We have different standards, and why should I have to work to your standards. That's unfair."

Meaning: If I begin to get bugged by the dirt and crap I will say, "This place sure is a sty" or "How can anyone live like this?" and wait for your reaction. I know that all women have a sore called "Guilt over a messy house" or "Household work is ultimately my responsibility." I know that men have caused that sore—if anyone visits and the place *is* a sty, they're not going to leave and say, "He sure is a lousy housekeeper." You'll take the rap in any case. I can outwait you.

Also Meaning: I can provoke innumerable scenes over the housework issue. Eventually doing all the housework yourself will be less painful to you than trying to get me to do half. Or I'll suggest we get a maid. She will do my share of the work. You will do yours. It's women's work.

"I've got nothing against sharing the housework, but you can't make me do it on your schedule."

Meaning: Passive resistance. I'll do it when I damned well please, if at all. If my job is doing dishes, it's easier to do them once a week. If taking out laundry, once a month. If washing the floors, once a year. If you don't like it, do it yourself oftener, and then I won't do it at all.

"I *hate* it more than you. You don't mind it so much."

Meaning: Housework is garbage work. It's the worst crap I've ever done. It's degrading and humiliating for someone of *my* intelligence to do it. But for someone of *your* intelligence . . .

"Housework is too trivial to even talk about."

Meaning: It's even more trivial to do. Housework is beneath my status. My purpose in life is to deal with matters of significance. Yours is to deal with matters of insignificance. You should do the housework.

"This problem of housework is not a man-woman problem! In any relationship between two people one is going to have a stronger personality and dominate."

Meaning: That stronger personality had better be *me.*

"In animal societies, wolves, for example, the top animal is usually a male even where he is not chosen for brute strength but on the basis of cunning and intelligence. Isn't that interesting?"

Meaning: I have historical, psychological, anthropological, and biological justification for keeping you down. How can you ask the top wolf to be equal?

"Women's liberation isn't really a political movement."

Meaning: The Revolution is coming too close to home.

Also meaning: I am only interested in how *I* am oppressed, not how I oppress others. Therefore the war, the draft, and the university are political. Women's liberation is not.

"Man's accomplishments have always depended on getting help from other people, mostly women. What great man would have accomplished what he did if he had to do his own housework?"

Meaning: Oppression is built into the System. I, as the white American male, receive the benefits of this System. I don't want to give them up.

I Want a Wife

BY JUDY (SYFERS) BRADY

Feminist writer Judy Brady wrote this humorous piece, which became an instant sensation, after a consciousness-raising session. Brady first read the piece during a 1970 rally for the Women's Strike for Equality. The piece was also published in a Bay Area feminist underground newspaper called *Tooth and Nail* and was reprinted in other feminist underground presses across the country before it was included in the first issue of *Ms.* magazine in 1971 under Brady's married name, Syfers. The feminist message couched in satirical humor spelled out the benefits of having a wife, outlining all the unpaid, unappreciated labor married women do daily that is all too often taken for granted. "I want a wife who will keep my house clean. A wife who will pick up after me. I want a wife who will keep my clothes clean, ironed, mended, replaced when need be, and who will see to it that my personal things are kept in their proper place so that I can find what I need the minute I need it," Brady writes. It is bittersweet that this piece still resonates in a world where women do the majority of the housework even when both spouses hold jobs outside of the home.

I belong to that classification of people known as wives. I am A Wife. And, not altogether incidentally, I am a mother.

Not too long ago a male friend of mine appeared on the scene fresh from a recent divorce. He had one child, who is, of course, with his ex-wife. He is obviously looking for another wife. As I thought about him while I was ironing one evening, it suddenly occurred to me that I, too, would like to have a wife. Why do I want a wife?

I would like to go back to school so that I can become economically independent, support myself, and, if need be, support those dependent upon me. I want a wife who will work and send me to school. And while I am going to school I want a wife to take care of my children. I want a wife to keep track of the children's doctor and dentist appointments. And to keep track of mine, too. I want a wife to make sure my children eat properly and are kept clean. I want a wife who will wash the children's clothes and keep them mended. I want a wife who is a good nurturant attendant to my children, who arranges for their schooling, makes sure that they have an adequate social life with their peers, takes them to the park, the zoo, etc. I want a wife who takes care of the children when they are sick, a wife who arranges to be around when the children need special care, because, of course, I cannot miss classes at school. My wife must arrange to lose time at work and not lose the job. It may mean a small cut in my wife's income from time to time, but I guess I can tolerate that. Needless to say, my wife will arrange and pay for the care of the children while my wife is working.

I want a wife who will take care of *my* physical needs. I want a wife who will keep my house clean. A wife who will pick up after me. I want a wife who will keep my clothes clean, ironed, mended, replaced when need be, and who will see to it that my personal things are kept in their proper place so that I can find what I need the minute I need it. I want a wife who cooks the meals, a wife who is a *good* cook. I want a wife who will plan the menus, do the necessary grocery shopping, prepare the meals, serve them pleasantly, and then do the cleaning up while I do my studying. I want a wife who will care for me when I am sick and sympathize with my pain and loss of time from school. I want a wife to go along when our family takes a vacation so that someone can continue to care for me and my children when I need a rest and change of scene.

I want a wife who will not bother me with rambling complaints about a wife's duties. But I want a wife who will listen to me when I feel the need to explain a rather difficult point I have come across in my course of studies. And I want a wife who will type my papers for me when I have written them.

I want a wife who will take care of the details of my social life. When my wife and I are invited out by my friends, I want a wife who will take care of the babysitting arrangements. When I meet people at school that I like and want to entertain, I want a wife who will have the house clean, will prepare a special meal, serve it to me and my friends, and not interrupt when I talk about things that interest me and my friends. I want a wife who will have arranged that the children are fed and ready for bed before my guests arrive so that the children do not bother us.

And I want a wife who knows that sometimes I need a night out by myself.

I want a wife who is sensitive to my sexual needs, a wife who makes love passionately and eagerly when I feel like it, a wife who makes sure that I am satisfied. And, of course, I want a wife who will not demand sexual attention when I am not in the mood for it. I want a wife who assumes the complete responsibility for birth control, because I do not want more children. I want a wife who will remain sexually faithful to me so that I do not have to clutter up my intellectual life with jealousies. And I want a wife who understands that *my* sexual needs may entail more than strict adherence to monogamy. I must, after all, be able to relate to people as fully as possible.

If, by chance, I find another person more suitable as a wife than the wife I already have, I want the liberty to replace my present wife with another one. Naturally, I will expect a fresh, new life; my wife will take the children and be solely responsible for them so that I am left free.

When I am through with school and have a job, I want my wife to quit working and remain at home so that my wife can more fully and completely take care of a wife's duties.

My God, who *wouldn't* want a wife?

Women and the
Myth of Consumerism

BY ELLEN WILLIS

Ellen Willis was the first pop music critic for *The New Yorker*, and later wrote for publications such as *The Village Voice*, *The Nation*, *Rolling Stone*, *Slate*, and *Salon*, as well as *Dissent*, where she was also on the editorial board. She was the author of several books of collected essays. Willis was a member of New York Radical Women and in 1969 co-founded the radical feminist group Redstockings with Shulamith Firestone. In "Women and the Myth of Consumerism," published in *Ramparts* in 1970, Willis calls out the Left for the facile argument (based on Freudian psychoanalysis) that women are easily manipulated by consumer culture and are therefore the unwitting base of predatory consumer culture. Willis argues that any understanding of consumer culture must examine the ways in which women are caught up in a capitalist, sexist system that forces them to be dependent upon the same system that oppresses them.

If white radicals are serious about revolution, they are going to have to discard a lot of bullshit ideology created by and for educated white middle-class males. A good example of what has to go is the popular theory of consumerism.

As expounded by many leftist thinkers, notably Marcuse, this theory maintains that consumers are psychically manipulated by the mass media to crave more and more consumer goods, and thus power an economy that depends on constantly expanding sales. The theory is said to be particularly applicable to women, for women do most of the actual buying, their consumption is often directly related to their oppression (e.g., makeup, soap flakes), and they are a special target of advertisers. According to this view, the society defines women as consumers, and the purpose of the prevailing media image of women as passive sexual objects is to sell products. It follows that the beneficiaries of this depreciation of women are not men but the corporate power structure.

Although the consumerism theory has, in recent years, taken on the invulnerability of religious dogma, like most dogmas its basic function is to defend the interests of its adherents—in this case, the class, sexual and racial privileges of Movement people.

First of all, there is nothing inherently wrong with consumption. Shopping and consuming are enjoyable human activities and the marketplace has been a center of social life for thousands of years. The profit system is oppressive not because relatively trivial luxuries are available, but because basic necessities are not. The locus of the oppression resides in the production function: people have no control over which commodities are produced (or services performed), in what amounts, under what conditions, or how these commodities are distributed. Corporations make these decisions and base them solely on their profit potential. It is more profitable to produce luxuries for the affluent (or for that matter for the poor, on exploitative installment plans) than to produce and make available food, housing, medical care, education, and recreational and cultural facilities according to the needs and desires of the people. We, the consumers, can accept the goods offered to us or we can reject them, but we cannot determine their quality or change the system's priorities.

As it is, the profusion of commodities is a genuine and powerful compensation for oppression. It is a bribe, but like all bribes it offers concrete benefits—in the average American's case, a degree of physical comfort unparalleled in history. Under present conditions, people are preoccupied with consumer goods not because they are brainwashed but because buying is the one pleasurable activity not only permitted but actively encouraged by our rulers. The pleasure of eating an ice cream cone may be minor compared to the pleasure of meaningful, autonomous work, but the former is easily available and the latter is not. A poor family would undoubtedly rather have a decent apartment than a new TV, but since they are unlikely to get the apartment, what is to be gained by not getting the TV?

————

Radicals who in general are healthily skeptical of facile Freudian explanations have been quick to embrace this theory of media manipulation based squarely on Freud, as popularized by market researchers and journalists like Vance Packard (Marcuse acknowledges Packard's influence in *One-Dimensional Man*). In essence, this theory holds that ads designed to create unconscious associations between merchandise and deep-seated fears, sexual desires, and needs for identity and self-esteem, induce people to buy products in search of gratifications no product can provide. Furthermore, the corporations, through the media, deliberately create fears and desires that their products can claim to fulfill. The implication is that women are not merely taken in by lies or exaggerations—as, say, by the suggestion that a certain perfume will make us sexually irresistible—but are psychically incapable of learning from experience and will continue to buy no matter how often we are disappointed, and that in any case our "need" to be sexually irresistible is programmed into us to keep us buying perfume. This hypothesis of psychic distortion is based on the erroneous assumption that mental health and anti-materialism are synonymous.

Although they have to cope with the gyppery inherent in the profit system, people for the most part buy goods for practical, self-interested reasons. A washing machine does make a housewife's work easier (in the absence of socialization of housework); Excedrin does make a headache go away; a car does provide transportation. If one is duped into buying a product because of misleading advertising, the process is called exploitation; it has nothing to do with brainwashing.

Advertising, in fact, is a how-to manual on the consumer economy, constantly reminding us of what is available and encouraging us to indulge ourselves. It works (that is, stimulates sales) *because* buying is the only game in town, not vice versa. Advertising does appeal to morbid fears (e.g., of body odors) and false hopes (of irresistibility) and shoppers faced with indistinguishable brands of a product may choose on the basis of an ad (what method is better?), but this is just the old game of caveat emptor. It thrives on naivete and people learn to resist it through experience. Other vulnerable groups are older people, who had no previous experience—individual or historical—to guide them when the consumer cornucopia suddenly developed after World War II, and poor people, who do not have enough money to learn through years of trial, error and disillusionment to be shrewd consumers. The constant refinement of advertising claims, visual effects and so on, shows that experience desensitizes. No one really believes that smoking Brand X cigarettes will make you sexy. (The function of sex in an ad is probably the obvious one—to lure people into paying closer attention to the ad—rather than to make them "identify" their lust with a product. The chief effect of the heavy sexual emphasis in advertising has been to stimulate a national preoccupation with sex, showing that you can't identify away a basic human drive as easily as all that.) Madison Avenue has increasingly de-emphasized "motivational" techniques in favor of aesthetic ones—TV commercials in particular have become incredibly inventive visually—and even made a joke out of the old motivational ploys (the phallic Virginia Slims ad, for instance, is blatantly campy). We can conclude from this that either the depth psychology approach never worked in the first place, or that it has stopped working as consumers have gotten more sophisticated.

The argument that the corporations create new psychological needs in order to sell their wares is equally flimsy. There is no evidence that propaganda can in itself create a desire, as opposed to bringing to consciousness a latent desire by suggesting that means of satisfying it are available. This idea is superstitious: it implies that the oppressor is diabolically intelligent (he has learned how to control human souls) and that the media have magic powers. It also mistakes effects for causes and drastically oversimplifies the relation between ideology and material conditions. We have not been taught to dislike our smell so that they can sell deodorants; deodorants sell because there are social consequences for smelling. And the negative attitude about our bodies that has made it feasible to invent and market deodorants is deeply rooted in our anti-sexual culture, which in turn has been shaped by exploitive modes of production and class antagonism between men and women.

The confusion between cause and effect is particularly apparent in the consumerist analysis of women's oppression. Women are not manipulated by the media into being domestic servants and mindless sexual decorations, the better to sell soap and hair spray. Rather, the image reflects women as they are forced by men in a sexist society to behave. Male supremacy is the oldest and most basic form of class exploitation; it was not invented by a smart ad man. The real evil of the media image of women is that it supports the sexist status quo. In a sense, the fashion, cosmetics and "feminine hygiene" ads are aimed more at men than at women. They encourage men to expect women to sport all the latest trappings of sexual slavery—expectations women must then fulfill if they are to survive. That advertisers exploit women's subordination rather than cause it can be clearly seen now that *male* fashions and toiletries have become big business. In contrast to ads for women's products, whose appeal is "use this and he will want you" (or "if you don't use this, he won't want you"), ads for the male counterparts urge, "You too can enjoy perfume and bright-colored clothes; don't worry, it doesn't make you feminine." Although advertisers are careful to emphasize how *virile* these products are (giving them names like "Brut," showing the man who uses them hunting or flirting with admiring women—who, incidentally, remain decorative objects when the sell is aimed directly at men), it is never claimed that the product is *essential* to masculinity (as makeup is essential to femininity), only *compatible* with it. To convince a man to buy, an ad must appeal to his desire for autonomy and freedom from conventional restrictions; to convince a woman, an ad must appeal to her need to please the male oppressor.

For women, buying and wearing clothes and beauty aids is not so much consumption as work. One of a woman's jobs in this society is to be an attractive sexual object, and clothes and makeup are tools of the trade. Similarly, buying food and household furnishings is a domestic task; it is the wife's chore to pick out the commodities that will be consumed by the whole family. Appliances and cleaning materials are tools that facilitate her domestic function. When a woman spends a lot of money and time decorating her home or herself, or hunting down the latest in vacuum cleaners, it is not idle self-indulgence (let alone the result of psychic manipulation) but a healthy attempt to find outlets for her creative energies within her circumscribed role.

There is a persistent myth that a wife has control over her husband's money because she gets to spend it. Actually, she does not have much more financial autonomy than the employee of a corporation who is delegated to buy office furniture or supplies. The husband, especially if he is rich, may allow his wife wide latitude in spending—he may reason that since she has to work in the home she is entitled to furnish it to her taste, or he may simply not want to bother with domestic details—but he retains the ultimate veto power. If he doesn't like the way his wife handles his money, she will hear about it. In most households, particularly in the working class, a wife cannot make significant expenditures, either personal or in her role as object-servant, without consulting her husband. And more often than not, according to statistics, it is the husband who makes the final decisions about furniture and appliances as well as about other major expenditures like houses, cars and vacations.

The consumerism theory is the outgrowth of an aristocratic, European-oriented anti-materialism based on upper-class resentment against the rise of the vulgar bourgeoisie. Radical intellectuals have been attracted to this essentially reactionary position (Herbert Marcuse's view of mass culture is strikingly similar to that of conservative theorists like Ernest van den Haag) because it appeals both to their dislike of capitalism and to their feeling of superiority to the working class. This elitism is evident in radicals' conviction that they have seen through the system, while the average working slob is brainwashed by the media. (Oddly, no one claims that the ruling class is oppressed by commodities; it seems that rich people consume out of free choice.) Ultimately this point of view leads to a sterile emphasis on individual solutions—if only the benighted would reject their "plastic" existence and move to East Village tenements—and the conclusion that people are oppressed because they are stupid or sick. The obnoxiousness of this attitude is compounded by the fact that radicals can only maintain their dropout existence so long as plenty of brainwashed workers keep the economy going.

Consumerism as applied to women is blatantly sexist. The pervasive image of the empty-headed female consumer constantly trying her husband's patience with her extravagant purchases contributes to the myth of male superiority: we are incapable of spending money rationally; all we need to make us happy is a new hat now and then. (There is an analogous racial stereotype—the black with his Cadillac and his magenta shirts.) Furthermore, the consumerism line allows Movement men to avoid recognizing that they exploit women by attributing women's oppression solely to capitalism. It fits neatly into already existing radical theory and concerns, saving the Movement the trouble of tackling the real problems of women's liberation. And it retards the struggle against male supremacy by dividing women. Just as in the male movement, the belief in consumerism encourages radical women to patronize and put down other women for trying to survive as best they can, and maintains individualist illusions.

If we are to build a mass movement we must recognize that no individual decision, like rejecting consumption, can liberate us. We must stop arguing about whose life style is better (and secretly believing ours is) and tend to the task of collectively fighting our own oppression and the ways in which we oppress others. When we create a political alternative to sexism, racism and capitalism, the consumer problem, if it is a problem, will take care of itself.

A Question of Class

BY DOROTHY ALLISON

Dorothy Allison is a writer and editor whose work—such as this essay, published in her 1994 collection *Skin: Talking about Sex, Class, and Literature*—focuses on class struggles, sexual abuse and violence, and sexuality through a feminist lens. Her personal experience with poverty, sexual abuse, and her lesbian identity informs all of her work. Her debut novel, *Bastard out of Carolina*, was a finalist for the National Book Award and won the Ferro-Grumley Award, an ALA Award for Lesbian and Gay Writing. It became a bestseller and was made into an award-winning movie. In "A Question of Class," Allison is trenchant as she articulates the seething rage of being poor in a world that believes "poverty is a voluntary condition." She grounds her interrogation of class in her own experiences as the daughter of an unwed teenage mother, and also explores what it means to always feel like there is no place for you in the world others assume you belong to. By the end, she demonstrates that we have a mythic cultural narrative about poverty that must be dismantled. Allison writes, "To resist destruction, self-hatred, or lifelong hopelessness, we have to throw off the conditioning of being despised, the fear of becoming the *they* that is talked about so dismissively, to refuse lying myths and easy moralities, to see ourselves as human, flawed, and extraordinary."

The first time I heard, "They're different than us, don't value human life the way we do," I was in high school in Central Florida. The man speaking was an army recruiter talking to a bunch of boys, telling them what the army was really like, what they could expect overseas. A cold angry feeling swept over me. I had heard the word they pronounced in that same callous tone before. *They*, those people over there, those people who are not us, they die so easily, kill each other so casually. They are different. "*We*," I thought. "*Me*."

When I was six or eight back in Greenville, South Carolina, I had heard that same matter-of-fact tone of dismissal applied to me. "Don't you play with her. I don't want you talking to them." Me and my family, we had always been *they*. "Who am I?" I wondered, listening to that recruiter. "Who are my people?" We die so easily, disappear so completely—we/they, the poor and the queer. I pressed my bony white trash fists to my stubborn lesbian mouth. The rage was a good feeling, stronger and purer than the shame that followed it, the fear and the sudden urge to run and hide, to deny, to pretend I did not know who I was and what the world would do to me.

My people were not remarkable. We were ordinary, but even so we were mythical. We were the *they* everyone talks about—the un-grateful poor. I grew up trying to run away from the fate that destroyed so many of the people I loved, and having learned the habit of hiding, I found I had also learned to hide from myself. I did not know who I was, only that I did not want to be *they*, the ones who are destroyed or dismissed to make the "real" people, the important people, feel safer. By the time I understood that I was queer, that habit of hiding was deeply set in me, so deeply that it was not a choice but an instinct. Hide, hide to survive, I thought, knowing that if I told the truth about my life, my family, my sexual desire, my history, I would move over into that un-known territory, the land of they, would never have the chance to name my own life, to understand it or claim it.

Why are you so afraid? my lovers and friends have asked me the many times I have suddenly seemed a stranger, someone who would not speak to them, would not do the things they believed I should do, simple things like applying for a job, or a grant, or some award they were sure I could acquire easily. Entitlement, I have told them, is a matter of feeling like we rather than they. You think you have a right to things, a place in the world, and it is so intrinsically a part of you that you cannot imagine people like me, people who seem to live in your world, who don't have it. I have explained what I know over and over, in every way I can, but I have never been able to make clear the degree of my fear, the extent to which I feel myself denied: not only that I am queer in a world that hates queers, but that I was born poor into a world that despises the poor. The need to make my world believable to people who have never experienced it is part of why I write fiction. I know that some things must be felt to be understood, that despair, for example, can never be adequately analyzed; it must be lived. But if I can write a story that so draws the reader in that she imagines herself like my characters, feels their sense of fear and uncertainty, their hopes and terrors, then I have come closer to knowing myself as real, important as the very people I have always watched with awe.

I have known I was a lesbian since I was a teenager, and I have spent a good twenty years making peace with the effects of incest and physical abuse. But what may be the central fact of my life is that I was born in 1949 in Greenville, South Carolina, the bastard daughter of a white woman from a desperately poor family, a girl who had left the seventh grade the year before, worked as a waitress, and was just a month past fifteen when she had me. That fact, the inescapable impact of being born in a condition of poverty that this society finds shameful, contemptible, and somehow deserved, has had dominion over me to such an extent that I have spent my life trying to overcome or deny it. I have learned with great difficulty that the vast majority of people believe that poverty is a voluntary condition.

I have loved my family so stubbornly that every impulse to hold them in contempt has sparked in me a countersurge of pride—complicated and undercut by an urge to fit us into the acceptable myths and theories of both mainstream society and a lesbian-feminist reinterpretation. The choice becomes Steven Spielberg movies or Erskine Caldwell novels, the one valorizing and the other caricaturing, or the patriarchy as villain, trivializing the choices the men and women of my family have made. I have had to fight broad generalizations from every theoretical viewpoint.

Traditional feminist theory has had a limited understanding of class differences and of how sexuality and self are shaped by both desire and denial. The ideology implies that we are all sisters who should only turn our anger and suspicion on the world outside the lesbian community. It is easy to say that the patriarchy did it, that poverty and social contempt are products of the world of the fathers, and often I felt a need to collapse my sexual history into what I was willing to share of my class background, to pretend that my life both as a lesbian and as a working-class escapee was constructed by the patriarchy. Or conversely, to ignore how much my life was shaped by growing up poor and talk only about what incest did to my identity as a woman and as a lesbian. The difficulty is that I can't ascribe everything that has been problematic about my life simply and easily to the patriarchy, or to incest, or even to the invisible and much-denied class structure of our society.

In my lesbian-feminist collective we had long conversations about the mind/body split, the way we compartmentalize our lives to survive. For years I thought that that concept referred to the way I had separated my activist life from the passionate secret life in which I acted on my sexual desires. I was convinced that the fracture was fairly simple, that it would be healed when there was time and clarity to do so—at about the same point when I might begin to understand sex. I never imagined that it was not a split but a splintering, and I passed whole portions of my life—days, months, years—in pure directed progress, getting up every morning and setting to work, working so hard and so continually that I avoided examining in any way what I knew about my life. Busywork became a trance slate. I ignored who I really was and how I became that person, continued in that daily progress, became an automaton who was what she did. I tried to become one with the lesbian-feminist community so as to feel real and valuable. I did not know that I was hiding, blending in for safety just as I had done in high school, in college. I did not recognize the impulse to forget. I believed that all those things I did not talk about, or even let myself think too much about, were not important, that none of them defined me. I had constructed a life, an identity in which I took pride, an alternative lesbian family in which I felt safe, and I did not realize that the fundamental me had almost disappeared.

It is surprising how easy it was to live that life. Everyone and everything cooperated with the process. Everything in our culture—books, television, movies, school, fashion—is presented as if it is being seen by one pair of eyes, shaped by one set of hands, heard by one pair of ears. Even if you know you are not part of that imaginary creature—if you like country music not symphonies, read books cynically, listen to the news unbelievingly, are lesbian not heterosexual, and surround yourself with your own small deviant community—you are still shaped by that hegemony, or your resistance to it. The only way I found to resist that homogenized view of the world was to make myself part of something larger than myself. As a feminist and a radical lesbian organizer, and later as a sex radical (which eventually became the term, along with pro-sex feminist, for those who were not anti-pornography but anti-censorship, those of us arguing for sexual diversity), the need to belong, to feel safe, was just as important for me as for any heterosexual, nonpolitical citizen, and sometimes even more important because the rest of my life was so embattled.

The first time I read the Jewish lesbian Irena Klepfisz's poems I experienced a frisson of recognition. It was not that my people had been "burned off the map" or murdered as hers had. No, we had been encouraged to destroy ourselves, made invisible because we did not fit the myths of the noble poor generated by the middle class. Even now, past forty and stubbornly proud of my family, I feel the draw of that mythology, that romanticized, edited version of the poor. I find myself looking back and wondering what was real, what was true. Within my family, so much was lied about, joked about, denied, or told with deliberate indirection, an undercurrent of humiliation or a brief pursed grimace that belied everything that had been said. What was real? The poverty depicted in books and movies was romantic, a backdrop for the story of how it was escaped.

The poverty portrayed by left-wing intellectuals was just as romantic, a platform for assailing the upper and middle classes, and from their perspective, the working-class hero was invariably male, righteously indignant, and inhumanly noble. The reality of self-hatred and violence was either absent or caricatured. The poverty I knew was dreary, deadening, shameful, the women powerful in ways not generally seen as heroic by the world outside the family.

My family's lives were not on television, not in books, not even comic books. There was a myth of the poor in this country, but it did not include us no matter how hard I tried to squeeze us in. There was an idea of the good poor—hard-working, ragged but clean, and intrinsically honorable. I understood that we were the bad poor: men who drank and couldn't keep a job; women, invariably pregnant before marriage, who quickly became worn, fat, and old from working too many hours and bearing too many children; and children with runny noses, watery eyes, and the wrong attitudes. My cousins quit school, stole cars, used drugs, and took dead-end jobs pumping gas or waiting tables. We were not noble, not grateful, not even hopeful. We knew ourselves despised. My family was ashamed of being poor, of feeling hopeless. What was there to work for, to save money for, to fight for or struggle against? We had generations before us to teach us that nothing ever changed, and that those who did try to escape failed.

My mama had eleven brothers and sisters, of whom I can name only six. No one is left alive to tell me the names of the others. It was my grandmother who told me about my real daddy, a shiftless pretty man who was supposed to have married, had six children, and sold cut-rate life insurance to poor Black people. My mama married when I was a year old, but her husband died just after my little sister was born a year later.

When I was five, Mama married the man she lived with until she died. Within the first year of their marriage Mama miscarried, and while we waited out in the hospital parking lot, my stepfather molested me for the first time, something he continued to do until I was past thirteen. When I was eight or so, Mama took us away to a motel after my stepfather beat me so badly it caused a family scandal, but we returned after two weeks. Mama told me that she really had no choice: she could not support us alone. When I was eleven I told one of my cousins that my stepfather was molesting me. Mama packed up my sisters and me and took us away for a few days, but again, my stepfather swore be would stop, and again we went back after a few weeks. I stopped talking for a while, and I have only vague memories of the next two years.

My stepfather worked as a route salesman, my mama as a

waitress, laundry worker, cook, or fruit packer. I could never understand, since they both worked so hard and such long hours, how we never had enough money, but it was also true of my mama's brothers and sisters who worked hard in the mills or the furnace industry. In fact, my parents did better than anyone else in the family. But eventually my stepfather was fired and we hit bottom—nightmarish months of marshals at the door, repossessed furniture, and rubber checks. My parents worked out a scheme so that it appeared my stepfather had abandoned us, but instead he went down to Florida, got a new job, and rented us a house. He returned with a U-Haul trailer in the dead of night, packed us up, and moved us south.

The night we left South Carolina for Florida, my mama leaned over the backseat of her old Pontiac and promised us girls, "It'll be better there." I don't know if we believed her, but I remember crossing Georgia in the early morning, watching the red clay hills and swaying grey blankets of moss recede through the back window. I kept looking at the trailer behind us, ridiculously small to contain everything we owned. Mama had packed nothing that wasn't fully paid off, which meant she had only two things of worth: her washing and sewing machines, both of them tied securely to the trailer walls. Throughout the trip I fantasized an accident that would burst that trailer, scattering old clothes and cracked dishes on the tarmac.

I was only thirteen. I wanted us to start over completely, to begin again as new people with nothing of the past left over. I wanted to run away from who we had been seen to be, who we had been. That desire is one I have seen in other members of my family. It is the first thing I think of when trouble comes—the geographic solution. Change your name, leave town, disappear, make yourself over. What hides behind that impulse is the conviction that the life you have lived, the person you are, is valueless, better off abandoned, that running away is easier than trying to change things, that change itself is not possible. Sometimes I think it is this conviction—more seductive than alcohol or violence, more subtle than sexual hatred or gender injustice—that has dominated my life and made real change so painful and difficult.

Moving to Central Florida did not fix our lives. It did not stop my stepfather's violence, heal my shame, or make my mother happy. Once there, our lives became controlled by my mother's illness and medical bills. She had a hysterectomy when I was about eight and endured a series of hospitalizations for ulcers and a chronic back problem. Through most of my adolescence she superstitiously refused to allow anyone to mention the word cancer. When she was not sick, Mama and my stepfather went on working, struggling to pay off what seemed an insurmountable load of debts.

By the time I was fourteen, my sisters and I had found ways to discourage most of our stepfather's sexual advances. We were not close, but we united against him. Our efforts were helped along when he was referred to a psychotherapist after he lost his temper at work, and was prescribed drugs that made him sullen but less violent. We were growing up quickly, my sisters moving toward dropping out of school while I got good grades and took every scholarship exam I could find. I was the first person in my family to graduate from high school, and the fact that I went on to college was nothing short of astonishing.

We all imagine our lives are normal, and I did not know my life was not everyone's. It was in Central Florida that I began to realize just how different we were. The people we met there had not been shaped by the rigid class structure that dominated the South Carolina Piedmont. The first time I looked around my junior high classroom and realized I did not know who those people were— not only as individuals but as categories, who their people were and how they saw themselves—I also realized that they did not know me. In Greenville, everyone knew my family, knew we were trash, and that meant we were supposed to be poor, supposed to have grim low-paid jobs, have babies in our teens, and never finish school. But Central Florida in the 1960s was full of runaways and immigrants, and our mostly white working-class suburban school sorted us out not by income and family background but by intelligence and aptitude tests. Suddenly I was boosted into the college-bound track, and while there was plenty of contempt for my inept social skills, pitiful wardrobe, and slow drawling accent, there was also something I had never experienced before: a protective anonymity, and a kind of grudging respect and curiosity about who I might become. Because they did not see poverty and hope-lessness as a foregone conclusion for my life, I could begin to imagine other futures for myself.

In that new country, we were unknown. The myth of the poor settled over us and glamorized us. I saw it in the eyes of my teach-ers, the Lion's Club representative who paid for my new glasses, and the lady from the Junior League who told me about the schol-arship I had won. Better, far better, to be one of the mythical poor than to be part of the *they* I had known before. I also experienced a new level of fear, a fear of losing what had never before been imaginable. Don't let me lose this chance, I prayed, and lived in terror that I might suddenly be seen again as what I knew myself to be.

As an adolescent I thought that my family's escape from South Carolina played like a bad movie. We fled the way runaway serfs might have done, with the sheriff who would have arrested my stepfather the imagined border guard. I am certain that if we had remained in South Carolina, I would have been trapped by my family's heritage of poverty, jail, and illegitimate children—that even being smart, stubborn, and a lesbian would have made no difference.

My grandmother died when I was twenty, and after Mama went home for the funeral, I had a series of dreams in which we still lived up in Greenville, just down the road from where Granny died. In the dreams I had two children and only one eye, lived in a trailer, and worked at the textile mill. Most of my time was taken up with deciding when I would finally kill my children and myself. The dreams were so vivid, I became convinced they were about the life I was meant to have had, and I began to work even harder to put as much distance as I could between my family and me. I copied the dress, mannerisms, attitudes, and ambitions of the girls I met in college, changing or hiding my own tastes, inter-ests, and desires, I kept my lesbianism a secret, forming a relation-ship with an effeminate male friend that served to shelter and disguise us both. I explained to friends that I went home so rarely because my stepfather and I fought too much for me to be com-fortable in his house. But that was only part of the reason I avoided home, the easiest reason. The truth was that I feared the person I might become in my mama's house, the woman of my dreams—hateful, violent, and hopeless.

It is hard to explain how deliberately and thoroughly I ran away from my own life. I did not forget where I came from, but I gritted my teeth and hid it. When I could not get enough scholarship money to pay for graduate school, I spent a year of rage working as a salad girl, substitute teacher, and maid. I finally managed to find a job by agreeing to take any city assignment where the Social Security Administration needed a clerk. Once I had a job and my own place far away from anyone in my family, I became sexually and politically active, joining the Women's Center support staff and falling in love with a series of middle-class women who thought my accent and stories thoroughly charming. The stories I told about my family, about South Carolina, about being poor itself, were all lies, carefully edited to seem droll or funny. I knew damn well that no one would want to hear the truth about poverty, the hopelessness and fear, the feeling that nothing I did would ever make any difference and the raging resentment that burned beneath my jokes. Even when my lovers and I formed an alternative lesbian family, sharing what we could of our resources, I kept the truth about my background and who I knew myself to be a carefully obscured mystery. I worked as hard as I could to make myself a new person, an emotionally healthy radical lesbian activist, and I believed completely that by remaking myself I was helping to remake the world.

For a decade, I did not go home for more than a few days at a time. When in the 1980s I ran into the concept of feminist sexuality, I genuinely did not know what it meant. Though I was, and am, a feminist, and committed to claiming the right to act on my sexual desires without tailoring my lust to a sex-fearing society, demands that I explain or justify my sexual fantasies have left me at a loss. How does anyone explain sexual need?

The Sex Wars are over, I've been told, and it always makes me want to ask who won. But my sense of humor may be a little obscure to women who have never felt threatened by the way most lesbians use and mean the words *pervert* and *queer*. I use the word queer to mean more than lesbian. Since I first used it in 1980 I have always meant it to imply that I am not only a lesbian but a transgressive lesbian-femme, masochistic, as sexually aggressive as the women I seek out, and as pornographic in my imagination and sexual activities as the heterosexual hegemony has ever believed.

My aunt Dot used to joke, "There are two or three things I know for sure, but never the same things and I'm never as sure as I'd like." What I know for sure is that class, gender, sexual preference, and prejudice—racial, ethnic, and religious—form an intricate lattice that restricts and shapes our lives, and that resistance to hatred is not a simple act. Claiming your identity in the cauldron of hatred and resistance to hatred is infinitely complicated, and worse, almost unexplainable.

I know that I have been hated as a lesbian both by "society" and by the intimate world of my extended family, but I have also been hated or held in contempt (which is in some ways more debilitating and slippery than hatred) by lesbians for behavior and sexual practices shaped in large part by class. My sexual identity is intimately constructed by my class and regional background, and much of the hatred directed at my sexual preferences is class hatred—however much people, feminists in particular, like to pretend this is not a factor. The kind of woman I am attracted to is invariably the kind of woman who embarrasses respectably middle-class, politically aware lesbian feminists. My sexual ideal is butch, exhibitionistic, physically aggressive, smarter than she wants you to know, and proud of being called a pervert. Most often she is working class, with an aura of danger and an ironic sense of humor. There is a lot of contemporary lip service paid to sexual tolerance, but the fact that my sexuality is constructed within, and by, a butch/femme and leather fetishism is widely viewed with distaste or outright hatred.

For most of my life I have been presumed to be misguided, damaged by incest and childhood physical abuse, or deliberately indulging in hateful and retrograde sexual practices out of a selfish concentration on my own sexual satisfaction. I have been expected to abandon my desires, to become the normalized woman who flirts with fetishization, who plays with gender roles and treats the historical categories of deviant desire with humor or gentle contempt but never takes any of it so seriously as to claim a sexual identity based on these categories. It was hard enough for me to shake off demands when they were made by straight society.

It was appalling when I found the same demands made by other lesbians.

One of the strengths I derive from my class background is that I am accustomed to contempt. I know that I have no chance of becoming what my detractors expect of me, and I believe that even the attempt to please them will only further engage their contempt, and my own self-contempt as well. Nonetheless, the relationship between the life I have lived and the way that life is seen by strangers has constantly invited a kind of self-mythologizing fantasy. It has always been tempting for me to play off of the stereotypes and misconceptions of mainstream culture, rather than describe a difficult and sometimes painful reality.

I am trying to understand how we internalize the myths of our society even as we resist them. I have felt a powerful temptation to write about my family as a kind of morality tale, with us as the heroes and middle and upper classes as the villains. It would be within the romantic myth, for example, to pretend that we were the kind of noble Southern whites portrayed in the movies, mill workers for generations until driven out by alcoholism and a family propensity for rebellion and union talk. But that would be a lie. The truth is that no one in my family ever joined a union.

Taken to its limits, the myth of the poor would make my family over into union organizers or people broken by the failure of the unions. As far as my family was concerned union organizers, like preachers, were of a different class, suspect and hated however much they might be admired for what they were supposed to be trying to achieve. Nominally Southern Baptist, no one in my family actually paid much attention to preachers, and only little children went to Sunday school. Serious belief in anything—any political ideology, any religious system, or any theory of life's meaning and purpose—was seen as unrealistic. It was an attitude that bothered me a lot when I started reading the socially conscious novels I found in the paperback racks when I was eleven or so. I particularly loved Sinclair Lewis's novels and wanted to imagine my own family as part of the working man's struggle.

"We were not joiners," my aunt Dot told me with a grin when I asked her about the union. My cousin Butch laughed at that, told me the union charged dues, and said, "Hell, we can't even be persuaded to toss money in the collection plate. An't gonna give it to no union man." It shamed me that the only thing my family whole-heartedly believed in was luck and the waywardness of fate. They held the dogged conviction that the admirable and wise thing to do was keep a sense of humor, never whine or cower, and trust that luck might someday turn as good as it had been bad— and with just as much reason. Becoming a political activist with an almost religious fervor was the thing I did that most outraged my family and the Southern working-class community they were part of.

Similarly, it was not my sexuality, my lesbianism, that my family saw as most rebellious; for most of my life, no one but my mama took my sexual preference very seriously. It was the way I thought about work, ambition, and self-respect. They were waitresses, laundry workers, counter girls. I was the one who went to work as a maid, something I never told any of them. They would have been angry if they had known. Work was just work for them, necessary. You did what you had to do to survive. They did not so much believe in taking pride in doing your job as in stubbornly enduring hard work and hard times. At the same time, they held that there were some forms of work, including maid's work, that were only for Black people, not white, and while I did not share that belief, I knew how intrinsic it was to the way my family saw the world. Sometimes I felt as if I straddled cultures and belonged on neither side. I would grind my teeth at what I knew was my family's unquestioning racism while continuing to respect their pragmatic endurance. But more and more as I grew older, what I felt was a deep estrangement from their view of the world, and gradually a sense of shame that would have been completely incomprehensible to them.

"Long as there's lunch counters, you can always find work," I was told by my mother and my aunts. Then they'd add, "I can get me a little extra with a smile." It was obvious there was supposed to be nothing shameful about it, that needy smile across a lunch counter, that rueful grin when you didn't have rent, or the half-provocative, half-pleading way my mama could cajole the man at the store to give her a little credit. But I hated it, hated the need for it and the shame that would follow every time I did it myself. It was begging, as far as I was concerned, a quasi-prostitution that I despised even while I continued to rely on it. After all, I needed the money.

"Just use that smile" my girl cousins used to joke, and I hated what I knew they meant. After college, when I began to support myself and study feminist theory, I became more contemptuous rather than more understanding of the women in my family. I told myself that prostitution is a skilled profession and my cousins were never more than amateurs. There was a certain truth in this, though like all cruel judgments rendered from the outside, it ignored the conditions that made it true. The women in my family, my mother included, had sugar daddies, not Johns, men who slipped them money because they needed it so badly. From their point of view they were nice to those men because the men were nice to them, and it was never so direct or crass an arrangement that they would set a price on their favors. Nor would they have described what they did as prostitution. Nothing made them angrier than the suggestion that the men who helped them out did it just for their favors. They worked for a living, they swore, but this was different.

I always wondered if my mother hated her sugar daddy, or if not him then her need for what he offered her, but it did not seem to me in memory that she had. He was an old man, half-crippled, hesitant and needy, and he treated my mama with enormous consideration and, yes, respect. The relationship between them was painful, and since she and my stepfather could not earn enough to support the family, Mama could not refuse her sugar daddy's money. At the same time the man made no assumptions about that money buying anything Mama was not already offering. The truth was, I think, that she genuinely liked him, and only partly because he treated her so well.

Even now, I am not sure whether there was a sexual exchange between them. Mama was a pretty woman, and she was kind to him, a kindness he obviously did not get from anyone else in his life. Moreover, he took extreme care not to cause her any problems with my stepfather. As a teenager, with a teenager's contempt for moral failings and sexual complexity of any kind, I had been convinced that Mama's relationship with that old man was contemptible. Also, that I would never do such a thing. But the first time a lover of mine gave me money and I took it, everything in my head shifted.

The amount was not much to her, but it was a lot to me and I needed it. While I could not refuse it, I hated myself for taking it and I hated her for giving it. Worse, she had much less grace about my need than my mama's sugar daddy had displayed toward her. All that bitter contempt I felt for my needy cousins and aunts raged through me and burned out the love. I ended the relationship quickly, unable to forgive myself for selling what I believed should only be offered freely—not sex but love itself.

When the women in my family talked about how hard they worked, the men would spit to the side and shake their heads. Men took real jobs—harsh, dangerous, physically daunting work. They went to jail, not just the cold-eyed, careless boys who scared me with their brutal hands, but their gentler, softer brothers. It was another family thing, what people expected of my mama's people, mine. "His daddy's that one was sent off to jail in Georgia, and his uncle's another. Like as not, he's just the same," you'd hear people say of boys so young they still had their milk teeth. We were always driving down to the county farm to see somebody, some uncle, cousin, or nameless male relation. Shaven-headed, sullen, and stunned, they wept on Mama's shoulder or begged my aunts to help. "I didn't do nothing, Mama," they'd say, and it might have been true, but if even we didn't believe them, who would? No one told the truth, not even about how their lives were destroyed.

One of my favorite cousins went to jail when I was eight years old, for breaking into pay phones with another boy. The other boy was returned to the custody of his parents. My cousin was sent to the boys' facility at the county farm. After three months, my mama took us down there to visit, carrying a big basket of fried chicken, cold cornbread, and potato salad. Along with a hundred others we sat out on the lawn with my cousin and watched him eat like he hadn't had a full meal in the whole three months. I stared at his near-bald head and his ears marked with fine blue scars from the carelessly handled razor. People were laughing, music was playing, and a tall, lazy, uniformed man walked past us chewing on toothpicks and watching us all closely. My cousin kept his head down, his face hard with hatred, only looking back at the guard when he turned away.

"Sons-a-bitches," he whispered, and my mama shushed him. We all sat still when the guard turned back to us. There was a long moment of quiet, and then that man let his face relax into a big wide grin.

"Uh-huh," he said. That was all he said. Then he turned and walked away. None of us spoke. None of us ate. He went back inside soon after, and we left. When we got back to the car, my mama sat there for a while crying quietly. The next week my cousin was reported for fighting and had his stay extended by six months.

My cousin was fifteen. He never went back to school, and after jail he couldn't join the army. When he finally did come home we never talked, never had to. I knew without asking that the guard had had his little revenge, knew too that my cousin would break into another phone booth as soon as he could, but do it sober and not get caught. I knew without asking the source of his rage, the way he felt about clean, well-dressed, contemptuous people who looked at him like his life wasn't as important as a dog's. I knew because I felt it too. That guard had looked at me and Mama with the same expression he used on my cousin. We were trash. We were the ones they built the county farm to house and break. The boy who was sent home was the son of a deacon in the church, the man who managed the hardware store.

As much as I hated that man, and his boy, there was a way in which I also hated my cousin. He should have known better, I told myself, should have known the risk he ran. He should have been more careful. As I grew older and started living on my own, it was a litany I used against myself even more angrily than I used it against my cousin. I knew who I was, knew that the most important thing I had to do was protect myself and hide my despised identity, blend into the myth of both the good poor and the reasonable lesbian. When I became a feminist activist, that litany went on reverberating in my head, but by then it had become a groundnote, something so deep and omnipresent I no longer heard it, even when everything I did was set to its cadence.

By 1975 I was earning a meager living as a photographer's assistant in Tallahassee, Florida. But the real work of my life was my lesbian-feminist activism, the work I did with the local women's center and the committee to found a women's studies program at Florida State University. Part of my role, as I saw it, was to be a kind of evangelical lesbian feminist, and to help develop a political analysis of this woman-hating society. I did not talk about class, except to give lip service to how we all needed to think about it, the same way I thought we all needed to think about racism. I was a determined person, living in a lesbian collective—all of us young and white and serious—studying each new book that purported to address feminist issues, driven by what I saw as a need to revolutionize the world.

Years later it's difficult to convey just how reasonable my life seemed to me at that time. I was not flippant, not consciously condescending, not casual about how tough a struggle remaking social relations would be, but like so many women of my generation, I believed absolutely that I could make a difference with my life, and I was willing to give my life for the chance to make that difference. I expected hard times, long slow periods of self-sacrifice and grinding work, expected to be hated and attached in public, to have to set aside personal desire, lovers, and family in order to be part of something greater and more important than my individual concerns. At the same time, I was working ferociously to take my desires, my sexuality, my needs as a woman and a lesbian more seriously. I believed I was making the personal political revolution with my life every moment, whether I was scrubbing the floor of the childcare center, setting up a new budget for the women's lecture series at the university, editing the local feminist magazine, or starting a women's bookstore. That I was constantly exhausted and had no health insurance, did hours of dreary unpaid work and still sneaked out of the collective to date butch women my housemates thought retrograde and sexist never interfered with my sense of total commitment to the feminist revolution. I was not living in a closet: I had compartmentalized my own mind to such an extent that I never questioned why I did what I did. And I never admitted what lay behind all my feminist convictions—a class-constructed distrust of change, a secret fear that someday I would be found out for who I really was, found out and thrown out. If I had not been raised to give my life away, would I have made such an effective, self-sacrificing revolutionary?

The narrowly focused concentration of a revolutionary shifted only when I began to write again. The idea of writing stories seemed frivolous when there was so much work to be done, but everything changed when I found myself confronting emotions and ideas that could not be explained away or postponed until after the revolution. The way it happened was simple and unexpected. One week I was asked to speak to two completely different groups: an Episcopalian Sunday school class and a juvenile detention center. The Episcopalians were all white, well-dressed, highly articulate, nominally polite, and obsessed with getting me to tell them (without their having to ask directly) just what it was that two women did together in bed. The delinquents were all women, 80 percent Black and Hispanic, wearing green uniform dresses or blue jeans and workshirts, profane, rude, fearless, witty, and just as determined to get me to talk about what it was that two women did together in bed.

I tried to have fun with the Episcopalians, teasing them about their fears and insecurities, and being as bluntly honest as I could about my sexual practices. The Sunday school teacher, a man who had assured me of his liberal inclinations, kept blushing and stammering as the questions about my growing up and coming out became more detailed. I stepped out into the sunshine when the meeting was over, angry at the contemptuous attitude implied by all their questioning, and though I did not know why, so deeply depressed I couldn't even cry.

The delinquents were another story. Shameless, they had me blushing within the first few minutes, yelling out questions that were part curiosity and partly a way of boasting about what they already knew. "You butch or femme?" "You ever fuck boys?" "You ever want to?" "You want to have children?" "What's your girlfriend like?" I finally broke up when one very tall, confident girl leaned way over and called out, "Hey, girlfriend! I'm getting out of here next weekend. What you doing that night?" I laughed so hard I almost choked. I laughed until we were all howling and giggling together. Even getting frisked as I left didn't ruin my mood. I was still grinning when I climbed into the waterbed with my lover that night, grinning right up to the moment when she wrapped her arms around me and I burst into tears.

That night I understood, suddenly, everything that had happened to my cousins and me, understood it from a wholly new and agonizing perspective, one that made clear how brutal I had been to both my family and myself. I grasped all over again how we had been robbed and dismissed, and why I had worked so hard not to think about it. I had learned as a child that what could not be changed had to go unspoken, and worse, that those who cannot change their own lives have every reason to be ashamed of that fact and to hide it. I had accepted that shame and believed in it, but why? What had I or my cousins done to deserve the contempt directed at us? Why had I always believed us contemptible by nature? I wanted to talk to someone about all the things I was thinking that night, but I could not. Among the women I knew there was no one who would have understood what I was thinking, no other working-class woman in the women's collective where I was living. I began to suspect that we shared no common language to speak those bitter truths.

In the days that followed I found myself remembering that afternoon long ago at the county farm, that feeling of being the animal in the zoo, the thing looked at and laughed at and used by the real people who watched us. For all his liberal convictions, that Sunday school teacher had looked at me with the eyes of my cousin's long-ago guard. I felt thrown back into my childhood, into all the fears I had tried to escape. Once again I felt myself at the mercy of the important people who knew how to dress and talk, and would always be given the benefit of the doubt, while my family and I would not.

I experienced an outrage so old I could not have traced all the ways it shaped my life. I realized again that some are given no quarter, no chance, that all their courage, humor, and love for each other is just a joke to the ones who make the rules, and I hated the rule-makers. Finally, I recognized that part of my grief came from the fact that I no longer knew who I was or where I belonged. I had run away from my family, refused to go home to visit, and tried in every way to make myself a new person. How could I be working class with a college degree? As a lesbian activist? I thought about the guards at the detention center. They had not stared at me with the same picture-window emptiness they turned on the girls who came to hear me, girls who were closer to the life I had been meant to live than I could bear to examine. The contempt in their eyes was contempt for me as a lesbian, different and the same, but still contempt.

While I raged, my girlfriend held me and comforted me and tried to get me to explain what was hurting me so bad, but I could not. She had told me so often about her awkward relationship with her own family, the father who ran his own business and still sent her checks every other month. She knew almost nothing about my family, only the jokes and careful stories I had given her. I felt so alone and at risk lying in her arms that I could not have explained anything at all. I thought about those girls in the detention center and the stories they told in brutal shorthand about their sisters, brothers, cousins, and lovers. I thought about their one-note references to those they had lost, never mentioning the loss of their own hopes, their own futures, the bent and painful shape of their lives when they would finally get free. Cried-out and dry-eyed, I lay watching my sleeping girlfriend and thinking about what I had not been able to say to her. After a few hours I got up and made some notes for a poem I wanted to write, a bare, painful litany of loss shaped as a conversation between two women, one who cannot understand the other, and one who cannot tell all she knows.

It took me a long tine to take that poem from a raw lyric of outrage and grief to a piece of fiction that explained to me something I had never let myself see up close before—the whole process of running away, of closing up inside yourself, of hiding. It has taken me most of my life to understand that, to see how and why those of us who are born poor and different are so driven to give ourselves away or lose ourselves, but most of all, simply to disappear as the people we really are. By the time that poem became the story "River of Names," I had made the decision to reverse that process: to claim my family, my true history, and to tell the truth not only about who I was but about the temptation to lie.

By the time I taught myself the basics of storytelling on the page, I knew there was only one story that would haunt me until I understood how to tell it—the complicated, painful story of how my mama had, and had not, saved me as a girl. Writing *Bastard Out of Carolina* became, ultimately, the way to claim my family's pride and tragedy, and the embattled sexuality I had fashioned on a base of violence and abuse.

The compartmentalized life I had created burst open in the late 1970s after I began to write what I really thought about my family. I lost patience with my fear of what the women I worked with, mostly lesbians, thought of who I slept with and what we did together. When schisms developed within my community; when I was no longer able to hide within the regular dyke network; when I could not continue to justify my life by constant political activism or distract myself by sleeping around; when my sexual promiscuity, butch/femme orientation, and exploration of sadomasochistic sex became part of what was driving me out of my community of choice—I went home again. I went home to my mother and my sisters, to visit, talk, argue, and begin to understand.

Once home I saw that as far as my family was concerned, lesbians were lesbians whether they wore suitcoats or leather jackets. Moreover, in all that time when I had not made peace with myself, my family had managed to make a kind of peace with me. My girlfriends were treated like slightly odd versions of my sisters' husbands, while I was simply the daughter who had always been difficult but was still a part of their lives. The result was that I started trying to confront what had made me unable really to talk to my sisters for so many years. I discovered that they no longer knew who I was either, and it took time and lots of listening to each other to rediscover my sense of family, and my love for them.

It is only as the child of my class and my unique family background that I have been able to put together what is for me a meaningful politics, to regain a sense of why I believe in activism, why self-revelation is so important for lesbians. There is no all-purpose feminist analysis that explains the complicated ways our sexuality and core identity are shaped, the way we see ourselves as parts of both our birth families and the extended family of friends and lovers we invariably create within the lesbian community. For me, the bottom line has simply become the need to resist that omnipresent fear, that urge to hide and disappear, to disguise my life, my desires, and the truth about how little any of us understand—even as we try to make the world a more just and human place. Most of all, I have tried to understand the politics of *they*, why human beings fear and stigmatize the different while secretly dreading that they might be one of the different themselves. Class, race, sexuality, gender—and all the other categories by which we categorize and dismiss each other—need to be excavated from the inside.

The horror of class stratification, racism, and prejudice is that some people begin to believe that the security of their families and communities depends on the oppression of others, that for some to have good lives there must be others whose lives are truncated and brutal. It is a belief that dominates this culture. It is what makes the poor whites of the South so determinedly racist and the middle class so contemptuous of the poor. It is a myth that allows some to imagine that they build their lives on the ruin of others, a secret core of shame for the middle class, a goad and a spur to the marginal working class, and cause enough for the homeless and poor to feel no constraints on hatred or violence. The power of the myth is made even more apparent when we examine how, within the lesbian and feminist communities where we have addressed considerable attention to the politics of marginalization, there is still so much exclusion and fear, so many of us who do not feel safe.

I grew up poor, hated, the victim of physical, emotional, and sexual violence, and I know that suffering does not ennoble. It destroys. To resist destruction, self-hatred, or lifelong hopelessness, we have to throw off the conditioning of being despised, the fear of becoming the *they* that is talked about so dismissively, to refuse lying myths and easy moralities, to see ourselves as human, flawed, and extraordinary. All of us—extraordinary.

The Advantages
of Being a Woman Artist

BY THE GUERRILLA GIRLS

Since 1984, the Guerrilla Girls have called out bigotry and gender discrimination in the art world in memorable, audacious ways. They've also demanded equal representation for women and nonwhite artists in major museums, plastering New York City with eye-catching posters attacking persistent sexism and racism in the art world. Today, the Guerrilla Girls—known for wearing gorilla masks and naming themselves for artists like Frida Kahlo and Gertrude Stein—continue to use humor, facts, and flamboyant visuals to expose gender and racial bias while emphasizing intersectional feminism's necessity in twenty-first-century art and society. The print outlining advantages of being a woman artist was made from a poster created in 1988. The thirteen items on the list are mostly tongue in cheek, reflecting the frustrating realities of the art world women have been forced to contend with, then and now. At the bottom of their poster was a mailing address where people could send money or comments and also the tag line "Conscience of the art world." And clearly, there was a significant void of moral clarity needing to be filled by the Guerrilla Girls' work.

THE ADVANTAGES OF BEING A WOMAN ARTIST:

Working without the pressure of success.

Not having to be in shows with men.

Having an escape from the art world in your 4 free-lance jobs.

Knowing your career might pick up after you're eighty.

Being reassured that whatever kind of art you make it will be labeled feminine.

Not being stuck in a tenured teaching position.

Seeing your ideas live on in the work of others.

Having the opportunity to choose between career and motherhood.

Not having to choke on those big cigars or paint in Italian suits.

Having more time to work after your mate dumps you for someone younger.

Being included in revised versions of art history.

Not having to undergo the embarrassment of being called a genius.

Getting your picture in the art magazines wearing a gorilla suit.

Please send $ and comments to:
Guerrilla Girls CONSCIENCE OF THE ART WORLD
Box lo56 CooperSta.NY,NY 10276

Men Explain Things to Me

BY REBECCA SOLNIT

Writer Rebecca Solnit is the author of more than twenty books and numerous essays and has been called "the voice of the resistance" by *The New York Times*. Solnit's 2008 essay "Men Explain Things to Me," from her collection of the same name, describes her experience at a party with a man who refused to hear that she had written the piece he was explaining to her. This short essay skewered one of the most prevalent forms of sexist trolling online and led to the coining of the term *mansplaining*, describing the ways in which some men silence women and diminish their expertise by assuming they themselves are experts on anything and everything. In her essay, Solnit is both droll and exasperated as she articulates an experience many women have endured. Beyond sharing an amusing albeit frustrating anecdote, Solnit also examines the broader, more pernicious issues surrounding the notion that men are experts and women are ingenues, at best. She writes that this dynamic, "trains us in self-doubt and self-limitation just as it exercises men's unsupported overconfidence."

I still don't know why Sallie and I bothered to go to that party in the forest slope above Aspen. The people were all older than us and dull in a distinguished way, old enough that we, at forty-ish, passed as the occasion's young ladies. The house was great—if you like Ralph Lauren–style chalets—a rugged luxury cabin at 9,000 feet complete with elk antlers, lots of kilims, and a wood-burning stove. We were preparing to leave, when our host said, "No, stay a little longer so I can talk to you." He was an imposing man who'd made a lot of money.

He kept us waiting while the other guests drifted out into the summer night, and then sat us down at his authentically grainy wood table and said to me, "So? I hear you've written a couple of books."

I replied, "Several, actually."

He said, in the way you encourage your friend's seven-year-old to describe flute practice, "And what are they about?"

They were actually about quite a few different things, the six or seven out by then, but I began to speak only of the most recent on that summer day in 2003, *River of Shadows: Eadweard Muybridge and the Technological Wild West*, my book on the annihilation of time and space and the industrialization of everyday life.

He cut me off soon after I mentioned Muybridge. "And have you heard about the *very important* Muybridge book that came out this year?"

So caught up was I in my assigned role as ingénue that I was perfectly willing to entertain the possibility that another book on the same subject had come out simultaneously and I'd somehow missed it. He was already telling me about the very important book—with that smug look I know so well in a man holding forth, eyes fixed on the fuzzy far horizon of his own authority.

Here, let me just say that my life is well sprinkled with lovely men, with a long succession of editors who have, since I was young, listened to and encouraged and published me, with my infinitely generous younger brother, with splendid friends of whom it could be said—like the Clerk in *The Canterbury Tales* I still remember from Mr. Pelen's class on Chaucer—"gladly would he learn and gladly teach." Still, there are these other men, too. So, Mr. Very Important was going on smugly about this book I should have known when Sallie interrupted him, to say, "That's her book." Or tried to interrupt him anyway.

But he just continued on his way. She had to say, "That's her book" three or four times before he finally took it in. And then, as if in a nineteenth-century novel, he went ashen. That I was indeed the author of the very important book it turned out he hadn't read, just read about in the *New York Times Book Review* a few months earlier, so confused the neat categories into which his world was sorted that he was stunned speechless—for a moment,

before he began holding forth again. Being women, we were politely out of earshot before we started laughing, and we've never
really stopped.

I like incidents of that sort, when forces that are usually so
sneaky and hard to point out slither out of the grass and are as obvious as, say, an anaconda that's eaten a cow or an elephant turd
on the carpet.

THE SLIPPERY SLOPE OF SILENCINGS

Yes, people of both genders pop up at events to hold forth on irrelevant things and conspiracy theories, but the out-and-out con-
frontational confidence of the totally ignorant is, in my experience,
gendered. Men explain things to me, and other women, whether
or not they know what they're talking about. Some men.

Every woman knows what I'm talking about. It's the presumption that makes it hard, at times, for any woman in any field; that
keeps women from speaking up and from being heard when they
dare; that crushes young women into silence by indicating, the
way harassment on the street does, that this is not their world. It
trains us in self-doubt and self-limitation just as it exercises men's
unsupported overconfidence.

I wouldn't be surprised if part of the trajectory of American
politics since 2001 was shaped by, say, the inability to hear Coleen
Rowley, the FBI woman who issued those early warnings about
al-Qaeda, and it was certainly shaped by a Bush administration to
which you couldn't tell anything, including that Iraq had no links
to al-Qaeda and no WMDs, or that the war was not going to be
a "cakewalk." (Even male experts couldn't penetrate the fortress
of its smugness.)

Arrogance might have had something to do with the war, but
this syndrome is a war that nearly every woman faces every day,
a war within herself too, a belief in her superfluity, an invitation
to silence, one from which a fairly nice career as a writer (with a
lot of research and facts correctly deployed) has not entirely freed
me. After all, there was a moment there when I was willing to let
Mr. Important and his overweening confidence bowl over my
more shaky certainty.

Don't forget that I've had a lot more confirmation of my right to think and speak than most women, and I've learned that a certain amount of self-doubt is a good tool for correcting, understanding, listening, and progressing—though too much is paralyzing and total self-confidence produces arrogant idiots. There's a happy medium between these poles to which the genders have been pushed, a warm equatorial belt of give and take where we should all meet.

More extreme versions of our situation exist in, for example, those Middle Eastern countries where women's testimony has no legal standing: so that a woman can't testify that she was raped without a male witness to counter the male rapist. Which there rarely is.

Credibility is a basic survival tool. When I was very young and just beginning to get what feminism was about and why it was necessary, I had a boyfriend whose uncle was a nuclear physicist. One Christmas, he was telling—as though it were a light and amusing subject—how a neighbor's wife in his suburban bomb-making community had come running out of her house naked in the middle of the night screaming that her husband was trying to kill her. How, I asked, did you know that he wasn't trying to kill her? He explained, patiently, that they were respectable middle-class people. Therefore, her-husband-trying-to-kill-her was simply not a credible explanation for her fleeing the house yelling that her husband was trying to kill her. That she was crazy, on the other hand. . . .

Even getting a restraining order—a fairly new legal tool—requires acquiring the credibility to convince the courts that some guy is a menace and then getting the cops to enforce it. Restraining orders often don't work anyway. Violence is one way to silence people, to deny their voice and their credibility, to assert your right to control over their right to exist. About three women a day are murdered by spouses or ex-spouses in this country. It's one of the main causes of death for pregnant women in the United States. At the heart of the struggle of feminism to give rape, date rape, marital rape, domestic violence, and workplace sexual harassment legal standing as crimes has been the necessity of making women credible and audible.

I tend to believe that women acquired the status of human

beings when these kinds of acts started to be taken seriously, when the big things that stop us and kill us were addressed legally from the mid-1970s on; well after, that is, my birth. And for anyone about to argue that workplace sexual intimidation isn't a life-or-death issue, remember that Marine Lance Corporal Maria Lauterbach, age twenty, was apparently killed by her higher-ranking colleague one winter's night while she was waiting to testify that he raped her. The burned remains of her pregnant body were found in the fire pit in his backyard.

Being told that, categorically, he knows what he's talking about and she doesn't, however minor a part of any given conversation, perpetuates the ugliness of this world and holds back its light. After my book *Wanderlust* came out in 2000, I found myself better able to resist being bullied out of my own perceptions and interpretations. On two occasions around that time, I objected to the behavior of a man, only to be told that the incidents hadn't happened at all as I said, that I was subjective, delusional, overwrought, dishonest—in a nutshell, female.

Most of my life, I would have doubted myself and backed down. Having public standing as a writer of history helped me stand my ground, but few women get that boost, and billions of women must be out there on this seven-billion-person planet being told that they are not reliable witnesses to their own lives, that the truth is not their property, now or ever. This goes way beyond Men Explaining Things, but it's part of the same archipelago of arrogance.

Men explain things to me, still. And no man has ever apologized for explaining, wrongly, things that I know and they don't. Not yet, but according to the actuarial tables, I may have another forty-something years to live, more or less, so it could happen. Though I'm not holding my breath.

GENDER CONSIDERATIONS

A Cyborg Manifesto

Science, Technology, and Socialist-Feminism in the Late Twentieth Century

BY DONNA J. HARAWAY

Donna Haraway is an American professor emerita in the History of Consciousness Department and Feminist Studies Department at the University of California, Santa Cruz. Her work focuses on the production of knowledge and taxonomies of identity, particularly in the sciences, which she views as inherently patriarchal and essentialist. Haraway's "Cyborg Manifesto" was first published in 1985 in the *Socialist Review* as a reaction to rigid binaries that dominate Western culture and also function to other marginalized groups. Much like Gloria Anzaldúa, Haraway's solution is hybridity, but one that includes nonhuman agents. Haraway explains that her "manifesto" is "an effort to build an ironic political myth faithful to feminism, socialism, and materialism." She suggests that there may be another way forward that moves beyond binaries. And thus, she introduces the idea of the cyborg, "a cybernetic organism, a hybrid of machine and organism, a creature of social reality as well as a creature of fiction."

AN IRONIC DREAM OF A COMMON LANGUAGE FOR WOMEN IN THE INTEGRATED CIRCUIT

This chapter is an effort to build an ironic political myth faithful to feminism, socialism, and materialism. Perhaps more faithful as blasphemy is faithful, than as reverent worship and identification.

Blasphemy has always seemed to require taking things very seriously. I know no better stance to adopt from within the secular-religious, evangelical traditions of United States politics, including the politics of socialist feminism. Blasphemy protects one from the moral majority within, while still insisting on the need for community. Blasphemy is not apostasy. Irony is about contradictions that do not resolve into larger wholes, even dialectically, about the tension of holding incompatible things together because both or all are necessary and true. Irony is about humor and serious play. It is also a rhetorical strategy and a political method, one I would like to see more honored within socialist-feminism. At the center of my ironic faith, my blasphemy, is the image of the cyborg.

A cyborg is a cybernetic organism, a hybrid of machine and organism, a creature of social reality as well as a creature of fiction. Social reality is lived social relations, our most important political construction, a world-changing fiction. The international women's movements have constructed "women's experience," as well as uncovered or discovered this crucial collective object. This experience is a fiction and fact of the most crucial, political kind. Liberation rests on the construction of the consciousness, the imaginative apprehension, of oppression, and so of possibility. The cyborg is a matter of fiction and lived experience that changes what counts as women's experience in the late twentieth century. This is a struggle over life and death, but the boundary between science fiction and social reality is an optical illusion.

Contemporary science fiction is full of cyborgs—creatures simultaneously animal and machine, who populate worlds ambiguously natural and crafted. Modern medicine is also full of cyborgs, of couplings between organism and machine, each conceived as coded devices, in an intimacy and with a power that was not generated in the history of sexuality. Cyborg "sex" restores some of the lovely replicative baroque of ferns and invertebrates (such nice organic prophylactics against heterosexism). Cyborg replication is uncoupled from organic reproduction. Modern production seems like a dream of cyborg colonization work, a dream that makes the nightmare of Taylorism seem idyllic. And modern war is a cyborg orgy, coded by C^3I, command-control-communication-intelligence, an $84 billion item in 1984's U.S. defense budget. I am making an argument for the cyborg as a fiction mapping our

social and bodily reality and as an imaginative resource suggesting some very fruitful couplings. Michel Foucault's biopolitics is a
flaccid premonition of cyborg politics, a very open field.

By the late twentieth century, our time, a mythic time, we are
all chimeras, theorized and fabricated hybrids of machine and organism; in short, we are cyborgs. The cyborg is our ontology; it
gives us our politics. The cyborg is a condensed image of both
imagination and material reality, the two joined centers structuring any possibility of historical transformation. In the traditions
of "Western" science and politics—the tradition of racist, male-
dominant capitalism; the tradition of progress; the tradition of the
appropriation of nature as resource for the productions of culture;
the tradition of reproduction of the self from the reflections of the
other—the relation between organism and machine has been a
border war. The stakes in the border war have been the territories
of production, reproduction, and imagination. This chapter is an
argument for *pleasure* in the confusion of boundaries and for *responsibility* in their construction. It is also an effort to contribute
to socialist-feminist culture and theory in a postmodernist, non-
naturalist mode and in the utopian tradition of imagining a world
without gender, which is perhaps a world without genesis, but
maybe also a world without end. The cyborg incarnation is outside salvation history. Nor does it mark time on an oedipal calen-
dar, attempting to heal the terrible cleavages of gender in an oral
symbiotic utopia or post-oedipal apocalypse. As Zoe Sofoulis argues in her unpublished manuscript on Jacques Lacan, Melanie
Klein, and nuclear culture, *Lacklein*, the most terrible and perhaps the most promising monsters in cyborg worlds are embodied
in non-oedipal narratives with a different logic of repression,
which we need to understand for our survival.

The cyborg is a creature in a post-gender world; it has no truck
with bisexuality, pre-oedipal symbiosis, unalienated labor, or
other seductions to organic wholeness through a final appropriation of all the powers of the parts into a higher unity. In a sense,
the cyborg has no origin story in the Western sense—a "final"
irony since the cyborg is also the awful apocalyptic *telos* of the
"West's" escalating dominations of abstract individuation, an ultimate self untied at last from all dependency, a man in space. An
origin story in the "Western," humanist sense depends on the

myth of original unity, fullness, bliss, and terror, represented by
the phallic mother from whom all humans must separate, the task
of individual development and of history, the twin potent myths
inscribed most powerfully for us in psychoanalysis and Marxism.
Hilary Klein has argued that both Marxism and psychoanalysis,
in their concepts of labor and of individuation and gender formation, depend on the plot of original unity out of which difference
must be produced and enlisted in a drama of escalating domination of woman/nature. The cyborg skips the step of original unity,
of identification with nature in the Western sense. This is its illegitimate promise that might lead to subversion of its teleology as
Star Wars.

The cyborg is resolutely committed to partiality, irony, intimacy, and perversity. It is oppositional, utopian, and completely
without innocence. No longer structured by the polarity of public
and private, the cyborg defines a technological polis based partly
on a revolution of social relations in the *oikos*, the household. Nature and culture are reworked; the one can no longer be the resource for appropriation or incorporation by the other. The
relationships for forming wholes from parts, including those of
polarity and hierarchical domination, are at issue in the cyborg
world. Unlike the hopes of Frankenstein's monster, the cyborg
does not expect its father to save it through a restoration of the
garden; that is, through the fabrication of a heterosexual mate,
through its completion in a finished whole, a city and cosmos. The
cyborg does not dream of community on the model of the organic
family, this time without the oedipal project. The cyborg would
not recognize the Garden of Eden; it is not made of mud and cannot dream of returning to dust. Perhaps that is why I want to see
if cyborgs can subvert the apocalypse of returning to nuclear dust
in the manic compulsion to name the Enemy. Cyborgs are not reverent; they do not remember the cosmos. They are wary of holism,
but needy for connection—they seem to have a natural feel for
united front politics, but without the vanguard party. The main
trouble with cyborgs, of course, is that they are the illegitimate
offspring of militarism and patriarchal capitalism, not to mention
state socialism. But illegitimate offspring are often exceedingly
unfaithful to their origins. Their fathers, after all, are inessential.

I will return to the science fiction of cyborgs at the end of this chapter, but now I want to signal three crucial boundary break-downs that make the following political-fictional (political-scientific) analysis possible. By the late twentieth century in United States scientific culture, the boundary between human and animal is thoroughly breached. The last beachheads of uniqueness have been polluted if not turned into amusement parks—language, tool use, social behavior, mental events, nothing really convincingly settles the separation of human and animal. And many people no longer feel the need for such a separation; indeed, many branches of feminist culture affirm the pleasure of connection of human and other living creatures. Movements for animal rights are not irrational denials of human uniqueness; they are a clear-sighted recognition of connection across the discredited breach of nature and culture. Biology and evolutionary theory over the last two centuries have simultaneously produced modern organisms as objects of knowledge and reduced the line between humans and animals to a faint trace re-etched in ideological struggle or professional disputes between life and social science. Within this framework, teaching modern Christian creationism should be fought as a form of child abuse.

Biological-determinist ideology is only one position opened up in scientific culture for arguing the meanings of human animality. There is much room for radical political people to contest the meanings of the breached boundary. The cyborg appears in myth precisely where the boundary between human and animal is transgressed. Far from signaling a walling off of people from other living beings, cyborgs signal disturbingly and pleasurably tight coupling. Bestiality has a new status in this cycle of marriage exchange.

The second leaky distinction is between animal-human (organism) and machine. Pre-cybernetic machines could be haunted; there was always the specter of the ghost in the machine. This dualism structured the dialogue between materialism and idealism that was settled by a dialectical progeny, called spirit or history, according to taste. But basically machines were not self-moving, self-designing, autonomous. They could not achieve man's dream, only mock it. They were not man, an author to himself, but only a caricature of that masculinist reproductive dream. To think they were otherwise was paranoid. Now we are not so sure. Late twentieth-century machines have made thoroughly ambiguous the difference between natural and artificial, mind and body, self-developing and externally designed, and many other distinctions that used to apply to organisms and machines. Our machines are disturbingly lively, and we ourselves frighteningly inert.

Technological determination is only one ideological space opened up by the reconceptions of machine and organism as coded texts through which we engage in the play of writing and reading the world. "Textualization" of everything in poststructuralist, postmodernist theory has been damned by Marxists and socialist feminists for its utopian disregard for the lived relations of domination that ground the "play" of arbitrary reading. It is certainly true that postmodernist strategies, like my cyborg myth, subvert myriad organic wholes (for example, the poem, the primitive culture, the biological organism). In short, the certainty of what counts as nature—a source of insight and promise of innocence—is undermined, probably fatally. The transcendent authorization of interpretation is lost, and with it the ontology grounding "Western" epistemology. But the alternative is not cynicism or faithlessness, that is, some version of abstract existence, like the accounts of technological determinism destroying "man" by the "machine" or "meaningful political action" by the "text." Who cyborgs will be is a radical question; the answers are a matter of survival. Both chimpanzees and artifacts have politics, so why shouldn't we?

The third distinction is a subset of the second: The boundary between physical and non-physical is very imprecise for us. Pop physics books on the consequences of quantum theory and the indeterminacy principle are a kind of popular scientific equivalent to Harlequin romances as a marker of radical change in American white heterosexuality: They get it wrong, but they are on the right subject. Modern machines are quintessentially microelectronic devices: They are everywhere and they are invisible. Modern machinery is an irreverent upstart god, mocking the Father's ubiquity and spirituality. The silicon chip is a surface for writing; it is etched in molecular scales disturbed only by atomic noise, the ultimate interference for nuclear scores. Writing, power, and technology are old partners in Western stories of the origin of civilization, but miniaturization has changed our experience of mechanism. Miniaturization has turned out to be about power; small is not so much beautiful as pre-eminently dangerous, as in cruise missiles. Contrast the TV sets of the 1950s or the news cameras of the 1970s with the TV wrist bands or hand-sized video cameras now advertised. Our best machines are made of sunshine; they are all light and clean because they are nothing but signals, electromagnetic waves, a section of a spectrum, and these machines are eminently portable, mobile—a matter of immense human pain in Detroit and Singapore. People are nowhere near so fluid, being both material and opaque. Cyborgs are ether, quintessence.

The ubiquity and invisibility of cyborgs is precisely why these sunshine-belt machines are so deadly. They are as hard to see politically as materially. They are about consciousness—or its simulation. They are floating signifiers moving in pickup trucks across Europe, blocked more effectively by the witch-weavings of the displaced and so unnatural Greenham women, who read the cyborg webs of power so very well, than by the militant labor of older masculinist politics, whose natural constituency needs defense jobs. Ultimately the "hardest" science is about the realm of greatest boundary confusion, the realm of pure number, pure spirit, C³I, cryptography, and the preservation of potent secrets. The new machines are so clean and light. Their engineers are sunworshippers mediating a new scientific revolution associated with the night dream of post-industrial society. The diseases evoked by these clean machines are "no more" than the minuscule coding changes of an antigen in the immune system, "no more" than the experience of stress. The nimble fingers of "Oriental" women, the old fascination of little Anglo-Saxon Victorian girls with doll's houses, women's enforced attention to the small take on quite new dimensions in this world. There might be a cyborg Alice taking account of these new dimensions. Ironically, it might be the unnatural cyborg women making chips in Asia and spiral dancing in Santa Rita jail whose constructed unities will guide effective oppositional strategies.

So my cyborg myth is about transgressed boundaries, potent fusions, and dangerous possibilities which progressive people might explore as one part of needed political work. One of my premises is that most American socialists and feminists see

deepened dualisms of mind and body, animal and machine, idealism and materialism in the social practices, symbolic formulations, and physical artifacts associated with "high technology"
and scientific culture. From *One-Dimensional Man* to *The Death
of Nature*, the analytic resources developed by progressives have
insisted on the necessary domination of technics and recalled us
to an imagined organic body to integrate our resistance. Another
of my premises is that the need for unity of people trying to resist
world-wide intensification of domination has never been more
acute. But a slightly perverse shift of perspective might better enable us to contest for meanings, as well as for other forms of
power and pleasure in technologically mediated societies.

From one perspective, a cyborg world is about the final imposition of a grid of control on the planet, about the final abstraction
embodied in a Star Wars apocalypse waged in the name of defense, about the final appropriation of women's bodies in a masculinist orgy of war. From another perspective, a cyborg world
might be about lived social and bodily realities in which people
are not afraid of their joint kinship with animals and machines,
not afraid of permanently partial identities and contradictory
standpoints. The political struggle is to see from both perspectives
at once because each reveals both dominations and possibilities
unimaginable from the other vantage point. Single vision produces worse illusions than double vision or many-headed monsters. Cyborg unities are monstrous and illegitimate; in our
present political circumstances, we could hardly hope for more
potent myths for resistance and recoupling. I like to imagine LAG,
the Livermore Action Group, as a kind of cyborg society, dedicated to realistically converting the laboratories that most fiercely
embody and spew out the tools of technological apocalypse, and
committed to building a political form that actually manages to
hold together witches, engineers, elders, perverts, Christians,
mothers, and Leninists long enough to disarm the state. Fission
Impossible is the name of the affinity group in my town. (Affinity:
related not by blood but by choice, the appeal of one chemical nuclear group for another, avidity.) . . .

The Woman-Identified Woman

BY RADICALESBIANS

In 1969, feminist Betty Friedan cautioned the National Organization for Women (NOW) to remain vigilant about the "lavender menace" she believed was threatening the women's movement. For Friedan, lesbians in the women's movement would compromise feminist credibility, and women in NOW would be dismissed as "man-haters," as if that's a bad thing. (I jest, mostly.) In 1970, a group of Gay Liberation Front women, including author Rita Mae Brown and scholar Karla Jay, crashed the Second Congress to Unite Women wearing "LAVENDER MENACE" T-shirts and distributing copies of a manifesto entitled "The Woman-Identified Woman." Written by Artemis March, Lois Hart, Rita Mae Brown, Ellen Shumsky, Cynthia Funk, and Barbara XX, the manifesto centered lesbianism in feminist politics as an identity of political, cultural, and erotic resistance to patriarchy. At the subsequent NOW conference in 1971, the congress adopted a resolution acknowledging the rights of lesbians as a "legitimate concern for feminism." The manifesto is now considered a critical text of feminism and gender politics. It is also a necessary reminder that feminism without genuine inclusivity is not really feminism at all.

What is a lesbian? A lesbian is the rage of all women condensed to the point of explosion. She is the woman who, often beginning at an extremely early age, acts in accordance with her inner compulsion to be a more complete and freer human being than her society—perhaps then, but certainly later—cares to allow her. These needs and actions, over a period of years, bring her into painful conflict with people, situations, the accepted ways of thinking, feeling and behaving, until she is in a state of continual war with everything around her, and usually with herself. She may not be fully conscious of the political implications of what for her began as personal necessity, but on some level she has not been able to accept the limitations and oppression laid on her by the most basic role of her society—the female role. The turmoil she experiences tends to induce guilt proportional to the degree to which she feels she is not meeting social expectations, and/or eventually drives her to question and analyze what the rest of her society more or less accepts. She is forced to evolve her own life pattern, often living much of her life alone, learning usually much earlier than her "straight" (heterosexual) sisters about the essential aloneness of life (which the myth of marriage obscures) and about the reality of illusions. To the extent that she cannot expel the heavy socialization that goes with being female, she can never truly find peace with herself. For she is caught somewhere between accepting society's view of her—in which case she cannot accept herself—and coming to understand what this sexist society has done to her and why it is functional and necessary for it to do so. Those of us who work that through find ourselves on the other side of a tortuous journey through a night that may have been decades long. The perspective gained from that journey, the liberation of self, the inner peace, the real love of self and of all women, is something to be shared with all women—because we are all women.

It should first be understood that lesbianism, like male homosexuality, is a category of behavior possible only in a sexist society characterized by rigid sex roles and dominated by male supremacy. Those sex roles dehumanize women by defining us as a supportive/serving caste in relation to the master caste of men, and emotionally cripple men by demanding that they be alienated from their own bodies and emotions in order to perform their economic/political/military functions effectively. Homosexuality is a by-product of a particular way of setting up roles (or approved patterns of behavior) on the basis of sex; as such it is an inauthentic (not consonant with "reality") category. In a society in which men do not oppress women, and sexual expression is allowed to follow feelings, the categories of homosexuality and heterosexuality would disappear.

But lesbianism is also different from male homosexuality, and serves a different function in the society. "Dyke" is a different kind of put-down from "faggot," although both imply you are not playing your socially assigned sex role . . . are not therefore a "real woman" or a "real man." The grudging admiration felt for the tomboy, and the queasiness felt around a sissy boy point to the same thing: the contempt in which women—or those who play a female role—are held. And the investment in keeping women in that contemptuous role is very great. Lesbian is a word, the label, the condition that holds women in line. When a woman hears this word tossed her way, she knows she is stepping out of line. She knows that she has crossed the terrible boundary of her sex role. She recoils, she protests, she reshapes her actions to gain approval. Lesbian is a label invented by the Man to throw at any woman who dares to be his equal, who dares to challenge his prerogatives (including that of all women as part of the exchange medium among men), who dares to assert the primacy of her own needs. To have the label applied to people active in women's liberation is just the most recent instance of a long history; older women will recall that not so long ago, any woman who was successful, independent, not orienting her whole life about a man, would hear this word. For in this sexist society, for a woman to be independent means she <u>can't be</u> a woman—she must be a dyke. That in itself should tell us where women are at. It says as clearly as can be said: women and person are contradictory terms. For a lesbian is not considered a "real woman." And yet, in popular thinking, there is really only one essential difference between a lesbian and other women: that of sexual orientation—which is to say, when you strip off all the packaging, you must finally realize that the essence of being a "woman" is to get fucked by men.

"Lesbian" is one of the sexual categories by which men have divided up humanity. While all women are dehumanized as sex objects, as the objects of men they are given certain compensations: identification with his power, his ego, his status, his protection (from other males), feeling like a "real woman," finding social acceptance by adhering to her role, etc. Should a woman confront herself by confronting another woman, there are fewer rationalizations, fewer buffers by which to avoid the stark horror of her dehumanized condition. Herein we find the overriding fear of many women toward being used as a sexual object by a woman, which not only will bring her no male-connected compensations, but also will reveal the void which is woman's real situation. This dehumanization is expressed when a straight woman learns that a sister is a lesbian; she begins to relate to her lesbian sister as her potential sex object, laying a surrogate male role on the lesbian. This reveals her heterosexual conditioning to make herself into an object when sex is potentially involved in a relationship, and it denies the lesbian her full humanity. For women, especially those in the movement, to perceive their lesbian sisters through this male grid of role definitions is to accept this male cultural conditioning and to oppress their sisters much as they themselves have been oppressed by men. Are we going to continue the male classification system of defining all females in sexual relation to some other category of people? Affixing the label lesbian not only to a woman who aspires to be a person, but also to any situation of real love, real solidarity, real primacy among women, is a primary form of divisiveness among women: it is the condition which keeps women within the confines of the feminine role, and it is the debunking/scare term that keeps women from forming any primary attachments, groups, or associations among ourselves.

Women in the movement have in most cases gone to great lengths to avoid discussion and confrontation with the issue of lesbianism. It puts people up-tight. They are hostile, evasive, or try to incorporate it into some "broader issue." They would rather not talk about it. If they have to, they try to dismiss it as a "lavender herring." But it is no side issue. It is absolutely essential to the success and fulfillment of the women's liberation movement that this issue be dealt with. As long as the label "dyke" can be used to frighten women into a less militant stand, keep her separate from her sisters, keep her from giving primacy to anything other than men and family—then to that extent she is controlled by the male culture. Until women see in each other the possibility of a primal commitment which includes sexual love, they will be denying themselves the love and value they readily accord to men, thus affirming their second-class status. As long as male acceptability is primary—both to individual women and to the movement as a whole—the term lesbian will be used effectively against women. Insofar as women want only more privileges within the system, they do not want to antagonize male power. They instead seek acceptability for women's liberation, and the most crucial aspect of the acceptability is to deny lesbianism—i.e., to deny any fundamental challenge to the basis of the female.

It should also be said that some younger, more radical women have honestly begun to discuss lesbianism, but so far it has been primarily as a sexual "alternative" to men. This, however, is still giving primacy to men, both because the idea of relating more completely to women occurs as a negative reaction to men, and because the lesbian relationship is being characterized simply by sex, which is divisive and sexist. On one level, which is both personal and political, women may withdraw emotional and sexual energies from men, and work out various alternatives for those energies in their own lives. On a different political/psychological level, it must be understood that what is crucial is that women begin disengaging from male-defined response patterns. In the privacy of our own psyches, we must cut those cords to the core. For irrespective of where our love and sexual energies flow, if we are male-identified in our heads, we cannot realize our autonomy as human beings.

But why is it that women have related to and through men? By virtue of having been brought up in a male society, we have internalized the male culture's definition of ourselves. That definition consigns us to sexual and family functions, and excludes us from defining and shaping the terms of our lives. In exchange for our psychic servicing and for performing society's non-profit-making functions, the man confers on us just one thing: the slave status which makes us legitimate in the eyes of the society in which we live. This is called "femininity" or "being a real woman" in our cultural lingo. We are authentic, legitimate, real to the extent that we are the property of some man whose name we bear. To be a woman who belongs to no man is to be invisible, pathetic, inauthentic, unreal. He confirms his image of us—of what we have to be in order to be acceptable by him—but not our real selves; he confirms our womanhood—as he defines it, in relation to him—but cannot confirm our personhood, our own selves as absolutes. As long as we are dependent on the male culture for this definition. For this approval, we cannot be free.

The consequence of internalizing this role is an enormous

reservoir of self-hate. This is not to say the self-hate is recognized or accepted as such; indeed most women would deny it. It may be experienced as discomfort with her role, as feeling empty, as numbness, as restlessness, as a paralyzing anxiety at the center. Alternatively, it may be expressed in shrill defensiveness of the glory and destiny of her role. But it does exist, often beneath the edge of her consciousness, poisoning her existence, keeping her alienated from herself, her own needs, and rendering her a stranger to other women. They try to escape by identifying with the oppressor, living through him, gaining status and identity from his ego, his power, his accomplishments. And by not identifying with other "empty vessels" like themselves. Women resist relating on all levels to other women who will reflect their own oppression, their own secondary status, their own self-hate. For to confront another woman is finally to confront one's self—the self we have gone to such lengths to avoid. And in that mirror we know we cannot really respect and love that which we have been made to be.

As the source of self-hate and the lack of real self are rooted in our male-given identity, we must create a new sense of self. As long as we cling to the idea of "being a woman," we will sense some conflict with that incipient self, that sense of I, that sense of a whole person. It is very difficult to realize and accept that being "feminine" and being a whole person are irreconcilable. Only women can give to each other a new sense of self. That identity we have to develop with reference to ourselves, and not in relation to men. This consciousness is the revolutionary force from which all else will follow, for ours is an organic revolution. For this we must be available and supportive to one another, give our commitment and our love, give the emotional support necessary to sustain this movement. Our energies must flow toward our sisters, not backward toward our oppressors. As long as woman's liberation tries to free women without facing the basic heterosexual structure that binds us in one-to-one relationship with our oppressors, tremendous energies will continue to flow into trying to straighten up each particular relationship with a man, into finding how to get better sex, how to turn his head around—into trying to make the "new man" out of him, in the delusion that this will allow us to be the "new woman." This obviously splits our energies and

commitments, leaving us unable to be committed to the construction of the new patterns which will liberate us.

It is the primacy of women relating to women, of women creating a new consciousness of and with each other, which is at the
heart of women's liberation, and the basis for the cultural revolution. Together we must find, reinforce, and validate our authentic
selves. As we do this, we confirm in each other that struggling,
incipient sense of pride and strength, the divisive barriers begin to
melt, we feel this growing solidarity with our sisters. We see ourselves as prime, find our centers inside of ourselves. We find reced-
ing the sense of alienation, of being cut off, of being behind a
locked window, of being unable to get out what we know is inside. We feel a real-ness, feel at last we are coinciding with ourselves. With that real self, with that consciousness, we begin a
revolution to end the imposition of all coercive identifications, and
to achieve maximum autonomy in human expression.

Women Like Me

BY WENDY ROSE

Wendy Rose writes poetry—such as this 2002 poem from her book *Itch Like Crazy*—and nonfiction. Her essays often call out the appropriation of Native American culture, including "whiteshamanism," the misuse of the shaman identity by white writers. Rose is an artist, writer, and anthropologist of Hopi, Miwok, and European descent whose work addresses identity, ecology, intersectional feminism, and colonialism. She earned her PhD in anthropology from the University of California, Berkeley. Rose is also the author of five poetry collections, one of which, 1980's *Lost Copper*, was nominated for a Pulitzer Prize. In "Women Like Me," as in most of her work, Rose foregrounds her identity and lived experience as a Native American woman. The poem has a sharp edge as she laments all her people have lost, and the questions she poses are existential. "Who should blossom? Who should receive pollen? / Who should be rooted, who pruned, / who watered, who picked?" Rose asks, knowing there are no easy answers.

> making promises they can't keep.
> For you, Grandmother, I said I would pull
> each invading burr and thistle from your skin,
> cut out the dizzy brittle eucalypt,
> take from the ground the dark oily poison—
> all to restore you happy and proud,
> the whole of you transformed
> and bursting into tomorrow.
> But where do I cut first?
> Where should I begin to pull?
> Should it be the Russian thistle
> down the hill where backhoes

have bitten? Or African senecio
or tumbleweed bouncing
above the wind? Or the middle finger
of my right hand? Or my left eye
or the other one? Or a slice
from the small of my back, a slab of fat
from my thigh? I am broken
as much as any native ground,
my roots tap a thousand migrations.
My daughters were never born, I am
as much the invader as the native,
as much the last day of life as the first.
I presumed you to be as bitter as me,
to tremble and rage against alien weight.
Who should blossom? Who should receive pollen?
Who should be rooted, who pruned,
who watered, who picked?
Should I feed the white-faced cattle
who wait for the death train to come
or comb the wild seeds from their tails?
Who should return across the sea
or the Bering Strait or the world before this one
or the Mother Ground? Who should go screaming
to some other planet, burn up or melt
in a distant sun? Who should be healed
and who hurt? Who should dry
under summer's white sky, who should shrivel
at the first sign of drought? Who should be remembered?
Who should be the sterile chimera of earth and of another
    place,
alien with a native face,
native with an alien face?

We Are All Works in Progress

BY LESLIE FEINBERG

Leslie Feinberg was a working-class, butch lesbian, trans-gender activist, communist, and author. Hir first novel, *Stone Butch Blues*, was published in 1993 and won a Lambda Literary Award and a 1994 American Library Association Literature Award. In 2019 Feinberg was one of the inaugural fifty American "pioneers, trailblazers, and heroes" inducted on the National LGBTQ Wall of Honor in the Stonewall National Monument. Feinberg's writing—notably *Stone Butch Blues* and hir 1996 book *Transgender Warriors*—laid the groundwork for much of the terminology and discourse around gender identity and sexuality and was instrumental in broadening aware-ness to a mainstream audience. This 1998 essay gives voice to the realities of trans discrimination and how bigotry exacts a price few are able to pay. Sie also writes about how trans liberation will, ultimately, liberate us all, noting that "our struggle will also help expose some of the harmful myths about what it means to be a woman or a man that have compartmentalized and dis-torted your life, as well as mine."

The sight of pink-blue gender-coded infant outfits may grate on your nerves. Or you may be a woman or a man who feels at home in those categories. Trans liberation defends you both.

Each person should have the right to *choose* between pink or blue tinted gender categories, as well as all the other hues of the palette. At this moment in time, that right is denied to us. But to-gether, we could make it a reality. . . .

I am a human being who would rather not be addressed as Ms. or Mr., ma'am or sir. I prefer to use gender-neutral pronouns like *sie* (pronounced like "*see*") and *hir* (pronounced like "*here*") to describe myself. I am a person who faces almost insurmountable difficulty when instructed to check off an "F" or an "M" box on identification papers.

I'm not at odds with the fact that I was born female-bodied. Nor do I identify as an intermediate sex. I simply do not fit the prevalent Western concepts of what a woman or man "should" look like. And that reality has dramatically directed the course of my life.

I'll give you a graphic example. From December 1995 to December 1996, I was dying of endocarditis—a bacterial infection that lodges and proliferates in the valves of the heart. A simple blood culture would have immediately exposed the root cause of my raging fevers. Eight weeks of round-the-clock intravenous antibiotic drips would have eradicated every last seedling of bacterium in the canals of my heart. Yet I experienced such hatred from some health practitioners that I very nearly died.

I remember late one night in December my lover and I arrived at a hospital emergency room during a snowstorm. My fever was 104 degrees and rising. My blood pressure was pounding dangerously high. The staff immediately hooked me up to monitors and worked to bring down my fever. The doctor in charge began physically examining me. When he determined that my anatomy was female, he flashed me a mean-spirited smirk. While keeping his eyes fixed on me, he approached one of the nurses, seated at a desk, and began rubbing her neck and shoulders. He talked to her about sex for a few minutes. After his pointed demonstration of "normal sexuality," he told me to get dressed and then he stormed out of the room. Still delirious, I struggled to put on my clothes and make sense of what was happening.

The doctor returned after I was dressed. He ordered me to leave the hospital and never return. I refused. I told him I wouldn't leave until he could tell me why my fever was so high. He said, "You have a fever because you are a very troubled person."

This doctor's prejudices, directed at me during a moment of catastrophic illness, could have killed me. The death certificate would have read: Endocarditis. By all rights it should have read: Bigotry.

As my partner and I sat bundled up in a cold car outside the emergency room, still reverberating from the doctor's hatred, I thought about how many people have been turned away from medical care when they were desperately ill—some because an apartheid "whites only" sign hung over the emergency room entrance, or some because their visible Kaposi sarcoma lesions kept personnel far from their beds. I remembered how a blemish that wouldn't heal drove my mother to visit her doctor repeatedly during the 1950s. I recalled the doctor finally wrote a prescription for Valium because he decided she was a hysterical woman. When my mother finally got to specialists, they told her the cancer had already reached her brain.

Bigotry exacts its toll in flesh and blood. And left unchecked and unchallenged, prejudices create a poisonous climate for us all. Each of us has a stake in the demand that every human being has a right to a job, to shelter, to health care, to dignity, to respect.

I am very grateful to have this chance to open up a conversation with you about why it is so vital to also defend the right of individuals to express and define their sex and gender, and to control their own bodies. For me, it's a life-and-death question. But I also believe that this discussion will have great meaning for you. All your life you've heard such dogma about what it means to be a "real" woman or a "real" man. And chances are you've choked on some of it. You've balked at the idea that being a woman means having to be thin as a rail, emotionally nurturing, and an airhead when it comes to balancing her checkbook. You know in your guts that being a man has nothing to do with rippling muscles, innate courage, or knowing how to handle a chain saw. These are really caricatures. Yet these images have been drilled into us through popular culture and education over the years. And subtler, equally insidious messages lurk in the interstices of these grosser concepts. These ideas of what a "real" woman or man should be straight-jacket the freedom of individual self-expression. These gender messages play on and on in a continuous loop in our brains, like commercials that can't be muted.

But in my lifetime I've also seen social upheavals challenge this sex and gender doctrine. As a child who grew up during the McCarthyite, Father-Knows-Best 1950s, and who came of age during the second wave of women's liberation in the United States, I've seen transformations in the ways people think and talk about what it means to be a woman or a man.

Today the gains of the 1970s women's liberation movement are under siege by right-wing propagandists. But many today who are too young to remember what life was like before the women's movement need to know that this was a tremendously progressive development that won significant economic and social reforms. And this struggle by women and their allies swung human consciousness forward like a pendulum.

The movement replaced the common usage of vulgar and diminutive words to describe females with the word *woman* and infused that word with strength and pride. Women, many of them formerly isolated, were drawn together into consciousness-raising groups. Their discussions—about the root of women's oppression and how to eradicate it—resonated far beyond the rooms in which they took place. The women's liberation movement sparked a mass conversation about the systematic degradation, violence, and discrimination that women faced in this society. And this consciousness-raising changed many of the ways women and men thought about themselves and their relation to each other. In retrospect, however, we must not forget that these widespread discussions were not just organized to *talk* about oppression. They were a giant dialogue about how to take action to fight institutionalized anti-woman attitudes, rape and battering, the illegality of abortion, employment and education discrimination, and other ways women were socially and economically devalued.

This was a big step forward for humanity. And even the period of political reaction that followed has not been able to overturn all the gains made by that important social movement.

Now another movement is sweeping onto the stage of history: Trans liberation. We are again raising questions about the societal treatment of people based on their sex and gender expression. This discussion will make new contributions to human consciousness. And trans communities, like the women's movement, are carrying out these mass conversations with the goal of creating a movement capable of fighting for justice—of righting the wrongs.

We are a movement of masculine females and feminine males, cross-dressers, transsexual men and women, intersexuals born on the anatomical sweep between female and male, gender-blenders, many other sex and gender-variant people, and our significant others. All told, we expand understanding of how many ways there are to be a human being.

Our lives are proof that sex and gender are much more complex than a delivery room doctor's glance at genitals can determine, more variegated than pink or blue birth caps. We are oppressed for not fitting those narrow social norms. We are fighting back.

Our struggle will also help expose some of the harmful myths about what it means to be a woman or a man that have compartmentalized and distorted your life, as well as mine. Trans liberation has meaning for you—no matter how you define or express your sex or your gender.

If you are a trans person, you face horrendous social punishments— from institutionalization to gang rape, from beatings to denial of child visitation. This oppression is faced, in varying degrees, by all who march under the banner of trans liberation. This brutalization and degradation strips us of what we could achieve with our individual lifetimes.

And if you do not identify as transgender or transsexual or intersexual, your life is diminished by our oppression as well. Your own choices as a man or a woman are sharply curtailed. Your individual journey to express yourself is shunted into one of two deeply carved ruts, and the social baggage you are handed is already packed.

So the defense of each individual's right to control their own body, and to explore the path of self-expression, enhances your own freedom to discover more about yourself and your potentialities. This movement will give you more room to breathe—to be yourself. To discover on a deeper level what it means to be yourself.

Together, I believe we can forge a coalition that can fight on behalf of your oppression as well as mine. Together, we can raise each other's grievances and win the kind of significant change we all long for. But the foundation of unity is understanding. So let me begin by telling you a little bit about myself.

I am a human being who unnerves some people. As they look at me, they see a kaleidoscope of characteristics they associate with both males and females. I appear to be a tangled knot of gender contradictions. So they feverishly press the question on me:

woman or man? Those are the only two words most people have as tools to shape their question.

"Which sex are you?" I understand their question. It sounds so simple. And I'd like to offer them a simple resolution. But merely answering woman or man will not bring relief to the questioner. As long as people try to bring me into focus using only those two lenses, I will always appear to be an enigma.

The truth is I'm no mystery. I'm a female who is more masculine than those prominently portrayed in mass culture. Millions of females and millions of males in this country do not fit the cramped compartments of gender that we have been taught are "natural" and "normal." For many of us, the words *woman* or *man, ma'am* or *sir, she* or *he*—in and of themselves—do not total up the sum of our identities or of our oppressions. Speaking for myself, my life only comes into focus when the word *transgender* is added to the equation.

Simply answering whether I was born female or male will not solve the conundrum. Before I can even begin to respond to the question of my own birth sex, I feel it's important to challenge the assumptions that the answer is always as simple as either-or. I believe we need to take a critical look at the assumption that is built into the seemingly innocent question: "What a beautiful baby—is it a boy or a girl?"

The human anatomical spectrum can't be understood, let alone appreciated, as long as female or male are considered to be all that exists. "Is it a boy or a girl?" Those are the only two categories allowed on birth certificates.

But this either-or leaves no room for intersexual people, born between the poles of female and male. Human anatomy continues to burst the confines of the contemporary concept that nature delivers all babies on two unrelated conveyor belts. So, are the birth certificates changed to reflect human anatomy? No, the U.S. medical establishment hormonally molds and shapes and surgically hacks away at the exquisite complexities of intersexual infants until they neatly fit one category or the other.

A surgeon decides whether a clitoris is "too large" or a penis is "too small." That's a highly subjective decision for anyone to make about another person's body. Especially when the person making the arbitrary decision is scrubbed up for surgery! And what is the criterion for a penis being "too small"? Too small for successful heterosexual intercourse. Intersexual infants are already being tailored for their sexuality, as well as their sex. The infants have no say over what happens to their bodies. Clearly the struggle against genital mutilation must begin here, within the borders of the United States.

But the question asked of all new parents: "Is it a boy or a girl?" is not such a simple question when transsexuality is taken into account, either. Legions of out-and-proud transsexual men and women demonstrate that individuals have a deep, developed, and valid sense of their own sex that does not always correspond to the cursory decision made by a delivery-room obstetrician. Nor is transsexuality a recent phenomenon. People have undergone social sex reassignment and surgical and hormonal sex changes throughout the breadth of oral and recorded human history.

Having offered this view of the complexities and limitations of birth classification, I have no hesitancy in saying I was born female. But that answer doesn't clear up the confusion that drives some people to ask me, "Are you a man or a woman?" The problem is that they are trying to understand my gender expression by determining my sex—and therein lies the rub! Just as most of us grew up with only the concepts of *woman* and *man*, the terms *feminine* and *masculine* are the only two tools most people have to talk about the complexities of gender expression.

That pink-blue dogma assumes that biology steers our social destiny. We have been taught that being born female or male will determine how we will dress and walk, whether we will prefer our hair shortly cropped or long and flowing, whether we will be emotionally nurturing or repressed. According to this way of thinking, masculine females are trying to look "like men," and feminine males are trying to act "like women."

But those of us who transgress those gender assumptions also shatter their inflexibility.

So, why do I sometimes describe myself as a masculine female? Isn't each of those concepts very limiting? Yes. But placing the two words together is incendiary, exploding the belief that gender expression is linked to birth sex like horse and carriage. It is the social contradiction missing from Dick-and-Jane textbook education.

I actually chafe at describing myself as masculine. For one thing, masculinity is such an expansive territory, encompassing boundaries of nationality, race, and class. Most importantly, individuals blaze their own trails across this landscape.

And it's hard for me to label the intricate matrix of my gender as simply masculine. To me, branding individual self-expression as simply feminine or masculine is like asking poets: Do you write in English or Spanish? The question leaves out the possibilities that the poetry is woven in Cantonese or Ladino, Swahili or Arabic. The question deals only with the system of language that the poet has been taught. It ignores the words each writer hauls up, hand over hand, from a common well. The music words make when finding themselves next to each other for the first time. The silences echoing in the space between ideas. The powerful winds of passion and belief that move the poet to write.

That is why I do not hold the view that gender is simply a social construct—one of two languages that we learn by rote from early age. To me, gender is the poetry each of us makes out of the language we are taught. When I walk through the anthology of the world, I see individuals express their gender in exquisitely complex and ever-changing ways, despite the laws of pentameter.

So how can gender expression be mandated by edict and enforced by law? Isn't that like trying to handcuff a pool of mercury? It's true that human self-expression is diverse and is often expressed in ambiguous or contradictory ways. And what degree of gender expression is considered "acceptable" can depend on your social situation, your race and nationality, your class, and whether you live in an urban or rural environment.

But no one can deny that rigid gender education begins early on in life—from pink and blue color-coding of infant outfits to gender-labeling toys and games. And those who overstep these arbitrary borders are punished. Severely. When the steel handcuffs tighten, it is human bones that crack. No one knows how many trans lives have been lost to police brutality and street-corner bashing. The lives of trans people are so depreciated in this society that many murders go unreported. And those of us who have survived are deeply scarred by daily run-ins with hate, discrimination, and violence.

Trans people are still literally social outlaws. And that's why I am willing at times, publicly, to reduce the totality of my self-expression to descriptions like masculine female, butch, bulldagger, drag king, cross-dresser. These terms describe outlaw status. And I hold my head up proudly in that police lineup. The word *outlaw* is not hyperbolic. I have been locked up in jail by cops because I was wearing a suit and tie. Was my clothing really a crime? Is it a "man's" suit if I am wearing it? At what point—from field to rack—is fiber assigned a sex?

The reality of why I was arrested was as cold as the cell's cement floor: I am considered a masculine female. That's a *gender* violation. My feminine drag queen sisters were in nearby cells, busted for wearing "women's" clothing. The cells that we were thrown into had the same design of bars and concrete. But when we—gay drag kings and drag queens—were thrown into them, the cops referred to the cells as bull's tanks and queen's tanks. The cells were named after our crimes: gender transgression. Actual statutes against cross-dressing and cross-gendered behavior still exist in written laws today. But even where the laws are not written down, police, judges, and prison guards are empowered to carry out merciless punishment for sex and gender "difference."

I believe we need to sharpen our view of how repression by the police, courts, and prisons, as well as all forms of racism and bigotry, operates as gears in the machinery of the economic and social system that governs our lives. As all those who have the least to lose from changing this system get together and examine these social questions, we can separate the wheat of truths from the chaff of old lies. Historic tasks are revealed that beckon us to take a stand and to take action.

That moment is now. And so this conversation with you takes place with the momentum of struggle behind it.

What will it take to put a halt to "legal" and extralegal violence against trans people? How can we strike the unjust and absurd laws mandating dress and behavior for females and males from the books? How can we weed out all the forms of transphobic and gender-phobic discrimination?

Where does the struggle for sex and gender liberation fit in relation to other movements for economic and social equality? How can we reach a point where we appreciate each other's differences, not just tolerate them? How can we tear down the electrified barbed wire that has been placed between us to keep us separated, fearful and pitted against each other? How can we forge a movement that can bring about profound and lasting change—a movement capable of transforming society?

These questions can only be answered when we begin to organize together, ready to struggle on each other's behalf. Understanding each other will compel us as honest, caring people to fight each other's oppression as though it was our own.

Girl

BY ALEXANDER CHEE

Alexander Chee is a novelist and essayist who is an associate professor at Dartmouth College. His work is widely published, and he is the author of two novels and an essay collection. Chee has received numerous awards for his work including the 2003 Whiting Award and a 2004 NEA fellowship. In Alexander Chee's essay "Girl," first published in *Guernica* in 2015, included in *Best American Essays 2016*, and excerpts of which are shared here, he uses personal experiences to interrogate the limitations of static identity categories and what it means to live at the intersections. Chee also reveals the underlying fluidity of gender and sexuality and how most of us seek refuge behind one kind of mask or another.

MY COUNTRY

I am half white, half Korean, or, to be more specific, Scotch-Irish, Irish, Welsh, Korean, Chinese, Mongolian. It is a regular topic, my whole life, this question of what I am. People are always telling me, like my first San Francisco hairdresser.

"Girl, you are mixed, aren't you? But you can pass," he said, as if this was a good thing.

"Pass as what?" I asked.

"White. You look white."

When people use the word "passing" in talking about race, they only ever mean one thing, but I still make them say it. He told me he was Filipino. "You could be one of us," he said. "But you're not."

Yes. I *could* be, but I am not. I am used to this feeling.

As a child in Korea, living in my grandfather's house, I was not to play in the street by myself: Amerasian children had no rights there generally, as usually no one knew who their father was, and they could be bought and sold as help or prostitutes, or both. No one would check to see if I was any different from the others.

"One day everyone will look like you," people say to me, all the time. I am a citizen of a nation that has only ever existed in the future, a nation where nationalism dies of confusion. And so I cringe when someone tells me I am a "fine mix," that it "worked well"; what if it hadn't?

After I read Eduardo Galeano's stories in *Century of Fire*, I mostly remember the mulatto ex-slaves in Haiti, obliterated when the French recaptured the island, the *mestiza* Argentinean courtesans—hated both by the white women for daring to put on wigs as fine as theirs, and by the Chilote slaves, who think the courtesans put on airs when they do so. The book is supposed to be a lyric history of the Americas, but it read more like a history of racial mixing.

I found in it a pattern for the history of half-breeds hidden in every culture: historically, we are allowed neither the privileges of the ruling class nor the community of those who are ruled. To each side that disowns us, we represent everything the other does not have. We only survive if we are valued, and we are valued only for strength, or beauty, sometimes for intelligence or cunning. As I read these stories of who survives and who does not, I know that I have survived in all of these ways and that these are the only ways I have survived so far.

This beauty I find when I put on drag then; it is made up of these talismans of power, a balancing act of the self-hatreds of at least two cultures, an act I've engaged in my whole life, here on the fulcrum I make of my face. That night, I find I want this beauty to last because it seems more powerful than any beauty I've had before. Being pretty like this is stronger than any drug I've ever tried.

But in my blond hair, I ask myself, are you really passing? Or is it just the dark, the night, people seeing what they want to see?

And what exactly are you passing as? And is that what we are really doing here?

Each time I pass that night it is a victory over these doubts, a hit off the pipe. This hair is all mermaid's gold and like anyone in a fairy tale I want it to be real when I wake up.

GIRL

My fascination with makeup started young. I remember the first time I wore lipstick in public. I was seven, eight years old at the time, with my mother at the Jordan Marsh makeup counter at the Maine Mall in South Portland, Maine. We were Christmas shopping, I think—it was winter, at least—and she was there trying on samples.

My mother is a beauty, from a family of Maine farmers who are almost all tall, long-waisted, thin, and pretty, the men and the women. Her eyes are Atlantic Ocean blue. She has a pragmatic streak, from being a farmer's daughter, that typically rules her, but she also loves fashion and glamour—when she was younger, she wore simple but chic clothes she often accessorized with cocktail rings, knee-high black leather boots, white sunglasses with black frames.

I had a secret from my mom, or at least I thought I did: I would go into her bathroom and try on her makeup, looking at myself in the mirror. I spent hours in front of my mother's bathroom mirror, rearranging my facial expressions—my face at rest looked unresolved to me, in between one thing and another. I would sometimes stare at my face and imagine it was either more white or more Asian. But makeup, I understood; I had watched the change that came over my mother when she put on makeup and I wanted it for myself. So while she was busy at the makeup counter, I reached up for one of the lipsticks, applied it, and then turned to her with a smile.

I thought it would surprise her, make her happy. I am sure the reddish-orange color looked clownish, even frightening, on my little face.

"Alexander," was all she said, stepping off the chair at the Clinique counter and sweeping me up. She pulled my ski mask over my head and led me out of the department store to the car, like I had stolen something. We drove home in silence, and once there, she washed the lipstick off my face and warned me to never do that again.

She was angry, upset, she felt betrayed by me. There was a line, and I had thought I could go back and forth across it, but it seemed I could not.

Until I could. Until I did.

I was not just mistaken for a member of other races, as a child. I was also often mistaken for a girl. What a beautiful little girl you have, people used to say to my mother at the grocery store when I was six, seven, eight. She had let my hair grow long.

I'm a boy, I would say each time. And they would turn red, or stammer an apology, or say, His hair is so long, and I would feel as if I had done something wrong, or she had.

I have been trying to convince people for so long that I am a real boy, it is a relief to stop—to run in the other direction.

Before Halloween night, I thought I knew some things about being a woman. I'd had women teachers, read women writers, women were my best friends growing up. But that night was a glimpse into a universe beside my own. Drag is its own world of experience—a theater of being female more than a reality. It isn't like being trans, either—it isn't, the more I think about it, like anything except what it is: costumes, illusion, a spell you cast on others and on yourself. But girl, girl is something else.

My friends in San Francisco at this time, we all call each other "girl," except for the ones who think they are too butch for such nellying, though we call them "girl" maybe most of all. My women friends call each other "girl" too, and they say it some-times like they are a little surprised at how much they like it. This, for me, began in meetings for ACT UP and Queer Nation, a little word that moved in on us all back then. When we say it, the word is like a stone we pass one to the other: the stone thrown at all of us. And the more we catch it and pass it, it seems like the less it can hurt us, the more we know who our new family is now. Who knows us, and who doesn't. It is something like a bullet turned into something like a badge of pride.

Later that night we go to a club, Club Uranus. John and Fred have removed their wigs and makeup. I have decided not to. Fred was uncomfortable—a wig is hot—and John wanted to get laid by a man as a man. I wasn't ready to let go. As we walked there, we passed heterosexual couples on the street. I walked with Fred, holding his arm, and noted the passing men who treated me like a woman—and the women who did also. Only one person let on that they saw through me—a man at a stoplight who leaned out his car window to shout, "Hey, Lola! Come back here, baby! I love you!"

My friend Darren is there, a thin blond boy done up as Marie Antoinette in hair nearly a foot tall and a professional costume rental dress, hoopskirts and all. On his feet, combat boots also. He raises his skirts periodically to show he is wearing nothing underneath.

Soon I am on the go-go stage by the bar. On my back, riding me, is a skinny white boy in a thong made out of duct tape, his body shaved. We are both sweating, the lights a crown of wet bright heat. The music is loud and very fast, and I roll my head like a lion, whipping the wig around for the cool air this lets in. People squeeze by the stage, staring and ignoring us alternately.

I see very little, but I soon spot Fred, who raises his hand and gives me a little wave from where he is standing. I want to tell him I know the boy on my back, and that it isn't anything he needs to worry about, but he seems to understand this. I wonder if he is jealous, but I tell myself he is not, that he knew what he was getting into with me—when we met, he mentioned the other stages he had seen me on around town. Tonight is one of those nights when I am growing, changing quickly, without warning, into new shapes and configurations, and I don't know where this all goes.

I feel more at home than I ever have in that moment, not in San Francisco, not on earth, but in myself. I am on the other side of something and I don't know what it is. I wait to find out.

REAL

I am proud for years of the way I looked real that night. I remember the men who thought I was a real woman, the straight guys in the cars whooping at me and their expressions when I said, "Thanks, guys," my voice my voice, and the change that rippled over their faces.

You wanted me, I wanted to say. You might still want me.

Real is good. Real is what you want. No one does drag to be a real woman, though. Drag is not the same as that. Drag knows it is different. But if you can pass as real, when it comes to drag, that is its own gold medal.

I'm also very aware of how that night was the first night I felt comfortable with my face. It makes me wary, even confused. I can feel the longing for the power I had. I jones for it like it's cocaine.

The little boy I used to be, in the mirror making faces, he was happy. But the process took so much work. I can't do that every day, though I know women who do. And that isn't the answer to my unhappiness, and I know it.

When my friend Danny gives me a photo from that night, I see something I didn't notice at the time. I look a little like my mom. I had put on my glasses for him—a joke about "girls who wear glasses"—and in that one picture, I see it all—the dark edges of my real hair sticking out, the cheapness of the wig, the smooth face, finally confident.

I send a copy to my sister and write, *This is what I would look like if I was your big sister.*

I can't skip what I need to do to love this face by making it over. I can't chase after the power I felt that night, the fleeting sense of finally belonging to the status quo, by making myself into something that looks like the something they want. Being real means being at home in this face, just as it is when I wake up.

I am not the person who appeared for the first time that night. I am the one only I saw, the one I had rejected until then, the one I needed to see, and didn't see until I had taken nearly everything about him away. His face is not half this or half that, it is all something else.

Sometimes you don't know who you are until you put on a mask.

A few months after Halloween, a friend borrows my wig. He has begun performing in drag on a regular basis. I have not. I bring it into the bookstore where we both work and pass it off to him. It looks like a burned-out thing, what's left in the wick of a candle after a long night.

I go to see my friend perform in the wig—he has turned it into the ponytail of a titanic hair sculpture, made from three separate wigs. He is beautiful beneath its impossible size, a hoopskirted vision, his face whited out, a beauty mark on his lip. Who was the first blond to dot a beauty mark on her upper lip? How far back in time do we have to go? It is like some spirit in the wig has moved on, into him.

He never gives me the wig back, and I don't ask for it back—it was never really mine.

Gender Outlaw

BY KATE BORNSTEIN

Kate Bornstein's life and work questions and complicates identity categories our culture takes as givens. Bornstein's anthology, *Gender Outlaws: The Next Generation*, co-edited with S. Bear Bergman, won Lambda Literary and Publishing Triangle Awards. Bornstein is also the author of a 2012 autobiography, *A Queer and Pleasant Danger: A Memoir* and 2013's *My New Gender Workbook: A Step-by-Step Guide to Achieving World Peace through Gender Anarchy and Sex Positivity*. Bornstein blends cultural criticism, humor, dramatic writing, performance art, and autobiography to reveal gender as a cultural rather than a biological or "natural" phenomenon. Bornstein's *Gender Outlaw*—published in 1994 and an excerpt of which is included here—challenged hegemonic gender binaries and the persistence of gender essentialism in the feminist movement. In particular, she examines some of the internalized biases she had to overcome when she first came out as trans and explores desire, what it means to want and be wanted when the contours of your identity are blurred.

NAMING ALL THE PARTS

For the first thirty-or-so years of my life, I didn't listen, I didn't ask questions, I didn't talk, I didn't deal with gender—I avoided the dilemma as best I could. I lived frantically on the edge of my white male privilege, and it wasn't 'til I got into therapy around the issue of my transsexualism that I began to take apart gender and really examine it from several sides. As I looked at each facet of gender, I needed to fix it with a definition, just long enough for me to realize that each definition I came up with was entirely inadequate and needed to be abandoned in search of deeper meaning.

Definitions have their uses in much the same way that road signs make it easy to travel: they point out the directions. But you don't get where you're going when you just stand underneath some sign, waiting for it to tell you what to do.

I took the first steps of my journey by trying to define the phenomenon I was daily becoming.

There's a real simple way to look at gender: Once upon a time, someone drew a line in the sands of a culture and proclaimed with great self-importance, "On this side, you are a man; on the other side, you are a woman." It's time for the winds of change to blow that line away. Simple.

Gender means *class*. By calling gender a system of classification, we can dismantle the system and examine its components. Suzanne Kessler and Wendy McKenna in their landmark 1978 book, *Gender: An Ethnomethodological Approach*, open the door to viewing gender as a social construct. They pinpoint various phenomena of gender, as follows:

Gender Assignment

Gender assignment happens when the culture says, "This is what you are." In most cultures, we're assigned a gender at birth. In our culture, once you've been assigned a gender, that's what you are; and for the most part, it's doctors who dole out the gender assignments, which shows you how emphatically gender has been medicalized. These doctors look down at a newly-born infant and say "It has a penis, it's a boy." Or they say, "It doesn't have a penis, it's a girl." It has little or nothing to do with vaginas. It's all penises or no penises: gender assignment is both phallocentric and genital. Other cultures are not or have not been so rigid.

In the early nineteenth century, Kodiak Islanders would occasionally assign a female gender to a child with a penis: this resulted in a woman who would bring great good luck to her husband, and a larger dowry to her parents. The European umbrella term for this and any other type of Native American transgendered person is *berdache*. Walter Williams in *The Spirit and the Flesh* chronicles nearly as many types of *berdache* as there were nations.

> *Even as early as 1702, a French explorer who lived for four years among the Illinois Indians noted that berdaches were known "from their childhood, when they are seen frequently picking up the spade, the spindle, the ax [women's tools], but making no use of the bow and arrow as all the other small boys do."*
>
> —Pierre Liette, *Memoir of Pierre Liette on the Illinois Country*

When the gender of a child was in question in some Navajo tribes, they reached a decision by putting a child inside a *tipi* with loom and a bow and arrow—female and male implements respectively. They set fire to the *tipi*, and whatever the child grabbed as he/she ran out determined the child's gender. It was perfectly natural to these Navajo that the child had some say in determining its own gender. Compare this method with the following modern example:

> *[The Montana Educational Telecommunications Network, a computer bulletin board,] enabled students in tiny rural schools to communicate with students around the world. Cynthia Denton, until last year a teacher at the only public school in Hobson, Montana (population 200), describes the benefit of such links. "When we got our first messages from Japan, a wonderful little fifth-grade girl named Michelle was asked if she was a boy or a girl. She was extraordinarily indignant at that, and said, 'I'm Michelle—I'm a girl of course.' Then I pointed out the name of the person who had asked the question and said, 'Do you know if this is a boy or a girl?' She said, 'No, how am I supposed to know that?' I said, 'Oh, the rest of the world is supposed to know that Michelle is a girl, but you have no social responsibility to know if this is a boy or a girl?' She stopped and said, 'Oh.' And then she rephrased her reply considerably."*
>
> —Jacques Leslie, *The Cursor Cowboy*, 1993

Is the determination of one another's gender a "social responsibility?"

Do we have the legal or moral right to decide and assign our own genders?

Or does that right belong to the state, the church, and the medical profession?

If gender is classification, can we afford to throw away the very basic right to classify ourselves?

Gender Identity

Gender identity answers the question, "who am I?" Am I a man or a woman or a what? It's a decision made by nearly every individual, and it's subject to any influence: peer pressure, advertising, drugs, cultural definitions of gender, whatever.

Gender identity is assumed by many to be "natural"; that is someone can feel "like a man," or "like a woman." When I first started giving talks about gender, this was the one question that would keep coming up: "Do you feel like a woman now?" "Did you ever feel like a man?" "How did you know what a woman would feel like?"

I've no idea what "a woman" feels like. I never did feel like a girl or a woman; rather, it was my unshakable conviction that I was not a boy or a man. It was the absence of a feeling, rather than its presence, that convinced me to change my gender.

What **does** a man feel like?
What does a woman feel like?
Do **you** feel "like a man?"
Do you feel "like a woman?"
I'd really like to know that from people.

Gender identity answers another question: "to which gender (class) do I want to belong?" Being and belonging are closely related concepts when it comes to gender. I felt I was a woman (being), and more importantly I felt I belonged with the other women (belonging). In this culture, the only two sanctioned gender clubs are "men" and "women." If you don't belong to one or the other, you're told in no uncertain terms to sign up fast.

Sweet Loretta Martin
Thought she was a woman
But she was another man.
All the girls around her
Thought she had it coming
But she gets it while she can.
Get back, get back,
Get back to where you once belonged.
Get back, Loretta.
—John Lennon and Paul McCartney, *Get Back*, 1969

I remember a dream I had when I was no more than seven or eight years old—I might have been younger. In this dream, two lines of battle were drawn up facing one another on a devastated plain: I remember the earth was dry and cracked. An army of men on one side faced an army of women on the other. The soldiers on both sides were exhausted. They were all wearing skins—I remember smelling the un-tanned leather in my dream. I was a young boy, on the side of the men, and I was being tied down to a roughly-hewn cart. I wasn't struggling. When I was completely secured, the men attached a long rope to the cart, and tossed the other end of the rope over to the women. The soldiers of the women's army slowly pulled me across the empty ground between the two armies, as the sun began to rise. I could see only the sun and the sky. When I'd been pulled over to the side of the women, they untied me, turned their backs to the men, and we all walked away. I looked back, and saw the men walking away from us. We were all silent.

I wonder about reincarnation. I wonder how a child could have had a dream like that in such detail. I told this dream to the psychiatrist at the army induction center in Boston in 1969—they'd asked if I'd ever had any strange dreams, so I told them this one. They gave me a I-Y, deferred duty due to psychiatric instability.

Gender Roles

Gender roles are collections of factors which answer the question, "How do I need to function so that society perceives me as belonging or not belonging to a specific gender?" Some people would include appearance, sexual orientation, and methods of communication

under the term, but I think it makes more sense to think in terms
of things like jobs, economic roles, chores, hobbies; in other
words, positions and actions specific to a given gender as defined
by a culture. Gender roles, when followed, send signals of membership in a given gender.

Gender Attribution

Then there's gender attribution, whereby we look at somebody
and say, "that's a man," or "that's a woman." And this is important because the way we perceive another's gender affects the way
we relate to that person. Gender attribution is the sneaky one. It's
the one we do all the time without thinking about it; kinda like
driving a sixteen-wheeler down a crowded highway . . . without
thinking about it.

In this culture, gender attribution, like gender assignment, is
phallocentric. That is, one is male until perceived otherwise. According to a study done by Kessler and McKenna, one can extrapolate that it would take the presence of roughly four female cues
to outweigh the presence of one male cue: one is assumed male
until proven otherwise. That's one reason why many women today get "sirred" whereas very few men get called "ma'am."

Gender attribution depends on cues given by the attributee, and
perceived by the attributer. The categories of cues as I have looked
at them apply to a man/woman bi-polar gender system, although
they could be relevant to a more fluidly-gendered system. I found
these cues to be useful in training actors in cross-gender role-
playing.

Physical cues include body, hair, clothes, voice, skin, and movement.

I'm nearly six feet tall, and I'm large-boned. Like most people born
"male," my hands, feet, and forearms are proportionally larger to
my body as a whole than those of people born "female." My hair
pattern included coarse facial hair. My voice is naturally deep—I
sang bass in a high school choir and quartet. I've had to study ways
and means of either changing these physical cues, or drawing

attention away from them if I want to achieve a female attribution from people.

Susan Brownmiller's book, *Femininity*, is an excellent analysis of the social impact of physical factors as gender cues.

Behavioral cues include manners, decorum, protocol, and deportment. Like physical cues, behavioral cues change with time and culture. *Dear Abby* and other advice columnists often freely dispense gender-specific manners. Most of the behavioral cues I can think of boil down to how we occupy space, both alone and with others.

Some points of manners are not taught in books of etiquette. They are, instead, signals we learn from one another, mostly signals acknowledging membership to an upper (male) or lower (female) class. But to commit some of *these* manners in writing in terms of gender-specific behavior would be an acknowledgment that gender exists as a class system.

Here's one: As part of learning to pass as a woman, I was taught to avoid eye contact when walking down the street; that looking someone in the eye was a male cue. Nowadays, sometimes I'll look away, and sometimes I'll look someone in the eye—it's a behavior pattern that's more fun to play with than to follow rigidly. A femme cue (not "woman," but "femme") is to meet someone's eyes (usually a butch), glance quickly away, then slowly look back into the butch's eyes and hold that gaze: great, hot fun, that one!

In many transsexual and transvestite meetings I attended, when the subject of the discussion was "passing," a lot of emphasis was given to manners: who stands up to shake hands? who exits an elevator first? who opens doors? who lights cigarettes? These are all cues I had to learn in order to pass as a woman in this culture. It wasn't 'til I began to read feminist literature that I began to question these cues or to see them as oppressive.

Textual cues include histories, documents, names, associates, relationships—true or false—which support a desired gender attribution. Someone trying to be taken for male in this culture might take the name Bernard, which would probably get a better male attribution than the name Brenda.

Changing my name from Al to Kate was no big deal in Pennsylvania. It was a simple matter of filing a form with the court and publishing the name change in some unobtrusive "notices" column of a court-approved newspaper. Bingo—done. The problems came with changing all my documents. The driver's license was particularly interesting. Prior to my full gender change, I'd been pulled over once already dressed as a woman, yet holding my male driver's license—it wasn't something I cared to repeat.

Any changes in licenses had to be done in person at the Department of Motor Vehicles. I was working in corporate America: Ford Aerospace. On my lunch break, I went down to the DMV and waited in line with the other folks who had changes to make to their licenses. The male officer at the desk was flirting with me, and I didn't know what to do with that, so I kept looking away. When I finally got to the desk, he asked "Well young lady, what can we do for you?"

"I've got to make a name change on my license," I mumbled.

"Just get married?" he asked jovially.

"Uh, no," I replied.

"Oh! Divorced!" he proclaimed with just a bit of hope in his voice, "Let's see your license." I handed him my old driver's license with my male name on it. He glanced down at the card, apparently not registering what he saw. "You just go on over there, honey, and take your test. We'll have you fixed up soon. Oh," he added with a wink, "if you need anything special, you just come back here and ask old Fred."

I left old Fred and joined the line for my test. I handed the next officer both my license and my court order authorizing my name change. This time, the officer didn't give my license a cursory glance. He kept looking at me, then down at the paper, then me, then the paper. His face grim, he pointed over to the direction of the testing booths. On my way over to the booths, old Fred called out, "Honey, they treating you all right?" Before I could reply, the second officer snarled at old Fred to "get his butt over" to look at all my paperwork.

I reached the testing booths and looked back just in time to see a quite crestfallen old Fred looking at me, then the paper, then me, then the paper.

Mythic cues include cultural and sub-cultural myths which support membership in a given gender. This culture's myths include archetypes like: weaker sex, dumb blonde, strong silent type, and better half. Various waves of the women's movement have had to deal with a multitude of myths of male superiority.

Power dynamics as cue include modes of communication, communication techniques, and degrees of aggressiveness, assertiveness, persistence, and ambition.

Sexual orientation as cue highlights, in the dominant culture, the heterosexual imperative (or in the lesbian and gay culture, the homosexual imperative). For this reason, many male heterosexual transvestites who wish to pass as female will go out on a "date" with another man (who is dressed as a man)—the two seem to be a heterosexual couple. In glancing at the "woman" of the two, an inner dialogue might go, "It's wearing a dress, and it's hanging on the arm of a man, so it must be a woman." For the same man to pass as a female in a lesbian bar, he'd need to be with a woman, dressed as a woman, as a "date."

I remember one Fourth of July evening in Philadelphia, about a year after my surgery. I was walking home arm in arm with Lisa, my lover at the time, after the fireworks display. We were leaning in to one another, walking like lovers walk. Coming toward us was a family of five: mom, dad, and three teenage boys. "Look, it's a coupla faggots," said one of the boys. "Nah, it's two girls," said another. "That's enough outa you," bellowed the father, "one of 'em's got to be a man. This is America!"

So sex (the act) and gender (the classification) are different, and depending on the qualifier one is using for gender differentiation, they may or may not be dependent on one another. There are probably as many types of gender (gender systems) as could be imagined. Gender by clothing, gender by divine right, gender by lottery—these all make as much sense as any other criteria, but in our Western civilization, we bow down to the great god Science. No other type of gender holds as much sway as:

Biological gender, which classifies a person through any combination of body type, chromosomes, hormones, genitals, reproductive organs, or some other corporal or chemical essence. Belief in biological gender is in fact a belief in the supremacy of the body in the determination of identity. It's biological gender that most folks refer to when they say *sex.* By calling something "sex," we grant it seniority over all the other types of gender—by some right of biology.

So, there are all these *types* of gender which in and of themselves are *not* gender, but criteria for systemic classification. And there's sex, which somehow winds up on top of the heap. Add to this room full of seeds the words *male, female, masculine, feminine, man, woman, boy, girl.* These words are not descriptive of any sexual act, so all these words fall under the category of gender and are highly subjective, depending on which system of gender one is following.

But none of this explains why there is such a widespread insistence upon the conflation of *sex* and *gender.* I think a larger question is why Eurocentric culture needs to see *so much* in terms of sex.

It's not like gender is the **only** thing we confuse with sex. As a culture, we're encouraged to equate sex (the act) with money, success, and security; and with the products we're told will help us attain money, success, and security. We live in a culture that succeeds in selling products (the apex of accomplishment in capitalism) by aligning those products with the attainment of one's sexual fantasies.

Switching my gender knocked me for a time curiously out of the loop of ads designed for men or women, gays or straights. I got to look at sex without the hype, and ads without the allure. None of them, after all, spoke to me, although all of them beckoned.

Kinds of Sex

"Can you orgasm with that vagina?"
—Audience member question for Kate
on the *Geraldo Rivera* show

It's important to keep *gender* and *sex* separated as, respectively, *system* and *function*. Since function is easier to pin down than system, sex is a simpler starting place than gender.

"Yah, the plumbing works and so does the electricity."
—Kate's answer

There are so many sex manuals on the market—the how-to kind—and depending on where you look, there's bound to be one that talks about what you like to do. That's great, and I own several of them, but it's beyond the scope of this book. The purpose of talking about sex here is to disentangle it from gender.

Sex does have a primary factor to it which is germane to a discussion of gender: *sexual orientation*, which is what people call it, if they believe you're born with it, or *sexual preference* which is what people call it if they believe you have more of a choice and more of a say in the matter.

[W]e do not need a sophisticated methodology or technology to confirm that the gender component of identity is the most important one articulated during sex. Nearly everyone (except for bisexuals, perhaps) regards it as the prime criterion for choosing a sex partner.
—Murray S. Davis, *Smut: Erotic Reality/Obscene Ideology*,
1983

The Basic Mix-Up

A gay man who lived in Khartoum
Took a lesbian up to his room.
They argued all night

Over who had the right
To do what, and with what, to whom.
                    —anonymous limerick

Here's the tangle that I found: sexual orientation/preference is based in this culture solely on the gender of one's partner of choice. Not only do we confuse the two words, we make them dependent on one another. The only choices we're given to determine the focus of our sexual desire are these:

- *Heterosexual model:* in which a culturally-defined male is in a relationship with a culturally-defined female.
- *Gay male model:* two culturally-defined men involved with each other.
- *Lesbian model:* two culturally-defined women involved with each other.
- *Bisexual model:* culturally-defined men and women who could be involved with either culturally-defined men or women.

Variants to these gender-based relationship dynamics would include heterosexual female with gay male, gay male with lesbian woman, lesbian woman with heterosexual woman, gay male with bisexual male, and so forth. People involved in these variants know that each dynamic is different from the other. A lesbian involved with another lesbian, for example, is a very different relationship than that of a lesbian involved with a bisexual woman, and *that's* distinct from being a lesbian woman involved with a heterosexual woman. What these variants have in common is that each of these combinations forms its own clearly-recognizable dynamic, and none of these are acknowledged by the dominant cultural binary of sexual orientation: heterosexuality/homosexuality.

Despite the non-recognition of these dynamics by the broader culture, *all these models depend on the gender of the partner.* This results in minimizing, if not completely dismissing, other dynamic models of a relationship which could be more important than gender and are often more telling about the real nature of someone's desire. There are so many factors on which we *could* base sexual orientation. Examples of alternate dynamic models include:

- *Butch/Femme model,* however that may be defined by its participants.

Butch style, whether worn by men or women, is a symbol of detachment. Dressing butch gives the wearer the protection of being the observer, not the object. A femme-y look, by contrast, suggests self-display, whether in a quietly demure or sexually flashy fashion. Butch is a style of understatement: "I don't need to show flesh because I am in a position to choose." Butch is no coy "come hither" look, but a challenge—"I see you and maybe I like what I see."

There is something about femme-y style that in itself produces insecurity, a sense of vulnerability and exposure. The femme invites the gaze and it takes a great deal of feminine self-confidence to risk that kind of scrutiny.

—Wendy Chapkis, *Beauty Secrets: Women and the Politics of Appearance*, 1986

- *Top/Bottom model* which can be further sub-classified as dominant/submissive or sadist/masochist.

The bottom is responsible for being obedient, for carrying out her top's orders with dispatch and grace, for being as aroused and sexually available and desirable as possible, and for letting her top know when she is physically uncomfortable or needs a break. . . . The top is responsible for constructing a scene that falls within the bottom's limits, although it is permissible to stretch her limit if she suddenly discovers the capacity to go further than she ever has before.

—Pat Califia, *Sapphistry: The Book of Lesbian Sexuality*, 1983

There are also:

Butch/Butch models
Femme/Femme models
Triad (or more) models
Human/Animal models
Adult/Child models
Same-aged models
Parent/Child models
Multiple partners models
Able-bodied models
Differently-abled bodies models

Reproductive models
Owner/Slave models
Monogamous models
Non-monogamous models

I'm sure I'm leaving models out of this, and someone is going to be really upset that I didn't think of them, but the point is there's more to sex (the act) than gender (one classification of identity).

Try making a list of ways in which sexual preference or orientation could be measured, and then add to that list (or subtract from it) every day for a month, or a year (or for the rest of your life). Could be fun!

Sex Without Gender

There are plenty of instances in which sexual attraction can have absolutely nothing to do with the gender of one's partner.

When Batman and Catwoman try to get it on sexually, it only works when they are both in their caped crusader outfits. Naked heterosexuality is a miserable failure between them. . . . When they encounter each other in costume however something much sexier happens and the only thing missing is a really good scene where we get to hear the delicious sound of Catwoman's latex rubbing on Batman's black rubber/leather skin. To me their flirtation in capes looked queer precisely because it was not heterosexual, they were not man and woman, they were bat and cat, or latex and rubber, or feminist and vigilante: gender became irrelevant and sexuality was dependent on many other factors. . . .

You could also read their sexual encounters as the kind of sex play between gay men and lesbians that we are hearing so much about recently: in other words, the sexual encounter is queer because both partners are queer and the genders of the participants are less relevant. Just because Batman is male and Catwoman is female does not make their interactions heterosexual—think about it, there is nothing straight about two people getting it on in rubber and latex costumes, wearing eyemasks and carrying whips and other accoutrements.

—Judith Halberstam, "Queer Creatures," *On Our Backs*, Nov/Dec, 1992

Sexual preference *could* be based on genital preference. (This is not the same as saying preference for a specific gender, unless you're basing your definition of gender on the presence or absence of some combination of genitals.) Preference could also be based on the kind of sex *acts* one prefers, and, in fact, elaborate systems exist to distinguish just that, and to announce it to the world at large. For example, here's a handkerchief code from the Samois Collective's *Coming To Power*. The code is used for displaying preference in sexual behavior. Colors mean active if worn on the left side, or passive if worn on the right.

LEFT SIDE	COLOR	RIGHT SIDE
Fist Fucker	Red	Fist Fuckee
Anal Sex, Top	Dark Blue	Anal Sex, Bottom
Oral Sex, Top	Light Blue	Oral Sex, Bottom
Light S/M, Top	Robin's Egg Blue	Light S/M, Bottom
Foot Fetish, Top	Mustard	Foot Fetish, Bottom
Anything Goes, Top	Orange	Anything Goes, Bottom
Gives Golden Showers	Yellow	Wants Golden Showers
Hustler, Selling	Green	Hustler, Buying
Uniforms/Military, Top	Olive Drab	Uniforms/Military, Bottom
Likes Novices, Chickenhawk	White	Novice (or Virgin)
Victorian Scenes	White Lace	Victorian Scenes, Bottom
Does Bondage	Grey	Wants to be put in Bondage
Shit Scenes, Top	Brown	Shit Scenes, Bottom
Heavy S/M & Whipping, Top	Black	Heavy S/M & Whipping, Bottom
Piercer	Purple	Piercee
Likes Menstruating Women	Maroon	Is Menstruating
Group Sex, Top	Lavender	Group Sex, Bottom
Breast Fondler	Pink	Breast Fondlee

I love this code! It gave me quite a few ideas when I first read it. But despite the many variations possible, sexual orientation/preference remains culturally linked to our gender system (and by extension to gender identity) through the fact that it's most usually based on the gender of one's partner. This link probably accounts for much of the tangle between sex and gender.

The confusion between sex and gender affects more than individuals and relationships. The conflation of sex and gender contributes to the linking together of the very different subcultures of gays, lesbians, bisexuals, leather sexers, sex-workers, and the transgendered.

> A common misconception is that male cross-dressers are both gay and prostitutes, whereas the truth of the matter is that most cross-dressers that I've met hold down more mainstream jobs, careers, or professions, are married, and are practicing heterosexuals.

A dominant culture tends to combine its subcultures into manageable units. As a result, those who practice non-traditional sex are seen by members of the dominant culture (as well as by members of sex and gender subcultures) as a whole with those who don non-traditional gender roles and identities. Any work to deconstruct the gender system needs to take into account the artificial amalgam of subcultures, which might itself collapse if the confusion of terms holding it together were to be settled.

In any case, if we buy into categories of sexual orientation based solely on gender—heterosexual, homosexual, or bisexual—we're cheating ourselves of a searching examination of our real sexual preferences. In the same fashion, by subscribing to the categories of gender based solely on the male/female binary, we cheat ourselves of a searching examination of our real gender identity. And now we can park sex off to the side for a while, and bring this essay back around to gender.

Desire

I was not an unattractive man. People's reactions to my gender change often included the remonstrative, "But you're such a good-looking guy!" Nowadays, as I navigate the waters between male and female, there are still people attracted to me. At first, my reaction was fear: "What kind of pervert," I thought, "would be attracted to a freak like me?" As I got over that internalized phobia of my transgender status, I began to get curious about the nature of desire, sex, and identity. When, for example, I talk about the need to do away with gender, I always get looks of horror from the audience: "What about desire and attraction!" they want to know, "How can you have desire with no gender?" They've got a good point: the concepts of sex and gender seem to overlap around the phenomenon of desire. So I began to explore my transgendered relationship to desire.

> About five months into living full-time as a woman, I woke up one morning and felt really good about the day. I got dressed for work, and checking the mirror before I left, I liked what I saw— at last! I opened the door to leave the building, only to find two workmen standing on the porch, the hand of one poised to knock on the door. This workman's face lit up when he saw me. "Well!" he said, "Don't you look beautiful today." At that moment, I realized I didn't know how to respond to that. I felt like a deer caught in the headlights of an oncoming truck. I really wasn't prepared for people to be attracted to me. To this day, I don't know how to respond to a man who's attracted to me—I never learned the rituals.

To me, desire is a wish to experience someone or something that I've never experienced, or that I'm not currently experiencing. Usually, I need an identity appropriate (or appropriately inappropriate) to the context in which I want to experience that person or thing. This context could be anything: a romantic involvement, a tennis match, or a boat trip up a canal. On a boat trip up the canal, I could appropriately be a passenger or a crew member. In a tennis match, I could be a player, an audience member, a concessionaire, a referee, a member of the grounds staff. In the context of a romantic involvement, it gets less obvious about what I need to be in order to have an appropriate identity, but I would need to have *some* identity. Given that most romantic or sexual involvements in this culture are defined by the genders of the partners, the *most* appropriate identity to have in a romantic relationship would be a gender identity, or something that passes for gender identity, like a gender role. A gender role might be butch, femme, top, and bottom—these are all methods of acting. So, even without a gender identity *per se*, some workable identity can be called up and put into motion within a relationship, and when we play with our identities, we play with desire. Some identities stimulate desire, others diminish desire. To make ourselves attractive to someone, we modify our identity, or at least the appearance of an identity—and this includes gender identity.

I love the idea of being without an identity, it gives me a lot of room to play around; but it makes me dizzy, having nowhere to hang my hat. When I get too tired of not having an identity, I take one on: it doesn't really matter what identity I take on, as long as it's recognizable. I can be a writer, a lover, a confidante, a femme, a top, or a woman. I retreat into definition as a way of demarcating my space, a way of saying "Step back, I'm getting crowded here." By saying "I am the (fill in the blank)," I also say, "You are *not*, and so you are not in my space." Thus, I achieve privacy. Gender identity is a form of self-definition: something into which we can withdraw, from which we can glean a degree of privacy from time to time, and with which we can, to a limited degree, manipulate desire.

Our culture is obsessed with desire: it drives our economy. We come right out and say we're going to stimulate desire for goods and services, and so we're bombarded daily with ads and commercial announcements geared to make us desire things. No wonder the emphasis on desire spills over into the rest of our lives. No wonder I get panicked reactions from audiences when I suggest we eliminate gender as a system; gender defines our desire, and we don't know what to do if we don't have desire. Perhaps the more importance a culture places on desire, the more conflated become the concepts of sex and gender.

As an exercise, can you recall the last time you saw someone whose gender was ambiguous? Was this person attractive to you? And if you knew they called themselves neither a man nor a woman, what would it make you if you're attracted to that person? And if you were to kiss? Make love? What would you be?

I remember one time at a gay and lesbian writers' conference in San Francisco, I was on a panel and asking these same questions. Because it was a specifically gay and lesbian audience, an audience that defined itself by its sexual orientation, I wanted to tweak them on that identity. I asked, "And what if I strapped on a dildo and made love to you: what would that make me?" Without missing a beat, panelist Carol Queen piped up, "Nostalgic."

Being Female

BY EILEEN MYLES

Eileen Myles is an award-winning poet, writer, performance artist, and activist who has published more than twenty books including *Chelsea Girls: A Novel*, *Inferno: A Poet's Novel*, *Afterglow: A Dog Memoir*, and many others. In their 2011 essay "Being Female," published in *The Awl*, they write about how women dominate the poetry world and still, men's work is disproportionately recognized, reviewed, and otherwise feted. They examine all the ways in which women are diminished in the poetry community and well beyond, and how, ultimately, they want to "be loved because I am. That's all." Indeed.

When I think about being female I think about being loved. What I mean by that: I have a little exercise I do when I present my work or speak publicly or even write (like this). In order to build up my courage I try to imagine myself deeply loved. Because there are men whose lives I've avidly followed—out of admiration for their work or their "way." Paolo Pasolini always comes to mind. I love his work, his films, his poetry, his writings on film and literature, his life, all of it, even his death. How did he do it—make such amazing work and stand up so boldly as a queer and a Marxist in a Catholic country in the face of so much (as his violent death proved) hate. I have one clear answer. He was loved. Pasolini's mother was wild about him. We joke about this syndrome—Oh she was an Italian mother, but she could just have well been a Jewish mother, an Irish mother, an African-American one. A mother loves her son. And so does a country. And that is much to count on. So I try to conjure that for myself particularly when I'm writing or saying something that seems both vulnerable and important so I don't have to be defending myself so hard. I try and act like it's mine. The culture. That I'm its beloved son. It's not an impossible conceit. But it's hard. Because a woman, reflexively, often feels unloved. When I saw the recent Vida pie charts that showed how low the numbers are of female writers getting reviewed in the mainstream press I just wasn't surprised at all though I did cringe. When you see your oldest fears reflected back at you in the hard bright light of day it doesn't feel good. Because a woman is someone who grew up observing that a whole lot more was being imagined by everyone for her brother and the boys around her in school. If she's a talented artist she's told that she could probably teach art to children when she grows up and then she hears the boy who's good in art get told by the same teacher that one day he could grow up to be a commercial artist. The adult doing the talking in these kinds of exchanges is most often female. And the woman who is still a child begins to wonder if her childhood is already gone because she has been already replaced in the future by a woman who will be teaching children like herself. And will she tell them that they too will not so much fail but vanish before their lives can even begin. These pie charts don't surprise me. They just demonstrate that a lot of us can easily become just a few of us or even just one of us. I am mildly curious about whether the situation in book reviewing (or even publishing) was actually better for a while during and right after the 70s, the heyday of feminism, but you know I'm not that curious. That thrilling rise then dogged fall would only underline the sad fact that the increased interest in women's writings for a decade or so was a kind of fleeting impulse, like the interest-in-incest moment, just "a thing," not a deep cultural shift like the comprehension that slavery or human sacrifice are wrong and we just won't ever go there again. But to have such a deep sea change in a culture and keep it you have put the reins of its institutions permanently in other hands and let them stay there. "They" would have to have become "you." And you (whether you were male or female) would have long concluded that women's writing is either just writing or no different than men's or equally interesting, or even better. And that perspective would by now be so embedded in our cultural sense of self that the Times or Harpers or The New York Review of Books would no more likely be short changing women's books today any more than they would pull quietly away from reviewing books written in English in order to uphold a belief that the only good work being written today is by African, South American or Icelandic authors. And think nobody would notice. Reasonable people of course would smile and insist that the NYRB be renamed The New York Review of African Books or South American Books or Icelandic. It would have to happen, the NYRB would have to own their bias eventually, what they were doing, the editor would have to issue a statement or else the publication would become a total joke. But to publish a review today that purportedly reviews "all" books yet in fact is dedicated to the project of mainly reviewing men's without acknowledging that kind of bias sort of begs the question—the operating presumption must be that "we" "all know" that men's writing is in fact better or more important than women's—is the real deal and the only thing disputing this is feminism and since that's "over" (phew) we are back to business as usual. When I say business I mean that there's just a whole lot of money talking. That's what's going on. The more culturally generous moment we're all missing (whether it ever truly happened or not) was tied to a booming economy. Men weren't actually sharing space in the 70s and 80s—the doors just got a little wider for a while. And now that there's less money to go around in book publishing and the surrounding media it seems like what's getting shoved out is women. That's what I believe is happening, don't you. I think we can do this, right? The editor might ask his staff holding up the cover of the next great all-male issue that dare not speak its name—and his staff probably includes a few females and queers—who want to be in on "the conversation." Who could blame them for that? Well I can. Can't you? I mean what are we doing here after all.

Is writing just a job. Writing books, writing poems. If it is then the message to women is to go elsewhere. But they can go to hell—these messengers, the collective whoever or whatever that is saying it. I don't believe that this is a job. I think writing is a passion. It's an urge as deep as life itself. It's sex. It's being and becoming. If you write, then writing is how you know. And when someone starts slowly removing women from the public reflection of this fact they are saying that she doesn't know. Or I don't care if she thinks she knows. She is not a safe bet.

Interestingly the poetry world is getting celebrated for its VIDA showing of nearly equal gender parity in reviewing etc. The problem there though is that the majority of the poets writing are female. It's true. That's who takes workshops, that's who gets MFAs, you can easily get some numbers there and frankly in the poetry scene the women are the ones who are generally doing the most exciting work. Why? Because the female reality is still largely unknown. And language is the thrill that holds the unknown in its vague and shifting ways. That's writing. But despite the fact that there are more females in the poetry world, more females writing their accounts somehow only a fraction of them are able to bob to top of the heap. So the poetry world is in effect performing a kind of affirmative action for men by giving their work a big push ahead, celebrating men's books at a much higher ratio to the amount and quality of work actually being produced. And I'm not entertaining for a moment that this is because male work is better. I'm female and I don't so much think female work is better. Female reality is not better. But female reality has consumed male reality abundantly—we have to in order just to survive so female reality always contains male and female. That seems interesting as hell so at the very least I think it's a lot more interesting than a monotonous male reality. Which seems just sort of staid and old. Tapped out. Female reality (and this goes for all the "other" realities as well—queer, black, trans—everyone else) is more interesting because it is wider, more representative of humanity—it's definitely more stylistically various because of all it has to carry and show. After all, style is practical. You do different things because you are different. Women are different. Maybe not the women who routinely get invited to take part in the men's monolith. They are another item. But women as a class are different. That's how I dispense with the quality question.

But here's the actual problem. If the poetry world celebrated its female stars at the true level of their productivity and influence poetry would wind up being a largely female world and the men would leave. Poetry would not seem to be the job for them. I think that's the fear. Losing daddy again! Plus women always need to support, I mean actively support male work in order to dispense with the revolting suggestion that they are feminists. I supported Hillary Clinton with my vote but did you notice she wasn't really a feminist until she was losing. Well what does feminism mean?

Well I think it means that you don't do much in your work except complain about injustice and describe the personal sphere and talk in a wide variety of ways about labias. You think I'm kidding. Cause I actually do that in my most recent novel—I thought well women in the art world are always celebrating their labias so maybe I should do that in writing. What a great, funny, even masculine idea. To use the pussy as material. So I wrote five pages of pussy wallpaper and gave it to the editors at VICE who did publish it but confided in me that the money people really had to be convinced that it was not entirely disgusting. With all the dirty and violent and racist things that VICE has done, this was um a little troubling. Do we really want to send that kind of message to our readers. What kind of message is that. I guess a wet hairy soft female one. I mean a big giant female hole you might fall into never to be heard from again. I mean and there's just always a danger if you're a feminist that you're also a lesbian (I am) and the only way to really make it clear that you are not that (or that "it" means nothing) is to firmly vote with the guys, kid with them, and be willing to laugh at other women (to demonstrate that you have "a sense of humor") and not push too hard to include women in anything. Speaking frankly as a lesbian I have to say that the salient fact about the danger zone I call home is the persistent experience of witnessing the quick revulsion of people who believe that because I love women I am a bottom feeder. I am desperately running toward what anyone in their right mind would be running away from. Which is femaleness, which is failure.

And one does after all want to be read as a man. As a man who is a woman perhaps. Can't we just all be men and some have these genitals and some have those. I heard that that's how they saw it in the middle ages. And some died after having thirteen children and some just got another wife. Women finally are all replaceable and that's the real truth. The more different we get the less likely we can fit our foot in the tiny shoe. And that's the gig. Not being female, but being small. But I want to be loved because I am. That's all.

Volcano Dreams

BY GABRIELLE BELLOT

Gabrielle Bellot, an essayist and staff writer for *Literary Hub*, uses her work to examine the ways identity is complicated by intersectional oppressions. Bellot interrogates cultural icons and movements and connects them to the personal and the body through an LGBTQIA+, immigrant, anti-racist, feminist lens; she also writes about global literature, literary history, the Caribbean, and what it means to navigate the world as a multiracial transgender woman. Her work has appeared in publications such as *The New Yorker*, *The New York Times*, *The Atlantic*, *The Guardian*, *Shondaland*, and *The Paris Review Daily*. In this 2018 essay "The Body Cannot Be One Simple Thing (Volcano Dreams)" first published in *Gay Magazine*, Bellot writes about being trans and reclaiming her womanhood. This is an essay about navigating what it means to live in an unruly body, and how, despite not always feeling whole, "transitioning has taught me that a body can encompass far more than we are usually taught, that there are many architectures of bodies a gender may possess."

I think this story begins at a bar in Greenwich late last year, when New York was under a record freeze. I was meeting an old friendly African acquaintance I hadn't seen in nearly a year. Some months before, he had messaged me on social media to say he might be in New York for Christmas and that we should meet if he came; to my surprise, in December, he contacted me again. He was visiting family in Long Island, the message declared, and suggested meeting up, ending with a grinning emoji. I knew, from old gossip with friends to whom he had sent flirtatious texts and DMs, that he seemed to enjoy casual hookups, but he had never shown any interest in me before, and I mused, on occasion, that my being trans had cloaked me with a kind of diaphanous sexual invisibility.

He had contacted just about every other woman in the circles of my old life before my move to Brooklyn—everyone but me, it seemed. I wasn't particularly attracted to him, though I thought him sweet and funny, and because I was from the Commonwealth of Dominica, I always held a soft spot in my heart for other people from former British colonies in America who understood things Americans often did not—how we spelt words, having digestive biscuits at teatime, teatime in general, the colonial holdovers in many of our governments and institutions. I was disinterested and yet vaguely, stupidly desired his desire, as if that would validate something of my womanhood—*no* but *yes*, an in-between uncertainty, like the grey smoky nightmares of a slumbering volcano. Still, I wondered what it would be like if, absurdly, he asked to go back to my place. I was in a dating rut then, feeling lonely, vulnerable, and like I had little future with love due to who and what I was.

I hadn't really thought we would have sex, but now that we were alone in the bar, he seemed to want it, seemed to exude a hunger that made me swallow more than usual. He had never been with a trans woman, but, he said, grinning in the chiaroscuro light like a hyena, that he wouldn't mind trying something with me. He told lurid smiling tales about the pythonic dimensions supposedly concealed in his pants; one woman, he insisted, had to tell him to stop because he was simply *too* monstrous. It was silly, crass braggadocio, but I liked feeling his desire tug at me in the candlelight. When I descended the bar's stairs into its bathroom, I almost expected him to follow me; if he had, I might have paused, grabbed him, and pulled him in, wrapping a leg around his waist and an arm around the crook of his brown neck.

He had no condoms, so we bought a box together at Target. In my apartment, he suddenly kissed me, eyes glazed. He unzipped his jeans. We undressed over to my room, which held the sad chaos of a shipwreck, hidden, thankfully, by the darkness. I had been with a variety of men, younger and older, and I could tell he seemed nervous. I couldn't tell if he was shy with me or if such trepidation was his signature, but we continued on. He asked me, again, "how it worked"—how one might have sex with a trans woman. At the bar, I had explained my simple preferences—anal sex—but said it again. Right before anything happened, he told me to lie down with him. He couldn't do it, he whispered; he didn't think he could sleep with a trans woman. I stared. My self-loathing and loneliness returned in a swirl. I had been rejected, I realized.

As we lay on my bed in the dark, I started to cry but tried to hide it behind my robe, not wanting him to feel bad, even as I felt like shit. *I still think you're amazing*, he said, and *we could be friends*, which only made my sense that I had been rejected for my body heavier. A sinuous fear had risen back up from the blue pools in me: that my body, by virtue of not being cisgender, was hideous, repulsive, lovable only in evanescent encounters. I had learned to accept my body as a woman's, yet the unceremonious rejection hit me hard.

I still walked him back to the subway near Barclays Center and waited to make sure he got on the train. My silence was a thick mist around me, like the dense, white rain-fog high in the Dominican mountains, where the primeval trees and ferns grow to half their normal height, and I knew he felt uncomfortable. Still, I hugged him before he left, texted to make sure he reached home safely, and even apologized for crying, because I have always been the kind of person who feels and desires to take away people's pain even if it means I begin to sink, like a wood-girl from a lost ship, under the pelagic weight of their hurt.

I cried again at home, hating my body, myself. My body, too ugly, too unruly.

But this isn't where the story begins. I don't know how to tell it. I am still trying to find the where and when, though I feel the why all around me.

Stories begin when and where we least expect, like a volcano's awakening.

My body, I sometimes think, like many bodies, is like Dominica's. *Waitukubuli*, the Caribs declared our island before the colonists came, a mountainous world named corporeally: *Tall is her body*. An unruly island, rainforest one moment, melancholy ramshackle zinc roofs rattling under the metallic drums of rain the next, stunted elfin woodland and lakes that perhaps once knew the world's earliest reptiles the next, and then patches of sandy scrubland peppered with cacti and agaves and reclusive ethereal scorpions, beaches of nothing but the grey stones a hurricane hurled with its roiling rolling arms like a furious crazed cricket bowler, a rough Atlantic beyond the fins of sharks or whales where fishermen in bright-painted dinghies occasionally venture under the spells of their insomniac mermaid dreams and never return. Dominica's body changes grandly, wider in potential than a Sargasso Sea, yet she is also one defined whole. Her shifting landscapes, for many who know her, are beautiful.

I wonder about the body.

A body tectonic, geologic, at times, volcanic, voltaic, vulpine, vulgar, geologic in that it follows the logic of the earth, its ceaseless tumult.

I have learned to embrace the kinky, difficult, tender black curls my mother told me for years represented "bad" hair and which, contrarily, friends often said represented "good" hair, even as they disavowed their own tighter curls. I have learned to embrace the amorphousness of my ethnicity, whereby I am part-black yet am as often read by strangers as Latina or simply one of an indeterminate brownness. I embrace the expansive pansexuality I denied for most of my life.

Yet I do not always feel whole.

What does it mean when your body cannot be one simple thing, whenever you want it to be? What does it mean when your womanhood, ever in question, terra incognita, is itself in rolling, roiling tumult?

Simple things I cannot do without my body reasserting itself, without my heart beating like hummingbird wings: use a bathroom with slats on the door or slits between door and wall, lest someone look in; try on clothes in a changing room with the same slats; buy a swimsuit to wear at a public beach or pool; speak on the phone without first practicing my voice's pitch, tone, and resonance, often in panic, and with multiple recordings to listen to; talk to a stranger who offers to buy me a drink because I am pretty, lest he learn what I am; use my Dominican passport, which contains both a name and gender that are not me and yet cannot be changed.

As a trans woman, I sometimes think I've experienced puberty twice. That a new life began at the genesis, opening chapter, of transitioning. *You have a second virginity to lose*, my best friend said with a grin after I came out.

The same body, it turns out, can lose its innocence twice, and more, even as it is also not the same body at all, just as we both are and are not our old photographs and mottling memories.

The body has no simple theology. We reinvent and realign our constellations as we wander; our old sailing stars will not do forever.

Transitioning has taught me that a body can encompass far more than we are usually taught, that there are many architectures of bodies a gender may possess. Some days, I stand, naked, in front a mirror and feel happy, understanding why someone might desire to hold a body like mine in the calm harbor of their arms; on other days, I tilt like a sailor who has not learned the language of the waves, and feel, despite my self-acceptance, a sharp, funneling frustration.

Perhaps this afflictive uncertainty can be redefined. Uncertainty can ground us, sometimes. We need arrogance in one hand and doubt in the other; we fail ourselves, fall into too zealous a body theology, with too great an imbalance of either.

For a week after the rejection, I fell into a grey, Goethean gloom, the kind of funk everyone could sense with vague dread, like the aspirational dreams of volcanoes. I seemed like I could blow at any moment. This newest, in-the-middle-of-it-all rejection just seemed to confirm, at my emotional nadir, my deep fear of unlovability.

Then I realigned. My body simply *is*, I reminded myself; I need someone who accepts that. I was still, after years of transitioning, letting others define me, letting others start and end my story. The way to tell the narrative, instead, is by accepting its messiness and, from there, weaving the sail myself.

I rededicated my search, chanting that I had to learn to not just accept but respect myself, curves and voice and curls and all. I would stop thinking of magma and smoke and more, instead, of ocean.

Perhaps self-love means accepting our blue, blue as the color that is as much depth as lightness, solitude-sadness as mirth, ocean as sky. Self-love means learning the shifting language of a body's rules—and then when to accept them and when to break them, and finding, through both, the beauty in our landscapes, seascapes, dreamscapes, even our blue deserts.

Self-love is not giving up, even when your body breaks the rules we fear it breaking most.

PART VI

BLACK FEMINISM(S)

The Combahee River Collective Statement

BY VARIOUS

Named for an action at the Combahee River led by Harriet Tubman that freed 750 enslaved people—the only woman-led military campaign in American history—the Combahee River Collective was active in Boston from 1974 to 1980. Founded by Black women responding to the racism of the mainstream (read: white) second wave feminist movement and the misogyny of the civil rights movement, the women of the Collective called out racism, classism and homophobia and created a blueprint for inclusivity to combat patriarchy, heteronormativity, and white supremacy. More than a decade before Kimberlé Crenshaw coined the term *intersectionality*, the Black women of the Combahee River Collective introduced the concept of interlocking systems of oppression, which would become key to intersectionality. They also coined the term *identity politics*, which has become a powerful tool in combatting oppressions that have been appropriated by conservative figures to criticize anything that highlights difference. The Combahee River Collective's statement became an essential text and a blueprint for feminists to combat multidimensional structures of oppression in which we are all entangled. It was an unequivocal clarion call recognizing that it is only through collective action that we can achieve a sustainable, truly inclusive feminist future.

COMBAHEE RIVER COLLECTIVE

We are a collective of Black feminists who have been meeting together since 1974. During that time we have been involved in the process of defining and clarifying our politics, while at the same time doing political work within our own group and in coalition with other progressive organizations and movements. The most general statement of our politics at the present time would be that we are actively committed to struggling against racial, sexual, heterosexual, and class oppression, and see as our particular task the development of integrated analysis and practice based upon the fact that the major systems of oppression are interlocking. The synthesis of these oppressions creates the conditions of our lives. As Black women we see Black feminism as the logical political movement to combat the manifold and simultaneous oppressions that all women of color face.

We will discuss four major topics in the paper that follows: (1) the genesis of contemporary Black feminism; (2) what we believe, i.e., the specific province of our politics; (3) the problems in organizing Black feminists, including a brief herstory of our collective; and (4) Black feminist issues and practice.

1. The Genesis of Contemporary Black Feminism

Before looking at the recent development of Black feminism we would like to affirm that we find our origins in the historical reality of Afro-American women's continuous life-and-death struggle for survival and liberation. Black women's extremely negative relationship to the American political system (a system of white male rule) has always been determined by our membership in two oppressed racial and sexual castes. As Angela Davis points out in "Reflections on the Black Woman's Role in the Community of Slaves," Black women have always embodied, if only in their physical manifestation, an adversary stance to white male rule and have actively resisted its inroads upon them and their communities in both dramatic and subtle ways. There have always been Black women activists—some known, like Sojourner Truth, Harriet Tubman, Frances E. W. Harper, Ida B. Wells Barnett, and Mary Church Terrell, and thousands upon thousands unknown—who have had a shared awareness of how their sexual identity combined with their racial identity to make their whole life situation and the focus of their political struggles unique. Contemporary Black feminism is the outgrowth of countless generations of personal sacrifice, militancy, and work by our mothers and sisters.

A Black feminist presence has evolved most obviously in connection with the second wave of the American women's movement beginning in the late 1960s. Black, other Third World, and working women have been involved in the feminist movement from its start, but both outside reactionary forces and racism and elitism within the movement itself have served to obscure our participation. In 1973, Black feminists, primarily located in New York, felt the necessity of forming a separate Black feminist group. This became the National Black Feminist Organization (NBFO).

Black feminist politics also have an obvious connection to movements for Black liberation, particularly those of the 1960s and 1970s. Many of us were active in those movements (Civil Rights, Black nationalism, the Black Panthers), and all of our lives Were greatly affected and changed by their ideologies, their goals, and the tactics used to achieve their goals. It was our experience and disillusionment within these liberation movements, as well as experience on the periphery of the white male left, that led to the need to develop a politics that was anti-racist, unlike those of white women, and anti-sexist, unlike those of Black and white men.

There is also undeniably a personal genesis for Black Feminism, that is, the political realization that comes from the seemingly personal experiences of individual Black women's lives. Black feminists and many more Black women who do not define themselves as feminists have all experienced sexual oppression as a constant factor in our day-to-day existence. As children we realized that we were different from boys and that we were treated differently. For example, we were told in the same breath to be quiet both for the sake of being "ladylike" and to make us less objectionable in the eyes of white people. As we grew older we became aware of the threat of physical and sexual abuse by men. However, we had no way of conceptualizing what was so apparent to us, what we knew was really happening.

Black feminists often talk about their feelings of craziness before becoming conscious of the concepts of sexual politics, patriarchal rule, and most importantly, feminism, the political analysis and practice that we women use to struggle against our oppression. The fact that racial politics and indeed racism are pervasive factors in our lives did not allow us, and still does not allow most Black women, to look more deeply into our own experiences and, from that sharing and growing consciousness, to build a politics that will change our lives and inevitably end our oppression. Our development must also be tied to the contemporary economic and political position of Black people. The post World War II generation of Black youth was the first to be able to minimally partake of certain educational and employment options, previously closed completely to Black people. Although our economic position is still at the very bottom of the American capitalistic economy, a handful of us have been able to gain certain tools as a result of tokenism in education and employment which potentially enable us to more effectively fight our oppression.

A combined anti-racist and anti-sexist position drew us together initially, and as we developed politically we addressed ourselves to heterosexism and economic oppression under capItalism.

2. What We Believe

Above all else, Our politics initially sprang from the shared belief that Black women are inherently valuable, that our liberation is a necessity not as an adjunct to somebody else's but because of our need as human persons for autonomy. This may seem so obvious as to sound simplistic, but it is apparent that no other ostensibly progressive movement has ever consIdered our specific oppression as a priority or worked seriously for the ending of that oppression. Merely naming the pejorative stereotypes attributed to Black women (e.g., mammy, matriarch, Sapphire, whore, bulldagger), let alone cataloguing the cruel, often murderous, treatment we receive, Indicates how little value has been placed upon our lives during four centuries of bondage in the Western hemisphere. We realize that the only people who care enough about us to work consistently for our liberation are us. Our politics evolve from a healthy love for ourselves, our sisters and our community which allows us to continue our struggle and work.

This focusing upon our own oppression is embodied in the concept of identity politics. We believe that the most profound and potentially most radical politics come directly out of our own identity, as opposed to working to end somebody else's oppression. In the case of Black women this is a particularly repugnant, dangerous, threatening, and therefore revolutionary concept because it is obvious from looking at all the political movements that have preceded us that anyone is more worthy of liberation than ourselves. We reject pedestals, queenhood, and walking ten paces behind. To be recognized as human, levelly human, is enough.

We believe that sexual politics under patriarchy is as pervasive in Black women's lives as are the politics of class and race. We also often find it difficult to separate race from class from sex oppression because in our lives they are most often experienced simultaneously. We know that there is such a thing as racial-sexual oppression which is neither solely racial nor solely sexual, e.g., the history of rape of Black women by white men as a weapon of political repression.

Although we are feminists and Lesbians, we feel solidarity with progressive Black men and do not advocate the fractionalization that white women who are separatists demand. Our situation as Black people necessitates that we have solidarity around the fact of race, which white women of course do not need to have with white men, unless it is their negative solidarity as racial oppressors. We struggle together with Black men against racism, while we also struggle with Black men about sexism.

We realize that the liberation of all oppressed peoples necessitates the destruction of the political-economic systems of capitalism and imperialism as well as patriarchy. We are socialists because we believe that work must be organized for the collective benefit of those who do the work and create the products, and not for the profit of the bosses. Material resources must be equally distributed among those who create these resources. We are not convinced, however, that a socialist revolution that is not also a feminist and anti-racist revolution will guarantee our liberation. We have arrived at the necessity for developing an understanding of class relationships that takes into account the specific class position of Black women who are generally marginal in the labor force, while at this particular time some of us are temporarily viewed as doubly desirable tokens at white-collar and professional levels. We need to articulate the real class situation of persons who are not merely raceless, sexless workers, but for whom racial and sexual oppression are significant determinants in their working/economic lives. Although we are in essential agreement with Marx's theory as it applied to the very specific economic relationships he analyzed, we know that his analysis must be extended further in order for us to understand our specific economic situation as Black women.

A political contribution which we feel we have already made is the expansion of the feminist principle that the personal is political. In our consciousness-raising sessions, for example, we have in many ways gone beyond white women's revelations because we are dealing with the implications of race and class as well as sex. Even our Black women's style of talking/testifying in Black language about what we have experienced has a resonance that is both cultural and political. We have spent a great deal of energy delving into the cultural and experiential nature of our oppression out of necessity because none of these matters has ever been looked at before. No one before has ever examined the multilayered texture of Black women's lives. An example of this kind of revelation/conceptualization occurred at a meeting as we discussed the ways in which our early intellectual interests had been attacked by our peers, particularly Black males. We discovered that all of us, because we were "smart" had also been considered "ugly," i.e., "smart-ugly." "Smart-ugly" crystallized the way in which most of us had been forced to develop our intellects at great cost to our "social" lives. The sanctions In the Black and white communities against Black women thinkers is comparatively much higher than for white women, particularly ones from the educated middle and upper classes.

As we have already stated, we reject the stance of Lesbian separatism because it is not a viable political analysis or strategy for us. It leaves out far too much and far too many people, particularly Black men, women, and children. We have a great deal of criticism and loathing for what men have been socialized to be in this society: what they support, how they act, and how they oppress. But we do not have the misguided notion that it is their maleness, per se—i.e., their biological maleness—that makes them what they are. As Black women we find any type of biological determinism a particularly dangerous and reactionary basis upon which to build a politic. We must also question whether Lesbian separatism is an adequate and progressive political analysis and strategy, even for those who practice it, since it so completely denies any but the sexual sources of women's oppression, negating the facts of class and race.

3. Problems in Organizing Black Feminists

During our years together as a Black feminist collective we have experienced success and defeat, joy and pain, victory and failure. We have found that it is very difficult to organize around Black feminist issues, difficult even to announce in certain contexts that we are Black feminists. We have tried to think about the reasons for our difficulties, particularly since the white women's movement continues to be strong and to grow in many directions. In this section we will discuss some of the general reasons for the organizing problems we face and also talk specifically about the stages in organizing our own collective.

The major source of difficulty in our political work is that we are not just trying to fight oppression on one front or even two, but instead to address a whole range of oppressions. We do not have racial, sexual, heterosexual, or class privilege to rely upon, nor do we have even the minimal access to resources and power that groups who possess any one of these types of privilege have.

The psychological toll of being a Black woman and the difficulties this presents in reaching political consciousness and doing political work can never be underestimated. There is a very low value placed upon Black women's psyches in this society, which is both racist and sexist. As an early group member once said, "We are all damaged people merely by virtue of being Black women." We are dispossessed psychologically and on every other level, and yet we feel the necessity to struggle to change the condition of all Black women. In "A Black Feminist's Search for Sisterhood," Michele Wallace arrives at this conclusion:

> We exist as women who are Black who are feminists, each stranded for the moment, working independently because there is not yet an environment in this society remotely congenial to our struggle—because,

being on the bottom, we would have to do what no one else has done: we would have to fight the world.

Wallace is pessimistic but realistic in her assessment of Black feminists' position, particularly in her allusion to the nearly classic isolation most of us face. We might use our position at the bottom, however, to make a clear leap into revolutionary action. If Black women were free, it would mean that everyone else would have to be free since our freedom would necessitate the destruction of all the systems of oppression.

Feminism is, nevertheless, very threatening to the majority of Black people because it calls into question some of the most basic assumptions about our existence, i.e., that sex should be a determinant of power relationships. Here is the way male and female roles were defined in a Black nationalist pamphlet from the early 1970s:

> We understand that it is and has been traditional that the man is the head of the house. He is the leader of the house/nation because his knowledge of the world is broader, his awareness is greater, his understanding is fuller and his application of this information is wiser . . . After all, it is only reasonable that the man be the head of the house because he is able to defend and protect the development of his home . . . Women cannot do the same things as men—they are made by nature to function differently. Equality of men and women is something that cannot happen even in the abstract world. Men are not equal to other men, i.e., ability, experience or even understanding. The value of men and women can be seen as in the value of gold and silver—they are not equal but both have great value. We must realize that men and women are a complement to each other because there is no house/family without a man and his wife. Both are essential to the development of any life.

The material conditions of most Black women would hardly lead them to upset both economic and sexual arrangements that seem to represent some stability in their lives. Many Black women have a good understanding of both sexism and racism, but because of the everyday constrictions of their lives, cannot risk struggling against them both.

The reaction of Black men to feminism has been notoriously negative. They are, of course, even more threatened than Black women by the possibility that Black feminists might organize around our own needs. They realize that they might not only lose valuable and hardworking allies in their struggles but that they might also be forced to change their habitually sexist ways of interacting with and oppressing Black women. Accusations that Black feminism divides the Black struggle are powerful deterrents to the growth of an autonomous Black women's movement.

Still, hundreds of women have been active at different times during the three-year existence of our group. And every Black woman who came, came out of a strongly-felt need for some level of possibility that did not previously exist in her life.

When we first started meeting early in 1974 after the NBFO first eastern regional conference, we did not have a strategy for organizing, or even a focus. We just wanted to see what we had. After a period of months of not meeting, we began to meet again late in the year and started doing an intense variety of consciousness-raising. The overwhelming feeling that we had is that after years and years we had finally found each other. Although we were not doing political work as a group, individuals continued their involvement in Lesbian politics, sterilization abuse and abortion rights work, Third World Women's International Women's Day activities, and support activity for the trials of Dr. Kenneth Edelin, Joan Little, and Inéz García. During our first summer when membership had dropped off considerably, those of us remaining devoted serious discussion to the possibility of opening a refuge for battered women in a Black community. (There was no refuge in Boston at that time.) We also decided around that time to become an independent collective since we had serious disagreements with NBFO's bourgeois-feminist stance and their lack of a clear politIcal focus.

We also were contacted at that time by socialist feminists, with whom we had worked on abortion rights activities, who wanted to encourage us to attend the National Socialist Feminist Conference in Yellow Springs. One of our members did attend and despite the narrowness of the ideology that was promoted at that particular conference, we became more aware of the need for us to understand our own economic situation and to make our own economic analysis.

In the fall, when some members returned, we experienced several months of comparative inactivity and internal disagreements which were first conceptualized as a Lesbian-straight split but which were also the result of class and political differences. During the summer those of us who were still meeting had determined the need to do political work and to move beyond consciousness-raising and serving exclusively as an emotional support group. At the beginning of 1976, when some of the women who had not wanted to do political work and who also had voiced disagreements stopped attending of their own accord, we again looked for a focus. We decided at that time, with the addition of new members, to become a study group. We had always shared our reading with each other, and some of us had written papers on Black feminism for group discussion a few months before this decision was made. We began functioning as a study group and also began discussing the possibility of starting a Black feminist publication. We had a retreat in the late spring which provided a time for both political discussion and working out interpersonal issues. Currently we are planning to gather together a collection of Black feminist writing. We feel that it is absolutely essential to demonstrate the reality of our politics to other Black women and believe that we can do this through writing and distributing our work. The fact that individual Black feminists are living in isolation all over the country, that our own numbers are small, and that we have some skills in writing, printing, and publishing makes us want to carry out these kinds of projects as a means of organizing Black feminists as we continue to do political work in coalition with other groups.

4. Black Feminist Issues and Projects

During our time together we have identified and worked on many issues of particular relevance to Black women. The inclusiveness of our politics makes us concerned with any situation that impinges upon the lives of women, Third World and working people. We are of course particularly committed to working on those struggles in which race, sex, and class are simultaneous factors in oppression. We might, for example, become involved in workplace organizing at a factory that employs Third World women or picket a hospital that is cutting back on already inadequate health care to a Third World community, or set up a rape crisis center in a Black neighborhood. Organizing around welfare and daycare concerns might also be a focus. The work to be done and the countless issues that this work represents merely reflect the pervasiveness of our oppression.

Issues and projects that collective members have actually worked on are sterilization abuse, abortion rights, battered women, rape and health care. We have also done many workshops and educationals on Black feminism on college campuses, at women's conferences, and most recently for high school women.

One issue that is of major concern to us and that we have begun to publicly address is racism in the white women's movement. As Black feminists we are made constantly and painfully aware of how little effort white women have made to understand and combat their racism, which requires among other things that they have a more than superficial comprehension of race, color, and Black history and culture. Eliminating racism in the white women's movement is by definition work for white women to do, but we will continue to speak to and demand accountability on this issue.

In the practice of our politics we do not believe that the end always justifies the means. Many reactionary and destructive acts have been done in the name of achieving "correct" political goals. As feminists we do not want to mess over people in the name of politics. We believe in collective process and a nonhierarchical distribution of power within our own group and in our vision of a revolutionary society. We are committed to a continual examination of our politics as they develop through criticism and self-criticism as an essential aspect of our practice. In her introduction to *Sisterhood Is Powerful* Robin Morgan writes:

> I haven't the faintest notion what possible revolutionary role white heterosexual men could fulfill, since they are the very embodiment of reactionary-vested-interest-power.

As Black feminists and Lesbians we know that we have a very definite revolutionary task to perform and we are ready for the lifetime of work and struggle before us.

Race, Gender, and the Prison Industrial Complex

BY ANGELA Y. DAVIS AND CASSANDRA SHAYLOR

Angela Y. Davis is an American political activist, philosopher, scholar, and author, and was a professor at the University of California, Santa Cruz, until her retirement. She is a founding member of Critical Resistance, an organization dedicated to prison abolition. Davis has received numerous awards, including the former Soviet Union's Lenin Peace Prize and was inducted into the National Women's Hall of Fame. Her co-writer Cassandra Shaylor is an activist lawyer who is also committed to prison abolition. In 1970, guns belonging to Davis were used in an armed takeover of a courtroom in Marin County, California, in which four people were killed. Davis was prosecuted for three capital felonies and held in jail for over a year before being acquitted in 1972. That experience informed much of her writing about the failures of the carceral state. With pieces like this article from 2001, Davis has since been a leading voice in the prison abolition movement. She takes an intersectional approach, examining how prisons reflect and reinforce the racist structures that shape our lives. She also identifies the myriad ways prisons fail the people held within them, from violence to inadequate healthcare to the erosion of human rights and dignity. And still, despite the carceral horrors the authors detail, Davis and Shaylor also highlight the ways women in prison want "to challenge the conditions of their confinement."

WOMEN'S RIGHTS AS HUMAN RIGHTS

A central achievement of the 1995 United Nations Fourth World Conference on Women in Beijing was the emphatic articulation of women's rights as human rights. In specifically identifying violence against women in both public and private life as an assault against women's human rights, the Beijing Conference helped to deepen awareness of violence against women on a global scale. Yet, even with this increasing attention, the violence linked to women's prisons remains obscured by the social invisibility of the prison. There, violence takes the form of medical neglect, sexual abuse, lack of reproductive control, loss of parental rights, denial of legal rights and remedies, the devastating effects of isolation, and, of course, arbitrary discipline.

Recent reports by international human rights organizations have begun to address the invisibility of women prisoners and to highlight the severity of the violence they experience. For example, Human Rights Watch and Amnesty International have specifically focused on the widespread problem of sexual abuse in United States' prisons. In 1999 the United Nations Special Rapporteur on Violence Against Women issued a report on her findings—which were even more disturbing than prison activists had predicted—from visits to eight women's prisons in the U.S. In general, although international human rights standards rarely have been applied within the context of the U.S., particularly in the legal arena, UN documents (such as the *International Covenant on Civil and Political Rights* and the *Standard Minimum Rules for the Treatment of Prisoners*) have been used productively by activists to underscore the gravity of human rights violations in women's prisons.

THE PRISON INDUSTRIAL COMPLEX

As prison populations have soared in the United States, the conventional assumption that increased levels of crime are the cause has been widely contested. Activists and scholars who have tried to develop more nuanced understandings of the punishment process—and especially racism's role—have deployed the concept of the "prison industrial complex" to point out that the proliferation of prisons and prisoners is more clearly linked to larger economic and political structures and ideologies than to individual criminal conduct and efforts to curb "crime." Indeed, vast numbers of corporations with global markets rely on prisons as an important source of profit and thus have acquired clandestine stakes in the continued expansion of the prison system. Because the overwhelming majority of U.S. prisoners are from racially marginalized communities, corporate stakes in an expanding apparatus of punishment necessarily rely on and promote old as well as new structures of racism.

Women especially have been hurt by these developments. Although women comprise a relatively small percentage of the entire prison population, they constitute, nevertheless, the fastest growing segment of prisoners. There are now more women in prison in the State of California alone than there were in the United States as a whole in 1970. Because race is a major factor in determining who goes to prison and who does not, the groups most rapidly increasing in number are black, Latina, Asian-American, and indigenous women.

Globalization of capitalism has precipitated the decline of the welfare state in industrialized countries, such as the U.S. and Britain, and has brought about structural adjustment in the countries of the southern region. As social programs in the U.S. have been drastically curtailed, imprisonment has simultaneously become the most self-evident response to many of the social problems previously addressed by institutions such as Aid to Families with Dependent Children (AFDC). In other words, in the era of the disestablishment of social programs that have historically served poor communities, and at a time when affirmative action programs are being dismantled and resources for education and health are declining, imprisonment functions as the default solution.

Especially for women of color, who are hardest hit by the withdrawing of social resources and their replacement with imprisonment, these draconian strategies—ever longer prison sentences for offenses that are often petty—tend to reproduce and, indeed, exacerbate the very problems they purport to solve.

There is an ironic but telling similarity between the economic impact of the prison industrial complex and that of the military industrial complex, with which it shares important structural features. Both systems simultaneously produce vast profits and social destruction. What is beneficial to the corporations, politicians, and state entities involved in these systems brings blight and death to poor and racially marginalized communities throughout the world. In the case of the prison industrial complex, the transformation of imprisoned bodies of color into consumers and/or producers of an immense range of commodities effectively transforms public funds into profit, leaving little in the way of social assistance to bolster the efforts of women and men who want to overcome barriers erected by poverty and racism. For example, when women who spend many years in prison are released, instead of jobs, housing, health care, and education, they are offered a small amount of release money, which covers little more than a bus ride and two nights in an inexpensive hotel. In the "free world," they are haunted by the stigma of imprisonment, which renders it extremely difficult for a "felon" to find a job. Thus they are inevitably tracked back into a prison system that in this era of the prison industrial complex has entirely dispensed with even a semblance of rehabilitation.

The emergence of a prison industrial complex means that whatever rehabilitative potential the prison may have previously possessed (as implied by the bizarre persistence of the term "corrections") is negated. Instead, the contemporary economics of imprisonment privilege the profitability of punishment at the expense of human education and transformation. State budgets increasingly are consumed by the costs of building and maintaining prisons, while monies dedicated to sustaining and improving communities are slashed. A glaring example of the misplaced financial investment in punishment is the decreasing state support for public education; for example, in California in 1995 the budget for prisons exceeded that for higher education.

Corporations are intimately linked to prison systems in both the public and the private sector. The trend toward privatization is only one manifestation of a growing involvement of corporations in the punishment process. While a myopic focus on private prisons in activist campaigns may tend to legitimate public prisons by default, placing this development within the context of a far-reaching prison industrial complex can enhance our under-standing of the contemporary punishment industry. In the U.S., there are currently twenty-six for-profit prison corporations that operate approximately 150 facilities in twenty-eight states. The largest of these companies, Corrections Corporations of America (CCA) and Wackenhut, control 76.4% of the private prison market globally. While CCA is headquartered in Nashville, Tennes-see, its largest shareholder is Sodexho Marriott, the multi-national headquartered in Paris, which provides catering services at many U.S. colleges and universities. Currently, CCA, Wackenhut and the other smaller private prison companies together bring in $1.5 to 2 billion a year.

Though private prisons represent a fairly small proportion of prisons in the U.S., the privatization model is quickly becoming the primary mode of organizing punishment in many other coun-tries. These companies have tried to take advantage of the ex-panding population of women prisoners, both in the U.S. and globally. In 1996, the first private women's prison was established by CCA in Melbourne, Australia. The government of Victoria

> adopted the U.S. model of privatization in which financing, design, construction, and ownership of the prison are awarded to one con-tractor and the government pays them back for construction over twenty years. This means that it is virtually impossible to remove the contractor because that contractor owns the prison.

However, to understand the reach of the prison industrial com-plex, it is not enough to evoke the looming power of the private prison business. Of course, by definition, those companies court the state inside and outside the U.S. for the purpose of obtaining prison contracts. They thus bring punishment and profit into a menacing embrace. Still, this is only the most visible dimension of the prison industrial complex, and it should not lead us to ignore the more comprehensive corporatization that is a feature of con-temporary punishment. As compared to earlier historical eras, the prison economy is no longer a small, identifiable and containable set of markets. Many corporations, whose names are highly rec-ognizable by "free-world" consumers, have discovered new possibilities for expansion by selling their products to correctional facilities.

> In the 1990s, the variety of corporations making money from prisons is truly dizzying, ranging from Dial Soap to Famous Amos cookies, from AT&T to health-care providers. . . . In 1995 Dial Soap sold $100,000 worth of its product to the New York City jail system alone. . . . When VitaPro Foods of Montreal, Canada, contracted to supply inmates in the State of Texas with its soy-based meat substitute, the contract was worth $34 million a year.

The point here is that even if private prison companies were prohibited—an unlikely prospect, indeed—the prison industrial complex and its many strategies for profit would remain intact.

Moreover, it is not only the private prison—CCA and Wackenhut in particular—that gets reproduced along the circuits of global capital and insinuates itself into the lives of poor people in various parts of the world. Connections between corporations and public prisons, similar to those in the U.S., are currently emerging throughout the world and are being reinforced by the contemporary idea, widely promoted by the U.S., that imprisonment is a social panacea. The most obvious effects of these ideas and practices on women can be seen in the extraordinary numbers of women arrested and imprisoned on drug charges throughout the world. The U.S.-instigated "war on drugs" has disproportionately claimed women as its victims inside the U.S., but also elsewhere in Europe, South America, the Caribbean, Asia, and Africa. In what can be seen as the penal equivalent of ambulance chasing, architectural firms, construction companies, and other corporations are helping to create new women's prisons throughout the world.

RACE, GENDER, AND THE PRISON INDUSTRIAL COMPLEX

Activist opposition to the prison industrial complex has insisted on an understanding of the ways racist structures and assumptions facilitate the expansion of an extremely profitable prison system, in turn helping to reinforce racist social stratification. This racism is always gendered, and imprisonment practices that are conventionally considered to be "neutral"—such as sentencing, punishment regimes, and health care—differ in relation to the ways race, gender, and sexuality intersect.

The women most likely to be found in U.S. prisons are black, Latina, Asian American, and Native American women. In 1998, one out of every 109 women in the U.S. was under the control of the criminal justice system. But where these women are located within the system differs according to their race: while about two thirds of women on probation are white, two thirds of women in prison are women of color. An African-American woman is eight times more likely to go to prison than a white woman; a Latina woman is four times more likely. African-American women make up the largest percentage of women in state prisons (48%) and federal detention centers (35%), even though they are only approximately 13% of the general population. As the population of Latinas in the U.S. grows, so does their number in prisons. In California, for example, though Latinas comprise 13% of the general population, they make up around 25% of women in prison. Though there is no official data maintained on the numbers of Native American women in prison, numerous studies document that they are arrested at a higher rate than whites and face discrimination at all levels of the criminal justice system.

Given the way in which U.S. government statistics fail to specify racial categories other than "white," "black," and "Hispanic" (figures regarding women who self-identify as Native American, Vietnamese, Filipina, Pacific Islander, or as from any other racially marginalized community, are consolidated into a category of "other"), it is difficult to provide precise numbers of women from these groups in prison. However, advocates for women prisoners report that the numbers of Asian women, including Vietnamese, Filipinas, and Pacific Islanders, are growing in women's prisons.

The vast increase in the numbers of women of color in U.S. prisons has everything to do with the "war on drugs." Two African-American women serving long federal sentences on questionable drug charges—Kemba Smith and Dorothy Gaines—were pardoned by President Bill Clinton during his last days in office. In the cases of both Smith, who received a twenty-four-and-a-half year sentence, and Gaines, whose sentence was nineteen years and seven months, their sole link to drug trafficking was their involvement with men who were accused traffickers.

Considering only the federal system, between 1990 and 1996, 84% of the increase in imprisoned women (2,057) was drug-related. In the entire complex of U.S. prisons and jails, drug-related convictions are largely to blame for the fact that black women are imprisoned at rates that are twice as high as their male counterparts and three times the rate of white women. Harsh sentencing laws, such as mandatory minimums attached to drug convictions and "three strikes" laws, which can result in a life sentence for a relatively minor drug offense, have created a trap door through which too many women of color have fallen into the ranks of disposable populations.

VIOLENCE AGAINST WOMEN IN PRISON

Dorothy Gaines and Kemba Smith were fortunate, but they are only two of the women incarcerated during the Clinton years, during which more women than ever were sentenced to prison. What happens to the vast numbers of women behind walls? In the first place, contrary to international human rights standards, imprisonment means much more than just a loss of freedom. Women's prisons are located on a continuum of violence that extends from the official practices of the state to the spaces of intimate relationships. Both public and private incarnations of this violence are largely hidden from public view. But while domestic violence increasingly is an issue of concern in public life, the violence of imprisonment rarely is discussed. Prisons are places within which violence occurs on a routine and constant basis; the functioning of the prison depends upon it. The threat of violence emanating from prison hierarchies is so ubiquitous and unpredictable that some women have pointed out the striking structural similarities between the experiences of imprisonment and battering relationships.

Though many women prisoners have indeed experienced intimate violence, the profile of "the woman prisoner" tends to imply that this victimization in the "free world" is the cause of imprisonment. Such a simplistic causal link fails to recognize the complex set of factors related to the social and political legitimation of violence against women, emphasizing *domestic* violence at the expense of an understanding of *state* violence—both in the "free world" and in the world of prison.

Violence in prison is directed at the psyche as well as the body. Increasingly, prisons in the U.S. are becoming a primary response to mental illness among poor people. The institutionalization of mentally ill people, historically, has been used more often against women than against men. However, for women who do not enter prison with mental problems, extended imprisonment is sure to create them. According to Penal Reform International,

> [l]ong term prisoners may develop mental and psychic disturbances by imprisonment itself and by being cut off from their families. Mental problems also arise and may become chronic in big prisons, where there is much overcrowding; where there are few activities; where prisoners have to stay a long time in their cells in daytime. . . .

Thus, this organization interprets the *Standard Minimum Rules for the Treatment of Prisoners* (SMR) as not only proscribing the incarceration of mentally ill persons in prisons, but as also calling for compassionate care by medical, psychological, and custodial staff of those who suffer mental and emotional problems as a consequence of imprisonment.

Most women in prison experience some degree of depression or post-traumatic stress disorder. Very often they are neither diagnosed nor treated, with injurious consequences for their mental health in and out of prison. Many women report that if they ask for counseling they are offered psychotropic medications instead. Despite legal challenges, prison regimes construct prisoners who suffer the effects of institutionalization as "sick" and in need of treatment with psychotropic drugs. Historically, this "medicalization model" has been most widely used against women.

As technologies of imprisonment become increasingly repressive and practices of isolation become increasingly routine, mentally ill women often are placed in solitary confinement, which can only exacerbate their condition. Moreover, women prisoners with significant mental illnesses frequently do not seek treatment because they fear harsh procedures (such as being placed in a "strip cell" if they say they are suicidal) and/or over-medication with psychotropic drugs. While women who have mental health concerns are mistreated, women with serious physical conditions often are labeled mentally ill in order to preempt their complaints—sometimes with grave consequences.

MEDICAL NEGLECT

At the historic legislative hearings recently conducted inside California women's prisons, prisoner Gloria Broxton declared: "They don't have the right to take my life because they thought I was worthless. I didn't come here to do my death sentence. I did a stupid thing, but I should not have to pay for it with my life." As Broxton's words indicate, she would probably not be dying of endometrial cancer today had she been granted earlier treatment. Violence is promoted by prison regimes, which also divest prisoners of the agency to contest them. The most salient example of this habitual violence is the lack of access to decent health care—in prison, medical neglect can result in death. Widely accepted interpretations of UN documents, such as the *Convention Against Torture, and Other Cruel, Inhuman or Degrading Treatment or Punishment*, and the *International Covenant on Civil and Political Rights*, and the *Standard Minimum Rules for the Treatment of Prisoners*, emphasize the importance of health care in prisons. "The level of health care in prison and medication should be at least equivalent to that in the outside community. It is a consequence of the government's responsibility for people deprived of their liberty and thus fully dependent on state authority."

Women in California prisons overwhelmingly have identified lack of access to medical information and treatment as their primary concern. At the hearings on conditions in women's prisons in California, witnesses reported that they often waited months to see a doctor and weeks for prescriptions to be refilled. For women with heart disease, diabetes, asthma, cancer, seizures, and HIV/AIDS, such delays in medication can cause serious medical complications or premature death. For example, Sherrie Chapman, an African-American woman imprisoned at the California Institution for Women, testified about extreme delays in treatment that led to the development of a terminal condition. Chapman sought diagnosis of breast lumps for ten years and was denied access to medical care. By the time she received treatment, she was subjected to a double mastectomy, and ten months later a hysterectomy. Despite the fact that at the time of the hearings her cancer had metastasized to her head and neck, she consistently was denied adequate pain management. As she testified: "I can't just go to the doctor and ask for help without being looked at and thought of as a manipulator, a drug seeker." Her requests for a compassionate release—in order to live with her mother until she dies—have been denied, and she will likely die in prison.

Tragically, all too often medical neglect in prison results in premature death. As Beverly Henry, a prisoner peer educator, testified:

> I have seen women die on my yard, women that I was very close to and women that I knew. If I could see that the whites of their eyes were as yellow as a caution sign, why couldn't somebody else? I watched a woman's waist grow from approximately 27 inches to 67 inches because her liver was cirrhoted [a sign of advanced liver failure]. She could not wear shoes, she looked nine months pregnant, and every day she asked me: "Am I gonna die here? Am I gonna die here? Do you think this is what is gonna happen to me?" And she died. And there was nothing we could do about it. And I know that something could have been done.

During an eight-week period at the end of 2000, nine women did, in fact, die in the Central California Women's Facility (CCWF) in Chowchilla, California. Though these women died of a variety of illnesses, all of their deaths were in some way attributable to severe medical neglect on the part of the prison. One of these women was Pamela Coffey, a forty-six-year-old African-American woman who complained of a mass on her side and swelling in her abdomen for several months but was denied medical treatment. On the night she died, she complained of extreme abdominal pain, swelling in her face and mouth, and numbness in her legs. Her roommates called for medical help, but for three hours no one came. She collapsed on the bathroom floor in her cell, and when a Medical Technical Assistant (MTA)—a guard with minimal medical training—finally arrived, he failed to examine her or to call for medical help. He left the cell, and Coffey's condition deteriorated. Her cellmates again called for help, but by the time the MTA arrived thirty minutes later, Coffey was dead. Prison staff then left her body in the cell for over an hour, further traumatizing her cellmates. Pamela Coffey's death exemplifies the severe medical neglect many women prisoners face, as well as the punishment all women are subjected to in an environment in which medical neglect is rampant. Many women are forced to watch other women deteriorate and sometimes die, and as a result must live in fear that they or someone they care about will be next.

Following the deaths, prison officials attempted to further criminalize the women who died by claiming that their deaths were attributable to illicit drug use in prison, despite the fact that there was no evidence to support such a claim. Prison administrators thus easily relied on widely circulating stereotypes of women prisoners as drug addicts—stereotypes fueled by the "war on drugs"—to demonize women who died as a result of medical neglect. Prison staff also instituted a new practice of treating the cell of a woman who called for medical help after hours as a "crime scene," which meant searching all of the women, upending the cell, and seizing property. Such a practice serves to make women fearful of calling for help because they or their cellmates will be punished. All of the women who died at CCWF were determined to have died of "natural" causes. Given that these premature deaths were preventable, they cannot be considered to be "natural." On the other hand, given that women prisoners are systematically denied appropriate health care leading to the development of serious illnesses and premature death, medical neglect and death in prison have become, sadly, all too "natural."

Women prisoners are consistently accused of malingering, and medical staff often use intimidation to dissuade them from seeking treatment. In order to complain about inadequate medical care, women must first file written grievances with the staff person with whom they have a problem. In other words, the recipient of the complaint is the only person who ostensibly can provide them with the care they need. Because there is only one doctor on each prison yard, women prisoners have told outside advocates that they rarely complain in order to avoid retaliation and the denial of treatment altogether. This process clearly violates the spirit of Rule thirty-six of the SMR, which encourages prison authorities to make confidential channels available to prisoners who decide to make complaints.

Beyond the ongoing epidemic of medical neglect of individual women prisoners, prisons also operate to create and exacerbate public health crises such as Hepatitis C Virus (HCV) and HIV. Lack of treatment and callous disregard for individual women's lives is even more frightening within the context of such massive infectious epidemics, HIV rates are at least ten times higher among prisoners than among people outside of prison, and the rate is higher among women prisoners than men. HCV has reached epidemic levels in California prisons—the California Department of Corrections estimates that 40% of the prison population is infected. Because the Department of Corrections regularly fails to test women for HCV or to provide information about prevention, advocates for women prisoners believe the numbers to be considerably higher. Not only is there a dearth of access to treatment but also to information about prevention. Women report that when they request to be tested for communicable diseases, they often do not get the results, even if they test positive. By virtue of this medical neglect, the prison promotes the spread of these diseases both inside prison and in the communities outside of prison to which women go when they are released.

Medical neglect in prison reflects and extends the lower value society places on the provision of preventative care and treatment to poor women of color outside of the prison. The abuse of women prisoners through medical neglect recapitulates a long history of inadequate healthcare for women, particularly women of color, which is often explicitly justified by sexist and racist ideologies.

REPRODUCTIVE RIGHTS

Reproductive health care in prisons is equally informed by these ideologies and often equally abysmal. Pregnant women are provided limited pre-natal care, and in several U.S. jurisdictions, women are shackled during labor. Women prisoners wait months, and sometimes years, to receive routine gynecological examinations that protect against the development of serious health conditions. For some women, these delays, combined with a consistent failure of prison medical staff to address treatable conditions early, result in the development of serious reproductive health problems. Theresa Lopez, a young Latina in her twenties, developed and died of cervical cancer, a condition that is easily treatable in its early stages, because prison medical staff failed to provide her with basic medical treatment.

In an interview with community activists recording women prisoners' oral histories, Davara Campbell described the politics of reproductive health in prisons:

> In the 1970s I was suffering severe menstrual cramps and a tilted uterus. As a young woman in the criminal justice system serving a life sentence complicated by medical female "disorders" and subject to misdiagnoses by questionable, unprofessional, unethical medical personnel, it was recommended I have a hysterectomy. I was maybe twenty-years-old. Having some enlightenment about genocide, I felt that the prospect of my being able to have a family was being threatened, so I escaped from prison to have a child. I had a son. He is now 28 years old, and I have four grandchildren who I would not have if I had given up my rights. Any imposition upon reproductive rights is an injustice against the well-being of family units—the rights of women, children, and grandchildren, or the promise of the future.

As this account highlights, gynecological and reproductive health services in prisons are inadequate at best, dangerous and life-threatening at worst. Inside prisons, women are subject to substandard gynecological care that sometimes results in loss of reproductive capacity or leads to premature death. Often this inadequate care amounts to practices of sterilization, as Campbell's analysis highlights. The use of sterilization as a "solution" to women's gynecological problems resonates with racist practices that women of color in the U.S. have experienced historically.

In the contemporary efforts to justify the abolition of welfare, continuing accusations of over-reproduction directed at African-American and Latina single mothers legitimize differential claims to reproductive rights. Racist ideologies circulating outside prisons then enable the kinds of assaults on women's reproductive capacities inside prisons that are reminiscent of earlier historical eras, such as the forced sterilization of Puerto Rican and Native American women and forced reproduction of enslaved black women. Thus prisons operate as sites where those reproductive rights putatively guaranteed to women in the "free world" are often systematically ignored, especially where women of color are concerned.

Gynecology is one of the most problematic areas in prison health care. Historical connections with racist gynecological practices continue to live on within the prison environment. More generally, to say that imprisonment deleteriously affects the health of women is clearly a criticism of health care in women's prisons, conditions that have been abundantly documented by legal and human rights organizations. But it is also to raise questions about the inertia that appears to prevent significant change in health care conditions, even when there is acknowledgment that such change is necessary. Why, for example, do accusations of sexual abuse continue to hover around medical regimes in women's prisons? Why have women prisoners complained for many decades about the difficulty of gaining access to skilled medical personnel? One of the ways to answer these questions is to look at the prison as a receptacle for obsolete practices—a site where certain practices, even when discredited in the larger society, acquire a second life.

There are children and families left behind in the "free world" on whom the imprisonment of women undoubtedly has a devastating impact. Almost 80% of women in prison have children for whom they were the primary caretakers before their imprisonment. The removal of a significant number of women of color, coupled with the alarming rates of incarceration for their male counterparts, has a disabling effect on the ability of poor communities to support families, whatever their constellation. When mothers are arrested, children are often placed in foster care and, in line with new laws, such as the Adoption and Safe Families Act of 1997, many are streamlined into adoption. All ties with birth mothers and extended families are thus systematically severed. In many instances, this process tracks children into juvenile detention centers and from there into adult prisons. For women who are reunited with their children upon release, the challenges for them are amplified by new welfare reform guidelines that prevent a former prisoner from receiving public benefits, including housing assistance. When previously imprisoned women are divested of their rights to social services—a move related to the political disenfranchisement of former prisoners in many states—they are effectively tracked back into the prison system. This is one of the modes of reproduction of the prison industrial complex.

SEXUAL HARASSMENT AND ABUSE

The development of putatively "feminist" campaigns by prison administrators has had deleterious consequences for women in prison. The assumption that formal gender equality inevitably leads to better conditions for women is contradicted by the recent pattern of modeling the architecture, regimes and staff of women's prisons after the men's counterparts. The current tendency, for example, is to place gun towers in women's maximum-security units in order to render them equal to similar men's units. The hiring of male custodial staff, who have visual access at all times to women's cells—even when they are changing clothes—and to the showers, creates a climate that invites sexual abuse. In U.S. women's prisons, the ratio of male to female corrections staff is often two to one and sometimes three to one. Though this disproportion alone does not inevitably lead to abuse, the administration and culture of the prison creates an environment in which sexual abuse thrives.

Partly as a result of these increasingly repressive models, and partly because of the rampant sexist and racist ideologies that support and sustain women's prisons, routine sexual abuse and harassment amount to a veritable climate of terror. Among the many abuses women prisoners have identified are inappropriate pat searches (male guards pat searching and groping women), illegal strip searches (male guards observing strip searches of women), constant lewd comments and gestures, violations of their right to privacy (male guards watching women in showers and toilets), and in some instances, sexual assault and rape.

According to international human rights standards, the rape of a woman in custody is an act of torture. Furthermore, violations of rights to privacy and preservation of human dignity are protected by the *International Covenant on Civil and Political Rights*. Recent studies by human rights organizations have confirmed that these international standards are routinely violated in U.S. prisons. Human Rights Watch, for example, found that sexual abuse is often related to perceived sexual orientations of prisoners. Sexual abuse is also frequently linked to medical practices. Many women in California prisons have indicated that they avoid much-needed medical treatment because male doctors can force them to submit to inappropriate pelvic examinations regardless of their symptoms. However, only a small proportion of sexually harassed women report these incidents to prison authorities, not only because staff perpetrators are rarely disciplined, but also because they themselves may suffer retaliation.

Sexual harassment and abuse are also linked to the new technologies of imprisonment. For example, the rapidly proliferating "supermax units," which isolate prisoners in individual cells for twenty-three out of twenty-four hours a day, render women even more vulnerable to sexual assault and harassment. In a legal interview, Regina Johnson, a thirty-six-year-old African-American woman in the Security Housing Unit at Valley State Prison for Women in Chowchilla, California, reported being required to expose her breasts to a male guard in order to obtain necessary hygiene supplies.

"Cell extractions," a practice linked to the "supermax," involve subduing a prisoner, usually by means of restraints, and performing a strip-search before removing her from her cell. The involvement of male guards—although female guards also participate—especially imbues cell extractions with a very real potential for sexual abuse.

In the State of Arizona, the sheriff in Maricopa County has installed video cameras in the women's holding and search cells in the county jail; he broadcasts live footage of women in these cells on the internet at <www.crime.com>. Though such prurient monitoring is unacceptable in any detention setting, it is particularly disturbing in the jail setting because many of these women are pre-trial detainees who have not been found guilty of any crime and, therefore, presumably are not yet to be subjected to any form of punishment.

POLICING SEXUALITY

Such sexual harassment of women, in the guise of being "tough on crime," illustrates the myriad ways in which prisons attempt to control women and their sexuality through sexual violence. In the sexualized environment of the prison, prison guards and staff learn not to fear sanctions for being sexually abusive to women. At the same time, women's sexuality, both inside and outside of prison, is policed and punished. A significant number of women enter the prison system as a direct result of the criminalization of sexual practices. Laws against sex work in most United States' jurisdictions result in the arrest and conviction of thousands of poor women. Sex workers most often arrested work the streets, as opposed to working in organized environments such as brothels, parlors, or escort services. Street workers, who are disproportionately women of color, are most likely to land in jail. In several states, there is now a charge of "felony prostitution" for sex workers with a known HIV-positive status, carrying a mandatory minimum sentence of four years. The criminalization of sex work creates a cycle of imprisonment: women are arrested, sentenced to jail time and often charged heavy fines and court fees, which then force them back onto the streets only to be arrested again.

Such criminalization of women's sexuality begins at a young age; girls are now the fastest growing population in the juvenile justice system. Most often these girls are arrested for "status offenses," which include truancy, underage drinking, breaking curfew, running away, and prostitution. Boys are less likely to be arrested for similar behavior, reflecting an obvious gender bias, but race determines which girls will actually end up in juvenile hall. As in the prison system, communities of color are represented disproportionately in juvenile justice systems. Almost half of girls in juvenile detention in the United States are African American and 13% are Latina. While seven out of ten cases involving white girls are dropped, only three out of ten cases involving African-American girls are dismissed. This increasing imprisonment of girls occurs despite the fact that the juvenile crime rate, particularly violent crime, has continued to decline since 1994. The targeting of girls of color for imprisonment in juvenile detention is a precursor to their later entrapment in women's prisons, because a majority of women in prison first entered the prison system as girls.

The anxieties about women's sexualities that circulate outside of the prison, and often lead to women's criminalization, are exacerbated and foregrounded within the prison. Guards and staff sexualize the space of the prison through their abuse of women, and in so doing not only cast women prisoners as criminal but also as sexually available.

At least since the publication of Rose Giallombardo's *Society of Women: A Study of a Women's Prison* (1966), the most salient characteristic of women's prisons is assumed to be women's intimate and sexual involvement with each other. Yet the ideological presumption of heterosexuality is policed more systematically than in the free world. Women's prisons have rules against "homosecting"—a term used within prisons to refer to same-sex sexual practices among prisoners. The racism and sexism associated with prison regimes intersect in the construction of women of color as hyper-deviant, and the addition of heterosexism means that lesbians of color face a triple jeopardy. A Latina lesbian couple at Valley State Prison for Women reported in a legal interview that masculine-identified prisoners are targeted for verbal harassment and sometime physical assault by male guards, while their feminine-identified partners are sexually harassed by those same guards. This gendered form of harassment exemplifies the ways in which gender identity is rigidly policed inside prisons.

ORGANIZING FOR CHANGE

Despite the significant obstacles encountered by those who want to challenge conditions of their confinement, especially through traditional legal methods, women prisoners find many ways to meaningfully organize and contest the injustices of imprisonment. In many states, women prisoners organize formal or informal peer networks that provide information and support on a wide range of issues, including health care prevention and treatment, child custody, labor conditions, and legal rights. In New York, women at Bedford Hills Correctional Facility organized a program called AIDS Counseling and Education (ACE), which provides prevention and treatment education and support to women in prison about HIV and AIDS. In California, peer educators have organized against the spread of HIV and HCV in prison and have provided health care information about a variety of medical conditions. Women prisoners have also filed individual and class action lawsuits demanding protection of their legal and human rights. In Washington, D.C., Massachusetts, and Michigan, for example, women successfully organized lawsuits challenging systemic sexual abuses in state prisons. The Legislative Hearings in October 2000 marked the first time in the history of California that proceedings were conducted inside women's prisons with prisoners serving as the primary witnesses. Approximately twenty women testified at two institutions on medical neglect, sexual assault, battered women's issues, and separation from their children and families. As a result of this testimony, two bills were introduced in the California legislature that will potentially have a far-reaching impact on health care in California prisons.

Advocates for women in prison are increasingly locating their efforts to ameliorate conditions of confinement within the frame of a broader resistance to the prison industrial complex. Human rights instruments are deployed to emphasize the systematic denial of human rights further exacerbated by the contemporary corporatization of punishment. However, the strategic goal of this work is not to create better prisons but rather to abolish prisons insofar as they function as a default solution for a vast range of social problems that need to be addressed by other institutions. It is within this context that the most far-reaching challenges are emerging to the racism that has been bolstered by the expansion of prisons. In California, for example, a number of groups work collaboratively to develop more radical approaches of working with and for women in prison. Justice Now is an organization that actively contests violence against women in prison and its connections to the prison industrial complex by training students, family members, and community members to provide direct services to women prisoners in California in conjunction with community-based education, media, and policy campaigns. The California Coalition for Women Prisoners organizes activist campaigns with and for women prisoners to raise awareness about inhumane conditions and advocate for positive changes. Legal Services for Prisoners with Children provides civil legal services to women prisoners, support to prisoner family members, and it also organizes in the communities from which prisoners come. California Prison Focus investigates and exposes human rights violations in California prisons, in particular those in Security Housing Units and supermax prisons. Critical Resistance (CR) builds national campaigns framed by analyses of the prison industrial complex that foreground the intersections of race, gender, and class. In the course of these campaigns, CR encourages people to envision social landscapes where ubiquitous state punishment will have been replaced by free education, health care, and drug rehabilitation, as well as affordable housing and jobs.

While national campaigns are rapidly advancing in the U.S., the World Conference Against Racism, Racial Discrimination, Xenophobia, and Related Intolerance provides a major opportunity to learn from and share experiences with organizations in other parts of the world. Greater emphasis must be placed on the global reach of the prison industrial complex and the further proliferation of the gendered racism it encourages. It is especially important that the punishment industry be seen as a significant component of the developing global political economy. An overarching recommendation for action thus calls for international networking among organizations that acknowledge the link between prisons and racism and that locate the important work of providing services to imprisoned women within a strong anti-corporate and anti-racist framework.

Further recommendations for action include the decriminalization of drug use and the establishment of free drug rehabilitation programs that are not tied to criminal justice agencies and procedures. This would drastically decrease the number of women in prison. In conjunction with these decarceration strategies, local and transnational campaigns to prevent the construction of new public and private prisons are also necessary. Legislation is needed that makes state and federal governments, as well as individual perpetrators, responsible for sexual abuse and harassment of women prisoners. In line with human rights standards, women's reproductive and family rights must be guaranteed. This means that civilian boards with enforcement powers should be established to review and act upon the grievances of women prisoners, especially those involving medical neglect, arbitrary discipline, and sexual abuse. In general, more widespread education and media campaigns are needed to expand and deepen awareness of the central role women's prisons play throughout the world in perpetuating misogyny, poverty, and racism.

The Uses of Anger

BY AUDRE LORDE

Audre Lorde was a brilliant American poet, essayist, novelist, librarian, and Black feminist activist. Lorde received numerous awards for her work, including a 1989 National Book Award for *A Burst of Light*. She and her work have been absolutely formative in my feminist evolution and growth as a writer. She was probably the first Black lesbian feminist I ever read, and in her writing, I found a way forward. I found connection. I understood I was not alone as a Black woman who loved women. Lorde's writing, from her poetry to essays and novels, examined identity through the lens of Lorde's experience as a Black lesbian daughter of Grenadian immigrants. Lorde was active in the women's rights and civil rights movements and spoke out against the racism and sexism in both movements. This 1981 essay, "The Uses of Anger," not only calls on women to see their anger as powerful at a time when patriarchal culture called for civil discourse and for women to be silent, but demands white women do the work necessary to understand racism as a fundamentally feminist issue.

Racism. The belief in the inherent superiority of one race over all others and thereby the right to dominance, manifest and implied.

Women respond to racism. My response to racism is anger. I have lived with that anger, on that anger, beneath that anger, on top of that anger, ignoring that anger, feeding upon that anger, learning to use that anger before it laid my visions to waste, for most of my life. Once I did it in silence, afraid of the weight of that anger. My fear of that anger taught me nothing. Your fear of that anger will teach you nothing, also.

Women responding to racism means women responding to

anger, the anger of exclusion, of unquestioned privilege, of racial distortions, of silence, ill-use, stereotyping, defensiveness, mis-naming, betrayal, and coopting.

My anger is a response to racist attitudes, to the actions and presumptions that arise out of those attitudes. If in your dealings with other women your actions have reflected those attitudes, then my anger and your attendant fears, perhaps, are spotlights that can be used for your growth in the same way I have had to use learning to express anger for my growth. But for corrective surgery, not guilt. Guilt and defensiveness are bricks in a wall against which we will all perish, for they serve none of our futures.

Because I do not want this to become a theoretical discussion, I am going to give a few examples of interchanges between women that I hope will illustrate the points I am trying to make. In the interest of time, I am going to cut them short. I want you to know that there were many more.

For example:

- I speak out of a direct and particular anger at a particular academic conference, and a white woman comes up and says, "Tell me how you feel but don't say it too harshly or I cannot hear you." But is it my manner that keeps her from hearing, or the message that her life may change?

- The Women's Studies Program of a southern university invites a Black woman to read following a week-long forum on Black and white women. "What has this week given to you?" I ask. The most vocal white woman says, "I think I've gotten a lot. I feel Black women really understand me a lot better now; they have a better idea of where I'm coming from." As if understanding her lay at the core of the racist problem. These are the bricks that go into the walls against which we will bash our consciousness, unless we recognize that they can be taken apart.

- After fifteen years of a women's movement which professes to address the life concerns and possible futures of all women, I still hear, on campus after campus, "How can we address the issues of racism? No women of Color attended." Or, the other side of that statement, "We have no one in our department equipped to teach their work." In other words, racism is a Black women's problem, a problem of women of Color, and only we can discuss it.

- After I have read from my work entitled "Poems for Women in Rage" a white woman asks me, "Are you going to do anything with how we can deal directly with *our* anger? I feel it's so important." I ask, "How do you use *your* rage?" And then I have to turn away from the blank look in her eyes, before she can invite me to participate in her own annihilation. Because I do not exist to feel her anger for her.

- White women are beginning to examine their relationships to Black women, yet often I hear you wanting only to deal with the little colored children across the roads of childhood, the beloved nursemaid, the occasional second-grade classmate; those tender memories of what was once mysterious and intriguing or neutral. You avoid the childhood assumptions formed by the raucous laughter at Rastus and Oatmeal, the acute message of your mommy's handkerchief spread upon the park bench because I had just been sitting there, the indelible and dehumanizing portraits of Amos and Andy and your Daddy's humorous bedtime stories.

  I wheel my two-year-old daughter in a shopping cart through a supermarket in Eastchester in 1967 and a little white girl riding past in her mother's cart calls out excitedly, "Oh look, Mommy, a baby maid!" And your mother shushes you, but she does not correct you. And so, fifteen years later, at a conference on racism, you can still find that story humorous. But I hear your laughter is full of terror and dis-ease.

- At an international cultural gathering of women, a well-known white American woman poet interrupts the reading of the work of women of Color to read her own poem, and then dashes off to an "important panel."

- Do women in the academy truly want a dialogue about racism? It will require recognizing the needs and the living contexts of other

women. When an academic woman says, for instance, "I can't afford it," she may mean she is making a choice about how to spend
her available money. But when a woman on welfare says, "I can't
afford it," she means she is surviving on an amount of money that
was barely subsistence in 1972, and she often does not have
enough to eat. Yet the National Women's Studies Association here
in 1981 holds a Convention in which it commits itself to responding to racism, yet refuses to waive the registration fee for poor
women and women of Color who wished to present and conduct
workshops. This has made it impossible for many women of
Color—for instance, Wilmette Brown, of Black Women for
Wages for Housework—to participate in this Convention. And so
I ask again: Is this to be merely another situation of the academy
discussing life within the closed circuits of the academy?

To all the white women here who recognize these attitudes as
familiar, but most of all, to all my sisters of Color who live and
survive thousands of such encounters—to my sisters of Color who
like me still tremble their rage under harness, or who sometimes
question the expression of our rage as useless and disruptive (the
two most popular accusations), I want to speak about anger, my
anger, and what I have learned from my travels through its do-
minions.

*Everything can be used, except what is wasteful. You will need
to remember this, when you are accused of destruction.*
Every woman has a well-stocked arsenal of anger potentially
useful against those oppressions, personal and institutional,
which brought that anger into being. Focused with precision it
can become a powerful source of energy serving progress and
change. And when I speak of change, I do not mean a simple
switch of positions or a temporary lessening of tensions, nor the
ability to smile or feel good. I am speaking of a basic and radical
alteration in all those assumptions underlining our lives.

I have seen situations where white women hear a racist remark,
resent what has been said, become filled with fury, and remain silent, because they are afraid. That unexpressed anger lies within
them like an undetonated device, usually to be hurled at the first
woman of Color who talks about racism.

But anger expressed and translated into action in the service of our vision and our future is a liberating and strengthening act of clarification, for it is in the painful process of this translation that we identify who are our allies with whom we have grave differences, and who are our genuine enemies.

Anger is loaded with information and energy. When I speak of women of Color, I do not only mean Black women. We are also Asian American, Caribbean, Chicana, Latina, Hispanic, Native American, and we have a right to each of our names. The woman of Color who charges me with rendering her invisible by assuming that her struggles with racism are identical with my own has something to tell me that I had better learn from, lest we both waste ourselves fighting the truths between us. If I participate, knowingly or otherwise, in my sister's oppression and she calls me on it, to answer her anger with my own only blankets the substance of our exchange with reaction. It wastes energy I need to join with her. And yes, it is very difficult to stand still and to listen to another woman's voice delineate an agony I do not share, or even one in which I myself may have participated.

We speak in this place removed from the more blatant reminders of our embattlement as women. This need not blind us to the size and complexities of the forces mounting against us and all that is most human within our environment. We are not here as women examining racism in a political and social vacuum. We operate in the teeth of a system for whom racism and sexism are primary, established, and necessary props of profit. Women responding to racism is a topic so dangerous that when the local media attempt to discredit this Convention they choose to focus upon the provision of Lesbian housing as a diversionary device—as if the Hartford *Courant* dare not mention the topic chosen for discussion here, racism, lest it become apparent that women are in fact attempting to examine and to alter all the repressive conditions of our lives.

Mainstream communication does not want women, particularly white women, responding to racism. It wants racism to be accepted as an immutable given in the fabric of existence, like evening time or the common cold.

So we are working in a context of opposition and threat, the cause of which is certainly not the angers which lie between us, but rather that virulent hatred leveled against all women, people of Color, Lesbians and gay men, poor people—against all of us who are seeking to examine the particulars of our lives as we resist our oppressions, moving toward coalition and effective action.

Any discussion among women about racism must include the recognition and the use of anger. It must be direct and creative, because it is crucial. We cannot allow our fear of anger to deflect us nor to seduce us into settling for anything less than the hard work of excavating honesty; we must be quite serious about the choice of this topic and the angers entwined within it, because, rest assured, our opponents are quite serious about their hatred of us and of what we are trying to do here.

And while we scrutinize the often painful face of each other's anger, please remember that it is not our anger which makes me caution you to lock your doors at night, and not to wander the streets of Hartford alone. It is the hatred which lurks in those streets, that urge to destroy us all if we truly work for change rather than merely indulge in our academic rhetoric.

This hatred and our anger are very different. Hatred is the fury of those who do not share our goals, and its object is death and destruction. Anger is the grief of distortions between peers, and its object is change. But our time is getting shorter. We have been raised to view any difference other than sex as a reason for destruction, and for Black women and white women to face each other's angers without denial or immobilization or silence or guilt is in itself a heretical and generative idea. It implies peers meeting upon a common basis to examine difference, and to alter those distortions which history has created around difference. For it is those distortions which separate us. And we must ask ourselves: Who profits from all this?

Women of Color in America have grown up within a symphony of anguish at being silenced, at being unchosen, at knowing that when we survive, it is in spite of a whole world out there that takes for granted our lack of humanness, that hates our very existence, outside of its service. And I say "symphony" rather than "cacophony" because we have had to learn to orchestrate those furies so that they do not tear us apart. We have had to learn to move through them and use them for strength and force and insight within our daily lives. Those of us who did not learn this difficult lesson did not survive. And part of my anger is always libation for my fallen sisters.

Anger is an appropriate reaction to racist attitudes, as is fury when the actions arising from those attitudes do not change. To those women here who fear the anger of women of Color more than their own unscrutinized racist attitudes, I ask: Is our anger more threatening than the woman-hatred that tinges all the aspects of our lives?

It is not the anger of other women that will destroy us, but our refusals to stand still, to listen to its rhythms, to learn within it, to move beyond the manner of presentation to the substance, to tap that anger as an important source of empowerment.

I cannot hide my anger to spare you guilt, nor hurt feelings, nor answering anger; for to do so insults and trivializes all our efforts. Guilt is not a response to anger; it is a response to one's own actions or lack of action. If it leads to change then it can be useful, since it becomes no longer guilt but the beginning of knowledge. Yet all too often, guilt is just another name for impotence, for defensiveness destructive of communication; it becomes a device to protect ignorance and the continuation of things the way they are, the ultimate protection for changelessness.

Most women have not developed tools for facing anger constructively. CR groups in the past, largely white, dealt with how to express anger, usually at the world of men. And these groups were made up of white women who shared the terms of their oppressions. There was usually little attempt to articulate the genuine differences between women, such as those of race, color, class, and sexual identity. There was no apparent need at that time to examine the contradictions of self, woman, as oppressor. There was work on expressing anger, but very little on anger directed against each other. No tools were developed to deal with other women's anger except to avoid it, deflect it, or flee from it under a blanket of guilt.

I have no creative use for guilt, yours or my own. Guilt is only another way of avoiding informed action, of buying time out of the pressing need to make clear choices, out of the approaching storm that can feed the earth as well as bend the trees. If I speak to you in anger, at least I have spoken to you; I have not put a gun to your head and shot you down in the street; I have not looked at your bleeding sister's body and asked, "What did she do to deserve it?" This was the reaction of two white women to Mary

Church Terrell's telling of the lynching of a pregnant Black woman whose baby was then torn from her body. That was in 1921, and Alice Paul had just refused to publicly endorse the enforcement of the Nineteenth Amendment for all women—excluding the women of Color who had worked to help bring about that amendment.

The angers between women will not kill us if we can articulate them with precision, if we listen to the content of what is said with at least as much intensity as we defend ourselves from the manner of saying. Anger is a source of empowerment we must not fear to tap for energy rather than guilt. When we turn from anger we turn from insight, saying we will accept only the designs already known, those deadly and safely familiar. I have tried to learn my anger's usefulness to me, as well as its limitations.

For women raised to fear, too often anger threatens annihilation. In the male construct of brute force, we were taught that our lives depended upon the good will of patriarchal power. The anger of others was to be avoided at all costs, because there was nothing to be learned from it but pain, a judgment that we had been bad girls, come up lacking, not done what we were supposed to do. And if we accept our powerlessness, then of course any anger can destroy us.

But the strength of women lies in recognizing differences between us as creative, and in standing to those distortions which we inherited without blame but which are now ours to alter. The angers of women can transform differences through insight into power. For anger between peers births change, not destruction, and the discomfort and sense of loss it often causes is not fatal, but a sign of growth.

My response to racism is anger. That anger has eaten clefts into my living only when it remained unspoken, useless to anyone. It has also served me in classrooms without light or learning, where the work and history of Black women was less than a vapor. It has served me as fire in the ice zone of uncomprehending eyes of white women who see in my experience and the experience of my people only new reasons for fear or guilt. And my anger is no excuse for not dealing with your blindness, no reason to withdraw from the results of your own actions.

When women of Color speak out of the anger that laces so many of our contacts with white women, we are often told that we are "creating a mood of hopelessness," "preventing white women from getting past guilt," or "standing in the way of trusting communication and action." All these quotes come directly from letters to me from members of this organization within the last two years. One woman wrote, "Because you are Black and Lesbian, you seem to speak with the moral authority of suffering." Yes, I am Black and Lesbian, and what you hear in my voice is fury, not suffering. Anger, not moral authority. There is a difference.

To turn aside from the anger of Black women with excuses or the pretexts of intimidation, is to award no one power—it is merely another way of preserving racial blindness, the power of unaddressed privilege, unbreached, intact. For guilt is only yet another form of objectification. Oppressed peoples are always being asked to stretch a little more, to bridge the gap between blindness and humanity. Black women are expected to use our anger only in the service of other people's salvation, other people's learning. But that time is over. My anger has meant pain to me but it has also meant survival, and before I give it up I'm going to be sure that there is something at least as powerful to replace it on the road to clarity.

What woman here is so enamored of her own oppression, her own oppressed status, that she cannot see her heelprint upon another woman's face? What woman's terms of oppression have become precious and necessary as a ticket into the fold of the righteous, away from the cold winds of self-scrutiny?

I am a Lesbian woman of Color whose children eat regularly because I work in a university. If their full bellies make me fail to recognize my commonality with a woman of Color whose children do not eat because she cannot find work, or who has no children because her insides are rotted from home abortions and sterilization; if I fail to recognize the Lesbian who chooses not to have children, the woman who remains closeted because her homophobic community is her only life support, the woman who chooses silence instead of another death, the woman who is terrified lest my anger trigger the explosion of hers; if I fail to recognize them as other faces of myself, then I am contributing not only to each of their oppressions but also to my own, and the anger which stands between us then must be used for clarity and mutual empowerment, not for evasion by guilt or for further separation.

I am not free while any woman is unfree, even when her shackles are very different from my own. And I am not free as long as one person of Color remains chained. Nor is any one of you.

I speak here as a woman of Color who is not bent upon destruction, but upon survival. No woman is responsible for altering the psyche of her oppressor, even when that psyche is embodied in another woman. I have suckled the wolf's lip of anger and I have used it for illumination, laughter, protection, fire in places where there was no light, no food, no sisters, no quarter. We are not goddesses or matriarchs or edifices of divine forgiveness; we are not fiery fingers of judgment or instruments of flagellation; we are women always forced back upon our woman's power. We have learned to use anger as we have learned to use the dead flesh of animals; and bruised, battered, and changing, we have survived and grown and, in Angela Wilson's words, we *are* moving on. With or without uncolored women. We use whatever strengths we have fought for, including anger, to help define and fashion a world where all our sisters can grow. Where our children can love, and where the power of touching and meeting another woman's difference and wonder will eventually transcend the need for destruction.

For it is not the anger of Black women which is dripping down over this globe like a diseased liquid. It is not my anger that launches rockets, spends over sixty thousand dollars a second on missiles and other agents of war and death, pushes opera singers off rooftops, slaughters children in cities, stockpiles nerve gas and chemical bombs, sodomizes our daughters and our earth. It is not the anger of Black women which corrodes into blind, dehumanizing power, bent upon the annihilation of us all unless we meet it with what we have, our power to examine and to redefine the terms upon which we will live and work; our power to envision and to reconstruct, anger by painful anger, stone upon heavy stone, a future of pollinating difference and the earth to support our choices.

We welcome all women who can meet us, face to face, beyond objectification and beyond guilt.

Holding My Sister's Hand

BY BELL HOOKS

During her lifetime, bell hooks published more than thirty books and numerous scholarly articles, appeared in documentary films, and participated in public lectures. She has held positions as professor of African American studies and English at Yale University, associate professor of women's studies and American literature at Oberlin College, and distinguished lecturer of English literature at the City College of New York. In 2014, she founded the bell hooks Center at Berea College in Berea, Kentucky. The focus of bell hooks's writing was the intersectionality of race, capitalism, and gender, and what she describes as their ability to produce and perpetuate systems of oppression. In "Holding My Sister's Hand," a chapter from her 1994 book *Teaching to Transgress: Education as the Practice of Freedom*, hooks calls out racism in feminist movements and asks feminists both Black and white to confront the systemic racism from enslavement to the present day, and the ways it intersects with gendered oppression. The only way to achieve solidarity, she suggests, is to actively and openly engage in this confrontation. Of Black feminists, she writes, "We believed that true sisterhood would not emerge without radical confrontation, without feminist exploration and discussion of white female racism and black female response." As you might expect, these confrontations have often been fraught, and the work of achieving feminist solidarity is ongoing.

Patriarchal perspectives on race relations have traditionally evoked the image of black men gaining the freedom to be sexual with white women as that personal relationship which best exemplifies the connection between public struggle for racial equality and the private politics of racial intimacy. Racist fears that socially sanctioned romantic relationships between black men and white women would dismantle the white patriarchal family structure historically heightened the sense of taboo even as individuals chose to transgress boundaries. But sex between black men and white women, even when legally sanctioned through marriage, did not have the feared impact. It did not fundamentally threaten white patriarchy. It did not further the struggle to end racism. Making heterosexual sexual experience—particularly the issue of black men gaining access to the bodies of white women—the quintessential expression of racial liberation deflected attention away from the significance of social relations between white and black women, and of the ways this contact determines and affects race relations.

As a teenager in the late sixties, living in a racially segregated Southern town, I knew that black men who desired intimacy with white women, and vice versa, forged bonds. I knew of no intimacy, no deep closeness, no friendship between black and white women. Though never discussed, it was evident in daily life that definite barriers separated the two groups, making close friendship impossible. The point of contact between black women and white women was one of servant-served, a hierarchal, power-based relationship unmediated by sexual desire. Black women were the servants, and white women were the served.

In those days, a poor white woman who might never be in a position to hire a black woman servant would still, in all her encounters with black women, assert a dominating presence, ensuring that contact between the two groups should always place white in a position of power over black. The servant-served relationship was established in domestic space, in the household, within a context of familiarity and commonality (the belief that it was the female's role to tend the home was shared by white and black women). Given this similarity of positioning within sexist norms, personal contact between the two groups was carefully constructed to reinforce difference in status based on race. Recognizing class difference was not enough of a division; white women wanted their racial status affirmed. They devised strategies both subtle and overt to reinforce racial difference, to assert their superior positions. This was especially the case in households where white women remained home during the day while black female servants worked. White women might talk about "niggers" or enact ritualized scenarios focusing on race in order to stress differentiation in status, Even a small gesture—like showing a black servant a new dress that she would not be able to try on in a store because of Jim Crow laws—reminded all concerned of the difference in status based on race.

Historically, white female efforts to maintain racial dominance were directly connected to the politics of heterosexism within a white supremacist patriarchy. Sexist norms, which deemed white women inferior because of gender, could be mediated by racial bonding. Even though males, white and black, may have been most concerned with policing or gaining access to white women's bodies, the social reality white women lived was one in which white males did actively engage in sexual relationships with black women. In the minds of most white women, it was not important that the overwhelming majority of these liaisons were forged by aggressive coercion, rape, and other forms of sexual assault; white women saw black women as competitors in the sexual marketplace. Within a cultural setting where a white woman's status was overdetermined by her relationship to white men, it follows that white women desired to maintain clear separations between their status and that of black women. It was crucial that black women be kept at a distance, that racial taboos forbidding legal relations between the two groups be reinforced either by law or social opinion. (In those rare cases where slaveholding white men sought divorces to legitimate liaisons with black slave women, they were most often judged insane.) In a white supremacist patriarchy, that relationship which most threatened to disrupt, challenge, and dismantle white power its concomitant social order was the legalized union between a white man and a black woman. Slave testimony, as well as the diaries of southern white women, record incidents of jealousy, rivalry, and sexual competition between white mistresses and enslaved black women. Court records document that individual white men did try to gain public recognition of their bonds with black women either through attempts to marry or through efforts to leave property and money in wills. Most of these cases were contested by white family members. Importantly, white females were protecting their fragile social positions and power within patriarchal culture by asserting their superiority over black women. They were not necessarily trying to prevent white men from engaging in sexual relations with black women, for this was not in their power—such is the nature of patriarchy. So long as sexual unions with black women and white men took place in a nonlegalized context, within a framework of subjugation, coercion, and degradation, the split between white female's status as "ladies" and black women's representation as "whores" could be maintained. Thus to some extent, white women's class and race privilege was reinforced by the maintenance of a system where black women were the objects of white male sexual subjugation and abuse.

Contemporary discussions of the historical relationship between white and black women must include acknowledgment of the bitterness black slave women felt toward white women. They harbored understandable resentment and repressed rage about racial oppression, but they were particularly aggrieved by the overwhelming absence of sympathy shown by white women in circumstances involving sexual and physical abuse of black women as well as situations where black children were taken away from their enslaved mothers. Again it was within this realm of shared concern (white women knew the horror of sexual and physical abuse as well as the depth of a mother's attachment to her children) that the majority of white women who might have experienced empathic identification turned their backs on black women's pain.

Shared understanding of particular female experiences did not mediate relations between most white mistresses and black slave women. Though there were rare exceptions, they had little impact on the overall structure of relations between black and white women. Despite the brutal oppression of black female slaves, many white women feared them. They may have believed that, more than anything, black women wanted to change places with them, to acquire their social status, to marry their men. And they must have feared (given white male obsessions with black women) that, were there no legal and social taboos forbidding legalized relations, they would lose their status.

The abolition of slavery had little meaningful positive impact on relations between white and black women. Without the structure of slavery, which institutionalized, in a fundamental way, the different status of white and black women, white women were all the more concerned that social taboos uphold their racial superiority and forbid legalized relations between the races. They were instrumental in perpetuating degrading stereotypes about black womanhood. Many of these stereotypes reinforced the notion that black women were lewd, immoral, sexually licentious, and lacking in intelligence. White women had a closeness with black women in the domestic household that made it appear that they knew what we were really like; they had direct contact. Though there is little published material from the early twentieth century documenting white female perceptions of black women and vice versa, segregation diminished the possibility that the two groups might develop a new basis of contact with one another outside the realm of servant-served. Living in segregated neighborhoods, there was little chance that white and black women would meet one another on common, neutral ground.

The black woman who traveled from her segregated neighborhood into "unsafe" white areas, to work in the homes of white families, no longer had a set of familial relations, however tenuous, that were visible and known by white women employers as had been the case under slavery. The new social arrangement was as much a context for dehumanization as the plantation household, with the one relief that black women could return home. Within the social circumstance of slavery, white mistresses were sometimes compelled by circumstance, caring feelings, or concern for property to enter the black female's place of residence and be cognizant of a realm of experience beyond the servant-served sphere. This was not the case with the white female employer.

Racially segregated neighborhoods (which were the norm in most cities and rural areas) meant that black women left poor neighborhoods to work in privileged white homes. There was little or no chance that this circumstance would promote and encourage friendship between the two groups. White women continued to see black women as sexual competitors, ignoring white male sexual assault and abuse of black females. Although they have written poignant memoirs which describe affectional bonds between themselves and black female servants, white women often failed to acknowledge that intimacy and care can coexist with domination. It has been difficult for white women who perceive black women servants to be "like one of the family" to understand that the servant might have a completely different understanding of their relationship. The servant may be ever mindful that no degree of affection or care altered differences in status—or the reality that white women exercised power, whether benevolently or tyrannically.

Much of the current scholarship by white women focusing on relationships between black women domestics and white female employers presents perspectives that highlight positives, obscuring the ways negative interaction in these settings have created profound mistrust and hostility between the two groups. Black female servants interviewed by white women often give the impression that their relationships with white women employers had many positive dimensions. They say what they feel is the polite and correct version of reality, often suppressing truths. Again it must be remembered that exploitative situations can also be settings where caring ties emerge even in the face of domination (feminists should know this from the evidence that care exists in heterosexual relationships where men abuse women). Hearing Susan Tucker give an oral presentation discussing her book *Telling Memories Among Southern Women: Domestic Workers Employers in the Segregated South*, I was struck by her willingness to acknowledge that as a white child cared for by black women she remembered overhearing them expressing negative feelings about white women. She was shocked by their expressions of rage, enmity, and contempt. We both remembered a common declaration of black women: "I've never met a white woman over the age of twelve that I can respect." In contrast to her memories, Tucker's contemporary discussion paints a much more positive picture of the subject. Studies of black and white women's relationships must cease to focus solely on whether interaction between black servants and white female employers was "positive." If we are to understand our contemporary relations, we must explore the impact of those encounters on black women's perceptions of white women as a whole. Many of us who have never been white women's servants have inherited ideas about them from relatives and kin, ideas which shape our expectations and interactions.

My memories and present day awareness (based on conversations with my mother, who works as a maid for white women, and the comments and stories of black women in our communities) indicate that in "safe" settings black women highlight the negative aspects of working as servants for white women. They express intense anger, hostility, bitterness, and envy—and very little affection or care—even when they are speaking positively. Many of these women recognize the exploitative nature of their jobs, identifying ways they are subjected to various unnecessary humiliations and degrading encounters. This recognition may be the most salient feature in a situation where a black woman may also have good feelings about her white employer (Judith Rollins's book, *Between Women*, is a useful and insightful discussion of these relationships).

Whether talking with black domestics or nonprofessional black women, I find that the overwhelming perceptions of white women are negative. Many of the black women who have worked as servants in white homes, particularly during the times when white women were not gainfully employed, see white women as maintaining childlike, self-centered postures of innocence and irresponsibility at the expense of black women. Again and again, it was pointed out that the degree to which white women are able to turn away from domestic reality, from the responsibilities of child care and housework, whether they are turning away for careers or to have greater leisure, is determined by the extent to which black women, or some other underclass group, are bound to that labor, forced by economic circumstance to pick up the slack, to assume responsibility.

I found it ironic that black women often critiqued white women from a nonfeminist standpoint, emphasizing the ways in which white women were not worthy of being on pedestals because they were shiftless, lazy, and irresponsible. Some black women seemed to feel a particular rage that their work was "overseen" by white women whom they saw as ineffectual and incapable of performing the very tasks they were presiding over. Black women working as servants in white homes were in positions similar to those assumed by cultural anthropologists seeking to understand a different culture. From this particular insider vantage point, black women learned about white lifestyles. They observed all the details in white households, from furnishings to personal encounters. Taking mental notes, they make judgments about the quality of life they witnessed, comparing it to black experience. Within the confines of segregated black communities, they shared their perceptions of the white "other." Often their accounts were most negative when they described white women; they were able to study them much more consistently than white men, who were not always present. If the racist white world represented black women as sluts, then black women examined the actions of white women to see if their sexual mores were different. Their observations often contradicted stereotypes. Overall, black women have come away from encounters with white women in the servant-served relationship feeling confident that the two groups are radically different and share no common language. It is this legacy of attitudes and reflections about white women that is shared from generation to generation, keeping alive the sense of distance and separation, feelings of suspicion and mistrust. Now that interracial relationships between whites and blacks are more common, black women see white women as sexual competitors—irrespective of sexual preference—often advocating continued separation in the private sphere despite proximity and closeness in work settings.

Contemporary discussions of relationships between black women and white women (whether scholarly or personal) rarely take place in integrated settings. White women writing about their impressions in scholarly and confessional work often ignore the depth of enmity between the two groups, or see it as solely a black female problem. Many times in feminist circles I have heard white women talk about a particular black woman's hostility toward white females as though such feelings are not rooted in historical relations and contemporary interactions. Instead of exploring the reasons such hostility exists, or giving it any legitimacy as an appropriate response to domination or exploitation, they see the black woman as being difficult, problematic, irrational, and "insane." Until white women can confront their fear and hatred of black women (and vice versa), until we can acknowledge the negative history which shapes and informs our contemporary interaction, there can be no honest, meaningful dialogue between the two groups. The contemporary feminist call for sisterhood, the radical white woman's appeal to black women and all women of color to join the feminist movement, is seen by many black women as yet another expression of white female denial of the reality of racist domination, of their complicity in the exploitation and oppression of black women and black people. Though the call for sisterhood was often motivated by a sincere longing to transform the present, expressing white female desire to create a new context for bonding, there was no attempt to acknowledge history, or the barriers that might make such bonding difficult, if not impossible. When black women responded to the evocation of sisterhood based on shared experience by calling attention to both the past of racial domination and its present manifestations in the structure of feminist theory and the feminist movement, white women initially resisted the analysis. They assumed a posture of innocence and denial (a response that evoked memories in black women of negative encounters, the servant-served relationship). Despite flaws and contradictions in her analysis, Adrienne Rich's essay "'Disloyal to Civilization': Feminism, Racism, and Gynephobia" was groundbreaking in that it ruptured that wall of denial, addressing the issue of race and accountability. White women were more willing to "hear" another white woman talk about racism, yet it is their inability to listen to black women that impedes feminist progress.

Ironically, many of the black women who were actively engaged with feminist movement were talking about racism in a sincere attempt to create an inclusive movement, one that would bring white and black women together. We believed that true sisterhood would not emerge without radical confrontation, without feminist exploration and discussion of white female racism and black female response. Our desire for an honorable sisterhood, one that would emerge from the willingness of all women to face our histories, was often ignored. Most white women dismissed us as "too angry," refusing to reflect critically on the issues raised. By the time white women active in the feminist movement were willing to acknowledge racism, accountability, and its impact on the relationships between white women and women of color, many black women were devastated and worn out. We felt betrayed; white women had not fulfilled the promise of sisterhood. That sense of betrayal continues and is intensified by the apparent abdication of interest in forging sisterhood, even though white women now show interest in racial issues. It seems at times as though white feminists working in the academy have appropriated discussions of race and racism, while abandoning the effort to construct a space for sisterhood, a space where they could examine and change attitudes and behavior toward black women and all women of color.

With the increasing institutionalization and professionalization of feminist work focused on the construction of feminist theory and the dissemination of feminist knowledge, white women have assumed positions of power that enable them to reproduce the servant-served paradigm in a radically different context. Now black women are placed in the position of serving white female desire to know more about race and racism, to "master" the subject. Curiously, most white women writing feminist theory that looks at "difference" and "diversity" do not make white women's lives, works, and experiences the subject of their analysis of "race," but rather focus on black women or women of color. White women who have yet to get a critical handle on the meaning of "whiteness" in their lives, the representation of whiteness in their literature, or the white supremacy that shapes their social status are now explicating blackness without critically questioning whether their work emerges from an aware antiracist standpoint. Drawing on the work of black women, work that they once dismissed as irrelevant, they now reproduce the servant-served paradigms in their scholarship. Armed with their new knowledge of race, their willingness to say that their work is coming from a white perspective (usually without explaining what that means), they forget that the very focus on race and racism emerged from the concrete political effort to forge meaningful ties between women of different race and class groups. This struggle is often completely ignored. Content with the appearance of greater receptivity (the production of texts where white women discuss race is given as evidence that there has been a radical shift in direction), white women ignore the relative absence of black women's voices, either in the construction of new feminist theory or at feminist gatherings.

Talking with groups of women about whether they thought feminist movement has had a transformative impact on relations between white and black women, I heard radically different responses. Most white women felt there had been a change, that they were more aware of race and racism, more willing to assume accountability and engage in antiracist work. Black women and women of color were adamant that little had changed, that despite recent white female focus on race, racist domination is still a factor in personal encounters. They felt that the majority of white women still assert power even as they address issues of race. As one black woman put it, "It burns me up to be treated like shit by white women who are busy getting their academic recognition, promotions, more money, et cetera, doing 'great' work on the topic of race." Some black women I spoke with suggested that it was fear that their resources would be appropriated by white women that led them to avoid participating in feminist movement.

Fear and anger about appropriation, as well as concern that we not be complicit in reproducing servant-served relationships, have led black women to withdraw from feminist settings where we must have extensive contact with white women. Withdrawal exacerbates the problem: it makes us complicit in a different way. If a journal is doing a special issue on Black Women's Studies and only white women submit work, then black women cannot effectively challenge their hegemonic hold on feminist theory. This is only one example of many. Without our voices in written work and in oral presentations there will be no articulation of our concerns. Where are our books on race and feminism and other aspects of feminist theory, works which offer new approaches and understanding? What do we do to further the development of a more inclusive feminist theory and practice? What do we presume our role to be in the mapping of future direction for feminist movement? Withdrawal is not the answer.

Even though practically every black woman active in any aspect of feminist movement has a long record of horror stories documenting the insensitivity and racist aggression of individual white women, we can testify as well to those encounters that are positive, that enrich rather than diminish. Granted, such encounters are rare. They tend to take place with white women who are not in positions where they can assert power (which may be why these are seen as exceptional rather than as positive signs indicating the overall potential for growth and change, for greater togetherness).

Perhaps we need to examine the degree to which white women (and all women) who assume powerful positions rely on conventional paradigms of domination to reinforce and maintain that power.

Talking with black women and women of color I wanted to know what factors distinguish these relationships we have with white feminists which we do not see as exploitative or oppressive. A common response was that these relationships had two important factors: honest confrontation, and dialogue about race, and reciprocal interaction. Within the servant-served paradigm, it is usually white women who are seeking to receive something from black women, even if that something is knowledge about racism. When I asked individual white women who have friendships and positive work relations with black women in feminist settings what were the conditions enabling reciprocity, they responded by emphasizing that they had not relied on black women to force them to confront their racism. Somehow, assuming responsibility for examining their own responses to race was a precondition for relations on an equal footing. These women felt they approach women of color with knowledge about racism, not with guilt, shame, or fear. One white woman said that she starts from the standpoint of accepting and acknowledging that "white people always have racist assumptions that we have to deal with." Readiness to deal with these assumptions certainly makes forming ties with nonwhite women easier. She suggests that the degree to which a white woman can accept the truth of racist oppression—of white female complicity, of the privileges white women receive in a racist structure—determines the extent to which they can be empathic with women of color. In conversations I found that feminist white women from nonmaterially privileged backgrounds often felt their understanding of class difference made it easier for them to hear women of color talk about the impact of race, of domination, without feeling threatened. Personally, I find many of my deepest friendships and feminist bonds are formed with white women who come from working-class backgrounds or who are working class and understand the impact of poverty and deprivation.

I talked about writing this essay with a group of white female colleagues—all of them English professors—and they emphasized the fear many privileged white women have of black women. We all remembered Lillian Hellman's frank comments about her relationship with the black woman servant who was in her employ for many years. Hellman felt that this woman really exercised enormous power over her, admitting that it made her fear all black women. We talked about the fact that what many white women fear is being unmasked by black women. One white woman, from a working-class background, pointed out that black women servants witnessed the gap between white women's words and their deeds, saw contradictions and inadequacies. Perhaps contemporary generations of white women who do not have black servants, who never will, have inherited from their female ancestors the fear that black women have the power to see through their disguises, to see the parts of themselves they want no one to see. Though most of the white women present at this discussion do not have close friendships with black women, they would welcome the opportunity to have more intimate contact. Often black women do not respond to friendly overtures by white women for fear that they will be betrayed, that at some unpredictable moment the white woman will assert power. This fear of betrayal is linked with white female fear of exposure; clearly we need feminist psychoanalytic work that examines these feelings and the relational dynamics they produce.

Often black female fear of betrayal is not present when an individual white woman indicates by her actions that she is committed to antiracist work. For example, I once applied for a job in the Women's Studies program at a white women's college. The committee reviewing my application was all white. During the review process one of the reviewers felt that racism was shaping the nature and direction of the discussions, and she intervened. One gesture of intervention she made was to contact the black woman affirmative action officer so that there would be nonwhite participation in the discussion. Her commitment to feminist process and antiracist work informed her actions. She extended herself even though there was no personal gain. (Let's face it: opportunism has prevented many academic feminists from taking action that would force them to go against the status quo and take a stand.) Her actions confirmed for me both the power of solidarity and sisterhood. She did not play it safe. To challenge, she had to separate herself from the power and privilege of the group. One of the most revealing insights she shared was her initial disbelief that white feminists could be so blatantly racist, assuming that everyone in the group shared a common bond in "whiteness," the common acceptance that in an all-white group it was fine to talk about black people in stereotypical racist ways. When this process ended (I was offered the job), we talked about her sense that what she witnessed was white female fear that in the presence of black female power, their authority would be diminished. We talked about ways feelings allow many white women to feel more comfortable with black women who appear victimized or needy. We focused on ways white feminists sometimes patronize black women by assuming that it is understandable if we are not "radical," if our work on gender does not have a feminist standpoint. This condescension further estranges black and white women. It is an expression of racism.

Now that many white women engaged in feminist thinking and practice no longer deny the impact of race on the construction of gender identity, the oppressive aspects of racial domination, and white female complicity, it is time to move on to an exploration of the particular fears that inhibit meaningful bonding with black women. It is time for us to create new models for interaction that take us beyond the servant-served encounter, ways of being that promote respect and reconciliation. Concurrently, black women need to explore our collective attachment to rage and hostility toward white women. It may be necessary for us to have spaces where some of that repressed anger and hostility can be openly expressed so that we can trace its roots, understand it, and examine possibilities for transforming internalized anger into constructive, self-affirming energy we can use effectively to resist white female domination and forge meaningful ties with white female allies. Only when our vision is clear will we be able to distinguish sincere gestures of solidarity from actions rooted in bad faith. It may very well be that some black female rage toward white women masks sorrow and pain, anguish that it has been so difficult to make contact, to impress upon their consciousness our subjectivity. Letting go of some of the hurt may create a space for courageous contact without fear or blame.

If black women and white women continue to express fear and

rage without a commitment to move on through these emotions in order to explore new grounds for contact, our efforts to build an inclusive feminist movement will fail. Much depends on the strength of our commitment to feminist process and feminist movement. There have been so many feminist occasions where differences surface, and with them expressions of pain, rage, hostility. Rather than coping with these emotions and continuing to probe intellectually and search for insight and strategies of confrontation, all avenues for discussions become blocked and no dialogue occurs. I am confident that women have the skills (developed in interpersonal relations where we confront gender difference) to make productive space for critical dissent dialogue even as we express intense emotions. We need to examine why we suddenly lose the capacity to exercise skill and care when we confront one another across race and class differences. It may be that we give up so easily with one another because women have internalized the racist assumption that we can never overcome the barrier separating white women and black women. If this is so then we are seriously complicit. To counter this complicity, we must have more written work and oral testimony documenting ways barriers are broken down, coalitions formed, and solidarity shared. It is this evidence that will renew our hope and provide strategies and direction for future feminist movement.

Producing this work is not the exclusive task of white or black women; it is collective work. The presence of racism in feminist settings does not exempt black women or women of color from actively participating in the effort to find ways to communicate, to exchange ideas, to have fierce debate. If revitalized feminist movement is to have a transformative impact on women, then creating a context where we can engage in open critical dialogue with one another, where we can debate and discuss without fear of emotional collapse, where we can hear and know one another in the difference and complexities of our experience, is essential. Collective feminist movement cannot go forward if this step is never taken. When we create this woman space where we can value difference and complexity, sisterhood based on political solidarity will emerge.

In the Name of Beauty

BY TRESSIE MCMILLAN COTTOM

Tressie McMillan Cottom is a writer, sociologist, Mac-Arthur Fellow, and *New York Times* columnist whose work examines the cultural intersections of racism, sexism, and capitalism. Her essays, op-eds, and columns have been published in *The Atlantic*, *Vanity Fair*, and *Slate*, among many others. She previously co-hosted a Black feminist podcast, *Hear to Slay*, which examined pop culture, politics, and American culture through an intersectional lens always centering Black women. Her 2019 essay "In the Name of Beauty" interrogates the ways in which "beauty" as a category is created by capitalists, reiterated by white women in the name of "self-love," but is actually one of many forms of oppression. "As long as the beautiful people are white, what is beautiful at any given time can be renegotiated without redistributing capital from white to nonwhite people," McMillan Cottom writes. Rather than trying to conform, she offers a different path, one where Black women do not have to internalize ideas of beauty that were never meant for us.

Miley Cyrus was going through her dangerous phase. She had tattoos and piercings and dildos and so, of course, she also had to have some black affect to complete the package. It is all part of the pop star toolkit. I decided to write about it. Now, it is pretty common for people, sometimes lots of them, to respond to things I write. Sometimes they share heartbreaking stories of recognition. Other times, angry diatribes about what I get wrong while being black, a woman, and popular. But of all the things I have written, nothing has inspired more direct, intense emotional engagement than what I wrote about post-Disney pop star Miley Cyrus. What had me stuck—momentarily—wasn't just the heightened emotions of those who took me to task, but rather who was leading the charge.

I am accustomed to men and white people being angry with me. That is par for the course. But when black women are mad at me it is a special kind of contrition, and I take the time to figure out my responsibility. Something clearly wasn't registering in this scenario, because black women were giving me the business.

Sisters weren't really angry about my breakdown of just how dangerous Miley Cyrus's performance on a televised award show actually was. They weren't exactly angry that I pointed out the size and shape of the black woman dancers behind her. What many black women were angry about was how I located myself in what I'd written. I said, blithely as a matter of observable fact, that I am unattractive. Because I am unattractive, the argument went, I have a particular kind of experience of beauty, race, racism, and interacting with what we might call the white gaze. I thought nothing of it at the time I was writing it, which is unusual. I can usually pinpoint what I have said, written, or done that will piss people off and which people will be pissed off. I missed this one entirely.

The comments were brutal and feedback wasn't confined to the internet. Things got personal. One black male colleague emailed me to say how a black woman friend told him she did not want to read some trash article about how ugly I am when my accompanying picture belied the claim. It was, she insinuated, an appeal for public validation of my physical attractiveness. I did not think that was true, but I was raised right. I told him that was fair and drank myself to sleep. Someone else sent me a link to a Facebook group where many women, but especially more than a few black women, took me to task for hating myself. The person who sent it did not know that I was already a member of the group and had been watching the carnage for days. I never mentioned it.

A few months after the essay had been published, I was scheduled to deliver the Mason Sankora Lecture for the Department of English at my alma mater, a historically black college. It was a brutal experience because an HBCU is a special place. I am not the first to acknowledge that, of course. You can learn all about the legacy, the culture, the challenges, and the faults of black colleges in books, articles, movies, television shows, and documentaries. But few of those things have ever described the primary reason why HBCUs are so special to me.

When I was eleven years old, my waist caved in and my breasts sprung out. I could not be left alone at the school bus stop anymore. It was dangerous because men can be dangerous. I had some preparation for that. My mother had been, I believe, sexually victimized as a child. She doesn't speak of it except when her sentences fade out in retelling certain stories. But it was there in how protective she was of me, an only child of a single mother. There were no men allowed in our house except for family and even then only under her direct guidance. "I wanted your home to be safe, made for children and not adults," she has told me. Only children learn to gauge their single parent's emotional needs. It is vital for your survival and, you eventually learn, necessary if you are going to help your only adult protection in the world keep you both safe. I intuited from my mother's caution that I should be cautious of men, defensive of whatever I was calling home at any given time—my heart, my mental health, my car, my bedroom, my checkbook, my dreams, my body. Decades before I valued myself enough to be careful for myself, I was careful so that my mother would not worry.

If I knew to be cautious of men, I did not learn early enough to be cautious of white woman. The first time a white woman teacher told me that my breasts were distracting was in the sixth grade. Over the years, white women with authority over me have told me how wrong or dangerous or deviant my body is. As with that teacher, many of their comments focus on my breasts as opposed to, say, my ass. The next year I entered middle school, where you learn the rules of sexual presentation. That is where I started to discover that while my breasts distracted some of the boys and men, all distractions were not created equally.

As part of the last generation of Carolinians to attend the integrated schools that *Brown v. Board of Education* ushered into existence, I went to school with a lot of white people. Because of the racial composition of the districts drawn in my then-progressive school district, I also went to school with many South Asian and Latino kids. That racial and ethnic integration mattered to the rules I learned about being sexual, desirable, visible, and unseen.

Unlike home, where much of my social world was filtered through my mother's preference for African American history and culture, at school I learned that nothing was more beautiful than blond. The first time it happened was middle school. I heard a white boy, a bit of a loser with a crooked haircut who acted out because he couldn't bear to be unseen, say "that's a real blonde" about a girl in class, and I was confused. The only hair coloring I knew of at fourteen years old was the kind my grandmother used to "fix her edges," where curly gray hairs did not blend in properly with her wig. I had no idea what a "real" or "fake" blonde was, but I could intuit, much like my mother's fears, that the slacker boy was communicating some valuable social fact.

Later, we watched the musical *Grease* in a high school English class. In the final scene, when Olivia Newton-John's Sandy shows up at the carnival in shiny skin-tight pants, all the black kids tittered. She looked funny! There was so much space between her legs! A white boy too tall to be in the tenth grade reared back and shouted, "My hot damn, Ms. Newton-John!" I remember the scene so clearly, because that was when I got it. A whole other culture of desirability had been playing out just above and beyond my awareness, while my mostly black and Latino friends traded jokes at gapped thighs, flat behinds, and never trusting a big butt and a smile. And when the teacher, a middle-aged white woman not unlike the one who once told me my breasts were too distracting, looked at the too-tall boy, she smiled at him and rolled her eyes, acknowledging his sexual appreciation of Sandy as normal if unmannerly. He smiled back and kind of shrugged as if to say, "I just can't help myself." The teacher and the too-tall boy were in cahoots. Sandy, that strange creature, was *beautiful.*

Middle school moments—school dances and lunchroom strategies and weekend sleepovers—start to shake out the racial segregation of even the most utopian integrated schools. The white kids were your school friends, never your home friends. You took the gifted math classes together but you would not be on the lake with them over the weekend. We took that as normal. When we were together, politely sociable in classrooms and hallways, I learned what was beautiful. By high school, I knew that I was not it.

All girls in high school have self-esteem issues. And most girls compare themselves to unattainable, unrealistic physical ideals. That is not what I am talking about. That is the violence of gender that happens to all of us in slightly different ways. I am talking about a kind of capital. It is not just the preferences of a too-tall boy, but the way authority validates his preferences as normal. I had high school boyfriends. I had a social circle. I had evidence that I was valuable in certain contexts. But I had also parsed that there was something powerful about blondness, thinness, flatness, and gaps between thighs. And that power was the context against which all others defined themselves. That was beauty. And while few young women in high school could say they felt like they lived up to beauty, only the nonwhite girls could never be beautiful. That is because beauty isn't actually what you look like; beauty is the preferences that reproduce the existing social order. What is beautiful is whatever will keep weekend lake parties safe from strange darker people.

When white feminists catalogue how beauty standards over time have changed, from the "curvier" Marilyn Monroe to the skeletal Twiggy to the synthetic-athletic Pamela Anderson, their archetypes belie beauty's true function: whiteness. Whiteness exists as a response to blackness. Whiteness is a violent sociocultural regime legitimized by property to always make clear who is black by fastidiously delineating who is officially white. It would stand to reason that beauty's ultimate function is to exclude blackness. That beauty also violently conditions white women and symbolically precludes the existence of gender nonconforming people is a bonus. Some of the white girls I went to high school with may not have been beautiful. They may be thin when they should be fit or narrow of jaw when it should be strong. But, should power need them to be, social, economic, and political forces could make those girls beautiful by reshaping social norms. As long as the beautiful people are white, what is beautiful at any given time can be renegotiated without redistributing capital from white to nonwhite people.

Feminists have chronicled the changing standards of female beauty over time. One of the more popular examples of this is reborn on the internet every couple of years. In the meme, readers are asked to guess what size dress Marilyn Monroe would wear today. One is supposed to gasp at the realization that the iconic popular culture beauty was a *size twelve*. Memes are just born-digital nuggets of cultural norms. Whether the LOLcat is funny or Marilyn is beautiful or a gif of a YouTube prank is gross all depends on the norms of the culture that produced the meme. In the case of Marilyn Monroe's dress size, the meme assumes a western U.S. iconography. Marilyn is not just beautiful; she defines the beauty ideals of an entire era in U.S. popular culture. If you do not recognize that belief as your own, the meme will make no sense. The expectation that you should be shocked by Marilyn's dress size also relies on an audience who will share an idea about who is fat. And the audience must share the notion that fat and beauty are antithetical. Of course, fat has not always been juxtaposed against beauty in white western culture. Artists point to the Rubenesque female bodies of the seventeenth century as an example of how fat bodies were once the beauty ideal. They are also an ideal meant to lionize a version of white western history.

Naomi Wolf made the idea of examining beauty ideals across time a white third wave feminist cause du jour. In *The Beauty Myth*, Wolf excises the expectations of female beauty from the economic context that produces them, holding both up for feminist critique. As others have noted, Wolf does not do much work on how economic and political conditions produce a white hegemonic body as the ultimate expression of beauty. More precisely, Wolf demonstrates that as the sociopolitical context of whiteness—the political, state-sanctioned regime—tussles with historical forces like falling stock markets, mass media, suburbanization, and war, it will reshape an acceptable beauty standard for women that adjusts for body types, but never for body color. That was not Wolf's argument, but the absence of such a critique rather proves the point: beauty is for white women. It is a white woman's problem, if you are a feminist, or a white woman's grace, if you are something else not feminist. Beauty, in a meme or in the beauty myth, only holds as a meaningful cultural artifact through which we can examine politics, economics, and laws, and identity if we all share the assumption that beauty *is* precisely *because* it excludes nonwhite women.

Black women have examined where we are located in the beauty myth, examining the political economy through our bodies. If we could never be assumed beautiful in white culture's memes, histories, and feminisms, we could create other standards. Like feminist critiques of Rubens's renderings of white jiggling flesh, we have turned to cultural production for evidence of how we can ever be beautiful. Patricia Hill Collins's *Black Sexual Politics* is the most notable shot across the bow. Collins does not exactly wade into the complicated depth of race, class, nationalism, culture, economics, and the politics of how black sexuality is refracted through the racial hierarchy that precludes black women from being beautiful. She is, however, critical to defining a school of intellectual thought that gives us tools to understand these dynamics. Some of her most strident critique is saved for the compromises inherent in hip-hop culture. Here is a cultural product where blackness can be a critical feedback loop to the white mass media images of black women as caricatures. What Collins finds instead is a space where black masculine ideas about black women create ever more hierarchies of desirability based on body type, for example. Those hierarchies rarely go so far as to challenge the supremacy of white female beauty.

Black hip-hop feminists brought a deeper engagement with the complexities of hip-hop culture to bear on Collins's critique. Joan Morgan's *When Chickenheads Come Home to Roost: A Hip-Hop Feminist Breaks It Down* locates a black feminist voice in hip-hop culture, however marginalized in mainstream media. Despite arguing that the generation I claim is "misguidedly over-protective, hopelessly male-identified, and all too often self-sacrificing," hip-hop era feminists excavate a cultural history where we have tried to claim a space for black beauty. In 2014, comedian Leslie Jones performed a skit on *Saturday Night Live* about the complexities of claiming that space. In the skit, she turns the pain of racist beauty hierarchies that academics on the order of Marcus Hunter have studied into the kind of joke that made Richard Pryor so great. For approximately three minutes Jones bemoans her singleness. It is a frequent well from which she draws in her comedy. The topic is the designation of Lupita Nyong'o as *People*'s Most Beautiful Woman. Jones says that she is "waiting for them to put out the Most Useful List because that's where I'm gonna shine." It is a painful comment but not unfathomable given what beauty means, even if it said to be embodied by dark-skinned Kenyan-Mexican actress Nyong'o.

Jones is flatly saying that she is not beautiful and cannot be beautiful but that she is useful. She is locating her value not in beauty but in her use value. The real criticism was directed at her turn to slavery: "back in the slave days I would've never been single. I am six feet tall and I am strong! I'm just saying back in the slave days my love life would have been way better. Massa would've hooked me up with the best brother on the plantation." It hurts to watch the video. It's the kind of humor located in pain, not unlike that mined by Richard Pryor a generation ago. But we allowed Pryor his pain. He was an addict with self-esteem issues. He could set himself on fire and turn "nigga" into an incantation, often for white audiences. But Jones was not allowed to talk about the pain of being undesirable.

Free but black in the white western beauty myth, Jones is laying bare how futile it can be to desire beauty as a black woman. Many people slammed Jones for making light of slavery, especially of the systematic rape of enslaved black women. The argument was that she was mining historical pain for white consumption on a program that its creator Lorne Michaels once intoned would never be an "urban" show. I recall watching the skit and the ensuing social media firestorm about it with dismay. Not a single black woman that I read or followed seemed to empathize with Jones's obvious pain, whereas I had not been able to watch the video clip without pausing several times. Where others saw insult, I saw injury. The joke was not on enslaved black women of yesteryear but on the idea that it would take a totalizing system of enslavement to counter the structural violence that beauty does to Jones in her life today. Perhaps I caught what others missed because I am something different than Patricia Hill Collins or Joan Morgan or other important black women scholars of black feminism.

I am dark, physically and culturally. My complexion is not close to whiteness and my family roots reflect the economic realities of generations of dark-complexioned black people. We are rural, even when we move to cities. Our mobility is modest. Our out-marriage rates to nonblack men are negligible. Our social networks do not connect to elite black social institutions. When we move around in the world, we brush up against the criminal justice system. I am not located at the top of hip-hop's attenuated beauty hierarchy. I am, at best, in the middle. As Michael Jackson once sang, when you're too high to get over it and too low to get under it, you are stuck in the middle and the pain is thunder.

We have yet to make strides toward fleshing out a theory of desirability, the desire to be desired, in black feminist theory or politics. There is indeed a philosophy in how Jones desires being desired. That Nyong'o was atop a list of the world's most beautiful people does not invalidate the reality for many dark-skinned black women any more than Mark Zuckerberg making a billion dollars as a college drop-out invalidates the value of college for millions. Indeed, any system of oppression must allow exceptions to validate itself as meritorious. How else will those who are oppressed by the system internalize their own oppression? This is what I did not yet understand that when I was watching Ms. Newton-John: I was not beautiful and could never—no matter what was in fashion to serve the interests of capital and power—become beautiful. That was the theory trapped in my bones when I left for my mecca, my HBCU.

My first night as a college freshman at my HBCU, I ordered a pizza. The man-boy who delivered it stared too long before he handed it over. I snapped and grabbed my pizza. As I did, he muttered something about my phone number. I would date him off and on for a decade. As I walked back into the lobby of Eagleson Hall, I turned just as the pizza man-boy caught the eye of our dorm supervisor, an older black man. The man gave him a look like the one the teacher had once given the too-tall boy overtaken by Olivia Newton-John's spandexed thighs. I was Sandy!

At this institution I could be a kind of beautiful: normal, normative, taken for granted as desirable. It is one of many reasons that I loved my HBCU. Not because I got a few phone numbers or had a few boyfriends, but because I wasn't being defined by a standard of beauty that, by definition, could not include someone who looked like me. Don't get me wrong, the standard is complicated. It has the same economic costs to perform it as the ones white feminists argue that the massive global beauty industry exacts from white women. The costs may be even higher, because black women have fewer resources to purchase the accoutrements of thin waists, thick hips, tattooed brows, elegant contouring, red-heeled shoes, and femme styling that contemporary black beauty standards require. Black women experience negative consequences for not performing it sufficiently, especially if they are not straight, cisgender, and otherwise normative. But, feeling desired opened up avenues of inclusion that shaped my sense of self.

That inclusion is what I was coming home to the day I delivered a lecture at my dear ol' NCC. After sixty minutes or so of talking about the things my hosts had asked me to discuss, I opened the floor to questions. The first one was from a young sister about halfway back and to my left. The lighting shadowed her face, but I could make out her body language. I speak black woman fluently. My body recognized hers and I stood up straighter as she took the microphone and said, "We read your thing in class and Miley Cyrus ain't even do all that. Just because you ugly don't mean all black women are ugly." The room lit up. It seems all the English professors in attendance had assigned that essay as an example of what I do. And everyone in attendance had thoughts and feelings about it.

I did a little verbal dancing, trying to explain how we critique popular culture, and then moved on to the next question. Another young woman, another comment on how black and white people are friends now, unlike back in the day. Those black women are Miley's friends—and the white women I have written about who touch me in public are apparently doing so because they want to be my friend. Again, the idea of my body's value in social contexts was the a priori issue. These students were saying, in as many ways as they could, that I could not be ugly because white people find me desirable.

They were also saying, in their insistence and with their bodies, what more seasoned black women were saying to me in response to my essay. They were saying we had fought too long, worked too hard, come too far to concede that what white people have said about us is true. White people, as a collective system of cultural and economic production that has colonized nonwhite people across the globe through military and ideological warfare, have said that black people are animalistic. But, as sister bell hooks and many others have pointed out, animals with dicks can be useful. They can be "tall, dark, and handsome" if not also dangerous. There is no ideological exception to anti-blackness for black women but through colorism. Mulatto, "mixed," high yellow, light—all euphemisms for black people whose phenotype signals that they may have some genetic proximity to whiteness. But, by definition, black women are not beautiful except for any whiteness that may be in them.

Black women have worked hard to write a counternarrative of our worth in a global system where beauty is the only legitimate capital allowed women without legal, political, and economic challenge. That last bit is important. Beauty is not *good* capital. It compounds the oppression of gender. It constrains those who identify as women against their will. It costs money and demands money. It colonizes. It hurts. It is painful. It can never be fully satisfied. It is not useful for human flourishing. Beauty is, like all capital, merely valuable.

Because it is valuable, black women have said that we are beautiful too. We have traveled the cultural imaginations of the world's nonwhite people assembling a beauty construct that does not exclude us. We create culture about our beauty. We negotiate with black men to legitimize our beauty. We try to construct something that feels like liberation in an inherently oppressive regime, balancing peace with our marginally more privileged lighter-skinned black women while refuting the global caste status of darker-skinned black women. Some of us try to include multiple genders and politics in our definition of beauty. This kind of work requires discursive loyalty. We must name it and claim it, because naming is about the only unilateral power we have.

When I say that I am unattractive, concede that I am ugly, the antithesis of beauty, I sound like I am internalizing a white standard of beauty that black women fight hard to rise above. But my truth is quite the opposite. When oppressed people become complicit in their oppression, joining the dominant class in their ideas about what we are, it is symbolic violence. Like all concepts, symbolic violence has a context that is important for using it to mean what we intend to mean. It is not just that internalizing the values of the dominant class violently stigmatizes us. Symbolic violence only makes sense if we accept its priors: all preferences in imperial, industrialized societies are shaped by the economic system. There aren't any "good" preferences. There are only preferences that are validated by others, differently, based on social contexts.

These contexts should not just be reduced to race, class, and gender, as important as those are. Institutions that legitimize the "right" ideas and behaviors also matter. That's why beauty can never be about preference. "I just like what I like" is always a capitalist lie. Beauty would be a useless concept for capital if it were only a preference in the purest sense. Capital demands that beauty be coercive. If beauty matters at all to how people perceive you, how institutions treat you, which rules are applied to you, and what choices you can make, then beauty must also be a structure of patterns, institutions, and exchanges that eats your preferences for lunch.

Internalizing your inferiority is violent. Psychologically it cleaves you in two, what W. E. B. Du Bois famously called the double veil. As our science becomes more advanced, we find that the violence may even show up in our bodies as stress. Structurally, that violence becomes coded in the social norms around respectability that we black people use to do the dominant culture's work of disciplining other black people's identities, behaviors, and bodies. It is rational to check me if I am doing this kind of work for the devil.

But lest we forget, the greatest trick the devil ever pulled was convincing us that he does not exist. That is why naming is political. Our so-called counternarratives about beauty and what they demand of us cannot be divorced from the fact that beauty is contingent upon capitalism. Even our resistance becomes a means to commodify, and what is commodified is always, always stratified. There is simply no other way. To coerce, beauty must exclude. Exclusion can be part of a certain kind of liberation, where one dominant regime is overthrown for another, but it cannot be universal.

I love us loving ourselves under the most difficult conditions, but I must also write into my idea of truth and freedom. From my perch, trying to fillet the thinnest sections of popular culture, history, sociology, and my own biography, there isn't any room for error. I have to call a thing a thing. And sometimes, when we are trapped in the race not to be complicit in our own oppression, self-definition masquerades as a notion of loving our black selves in white terms. More than that, critique that hides the power being played out in the theater of our everyday lives only serves that power. It doesn't actually challenge it.

When I say that I am unattractive or ugly, I am not internalizing the dominant culture's assessment of me. I am naming what has been done to me. And signaling who did it.

I am glad that doing so unsettles folks, including the many white women who wrote to me with impassioned cases for how beautiful I am. They offered me neoliberal self-help nonsense that borders on the religious. They need me to believe beauty is both achievable and individual, because the alternative makes them vulnerable. If you did not earn beauty, never had the real power to reject it, then you are as much a vulnerable subject as I am in your own way. Deal with that rather than dealing with me. Compared with the forms of oppression they can now see via their proximity to me, it may seem to privileged people that it is easier to fix me than it is to fix the world. I live to disabuse people of that notion.

But it is interesting to think about why many white women, a handful of white men, and a few black men rejected my claim. Their interests cannot be the same as those of black women, whose stake in my claim that beauty excludes me is deeply intimate.

White women, especially white feminists, need me to lean in to pseudoreligious consumerist teachings that beauty is democratic and achievable. Beauty must be democratic. If it is not, then beauty becomes a commodity, distributed unequally and, even worse, at random. This is a notion often ascribed to a type of feminism, be it neoliberal feminism, marketplace feminism, or consumption feminism. But well-meaning white women also need me to believe because accessing beauty is about the totalizing construct of gender, in this case femininity, in a world where other forms of lifestyle consumption are splintering.

You can use an app to buy the foods of the rich, the music of the cool, the art of the revolutionary, and the look of the aspirational. But femininity is resistant to appification and frictionless consumption. Femininity is not about biological sex, but about the traits that have become ascribed to biological sex. And this set of traits carries a set of ideas and histories contingent upon the economics and politics of any given time. You cannot separate what it means to be a "woman," often used to mean a performance of acceptable femininity, from the conditions that decide what is and is not acceptable across time and space. We all do this kind of performance of ourselves, be it our gender or race or social class or national identity or culture. As we are doing it, we are always negotiating with powerful ideas about what constitutes a woman.

Beauty has an aesthetic, but it is not the same as aesthetics, not when it can be embodied, controlled by powerful interests, and when it can be commodified. Beauty can be manners, also a socially contingent set of traits. Whatever power decides that beauty is, it must always be more than reducible to a single thing. Beauty is a wonderful form of capital in a world that organizes everything around gender and then requires a performance of gender that makes some of its members more equal than others.

Beauty would not be such a useful distinction were it not for the economic and political conditions. It is trite at this point to point out capitalism, which is precisely why it must be pointed out. Systems of exchange tend to generate the kind of ideas that work well as exchanges. Because it can be an idea *and* a good *and* a body, beauty serves many useful functions for our economic system. Even better, beauty can be political. It can exclude and include, one of the basic conditions of any politics. Beauty has it all. It can be political, economic, external, individualized, generalizing, exclusionary, and perhaps best of all a story that can be told. Our dominant story of beauty is that it is simultaneously a blessing, of genetics or gods, and a site of conversion. You can *become* beautiful if you accept the right prophets and their wisdoms with a side of products thrown in for good measure. Forget that these two ideas—unique blessing and earned reward—are antithetical to each other. That makes beauty all the more perfect for our (social and political) time, itself anchored in paradoxes like freedom *and* property, opportunity *and* equality.

There is now an entire shelf among the periodicals at my nearby chain bookstore filled with magazines that will give me five meditations or three coloring book pages or nine yoga retreats or fourteen farmhouse ideas or nineteen paper-crafting inspirations that, if purchased, will acculturate me to achievable "inner beauty." Mind you, the consumption is always external and public. These are quite literally called "lifestyle" magazines, which begs the question "Whose lifestyle?" These are ways of expressing a kind of femininity, a kind of woman, for whom beauty is defined to selectively include or exclude. These are consumption goods made for a lifestyle associated with white western women of a certain status, class, profession, and disposition. These are for women who *can* be beautiful, if only conditionally, and contingent upon the needs of markets and states—and the men whom states and markets serve most and best. All of the admonishments that I should "love myself" and am "as cute as a button" from well-intentioned white women stem from their need for me to consume what is produced for them.

What those white women did not know or could not admit to knowing is that I cannot, by definition, ever be that kind of beautiful. In the way that gender has so structured how we move through the intersecting planes of class and status and income and wealth that shape our world and our selves, so does race. Rather, I should say, so does blackness, because everyone—including white women—have "race." It is actually blackness, as it has been created through the history of colonization, imperialism, and domination, that excludes me from the forces of beauty. For beauty to function as it should, it must exclude me. Big Beauty—the structure of who can be beautiful, the stories we tell about beauty, the value we assign beauty, the power given to those with beauty, the disciplining effect of the fear of losing beauty you might possess—definitionally excludes the kind of blackness I carry in my history and my bones. Beauty is for white women, if not for all white women. If beauty is to matter at all for capital, it can never be for black women.

But if I *believe* that I can become beautiful, I become an economic subject. My desire becomes a market. And my faith becomes a salve for the white women who want to have the right politics while keeping the privilege of never having to live them. White women need me to believe I can earn beauty, because when I want what I cannot have, what they have becomes all the more valuable.

I refuse them.

I also refuse the men. Oh, the men. I wish I could save this for another essay that I would promise to write but never do. Women's desire for beauty is a powerful weapon for exploitation. Even if the desire is natural, in that it is rational and also subconsciously coercive, open wanting against a backdrop of predatory constructs of cross-gender interactions is dangerous for women. There is an entire industry of men, self-proclaimed pickup artists, who sell their strategies for landing women. One of the most common techniques involves negging. This is when a man approaches a woman whose embodied beauty exceeds his own status. She is "out of his league." His league is typically determined by height, penis size, sexual experience, body type, and money, but also can take into account tastes and preferences. Some men say they turn to pickup artistry when the preferences so well suited to their social position—say, voting for a reviled political candidate or playing certain types of video games—are devalued in mate markets. Once a woman is identified the pickup artist might compliment her style, but mention that her teeth are imperfect. This is supposed to destabilize the woman, make her question what power she holds in the exchange, and eventually mold her into a more docile subject for sexual conquest.

Good men love to mock pickup artists and negging as evidence of their goodness. But good men also consume beauty, contributing much to its value. Without good men, the socio-cultural institution of Big Beauty could not be as powerful as it is. Big Beauty encompasses the norms that shape desirable traits in a romantic partner but also acceptable presentations of women in work, at play, and in public. It is the industrial complex of cosmetics, enhancements and services that promise individual women beauty. The idea that Big Beauty is evil but good men are nice is part of Big Beauty's systematic charm.

Big Beauty is just negging without the slimy actor. The constant destabilization of self is part and parcel of beauty's effectiveness as a social construct. When a woman must consume the tastes of her social position to keep it, but cannot control the tastes that define said position, she is suspended in a state of being negged. A good man need only then to come along and capitalize on the moment of negging, exploit the value of negged women, and consume the beauty that negs. It is really quite neat, if you think about it.

For black women who are engaging black men with the assumption that sexual engagement is within the realm of possibility, negging develops a new depth. I suspect this is true of all nonwhite male-female interactions shaped by sexual potential.

They may be moderated by their proximity to whiteness—a fair-skinned Latina might have a different depth of this experience than a darker-skinned Afro-Latina—but the relations still hold: women who are not white must contend with beauty through the gaze of white men *and* nonwhite men. This is perhaps the hardest of all these situations for me to describe. How do I distill something that is so diffuse across my life? That is what the relationship between my agency, the constraints of beauty, and the structure of race feels like—it has always been a part of the threads that are stitching me.

What these black men seemed to have wanted is the easiest way to suspend me between their wanting and my own. They needed me to reflect the duality of beauty regimes that exist in their corner of the social world. That's the corner where heterosexual masculinity does to them similar things that heterosexual femininity does to me but differently, at variable rates and with distinct political consequences. But unlike the space from which I emerge, these black men can poke holes in the walls that for me are impenetrable. They must travel through sexual ideologies about bulls and bucks, losing some skin as they scrape through the walls that beauty erects around social status. That is why it is so important for me, a sister and a sista, to reflect back at them the dominant beauty structure of white femininity *and* the subordinate beauty structure of black womanhood.

Black women have to both aspire to the unattainable paradox of white beauty and cultivate its counterparadox *because both must exist for black masculinity to retain the privilege of moving between two social spaces of potential mates*. If I reinforce the white beauty norm, then I reproduce it in a way that benefits white women. If black masculinity can or may or does benefit from having the option of hitching its star to white beauty, then it needs black women to play our part. But where there is dominance, there is also subordination. Black people have a whole structure of class and income and wealth and tastes and preferences. It stands to reason that we also have a construct of beauty that shapes and stratifies good black women and bad black women, and so on. If black masculinity benefits from the option of hooking up with black women, then it has to value at least the performance of black beauty. Playing my part would look like espousing what a thick black stallion I am, while coveting the beautiful white woman I could never become. If I play my part, black masculinity benefits. White women needed me to neg myself and black men needed me to neg them at the expense of myself. Either way, I was losing and I knew it.

Repeatedly people have said to me in their own way, from within their own stratified statuses, that I need to believe I am beautiful or can become beautiful—not for my own benefit, but because it serves so many others. I reject the implicit bid for solidarity from every single white woman and I reject every overture from a man who wants to convince me that I am beautiful. I want nice people with nice-enough politics to look at me, reason for themselves that I am worthy, and feel convicted when the world does not agree. God willing they may one day extrapolate my specific case to the general rule, seeing the way oppression marginalizes others to their personal benefit.

I do not have any issues of self-worth—well, no more than anyone who used to be young and now is not. I am sensible. I know the streets in pregentrified communities where old men will still look twice and someone behind a counter might give me an extra piece of something for free. I know that cute and attractive are categories that exist, with their own attended privileges. But none of these things negates the structural apparatus that controls access to resources and ad hoc designates those with capital as beauty's gate-keepers. When beauty is white and I am dark, it means that I am more likely to be punished in school, to receive higher sentences for crimes, less likely to marry, and less likely to marry someone with equal or higher economic status. Denying these empirical realities is its own kind of violence, even when our intentions are good.

They say that beauty is in the eye of the beholder and that ugly is as ugly does. Both are lies. Ugly is everything done to you in the name of beauty.

Knowing the difference is part of getting free.

The Problem with Sass

BY BRITTNEY COOPER

Brittney Cooper is an American author, professor at Rutgers University, activist, cultural critic, and co-founder of the Crunk Feminist Collective. Along with work on black female public intellectuals, Dr. Cooper studies Black women's organizations as sites for the production of intellectual thought. Like Audre Lorde, Cooper recognizes that anger can be a productive site of change. Cooper is the author of the 2018 essay collection *Eloquent Rage: A Black Feminist Discovers Her Superpower,* which examines the ways in which Black women have theorized racial identity and gender politics and the methods they used to bring theory into practice to empower Black communities. In this chapter from the collection, Cooper critiques the common trope of the sassy Black woman as a method of diminishing their power and righteous anger. In this chapter and in all her writing, Cooper reminds us that we should not have to diminish ourselves to be treated with dignity and respect.

This is a book by a grown-ass woman written for other grown-ass women. This is a book for women who expect to be taken seriously and for men who take grown women seriously. This is a book for women who know shit is fucked up. These women want to change things but don't know where to begin.

To be clear, I'm not really into self-help books, so I don't have one of those catchy three-step plans for changing the world. What I have is anger. Rage, actually. And that's the place where more women should begin—with the things that make us angry.

When it comes to Black women, sometimes Americans don't

recognize that sass is simply a more palatable form of rage. Americans adore sassy Black women. You know, those caricatures of finger-waving, eye-rolling Black women at whom everyone loves to laugh—women like Tyler Perry's Madea, Mammy in *Gone with the Wind*, or Nell from that old eighties sitcom *Gimme a Break!* These kinds of Black women put white folks at ease.

In my first terrible job after college, my boss, an older white woman, told me that the students at the predominantly Black school at which we worked had deemed her an honorary Black woman. When I looked at her with question marks in my eyes, she said, "You know, they mean the way I talk to them and roll my neck," and demonstrated it for me. I went on back to my desk.

Years after that, I was doing a summer abroad in South Korea. My Malaysian roommate, who had seen many episodes of the old nineties sitcom *Family Matters*, told me that she loved Black women because we were sassy like Harriette and Laura Winslow, the main Black female characters on that show. To her, these stereotypical portrayals made Black folks seem understandable, even though to me, her descriptions felt like we were exotic others. She loved it, she said, when Black women put their hands on their hips and swiveled their necks in protest. Not wanting to offend this woman who I otherwise really liked, I simply said, "We're not all like that." She looked disappointed.

I am fat, Black, and Southern. But this is not a sassy Black girl's tale. Black women turn to sass when rage is too risky—because we have jobs to keep, families to feed, and bills to pay. Black women who hold their communities together also hold our broader American community together. But it's unclear whether we are really being taken seriously.

Owning anger is a dangerous thing if you're a fat Black girl like me. Angry Black Women get dismissed all the time. We are told we are irrational, crazy, out of touch, entitled, disruptive, and not team players. The story goes that Angry Black Women scare babies, old people, and grown men. This is absurd. And it is a lie. If you have the nerve to be fat *and* angry, then you are treated as a bully even if you are doing nothing aggressive at all. The truth is that Angry Black Women are looked upon as entities to be contained, as inconvenient citizens who keep on talking about their rights while refusing to do their duty and smile at everyone. Don't you just hate when folks yell at you to "Smile!"? I told the last man who said that shit to me, "*You* smile!"

Some years ago, I ran into a former student on the college campus where I was teaching. Erica was a brilliant Black girl who wrote great papers and asked really smart questions. As we were standing around with a group of others, chatting, she said, "I loved having you as my professor. Your lectures were filled with rage. But it was, like, the most eloquent rage ever." I immediately felt defensive. What did she mean by *rage*? "I'm not angry," I told her. "I'm passionate." By then, I was wary of the Angry Black Woman stereotype. Even though I was only in my mid-twenties at the time, I had already experienced many years of white people doing that thing they do to articulate Black women—always asking us "Why are you so angry?" I hated the accusation from others, usually white people, because it was unfair, a way to discredit the legitimacy of the things Black women say by calling them emotional and irrational. But Erica was a Black girl. She fixed me with a telltale look that only another Black woman can give you, a look that said, *Girl, be for real.* And then she said, "Brittney, you know you're angry." I felt exposed. I couldn't even say anything. She had seen through the veneer, seen the lie I was telling. It was devastating. And life-changing.

I *was* angry. As hell. And I was fooling no one.

Black women have the right to be mad as hell. We have been dreaming of freedom and carving out spaces for liberation since we arrived on these shores. There is no other group, save Indigenous women, that knows and understands more fully the soul of the American body politic than Black women, whose reproductive and social labor have made the world what it is. This is not mere propaganda. Black women know what it means to love ourselves in a world that hates us. We know what it means to do a whole lot with very little, to "make a dollar out of fifteen cents," as it were. We know what it means to snatch dignity from the jaws of power and come out standing. We know what it means to face horrific violence and trauma from both our communities and our nation-state and carry on anyway. But we also scream, and cry, and hurt, and mourn, and struggle. We get heartbroken, our feelings get stepped on, our dreams get crushed. We get angry, and we express that anger. We know what it means to feel invisible.

———————

I know what it means to feel invisible. To be picked on, bullied, misunderstood, and dismissed. But when Erica called me out on my anger, it was clear that she saw me in a way that I wasn't particularly interested in being seen. She helped me to realize that my anger could be a powerful force for good. She had called my rage *eloquent*. Clear. Expressive. To the point. In her estimation, it had made me a good teacher, and it had inspired her and other students.

Over and over again, Black girls have called me out and demanded that I get my shit together, around my rage, around my work in the world, and around my feminism. Those Black-girl callouts, or "homegirl interventions," as I call them in this book, have come from my grandmama, my mama, and my girls. And they have saved my life.

America needs a homegirl intervention in the worst way. So in this book, I am doing what Black women do best. I'm calling America out on her bullshit about racism, sexism, classism, homophobia, and a bunch of other stuff.

And I'm using feminism to stage this homegirl intervention. I'm here for picket signs, pussy hats (as long as there are plenty of brown ones in the mix), and patchouli. My picket signs are as likely to say FUCK THE POLICE as they are to say FUCK THE PATRIARCHY. Black-girl feminism is all the rage, and we need all the rage. Feminism can give us a common language for thinking about how sexism, and racism, and classism work together to fuck shit up for everybody.

Like many other feminists, I used to carry around Audre Lorde's book *Sister Outsider* like it was the feminist bible. Her essay "The Uses of Anger: Women Responding to Racism" taught me that rage is a legitimate political emotion. She writes, "Focused with precision, it can become a powerful source of energy serving progress and change."

Here's the thing: My anger and rage haven't always been "focused with precision." The process, of both becoming a feminist and becoming okay with rage as a potential feminist superpower, has been messy as hell. We need to embrace our messiness more. We need to embrace the ways we are in process more. Very often

Black girls don't get the opportunity to be in process. So just know that you don't have to have everything figured out to read and enjoy this book.

For more than a decade, since Erica named for me my superpower—eloquent rage—I've been trying to figure out how to focus it with precision.

When I watch the Williams sisters—Venus and Serena—use their power on a tennis court, I feel like they are a case study in how to use rage with precision. Born six months after Venus and nine months before Serena, I feel like I grew up with the Williams sisters. When they first began to win major tournaments in the late 1990s, sportscasters derisively referred to the "power tennis" they played. These strong, athletic Black girls had serves with speeds of more than 120 miles per hour and they scared the shit out of white girls. Until they learned how to use their power, it often became a liability, causing them to make lots of mistakes on and off the court.

But in the nearly twenty years since they have come to dominate tennis, both sisters have figured out how to corral all that power into precise serves and shots that are nearly unmatched. They have created this kind of alchemy that uses their physical strength and strategic prowess on the court, together with all the racial slurs and insults they have endured over the years—being called the N-word, being called ugly, being told their bodies were too manly—to create something that looks magical to the rest of us. Watching Venus play, particularly on grass courts, is like watching a Black girl perform in a ballet. She is an elegant player. Watching Serena play, particularly when she's beating white women, is like watching eloquent rage personified. Her shots are clear and expressive. Her wins are exultant. Her victories belong to all of us, even though she's the one who does all the work.

That's kind of how it feels to be a Black woman. Like our victories belong to everyone, even though we do all the work. But here's the thing—if I can master any force in my life and slay it like Serena slays tennis balls on the court, then I'm happy to share the wealth.

The Meaning of Serena Williams

BY CLAUDIA RANKINE

Claudia Rankine is a poet, essayist, playwright, and editor whose work examines whiteness and white supremacy, particularly the ways it intersects with sexism. Rankine has received numerous awards including the Poets & Writers Jackson Poetry Prize, fellowships from the Guggenheim Foundation, the MacArthur Foundation, United States Artists, and the National Endowment of the Arts. Rankine's books *Citizen: An American Lyric* and *Don't Let Me Be Lonely: An American Lyric* explore the ways in which racism operates, from personal racist microaggressions to endemic state violence against Black people. Rankine's 2015 article in *The New York Times Magazine*, "The Meaning of Serena Williams: On Tennis and Black Excellence," examines the racism tennis great Serena Williams has battled on and off the court and how she is forging her own path through her career that will not be constrained by the bigotry of low expectations. Rankine concludes that "Serena is providing a new script, one in which winning doesn't carry the burden of curing racism, in which we win just to win."

There is no more exuberant winner than Serena Williams. She leaps into the air, she laughs, she grins, she pumps her fist, she points her index finger to the sky, signaling she's No. 1. Her joy is palpable. It brings me to my feet, and I grin right back at her, as if I've won something, too. Perhaps I have.

There is a belief among some African-Americans that to defeat racism, they have to work harder, be smarter, be *better*. Only after they give 150 percent will white Americans recognize black excellence for what it is. But of course, once recognized, black excellence is then supposed to perform with good manners and forgiveness in the face of any racist slights or attacks. Black excellence is not supposed to be emotional as it pulls itself together to win after questionable calls. And in winning, it's not supposed to swagger, to leap and pump its fist, to state boldly, in the words of Kanye West, "That's what it is, black excellence, baby."

Imagine you have won 21 Grand Slam singles titles, with only four losses in your 25 appearances in the finals. Imagine that you've achieved two "Serena Slams" (four consecutive Slams in a row), the first more than 10 years ago and the second this year. A win at this year's U.S. Open would be your fifth and your first calendar-year Grand Slam—a feat last achieved by Steffi Graf in 1988, when you were just 6 years old. This win would also break your tie for the most U.S. Open titles in the Open era, surpassing the legendary Chris Evert, who herself has called you "a phenomenon that once every hundred years comes around." Imagine that you're the player John McEnroe recently described as "the greatest player, I think, that ever lived." Imagine that, despite all this, there were so many bad calls against you, you were given as one reason video replay needed to be used on the courts. Imagine that you have to contend with critiques of your body that perpetuate racist notions that black women are hypermasculine and unattractive. Imagine being asked to comment at a news conference before a tournament because the president of the Russian Tennis Federation, Shamil Tarpischev, has described you and your sister as "brothers" who are "scary" to look at. Imagine.

The word "win" finds its roots in both joy and grace. Serena's grace comes because she won't be forced into stillness; she won't accept those racist projections onto her body without speaking back; she won't go gently into the white light of victory. Her excellence doesn't mask the struggle it takes to achieve each win. For black people, there is an unspoken script that demands the humble absorption of racist assaults, no matter the scale, because whites need to believe that it's no big deal. But Serena refuses to keep to that script. Somehow, along the way, she made a decision to be excellent while still being Serena. She would feel what she feels in front of everyone, in response to anyone. At Wimbledon this year, for example, in a match against the home favorite Heather Watson, Serena, interrupted during play by the deafening support of Watson, wagged her index finger at the crowd and said, "Don't try me." She will tell an audience or an official that they are disrespectful or unjust, whether she says, simply, "No, no, no" or something much more forceful, as happened at the U.S. Open in 2009, when she told the lineswoman, "I swear to God I am [expletive] going to take this [expletive] ball and shove it down your [expletive] throat." And in doing so, we actually see her. She shows us her joy, her humor and, yes, her rage. She gives us the whole range of what it is to be human, and there are those who can't bear it, who can't tolerate the humanity of an ordinary extraordinary person.

In the essay "Everybody's Protest Novel," James Baldwin wrote, "our humanity is our burden, our life; we need not battle for it; we need only to do what is infinitely more difficult—that is, accept it." To accept the self, its humanity, is to discard the white racist gaze. Serena has freed herself from it. But that doesn't mean she won't be emotional or hurt by challenges to her humanity. It doesn't mean she won't battle for the right to be excellent. There is nothing wrong with Serena, but surely there is something wrong with the expectation that she be "good" while she is achieving greatness. Why should Serena not respond to racism? In whose world should it be answered with good manners? The notable difference between black excellence and white excellence is white excellence is achieved without having to battle racism. Imagine.

Two years ago, recovering from cancer and to celebrate my 50th birthday, I flew from LAX to J.F.K. during Serena's semifinal match at the U.S. Open with the hope of seeing her play in the final. I had just passed through a year when so much was out of my control, and Serena epitomized not so much winning as the pure drive to win. I couldn't quite shake the feeling (I still can't quite shake it) that my body's frailty, not the cancer but the depth of my exhaustion, had been brought on in part by the constant onslaught of racism, whether something as terrible as the killing of Trayvon Martin or something as mundane as the guy who let the door slam in my face. The daily grind of being rendered invisible, or being attacked, whether physically or verbally, for being visible, wears a body down. Serena's strength and focus in the face of the realities we shared oddly consoled me.

That Sunday in Arthur Ashe Stadium at the women's final,

though the crowd generally seemed pro-Serena, the man seated next to me was cheering for the formidable tall blonde Victoria Azarenka. I asked him if he was American. "Yes," he said.

"We're at the U.S. Open. Why are you cheering for the player from Belarus?" I asked.

"Oh, I just want the match to be competitive," he said.

After Serena lost the second set, at the opening of the third, I turned to him again, and asked him, no doubt in my own frustration, why he was still cheering for Azarenka. He didn't answer, as was his prerogative. By the time it was clear that Serena was likely to win, his seat had been vacated. I had to admit to myself that in those moments I needed her to win, not just in the pure sense of a fan supporting her player, but to prove something that could never be proven, because if black excellence could cure us of anything, black people—or rather this black person—would be free from needing Serena to win.

"You don't understand me," Serena Williams said with a hint of impatience in her voice. "I'm just about winning." She and I were facing each other on a sofa in her West Palm Beach home this July. She looked at me with wariness as if to say, Not you, too. I wanted to talk about the tennis records that she is presently positioned either to tie or to break and had tried more than once to steer the conversation toward them. But she was clear: "It's not about getting 22 Grand Slams," she insisted. Before winning a calendar-year Grand Slam and matching Steffi Graf's record of 22 Slams, Serena would have to win seven matches and defend her U.S. Open title; *those* were the victories that she was thinking about.

She was wearing an enviable pink jumpsuit with palm trees stamped all over it as if to reflect the trees surrounding her estate. It was a badass outfit, one only someone of her height and figure could rock. She explained to me that she learned not to look ahead too much by looking ahead. As she approached 18 Grand Slam wins in 2014, she said, "I went too crazy. I felt I had to even up with Chris Evert and Martina Navratilova." Instead, she didn't make it past the fourth round at the Australian Open, the second at the French Open or the third at Wimbledon. She tried to change her tactics and focused on getting only to the quarterfinals of the U.S. Open. Make it to the second week and see what happens, she thought. "I started thinking like that, and then I got to 19. Actually I got to 21 just like that, so I'm not thinking about 22." She raised her water bottle to her lips, looking at me over its edge, as if to give me time to think of a different line of questioning.

Three years ago she partnered with the French tennis coach Patrick Mouratoglou, and I've wondered if his coaching has been an antidote to negotiating American racism, a dynamic that informed the coaching of her father, Richard Williams. He didn't want its presence to prevent her and Venus from winning. In his autobiography, "Black and White: The Way I See It," he describes toughening the girls' "skin" by bringing "busloads of kids from the local schools into Compton to surround the courts while Venus and Serena practiced. I had the kids call them every curse word in the English language, including 'Nigger,'" he writes. "I paid them to do it and told them to 'do their worst.'" His focus on racism meant that the sisters were engaged in two battles on and off the court. That level of vigilance, I know from my own life, can drain you. It's easier to shut up and pretend it's not happening, as the bitterness and stress build up.

Mouratoglou shifted Serena's focus to records (even if, as she prepares for a Slam, she says she can't allow herself to think about them). Perhaps it's not surprising that she broke her boycott against Indian Wells, where the audience notoriously booed her with racial epithets in 2001, during their partnership. Serena's decisions now seem directed toward building her legacy. Mouratoglou has insisted that she can get to 24 Grand Slams, which is the most won by a single player—Margaret Court—to date. Serena laughed as she recalled one of her earliest conversations with Mouratoglou. She told him: "I'm cool. I want to play tennis. I hate to lose. I want to win. But I don't have numbers in my head." He wouldn't allow that. "Now we are getting numbers in your head," he told her.

I asked how winning felt for her. I was imagining winning as a free space, one where the unconscious racist shenanigans of umpires, or the narratives about her body, her "unnatural" power, her perceived crassness no longer mattered. Unless racism destroyed the moment of winning so completely, as it did at Indian Wells, I thought it had to be the rare space free of all the stresses of black life. But Serena made it clear that she doesn't desire to dissociate from her history and her culture. She understands that even when she's focused only on winning, she is still representing. "I play for me," Serena told me, "but I also play and represent something much greater than me. I embrace that. I love that. I want that. So ultimately, when I am out there on the court, I am playing for me."

Her next possible victory is at the U.S. Open, the major where she has been involved in the most drama—everything from outrageous line calls to probations and fines. Serena admitted to losing her cool in the face of some of what has gone down there. In 2011, for example, a chair umpire, Eva Asderaki, ruled against Serena for yelling "Come on" before a point was completed, and as Serena described it to me, she "clutched her pearls" and told Asderaki not to look at her. But she said in recent years she finally felt embraced by the crowd. "No more incidents?" I asked. Before she could answer, we both laughed, because of course it's not wholly in her control. Then suddenly Serena stopped. "I don't want any incidents there," she said. "But I'm always going to be myself. If anything happens, I'm always going to be myself, true to myself."

I'm counting on it, I thought. Because just as important to me as her victories is her willingness to be an emotionally complete person while also being black. She wins, yes, but she also loses it. She jokes around, gets angry, is frustrated or joyous, and on and on. She is fearlessly on the side of Serena, in a culture that that has responded to living while black with death.

This July, the London School of Marketing (L.S.M.) released its list of the most marketable sports stars, which included only two women in its Top 20: Maria Sharapova and Serena Williams. They were ranked 12th and 20th. Despite decisively trailing Serena on the tennis court (Serena leads in their head-to-head matchups 18–2, and has 21 majors and 247 weeks at No. 1 to Sharapova's five majors and 21 weeks at number 1), Sharapova has a financial advantage off the court. This month Forbes listed her as the highest-paid female athlete, worth more than $29 million to Serena's $24 million.

When I asked Chris Evert about the L.S.M. list, she said, "I think the corporate world still loves the good-looking blond girls." It's a preference Evert benefited from in her own illustrious career. I suggested that this had to do with race. Serena, on occasion, has herself been a blonde. But of course, for millions of consumers, possibly not the right kind of blonde. "Maria was very aware of business and becoming a businesswoman at a much younger stage," Evert told me, adding, "She works hard." She also suggested that any demonstration of corporate preference is about a certain "type" of look or image, not whiteness in general. When I asked Evert what she made of Eugenie Bouchard, the tall, blond Canadian who has yet to really distinguish herself in the sport, being named the world's most marketable athlete by the British magazine SportsPro this spring, she said, with a laugh, "Well, there you have it." I took her statement to be perhaps a moment of agreement that Serena probably could not work her way to Sharapova's spot on Forbes's list.

"If they want to market someone who is white and blond, that's their choice," Serena told me when I asked her about her ranking. Her impatience had returned, but I wasn't sure if it was with me, the list or both. "I have a lot of partners who are very happy to work with me." JPMorgan Chase, Wilson Sporting Goods, Pepsi and Nike are among the partners she was referring to. "I can't sit here and say I should be higher on the list because I have won more." As for Sharapova, her nonrival rival, Serena was diplomatic: "I'm happy for her, because she worked hard, too. There is enough at the table for everyone."

There is another, perhaps more important, discussion to be had about what it means to be chosen by global corporations. It has to do with who is worthy, who is desirable, who is associated with the good life. As long as the white imagination markets itself by equating whiteness and blondness with aspirational living, stereotypes will remain fixed in place. Even though Serena is the best, even though she wins more Slams than anyone else, she is only superficially allowed to embody that in our culture, at least the marketable one.

But Serena was less interested in the ramifications involved in being chosen, since she had no power in this arena, and more interested in understanding her role in relation to those who came before her: "We have to be thankful, and we also have to be positive about it so the next black person can be No. 1 on that list," she told me. "Maybe it was not meant to be me. Maybe it's meant to be the next person to be amazing, and I'm just opening the door. Zina Garrison, Althea Gibson, Arthur Ashe and Venus opened so many doors for me. I'm just opening the next door for the next person."

I was moved by Serena's positioning herself in relation to other African-Americans. A crucial component of white privilege is the idea that your accomplishments can be, have been, achieved on your own. The private clubs that housed the tennis courts remained closed to minorities well into the second half of the 20th century. Serena reminded me that in addition to being a phenomenon, she has come out of a long line of African-Americans who battled for the right to be excellent in such a space that attached its value to its whiteness and worked overtime to keep it segregated.

Serena's excellence comes with the ability to imagine herself achieving a new kind of history for all of us. As long as she remains healthy, she will most likely tie and eventually pass Graf's 22 majors, regardless of what happens at the U.S. Open this year. I want Serena to win, but I know better than to think her winning can end something she didn't start. But Serena is providing a new script, one in which winning doesn't carry the burden of curing racism, in which we win just to win—knowing that it is simply her excellence, baby.

Black Girls Don't
Get to Be Depressed

BY SAMANTHA IRBY

Samantha Irby is an essayist and television writer who
has authored the books *Meaty*; *We Are Never Meeting
in Real Life*; *Wow, No Thank You*; and *Quietly Hostile*.
She has written critically acclaimed episodes of Hulu's
Shrill and HBO's *And Just Like That . . .* In her 2015 essay "Black Girls Don't Get to Be Depressed," Irby writes
about navigating anxiety and depression as a Black
woman because depression was "something that happened to white people on television, not a thing that
could take down a Strong Black Woman." With wit and
characteristic humor, she lays bare her humanity and
reminds us that Black women need the space to be vulnerable as much as any other women.

When I was young I was frequently described as "moody." Or dismissed as "angry." According to the social worker who routinely
pulled me out of class, I was intellectually bright but "quietly hostile." Never mind that I was basically living in squalor with my
mother's half-dead body, subsisting on the kind of cereal that
comes in a 5-pound bag and whatever meals were being served for
free hot lunch; I was diagnosed as having "an attitude problem."
So I rocked with that. When you're a kid, it's sometimes just easier
to go along with other people's definitions of who you are. They're
adults, right? So they're smarter? I would listen to this Faith No
More tape on my Walkman (do young people understand what
those words even mean) over and over while sulking and looking
morose, or whatever it is poor kids do when we have no access to
semiautomatic firearms or prescription drugs. It was the only
thing I could do to make it to the next day.

No one in my house was talking about depression. That's

something that happened to white people on television, not a thing that could take down a Strong Black Woman. Which also fucked with me on the "Why are you listening to Smashing Pumpkins instead of [*insert name of popular R+B artist*]? Are you even black?!" level. *Sigh.* So I was (1) super fucking depressed, (2) super fucking depressed with no one to talk to about it who wasn't going to immediately suggest child services remove me from my home, and (3) super fucking depressed while clocking in on the low end of my skinfolk's negrometers because I identified hard with Courtney Love and read *Sassy* magazine. Depression seemed like just another way I was desperately trying to be white.

I tried to take my own life in 1993 and the general response when it failed was basically LOL, TOUGHEN UP. I just slept straight through the rest of the weekend and went back to school the next Monday and kept doing the same shit I'd always been doing. I figured that if I wanted to try again, I needed to wait until I was old enough to get a car and drive it off one of suburban Chicago's many cliffs. I think my mom started watching me a little more closely, but what was she really going to do? She was severely disabled and my being hopeless all the time was trumped by "You know I can't walk, right?" and I get that. I was a kid, it was my job to go to school, so I did my job. I would deal with it when I was off Medicare and making enough money to pay for therapy myself. BAHAHAHAHAHA *choke sob* AHAHAHAHAHA!

Even when my parents died five years later when I was 18, and I had an actual thing I could point to as a source of my depression, I played it off. I come from the kind of people whose response to "Hey man, I'm pretty bummed out" is "Shut up, there's nothing wrong with you." Or "You just sleep all of the time because you're lazy." If it isn't broken or hemorrhaging, you need to bury it under these Dollar Store snack foods and work it out by your fucking self. Oh, OK, cool.

I developed very glamorous coping mechanisms like covering myself with grisly death tattoos and eating food out of the trash. And then, because I wasn't actively trying to kill myself and could keep a job and make friends and pay my rent and not do heroin, I made peace with it. This is just how I am. I'm fine. It was easy to ignore because it doesn't bother me that much. And I don't want to be some shiny, happy idiot. This is gritty, this is real.

I am just an old garbage bag full of blood patiently waiting for death to rescue me, but sometimes when I tell people that, their immediate response is, "How can you be sad, you're hilarious!!!!!" And then for five seconds I'm like, "This asshole who has never met me before is correct. I'm so funny I should stop thinking life is a trash can." Until five seconds after that, some human roadkill yells at the grocery store bagger or pulls his scrotum out on the train, and I get the urge to peel my skin off like the layers of an onion and jam my thumbs into my eye sockets. And then it's easy to just write the depression off as an irritation at the dummies I have to share the planet with. "I'm not depressed; dudes who ride unicycles in rush hour traffic are fucking idiots," or, "Nothing is wrong with me; the real problem is all these people mindlessly texting while their dogs shit in the middle of the G.D. sidewalk."

Two things forced me to finally have the "Sometimes I have a disproportionately rage-filled response to otherwise harmless shit" talk with my doctor. I was working my usual shift at the front desk of the animal hospital and the worst person in the world came in to buy dog food. She asked an unending stream of questions that I couldn't possibly answer as she emptied the entire contents of her handbag onto the counter in front of me. I hate the "please don't write a negative Yelp review of this business" trap that requires I stand there trying to look engaged while this woman uses me as a sounding board for questions like, "Is [redacted] going to eat three cans or maybe should I just get one?" She's not asking me, but she's not *not* asking me. And I have to wait there, held hostage because one of these questions pouring like vomit from her toothless maw might be one I can actually answer. "Can I really carry a 17-pound bag up my stairs?" (Well, not that one.) "I wonder if the dog really wants me to switch back to his old food." (Yeah, not that one either.) I could feel the familiar rageheat scratching at the backs of my eyeballs. And as she kept rambling nonsensically to herself, I calmly raised my hands to my ears and used my forefingers to hold them closed and said, "You have to get the fuck out of here or I will destroy you." So much for that stellar Yelp review.

A week later, I had the kind of anxiety attack that makes you feel like you're going to die on the spot in the parking lot of a combination gas station and Subway. I tossed my sandwich (tuna, plain, whole wheat because duh, I'm a health nut) onto the passenger seat and pawed at my chest while trying to catch my breath. What a depressing place to die, I thought. I assumed I was having a heart attack and I went straight to the hospital, smelling like old-ass Subway tuna fish.

I know when you feel a panic attack coming on, you're supposed to relax and do your breathing exercises, but in that moment, it feels like if I lie down and close my eyes for even a second, I will never open them again. And most of the time I'm down with that, but this shit always happens when my sheets need changing or my garbage can is full of freezer-burned Hot Pockets, and I get even more stressed out by the thought of whomever finds my corpse discovering the last thing I Googled was "Shark Tank bonus clips." Not being able to deal with your life is humiliating. It makes you feel weak. And if you're African-American and female, not only are you expected to be resilient enough to just take the hits and keep going, but if you can't, you're a black bitch with an attitude. *Rolls eyes for sarcastic effect.* You're not mentally ill, you're ghetto. Sitting in that hospital bed with a 23-year-old dude who looked like he was playing doctor with his father's stethoscope looped around his neck, I was so embarrassed, ashamed to be talking to him about being *so sad* as he dumped a syringe full of Ativan into my arm. I was sure I was letting Rosa Parks and Harriet Tubman down by talking about my silly little feelings.

All this might be easier if I could punch shit, but I'm not a punching-shit kind of person. I'm a sit-in-the-dark-in-the-bathroom-with-a-package-of-sharp-cheddar-cheese-slices person. The world is scary and terrible, and motherfuckers out here don't want Obamacare to fix a paper cut, let alone offer some discounted mental health care, so what can we do? Talk about it? Stop being afraid of it? Shut down dudes who want to dismiss us as fragile or crazy? I went on Lexapro, but after three weeks, it made me stop sleeping and fuck that. I'd rather be angry and well-rested than tired and happy. Or "happy." I have generic Klonopin and Ativan, and I learned how to do this 4-7-8 breathing technique that's supposed to switch your body from fight-or-flight to a passive response, but come on, bro. The only time it even occurs to me to do it is when I'm sweating and trying to dry-swallow some of these benzos. If I ever have more than $37 in my pocket, I'm going to open a school for girls with bad attitudes where we basically talk to therapists all day while wearing soft pants and occasionally taking a field trip to the nearest elote cart. And if that doesn't work, I'll just tell some jokes. Good thing I'm hilarious.

PART VII

SEXUAL POLITICS

Manifesto of the 343 Sluts

BY SIMONE DE BEAUVOIR

At a time when abortion was illegal in France, 343 women signed a petition stating that they had an abortion as an act of civil disobedience. By signing the petition, every woman was confessing to a crime and exposing themselves to prosecution. One of those signatories was Simone de Beauvoir, who also authored the manifesto published in *Le Nouvel Observateur* on April 5, 1971. It called for the legalization of abortion and free access to contraception. This act of civil disobedience resulted in the 1974 "Veil law" that repealed the penalty for the voluntary termination of a pregnancy in the first ten weeks and also paved the way for birth control in France. Known for her groundbreaking feminist text *The Second Sex*, de Beauvoir was not just an intellectual and philosopher but also a feminist activist who used her writing to break down gendered stereotypes and to challenge laws prohibiting women's bodily autonomy.

One million women in France have abortions every year.

Condemned to secrecy they do so in dangerous conditions, while under medical supervision this is one of the simplest procedures.

We are silencing these millions of women.

I declare that I am one of them. I declare that I have had an abortion.

Just as we demand free access to contraception, we demand the freedom to have an abortion.

Abortion

A word which seems to express and define the feminist fight

once and for all. To be a feminist is to fight for free abortion on demand.

Abortion

It's a women's thing, like cooking, diapers, something dirty. The fight to obtain free abortion on demand feels somehow ridiculous or petty. It can't shake the smell of hospitals or food, or of poo behind women's backs.

The complexity of the emotions linked to the fight for abortion precisely indicate our difficulty in being, the pain that we have in persuading ourselves that it is worth the trouble of fighting for ourselves.

It goes without saying that we do not have the right to choose what we want to do with our bodies, as other human beings do. Our wombs, however, belong to us.

Free abortion on demand is not the ultimate goal of women's plight. On the contrary, it is but the most basic necessity, without which the political fight cannot even begin. It is out of vital necessity that women should win back control and reintegrate their bodies. They hold a unique status in history: human beings who, in modern societies, do not have unfettered control over their own bodies. Up until today it was only slaves who held this status.

The scandal continues. Each year 1,500,000 women live in shame and despair. 5,000 of us die. But the moral order remains steadfast. We want to scream.

Free abortion on demand is:

Immediately ceasing to be ashamed of your body, being free and proud in your body just as everyone up until now who has had full use of it;

no longer being ashamed of being a woman.

An ego broken into tiny fucking pieces, that's what all women who have to undergo a clandestine abortion experience; just being yourself all the time, no longer having that ignoble fear of being "taken," taken into a trap, being double and powerless with a sort of tumor in your belly;

a thrilling fight, insofar as if I win I only begin to belong to myself and no longer to the State, to a family, to a child I do not want;

a step along the path to reaching full control over the production of children. Women, like all other producers, have in fact got the absolute right to control all of their productions. This control implies a radical change in women's mental configuration, and a no less radical change in social structures.

1. I will have a child if I want one, and no moral pressure, institution or economic imperative will compel me to do so. This is my political power. As any kind of producer, I can, while waiting for improvement, put pressure on society through my production (child strike).

2. I will have a child if I want one and if the society I will be bringing it into is suitable for me, if it will not make me a slave to that child, its nurse, its maid, its punchbag.

3. I will have a child if I want one, if society is suitable for both me and it, I am responsible for it, no risk of war, no work subject to whims.

No to supervised freedom.
The battle that has risen up around the subject of abortion goes over the heads of those it is most relevant to—women. The issue of whether the law should be made more liberal, the issue of when abortion can be permitted, basically the issue of therapeutic abortion does not interest us because it does not concern us.

Therapeutic abortion requires "good" reasons to receive "permission" to have an abortion. To put it plainly, this means that we must earn the right to not have children. That the decision as to whether to have them or not does not belong to us now any more than it did before.

The principle remains that it is legitimate to force women to have children.

A modification to the law, allowing exceptions to this principle, would do nothing other than reinforce it. The most liberal of laws would still be regulating how our bodies can be used. And how our bodies should be used is not something which should be regulated. We do not want tolerance, scraps of what other humans are born with: the freedom to use their bodies as they wish. We are as opposed to the Peyret Law or the ANEA project as to the current law, since we are opposed to all laws which claim to regulate any aspect of our bodies. We do not want a better law, we want it to be removed, pure and simple. We are not asking for charity, we want justice. There are 27,000,000 of us here alone. 27,000,000 "citizens" treated like cattle.

To fascists of all kinds—who admit that is what they are and lay into us, or who call themselves Catholics, fundamentalists, demographers, doctors, experts, jurists, "responsible men," Debré, Peyret, Lejeune, Pompidou, Chauchard, the Pope—we say that we have uncovered them.

We should call them assassins of the people. We should forbid them to use the term "respect for life" which is an obscenity in their mouths. There should be 27,000,000 of us. We should fight until the end because we want nothing more than our right: the free use of our bodies.

The ten commandments of the Bourgeois State:

You choose a fetus over a human being when that human is female.

No woman will have an abortion while Debré wants 100 million more French people.

You will have 100 million French people, as long as it costs you nothing.

You will be particularly severe with poor females who cannot go to England.

As such you will have a wheel of unemployment to make your capitalists happy.

You will be very moralistic, because God knows what "we" women would do if we had such freedom.

You will save the fetus, since it's more interesting to kill them off aged 18, the age of conscription. You will really need them as you pursue your imperialist politics.

You use contraception yourself, to send just a few children to the Polytechnique or the ENA because your flat only has 10 rooms.

As for the others, you will disparage the pill, because that's the only thing missing.

Signatures:

J. Abba-Sidick	Monique Anfredon	Maryse Arditi
Janita Abdalleh	Catherine Arditi	Hélène Argellies

Françoise Arnoul
Florence Asie
Isabelle Atlan
Brigitte Auber
Stéphane Audran
Colette Audry
Tina Aumont
L. Azan
Jacqueline Azim
Micheline Baby
Geneviève Bachelier
Cécile Ballif
Néna Baratier
D. Bard
E. Bardis
Anna de Bascher
C. Batini
Chantal Baulier
Hélène de Beauvoir
Simone de Beauvoir
Colette Bec
M. Bediou
Michèle Bedos
Anne Bellec
Lolleh Bellon
Edith Benoist
Anita Benoit
Aude Bergier
Dominique Bernabe
Jocelyne Bernard
Catherine Bernheim
Nicole Bernheim
Tania Bescomd
Jeannine Beylot
Monique Bigot
Fabienne Biguet
Nicole Bize
Nicole de Boisanger
Valérie Boisgel
Y. Boissaire
Silvina Boissonnade
Martine Bonzon
Françoise Borel

Ginette Bossavit
Olga Bost
Anne-Marie Bouge
Pierrette Bourdin
Monique Bourroux
Bénédicte Boysson-
Bardies
M. Braconnier-Leclerc
M. Braun
Andrée Brumeaux
Dominique Brumeaux
Marie-Françoise
Brumeaux
Jacqueline Busset
Françoise De Camas
Anne Camus
Ginette Cano
Ketty Cenel
Jacqueline Chambord
Josiane Chanel
Danièle Chinsky
Claudine Chonez
Martine Chosson
Catherine Claude
M.-Louise, Clave
Françoise Clavel
Iris Clert
Geneviève Cluny
Annie Cohen
Florence Collin
Anne Cordonnier
Anne Cornaly
Chantal Cornier
J. Corvisier
Michèle Cristofari
Lydia Cruse
Christiane Dancourt
Hélène Darakis
Françoise Dardy
Anne-Marie Daumont
Anne Dauzon
Martine Dayen
Catherine Dechezelle

Marie Dedieu
Lise Deharme
Claire Delpech
Christine Delphy
Catherine Deneuve
Dominique Desanti
Geneviève Deschamps
Claire Deshayes
Nicole Despiney
Catherine Deudon
Sylvie Dlarte
Christine Diaz
Arlette Donati
Gilberte Doppler
Danièle Drevet
Evelyne Droux
Dominique Dubois
Muguette Dubois
Dolorès Dubrana
C. Dufour
Elyane Dugny
Simone Dumont
Christiane Duparc
Pierrette Duperray
Annie Dupuis
Marguerite Duras
Françoise d'Eaubonne
Nicole Echard
Isabelle Ehni
Myrtho Elfort
Danièle El-Gharbaoui
Françoise Elie
Arlette Elkaim
Barbara Enu
Jacqueline d'Estree
Françoise Fabian
Anne Fabre-Luce
Annie Fargue
J. Foliot
Brigitte Fontaine
Antoinette Fouque-
Grugnardi
Eléonore Friedmann

Françoise Fromentin
J. Fruhling
Danièle Fulgent
Madeleine Gabula
Yamina Gacon
Luce Garcia-Ville
Monique Garnier
Micha Garrigue
Geneviève Gasseau
Geneviève Gaubert
Claude Genia
Elyane Germain-Horelle
Dora Gerschenfeld
Michèle Girard
F. Gogan
Hélène Gonin
Claude Gorodesky
Marie-Luce Gorse
Deborah Gorvier
Martine Gottlib
Rosine Grange
Rosemonde Gros
Valérie Groussard
Lise Grundman
A. Guerrand-Hermes
Françoise de Gruson
Catherine Guyot
Gisèle Halimi
Herta Hansmann
Noëlle Henry
M. Hery
Nicole Higelin
Dorinne Horst
Raymonde Hubschmid
Y. Imbert
L. Jalin
Catherine Joly
Colette Joly
Yvette Joly
Hemine Karagheuz
Ugne Karvelis
Katia Kaupp
Nenda Kerien

F. Korn
Hélène Kostoff
Marie-Claire Labie
Myriam Laborde
Anne-Marie Lafaurie
Bernadette Lafont
Michèle Lambert
Monique Lange
Maryse Lapergue
Catherine Larnicol
Sophie Larnicol
Monique Lascaux
M.-T. Latreille
Christiane Laurent
Françoise Lavallard
G. Le Bonniec
Danièle Lebrun
Annie Leclerc
M.-France Le Dantec
Colette Le Digol
Violette Leduc
Martine Leduc-Amel
Françoise Le Forestier
Michèle Leglise-Vian
M. Claude Lejaille
Mireille Lelièvre
Michèle Lemonnier
Françoise Lentin
Joëlle Lequeux
Emmanuelle de Lesseps
Anne Levaillant
Dona Levy
Irène Lhomme
Christine Llinas
Sabine Lods
Marceline Loridan
Edith Loser
Françoise Lugagne
M. Lyleire
Judith Magre
C. Maillard
Michèle Manceaux
Bona de Mandiargues

Michèle Marquais
Anne Martelle
Monique Martens
Jacqueline Martin
Milka Martin
Renée Marzuk
Colette Masbou
Cella Maulin
Liliane Maury
Edith Mayeur
Jeanne Maynial
Odile du Mazaubrun
Marie-Thérèse Mazel
Gaby Memmi
Michèle Meritz
Marie-Claude Mestral
Maryvonne Meuraud
Jolaine Meyer
Pascale Meynier
Charlotte Millau
M. de Miroschodji
Geneviève Mnich
Ariane Mnouchkine
Colette Moreau
Jeanne Moreau
Nelly Moreno
Michèle Moretti
Lydia Morin
Mariane Moulergues
Liane Mozere
Nicole Muchnik
C. Muffong
Véronique Nahoum
Eliane Navarro
Henriette Nizan
Lila de Nobili
Bulle Ogier
J. Olena
Janine Olivier
Wanda Olivier
Yvette Orengo
Iro Oshier
Gege Pardo

Elisabeth Pargny
Jeanne Pasquier
M. Pelletier
Jacqueline Perez
M. Perez
Nicole Perrottet
Sophie Pianko
Odette Picquet
Marie Pillet
Elisabeth Pimar
Marie-France Pisier
Olga Poliakoff
Danièle Poux
Micheline Presle
Anne-Marie Quazza
Marie-Christine
Questerbert
Susy Rambaud
Gisèle Rebillion
Gisèle Reboul
Arlette Reinert
Arlette Repart
Christiane Ribeiro
M. Ribeyrol
Delya Ribes
Marie-Françoise Richard
Suzanne Rigail-Blaise
Marcelle Rigaud
Laurence Rigault
Danièle Rigaut
Danielle Riva
M. Riva
Claude Rivière

Marthe Robert
Christiane Rochefort
J. Rogaldi
Chantal Rogeon
Francine Rolland
Christiane Rorato
Germaine Rossignol
Hélène Rostoff
G. Roth-Bernstein
C. Rousseau
Françoise Routhier
Danièle Roy
Yvette Rudy
Françoise Sagan
Rachel Salik
Renée Saurel
Marie-Ange Schiltz
Lucie Schmidt
Scania de Schonen
Monique Selim
Liliane Sendyke
Claudine Serre
Colette Sert
Jeanine Sert
Catherine de Seyne
Delphine Seyrig
Sylvie Sfez
Liliane Siegel
Annie Sinturel
Michèle Sirot
Michèle Stemer
Cécile Stern
Alexandra Stewart

Gaby Sylvia
Francine Tabet
Danièle Tardrew
Anana Terramorsi
Arlette Tethany
Joëlle Thevenet
Marie-Christine
Theurkauff
Constance Thibaud
Josy Thibaut
Rose Thierry
Suzanne Thivier
Sophie Thomas
Nadine Trintignant
Irène Tunc
Tyc Dumont
Marie-Pia Vallet
Agnès Van-Parys
Agnès Varda
Catherine Varlin
Patricia Varod
Cleuza Vernier
Ursula Vian-Kubler
Louise Villareal
Marina Vlady
A. Wajntal
Jeannine Weil
Anne Wiazemsky
Monique Wittig
Josée Yanne
Catherine Yovanovitch
Annie Zelensky

The list of signatures is a first act of revolt. For the first time, women have decided to lift the taboo weighing down on their wombs: women of the Women's Liberation Movement, the Free Abortion Movement, women who work, women who stay at home.

At the Women's Liberation Movement we are neither a party, nor an organization, nor an association, and even less so their women's subsidiary. This is an historic movement which does not only bring together women who come to the Women's Liberation Movement, this is the movement for all women, wherever they live, wherever they work, who have decided to take their lives and their freedom into their own hands. Fighting against our oppression means shattering all of society's structures, especially the most routine ones. We do not want any part or any place in this society which has been built without us and at our expense.

When womankind, the sector of humanity that has been lurking in the shadows, takes its destiny into its own hands, that's when we can start talking about a revolution.

A Free Abortion Movement has been set up, bringing together all those who are prepared to fight to the end for free abortions. The goal of this movement is to stir up local and corporate groups, to coordinate an explanatory and informative campaign, to become the only mass movement capable of demanding our right to decide for ourselves.

Thinking Sex

Notes for a Radical Theory
of the Politics of Sexuality

BY GAYLE S. RUBIN

Gayle S. Rubin is an associate professor of anthropology at the University of Michigan and recipient of the Woman of the Year Award from the National Leather Association. Rubin's assertion that gender is a cultural construct and not an essential or biological truth made her 1975 essay "The Traffic in Women" an important feminist text. In this excerpt from her 1984 essay "Thinking Sex," Rubin examined how certain sexual behaviors are constructed as moral or natural and others as unnatural. "Moral panics," she writes, "rarely alleviate any real problem because they are chimeras and signifiers." These moral panics seek to create cultural divisions between good and bad, deviant and normal, and to what end? "Thinking Sex" has become a foundational text of queer theory, lesbian history, the feminist sex wars, the politics of sadomasochism, crusades against prostitution and pornography, and the historical development of sexual knowledge.

SEXUAL THOUGHTS

"You see, Tim," Phillip said suddenly, "your argument isn't reasonable. Suppose I granted your first point that homosexuality is justifiable in certain instances and under certain controls. Then there is the catch: where does justification end and degeneracy begin? Society must condemn to protect. Permit even the intellectual homosexual a place of respect and the first bar is down. Then comes the next

and the next until the sadist, the flagellist, the criminally insane demand their places, and society ceases to exist. So I ask again: where
is the line drawn? Where does degeneracy begin if not at the beginning of individual freedom in such matters?"

[Fragment from a discussion between two gay men trying to
decide if they may love each other]

A radical theory of sex must identify, describe, explain, and denounce erotic injustice and sexual oppression. Such a theory needs
refined conceptual tools which can grasp the subject and hold it in
view. It must build rich descriptions of sexuality as it exists in society and history. It requires a convincing critical language that
can convey the barbarity of sexual persecution.

Several persistent features of thought about sex inhibit the development of such a theory. These assumptions are so pervasive in
Western culture that they are rarely questioned. Thus, they tend
to reappear in different political contexts, acquiring new rhetorical expressions but reproducing fundamental axioms.

One such axiom is sexual essentialism—the idea that sex is a
natural force that exists prior to social life and shapes institutions.
Sexual essentialism is embedded in the folk wisdoms of Western
societies, which consider sex to be eternally unchanging, asocial,
and transhistorical. Dominated for over a century by medicine, psychiatry, and psychology, the academic study of sex has reproduced
essentialism. These fields classify sex as a property of individuals.
It may reside in their hormones or their psyches. It may be construed as physiological or psychological. But within these ethno-
scientific categories, sexuality has no history and no significant
social determinants.

During the last five years, a sophisticated historical and theoretical scholarship has challenged sexual essentialism both explicitly
and implicitly. Gay history, particularly the work of Jeffrey Weeks,
has led this assault by showing that homosexuality as we know it is
a relatively modern institutional complex. Many historians have
come to see the contemporary institutional forms of heterosexuality as an even more recent development. An important contributor
to the new scholarship is Judith Walkowitz, whose research has
demonstrated the extent to which prostitution was transformed
around the turn of the century. She provides meticulous descrip-

tions of how the interplay of social forces such as ideology, fear, political agitation, legal reform, and medical practice can change the structure of sexual behavior and alter its consequences.

Michel Foucault's *The History of Sexuality* (1978) has been the most influential and emblematic text of the new scholarship on sex. Foucault criticizes the traditional understanding of sexuality as a natural libido yearning to break free of social constraint. He argues that desires are not pre-existing biological entities, but rather that they are constituted in the course of historically specific social practices. He emphasizes the generative aspects of the social organization of sex rather than its repressive elements by pointing out that new sexualities are constantly produced. And he points to a major discontinuity between kinship-based systems of sexuality and more modern forms.

The new scholarship on sexual behavior has given sex a history and created a constructivist alternative to sexual essentialism. Underlying this body of work is an assumption that sexuality is constituted in society and history, not biologically ordained. This does not mean the biological capacities are not prerequisites for human sexuality. It does mean that human sexuality is not comprehensible in purely biological terms. Human organisms with human brains are necessary for human cultures, but no examination of the body or its parts can explain the nature and variety of human social systems. The belly's hunger gives no clues as to the complexities of cuisine. The body, the brain, the genitalia, and the capacity for language are necessary for human sexuality. But they do not determine its content, its experiences, or its institutional forms. Moreover, we never encounter the body unmediated by the meanings that cultures give to it. To paraphrase Lévi-Strauss, my position on the relationship between biology and sexuality is a "Kantianism without a transcendental libido."

It is impossible to think with any clarity about the politics of race or gender as long as these are thought of as biological entities rather than as social constructs. Similarly, sexuality is impervious to political analysis as long as it is primarily conceived as a biological phenomenon or an aspect of individual psychology. Sexuality is as much a human product as are diets, methods of transportation, systems of etiquette, forms of labor, types of entertainment, processes of production, and modes of oppression. Once sex is understood in terms of social analysis and historical understanding, a more realistic politics of sex becomes possible. One may then think of sexual politics in terms of such phenomena as populations, neighborhoods, settlement patterns, migration, urban conflict, epidemiology, and police technology. These are more fruitful categories of thought than the more traditional ones of sin, disease, neurosis, pathology, decadence, pollution, or the decline and fall of empires.

By detailing the relationships between stigmatized erotic populations and the social forces which regulate them, work such as that of Allan Bérubé, John D'Emilio, Jeffrey Weeks, and Judith Walkowitz contains implicit categories of political analysis and criticism. Nevertheless, the constructivist perspective has displayed some political weaknesses. This has been most evident in misconstructions of Foucault's position.

Because of his emphasis on the ways that sexuality is produced, Foucault has been vulnerable to interpretations that deny or minimize the reality of sexual repression in the more political sense. Foucault makes it abundantly clear that he is not denying the existence of sexual repression so much as inscribing it within a large dynamic. Sexuality in western societies has been structured within an extremely punitive social framework, and has been subjected to very real formal and informal controls. It is necessary to recognize repressive phenomena without resorting to the essentialist assumptions of the language of libido. It is important to hold repressive sexual practices in focus, even while situating them within a different totality and a more refined terminology.

Most radical thought about sex has been embedded within a model of the instincts and their restraints. Concepts of sexual oppression have been lodged within that more biological understanding of sexuality. It is often easier to fall back on the notion of a natural libido subjected to inhumane repression than to reformulate concepts of sexual injustice within a more constructivist framework. But it is essential that we do so. We need a radical critique of sexual arrangements that has the conceptual elegance of Foucault and the evocative passion of Reich.

The new scholarship on sex has brought a welcome insistence that sexual terms be restricted to their proper historical and social contexts, and a cautionary skepticism toward sweeping generalizations. But it is important to be able to indicate groupings of erotic behavior and general trends within erotic discourse. In addition to sexual essentialism, there are at least five other ideological formations whose grip on sexual thought is so strong that to fail to discuss them is to remain enmeshed within them. These are sex negativity, the fallacy of misplaced scale, the hierarchical valuation of sex acts, the domino theory of sexual peril, and the lack of a concept of benign sexual variation.

Of these five, the most important is sex negativity. Western cultures generally consider sex to be a dangerous, destructive, negative force. Most Christian tradition, following Paul, holds that sex is inherently sinful. It may be redeemed if performed within marriage for procreative purposes and if the pleasurable aspects are not enjoyed too much. In turn, this idea rests on the assumption that the genitalia are an intrinsically inferior part of the body, much lower and less holy than the mind, the "soul," the "heart," or even the upper part of the digestive system (the status of the excretory organs is close to that of the genitalia). Such notions have by now acquired a life of their own and no longer depend solely on religion for their perseverance.

This culture always treats sex with suspicion. It construes and judges almost any sexual practice in terms of its worst possible expression. Sex is presumed guilty until proven innocent. Virtually all erotic behavior is considered bad unless a specific reason to exempt it has been established. The most acceptable excuses are marriage, reproduction, and love. Sometimes scientific curiosity, aesthetic experience, or a long-term intimate relationship may serve. But the exercise of erotic capacity, intelligence, curiosity, or creativity all require pretexts that are unnecessary for other pleasures, such as the enjoyment of food, fiction, or astronomy.

What I call the fallacy of misplaced scale is a corollary of sex negativity. Susan Sontag once commented that since Christianity focused "on sexual behavior as the root of virtue, everything pertaining to sex has been a 'special case' in our culture." Sex law has incorporated the religious attitude that heretical sex is an especially heinous sin that deserves the harshest punishments. Throughout much of European and American history, a single act of consensual anal penetration was grounds for execution. In some states, sodomy still carries twenty-year prison sentences.

Outside the law, sex is also a marked category. Small differences in value or behavior are often experienced as cosmic threats. Although people can be intolerant, silly, or pushy about what constitutes proper diet, differences in menu rarely provoke the kinds of rage, anxiety, and sheer terror that routinely accompany differences in erotic taste. Sexual acts are burdened with an excess of significance.

Modern Western societies appraise sex acts according to a hierarchical system of sexual value. Marital, reproductive heterosexuals are alone at the top erotic pyramid. Clamoring below are unmarried monogamous heterosexuals in couples, followed by most other heterosexuals. Solitary sex floats ambiguously. The powerful nineteenth-century stigma on masturbation lingers in less potent, modified forms, such as the idea that masturbation is an inferior substitute for partnered encounters. Stable, long-term lesbian and gay male couples are verging on respectability, but bar dykes and promiscuous gay men are hovering just above the groups at the very bottom of the pyramid. The most despised sexual castes currently include transsexuals, transvestites, fetishists, sadomasochists, sex workers such as prostitutes and porn models, and the lowliest of all, those whose eroticism transgresses generational boundaries.

Individuals whose behavior stands high in this hierarchy are rewarded with certified mental health, respectability, legality, social and physical mobility, institutional support, and material benefits. As sexual behaviors or occupations fall lower on the scale, the individuals who practice them are subjected to a presumption of mental illness, disreputability, criminality, restricted social and physical mobility, loss of institutional support, and economic sanctions.

Extreme and punitive stigma maintains some sexual behaviors as low status and is an effective sanction against those who engage in them. The intensity of this stigma is rooted in Western religious traditions. But most of its contemporary content derives from medical and psychiatric opprobrium.

The old religious taboos were primarily based on kinship forms of social organization. They were meant to deter inappropriate unions and to provide proper kin. Sex laws derived from Biblical pronouncements were aimed at preventing the acquisition of the wrong kinds of affinal partners: consanguineous kin (incest), the same gender (homosexuality), or the wrong species (bestiality). When medicine and psychiatry acquired extensive powers over sexuality, they were less concerned with unsuitable mates than with unfit forms of desire. If taboos against incest best characterized kinship systems of sexual organization, then the shift to an emphasis on taboos against masturbation was more apposite to the newer systems organized around qualities of erotic experience.

Medicine and psychiatry multiplied the categories of sexual misconduct. The section on psychosexual disorders in the *Diagnostic and Statistical Manual of Mental and Physical Disorders* (DSM) of the American Psychiatric Association (APA) is a fairly reliable map of the current moral hierarchy of sexual activities. The APA list is much more elaborate than the traditional condemnations of whoring, sodomy, and adultery. The most recent edition, *DSM-III*, removed homosexuality from the roster of mental disorders after a long political struggle. But fetishism, sadism, masochism, transsexuality, transvestism, exhibitionism, voyeurism, and pedophilia are quite firmly entrenched as psychological malfunctions. Books are still being written about the genesis, etiology, treatment, and cure of these assorted "pathologies."

Psychiatric condemnation of sexual behaviors invokes concepts of mental and emotional inferiority rather than categories of sexual sin. Low-status sex practices are vilified as mental diseases or symptoms of defective personality integration. In addition, psychological terms conflate difficulties of psycho-dynamic functioning with modes of erotic conduct. They equate sexual masochism with self-destructive personality patterns, sexual sadism with emotional aggression, and homoeroticism with immaturity. These terminological muddles have become powerful stereotypes that are indiscriminately applied to individuals on the basis of their sexual orientations.

Popular culture is permeated with ideas that erotic variety is dangerous, unhealthy, depraved, and a menace to everything from small children to national security. Popular sexual ideology is a noxious stew made up of ideas of sexual sin, concepts of psychological inferiority, anti-communism, mob hysteria, accusations of witchcraft, and xenophobia. The mass media nourish these attitudes with relentless propaganda. I would call this system of erotic stigma the last socially respectable form of prejudice if the old forms did not show such obstinate vitality, and new ones did not continually become apparent.

All these hierarchies of sexual value—religious, psychiatric, and popular—function in much the same ways as do ideological systems of racism, ethnocentrism, and religious chauvinism. They rationalize the well-being of the sexually privileged and the adversity of the sexual rabble.

Figure 9.1 diagrams a general version of the sexual value system. According to this system, sexuality that is "good," "normal," and "natural" should ideally be heterosexual, marital, monogamous, reproductive, and non-commercial. It should be coupled, relational, within the same generation, and occur at home. It should not involve pornography, fetish objects, sex toys of any sort, or roles other than male and female. Any sex that violates these rules is "bad," "abnormal," or "unnatural." Bad sex may be homosexual, unmarried, promiscuous, non-procreative, or commercial. It may be masturbatory or take place at orgies, may be casual, may cross generational lines, and may take place in "public," or at least in the bushes or the baths. It may involve the use of pornography, fetish objects, sex toys, or unusual roles.

Figure 9.2 diagrams another aspect of the sexual hierarchy: the need to draw and maintain an imaginary line between good and bad sex. Most of the discourses on sex, be they religious, psychiatric, popular, or political, delimit a very small portion of human sexual capacity as sanctifiable, safe, healthy, mature, legal, or politically correct. The "line" distinguishes these from all other erotic behaviors, which are understood to be the work of the devil, dangerous, psychopathological, infantile, or politically reprehensible. Arguments are then conducted over "where to draw the line," and to determine what other activities, if any, may be permitted to cross over into acceptability.

All these models assume a domino theory of sexual peril. The line appears to stand between sexual order and chaos. It expresses the fear that if anything is permitted to cross this erotic DMZ, the barrier against scary sex will crumble and something unspeakable will skitter across.

Most systems of sexual judgment—religious, psychological,

feminist, or socialist—attempt to determine on which side of the line a particular act falls. Only sex acts on the good side of the line are accorded moral complexity. For instance, heterosexual encounters may be sublime or disgusting, free or forced, healing or destructive, romantic or mercenary. As long as it does not violate other rules, heterosexuality is acknowledged to exhibit the full range of human experience. In contrast, all sex acts on the bad side of the line are considered utterly repulsive and devoid of all emotional nuance. The further from the line a sex act is, the more it is depicted as a uniformly bad experience.

As a result of the sex conflicts of the last decade, some behavior near the border is inching across it. Unmarried couples living together, masturbation, and some forms of homosexuality are moving in the direction of respectability. Most homosexuality is still on the bad side of the line. But if it is coupled and monogamous, the society is beginning to recognize that it includes the full range of human interaction. Promiscuous homosexuality, sadomasochism, fetishism, transsexuality, and cross-generational encounters are still viewed as unmodulated horrors incapable of involving affection, love, free choice, kindness, or transcendence.

This kind of sexual morality has more in common with ideologies of racism than with true ethics. It grants virtue to the dominant groups, and relegates vice to the underprivileged. A democratic morality should judge sexual acts by the way partners treat one another, the level of mutual consideration, the presence or absence of coercion, and quantity and quality of the pleasures they provide. Whether sex acts are gay or straight, coupled or in groups, naked or in underwear, commercial or free, with or without video, should not be ethical concerns.

It is difficult to develop a pluralistic sexual ethics without a concept of benign sexual variation. Variation is a fundamental property of all life, from the simplest biological organisms to the most complex human social formations. Yet sexuality is supposed to conform to a single standard. One of the most tenacious ideas about sex is that there is one best way to do it, and that everyone should do it that way.

Most people find it difficult to grasp that whatever they like to do sexually will be thoroughly repulsive to someone else, and that whatever repels them sexually will be the most treasured delight of someone, somewhere. One need not like or perform a particular sex act in order to recognize that someone else will, and that this difference does not indicate a lack of good taste, mental health, or intelligence in either party. Most people mistake their sexual preferences for a universal system that will or should work for everyone.

This notion of a single ideal sexuality characterizes most systems of thought about sex. For religion, the ideal is procreative marriage. For psychology, it is mature heterosexuality. Although its content varies, the format of a single sexual standard is continually reconstituted within other rhetorical frameworks, including feminism and socialism. It is just as objectionable to insist that everyone should be lesbian, non-monogamous, or kinky, as to believe that everyone should be heterosexual, married, or vanilla—though the latter set of opinions are backed by considerably more coercive power than the former.

Progressives who would be ashamed to display cultural chauvinism in other areas routinely exhibit it toward sexual differences. We have learned to cherish different cultures as unique expressions of human inventiveness rather than as the inferior or disgusting habits of savages. We need a similarly anthropological understanding of different sexual cultures.

Empirical sex research is the one field that does incorporate a positive concept of sexual variation. Alfred Kinsey approached the study of sex with the same uninhibited curiosity he had previously applied to examining a species of wasp. His scientific detachment gave his work a refreshing neutrality that enraged moralists and caused immense controversy. Among Kinsey's successors, John Gagnon and William Simon have pioneered the application of sociological understandings to erotic variety. Even some of the older sexology is useful. Although his work is imbued with unappetizing eugenic beliefs, Havelock Ellis was an acute and sympathetic observer. His monumental *Studies in the Psychology of Sex* is resplendent with detail.

Much political writing on sexuality reveals complete ignorance of both classical sexology and modern sex research. Perhaps this is because so few colleges and universities bother to teach human sexuality, and because so much stigma adheres even to scholarly investigation of sex. Neither sexology nor sex research has been immune to the prevailing sexual value system. Both contain assumptions and information which should not be accepted uncritically. But sexology and sex research provide abundant detail, a welcome posture of calm, and a well-developed ability to treat sexual variety as something that exists rather than as something to be exterminated. These fields can provide an empirical grounding for a radical theory of sexuality more useful than the combination of psychoanalysis and feminist first principles to which so many texts resort.

THE LIMITS OF FEMINISM

We know that in an overwhelmingly large number of cases, sex crime is associated with pornography. We know that sex criminals read it, are clearly influenced by it. I believe that, if we can eliminate the distribution of such items among impressionable children, we shall greatly reduce our frightening sex-crime rate.

—J. Edgar Hoover, cited in Hyde, 1965, p. 31

In the absence of a more articulated radical theory of sex, most progressives have turned to feminism for guidance. But the relationship between feminism and sex is complex. Because sexuality is a nexus of relationships between genders, much of the oppression of women is borne by, mediated through, and constituted within, sexuality. Feminism has always been vitally interested in sex. But there have been two strains of feminist thought on the subject. One tendency has criticized the restrictions on women's sexual behavior and denounced the high costs imposed on women for being sexually active. This tradition of feminist sexual thought has called for a sexual liberation that would work for women as well as for men. The second tendency has considered sexual liberalization to be inherently a mere extension of male privilege. This tradition resonates with conservative, anti-sexual discourse. With the advent of the anti-pornography movement, it achieved temporary hegemony over feminist analysis.

The anti-pornography movement and its texts have been the most extensive expression of this discourse. In addition, proponents of this viewpoint have condemned virtually every variant of sexual expression as anti-feminist. Within this framework, monogamous lesbianism that occurs within long-term, intimate relationships and which does not involve playing with polarized roles, has replaced married, procreative heterosexuality at the top of the value hierarchy. Heterosexuality has been demoted to somewhere in the middle. Apart from this change, everything else looks more or less familiar. The lower depths are occupied by the usual groups and behaviors: prostitution, transsexuality, sadomasochism, and cross-generational activities. Most gay male conduct, all casual sex, promiscuity, and lesbian behavior that does involve roles or kink or non-monogamy are also censured. Even sexual fantasy during masturbation is denounced as a phallocentric holdover.

This discourse on sexuality is less a sexology than a demonology. It presents most sexual behavior in the worst possible light. Its descriptions of erotic conduct always use the worst available example as if it were representative. It presents the most disgusting pornography, the most exploited forms of prostitution, and the least palatable or most shocking manifestations of sexual variation. This rhetorical tactic consistently misrepresents human sexuality in all its forms. The picture of human sexuality that emerges from this literature is unremittingly ugly.

In addition, this anti-porn rhetoric is a massive exercise in scapegoating. It criticizes non-routine acts of love rather than routine acts of oppression, exploitation, or violence. This demon sexology directs legitimate anger at women's lack of personal safety against innocent individuals, practices and communities. Anti-porn propaganda often implies that sexism originates within the commercial sex industry and subsequently infects the rest of society. This is sociologically nonsensical. The sex industry is hardly a feminist utopia. It reflects the sexism that exists in the society as a whole. We need to analyze and oppose the manifestations of gender inequality specific to the sex industry. But this is not the same as attempting to wipe out commercial sex.

Similarly, erotic minorities such as sadomasochists and transsexuals are as likely to exhibit sexist attitudes or behavior as any other politically random social grouping. But to claim that they are inherently anti-feminist is sheer fantasy. A good deal of current feminist literature attributes the oppression of women to graphic representations of sex, prostitution, sex education, sadomasochism, male homosexuality, and transsexualism. Whatever happened to the family, religion, education, child-rearing practices, the media, the state, psychiatry, job discrimination, and unequal pay?

Finally, this so-called feminist discourse recreates a very conservative sexual morality. For over a century, battles have been waged over just how much shame, distress, and punishment should be incurred by sexual activity. The conservative tradition has promoted opposition to pornography, prostitution, homosexuality, all erotic variation, sex education, sex research, abortion, and contraception. The opposing, pro-sex tradition has included individuals like Havelock Ellis, Magnus Hirschfeld, Alfred Kinsey, and Victoria Woodhull, as well as the sex education movement, organizations of militant prostitutes and homosexuals, the reproductive rights movement, and organizations such as the Sexual Reform League of the 1960s. This motley collection of sex reformers, sex educators, and sexual militants has mixed records on both sexual and feminist issues. But surely they are closer to the spirit of modern feminism than are moral crusaders, the social purity movement, and anti-vice organizations. Nevertheless, the current feminist sexual demonology generally elevates the anti-vice crusaders to positions of ancestral honor, while condemning the more liberatory tradition as antifeminist. In an essay that exemplifies some of these trends, Sheila Jeffreys blames Havelock Ellis, Edward Carpenter, Alexandra Kollontai, "believers in the joy of sex of every possible political persuasion," and the 1929 congress of the World League for Sex Reform for making "a great contribution to the defeat of militant feminism."

The anti-pornography movement and its avatars have claimed to speak for all feminism. Fortunately, they do not. Sexual liberation has been and continues to be a feminist goal. The women's movement may have produced some of the most retrogressive sexual thinking this side of the Vatican. But it has also produced an exciting, innovative, and articulate defense of sexual pleasure and erotic justice. This "pro-sex" feminism has been spearheaded by lesbians whose sexuality does not conform to movement standards of purity (primarily lesbian sadomasochists and butch/femme dykes), by unapologetic heterosexuals, and by women who adhere to classic radical feminism rather than to the revisionist celebrations of femininity which have become so common. Although the antiporn forces have attempted to weed anyone who disagrees with them out of the movement, the fact remains that feminist thought about sex is profoundly polarized.

Whenever there is polarization, there is an unhappy tendency to think the truth lies somewhere in between. Ellen Willis has commented sarcastically that "the feminist bias is that women are equal to men and the male chauvinist bias is that women are inferior. The unbiased view is that the truth lies somewhere in between." The most recent development in the feminist sex wars is the emergence of a "middle" that seeks to evade the dangers of anti-porn fascism, on the one hand, and a supposed "anything goes" libertarianism, on the other. Although it is hard to criticize a position that is not yet fully formed, I want to draw attention to some incipient problems.

The emergent middle is based on a false characterization of the poles of debate, construing both sides as equally extremist. According to B. Ruby Rich, "the desire for a language of sexuality has led feminists into locations (pornography, sadomasochism) too narrow or overdetermined for a fruitful discussion. Debate has collapsed into a rumble." True, the fights between Women Against Pornography (WAP) and lesbian sadomasochists have resembled gang warfare. But the responsibility for this lies primarily with the anti-porn movement, and its refusal to engage in principled discussion. S/M lesbians have been forced into a struggle to maintain their membership in the movement, and to defend themselves against slander. No major spokeswoman for lesbian S/M has argued for any kind of S/M supremacy, or advocated that everyone should be a sadomasochist. In addition to self-defense, S/M lesbians have called for appreciation for erotic diversity and more open discussion of sexuality. Trying to find a middle course between WAP and Samois is a bit like saying that the truth about homosexuality lies somewhere between the positions of the Moral Majority and those of the gay movement.

In political life, it is all too easy to marginalize radicals, and to attempt to buy acceptance for a moderate position by portraying others as extremists. Liberals have done this for years to communists. Sexual radicals have opened up the sex debates. It is shameful to deny their contribution, misrepresent their positions, and further their stigmatization.

In contrast to cultural feminists, who simply want to purge sexual dissidents, the sexual moderates are willing to defend the rights of erotic non-conformists to political participation. Yet this defense of political rights is linked to an implicit system of ideological condescension. The argument has two major parts. The first is an accusation that sexual dissidents have not paid close enough attention to the meaning, sources, or historical construction of their sexuality. This emphasis on meaning appears to function in much the same way that the question of etiology has functioned in discussions of homosexuality. That is, homosexuality, sadomasochism, prostitution, or boy-love are taken to be mysterious and problematic in some way that more respectable sexualities are not. The search for a cause is a search for something that could change so that these "problematic" eroticisms would simply not occur. Sexual militants have replied to such exercises that although the question of etiology or cause is of intellectual interest, it is not high on the political agenda and that, moreover, the privileging of such questions is itself a regressive political choice.

The second part of the "moderate" position focuses on questions of consent. Sexual radicals of all varieties have demanded the legal and social legitimation of consenting sexual behavior. Feminists have criticized them for ostensibly finessing questions about "the limits of consent" and "structural constraints" on consent. Although there are deep problems with the political discourse of consent, and although there are certainly structural constraints on sexual choice, this criticism has been consistently misapplied in the sex debates. It does not take into account the very specific semantic content that consent has in sex law and sex practice.

As I mentioned earlier, a great deal of sex law does not distinguish between consensual and coercive behavior. Only rape law contains such a distinction. Rape law is based on the assumption, correct in my view, that heterosexual activity may be freely chosen or forcibly coerced. One has the legal right to engage in heterosexual behavior as long as it does not fall under the purview of other statutes and as long as it is agreeable to both parties.

This is not the case for most other sexual acts. Sodomy laws, as I mentioned above, are based on the assumption that the forbidden acts are an "abominable and detestable crime against nature." Criminality is intrinsic to the acts themselves, no matter what the desires of the participants. "Unlike rape, sodomy or an unnatural or perverted sexual act may be committed between two persons both of whom consent, and, regardless of which is the aggressor, both may be prosecuted." Before the consenting adults statute was passed in California in 1976, lesbian lovers could have been prosecuted for committing oral copulation. If both participants were capable of consent, both were equally guilty.

Adult incest statutes operate in a similar fashion. Contrary to popular mythology, the incest statutes have little to do with protecting children from rape by close relatives. The incest statutes themselves prohibit marriage or sexual intercourse between adults who are closely related. Prosecutions are rare, but two were reported recently. In 1979, a 19-year-old Marine met his 42-year-old mother, from whom he had been separated at birth. The two fell in love and got married. They were charged and found guilty of incest, which under Virginia law carries a maximum ten-year sentence. During their trial, the Marine testified, "I love her very much. I feel that two people who love each other should be able to live together." In another case, a brother and sister who had been raised separately met and decided to get married. They were arrested and pleaded guilty to felony incest in return for probation. A condition of probation was that they not live together as husband and wife. Had they not accepted, they would have faced twenty years in prison. In a famous S/M case, a man was convicted of aggravated assault for a whipping administered in an S/M scene. There was no complaining victim. The session had been filmed and he was prosecuted on the basis of the film. The man appealed his conviction by arguing that he had been involved in a consensual sexual encounter and had assaulted no one. In rejecting his appeal, the court ruled that one may not consent to an assault or battery "except in a situation involving ordinary physical contact or blows incident to sports such as football, boxing, or wrestling." The court went on to note that the "consent of a person without legal capacity to give consent, such as a child or insane person, is ineffective," and that "It is a matter of common knowledge that a normal person in full possession of his mental faculties does not freely consent to the use, upon himself, of force likely to produce great bodily injury." Therefore, anyone who would consent to a whipping would be presumed *non compos mentis* and legally incapable of consenting. S/M sex generally involves a much lower level of force than the average football game, and results in far fewer injuries than most sports. But the court ruled that football players are sane, whereas masochists are not.

Sodomy laws, adult incest laws, and legal interpretations such as the one above clearly interfere with consensual behavior and impose criminal penalties on it. Within the law, consent is a privilege enjoyed only by those who engage in the highest-status sexual behavior. Those who enjoy low-status sexual behavior do not have the legal right to engage in it. In addition, economic sanctions, family pressures, erotic stigma, social discrimination, negative ideology, and the paucity of information about erotic behavior, all serve to make it difficult for people to make unconventional sexual choices. There certainly are structural constraints that impede free sexual choice, but they hardly operate to coerce anyone into being a pervert. On the contrary, they operate to coerce everyone toward normality.

The "brainwash theory" explains erotic diversity by assuming that some sexual acts are so disgusting that no one would willingly perform them. Therefore, the reasoning goes, anyone who does so must have been forced or fooled. Even constructivist sexual theory has been pressed into the service of explaining away why otherwise rational individuals might engage in variant sexual behavior. Another position that is not yet fully formed uses the ideas of Foucault and Weeks to imply that the "perversions" are an especially unsavory or problematic aspect of the construction of modern sexuality. This is yet another version of the notion that sexual dissidents are victims of the subtle machinations of the social system. Weeks and Foucault would not accept such an interpretation, since they consider all sexuality to be constructed, the conventional no less than the deviant.

Psychology is the last resort of those who refuse to acknowledge that sexual dissidents are as conscious and free as any other group of sexual actors. If deviants are not responding to the manipulations of the social system, then perhaps the source of their incomprehensible choices can be found in a bad childhood, unsuccessful socialization, or inadequate identity formation. In her essay on erotic domination, Jessica Benjamin draws upon psychoanalysis and philosophy to explain why what she calls "sadomasochism" is alienated, distorted, unsatisfactory, numb, purposeless, and an attempt to "relieve an original effort at differentiation that failed." This essay substitutes a psycho-philosophical inferiority for the more usual means of devaluing dissident eroticism. One reviewer has already construed Benjamin's argument as showing that sadomasochism is merely an "obsessive replay of the infant power struggle."

The position which defends the political rights of perverts but which seeks to understand their "alienated" sexuality is certainly preferable to the WAP-style bloodbaths. But for the most part, the sexual moderates have not confronted their discomfort with erotic choices that differ from their own. Erotic chauvinism cannot be redeemed by tarting it up in Marxist drag, sophisticated constructivist theory, or retro-psychobabble.

Whichever feminist position on sexuality—right, left, or center—eventually attains dominance, the existence of such a rich discussion is evidence that the feminist movement will always be a source of interesting thought about sex. Nevertheless, I want to challenge the assumption that feminism is or should be the privileged site of a theory of sexuality. Feminism is the theory of gender oppression. To assume automatically that this makes it the theory of sexual oppression is to fail to distinguish between gender, on the one hand, and erotic desire, on the other.

In the English language, the word "sex" has two very different meanings. It means gender and gender identity, as in "the female sex" or "the male sex." But sex also refers to sexual activity, lust, intercourse, and arousal, as in "to have sex." This semantic merging reflects a cultural assumption that sexuality is reducible to sexual intercourse and that it is a function of the relations between women and men. The cultural fusion of gender with sexuality has given rise to the idea that a theory of sexuality may be derived directly out of a theory of gender.

In an earlier essay, "The Traffic in Women," I used the concept of sex/gender system, defined as a "set of arrangements by which a society transforms biological sexuality into products of human activity." I went on to argue that "Sex as we know it—gender identity, sexual desire and fantasy, concepts of childhood—is itself a social product." In that essay, I did not distinguish between lust and gender, treating both as modalities of the same underlying social process.

"The Traffic in Women" was inspired by the literature on kinbased systems of social organization. It appeared to me at the time that gender and desire were systematically intertwined in such social formations. This may or may not be an accurate assessment of the relationship between sex and gender in tribal organizations. But it is surely not an adequate formulation for sexuality in Western industrial societies. As Foucault has pointed out, a system of sexuality has emerged out of earlier kinship forms and has acquired significant autonomy.

> Particularly from the eighteenth century onward, Western societies created and deployed a new apparatus which was superimposed on the previous one, and which, without completely supplanting the latter, helped to reduce its importance. I am speaking of the deployment of sexuality . . . For the first [kinship], what is pertinent is the link between partners and definite statutes; the second [sexuality] is concerned with the sensations of the body, the quality of pleasures, and the nature of impressions.

The development of this sexual system has taken place in the context of gender relations. Part of the modern ideology of sex is that lust is the province of men, purity that of women. It is no accident that pornography and perversions have been considered part of the male domain. In the sex industry, women have been excluded from most production and consumption, and allowed to participate primarily as workers. In order to participate in the "perversions," women have had to overcome serious limitations on their social mobility, their economic resources, and their sexual freedoms. Gender affects the operation of the sexual system, and the sexual system has had gender-specific manifestations. But although sex and gender are related, they are not the same thing, and they form the basis of two distinct arenas of social practice.

In contrast to my perspective in "The Traffic in Women," I am now arguing that it is essential to separate gender and sexuality analytically to reflect more accurately their separate social existence. This goes against the grain of much contemporary feminist thought, which treats sexuality as a derivation of gender. For instance, lesbian feminist ideology has mostly analyzed the oppression of lesbians in terms of the oppression of women. However, lesbians are also oppressed as queers and perverts, by the operation of sexual, not gender, stratification. Although it pains many lesbians to think about it, the fact is that lesbians have shared many of the sociological features and suffered from many of the same social penalties as have gay men, sadomasochists, transvestites, and prostitutes.

Catharine MacKinnon has made the most explicit theoretical attempt to subsume sexuality under feminist thought. According to MacKinnon, "Sexuality is to feminism what work is to marxism . . . the moulding, direction, and expression of sexuality organizes society into two sexes, women and men." This analytic strategy in turn rests on a decision to "use sex and gender relatively interchangeably." It is this definitional fusion that I want to challenge.

There is an instructive analogy in the history of the differentiation of contemporary feminist thought from Marxism. Marxism is probably the most supple and powerful conceptual system extant for analyzing social inequality. But attempts to make Marxism the sole explanatory system for all social inequalities have been dismal exercises. Marxism is most successful in the areas of social life for which it was originally developed—class relations under capitalism.

In the early days of the contemporary women's movement, a theoretical conflict took place over the applicability of Marxism to gender stratification. Since Marxist theory is relatively powerful, it does in fact detect important and interesting aspects of gender oppression. It works best for those issues of gender most closely related to issues of class and the organization of labor. The issues more specific to the social structure of gender were not amenable to Marxist analysis.

The relationship between feminism and a radical theory of sexual oppression is similar. Feminist conceptual tools were developed to detect and analyze gender-based hierarchies. To the extent that these overlap with erotic stratifications, feminist theory has some explanatory power. But as issues become less those of gender and more those of sexuality, feminist analysis becomes misleading and often irrelevant. Feminist thought simply lacks angles of vision which can fully encompass the social organization of sexuality. The criteria of relevance in feminist thought do not allow it to see or assess critical power relations in the area of sexuality.

In the long run, feminism's critique of gender hierarchy must be incorporated into a radical theory of sex, and the critique of sexual oppression should enrich feminism. But an autonomous theory and politics specific to sexuality must be developed.

It is a mistake to substitute feminism for Marxism as the last word in social theory. Feminism is no more capable than Marxism of being the ultimate and complete account of all social inequality. Nor is feminism the residual theory which can take care of everything to which Marx did not attend. These critical tools were fashioned to handle very specific areas of social activity. Other areas of social life, their forms of power, and their characteristic modes of oppression, need their own conceptual implements. In this essay, I have argued for theoretical as well as sexual pluralism.

The Sexual Geopolitics of Popular Culture and Transnational Black Feminism

BY JANELL HOBSON

Janell Hobson is a scholar, writer, critic, essayist, professor and chair of the Department of Women's, Gender, and Sexuality Studies at the University at Albany, and a contributing writer at *Ms.* magazine. In her writing, she uses a transnational lens to highlight women's iconography and experiences in the African Diaspora. Hobson is also the author of *Venus in the Dark: Blackness and Beauty in Popular Culture* (2005) and *Body as Evidence: Mediating Race, Globalizing Gender* (2012). Hobson frequently writes about pop culture and the problematic nature of popular music which simultaneously appropriates two thirds of world music traditions and extends the reach of that music and its feminist messages. In the 2014 essay, "The Sexual Geopolitics of Popular Culture and Transnational Black Feminism," Hobson focuses on R & B artist Beyoncé and how she complicates cultural appropriation by drawing from diasporic influences in her music. She also traces precedents through the work of Zora Neale Hurston, Josephine Baker, and others.

While the debate raged on toward the end of 2013 concerning Beyoncé's feminist politics—especially in her sampling of celebrated Nigerian author Chimamanda Ngozi Adichie's "We Should All Be Feminists" TED speech in her song "***Flawless," featured on her fast-selling *BEYONCÈ: The Visual Album*—few have contributed conversations on the potential for a transnational black feminist consciousness that this sampling promises.

Notably, Aljazeera America mapped out the global trend of the Twitter hashtag #BlackFemMusic, which prompted a lively conversation on the importance of feminist consciousness in African American women's music in the wake of Beyoncé's fifth solo album release, with other artists—from Billie Holiday to Nina Simone to Missy Elliott—receiving shout outs. This globally trending online conversation in some ways parallels the transnational dialogue that is sonically created in Beyoncé's deliberate selection of Adichie as the voice of feminism, which is also visually explored in the Black Atlantic spaces of Puerto Rico and Brazil in the music videos for "Heaven" and "Blue" respectively. Indeed, as Emily J. Lordi describes about the song and video for "Blue": "Despite the title, Beyoncé's own child is not the focus but is rather the catalyst for Beyoncé's appreciation of the wider world. *When I look in your eyes, I feel alive.* Blue opens her mother to newness."

It is this newness of the wider world that is found in her Diasporic videos, which capture rich colors and expansive landscapes—compared to the interior, enclosed narrow spaces of her sex-themed videos—and that does intricate work in geographically and psychically expanding cultural spaces allowed for female bonding—female friendships in "Heaven" and the bond between mothers and daughters in "Blue." In the bonus video "Grown Woman," the African-influenced "welele" chants, dance styles reminiscent of popular "twerk" gyrations, and the imagery of Beyoncé's mother, juxtaposed with her own identity as both literal and "global" mother holding racially diverse babies on her lap, create a visual collage and mashup around images and sounds of black womanhood. Lyrically, musically and visually, Beyoncé crosses national borders and fuses musical cultures in this millennial expression of black feminism.

This isn't to suggest that such cultural samplings aren't fraught with unequal power relations, given the pop-star, multimillionaire U.S. citizen status of Beyoncé in relation to other black women locally (in her appropriation of low-income black "ratchet girl" culture) and globally (in her heavy borrowing "simplistic, procapitalist, structurally violent sampling of feminism," a sampling practice earlier criticized by *Racialicious* guest blogger Isaac Miller who drew parallels between Beyoncé's sampling of Third World (or Two-Thirds World) music and dance in her 2011 single and video

"Run the World (Girls)" and white remix deejay Diplo, who provided her with the "Pon de Floor" dancehall remix heard in this hit song. Diplo is often accused of cultural imperialism with his well-known travels around the world for what some artists of color (most infamously Venus Iceberg X and her Ghe2o Goth1k Crew) perceive as sonic piracy of Two-Thirds World music cultures.

However, I would argue that, even though Beyoncé also travels the world like Diplo—currently with her "Mrs. Carter" world tour—her position as a black woman (and her complex integration of whiteness and blackness in her beautification practices) necessarily complicates these politics. This isn't simply "cultural appropriation" (as with Miley Cyrus's twerking or Katy Perry's "geisha" performances), not least of which is due to the very different ways that white male and black female bodies move around the world—despite Beyoncé's more obvious global and pop stardom success in comparison to Diplo. The body (geo) politic reads their personas in distinct ways, in which Diplo seems a "musical Columbus" while Beyoncé seemingly engages in Black Diasporic exchange. Of course, this represents a much longer history of what Paul Gilroy calls Black Atlantic cultural expression, political consciousness, and the complexities of African American identity within the larger spheres of the Diaspora.

HISTORICAL PRECEDENTS: CULTURAL IMPERIALISM OR CULTURAL EXCHANGE?

Early twentieth-century African American women artists like Zora Neale Hurston, Katherine Dunham, and Loïs Mailou Jones developed a Black Diasporic consciousness as a counterpoint to the larger discourse of "black primitivism" prevalent during this era of racial debates. However, these artists also accessed the Caribbean courtesy of U.S. occupation in Haiti and other foreign policies concerning the rest of the Caribbean and Latin America. Within these geopolitical spheres of cultural imperialism and cultural exchange, the African American artist is precariously positioned in ways that perpetuate racial essentialism while simultaneously suggesting transnational solidarity.

Consider the African American pop star Josephine Baker in Paris in the 1920s. Alluded to in Beyoncé's "Partition" music video, Baker occupied a similar position as sex symbol during her era. Improvising upon the "exotic" iconography of France's colonial rendering of "African nudes" and "savage dance," Baker spectacularly crafted a "modern primitive" fusing improvisatory jazz notions of the "nude savage" with her own expression of black female sexuality and her colonial "stand-in" for France's colonial subjects throughout Africa and the Antilles. Curiously, the same year that Baker returned from a world tour, where her earlier celebrated black sexualized performances met with white supremacist resistance and rioting in places like Vienna and Budapest, women in Nigeria protested against British colonial laws, which sought to curtail their local power, with the infamous "naked protest" in 1929, also called the "Women's War." Just as Baker's nude "danse sauvage" met with resistance in different European cities beyond Paris, the Nigerian women's naked protest—which is a traditional form of African women's resistance that relies on their embodied powers of "cursing"—was violently subverted by a white colonial gaze that recast the women as hypersexual, indecent "primitives" and "savages." This fear of black sexuality similarly framed the public reception of Josephine Baker and black jazz musicians, whose culture would later be denounced in Nazi Germany's "Degenerate Art" exhibit in 1937, just as the culture was denounced earlier in the U.S. as "devil's music" (and much like hip-hop, ratchet culture, and twerking are denounced today).

Another critical moment in 1929 also took place, which is worth remembering. Here I refer to the Universal Negro Improvement Association and African Communities League international convention that Marcus Garvey held in Jamaica, after he was deported from the United States, where he had been imprisoned while his wife Amy Jacques Garvey sustained their Pan-Africanist movement, which influenced and was equally influenced by various anticolonial movements in India, South Africa, Kenya, Cuba, and Brazil. These politics certainly seeped into the popular spheres of black "soul power" music of the 1970s, which had a global reach and subsequent impact on hip-hop.

In *Nomadic Identities: The Performance of Citizenship*, May Joseph wrote this about black soul music: "Operating ambivalently within the seductive and exploitative boundaries of U.S.

imperialism—consumerism being the new face of imperial expansion—soul prompted an international as well as local resurgence of Pan-African desire . . . The circulation of Afro-American popular culture through dramatically different ideological and geographical terrain beyond its national context foregrounds the complexities of transnationalism." Despite the perpetuation of consumer culture and capitalist endeavors—which Beyoncé's pop-star status and narratives promote—there is still the potential for a complex transnational conversation. Black popular music and dance, which created viable spaces for cultural and embodied resistance in the past, still has this potential today.

Moreover, there are other complex questions to consider. How much of African American culture is simply "U.S. culture," especially given the way African Americans are constantly positioned as "outsiders within," to paraphrase Patricia Hill Collins? How much of this culture is "already global"? Consider hip-hop, one of the most successful U.S. global exports with its roots in the South Bronx already expressing the transnational fusion of cultures represented by African Americans living (and partying) in close proximity with other black and immigrant communities from the Caribbean in these low-income urban locations. Do such pop stars as Beyoncé, Rihanna, and Nicki Minaj (the latter two with roots in Barbados and Trinidad respectively) and their engagements with Jamaican deejay and dancehall traditions, part of hip-hop's origins, represent "cultural appropriation" or the reclamation of black migratory roots returning home?

IS "SISTAHOOD" GLOBAL?
MAPPING TRANSNATIONAL BLACK FEMINISM

In her essay, "Globalization of the Local/Localization of the Global," Indian feminist Amrita Basu describes the importance of women of color in reshaping U.S. feminist discourse, which she believes reduced tensions in the sphere of global feminist movements. As she posits, "Recall that some of the earliest and most important critiques of feminist universalism came from African American and Latina women in the United States. Years later, in preparation for the 1995 Beijing women's conference, American women of color formed a coalition with women from the South and drafted language for the platform document about women who face multiple forms of discrimination." Such transnational developments can also be traced beyond the political spheres of NGOs, UN international conferences, and activist work and policy-making. We could argue that the popular sphere contributes to these narratives by reimagining these global and transnational connections—especially in articulations of women's power, sexual desire, and questions around solidarity and how our different rhetorics travel across academic, artistic, and grassroots divides.

Engaging the popular doesn't always have to mean a distraction from the larger global politics of women's oppression and resistance to these systems. Rather, popular culture makes legible these struggles—precisely because they enter into those spaces of leisure, fun, and pleasure. It is these spaces where we need to be reenergized from our daily struggles and to imagine and create different dreams for ourselves and the world at large—whether those visions are affirmed or contradicted in popular narratives.

Just as Queen Latifah created a transnational dialogue with London-based emcee Monie Love and addressed the South African apartheid struggle in the video for her nominal "Ladies First" hip-hop feminist anthem, the global stage performances of strip culture "twerking" or Jamaican dancehall (infused with Hindu goddess imagery of Durga and Indian pop music samplings)—make it possible to disrupt white supremacist visions of female beauty, sexuality, and feminist politics. There is a reason why mainstream American audiences are made uncomfortable by the "too sexy" performances that such booty-emphasizing dances convey. The (white) body politic is being challenged and such spectacles—coupled with feminist rhetorics *not* emerging from the institutional sphere of academic (usually white) feminism—pushes the boundaries around which bodies, which aesthetics, and which politics are valid. Sampling Nigerian-born Adichie alongside her African, Caribbean, and Latin-influenced music and videos, Beyoncé and other women of color artists doing similar work continue in a tradition of Diasporic and transnational articulations of black feminism. It is a far from "flawless" version of sisterhood but one that nonetheless suggests the possibilities and potential for transnational solidarity.

Rape Joke

BY PATRICIA LOCKWOOD

Patricia Lockwood is a poet, novelist, essayist, and social critic whose work simultaneously makes use of and interrogates social media platforms such as Twitter. Lockwood is a contributing editor to the *London Review of Books*, and her memoir, *Priestdaddy*, was named one of the ten best books of 2017 by *The New York Times Book Review*. In her poem "Rape Joke," published in *The Awl* in 2013, Lockwood calls out rape culture and the ways that culture is reproduced through small, supposedly meaningless acts like jokes. "Rape Joke" was selected for the 2014 edition of the *Best American Poetry*, won a Pushcart Prize, and has been translated into more than twenty languages. When I first read "Rape Joke," I admired the way Lockwood is in conversation with the idea of rape jokes and the expectation that victims of sexual violence should be able to find humor in something that is far from humorous. The repetition of the phrase *rape joke* in this poem is relentless and with sharp words, Lockwood manages to tell a haunting story. Toward the end, she writes, "The rape joke cries out for the right to be told," and, indeed, it does.

The rape joke is that you were 19 years old.

The rape joke is that he was your boyfriend.

The rape joke it wore a goatee. A goatee.

Imagine the rape joke looking in the mirror, perfectly reflecting back itself, and grooming itself to look more like a rape joke. "Ahhhh," it thinks. "Yes. *A goatee*."

No offense.

The rape joke is that he was seven years older. The rape joke is that you had known him for years, since you were too young to be interesting to him. You liked that use of the word *interesting*, as if you were a piece of knowledge that someone could be desperate to acquire, to assimilate, and to spit back out in different form through his goateed mouth.

Then suddenly you were older, but not very old at all.

The rape joke is that you had been drinking wine coolers. Wine coolers! Who drinks wine coolers? People who get raped, according to the rape joke.

The rape joke is he was a bouncer, and kept people out for a living.

Not you!

The rape joke is that he carried a knife, and would show it to you, and would turn it over and over in his hands as if it were a book.

He wasn't threatening you, you understood. He just really liked his knife.

The rape joke is he once almost murdered a dude by throwing him through a plate-glass window. The next day he told you and he was trembling, which you took as evidence of his sensitivity.

How can a piece of knowledge be stupid? But of course you were so stupid.

The rape joke is that sometimes he would tell you you were going on a date and then take you over to his best friend Peewee's house and make you watch wrestling while they all got high.

The rape joke is that his best friend was named Peewee.

OK, the rape joke is that he worshiped The Rock.

Like the dude was completely in love with The Rock. He thought it was so great what he could do with his eyebrow.

The rape joke is he called wrestling "a soap opera for men." Men love drama too, he assured you.

The rape joke is that his bookshelf was just a row of paperbacks about serial killers. You mistook this for an interest in history, and laboring under this misapprehension you once gave him a copy of Günter Grass's *My Century*, which he never even tried to read.

It gets funnier.

The rape joke is that he kept a diary. I wonder if he wrote about the rape in it.

The rape joke is that you read it once, and he talked about another girl. He called her Miss Geography, and said "he didn't have those urges when he looked at her anymore," not since he met you. Close call, Miss Geography!

The rape joke is that he was your father's high-school student—your father taught World Religion. You helped him clean out his classroom at the end of the year, and he let you take home the most beat-up textbooks.

The rape joke is that he knew you when you were 12 years old. He once helped your family move two states over, and you drove from Cincinnati to St. Louis with him, all by yourselves, and he was kind to you, and you talked the whole way. He had chaw in his mouth the entire time, and you told him he was disgusting and he laughed, and spat the juice through his goatee into a Mountain Dew bottle.

The rape joke is that *come on*, you should have seen it coming. This rape joke is practically writing itself.

The rape joke is that you were facedown. The rape joke is you were wearing a pretty green necklace that your sister had made for you. Later you cut that necklace up. The mattress felt a specific way, and your mouth felt a specific way open against it, as if you were speaking, but you know you were not. As if your mouth were open ten years into the future, reciting a poem called Rape Joke.

The rape joke is that time is different, becomes more horrible and more habitable, and accommodates your need to go deeper into it.

Just like the body, which more than a concrete form is a capacity.

You know the body of time is *elastic*, can take almost anything you give it, and heals quickly.

The rape joke is that of course there was blood, which in human beings is so close to the surface.

The rape joke is you went home like nothing happened, and laughed about it the next day and the day after that, and when you told people you laughed, and that was the rape joke.

It was a year before you told your parents, because he was like a son to them. The rape joke is that when you told your father, he made the sign of the cross over you and said, "I absolve you of your sins, in the name of the Father, and of the Son, and of the

Holy Spirit," which even in its total wrongheadedness, was so completely sweet.

The rape joke is that you were crazy for the next five years, and had to move cities, and had to move states, and whole days went down into the sinkhole of thinking about why it happened. Like you went to look at your backyard and suddenly it wasn't there, and you were looking down into the center of the earth, which played the same red event perpetually.

The rape joke is that after a while you weren't crazy anymore, but close call, Miss Geography.

The rape joke is that for the next five years all you did was write, and never about yourself, about anything else, about apples on the tree, about islands, dead poets and the worms that aerated them, and there was no warm body in what you wrote, it was elsewhere.

The rape joke is that this is finally artless. The rape joke is that you do not write artlessly.

The rape joke is if you write a poem called Rape Joke, you're asking for it to become the only thing people remember about you.

The rape joke is that you asked why he did it. The rape joke is he said he didn't know, like what else would a rape joke say? The rape joke said YOU were the one who was drunk, and the rape joke said you remembered it wrong, which made you laugh out loud for one long split-open second. The wine coolers weren't Bartles & Jaymes, but it would be funnier for the rape joke if they were. It was some pussy flavor, like Passionate Mango or Destroyed Strawberry, which you drank down without question and trustingly in the heart of Cincinnati Ohio.

Can rape jokes be funny at all, is the question.

Can any part of the rape joke be funny. The part where it ends—haha, just kidding! Though you did dream of killing the rape joke for years, spilling all of its blood out, and telling it that way.

The rape joke cries out for the right to be told.

The rape joke is that this is just how it happened.

The rape joke is that the next day he gave you Pet Sounds. No really. Pet Sounds. He said he was sorry and then he gave you Pet Sounds. Come on, that's a little bit funny.

Admit it.

If Men Could Menstruate

BY GLORIA STEINEM

Gloria Steinem is a feminist icon, journalist, and politi-cal activist whose work spans decades. In 1971, she co-founded the National Women's Political Caucus and the Women's Action Alliance, and in 2005, she established the Women's Media Center. She was also a co-founder of *Ms.* magazine. In 1978, Steinem wrote a semi-satirical essay for *Cosmopolitan* titled "If Men Could Menstru-ate." She concludes that in such a world, menstruation would become a badge of honor, with men comparing their relative sufferings, rather than the source of shame it has historically been for women. The essay became an instant sensation and is still invoked in memes such as "If Men Could Get Pregnant" and the hashtag #If-MenHadPeriods that call out the different ways systemic sexism restricts the bodily autonomy of women while privileging white men.

A white minority of the world has spent centuries conning us into thinking that a white skin makes people superior—even though the only thing it really does is make them more subject to ultravi-olet rays and to wrinkles. Male human beings have built whole cultures around the idea that penis-envy is "natural" to women—though having such an unprotected organ might be said to make men vulnerable, and the power to give birth makes womb-envy at least as logical.

In short, the characteristics of the powerful, whatever they may be, are thought to be better than the characteristics of the powerless—and logic has nothing to do with it.

What would happen, for instance, if suddenly, magically, men could menstruate and women could not?

The answer is clear—menstruation would become an enviable, boast-worthy, masculine event:

Men would brag about how long and how much.

Boys would mark the onset of menses, that longed-for proof of manhood, with religious ritual and stag parties.

Congress would fund a National Institute of Dysmenorrhea to help stamp out monthly discomforts.

Sanitary supplies would be federally funded and free. (Of course, some men would still pay for the prestige of commercial brands such as John Wayne Tampons, Muhammad Ali's Rope-a-dope Pads, Joe Namath Jock Shields—"For Those Light Bachelor Days," and Robert "Baretta" Blake Maxi-Pads.)

Military men, right-wing politicians, and religious fundamentalists would cite menstruation ("menstruation") as proof that only men could serve in the Army ("you have to give blood to take blood"), occupy political office ("can women be aggressive without that steadfast cycle governed by the planet Mars?"), be priests and ministers ("how could a woman give her blood for our sins?") or rabbis ("without the monthly loss of impurities, women remain unclean").

Male radicals, left-wing politicians, mystics, however, would insist that women are equal, just different, and that any woman could enter their ranks if she were willing to self-inflict a major wound every month ("you MUST give blood for the revolution"), recognize the preeminence of menstrual issues, or subordinate her selfness to all men in their Cycle of Enlightenment. Street guys would brag ("I'm a three pad man") or answer praise from a buddy ("Man, you lookin' good!") by giving fives and saying, "Yeah, man, I'm on the rag!" TV shows would treat the subject at length. ("Happy Days": Richie and Potsie try to convince Fonzie that he is still "The Fonz," though he has missed two periods in a row.) So would newspapers. (SHARK SCARE THREATENS MENSTRUATING MEN. JUDGE CITES MONTHLY STRESS IN PARDONING RAPIST.) And movies. (Newman and Redford in "Blood Brothers"!)

Men would convince women that intercourse was more pleasurable at "that time of the month." Lesbians would be said to fear blood and therefore life itself—though probably only because they needed a good menstruating man.

Of course, male intellectuals would offer the most moral and logical arguments. How could a woman master any discipline that demanded a sense of time, space, mathematics, or measurement, for instance, without that in-built gift for measuring the cycles of the moon and planets—and thus for measuring anything at all? In the rarefied fields of philosophy and religion, could women compensate for missing the rhythm of the universe? Or for their lack of symbolic death-and-resurrection every month?

Liberal males in every field would try to be kind: the fact that "these people" have no gift for measuring life or connecting to the universe, the liberals would explain, should be punishment enough.

And how would women be trained to react? One can imagine traditional women agreeing to all arguments with a staunch and smiling masochism. ("The ERA would force housewives to wound themselves every month": Phyllis Schlafly. "Your husband's blood is as sacred as that of Jesus—and so sexy, too!" Marabel Morgan.) Reformers and Queen Bees would try to imitate men, and pretend to have a monthly cycle. All feminists would explain endlessly that men, too, needed to be liberated from the false idea of Martian aggressiveness, just as women needed to escape the bonds of menses envy. Radical feminists would add that the oppression of the nonmenstrual was the pattern for all other oppressions ("Vampires were our first freedom fighters!") Cultural feminists would develop a bloodless imagery in art and literature. Socialist feminists would insist that only under capitalism would men be able to monopolize menstrual blood. . . .

In fact, if men could menstruate, the power justifications could probably go on forever.

If we let them.

Assume the Position

BY PATRICIA HILL COLLINS

Patricia Hill Collins is an award-winning American scholar, social theorist, and emeritus professor of sociology at the University of Maryland. Dr. Collins was also the one hundredth president of the American Sociological Association (ASA) and the first Black woman elected to this position. In 1990, Collins published *Black Feminist Thought: Knowledge, Consciousness, and the Politics of Empowerment*, which examined power through the work of Angela Davis, Alice Walker, and Audre Lorde and asserted the importance of marginalized forms of knowledge and counternarratives that challenge the mainstream ideological framing of identity on the basis of race, class, gender, sexuality, and nationality. Collins uses Crenshaw's theory of intersectionality to interrogate the unique position of Black women within a "matrix of domination" through a sociological lens. This incisive excerpt from the chapter "Assume the Position" from her 2004 book *Black Sexual Politics: African Americans, Gender, and the New Racism* examines the ways sexual violence is used to oppress Black women.

At the center of the table sat a single microphone, a glass of water, and a name card: "Professor Anita Hill." I sat down at the lone chair at the table. . . . In front of me, facing me and the bank of journalists, was the Senate Judiciary Committee—fourteen white men dressed in dark gray suits. I questioned my decision to wear bright blue linen, though it hadn't really been a decision; that suit was the only appropriate and clean suit in my closet when I hastily packed for Washington two days before. In any case, it offered a fitting contrast.

By now, the outcome of Anita Hill's 1991 testimony at the confirmation hearings of Supreme Court Justice Clarence Thomas is well known. In a calm, almost flat manner and before a packed room that contained twelve family members, including both of her parents, Hill recounted how Thomas had sexually harassed her when he headed the Equal Employment Opportunity Commission ten years earlier. Although she passed a lie detector test, her testimony did not affect the upshot of the hearings. The Senate Judiciary Committee simply did not believe her. Hill was no match for the fourteen White men in dark gray suits, many of whom had made up their minds before hearing her testimony. Thomas's opportunistic claim that the senators were engaged in a "high-tech lynching" sealed the outcome. Because lynching had been so associated with the atrocities visited upon Black men, it became virtually impossible for the senators to refute Thomas's self-presentation without being branded as racists. The combination of male dominance and the need to avoid any hint of racism made the choice simple. Believing Thomas challenged racism. Doubting Thomas supported it. Thomas won. Hill lost.

But was it really this simple? Certainly not for African Americans. For Black women and men, the Thomas confirmation hearings catalyzed two thorny questions. Why did so many African Americans join the "fourteen white men dressed in dark gray suits" and reject Hill's allegations of sexual harassment? Even more puzzling, why did so many African Americans who believed Anita Hill criticize her for coming forward and testifying? Critical race theorist Kimberlé Crenshaw offers one reason why the hearings proved to be so difficult: "In feminist contexts, sexuality represents a central site of the oppression of women; rape and the rape trial are its dominant narrative trope. In antiracist discourses, sexuality is also a central site upon which the repression of Blacks has been premised; the lynching narrative is embodied as its trope. (Neither narrative tends to acknowledge the legitimacy of the other)."

Crenshaw joins a prestigious group of African American women and men who, from Ida B. Wells-Barnett through Angela Davis, have examined how discourses of rape and lynching have historically influenced understandings of race, gender, and sexuality within American society. In American society, sexual violence has served as an important mechanism for controlling

African Americans, women, poor people, and gays and lesbians, among others. In the post-emancipation South, for example, institutionalized lynching and institutionalized rape worked together to uphold racial oppression. Together, lynching and rape served as gender-specific mechanisms of sexual violence whereby men were victimized by lynching and women by rape. Lynching and rape also reflected the type of binary thinking associated with racial and gender segregation mandating that *either* race *or* gender was primary, but not both. Within this logic of segregation, race and gender constituted separate rather than intersecting forms of oppression that could not be equally important. One was primary whereas the other was secondary. As targets of lynching as ritualized murder, Black men carried the more important burden of race. In contrast, as rape victims, Black women carried the less important burden of gender.

African American politics have been profoundly influenced by a Black gender ideology that ranks race and gender in this fashion. Lynching and rape have not been given equal weight and, as a result, social issues seen as affecting Black men, in this case lynching, have taken precedence over those that seemingly affect only Black women (rape). Within this logic, lynchings, police brutality, and similar expressions of state-sanctioned violence visited upon African American men operate as consensus issues within African American politics. Lynching was not a random act; instead, it occurred *in public*, was sanctioned by government officials, and often served as a unifying event for entire communities. In this sense, lynching can be defined as ritualized murder that took a particular form in the post-emancipation South. In that context, through its highly public nature as spectacle, lynching was emblematic of a form of institutionalized, ritualized murder that was visited upon Black men in particular. African American antiracist politics responded vigorously to the public spectacle of lynching by protesting against it as damage done to Black men as representatives of the "race." Because African American men were the main targets of this highly public expression of ritualized murder, the lynching of Black men came to symbolize the most egregious expressions of racism.

In contrast, the sexual violence visited upon African American women has historically carried no public name, garnered no significant public censure, and has been seen as a crosscutting gender issue that diverts Black politics from its real job of fighting racism. Black women were raped, yet their pain and suffering remained largely invisible. Whereas lynching (racism) was public spectacle, rape (sexism) signaled *private* humiliation. Black male leaders were not unaware of the significance of institutionalized rape. Rather, their political solution of installing a Black male patriarchy in which Black men would protect "their" women from sexual assault inadvertently supported ideas about women's bodies and sexuality as men's property. Stated differently, Black women's suffering under racism would be eliminated by encouraging versions of Black masculinity whereby Black men had the same powers that White men had long enjoyed.

By 1991, the Thomas confirmation hearings made it painfully obvious that these antiracist strategies of the past were no match for the new racism. Ranking either lynching or rape as more important than the other offered a painful lesson about the dangers of choosing race over gender or vice versa as the template for African American politics. What is needed is a progressive Black sexual politics that recognizes not only how important both lynching and rape were in maintaining historical patterns of racial segregation but that also questions how these practices may be changed and used to maintain the contemporary color-blind racism. Rather than conceptualizing lynching and rape as either race or gender-specific mechanisms of social control, another approach views institutionalized rape and lynching as *different* expressions of the *same* type of social control. Together, both constitute dominance strategies that uphold the new racism. Both involve the threat or actual physical violence done to the body's exterior, for example, beating, torture, and/or murder. Both can involve the threat of or actual infliction of violence upon the body's interior, for example, oral, anal, or vaginal penetration against the victim's will. Both strip victims of agency and control over their own bodies, thus aiming for psychological control via fear and humiliation. Moreover, within the context of the post–civil rights era's desegregation, these seemingly gender-specific forms of social control converge. Stated differently, just as the post–civil rights era has seen a crossing and blurring of boundaries of all sorts, lynching and rape as forms of state-sanctioned violence are not now and never were as gender-specific as once thought.

REVISITING THE FOUNDATION: LYNCHING AND RAPE AS TOOLS OF SOCIAL CONTROL

Lynching and rape both served the economic needs of Southern agriculture under racial segregation. In the American South during the years 1882 to 1930 the lynching of Black people for "crimes" against Whites was a common spectacle—mob violence was neither random in time nor geography. Like many other violent crimes, lynchings were more frequent during the summer months than in cooler seasons, a reflection of the changing labor demands of agricultural production cycles. One function of lynchings may well have been to rid White communities of Black people who allegedly violated the moral order. But another function was to maintain control over the African American population, especially during times when White landowners needed Black labor to work fields of cotton and tobacco.

Lynching also had political dimensions. This tool of gendered, racial violence was developed to curtail the citizenship rights of African American men after emancipation. Because Black women could not vote, Black men become targets for political repression. Explaining the power of lynching as a spectacle of violence necessary to maintain racial boundaries and to discipline populations, literary critic Trudier Harris describes the significance of violence to maintaining fixed racial group identities:

> When one Black individual dared to violate the restrictions, he or she was used as an example to reiterate to the entire race that the group would continually be held responsible for the actions of the individual. Thus an accusation of rape could lead not only to the accused Black man being lynched and burned, but to the burning of Black homes and the whipping or lynching of other Black individuals as well.

This is why lynchings were not private affairs, but were public events, often announced well in advance in newspapers: "To be effective in social control, lynchings had to be visible, with the killing being a public spectacle or at least minimally having the corpse on display for all to witness. Whereas a murder—even a racially motivated one—might be hidden from public scrutiny, lynchings were not."

The ritualized murders of lynching not only worked to terrorize the African American population overall but they also helped to install a hegemonic White masculinity over a subordinated Black masculinity. Lynching symbolized the type of violence visited upon African American men that was grounded in a constellation of daily micro-assaults on their manhood that achieved extreme form through the actual castration of many Black male lynch victims. Although Black women were also lynched, Black men were lynched in far greater numbers. Thus, lynching invokes ideas of Black male emasculation, a theme that persists within the contemporary Black gender ideology thesis of Black men as being "weak." The myth of Black men as rapists also emerged under racial segregation in the South. Designed to contain this newfound threat to White property and democratic institutions, the sexual stereotype of the newly emancipated, violent rapist was constructed on the back of the Black buck. No longer safely controlled under slavery, Black men could now go "buck wild."

Wide-scale lynching could only emerge after emancipation because murdering slaves was unprofitable, for their owners. In contrast, the institutionalized rape of African American women began under slavery and also accompanied the wide-scale lynching of Black men at the turn of the twentieth century. Emancipation constituted a continuation of actual practices of rape as well as the shame and humiliation visited upon rape victims that is designed to keep them subordinate. Black domestic workers reported being harassed, molested, and raped by their employers. Agricultural workers, especially those women who did not work on family farms, were also vulnerable. In the South, these practices persisted well into the twentieth century. For example, in the 1990s, journalist Leon Dash interviewed Washington, D.C., resident Rosa Lee. It took many conversations before Lee could share family secrets of stories of sexual abuse that had occurred in rural North Carolina. Because the experiences were so painful, she herself had learned about them only in bits and pieces from stories told to her by her grandmother and aunt. Rosa Lee came to understand the harsh lives endured by her mother Rosetta and her grandmother Lugenia at the bottom of the Southern Black class structure. Describing how White men would come and look over young Black girls, Rosa Lee recounted her family's stories:

> "You could tell when they wanted something. They all would come out there. Come out there in the field while everybody was working. And they're looking at the young girls. Her mouth. Teeth. Arms. You know, like they're looking at a horse. Feeling her breasts and everything. The white men would get to whispering."
>
> "And the mothers let them men do that?" Rosa Lee asked her grandmother.
>
> "What the hell do you think they could do?" Lugenia answered. "Couldn't do nothing!"

The overseers apparently preferred light-skinned Black girls, often the children of previous rapes, but dark-skinned girls did not escape White male scrutiny. In exchange for the girls, mothers received extra food or a lighter load. The costs were high for the girls themselves. Because Rosetta developed early, her mother tried to hide her when the men came. But after a while, it was hopeless. Rosetta did not escape the rapes:

> "Your mama was put to auction so many times," Lugenia told Rosa Lee. "They just kept wanting your mother." The overseers would assign the girls they wanted sexually to work in isolated parts of the farm, away from their families. The girls would try to get out of the work detail. "It never worked," Lugenia said. "Those men always got them."

Lugenia continued her tale by sharing how two White overseers had raped her when she was fourteen, and how two of her daughters, including Rosetta, had suffered the same fate. Only one daughter was spared, "because she was so fat," explained Lugenia. As for the children who were conceived, they were left with their mothers. Once a girl was pregnant, she was generally never bothered again. As Lugenia recalled: "They only wanted virgins. . . . They felt they'd catch diseases if they fooled with any girl that wasn't a virgin."

These social practices of institutionalized lynching and institutionalized rape did not go uncontested. Ida B. Wells-Barnett's antilynching work clearly rejected both the myth of the Black male rapist as well as the thesis of Black women's inherent immorality and advanced her own highly controversial interpretation. Not only did Wells-Barnett spark a huge controversy when she dared to claim that many of the sexual liaisons between White women and Black men were in fact consensual, she indicted White men as the actual perpetrators of crimes of sexual violence *both* against African American men (lynching) *and* against African American women (rape). Consider how her comments in *Southern Horrors* concerning the contradictions of laws forbidding interracial marriage place blame on White male behavior and power: "the miscegenation laws of the South only operate against the legitimate union of the races: they leave the white man free to seduce all the colored girls he can, but is death to the colored man who yields to the force and advances of a similar attraction in white women. White men lynch the offending Afro-American, not because he is a despoiler of virtue, but because he succumbs to the smiles of white women." In this analysis, Wells-Barnett reveals how ideas about gender difference—the seeming passivity of women and the aggressiveness of men—are in fact deeply racialized constructs. Gender had a racial face, whereby African American women, African American men, White women, and White men occupied distinct race/gender categories within an overarching social structure that proscribed their prescribed place. Interracial sexual liaisons violated racial and gender segregation.

Despite Wells-Barnett's pioneering work in analyzing sexual violence through an intersectional framework of race, gender, class, and sexuality, African American leaders elevated race over gender. Given the large numbers of lynchings from the 1890s to the 1930s, and in the context of racial segregation that stripped all African Americans of citizenship rights, this emphasis on antilynching made sense. Often accused of the crime of raping White women, African American men were lynched, and, in more gruesome cases, castrated. Such violence was so horrific that, catalyzed by Ida B. Wells-Barnett's tireless antilynching crusade, and later taken up by the NAACP and other major civil rights organizations, antilynching became an important plank in the Black civil rights agenda.

In large part due to this advocacy, lynchings have dwindled to a few, isolated albeit horrific events today. This does not mean that the use of lynching as a symbol of American racism has abated. Rather, Black protest still responds quickly and passionately to contemporary incidents of lynching and/or to events that can be recast through this historic framework. For example, the 1955 murder of fourteen-year-old Emmett Till in Mississippi was described in the press as a lynching and served as an important catalyst for the modern civil rights movement. The 1989 murder of sixteen-year-old Yusef Hawkins in the Bensonhurst section of New York City also was described as a lynching. When Hawkins and three friends came to their neighborhood to look at a used car, about thirty White youths carrying bats and sticks (one with a gun) immediately approached them. Furious that the ex-girlfriend of one of the group members had invited Black people to her eighteenth birthday party, the White kids thought that Hawkins and his friends were there for the party and attacked them, shooting Hawkins dead. In 1998, three White men in Jasper, Texas, chained a Black man named James Byrd, Jr. to a pick-up truck and dragged him to his death, an event likened to a modern-day lynching. Events such as these are publicly censured as unacceptable in a modern democracy. These modern lynchings served as rallying cries for the continuing need for an antiracist African American politics.

Unfortunately, this placement of lynching at the core of the African American civil rights agenda has also minimized the related issue of institutionalized rape. Even Ida Wells-Barnett, who clearly saw the connections between Black men's persecution as victims of lynching and Black women's vulnerability to rape, chose to advance a thesis of Black women's rape through the discourse on Black men's lynching. In the postbellum period, the rape of free African American women by White men subsisted as a "dirty secret" within the *private* domestic spheres of Black families and of Black civil society. Speaking out against their violation ran a dual risk—it reminded Black men of their inability to protect Black

women from White male assaults and it potentially identified
Black men as rapists, the very group that suffered from lynching.
The presence of biracial Black children was tangible proof of
Black male weakness in protecting Black women and of Black
women's violation within a politics of respectability. Because
rapes have been treated as crimes against women, the culpability
of the rape victim has long been questioned. Her dress, her de-
meanor, where the rape occurred, and her resistance all become
evidence for whether a woman was even raped at all. Because Black
women as a class emerged from slavery as collective rape victims,
they were encouraged to keep quiet in order to refute the thesis of
their wanton sexuality. In contrast to this silencing of Black
women as rape victims, there was no shame in lynching and no
reason except fear to keep quiet about it. In a climate of racial violence, it was clear that victims of lynching were blameless and
murdered through no fault of their own.

Because the new racism contains the past-in-present elements of
prior periods, African American politics must be vigilant in analyzing how the past-in-present practices of Black sexual politics
also influence contemporary politics. Clarence Thomas certainly
used this history to his advantage. Recognizing the historical importance placed on lynching and the relative neglect of rape,
Thomas successfully pitted lynching and rape against one another
for his gain and to the detriment of African Americans as a group.
Shrewdly recognizing the logic of prevailing Black gender ideology that routinely elevates the suffering of Black men as more important than that of Black women, Thomas guessed correctly that
Black people would back him no matter what. If nothing else
comes of the Thomas hearings, they raise the very important
question of how sexual violence that was a powerful tool of social
control in prior periods may be an equally important factor in the
new racism.

African Americans need a more progressive Black sexual politics dedicated to analyzing how state-sanctioned violence, especially practices such as lynching (ritualized murder) and rape,
operate as forms of social control. Michel Foucault's innovative
idea that oppression can be conceptualized as normalized war
within one society as opposed to between societies provides a
powerful new foundation for such an analysis. Mass media

images of a multiethnic, diverse, color-blind America that mask deeply entrenched social inequalities mean that open warfare on American citizens (the exact case that lynching Black men presented in the past), is fundamentally unacceptable. Many Americans were horrified when they saw the 1992 videotape of Rodney King being beaten by the Los Angeles police. Fictional attacks on Black men in movies are acceptable, assaults on real ones, less so. Managing contemporary racism relies less on visible warfare between men than on social relations among men and between women and men that are saturated with relations of war. In this context, rape as a tool of sexual violence may increase in importance because its association with women and privacy makes it an effective domestic tool of social control. The threat of rape as a mechanism of control can be normally and routinely used against American citizens because the crime is typically hidden and its victims are encouraged to remain silent. New configurations of state-sanctioned violence suggest the workings of a rape culture may affect not just Black women but also Black men far more than is commonly realized. Given the significance of these tools of social control, what forms of sexual violence do African American women and men experience under the new racism? Moreover, how do these forms draw upon the ideas and practices of lynching and rape?

AFRICAN AMERICAN WOMEN AND SEXUAL VIOLENCE

Racial segregation and its reliance on lynching and rape as gender-specific tools of control have given way to an unstable desegregation under the new racism. In this context, the sexual violence visited upon African American women certainly continues its historical purpose, but may be organized in new and unforeseen ways. The terms *institutionalized rape* and *rape culture* encompass the constellation of sexual assaults on Black womanhood. From the sexual harassment visited upon Anita Hill and Black women in the workplace to sexual extortion to acquaintance, marital, and stranger rapes to how misogynistic beliefs about women create an interpretive framework that simultaneously creates the conditions in which men rape women and erase the crime of rape itself to the lack of punishment meted out by the state to Black women's rapists, sexual violence is much broader than any specific acts. Collectively, these practices comprise a rape culture that draws energy from the ethos of violence that saturates American society. African American essayist Asha Bandele describes the persistent sexual harassment she experienced during her teenaged years as part of growing up in a rape culture: "although the faces may have changed, and the places may have also, some things could always be counted on to remain the same: the pulling, and grabbing, and pinching, and slapping, and all those dirty words, and all those bad names, the leering, the propositions." It is important to understand how a rape culture affects African American women because such understanding may help with antirape initiatives. It also sheds light on Black women's reactions to sexual violence, and it demonstrates how this rape culture affects other groups, namely, children, gay men, and heterosexual men.

Rape is part of a system of male dominance. Recall that hegemonic masculinity is predicated upon a pecking order among men that is dependent, in part, on the sexual and physical domination of women. Within popular vernacular, "screwing" someone links ideas about masculinity, heterosexuality, and domination. Women, gay men, and other "weak" members of society are figuratively and literally "screwed" by "real" men. Regardless of the gender, age, social class, or sexual orientation of the recipient, individuals who are forcibly "screwed" have been "fucked" or "fucked over." "Freaks" are women (and men) who enjoy being "fucked" or who "screw" around with anyone. Because the vast majority of African American men lack access to a Black gender ideology that challenges these associations, they fail to see the significance of this language let alone the social practices that it upholds. Instead, they define heterosexual sex acts within a framework of "screwing" and "fucking" women and, by doing so, draw upon Western ideologies of Black hyper-heterosexuality that defines Black masculinity in terms of economic, sexual, and physical dominance. In this interpretive context, for some men, violence (including the behaviors that comprise the rape culture) constitutes the next logical step of their male prerogative.

Currently, one of the most pressing issues for contemporary Black sexual politics concerns violence against Black women at the hands of Black men. Much of this violence occurs within the context of Black heterosexual love relationships, Black family life, and within African American social institutions. Such violence takes many forms, including verbally berating Black women, hitting them, ridiculing their appearance, grabbing their body parts, pressuring them to have sex, beating them, and murdering them. For many Black women, love offers no protection from sexual violence. Abusive relationships occur between African American men and women who may genuinely love one another and can see the good in each other as individuals. Black girls are especially vulnerable to childhood sexual assault. Within their families and communities, fathers, stepfathers, uncles, brothers, and other male relatives are part of a general climate of violence that makes young Black girls appropriate sexual targets for predatory older men.

Because Black male leaders have historically abandoned Black women as collective rape victims, Black women were pressured to remain silent about these and other violations at the hands of Black men. Part of their self-censorship certainly had to do with reluctance to "air dirty laundry" in a White society that viewed Black men as sexual predators. As Nell Painter points out, "because discussion of the abuse of Black women would not merely implicate Whites, Black women have been reluctant to press the point." Until recently, Black women have been highly reluctant to speak out against rape, especially against Black male rapists, because they felt confined by the strictures of traditional Black gender ideology. Describing herself and other Black women rape victims as "silent survivors," Charlotte Pierce-Baker explains her silence: "I didn't want my nonblack friends, colleagues, and acquaintances to know that I didn't trust my own people, that I was afraid of black men I didn't know. . . . I felt responsible for upholding the image of the strong black man for our young son, *and* for the white world with whom I had contact. I didn't want my son's view of sex to be warped by this crime perpetrated upon his mother by men the color of him, his father, and his grandfathers." African American women grapple with long-standing sanctions within their communities that urge them to protect African

American men at all costs, including keeping "family secrets" by remaining silent about male abuse.

Black women also remain silent for fear that their friends, family, and community will abandon them. Ruth, a woman who, at twenty years old, was raped on a date in Los Angeles, points out: "You can talk about being mugged and boast about being held up at knife point on Market Street Bridge or something, but you can't talk about being raped. And I know if I do, I can't count on that person ever being a friend again. . . . People have one of two reactions when they see you being needy. They either take you under their wing and exploit you or they get scared and run away. They abandon you." Black women recount how they feel abandoned by the very communities that they aim to protect, if they speak out. Theologian Traci West describes how the very visibility of Black female rape victims can work to isolate them: "When sexual violation occurs within their families or by any member of 'their' community, black women may confront the profound injury of being psychically severed from the only source of trustworthy community available to them. Because of the ambiguities of their racial visibility, black women are on exhibit precisely at the same time as they are confined to the invisible cage."

Contemporary African American feminists who raise issues of Black women's victimization must tread lightly through this minefield of race, gender, and sex. This is especially important because, unlike prior eras when White men were identified as the prime rapists of Black women, Black women are now more likely to be raped by Black men. Increasingly, African American women have begun to violate long-standing norms of racial solidarity counseling Black women to defend Black men's actions at all costs and have begun actively to protest the violent and abusive behavior of some African American men. Some African American women now openly identify Black men's behavior toward them as abuse and wonder why such men routinely elevate their own suffering as more important than that experienced by African American women: "Black women do not accept racism as the reason for sorry behavior—they have experienced it firsthand, and for them it is an excuse, not a justification."

Since 1970, African American women have used fiction, social science research, theology, and their writings to speak out about violence against Black women. Many African American women have not been content to write about sexual violence—some have taken to the streets to protest it. Determined not to duplicate the mistakes made during the Thomas confirmation hearings, many Black women were furious when they found out that a homecoming parade had been planned for African American boxer and convicted rapist Mike Tyson upon his release from prison. The Mike Tyson rape case catalyzed many Black women to challenge community norms that counseled it was a Black women's duty as strong Black women to "assume the position" of abuse. Within this logic, a Black woman's ability to absorb mistreatment becomes a measure of strength that can garner praise. In efforts to regulate displays of strong Black womanhood, some Black people apparently believed that prominent Black men like Mike Tyson were, by virtue of their status, incapable of sexual harassment or rape. "Many apparently felt that Washington [Tyson's victim] should have seen it as her responsibility to endure her pain in order to serve the greater good of the race," observes cultural critic Michael Awkward. Rejecting this position that views sexual violence against Black women as secondary to the greater cause of racial uplift (unless, of course, sexual violence is perpetrated by White men), Black women in New York staged their own counterdemonstration and protested a homecoming celebration planned for a man who had just spent three years in prison on a conviction of rape.

ASSUME THE POSITION: BLACK WOMEN AND RAPE

Rape is a powerful tool of sexual violence because women are forced to "assume the position" of powerless victim, one who has no control over what is happening to her body. The rapist imagines absolute power over his victim; she (or he) is the perfect slave, supine, legs open, willing to be subdued or "fucked," and enjoying it. Rape's power also stems from relegating sexual violence to the private, devalued, domestic sphere reserved for women. The ability to silence its victims also erases evidence of the crime. These dimensions of rape make it a likely candidate to become an important form of social control under the new racism.

We have learned much from African American women both about the meaning of rape for women and how it upholds systems of oppression. For one, female rape victims often experience a form of posttraumatic stress disorder, a rape trauma syndrome of depression, anxiety, and despair, with some attempting suicide that affects them long after actual assaults. Women who survived rape report effects such as mistrust of men or of people in general, continued emotional distress in connection with the abuse, specific fears such as being left alone or being out at night, and chronic depression that lasted an average of five and a half years after the assault. This climate harms all African American women, but the damage done to women who survive rape can last long after actual assaults. Yvonne, who was molested by an "uncle" when she was eight and raped at age twelve, describes how the rape and sexual molestation that she endured as a child affected her subsequent attitudes toward sexuality: "I didn't take pride in my body after the rape. After it happened, I became a bit promiscuous. . . . Everyone *thought* I was bad; so I thought, I should just *be* bad. After the rape it was like sex really didn't matter to me. It didn't seem like anything special because I figured if people could just take it, . . . if they just had to have it enough that they would take a little girl and put a knife to her neck and *take* it, . . . that it had nothin' to do with love." Yvonne's experiences show how as an act of violence, rape may not leave the victim physically injured—emotional damage is key. The rape itself can temporarily destroy the victim's sense of self-determination and undermines her integrity as a person. Moreover, when rape occurs in a climate that already places all Black women under suspicion of being prostitutes, claiming the status of rape victim becomes even more suspect.

Black women are just as harmed by sexual assault as all women, and may be even more harmed when their abusers are African American men within Black neighborhoods. Gail Wyatt's research on Black women's sexuality provides an important contribution in furthering our understanding of Black women and rape. Wyatt found little difference in the effects of rape on Black and

White women who reported being rape victims. One important finding concerns the effects of *repeated* exposure to sexual violence on people who survive rape: "Because incidents of attempted and completed rape for Black women were slightly more likely to be repeated, their victimization may have a more severe effect on their understanding of the reasons that these incidents occurred, and some of these reasons may be beyond their control. As a consequence, they may be less likely to develop coping strategies to facilitate the prevention rather than the recurrence of such incidents." Stated differently, African American women who suffer repeated abuse (e.g., participate in a rape culture that routinely derogates Black women more than any other group) might suffer more than women (and men) who do not encounter high levels of violence, especially sexual violence, as a daily part of their everyday lives. For example, being routinely disbelieved by those who control the definitions of violence (Anita Hill), encountering mass media representations that depict Black women as "bitches," "hoes," and other controlling images, and/or experiencing daily assaults such as having their breasts and buttocks fondled by friends and perfect strangers in school, the workplace, families, and/or on the streets of African American communities may become so routine that African American women cannot perceive their own pain.

Within the strictures of dominant gender ideology that depict Black women's sexuality as deviant, African American women often have tremendous difficulty speaking out about their abuse because the reactions that they receive from others deters them. Women may be twice victimized—even if they are believed, members of their communities may punish them for speaking out. As Yvonne points out, "where I lived in the South, any time a black woman said she had been raped, she was never believed. In my community, they always made her feel like she did something to deserve it—or she was lying." Adrienne, a forty-year-old Black woman who had been raped twice, once by a much older relative when she was seven and again by her mother's boyfriend when she was twelve, observes, "Black woman tend to keep quiet about rape and abuse . . . If you talk about it, a man will think it was your fault, or he'll think less of you. I think that's why I never told the men in my life, because I've always been afraid they would not look at me in the same way. We all live in the same neighborhood. If something happens to you, *everybody* knows."

One important feature of rape is that, contrary to popular opinion, it is more likely to occur between friends, loved ones, and acquaintances than between strangers. Black women typically know their rapists, and they may actually love them. Violence that is intertwined with love becomes a very effective mechanism for fostering submission. In a sense, Black women's silences about the emotional, physical, and sexual abuse that they experience within dating, marriage, and similar love relationships resembles the belief among closeted LGBT people that their silence will protect them. Just as the silence of LGBT people enables heterosexism to flourish, the reticence to speak out about rape and sexual violence upholds troublesome conceptions of Black masculinity. Within the domestic sphere, many Black men treat their wives, girlfriends, and children in ways that they would never treat their mothers, sisters, friends, workplace acquaintances, or other women. Violence and love become so intertwined that many men cannot see alternative paths to manhood that do not involve violence against women. Black feminist theologian Traci C. West uses the term "domestic captivity" to describe women who find themselves in this cycle of love and violence: "Although they are invisible, the economic, social, and legal barriers to escape that entrap women are extremely powerful. This gendered denial of rights and status compounds the breach with community. Being confined in a cage that seems invisible to everyone else nullifies a woman's suffering and exacerbates her isolation and alienation."

As Barbara Omolade observes, "Black male violence is even more poignant because Black men both love and unashamedly depend on Black women's loyalty and support. Most feel that without the support of a 'strong sister' they can't become 'real' men." But this may be the heart of the problem—if African American men need women to bring their Black masculinity into being, then women who seemingly challenge that masculinity become targets for Black male violence. Educated Black women, Black career women. Black women sex workers, rebellious Black girls, and Black lesbians, among others who refuse to submit to male power, become more vulnerable for abuse. Violence against "strong" Black women enables some African American men to recapture a lost masculinity and to feel like "real" men. By describing why he continued to financially exploit women, and why he hit his girlfriend, Kevin Powell provides insight into this process:

> I, like most Black men I know, have spent much of my life living in fear. Fear of White racism, fear of the circumstances that gave birth to me, fear of walking out my door wondering what humiliation will be mine today. Fear of Black women—of their mouths, their bodies, of their attitudes, of their hurts, of their fear of us Black men. I felt fragile, fragile as a bird with clipped wings, that day my ex-girlfriend stepped up her game and spoke back to me. Nothing in my world, nothing in my self-definition prepared me for dealing with a woman as an equal. My world said women were inferior, that they must, at all costs, be put in their place, and my instant re-action was to do that. When it was over, I found myself dripping with sweat, staring at her back as she ran barefoot out of the apartment.

Powell's narrative suggests that the connections among love, sexuality, and violence are much more complicated that the simple linear relationship in which African American men who are victimized by racism use the power that accrues to them as men to abuse African American women (who might then use their power as adults to beat African American children). Certainly one can trace these relations in love relationships, but the historical and contemporary interconnections of love, sexuality, violence, and male dominance in today's desegregated climate are infinitely more complex.

In these contexts, it may be possible for African American women and men to get caught up in a dynamics of love, sexuality, and dominance whereby the use of violence and sexuality resemble addiction. In other words, if Black masculinity and Black femininity can be achieved only via sexuality and violence, sexuality, violence, and domination become implicated in the very definitions themselves. Once addicted, there is no way to be a man or a woman without staying in roles prescribed by Black gender ideology. Men and women may not engage in open warfare, but they do engage in mutual policing that keeps everyone in check. As a form of sexual violence, actual rapes constitute the tip of the iceberg. Rape joins sexuality and violence as a very effective tool to routinize and normalize oppression.

The effectiveness of rape as a tool of control against Black women does not mean that they have escaped other forms of social control that have disproportionately affected Black men. Working jobs outside their homes heightens African American women's vulnerability to other forms of state-sanctioned violence. For example, Black women are vulnerable to physical attacks, and some Black women are murdered. But unlike the repetitive and ritualized form of male lynching to produce a horrific spectacle for White and Black viewers, Black women neither served as symbols of the race nor were their murders deemed to be as significant. There is evidence that forms of social control historically reserved for Black men are also impacting Black women. For example, in the post–civil rights era, African American women have increasingly been incarcerated, a form of social control historically reserved for African American men. Black women are seven times more likely to be imprisoned than White women and, for the first time in American history, Black women in California and several other states are being imprisoned at nearly the same rate as White men. Incarcerating Black women certainly shows an increasing willingness to use the tools of state-sanctioned violence historically reserved for Black men against Black women. But is there an increasing willingness to use tools of social control that have been primarily applied to women against Black men? If institutionalized rape and institutionalized lynching constitute *different* expressions of the *same* type of social control, how might they affect Black men?

AFRICAN AMERICAN MEN, MASCULINITY, AND SEXUAL VIOLENCE

African American men's experiences with the criminal justice system may signal a convergence of institutionalized rape and institutionalized murder (lynching) as state-sanctioned forms of sexual violence. Since 1980, a growing prison-industrial complex has incarcerated large numbers of African American men. Whatever measures are used—rates of arrest, conviction, jail time, parole, or types of crime—the record seems clear that African American men are more likely than White American men to encounter the criminal justice system. For example, in 1990, the nonprofit Washington, D.C.–based Sentencing Project released a survey result suggesting that, on an average day in the United States, one in every four African American men aged 20 to 29 was either in prison, jail, or on probation/parole. Practices such as unprovoked police brutality against Black male citizens, many of whom die in police custody, and the disproportionate application of the death penalty to African American men certainly suggest that the state itself has assumed the functions of lynching. Because these practices are implemented by large, allegedly impartial bureaucracies, the high incarceration rates of Black men and the use of capital punishment on many prisoners becomes seen as natural and normal.

But how does one manage such large populations that are incarcerated in prison and also in large urban ghettos? The ways in which Black men are treated by bureaucracies suggests that the disciplinary practices developed primarily for controlling women can be transferred to new challenges of incarcerating so many men. In particular, the prison-industrial complex's treatment of male inmates resembles the tactics honed on women in a rape culture, now operating not between men and women, but among men. These tactics begin with police procedures that disproportionately affect poor and working-class young Black men. Such men can expect to be stopped by the police for no apparent reason and asked to "assume the position" of being spread-eagled over a car hood, against a wall, or face down on the ground. Rendering Black men prone is designed to make them submissive, much like a female rape victim. The videotape of members of the Los Angeles Police Department beating motorist Rodney King provided a mass media example of what can happen when Black men refuse to submit. Police treatment of Black men demonstrates how the command to "assume the position" can be about much more than simple policing.

Rape while under custody of the criminal justice system is a visible yet underanalyzed phenomenon, only recently becoming the subject of concern. Because rape is typically conceptualized within a frame of heterosexuality and with women as rape

victims, most of the attention has gone to female inmates assaulted by male guards. Yet the large numbers of young African
American men who are in police custody suggest that the relationships among prison guards and male inmates from different race
and social class backgrounds constitutes an important site for negotiating masculinity. Moreover, within prisons, the connections
among hegemonic and subordinated masculinities, violence, and
sexuality may converge in ways that mimic and help structure the
"prison" of racial oppression. Because prisons rely on surveillance, being raped in prison turns private humiliation into public
spectacle. The atmosphere of fear that is essential to a rape culture
as well as the mechanisms of institutionalized rape function as
important tools in controlling Black men throughout the criminal
justice system. Whereas women fear being disbelieved, being
abandoned, and losing the love of their families, friends, and communities, men fear loss of manhood. Male rape in the context of
prison signals an emasculation that exposes male rape victims to
further abuse. In essence, a prison-industrial complex that con-
dones and that may even foster a male rape culture attaches a very
effective form of disciplinary control to a social institution that
itself is rapidly becoming a new site of slavery for Black men.

Drawing upon a national sample of prisoners' accounts and on
a complex array of data collected by state and federal agencies,
No Escape: Male Rape in U.S. Prisons, a 2001 publication by
Human Rights Watch, claims that male prisoner-on-prisoner sexual abuse is not an aberration; rather, it constitutes a deeply
rooted systemic problem in U.S. prisons. They note, "judging by
the popular media, rape is accepted as almost a commonplace of
imprisonment, so much so that when the topic of prison arises, a
joking reference to rape seems almost obligatory." Prison authorities claim that male rape is an exceptional occurrence. The narratives of prisoners who wrote to Human Rights Watch say
otherwise. Their claims are backed up by independent research
that suggests high rates of forced oral and anal intercourse. In one
study, 21 percent of inmates had experienced at least one episode
of forced or coerced sexual contact since being incarcerated, and
at least 7 percent reported being raped. Certain prisoners are targeted for sexual assault the moment they enter a penal facility. A
broad range of factors correlate with increased vulnerability to

rape: "youth, small size, and physical weakness; being white, gay, or a first offender; possessing 'feminine' characteristics such as long hair or a high voice; being unassertive, unaggressive, shy, intellectual, not street-smart, or 'passive'; or having been convicted of a sexual offense against a minor."

As is the case of rape of women, prisoners in the Human Rights Watch study, including those who had been forcibly raped, reported that the *threat* of violence is a more common factor than actual rape. A rape culture is needed to condone the actual practices associated with institutionalized rape. Once subject to sexual abuse, prisoners can easily become trapped into a sexually subordinate role. Prisoners refer to the initial rape as "turning out" the victim. Rape victims become stigmatized as "punks:" "Through the act of rape, the victim is redefined as an object of sexual abuse. He has been proven to be weak, vulnerable, 'female,' in the eyes of other inmates." Victimization is public knowledge, and the victim's reputation will follow him to other units and even to other prisons. In documenting evidence that sounds remarkably like the property relations of chattel slavery, Human Rights Watch reports on the treatment of male rape victims:

> Prisoners unable to escape a situation of sexual abuse may find themselves becoming another inmate's "property." The word is commonly used in prison to refer to sexually subordinate inmates, and it is no exaggeration. Victims of prison rape, in the most extreme cases, are literally the slaves of their perpetrators. Forced to satisfy another man's sexual appetites whenever he demands, they may also be responsible for washing his clothes, massaging his back, cooking his food, cleaning his cell, and myriad other chores. They are frequently "rented out" for sex, sold, or even auctioned off to other inmates. . . . Their most basic choices, like how to dress and whom to talk to, may be controlled by the person who "owns" them. Their name may be replaced by a female one. Like all forms of slavery, these situations are among the most degrading and dehumanizing experiences a person can undergo.

Prison officials condone these practices, leaving inmates to fend for themselves. Inmates reported that they received no protection from correctional staff, even when they complained.

Analyzing the connections among imprisonment, masculinity, and power, legal scholar Teresa Miller points out that "for most male prisoners in long-term confinement, the loss of liberty suffered during incarceration is accompanied by a psychological loss of manhood." In men's high-security prisons and large urban jails, for example, sexist, masculinized subcultures exist where power is allocated on the basis of one's ability to resist sexual victimization (being turned into a "punk"). Guards relate to prisoners in sexually derogatory ways that emphasize the prisoners' subordinate position. For example, guards commonly address male prisoners by sexually belittling terms such as *pussy*, *sissy*, *cunt*, and *bitch*. Moreover, the social pecking order among male prisoners is established and reinforced through acts of sexual subjugation, either consensual or coerced submission to sexual penetration. The theme of dominating women has been so closely associated with hegemonic masculinity that, when biological females are unavailable, men create "women" in order to sustain hierarchies of masculinity.

Miller reports that the pecking order of prisoners consists of three general classes of prisoners: men, queens, and punks. "Men" rule the joint and establish values and norms for the entire prison population. They are political leaders, gang members, and organizers of the drug trade, sex trade, protection rackets, and smuggled contraband. A small class of "queens" (also called bitches, broads, and sissies) exists below the "men." A small fraction of the population, they seek and are assigned a passive sexual role associated with women. As Miller points out, "the queen is the foil that instantly defined his partner as a 'man.'" However, "queens" are denied positions of power within the inmate economy. "Punks" or "bitches" occupy the bottom of the prison hierarchy. "Punks" are male prisoners who have been forced into sexual submission through actual or threatened rape. As Miller points out, "punks are treated as slaves. Sexual access to their bodies is sold through prostitution, exchanged in satisfaction of debt and loaned to others for favors." In essence, "punks" are sexual property. A prisoner's position within this hierarchy simultaneously defines his social and sexual status.

Male rape culture has several features that contribute to its effectiveness as a tool of social control. For one, in the prison context, maintaining masculinity is always in play. Miller points to the fluid nature of masculine identity: "Because status within the hierarchy is acquired through the forcible subjugation of others, and one's status as a man can be lost irretrievably through a single incident of sexual submission, 'men' must constantly demonstrate their manhood through sexual conquest. Those who do not vigorously demonstrate their manhood through sexual conquest are more apt to be challenged and be potentially overpowered. Hence, the surest way to minimize the risk of demotion is to aggressively prey on other prisoners." Consensual and forced sexual contact among men in prison has become more common. Because masculinity is so fluid and is the subject of struggle, it is important to note that sexual relations between men does not mean that they are homosexuals. Rather, sexual dominance matters. Those men who are treated as if they were women, for example, the "queens" who voluntarily submit to the sexual advances of other men and are orally or anally "penetrated" like women, may become lesser, less "manly" men in prison but need not be homosexuals. Moreover, those men who are forcibly penetrated and labeled "punks" may experience a subordinated masculinity in prison, but upon release from prison, they too can regain status as "men." Engaging in sexual acts typically reserved for women (being penetrated) becomes the mark of subordinated masculinity. In contrast, those men who are "on top" or who are serviced by subordinate men retain their heterosexuality, in fact, their masculinity may be enhanced by a hyper-masculinity that is so powerful that it can turn men into women.

Another important feature of male rape culture in prison concerns its effects on sexual identities. Since male prisoner-on-prisoner rape involves persons of the same sex, it is often misnamed "homosexual rape" that is thought to be perpetrated by "homosexual predators." This terminology ignores the fact that the vast majority of prison rapists do not view themselves as being gay. Rather, they are heterosexuals who see their victim as substituting for a woman. Because sexual identities as heterosexual or homosexual constitute fluid rather than fixed categories, masculinity in the prison context is performed and constructed." The sexual practices associated with rape—forced anal and oral penetration—determine sexual classification as "real" men or "punks," not biological maleness. In this predatory environment, it is important to be the one who "fucks with" others, not the one who "sucks dick" or who is "fucked in the ass." As one Illinois prisoner explains it: "the theory is that you are not gay or bisexual as long as YOU yourself do not allow another man to stick his penis into your mouth or anal passage. If you do the sticking, you can still consider yourself to be a macho man/heterosexual." The meaningful distinction in prison is not between men who engage in sex with men and in sex with women, but between what are deemed "active" and "passive" participants in the sexual act.

Installing a male rape culture in prison has the added important feature of shaping racial identities. White men rarely rape Black men. Instead, African American men are often involved in the rape of White men who fit the categories of vulnerability. One Texas prisoner describes the racial dynamics of sexual assault: "Part of it is revenge against what the non-white prisoners call, 'The White Man,' meaning authority and the justice system. A common comment is, 'ya'll may run it out there, but this is our world!'" Another prisoner sheds additional light on this phenomenon: "In my experience having a 'boy' (meaning white man) to a Negro in prison is sort of a 'trophy' to his fellow black inmates. And I think the root of the problem goes back a long time ago to when the African Americans were in the bonds of slavery. They have a favorite remark: 'It ain't no fun when the rabbit's got the gun, is it?'" Drawing upon psychoanalytic theory, William Pinar offers one explanation for these racial patterns: "Straight black men could have figured out many kinds of revenge, could they not: physical maiming for one, murder for another. But somehow black men knew exactly what form revenge must be once they were on 'top,' the same form that 'race relations' have taken (and continues to take) in the United States. 'Race' has been about getting fucked, castrated, made into somebody's 'punk,' politically, economically, and, yes, sexually."

Yet another important feature of male rape culture in prison that shows the effectiveness of this form of sexual violence concerns its effects on male victims/survivors. Men who are raped often describe symptoms that are remarkably similar to those of female rape victims, namely, a form of posttraumatic stress disorder described as a rape trauma syndrome. Men expressed depression, anxiety, and despair, with some attempting suicide. Another devastating consequence is the transmission of HIV. However, because male rape victims are men, they still have access to masculinity and male power, if they decide to claim it. As one Texas prisoner described his experiences in the rape culture: "It's fixed where if you're raped, the only way you [can escape being a punk is if] you rape someone else. Yes I know that's fully screwed, but that's how your head is twisted. After it's over you may be disgusted with yourself, but you realize that you're not powerless and that you can deliver as well as receive pain." Because prison authorities typically deny that male rape is a problem, this inmate's response is rational. As one inmate in a Minnesota prison points out, "When a man gets raped nobody gives a damn. Even the officers laugh about it. I bet he's going to be walking with a limp ha ha ha. I've heard them."

It is important to remember that the vast majority of African American men are not rapists nor have they been raped. However, male rape in prison as a form of sexual dominance and its clear ties to constructing the masculine pecking order within prisons do have tremendous implications for African American male prisoners, their perceptions of Black masculinity, and the gendered relationships among all African Americans. First and foremost, such a large proportion of African American men are either locked up in state and federal prisons and/or know someone who has been incarcerated, large numbers of African American men are exposed to conceptions of Black masculinity honed within prison rape culture. Among those African American men who are incarcerated, those who fit the profile of those most vulnerable to abuse run the risk of becoming rape victims. In this context of violence regulated by a male rape culture, achieving Black manhood requires *not* fitting the profile and *not* assuming the position. In a sense, surviving in this male rape culture and avoiding victimization require at most becoming a predator and victimizing others and, at the least, becoming a silent witness to the sexual violence inflicted upon other men.

Second, so many African American men are in prison on any given day that we fail to realize that the vast majority of these very same men will someday be released. Black men cannot be easily classified in two types, those who are "locked up" in prison and those who remain "free" outside it. Instead, prison culture and street culture increasingly reinforce one another, and the ethos of violence that characterizes prison culture flows into a more general ethos of violence that affects all Black men. For many poor and working-class Black men, prison culture and street culture constitute separate sides of the same coin. Sociologist Elijah Anderson's "code of the streets" has become indistinguishable from the violent codes that exist in most of the nation's jails, prisons, reform schools, and detention centers. Describing young Black men's encounters with the criminal justice system as "peculiar rites of passage," criminologist Jerome Miller contends: "So many young black males are now routinely socialized to the routines of arrest, booking, jailing, detention, and imprisonment that it should come as no surprise that they bring back into the streets the violent ethics of survival which characterize these procedures." For middle-class Black men who lack the actual experiences of prison and street culture, mass media representations of gangstas as authentic symbols of Black masculinity help fill the void. They may not be actual gangstas, but they must be cognizant that they could easily be mistaken as criminals. Varieties of Black masculinity worked through in prisons and on the streets strive to find some place both within and/or respite from this ethos of violence.

Black men who have served time in prison and are then released bring home this ethos of violence and its culpability in shaping Black masculinity. Certainly these men are denied access to full citizenship rights, for example, having a prison record disqualifies large numbers of Black men from getting jobs, ever holding jobs as police officers, or even voting. But an equally damaging effect lies in the views of Black masculinity that these men carry with them through the revolving doors of street and prison culture, especially when being victims or perpetrators within a male rape culture frames their conceptions of gender and sexuality. One wonders what effects these forms of Black masculinity are having on African American men, as well as their sexual partners, their children, and African American communities.

As sociologist Melvin Oliver points out in *The Violent Social World of Black Men*, African American men live in a climate of violence. Because the American public routinely perceives African

American men as actual or potential criminals, it often overlooks the climate of fear that affects Black boys, Black men on the street, and Black men in prison. In his memoir titled *Fist, Stick, Knife, Gun: A Personal History of Violence in America*, Geoffrey Canada details how he and his brothers had to work out elaborate strategies for negotiating the streets of their childhood, all in efforts to arrive safely at school, or buy items at the grocery store. As children of a single mother, they lacked the protection of an older Black man, thus making them vulnerable in the pecking order among Black men. All Black boys must negotiate this climate of fear, yet it often takes an especially tragic incident to arouse public protest about Black boys who victimize one another. For example, in 1994, five-year-old Eric Morse was dropped from a fourteenth floor apartment window to his death in the Ida B. Wells public housing project in Chicago. His tormentors allegedly threw him down a stairwell, stabbed him, and sprayed him with Mace before dropping him from the window. The two boys convicted of murdering him were ten and eleven years old.

The question of how the ethos of violence affects Black male adolescents is of special concern. In many African American inner-city neighborhoods, the presence of gang violence demonstrates a synergistic relationship between Black masculinity and violence. Research on Black male youth illustrates an alarming shift in the meaning of adolescence for men in large, urban areas. Autobiographical work by David Dawes on the Young Lords of Chicago, Nathan McCall recalling his youth in a small city in Virginia, and Sanyika Shakur's chilling autobiography that details how his involvement in gang violence in Los Angeles earned him the nickname "Monster" all delineate shocking levels of Black male violence. As revealed in these works, many young Black men participate in well-armed street gangs that resemble military units in which they are routinely pressured to shoot and kill one another. In these conditions, it becomes very difficult for Black boys to grow up without fear of violence and become men who refuse to use violence against others.

Only recently have scholars turned their attention to the effects that living in fear in climates of violence might have both on the quality of African American men's lives and on their conceptions of Black masculinity. Sociologist Al Young conducted extensive interviews with young Black men who were in their twenties, with some surprising findings. The men in his study did not exhibit the swagger and bravado associated with glorified hip-hop images of gangstas, thugs, and hustlers. Instead, these men shared stories of living in fear of being victimized, of dropping out of school because they were afraid to go, of spending considerable time figuring out how to avoid joining gangs, and, as a result, becoming cut off from all sorts of human relationships. Some suggest that Black men have given up hope, or as columnist Joan Morgan states: "When brothers can talk so cavalierly about killing each other and then reveal that they have no expectation to see their twenty-first birthday, that is straight-up depression masquerading as machismo."

Unlike Young's work, the effects of violence on African American men, especially those with firsthand knowledge of a prison male rape culture, have been neglected within social science research. Moreover, the effects of sexual violence on African American men also generates new social problems for African American families, communities, and American society overall. As the graphic discussion of the male "slaves" as property within the penal system indicates, many Black men victimize one another and strive to reproduce the same male pecking order *within* African American communities that they learn and understand as masculine within prison. These men victimize not just women and children; they harm other men and place all in a climate of fear.

SEXUAL VIOLENCE REVISITED

The new racism reflects changes in mechanisms of social control of the post–civil rights era. Lynching and rape as forms of violence still permeate U.S. society, but because they no longer are as closely associated with the binary thinking of the logic of segregation, these seemingly gender-specific practices of sexual violence are organized in new ways. First, movies, films, music videos, and other mass media spectacles that depict Black men as violent and that punish them for it have replaced the historical spectacles provided by live, public lynchings. When combined with the criminalization of Black men's behavior that incarcerates so many men, the combination of mass media images and institutional practices justifies these gender-specific mechanisms of control. For example, as vicarious participants in spectator sports, audience members can watch as men in general, and African American men in particular, get beaten, pushed, trampled, and occasionally killed, primarily in football arenas and boxing rings. The erotic arousal that many spectators might feel from viewing violence that historically came in attending live events (the violence visited upon the lynch victim being one egregious example of this situation) can be experienced vicariously in the anonymity of huge sports arenas and privately via cable television. Films and other forms of visual media provide another venue for framing societal violence. Contemporary films, for example, the slasher horror films targeted to adolescents, produce images of violence that rival the most gruesome lynchings of the past. Lynching is no longer a live show confined to African American men, but, as is the case with other forms of entertainment, has moved into the field of representations and images. Thus, there is the same ability to watch killing, but in the safety of one's living room, with DVD technology allowing the scene to be replayed. Both of these mass media spectacles fit nicely with the lack of responsibility associated with the new racism. Viewers need not "know" their victims, and violence can be blamed on the "bad guys" in the film or on governmental or corporate corruption. Witnessing beatings, tortures, and murders as spectator sport fosters a curious community solidarity that feeds back into a distinctly American ethos of violence associated with the frontier and slavery. Black men are well represented within this industry of media violence, typically as criminals whose death should be celebrated, and often as murder victims who are killed as "collateral damage" to the exploits of the real hero.

Second, in this new context of mass media glorification of violence, rape of women (but not of men) along with the constellation of practices and ideas that comprise rape culture has been moved from the hidden place of privacy of the past and also displayed as spectacle. Whether in Hollywood feature films, independent films such as Spike Lee's *She's Gotta Have It*, or the explosion of pornography as lucrative big business, viewers can now see women raped, beaten, tortured, and killed. Clearly, the ideas of a rape culture persist as a fundamental form of sexual dominance that affects African American women. As feminists remind us, thinking about rape not as a discrete act of violence but as part of a systemic pattern of violence reveals how social institutions and the idea structures that surround rape work to control actual and potential victims. Not every women needs to be raped to have the *fear* of rape function as a powerful mechanism of social control in everyday life. Women routinely adjust their behavior for fear of being raped. The workings of a rape culture, the privacy of the act, the secrecy, the humiliation of being a rape victim, seem especially well suited to the workings of routinization of violence as a part of the "normalized war" that characterizes desegregation. Rape becomes more readily available as a public tool of sexual dominance. At the same time, prison rape of men is not taken seriously and does not routinely appear as entertainment.

Third, the mechanisms of social control associated with a rape culture and with institutionalized rape might be especially effective in maintaining a new racism grounded in advancing myths of integration that mask actual social relations of segregation. Both Black men and Black women are required to "assume the position" of subordination within a new multicultural America, and the practices of a rape culture help foster this outcome. Most Americans live far more segregated lives than mass media leads them to believe. The vast majority of men and women, Blacks and Whites, and straights and gays still fit into clearly identifiable categories of gender, race, and sexuality, the hallmark of a logic of segregation. At the same time, the increased visibility and/or vocality of individuals and groups that no longer clearly fit within these same categories have changed the political and intellectual landscape. For example, many middle-class African Americans now live in the unstable in-between spaces of racially desegregated neighborhoods; lesbian, gay, bisexual, and transgendered (LGBT) people who have come out of the closet undercut the invisibility required for assumptions of heterosexism; some working-class kids of all races now attend elite universities; and biracial children of interracial romantic relationships have challenged binary understandings of race. Crossing borders, dissolving boundaries, and other evidence of an imperfect desegregation does characterize the experiences of a substantial minority of the American population.

When it comes to African Americans, focusing too closely on these important changes can leave the impression that much more change is occurring than actually is. The record on African American racial desegregation is far less rosy. This illusion of racial integration, especially that presented in a powerful mass media, masks the persistence of racial segregation for African Americans, especially the racial hypersegregation of large urban areas. Maintaining racial boundaries in this more fluid, desegregated situation requires not just revised representations of Black people in mass media but also requires new social practices that maintain social control yet do not have the visibility of past practices. Institutionalized rape serves as a mechanism for maintaining gender hierarchies of masculinity and femininity. But institutionalized rape and the workings of rape culture can also serve as effective tools of social control within racially desegregated settings precisely because they intimidate and silence victims and encourage decent people to become predators in order to avoid becoming victims. In this sense, the lessons from a rape culture become important in a society that is saturated with relations of war against segments of its own population but that presents itself as fair, open, and without problems.

Finally, these emerging modes of social control have important implications for antiracist African American politics generally and for developing a more progressive Black sexual politics in particular. Violence constitutes a major social problem for African Americans. State violence is certainly important, but the violence that African Americans inflict upon one another can do equal if not more damage. When confronting a social problem of this magnitude, rethinking Black gender ideology, especially the ways in which ideas about masculinity and femininity shape Black politics becomes essential. As the Clarence Thomas confirmation revealed, African Americans' failure to understand the gendered contours of sexual violence led them to choose race over gender. Incidents such as this suggest that Black leaders have been unable to help either Black women or Black men deal with the structural violence of the new racism because such leaders typically fail to question prevailing Black gender ideology. What happens when men incorporate ideas about violence (as an expression of dominance) into their definitions of Black masculinity? Can they remain "real" men if they do not engage in violence? How much physical, emotional, and/or sexual abuse should a "strong" Black woman absorb in order to avoid community censure? Stopping the violence will entail much more than Black organizations who protest state-sanctioned violence by White men against Black ones. Because violence flows from social injustices of race, class, gender, sexuality, and age, for African American women and men, eradicating violence requires a new Black sexual politics dedicated to a more expansive notion of social justice.

Hooters Chicken

BY LIZZ HUERTA

Lizz Huerta is a first-generation American writer of Mexican and Puerto Rican descent who identifies as "Mexi-Rican." Her fiction and essays have appeared in *The Rumpus*, *The Cut*, and the anthology *A People's Future of the United States*. Huerta is a five-time VONA fellow and the winner of the *Lumina* fiction contest. She has published three chapbooks, and her first novel, *The Lost Dreamer*, was published in March 2022. In "Hooters Chicken," published in *The Rumpus* in 2017, Huerta examines the ways in which performing for the male gaze as a waitress at Hooters altered not only her understanding of gender as a performance, but of sexuality as well. And then the essay delves deeper, into how working at Hooters "had given me a glimpse of what I thought was power," and how that power was constrained to "that tiny space allotted by the male gaze."

I applied for a job at Hooters on a dare a few weeks before my nineteenth birthday. A shoe salesman who worked across from me at the mall told me he'd pay me twenty dollars to apply. He told me what to wear: denim shorts, tennis shoes, a white tank top, and my best bra. Twenty dollars was four hours of trying to sell cheap makeup to mall walkers. I bought a white tank top.

There was a large table shaped like the state of California filled with raucous men in golf gear. They turned to me as I walked through the doors into the funk of fryer grease and stale beer. They whooped at me as I blushed and asked the bartender for an application. I sat at a corner table, my long hair a shield around my face as I filled out the form. Twenty dollars, I promised myself, some creepy men and twenty dollars. The manager snapped up my application, gave me a once over, and led me to a table in the middle of the restaurant for an interview.

Later, I learned the bartender was the lookout for potential hires. There was a tiny Hooters Owl on the upper right hand corner of the application. If the bartender thought an applicant was appropriate (cute, pretty, sexy, perky in the right ways) she would fill in the eyes of the owl before handing the application over. She was the first gatekeeper. The manager had what I would one day come to recognize as the broken blood vessels of an alcoholic striated across his face. He asked me a few questions. I did my best. I was less than a year out of high school and had been the president of the thespian society and a community college drama major. I could fake it. I faked it. I blinked like an ingénue and answered. When he asked me why I wanted to be a Hooters girl I paused, looked around at the tables full of lunch break men, the servers laughing and sending their orders to the kitchen via a type of wire and pulley system, and said, "It looks interesting." The manager laughed and told me most girls said it looked like fun.

He'd call me.

Before I had time to get up from my seat, one of the men from the California table approached and asked if I was being considered for the job. The manager nodded and the business man put a heavy, hot hand on my back and held out a roll of cash to me. "Is it okay if I give her her first tip on account of how pretty she is?" he drawled.

The manager shrugged.

"Good luck," the man said and handed me the roll. I stayed in character, acted charmed, thanked the man, and rushed out. In my Ford Festiva I unrolled the cash and counted it. Eighty-seven dollars, plus the twenty from the shoe salesman. It felt like a ton of money, maybe more money than I had ever held at once that was mine. I decided if they called me back, I would be a Hooters girl.

———

And then I became a Hooters girl. I stared at my breasts in the mirror. My large, matrilineal breasts were high on my chest, enhanced by the Lycra of the uniform.

My mother has large breasts, heavy and low, though they don't quite sit in her lap yet. She couldn't breastfeed any of her children but still they lengthened and dropped.

She hated her breasts. She hated her body. When I was a kid I watched her constantly diet, constantly try on different types of body slimmers, reduction bras. When my breasts came in she told me appreciate them while I could, before gravity and weight took over.

I stared at my mom's breasts when I told her about my job. My mom cried, scared that it would lead to stripping, followed by porn, sex work, and her having to swoop in and rescue me like the fierce, fearless mother from a Lifetime movie.

I told her, "Jesus mom, I'm serving chicken wings. Get over it."

She got over it. I wore all black back then, had for years, a gothling with Wiccan tendencies. Every Wednesday and Saturday night I would follow my favorite band to Tijuana, drink and sing along with Rockeros. We smoked clove cigarettes in tiny bars, and I wore the darkest lipstick I could find with tight black shirts, cigarette legged pants, and Doc Martens. Sandy at the end of *Grease*, but Mexi-Rican with a penchant for doing animal impressions when I was buzzed or nervous.

But at work, I ditched the black and went full-color.

———

My first week at Hooters I failed at acting anything but bewildered when the customers pretended not to look at my breasts while I asked mild medium or hot. Late into one shift the place was emptying out and I was parked at the wait-station with a group of other servers. I felt like the ultimate dork. The other girls were sorority girls or bikini models, and they had flat bellies and pierced navels. (I had a pierced belly button for about four hours until my mom cried, "How could you desecrate the part of your body where we were connected?") One of the servers was imitating the sound her puppy made when she left. I, socially inept after acting vapid for hours, decided that meant it was time for animal sounds. I dove into my barnyard chicken impression. I bent my arms, went wall-eyed, and began clucking loudly, scratching at the ground with my foot like I was searching for seeds. I thought, as I always fucking thought, they were laughing with me. The cooks came out of the kitchen, the manager came out of his office and guffawed. A few days later I came into work and there was a new name tag for me: Chicken Girl. I don't think anyone called me by my real name, Lizz, at that joint.

I was not only a Hooters girl, I was the jester and I fell into the role with relief. I didn't have to be a sexpot; I could stay in the skin of drama kid. I performed for other servers and the customers. I clucked. I learned how to pour a pitcher of beer while climbing a stool, simultaneously hula-hooping and making crude jokes about the head of the beer. My days were filled with community college theater classes, while nights I was Chicken Girl. After school I changed into the costume of sex kitten with wings, a side show. After work I was never invited to hang out with the other servers; they had tight cliques, hierarchies. I was the weird brown girl who quoted Kahlil Gibran. I didn't drink. I didn't party. I lived with my parents.

My first month on the job, a sexy long-haired cook asked me out; he was brown, too. He didn't tell me he had a girlfriend, one of the woman who had trained me. I saw them arguing, I heard my name. I was terrified; I hadn't known. To prove how harmless I was I began to play myself as absurd, a little off. It wasn't far from the truth. I wrote poetry on my breaks, I started smoking regular cigarettes instead of cloves so as not to have to see the wrinkled noses and side-eye at the sweet blue smoke of my Djarums. I had never been the other woman before. Another identity, claimed.

———

There were lessons from those days of orange shorts and push-up bras. My first lesson: how to wear thong underwear. My first day I noticed a bunch of servers whispering and giggling. One beckoned me over and told me my panties were bigger than my shorts. My full-bottomed, cotton crotch panties were hanging out of my shorts, under my pantyhose. After work I went and bought my first thong underwear. I practiced wearing them outside of work to get used to the discomfort of having a piece of cloth up my ass. *Discomfort is growth*, I told myself. I began mimicking the other servers in small ways, I bought a flat iron and Reeboks high tops with the double velcro straps. I started wearing low-cut tops in public outside of work. I felt powerful stepping into the role of sexpot, flirt, vixen. The sexual self-confidence was intoxicating and terrifying.

I was groped once, at a secondhand record store. I said, "Hey, that's not cool," and the perpetrator told me I should keep my tits covered then.

I complained to the record store manager and he glanced at my cleavage and said, "Maybe you shouldn't dress like that."

I was angry but hadn't yet developed the confidence to tell someone to fuck off out loud instead of in my head. That skill came much later in life. I had been raised with a God who was a man and wary of women. My family had been Jehovah's Witnesses and then we were not—but even when we changed affiliation and identity, some tenets remained, just as it did with Hooters.

———

There were girls who got gifts. A few well-off regulars would show up with bags from Bebe or Ed Hardy and hand them out to their favorites. My regulars were different. My nerd heart and animal impressions brought me a small but faithful group. A comic book artist always ordered a Coke with no ice, tipped a dollar, and sat in my section drawing large-breasted faeries. A sweet high school janitor obsessed with basketball and pro-wrestling would weekly bring me sock puppets in honor of his favorite wrestler, Mankind, and his powerful sock puppet, Mr. Socko. He brought me so many sock puppets that I started wearing them as socks under my Reeboks. He never noticed. I had a silent regular who came in with photo albums of Hooters girls from all over the world and asked me to pose for him. I did. I collected these gentle weirdos the same way I collected bad relationships, always looking for the granule of goodness and beauty. I wanted to prove I was beautiful on the inside.

———

At twenty-two, I decided I was done. I was bored. I'd spent three years serving wings and beer and glimpses at my cleavage. I

wanted to travel. I was tired of plastering on a fake smile, tired of
the mundane flirtation, the eye candy/male gaze relationship. I
gave my notice. I threw away dozens of pairs of suntan pantyhose
and a few pair of grease-soled Reeboks. I didn't put the uniform
on anymore but I kept the swagger it allowed me. I was still new
in my sexual confidence but my days in the orange shorts had
given me a glimpse of what I thought was power.

———————

I glided through the rest of my twenties with uncareful confidence. I swooped through dalliances and interludes with ease. I
had boyfriends. I cheated. I was the other woman, just as I was the
other woman at Hooters. I was cheated on. I played horrible
power games, fucking a married man who swore he was a bohe-
mian trapped in an ordinary marriage. I fucked his best friend to
test the theory. It was the first time I made a man cry. Another
power in my arsenal, cruelty. I peacocked, but whatever satisfac-
tions my body brought, I wanted something real. I still was
clothed in the remnants of the performative sexual swagger I'd
learned to inhabit in my orange shorts. I didn't know how to be
myself, how to be genuine. I didn't want to believe being a Hooters girl had changed me. It took years to stop leaning hard into the
hard flirt, into the innuendo. I knew the power of lust; I wanted to
know desire. I grieved the woman I knew I was underneath the
performance that had rooted in my body. My mother, it turned
out, was not wrong. I had not emerged unscathed. It was grief
that had me covering my body more and more. The uniform had
left its mark, and what I did was bury it. Baggy shirts over long
pants, an array of hoodies. I cocooned into my thirties, sick of
men coming for my body. I decided my mind and my creativity
were more important than my body. Instead of showing flesh in
person I began showing flesh on paper. I entered into a series of
romantic, platonic relationships. Sex, touching, intimacy of the
corporeal disappeared but my mind was getting freaky. My mind
was getting licked and loved, nibbled on—until the uniform was
eaten away. I engaged in orgies of thoughts and ideas; I was riled
up on intellectual exchanges then fell asleep next to my partners,
my foot maybe touching a leg, as close to touching as it came.

I had been Chicken Girl in a Hooters uniform, performance on top of performance, being rewarded with cash by men. I took that cash and bought myself vacations, started my business. I took the experience and spent years peeling off the uniform. Until I stopped performing.

Sometimes when rummaging, I'll come across my Hooters uniform in the bottom dresser drawer with other items of clothing I can't throw away. Memory cloth. I wonder how I ever fit into those tiny shorts, my ass chafed from running around in thong underwear. All the panties I wear now are bigger than those orange shorts.

But I keep them. They remind me of how I've literally and figuratively grown out of that young woman and that space, that tiny space allotted by the male gaze. And yet there is a part of her I want to reclaim: wildness.

I Used to Give Men Mercy

BY TERESE MAILHOT

Terese Mailhot is an award-winning writer from Seabird Island Band in British Columbia on the Seabird Island First Nation reservation. She has served on the faculty at the Institute of American Indian Arts and was a tenure-track professor at Purdue University. Mailhot was Saturday editor at *The Rumpus* and a columnist at *Indian Country Today*. Her work has appeared in the *Los Angeles Times*, *The Guardian*, *Mother Jones*, and Best American Essays. She is the author of *Heart Berries: A Memoir*. Her writing—including this 2018 essay first published in *Guernica*—interrogates sexual abuse, intergenerational trauma, and poverty through a feminist and Indigenous lens. Mailhot's work reframes her experiences through Indigenous myths and spirituality in an attempt to decolonize her narrative and the prevailing narratives regarding Indigenous people that persist in our culture.

I believe in Oprah. I see pictures of her every day. I pay attention to the way she smokes a turkey on Thanksgiving, and to the fact that she still loves bread. Because of Oprah, I tell myself, "The world is right there: take it."

In the hospital, after my second or third breakdown, I watched OWN as often as I could. There was an evening of programming dedicated to Maya Angelou. I took a risk watching TV, because the nurses considered it a symptom of depression. But I needed to hear Maya speak. She said, "Let me tell so much truth—not facts. Because facts can obscure the truth."

And I tell the truth as an expedient thing, for the reader and myself. I don't obscure the truth with the mundane. I don't build my work on the aesthetic I learned in the MFA classes at school, on suggestions that I slow down, that I remove the poetry and ambiguity from my prose, that I produce competent writing. Long before I graduated with my first degree, I was tired of competent writing. Competent books, with protagonists with names like Siobhán, who live in brownstone apartments and are never gratuitous or explicit or poor. I can't afford to let white academia drag me into mediocrity.

But it's hard to articulate how one goes from a server to a cam-girl to a master's student to someone holding a degree in her hands so tightly the paper became wet and she had to throw it away. Because I've existed in extremes for much of my life, I'm reticent to write from a middle place, where there is no urgency. I can hear my graduate program's workshop facilitator, a white man, saying, "Terese, slow down." He wants the tourist experience. He wants me to curate pain and titillation, and tell what each room looks like, because, without that, my work is not enough. He doesn't believe that these experiences felt this fast, but they did. He wants to see the struggle, but he doesn't deserve it.

Camgirl writes a story, and publishes it. It's about a gluttonous, sexually expressive Native woman—and a white man. It's about taking the pain of loving him and straddling it.

The dumb Indian becomes a community college instructor. I walk in to apply for a tutoring job, and they tell me I'm overqualified. They tell me I should be a teacher. People back home, on the rez, are proud. They are so proud, and it hurts to shine this bright when the inside still feels dim and dumb.

The dumb Indian is accepted to both MFA programs she applies to. Sherman Alexie is faculty at the Institute of American Indian Arts, and who can resist?

The same hustle I applied to waiting tables and to camming—to contorting my body—I apply it to my work and outrun any expectation I had for myself. This is exceptionalism. The year after graduation, Sherman Alexie is sending me excerpts from his forthcoming memoir as he writes them. I'm completing my own memoir and editing a literary magazine. When I finish the book, it sells immediately. I become the first Tecumseh Postdoctoral Fellow at Purdue University. I become faculty at the Institute of American Indian Arts. Camgirl makes good. It's also a love story, because now I have another baby. But I have three kids with three different last names. I'm still rez.

You can write the truth explicitly. Like the cold cracking open a healing wound, the truth can be that way. Nothing is too ugly for this world.

———

When I was a webcam model, a man wanted to fly me to New York. It wasn't explicitly sexual. He told me he was deeply unhappy at his job.

"That's familiar," I said.

He didn't know what I meant.

"If I was writing this story, they would call your use of my time a cliché. The deeply unhappy man is lonely, and pays a woman to listen to him."

"Can I fly you here?"

When I considered telling the man my real name, I quit. I still receive notifications from the website, telling me it's been a while since I've earned.

I called myself "Baby." My sister Viva calls me Baby. "I think I'm going to commit myself again," I say. "Baby," she says, every time.

I was packing up my apartment after being evicted—I wanted to leave behind the mattress I was raped on. I remember, before I closed the door behind me, I said, "Baby, do you want a better job? It's yours." I wanted fancy dinners, so I worked to buy them for myself. After so many years of hustle—of men telling me I was a "good look," or that I could be someone underneath them—I told myself I could have it. I gave myself what I wanted. Nobody has given it to me better—and nobody ever will.

———

The man snoring on my couch used to be my lover. He forgets I am pretty. I don't. He forgets many things, but he cannot forget that I am venerable now. Every day, as my book is rolling out, there is news, and money, compliments from other people. He cannot forget I am venerable because the world won't let him.

I supplement his lack, buying myself flowers and food and jewelry and clothing. I've supplemented his lack by becoming a good partner to myself. It's left me feeling successful, fulfilled, and lonely.

My husband is not all lack. Sometimes he smells like the parts of my childhood that were good. Like the river. Like sawdust and small animals, even though he is large. He used to play football. I'm familiar with every story of those days. We drive through his old town and see the fields and schools where he played, where someone with a name like Jimmy Wilkins fell through the roof, where his mother was always late to pick him up, where the children pushed themselves to extreme limits, terrified to let big people down. We drive past these monuments, and I've learned to start telling the story before he can. Only I add details he never told: Jimmy Wilkins didn't just walk on the roof and fall through it, but part of my husband's childhood remains on that roof, waiting for everything to collapse. These elaborations are how I show I care. This is how my people show they love each other.

In couples' therapy, the man tells me to stop calling bipolar disorder an illness. He tells me to stop nagging, because my husband is trying to quit smoking, and quitting smoking is hard enough. He looks like Terry Richardson, with pleated pants and cashmere sweaters. It's disconcerting. I don't like men, mostly. We change therapists.

The next therapist makes us do homework. Love is homework. We have to pick a safe word to use when we begin to feel afraid of what is about to be said. The unsaid is something we fear for different reasons. He fears saying it, and I fear hearing it. The safe word is "Allen," the name of a boy who wrote a story for my MFA workshop in which he likened breasts to milk jugs, and there was a wench, or a maid, and maybe a dragon. We, the women in the classroom, could not contain ourselves. We could not contain our laughter as he got into his sports car, and out of it, and never said hello. Lechery is not funny; bad writing is.

"I think you neglect me emotionally. I feel like you don't love me. I want a divorce."

"Allen."

I want to illustrate a tree so well that someone finds it. It's the snowball tree in my old yard on Seabird Island, on forty acres of land, surrounded by raspberry bushes and apple trees and overgrown grass. It's the largest snowball tree I've ever seen. I couldn't see it when I went home last because I was afraid of the wild dogs. The tree is not a metaphor; it's real. I'd like to be buried there.

At Little Grand Rapids First Nation, Donnelly Rose Eaglestick was mauled to death by a pack of dogs. There was a cull, twenty-five dollars a head. The white people said it wouldn't solve the problem. What do they know about walking home, scared to be torn apart?

———

I'm in a partial hospitalization program for fifteen days, to prepare myself emotionally for book touring and interviews. In our group therapy, we're asked to draw a tree.

"Everything about it is a metaphor."

We must illustrate the roots, which symbolize where we're from. And if I can't remember some of it, I can leave some roots missing. The tree I draw wouldn't be a good map for someone looking for the literal tree I want to be buried near. The tree I draw is all metaphor.

There are the roots of my grandmother, whose root caps are swelling hearts.

The middle roots are absent. I've drawn a blue corridor instead. The lack of roots is my father. The space where the roots should be is dark.

The absorbing roots and trunk flare are my mother, my brothers, my sister and her children: they compensate for the blue corridor.

The ground beneath the roots represents my present life. I want to draw something to symbolize the visibility I feel.

"If you want to practice being interviewed, we can help with that," my publicists say, before I tell them about the fifteen-day program I signed up for, before I tell them I didn't expect to talk so much, that I wrote the things so that I wouldn't need to speak them again.

The trunk is supposed to symbolize my skill. I don't know how to illustrate my skill. I make the trunk thin, but fill it with hearts. The branches are my hopes and dreams.

One side of my tree is a cedar tree and the other is the snowball tree. My mother washed cedar boughs in the river and hung them in our entryways to purify whatever entered and whatever left. The snowball tree was planted by my ancestors.

After group therapy, I go to bed exhausted and wake up in the morning to write a résumé for my friend's little brother. You should be able to describe the emotional work a prep cook does. You should be able to illustrate what it takes to get to work when you have kids and no car. You should be able to apply for a job with a tree in your hand.

————

Every day they ask you to speak what you are thankful for. Instead of saying "platitudes," I say "vegetables," because I feel good when I eat them.

"Your appetite is back?" the counselor asks.

I forget that she monitors me. I feel good knowing someone is monitoring me. If I had said "platitudes," it would have been out of righteous indignation. It would have been because this whole program is about platitudes: letting go, what we can handle, how time heals, what we deserve, that we'll be okay. If I had said "platitudes," I wouldn't have known someone cared what I was eating.

I am actively trying not to be diagnosed with a personality disorder. I am content with bipolarity and PTSD. I like polarity. I like the feeling of a swinging heart.

————

There are two types of anger, but the counselor doesn't explicitly name them. Instead, she plays "Dear Mr. Jesus" on YouTube. She wants us to be upset when we hear a little girl singing to Mr. Jesus, asking him to look out for a child from the evening news who was badly beaten by her parents. The little girl prays for Jesus to take the child up to heaven, or spare her life, and then the singer signs off, "My mommy hits me, too." I'm upset, but mostly at the little girl's coyness. In creative writing workshop we learned that coy reveals cheapen a story.

The counselor's point is that one can use anger to do good things. People can be compelled by anger to act righteously. She also says that anger is normal for people recovering from trauma.

We create an illustration of anger. Anger is an iceberg, and all of us together must list a hundred underlying reasons—reasons we become angry. She writes our reasons beneath the iceberg. I want to name the native women who shouldn't have died the way they did: Cindy Gladue, who died with an eleven-centimeter blunt force injury to her vagina, whose vagina was then cut from her body and preserved so it could be shown to the court—which was unprecedented. Barbara Kentner, who died slowly after a white man threw a trailer hitch at her from his moving vehicle. Savanna LaFontaine-Greywind, who was found wrapped in plastic in the Red River, her child having been cut from her womb. Joey English, who was not yet buried before the man who dismembered her was granted bail, twice. I want to name these women, not to posture but for naming's sake. In some cultures, you cannot speak the names of your dead. In some cultures, you rest the names of your dead, so you do not call them back to the world of the living. To play along, I tell the counselor to write "injustice," "bureaucracy," and "racism" under the iceberg. The white people suggest adding "bad weather" and "being misunderstood."

The counselor says, "What about you, Terese?" It's not much of a question, or I'm not sure what she's asking, but the topic is anger.

I start to cry and I believe I sound like a child. I recall the day my husband drove me to work and we fought. I cried and held my phone and told him that I could not go to work "like this." He said that I needed to, because he couldn't stand to speak to me any longer. I got out of the car and walked alone in a neighborhood I did not know. He left the parking lot, and I considered that I could go missing, like so many women I love.

Before him, I gave men mercy. Another man raped me because I cheated on him, and then I went to our counseling appointments to see if we could still make it work. One therapist (a man) said my rapist had a right to look through my phone, and another therapist (a woman) said we could get through it, that the man who raped me was profoundly broken. She suggested that my rapist listen to the song "If I Were a Boy," by Beyoncé. She suggested, because we had budgeting issues, that we sneak homemade popcorn into movie theaters. I forget why they trivialized the fact that this man raped me. I forget if I mitigated everything that happened, until all we could talk about was saving money. I explain that I cry when I'm angry.

When I get home, I email the old therapy center to ask if they have any record of him admitting that he raped me. I wonder what good it could possibly do to know something I know.

I talk in the group session like a child. "What is it about me?" And I'm really asking.

The women in the group whisper, "It's not you."

———

We never show our trees to each other. They sit in a desk. It's okay because the trees were for ourselves.

The other tree, the real one—it's waiting for any person to find it. What do words matter if they don't carry someone to something literal? I believe I write the places I can't arrive at alone. What good is one more illustration if it doesn't carry me somewhere? What I wouldn't give for something literal to come from me, not just words.

Is it too perfect that, where I'm from, when we become women, they plant you a tree? All the women form a circle, and each one says something. The tree is a metaphor and it is growing. If you walk across the tracks from old Haig Highway, down the gravel road to a burned-down house at the end of a circular driveway, you will find the snowball tree, and near Stein Valley there is a whole forest of women's trees—and where are the women? I need to know that you will look for us. But you don't give us any credit. You don't even give us humanity.

———

When I graduate from the partial hospitalization program, I'll receive a medallion. The people in group will adorn me with compliments and kind wishes. Then I will get on a plane and perform the persona of a successful author—a feature, interviews, a book tour. The medallion will be inside of my jacket pocket, between my fingertips. My hands will smell like a coin, and my nervous laughter will be amplified by a microphone, and women will line up to adorn me with kind wishes, and they'll tell me they've been hurt too, and I'm scared I'll reach out to hold them and the coin will fall out of my pocket like the secrets I don't tell. The coin will fall out and I'll have to admit that I'm a dumb Indian—and maybe that's what they need to hear. You can't obscure the truth with the mundane. You can't illustrate pain for tourists.

Maybe I'll wear the coin like a talisman, or be in the hospital again.

———————

At the mental health facility, we have a class on humor and the benefits of laughter. A man in recovery looks at me and says, "What do you get when a hooker dies in your hotel room?"

I say, "No."

The facilitator doesn't speak.

The man says, "One hour free."

The same man reaches over me at lunch to get a spoon, and I hold up my hand to guard my breasts. I could tell him that Cindy Gladue's killer told the court that he paid her sixty dollars for services rendered the night he murdered her, and that she died alone in a bathtub from her injuries. I could tell him that I did things for money, often, and that it didn't make me less of a human—but it doesn't matter. I don't want to tell him that I was raped and filmed and that I am someone different now, but the same woman. I don't want to tell him about the beauty of the women where I'm from, and that there is a forest of trees who are women. I don't want to tell him anything. I owe him as much as I owe the workshop facilitators, who taught me nothing of craft and everything of whiteness and men.

When the man looks at me in the hallway, he cowers, and I believe he is ashamed. I think it's because I use words like "effusive," and because I question the research in our handouts on the benefits of laughter. He believes I am venerable; he thinks I am beyond being cut open in a bathtub and left for dead. He thinks I am not desperate to tell someone to find my tree. He believes I am someone, and I must, too.

Everything I ever wanted, I have taken for myself. But still there is the sinking feeling that I will step into the undertow of everything around me and be lost. There is the sinking feeling that if I don't illustrate the tree, nobody will ever see me as human.

Happy Hookers

BY MELISSA GIRA GRANT

Melissa Gira Grant is an American journalist and former sex worker whose writing covers the intersection of sex, politics, and technology. Grant is the author of *Playing the Whore: The Work of Sex Work* (2014) and a staff writer at *The New Republic*. Her feature reporting has been published by *BuzzFeed News* and *The Guardian*, and her commentary and criticism have appeared in *The Washington Post*, *The New York Times*, *Bookforum*, and *The New York Review of Books*. Her essays are collected in *Best Sex Writing 2013*, *The Feminist Utopia Project*, and *Where Freedom Starts: Sex Power Violence #MeToo*. Grant's work complicates and interrogates our cultural understanding of sex work and the people who do it, an understanding that comes from pundits, writers, and feminists who rarely have experience with sex work, and whose aim is criminalizing sex workers in the name of saving them. Grant's "Happy Hookers," published in *Jacobin* in 2012, examines the difference between the myth and the reality of sex work, the dispute over shutting down Backpage, and the disconnects between the vantage point of self-appointed "saviors" and avowed feminists who did not have firsthand knowledge of sex work and the lived experience of sex workers themselves.

The following books were not published in 1972: *The Happy Secretary*, *The Happy Nurse*, *The Happy Napalm Manufacturer*, *The Happy President*, *The Happy Yippie*, *The Happy Feminist*. The memoir of a Manhattan madam was. *The Happy Hooker* climbed best-seller lists that year, selling over sixteen million copies.

When it reached their top five, the *New York Times* described the book as "liberally dosed with sex fantasies for the retarded." The woman who wrote them and lived them, Xaviera Hollander, became a folk hero. She remains the accidental figurehead of a class of women who may or may not have existed before she lived and wrote. Of course, they must have existed, but if they hadn't, say the critics of hooker happiness, we would have had to invent them.

Is prostitution so wicked a profession that it requires such myths?

We may remember the legend, but the particulars of the happy hooker story have faded. Hollander and the characters that grew up around her are correctly recalled as sexually omnivorous, but desire alone didn't make her successful as a prostitute. She realized that the sex trade is no underworld, that it is intimately entangled in city life, in all the ways in which we are economically interdependent. Hollander was famous for being able to sweep through the lobby of the Palace Hotel, unnoticed and undisturbed, on her way to an assignation, not because she didn't "look like" a working girl, but because she knew that too few people understood what a working girl really looked like.

In *The Happy Hooker Goes to Washington*, a 1977 film adapted from Hollander's memoir, a scene opens with teletype bashing the screen with Woodward-and-Bernstein urgency. Flashlights sweep a darkened hall. Inside an unlocked office, a criminal scene is revealed: a senator embracing a prostitute. Hollander is called before Congress to testify. When the assembled panel interrogates her career, attacking her morals, she is first shameless, then spare but sharp in pointing out the unsurprising fact that these men are patrons of the very business they wish to blame for America's downfall.

What's on trial in the film is ridiculous, but the questions are real. What value does a prostitute bring to society? Or is hooking really not so grandiose as all that? Could it be just another mostly tedious way to take ownership over something all too few of us are called before Congress to testify on (the conditions of our work)?

———

"Did you know that 89 percent of the women in prostitution want to escape?" a young man told me on the first day of summer this year, as he protested in front of the offices of the *Village Voice*. He wanted me to understand that it is complicit in what he calls "modern-day slavery." The *Village Voice* has moved the bulk of the sex-related ads it publishes onto the website Backpage.com. This young man, the leader of an Evangelical Christian youth group, wanted to hasten the end of "sex slavery" by shutting Backpage .com down. What happens to the majority of people who advertise willingly on the site, who rely on it to draw an income? "The reality is," the man said to me, not knowing I had ever been a prostitute, "almost all of these women don't really want to be doing it."

Let's ask the people around here, I wanted to say to him: the construction workers who dug up the road behind us, the cabbies weaving around the construction site, the cops over there who have to babysit us, the Mister Softee guy pulling a double shift in the heat, the security guard outside a nearby bar, the woman working inside, the receptionist upstairs. The freelancers at the *Village Voice*. The guys at the copy shop who printed your flyers. The workers at the factory that made the water bottles you're handing out. Is it unfair to estimate that 89 percent of New Yorkers would rather not be doing what they have to do to make a living?

"True, many of the prostitution ads on Backpage are placed by adult women acting on their own without coercion," writes *New York Times* columnist and professional prostitute savior Nicholas Kristof. But, he continues, invoking the happy hooker trope, "they're not my concern." He would like us to join him in separating women into those who chose prostitution and those who were forced into it; those who view it as business and those who view it as exploitation; those who are workers and those who are victims; those who are irremediable and those who can be saved. These categories are too narrow. They fail to explain the reality of one woman's work, let alone a class of women's labor. In this scheme, a happy hooker is apparently unwavering in her love of fucking and will fuck anyone for the right price. She has no grievances, no politics.

But happy hookers, says Kristof, don't despair, this isn't about women like you—we don't really mean to put you out of work. Never mind that shutting down the businesses people in the sex trade depend on for safety and survival only exposes all of them to danger and poverty, no matter how much choice they have. Kristof and the Evangelicals outside the *Village Voice* succeed only in taking choices away from people who are unlikely to turn up outside the *New York Times*, demanding that Kristof's column be taken away from him.

Even if they did, with the platform he's built for himself as the true expert on sex workers' lives, men like Kristof can't be run out of town so easily. There's always another ted conference, another women's rights organization eager to hire his expertise. Kristof and those like him, who have made saving women from themselves their pet issue and vocation, are so fixated on the notion that almost no one would ever choose to sell sex that they miss the dull and daily choices that all working people face in the course of making a living. Kristof himself makes good money at this, but to consider sex workers' equally important economic survival is inconvenient for him.

———

This business of debating sex workers' choices and whether or not they have them has only become more profitable under what sociologist Elizabeth Bernstein terms "post-industrial prostitution."

After the vigilant anti-prostitution campaigns of the last century, which targeted red-light districts and street-based prostitution, sex work has moved mostly indoors, into private apartments and gentlemen's clubs, facilitated by the internet and mobile phones. The sex economy exists in symbiosis with the leisure economy: personal services, luxury hotels, all increasingly anonymous and invisible. At the same time, more young people find themselves without a safety net, dependent on informal economies. Sex work now isn't a lifestyle; it's a gig, one of many you can select from a venue like Backpage or Craigslist.

Recall the favored slogan of prostitution prohibitionists that on the internet, they could buy a sofa and "a girl." It's not the potential purchase of a person that's so outrageous; it's the proximity of that person to the legitimate market.

Bernstein calls these "slippery borders," and asks us to observe the feelings provoked by them, and how they are transferred. Anxieties about slippery market borders become "anxieties about slippery moral borders," which are played out on the bodies of sex workers.

The anxiety is that sex work may be legitimate after all. In a sense, the prohibitionists are correct: people who might have never gotten into the sex trade before can and are. Fighting what they call "the normalizing of prostitution" is the focus of anti-sex work feminists. In this view, one happy hooker is a threat to all women everywhere.

"It's sad," said the speaker from the women's-rights NGO Equality Now in protest outside the *Village Voice*. She directed her remarks at the cluster of sex workers who had turned out in counterprotest. "Backpage is able to be a pimp. They're so normalizing this behavior that a group of Backpage advertisers have come out today to oppose us." So a prostitute's dissent is only possible if, as they understand prostitution itself, she was forced into it.

"Why did it take so long for the women's movement to genuinely consider the needs of whores, of women in the sex trades?" asks working-class queer organizer and ex-hooker Amber L. Hollibaugh, in her book *My Dangerous Desires*. "Maybe because it's hard to listen to—I mean really pay attention to—a woman who, without other options, could easily be cleaning your toilet? Maybe because it's intolerable to listen to the point of view of a woman who makes her living sucking off your husband?"

Hollibaugh points to this most difficult place, this politics of feelings performed by some feminists, in absence of solidarity. They imagine how prostitution must feel, and how that in turn makes them feel, despite all the real-life prostitutes standing in front of them to dispute them.

———

It didn't used to be that people opposed to prostitution could only get away with it by insisting that "happy" prostitutes didn't really exist. From Gilgamesh to the Gold Rush days, right up until Ms. Hollander's time, being a whore was reason enough for someone to demand you be driven out of town. Contemporary prostitution prohibitionists consider the new reality, in which they deny the existence of anyone with agency in prostitution, a form of victory for women. We aren't ruined now. We're victims.

Your Ass or Mine?

BY VIRGINIE DESPENTES

Virginie Despentes is a French writer, activist, and film-maker whose work examines marginalization, sexual violence, and injustice. Her 1993 novel, *Baise-moi,* or *Rape Me*, about a sex worker who is gang-raped and seeks revenge, was adapted into a film directed by Despentes in 2000. The English translation of her novel *Vernon Subutex 1* was short-listed for the 2018 International Booker Prize. The 2010 English translation of Despentes's wildly influential 2006 book *King Kong Theory* is a collection of essays drawn from personal experience to confront issues like rape, sex work, capitalism, and pornography that is ultimately about who gets to frame the narratives that become cultural norms. In the essay "Your Ass or Mine?" Despentes considers the backlash to the sexual revolution and its effect on women. She uses psychoanalysis to examine "the flood of 'slut-chic' in contemporary popular culture" as a "way of apologizing, of reassuring men" that all women want is to please them and be saved.

For some time now, in France, we've been getting shit about the 1970s. How we took the wrong turn, how we fucked things up with the sexual revolution, do we think we're men or what, and with all our PC bullshit you have to wonder what the hell's happened to the good old-fashioned masculinity of Dad and Granddad, who knew how to die on a battlefield and run a household with wholesome discipline. And with the law to back them up. We're getting shit because men are scared. As though this is somehow our fault. It's pretty amazing, and a very modern take, to say the least, for Dom to go bitching that the Sub isn't pulling her weight . . . Is the white man really laying into women, or is he just trying to express his surprise at the down-turn in his stock around the world? One way or the other, the way we're being skewered, called to order, and controlled is beyond belief. One minute, we're accused of constantly playing the victim, the next we're told we're fucking the wrong way, too slutty or too lovey-dovey, whatever we're doing, we're getting it wrong, too hard-core or not sensual enough . . . Obviously, this whole sexual revolution was just pearls before bimbos. Whatever we do, there'll always be someone who'll take the trouble to tell us it's crap. Essentially: things were better before. Oh, really?

I was born in '69. I went to a co-ed school. From my first year in primary school I knew that girls and boys were no different in terms of intelligence. I wore short skirts and no one in my family worried about what the neighbors would think. I was on the pill at fourteen, and it was no big deal. I was fucking as soon as I got the chance, I really enjoyed it at the time, and twenty years later the only thing I can think to say is "bully for me." I left home at seventeen and I had the right to live on my own, no one could criticize me for it. I always knew I'd work, that I'd never put up with some guy just so he'd pay the rent. I opened a bank account in my own name, completely unaware that I was part of the first generation of women to be able to do so without a father or a husband as guarantor. I was a late starter when it came to masturbation, though I knew the word, having read it in books that were completely clear on the subject: I wasn't some antisocial monster because I played with myself, in fact what I did with my pussy was nobody's business but mine. I slept with hundreds of guys without ever getting pregnant, in any case, I knew where to get an abortion without anyone's permission and without risking my life. I became a whore, I strutted the streets in high-heeled shoes and low-cut tops, without having to account to anyone—every cent I earned I kept and I spent. I went hitchhiking, I was raped, I went hitchhiking again. I wrote a first novel, signed it with my own name, a girl's name, without ever worrying that, when it was published, I'd have people reading me the riot act about the lines I shouldn't cross. Women my age are the first to be able to live life without sex, without having to go straight to a nunnery. Forced marriage has become shocking. Conjugal rights are no longer a given. For years, I was a million miles from feminism, not out of a lack of solidarity or awareness, but because, for a long time, my gender didn't really stop me from doing much of anything. Since I wanted a man's life, I lived a man's life. So the feminist revolution really did take place. People need to quit telling us that we were more fulfilled before. Horizons unfurled, vast territories were brutally opened up, as though it had always been this way.

Okay, so contemporary France is not exactly Arcadia for everyone. People aren't happy here, not women, not men. But it has nothing to do with the traditional ideas of gender. We could all stay home in the kitchen in our aprons squeezing out a baby every time we fuck, but it would do nothing to change the crises of employment, neoliberalism, Christianity, or ecological balance.

The women I know all earn less than the men, they have more junior roles, they think it's par for the course to be unappreciated when they achieve something. They have a drudge's pride at having to succeed against the odds, as though it was expedient, enjoyable, or sexy. A servile pleasure at the thought of being used as a doormat. We women are embarrassed by our powers. Constantly policed by men who keep sticking their noses into our business, telling us what's good for us and bad for us, but especially by other women, through the family, through women's magazines and public discourse. We are expected to play down our power, a trait that is never prized in women: "competent" still means "masculine."

In 1929, Joan Riviere, an early-twentieth-century psychoanalyst, wrote "Womanliness as a Masquerade," in which she discusses the case of an "intermediate type"—a heterosexual but masculine woman—who suffers from the fact that every time she expresses herself in public, she is overcome by a terrible dread that causes her to lose control and manifests itself as an obsessive, humiliating need to attract the attention of men.

Analysis then revealed that the explanation of her compulsive ogling and coquetting . . . was as follows: it was an unconscious attempt to ward off the anxiety which would ensue on account of the reprisals she anticipated from the father-figures after her intellectual performance. The exhibition in public of her intellectual proficiency, which was in itself carried through successfully, signified an exhibition of herself in possession of her father's penis, having castrated him. The display once over, she was seized by horrible dread of the retribution the father would then exact. Obviously, it was a step towards propitiating the avenger to endeavour to offer herself to him sexually.

This analysis offers a key to the tsunami of "slut-chic" in pop culture right now. Anyone walking the streets, watching MTV or some prime-time piece of light entertainment, or leafing through a women's magazine, will be struck by the rise of the slutty-bitch look—pretty hot as it goes—embraced by a lot of young women. In fact, it is a way of apologizing, of reassuring men: "See how sexy I am?" these girls in G-strings seem to proclaim. "For all my autonomy, my education, my intelligence, my only goal in life is to please you." I could have a different life, but I've settled on alienation via the most effective seduction strategies.

At first glance, it might seem surprising that girls would enthusiastically embrace the traits of woman-as-object, mutilating their bodies and flaunting them outrageously, while at the same time the younger generation venerates "respectable woman," which is a far cry from party sex. But the paradox is superficial. Women are sending men a message of reassurance: "Don't be scared of us." It makes it worth it to wear uncomfortable clothes and shoes you can barely walk in, to have your nose reshaped or your tits pumped up, to starve yourself half to death. No society has ever demanded such complete submission to aesthetic diktats, so many body modifications that purport to feminize the body. Yet at the same time, no society has ever offered women such physical and intellectual freedom of movement. The overmarketing of femininity seems like an apology to men for the loss of their prerogatives, a way of reassuring ourselves by reassuring them. "We want to be liberated, but not too much. We want to play the game, we don't want the powers associated with the phallus, we don't want to scare anyone." Women instinctively put themselves down, conceal the freedoms they've only just acquired, play the role of the seductress, take up their former role all the more outrageously since—deep down—they know that these days it's nothing more than a charade. Access to traditionally male powers is mingled with the fear of punishment. Since the dawn of time, stepping outside the cage has been met with brutal penalties.

It is not so much the notion of our own inferiority that we women have internalized—whatever the brutality of the instruments of control, day-to-day life has shown us that men, by nature, are neither inherently superior, nor particularly different from women. It is the idea that our independence is destructive that has penetrated to the marrow of our bones. And it's relentlessly repeated in the media: in the past twenty years, how many articles have been published about women who frighten men, about women who find themselves alone, punished for their ambition or their individualism? As though being a widow, being abandoned, abused, or alone in time of war were a recent invention. We've always had to muddle through without help. To claim that men and women understood each other better before the 1970s is historical revisionism. We simply spent less time with each other.

Similarly, motherhood has become the quintessential female experience, prized above all else: giving life is awesome. Rarely has "pro-motherhood" propaganda been so blatant. It's complete bullshit, the systematic modern use of the double bind: "Have kids, it's amazing, you'll feel more feminine and more fulfilled than ever before," but do it in a society in utter collapse, in which having a salaried position is a precondition of social survival, but is not guaranteed to anyone, especially not women. Have kids in cities where housing is substandard, where schools have thrown in the towel, where children are subject to the most vicious mental abuse through advertising, TV, the internet, companies hawking junk food and soft drinks. No kids = no fulfillment as a woman, but bringing up kids in half-decent conditions is virtually impossible. One way or another, women must be made to feel like failures. Whatever women do, someone feels obliged to prove that we've gone about it the wrong way. There is no correct response, whatever choice we make is necessarily wrong, and we are blamed for a failure that is, in fact, collective and involves both men and women. The weapons used against our gender may be specific, but the method also applies to men. The only good consumer is an anxious consumer.

A shocking and profoundly revealing fact: the feminist revolution of the seventies didn't result in any restructuring of childcare arrangements. Nor in dealing with housework. Unpaid work = women's work. We're still stuck in the do-it-yourself era. Politically as much as economically, we haven't occupied the public space, we haven't taken it over. We haven't set up the day care centers and the childcare facilities we need; we haven't created the technological solutions for domestic housework that would emancipate us. We haven't invested in these financially viable economic sectors either for profit or as a service to our communities. Why has no one come up with an equivalent of Ikea for childcare, an equivalent of Microsoft for housework? The public sphere has remained resolutely male. We worry that we lack the legitimacy to launch ourselves into the political sphere—that's the least of our problems, given the physical and moral campaign of terror we face because of our gender. As though others are going to deal appropriately with our problems, as though our specific concerns are not terribly important. We are wrong. While it is patently obvious that power corrupts and degrades women just as it does men, it is unarguable that certain considerations are specifically feminine. Relinquishing the political sphere as we have is indicative of our misgivings about emancipation. Granted, to fight and win in politics means being prepared to sacrifice our femininity, because we have to be prepared to brawl, to conquer, to make a show of strength. It means we have to forget about being gentle, sweet, considerate, we have to allow ourselves to publicly dominate the other. To get by without approval, to wield power aggressively, with no simpering, no apologizing, because there aren't many opponents prepared to congratulate you on thrashing them.

Motherhood has become the most venerated aspect of the female condition. In the West, it is also the sphere in which a woman's power has increased. The complete power mothers have long wielded over their daughters is now also true of their sons. A mother knows what's best for her child, we're constantly told, as though she innately carried this astounding wisdom within her. It is a domestic echo of what is happening in society: the surveillance state knows better than we do what we should eat, drink, smoke, ingest, what's appropriate for us to watch, to read, to understand, how we should travel, spend our money, entertain ourselves. When Nicolas Sarkozy calls for cops in schools, when Ségolène Royal calls for soldiers on the streets of certain neighborhoods, they're not presenting children with some macho figure of law and order, but an extension of the mother's absolute power. She alone knows how to discipline, to train, to take in hand these overgrown babies. A government that sets itself up as an all-powerful mother is a fascistic government. Citizens of a dictatorship revert to being babies: they are fed, changed, and kept in a crib by an ever-present power that knows everything, is capable of anything, and wields complete power over them for their own good. Individuals are stripped of their autonomy, of their right to make mistakes, to put themselves in harm's way. This is where our society is headed, probably because our glory days are long behind us and we are regressing toward organization models that infantilize the individual. Traditionally, masculine values are those of discovery, of risk-taking, of cutting ties with the family. Men would be wrong to cheer or take comfort when they see any trace of masculinity in women scorned, shackled, and considered toxic. It's their autonomy as much as ours that's being called into question. In a capitalist surveillance society, man is just another consumer, and it is disadvantageous for him to have significantly greater powers than a woman.

The collective body functions in the same way as the individual body: if the system is overanxious, it spontaneously gives rise to self-destructive patterns. When the collective unconscious, through the media and the entertainment industry, glorifies motherhood, it is not out of a love for the feminine or a global sense of benevolence. To invest the mother with every virtue is to prepare the collective body for a return to fascism. Powers granted by a sick state are necessarily suspect.

These days, we hear men bitching that women's liberation is emasculating them. They yearn for a status quo ante, when their power was rooted in the oppression of women. They forget that the political advantages they enjoyed always came at a cost: women's bodies belonged to men only inasmuch as men's bodies belonged to the means of production in peace time, and to the state in time of war. The expropriation of the female body coincided with the expropriation of the male body. There are no winners in this deal, aside from a handful of big shots.

The most famous soldier who fought in the Iraq War is a woman. Nowadays, states dispatch their poor to the front lines. Battlefields are now equal opportunity. Increasingly, the real disparity is one of social class.

Men vehemently denounce social or racial injustices, but are tolerant and understanding when it comes to macho bigotry. Many of them feel obliged to explain that the feminist struggle is secondary, a hobby for the rich that is neither significant nor urgent. You'd have to be a complete fuckwit, or deeply dishonest, to consider one form of oppression intolerable and another deeply poetic.

Similarly, women would be well-advised to rethink the advantages of men becoming more active parents instead of exploiting the power conferred on them politically by the glorification of the maternal instinct. In child-rearing, the paternal gaze is potentially revolutionary. In particular, fathers can make it clear to their daughters that they have an existence independent of the meat market of seduction, that they are capable of physical strength, of entrepreneurship, of independence, and they can teach them to value that strength without fear of sanction. They can teach their sons that the macho tradition is a trap, a brutal emotional inhibition in the service of the army and the state. Because traditional masculinity is just as destructive as prescribed femininity. What exactly does it take to be a real man? He always has to suppress his emotions. Bottle up his feelings. Be ashamed of his sensitivity and his vulnerability. Leave childhood behind, abruptly and definitively: the man-child doesn't get good press. Worry about the size of his prick. Know how to make a woman come without her knowing or indicating how to go about it. Muzzle his sensuality. Always dress in the same drab colors, the same clumpy shoes, never toy with his hair, or wear too much jewelry or any makeup. Make the first move, always. Have no knowledge of sexuality that might enhance his own orgasm. Be brave, even if he doesn't want to be. Value power, regardless of the form it takes. Show aggression. Have limited involvement in parenting. Be successful, to be able to afford the best women. Fear homosexuality, since a man, a real man, must never be penetrated. Not play with dolls as a kid, but make do with toy cars and hideous plastic guns. Don't lavish too much attention on your body. Accept the brutality of other men without complaint. Know how to defend himself, even if he's gentle. Be cut off from his feminine side, just as women give up their masculine side, not to meet the needs of a situation or a character but in accordance with the collective body dictates. So that women will keep providing children to fight wars, and men will keep getting themselves killed to protect the interests of a handful of shortsighted fuckwits.

If we do not push on toward the unknown that is the gender revolution, we know exactly what we will be slipping back toward. An all-powerful state that infantilizes us, meddles in our every decision, for our own good—keeping us in a state of childhood, of ignorance, fearful of punishment, of exclusion. The special treatment so far reserved for women, using shame as the primary tool to enforce their isolation, their docility, their inability to act, could be extended to everyone. To understand the mechanics of how we, as women, have been made to feel inferior, and been trained to become a crack team that polices itself, is to understand the mechanics of control of the population as a whole. Capitalism is an equal-opportunity religion in the sense that it subjugates us all, and leads each of us to feel trapped, as all women are.

To the Man Who Shouted "I Like Pork Fried Rice" at Me on the Street

BY FRANNY CHOI

Franny Choi is the author of the poetry collections *The World Keeps Ending, and the World Goes On*, *Soft Science*, and *Floating, Brilliant, Gone*. Their writing has also appeared in *The New York Times*, *Poetry*, *The Atlantic*, *The New Republic*, and many others. They are a Kundiman Fellow and a 2019 Ruth Lilly and Dorothy Sargent Rosenberg Poetry Fellow. Their work deals with identity and institutionalized racism and misogyny as well as grassroots activism. In this 2014 poem, which first appeared in *Poetry*, Choi situates themself at the intersections of racism, misogyny, and street harassment. The poem is visceral in how it positions woman as object, as something to be consumed by the male gaze, male appetites. "you want to eat me right out / of these jeans & into something / a little cheaper. more digestible. / more bite-sized. more *thank you*," they write, reminding us of how, all too often, this is how our society prefers women.

> you want to eat me
> out. right. *what does it taste like*
> you want to eat me right out
> of these jeans & into something
> a little cheaper. more digestible.
> more bite-sized. more *thank you*
>
> *come*: i am greasy
> for you. i slick my hair with MSG
> every morning. i'm bad for you.
> got some red-light district between

your teeth. *what does it*
taste like: a takeout box
between my legs.
plastic bag lady. flimsy white fork
to snap in half. dispose of me.

taste like dried squid. lips puffy
with salt. lips brimming
with foreign so call me
pork. curly-tailed obscenity
been playing in the mud. dirty meat.
worms in your stomach. give you

a fever. dead meat. butchered girl
chopped up & cradled
in styrofoam. you candid cannibal.
you want me bite-sized
no eyes clogging your throat.

but i've been watching
from the slaughterhouse. ever since
you named me edible. tossed in
a cookie at the end. lucky man.
go & take what's yours.
name yourself archaeologist   but

listen carefully
to the squelches in
your teeth & hear my sow squeal
scream murder between
molars. watch salt awaken
writhe, synapse.

watch me kick
back to life. watch me tentacles
& teeth. watch me
resurrected electric.

    what does it
           taste like: revenge
squirming alive in your mouth
strangling you quiet
from the inside out.

PART VIII

FEMINIST PRAXIS

Ecofeminism

Toward Global Justice and Planetary Health

BY GRETA GAARD AND LORI GRUEN

Greta Gaard is a professor of English and served as founding coordinator of the Sustainability Faculty Fellows at the University of Wisconsin-River Falls. Gaard's current research advances conversations across the fields of critical ecofeminism and climate justice, mindfulness pedagogy, happiness studies, writing pedagogy, and the environmental humanities. She is the author or editor of six books. Lori Gruen is the William Griffin professor of philosophy at Wesleyan University, where she coordinates Wesleyan animal studies. She is also a professor of feminist, gender, and sexuality studies and science in society and is the author or editor of eleven books. Gaard and Gruen's work on ecofeminism—highlighted in this 1993 article—has broadened the discourse on climate change to consider climate change through a feminist, queer theory lens. In ecofeminism, we recognize the importance of the natural world and our relationship to it. It creates space for the feminist project to include animals and the planet we all share within the sphere of our activism. In this piece, Gaard and Gruen conclude that "nothing less than the future of the earth and all of its inhabitants may well depend on how effectively we all can work together to achieve global justice and planetary health."

DEVELOPING AN ECOFEMINIST
FRAMEWORK

Much like US socialist feminists who, in the 1970s, began analyzing the oppression of women in terms not just of patriarchy or
capitalism, but both, ecofeminists are developing a "multi-systems"
approach to understanding the interconnected forces that operate
to oppress women and the natural world. Drawing heavily on
the initial insights of socialist feminist theories as well as the experiences of activists in the peace, anti-nuclear, anti-racist, anti-
colonialist, environmental, and animal liberation movements,
ecofeminist theory provides a historical, contextualized, inclusive
approach for solving the problems discussed above. Ecofeminists
believe that the current global crises are the result of the mutually
reinforcing ideologies of racism, sexism, classism, imperialism,
naturism, and speciesism. These ideologies, while conceptually
isolatable, are best understood, according to ecofeminists, as force
fields that intersect one another (to greater or lesser extents, depending on the actual context) to create complex systems of oppression.

To illustrate how an ecofeminist analysis differs from, yet draws
on, other theories, we will examine one particular issue—intensive
animal agriculture, a system of keeping animals indoors, in large
sheds, where every aspect of their existence can be regulated to
produce maximum output at minimum cost—through the theoretical lens of a number of distinct approaches. These analyses are
necessarily brief and are meant simply to indicate how different
theorists, using different arguments and points of reference, come
to sometimes different, although not incompatible, conclusions
about the same issue.

Feminists might respond to the practice of intensive animal agriculture in a variety of ways. From a liberal feminist perspective,
for example, the use of animals for food, however the animals are
raised, may be unproblematic. For liberal feminists, moral consid-
erability is grounded on the ability to reason, an ability that presumably animals lack. The traditional liberal split between culture
and nature is preserved with this view. Their primary concerns
are that women be recognized as fully rational creatures and thus
allowed the full privilege of participation in human culture.

Animals, like the natural world, are outside of the realm of culture; they can be used to further human ends. In addition, the liberal feminist would focus on the autonomy of individual humans to choose what they eat. According to liberal theory, individuals can do whatever they find pleasurable or fulfilling, as long as no humans are harmed by such action. Since animals are excluded from consideration, the concern a liberal feminist would have with intensive animal agriculture would be one that focuses on the inequitable distribution of animal protein and the effect such a distribution would have on women's lives, rather than on the effects factory farming has on animal lives.

Socialist feminists also traditionally have focused exclusively on humans. Yet their analysis of intensive animal agriculture would have a different emphasis than that of the liberal feminists. The socialist feminist criticism of animal rearing practices and the consumption of factory farmed animal protein would focus on the patriarchal capitalist nature of animal production. They might point out, for example, that in the United States, eight corporations, responsible for the deaths of 5.3 million birds annually, control over 50 percent of the chicken market. They might also point out that 95 percent of all poultry workers are black women who are required to scrape the insides out of 5000 chickens per hour and as a result suffer various disorders caused by repetitive motion and stress. Those who profit from industrialized animal production do so by exploiting traditionally underprivileged groups, namely working-class white women and people of color. The socialist feminist analysis might also include an examination of the commodification of animal bodies and the marketing of these bodies to women who are represented culturally as those responsible for the reproduction of raw flesh into dinner for husbands and children. In addition, these feminists would undoubtedly examine the social status that is associated with those who, in this country for example, can afford to consume filet mignon as opposed to ground beef and brisket and the implications such consumption patterns have for broader socioeconomic relationships between classes.

Environmental theorists view human consumption of animals as an integral part of the ecological food chain: "the natural world as actually constituted is one in which one being lives at the expense of others." Environmental theorists concentrate on holistic, biocentric analyses and thus reject vegetarianism as a choice that removes human beings from the workings of nature. That is not to say, however, that all environmental theorists would approve of intensive animal agriculture. Quite the contrary. However, their analysis of such practices focuses on "the transmogrification of organic to mechanical processes."

What is objectionable about industrialized animal agriculture is the process whereby organic creatures are domesticated, manipulated through breeding and biotechnological intervention, and ultimately reduced to food-producing units. In addition, the very process of industrialized food production, which requires massive amounts of energy, water, and grazing land and produces large quantities of waste, is environmentally destructive in itself.

A Third World analysis of industrial animal production would focus on this institution as one of the many that contribute to overconsumption in the North. As we indicated earlier, this type of analysis would examine the ways in which intensive animal production wastes vast amounts of protein that could otherwise be used to feed the millions of people around the globe who go to sleep hungry. Only about 17 percent of the grain and food energy that is fed to dairy cows is recovered in milk, while only about 6 percent is recovered from beef. In addition, a Third World analysis might link the rise of industrialized animal agriculture to other problematic economic developments that occurred after the second World War when multinational agribusiness corporations began exploiting the Third World by instituting certain agricultural policies such as cash cropping, monoculture, and consolidation. These policies led to a state of affairs in which small independent food producers lost their autonomy and could no longer afford to produce. This situation parallels that which is presently going on in first world intensive agriculture, where small "mom and pop" farms are going out of business because they simply cannot compete. In addition, agribusiness conglomerates go into Third World countries, cut down their forests, displace their people, and disrupt their economic system, in order to usurp land for intensive animal production.

The animal liberation perspective is one that would suggest that factory farming is immoral in itself. Animal proponents argue that nonhuman animals are beings whose lives can go better or worse, who can feel pain and experience pleasure, and who have interests in living free from confinement. Conditions on factory farms ignore the animals' most basic needs and interests, and because of this humans should refrain from consuming factory farmed food products and become vegetarians. While philosophically there are differences in the arguments that are advanced on behalf of animals, there is a rough consensus that because animals are enough like humans in morally relevant ways, their interests should not be excluded from ethical deliberations. To fail to morally consider the fate that animals suffer on factory farms would be "speciesist," a position that maintains that nonhuman animals are inherently less worthy of consideration simply because they are not human.

These analyses of animal agriculture are not mutually exclusive. A socialist feminist, for example, may also be inspired by an environmental perspective and/or a Third World analysis. Animal liberationists are informed by the environmental perspective insofar as factory farming affects not just domestic animals but wild animals whose habitats are destroyed by it. The point we are trying to highlight is that each of these different approaches focuses on one or two elements of oppression as primary in its analysis. An ecofeminist framework will view *all* of the various forms of oppression as central to an understanding of particular institutions. So, for example, an ecofeminist analysis of factory farming is one which would examine the way in which the logic of domination supports this institution not only as it affects animals' lives, but also as it affects workers, women, and nature.

By examining the connections between these various oppressions, ecofeminists provide a distinct critique of institutionalized animal agriculture. It is interesting to note that as far back as 1964 the beginnings of just such an analysis appeared in Ruth Harrison's *Animal Machines*, which offered the first major exposé of factory farming. Her book was heralded by ecofeminist forerunner Rachel Carson, who wrote in the foreword, "wherever [*Animal Machines*] is read it will certainly provoke feelings of dismay, revulsion, and outrage." More recently, ecofeminists have argued for a contextual moral vegetarianism, one that is capable of accounting for the injustices associated with factory farming while at the same time allowing for the moral justifiability of traditional food practices of indigenous people.

Focusing on context and diversity is one of the strengths of ecofeminist theorizing. However, during the past decade or so, the polyphony of perspectives known as ecofeminism has created interesting theoretical tensions. For example, not all ecofeminists agree about the importance of taking the suffering of animals seriously. Another area of some controversy involves the place of spirituality in ecofeminist theory. Some consider spirituality to be historically significant and personally empowering, while others have maintained that spirituality is not a necessary condition of ecofeminist theory. The use of feminized and sexualized metaphors for nature, such as "mother nature" and "the rape of the wild," has also been a topic of constructive debate. Clearly, ecofeminist theory is theory in process. What is thought to be important at this particular historical and cultural moment may not be important to ecofeminists in another place at another time. Although the vision of a just and sustainable future for all is shared by ecofeminists, what this future looks like and how it is to be arrived at varies according to the diverse voices and experiences of those people engaged in developing ecofeminist theories.

Indeed, ecofeminist theory is theory built on community-based knowing and valuing, and the strength of this knowledge is dependent on the inclusivity, flexibility, and reflexivity of the community in which it is generated. Ecofeminist theory grows out of dialogue and focuses on reaching consensus. One method for accomplishing this is to focus on commonality while at the same time respecting difference, building coalitions with any number of individuals or groups struggling against oppression—such as deep ecologists, social ecologists, bioregionalists, Native American traditionalists, anti-imperialists, ecosocialists, greens, and others. In solidarity, these efforts to encourage dialogue across difference must emphasize a principled unity-in-diversity. Nothing less than the future of the earth and all of its inhabitants may well depend on how effectively we all can work together to achieve global justice and planetary health.

Gendered Geographies
and Narrative Markings

BY MISHUANA GOEMAN

Dr. Mishuana Goeman, of the Tonawanda Band of Seneca, is an associate professor of gender studies, chair of the American Indian studies interdepartmental program, associate director of the American Indian Studies Center, and the special advisor to the chancellor on Native American and Indigenous affairs at the University of California, Los Angeles. In work such as this 2013 introduction to her book *Mark My Words: Native Women Mapping Our Nations*, Goeman examines spatiality through a feminist, Indigenous lens to interrogate how maps and Western spatial imaginings such as states, nations, and borders are inherently oppressive and a tool of imperialism. By studying narratives created by Indigenous women, Goeman challenges the colonized notion of place and urges those in struggle to resist using the tools and language of the oppressor and instead adopt alternative languages and maps of resistance.

This project would begin before I was even cognizant of the power of place and its relationship to colonialism, race, and gender. Yet, even as young children, many of us learn the constraints and limitations of the socially constructed spaces we find ourselves in. While I may not have known the history of how reservations came to be or how colonial governments enacted power in that space, I was deeply aware of the difference when I passed the lines of trees that mark the territories between off-reservation and on-reservation. I knew, on a deeply emotional level, that this was sovereign land without knowing the precise legal history. In my childhood migrations, I learned at a young age what it meant to be and how to act as a young Native girl in small-town rural Maine, or white suburban Connecticut, or a predominately black part of the city of Apex, North Carolina—and I knew it required adaptability and awareness of my own embodiment as I moved through tumultuous geographies constructed around differing and constantly shifting power structures. Yet I would not consciously reflect on these geographies and what they meant for years to come, even as I navigated them throughout the various stages of my life. In many ways this book theorizes my encounters within these spaces and what the geographies and maps we have created mean for the past, present, and future of not only Native people, but all of us.

In this book, I interrogate the use of historical and culturally situated spatial epistemologies, geographic metaphors, and the realities they produce; examine the discourse of spatial decolonization; and trace a trajectory of spatial configuration in Native women's writing. Yet this is not a treatise on Native women's construction of self, nor do I believe that such a text would be appropriate apart from a lengthy discussion of individual cultural construction that coincides with tribal specificities as well as those that interrogate how the United States, Mexico, and Canada map difference. The texts with which I have chosen to work are documents: they provide evidence of the reality of Native people. Rather than stand on the periphery, Native women are at the center of how our nations, both tribal and nontribal, have been imagined. The Native literature I discuss reorganizes a space that was never blank or fixed in time or space. Examining discourses of spatialized power dynamics in literature was a strategic move on my part. The imaginative possibilities and creations offered in the play of a poem, imagery of a novel, or complex relationships set up in a short story provide avenues beyond a recovery of a violent history of erasure and provide imaginative modes to unsettle settler space. That is, the literary (as opposed to other forms of discourse, such as journalism, surveys, BIA/field reports, Indian agents' diaries, etc., in which Native women are continually a shadow presence) tenders an avenue for the "imaginative" creation of new possibilities, which must happen through imaginative modes precisely because the "real" of settler colonial society is built on the violent erasures of alternative modes of mapping and geographic understandings. The Americas as a social, economic, political, and inherently spatial construction has a history and a relationship to people who have lived here long before Europeans arrived. It also has a history of colonization, imperialism, and nation-building.

The authors I examine in this project employ elements of Native conceptions of space in their narratives to (re)map a history of what Mary Louise Pratt terms a "European planetary consciousness," a consciousness that is deeply patriarchal in nature. This "planetary consciousness," which still largely orders the world, has had major implications for Native and non-Native communities alike. It has its historic roots in early geography and travel writing, a point I attend to in my last chapter, on Leslie Marmon Silko's *Almanac of the Dead*. Colonization resulted in a sorting of space based on ideological premises of hierarchies and binaries, and Indigenous women did not fare well in these systems of inequity. Settler colonialism continues to depend on imposing a "planetary consciousness" and naturalizing geographic concepts and sets of social relationships. Yet geography and the language we use to order space are formed in a "contact zone" in which various cultures interact. A main point of this book is to examine Native narratives that mediate and refute colonial organizing of land, bodies, and social and political landscapes.

(Re)mapping, as a powerful discursive discourse with material groundings, rose as the principal method in which I would address the unsettling of imperial and colonial geographies. The various intersections constructed by the colonial geographies enframe the boundaries of the state and manage its population, thus affecting our current actions in the world. Aboriginal scholar Linda Tuhiwai Smith reminds us about the connection among policy, people, and the mapping of space: "Imperialism and colonialism brought complete disorder to colonized peoples, disconnecting them from their histories, their landscapes, their languages, their social relations and their own ways of thinking, feeling, and interacting with the world." The relationships among Native peoples and between others begin to be ordered along gender, sexuality, and racial regimes that exert power and bring into being sets of social, political, and economic relationships. (Re)mapping, as I define it throughout this text and in my previous work, is the labor Native authors and the communities they write within and about undertake, in the simultaneously metaphoric and material capacities of map making, to generate new possibilities. The framing of "re" with parentheses connotes the fact that in (re)mapping, Native women employ traditional and new tribal stories as a means of continuation or what Gerald Vizenor aptly calls stories of survivance.

My objective to chart women's efforts to define themselves and their communities by interrogating the possibilities of spatial interventions, such as those found in literary mappings, reflects my belief that power inheres in our stories. My aim here, however, should not be mistaken as utopian recovery of land through mapping pure ideas of indigeneity (which I find troublesome) on top of colonial maps. Even if we were to recover the historical and legal dimensions of territory, for instance, I am not so sure that this alone would unsettle colonialism. Recovery has a certain saliency in Native American studies; it is appealing to people who have been dispossessed materially and culturally. I contend, however, that it is also our responsibility to interrogate our ever-changing Native epistemologies that frame our understanding of land and our relationships to it and to other peoples. In this vein, (re)mapping is not just about regaining that which was lost and returning to an original and pure point in history, but instead understanding the processes that have defined our current spatialities in order to sustain vibrant Native futures. I will examine the consequential geographies, a term Edward Soja uses to foreground a concept of spatial justice, albeit one that problematically does not address settler colonialism, in order to examine "spatial expression that is more than just a background reflection or set of physical attributes to be descriptively mapped." As such, my interests lie in examining the theoretical dimensions of power that struggle over geography's hold, rather than a recovery project. What are the relationships set forth during colonialism that continue to mark us today? What happens when non-normative geographies are examined? I use the parentheses in (re)mapping deliberately to avoid the pitfalls of recovery or a seeming return of the past to the present. (Re)mapping is about acknowledging the power of Native epistemologies in defining our moves toward spatial decolonization, a specific form of spatial justice I address throughout. It is about recognizing that "our geographies, like our histories, take on a material form as social relations become spatial but are also creatively represented in images, ideas, and imaginings."

For me, Native women's literature presents ways of thinking through the contradictions that arise from the paradoxes and contradictions that colonialism presents and that Native people experience on a daily basis. Whether it was within the crisp white pages of Joy Harjo's book *How We Became Human*, or my musty working copy of Leslie Marmon Silko's *Almanac of the Dead*, which traveled with me across the country four times, accruing black coffee stains, strange smells, and creased corners, I begin to see a pattern of confronting the epistemologies that sought to incorporate Native people through their disappearance or social deaths. As I wrote the chapter on *Almanac* (particularly on the "Five Hundred Year Map"), I began to unravel more of my own stories. As a Seneca woman from a family that moved and migrated around the East Coast, these experiences made the nodes, centers, and webs formed in *Almanac* comprehensible. The layered geographies in Native literature intersect with many of my own experiences and understanding of social, cultural, and political space. My dad, a "traditional" Iroquois ironworker, would pack up our gray Chevy pickup and make my brother and me a cozy spot in the bed of the truck among all our belongings: our clothes, my mom's cookware and beadwork, my dad's tools, and an odd piece of furniture or two that always changed with each move. We would drive for hours huddled up in the back of the truck, fighting and playing until we arrived at a new destination or one of our home bases. We would go either to Tonawanda or, more frequently, to northern rural Maine, a place called Twelve Corners named and claimed by my grandfather. Much of this depended on where my father had a paying job. The literary narratives involved in Silko's compiling a story about History (capital H intended) and its visual representation catalyzed my introspection into the geographies that prevail in my own life and my navigation through these very different terrains. Unlike the maps that designate Indian land as existing only in certain places, wherever we went there were Natives and Native spaces, and if there weren't, we carved them out.

Critical explorations of space, as figured in feminist geographer

Doreen Massey's book *For Space*, delineate the possibilities that space holds rather than glance over it as a surface upon which we act. Much about Native mobility sees space as such, whereas in my experience we literally influenced the spaces and people around us as much as these spaces imprinted upon us. So, what exactly is space, and how do we pin down a definition when we have been conditioned to think of it as a surface of expanse and enormousness? Even if we delimit our definition by the modifier of Native spaces the term still holds up as boundlessness. In fact, I struggled with constraining the geographies in this book until I settled for a discussion of the spaces between Mexico's northern border and Canada's southern border for pragmatic reasons, but I am well aware that these spaces are influenced by and intersect with much broader spaces. Massey's turn to uprooting normative modes of thinking of space defined as that which becomes "obvious" in the "tellings" that position space as "an expanse we travel across" is helpful as we progress throughout this text that wishes to (re)map our geographical knowledges. In order to reconceive space, Massey opens with a telling of arrival to "new" spaces that will be named the Americas, formed through the "crossing and conquering [of] space." Specifically, she begins her exploration with stories of the Spanish conquistadors and the positioned narratives of "discovery." The "we" implied in this instance is that of Europeans, for as Massey's analysis of this moment continues, this depiction of space "immobilizes" and "differentiates" Europeans as the history and mapmakers carrying with it "social and political effects." Massey asks to reimagine space and "to question that habit of thinking of space as surface" and instead think of it as a "meeting up of histories." In many ways this project is interested in the constant meetings that compose space: meeting between Native peoples, between Native and non-Native peoples, between people of color, between different migrating populations and especially meetings of different conceptions of land and ways of being in the world. As such, Massey's work with space is incorporated throughout the following chapters as she distills space into three functions that I posit are of utmost importance in decolonization projects: first, space can be defined "as the product of interrelations"; second, "as the spheres of possibility"; and third, "as always under construction" or a "simultaneity of stories-so-far." This definition moves us from essentialism, a common accusation made of Native scholars as we labor to maintain tribal traditions, political ground, and our lands, in that alternative spatialities are not mired in individual liberalism, but maintain their political viability. Alternative spatialities that I examine in this book imagine that many histories and ways of seeing and mapping the world can occur at the same time, and most importantly that our spatialities were and continue to be in process. As Massey effectively contends, "only if the future is open is there any ground for a politics which can make a difference."

As I thought through space, I kept returning to Silko's map of characters, Tucson, and the borderlands that in no way present as a realist map, one that we too often take for a transparent form or depiction of objective reality, nor did the "Five Hundred Year Map" act as a stabilizer of space-time. That is the map itself made no gestures toward veracity or Truth (intended with a capital T) in its representation. The map and its accompanying text complicated the narratives of what it means to live in this land. The spatialities I navigated through daily were complicated as well—the maps of my experience did not reflect those learned in grammar school or mediated through pop culture. What would a map of my trajectory look like if I set aside prescribed notions of what it means to be Indian, a woman, light-skinned, non–Seneca speaking, and other such constructed but materially real modifiers? How would the multiple histories it would take to create a representative map affect its comprehension? What power structures have deterred certain maps and produced others through the choices I have made or through others with whom I have come into contact or through those who have preceded me? Most importantly, I questioned what it would mean not to have the stories to accompany a map that represented my location.

I am the daughter of a Seneca man whose job as an ironworker resulted in migratory patterns of movement on and off our home bases. Gender was a significant aspect of our family's movement and tribal histories. We did not live on the reservation, as my mom was white, and in my Nation, women largely govern the land. So we—and I mean entire sections of my family—moved from city to city to rural areas, from place to place. Unlike many narratives would have us believe, I did not feel isolation from

Native communities, even though I lived on my small reservation of Tonawanda in upstate New York only briefly when my father's job site was near, or when my aunt invited us. I was encircled by extended family, adopted uncles, and many, many cousins who also moved to their fathers' ironwork sites, or I was surrounded by the Natives who already lived in the area who gravitated toward hanging out with other Natives. This experience reflects the fact that in these cities and places are many Native people, often only brought up in our field of study in relation to the 1950s construction of the urban Native. According to the 2000 census, 60 percent of Native people reside in areas off-reservation, but many of the models map research into tight constraints of reservation bases or urban relocation centers. Our family's mobility causes me not only to pause at the dichotomy of the urban/reservation Native, as we exist somewhere outside that paradigm, but also to question the very acceptance of colonial spatialities that, rather than reflect deeper meanings of spatialities, look at distance and closeness in terms of dichotomous differences.

My own "directional memory," a term coined by Esther Belin that I address in the second chapter, (re)maps my trajectories and was formed from early migratory patterns. Most importantly, the stories I heard about who we were provided me strength and remained with me as we moved from place to place. The stories we continue to make reflect these earlier stories and influence our everyday practices. I start with this reminiscence about the origins of this project and its personal trajectory, because, like Native writer and academic Gloria Bird, "I am motivated . . . by the belief that it is only through critique of where I come from that the act of witnessing and the testimony I offer can become a decolonizing strategy." Addressing the way the literal and figurative production of space constructs my realities quickly arose as a primary concern in this book. Rather than my story not fitting the mold of geographical imagining of Native people—or at times even Native peoples' imaginings—I instead believe it is a story much more prominent than the mapping of Native bodies and place reveals in the current research. Much of the work in Native literary studies did not present an analysis of intricate mobility and only now is beginning to do so.

To further complicate ideas of space that figure so prominently in the way Native people construct their politics, identity, and strategies for dealing with the pressures of colonization, there were my grandparents, Vera Swanson and Theodore Goeman. Originally from Minnesota, they imagined and constructed their own Native landscapes in Penobscot territory, or what is now known as Maine. In the mid-1960s, my grandfather bought two hundred acres of land and proceeded to build a house for his family—my great-grandmother and my several aunts and uncles. It was a tarpaper house with cement floors, built briskly and not very well, and thus holding an air of impermanency around it. There was a kitchen, one back room, and the living room—no bathroom, as we hauled our water from the undrinkable well about six hundred yards away at the bottom of the hill. In this small house lived multiple families and multiple generations—it was never quiet or a place of respite; one went into the woods to play, hunt, fish, or wander for that. Eventually, another room was added, meant to be an Indian jewelry store, which then turned into a convenience store. This capitalist endeavor best describes a meeting space in which we interacted with old Mainers, other Indians, tourists, or Europeans who fascinated me with their strange ways. These failed endeavors lapsed either when Indians went out of fashion in the 1980s or because it was too provisional to make any money. The room was then used to accommodate new cousins and eventually my great-grandmother as she grew elderly and needed care. This was the only room built with wood floors, a place where we huddled to avoid the lightning strikes that bombarded the bottom of the valley and the bottom of our feet on cold cement. Twelve Corners drew many forms of lightning to it.

Twelve Corners was the most vivid place of my childhood memories and consciousness of who I was as a young Indian girl. It was our imagined space of the rez, complete with aunts and uncles who eventually built on various sections of the land and whose land was invariably lost after my grandfather's passing when it was sectioned into private lots. In the early 1970s, a large canvas hung in the front, prominently displayed with its red-lettered words on white backdrop that stated my family's politics, "WE SUPPORT WOUNDED KNEE." It looked like the rez, too, with its beat-up cars, free-ranging dogs, and unwelcome cats. It was a safe space for Indians traveling from Canada down to Boston or New York in the 1960s and 1970s, or wandering hitchhikers from Europe, or drifting hippies enthusiastic to be picked up by one of my long-haired, good-looking Native family members, who would bring them home and play with their imaginings of Indians. It was a place of stories, laughter, anger, incredible turmoil, unimagined strength, and a deep sadness that spanned generations. In all aspects, it wasn't just a surface we crossed, but a place built through intersecting histories, longings, and belongings.

This home base for me in rural Maine provided much of the little stability and simultaneous instability I felt growing up. Twelve Corners, while it was marked as individual property by state authorities, was more than a piece of land owned or occupied. It was a stretch of land I knew completely and a place to which family would always return even if they left for a while. Native people from Canada and the United States, from a number of tribes, stayed with us at various times. Passamaquoddy and Penobscot folks from the reservations closest to us, whose lands constitute what is now Maine, would stop by and swap goods for artwork or stories for laughter. The decade of my first memories was a politicized time, and my aunts and uncles were young and hopeful about changing the world in which we lived. Before coming to Maine, where my parents had met, they had lived in cities and Indian ghettos as well as on Tonawanda until my grandparents split. Maine was supposed to be a place to get away, but upon arrival, with their long hair and tough beauty, they quickly realized the inherent racism that knew no borders or specificity in place. My family was the closest most people in Maine would come to encountering the racial conflict that was taking place on a national level. This was a time when Native people were organizing across national borders (both in terms of the larger nation-states of Canada and the United States and in terms of tribal Nations' borders), and my family was quick to participate. Even as a young child, I felt the tension, excitement, and air of possibility.

While place here references the point on the map in terms of latitude and longitude as well as a locale, or a definition of place where material setting provides a mechanism for social relations to take place, I conceive of Twelve Corners as a place of belonging connected to other such places of belonging, such as Tonawanda.

This sense of place becomes more than a fraction of space and/or a historical or material construction. Yet my affective attachment to this place is also accompanied by an acute awareness of what it meant to grow up in rural, predominately white, poverty-stricken Maine where everyone knows who belongs and who doesn't. In this spatial schema, Twelve Corners was criminalized in the outer community. At play here was more than the material location or even more than the present material social relations; instead evident here was the idea of Indians as criminals already, in a long history of colonial/Native relationships. All the same, this made my family's attachment to place, to Twelve Corners specifically, all the stronger, as it was protection against violence that accompanied us outside of these lines, even while at times violence took place within them. Place, and the way I will speak of it throughout this book, follows along the lines of geographers who have worked to expound the boundaries of place as more than just the point on a graph or locale, but that which carries with it a "way of being-in-the world." As mobile Indian bodies, we did traverse the safe—and at times not so safe—parameters and boundaries of the reservation or Twelve Corners, carrying with us these epistemologies that helped us navigate settler terrains. In a state where the murder rates are continually in the lowest one-eighth in the United States, two of my uncles have been brutally murdered and their aggressors received minimum jail sentences. Racialized violence was a common occurrence in my family's experience, and often still is as we were the only people of "difference" from the 1960s through the 1980s. Understanding spatiality and the places you occupied were and continue to be a significant means of survival. The demographic makeup of this area would evolve as changes were implemented in urban and immigration policies in the 1980s, which I discuss in relation to Joy Harjo's work. I use the personal here, to theorize place in terms of humanistic geographers, because it complicates notions of place as purely locale and the site of our identity formations, a mutually constitutive definition particularly problematic for hyperspatialized Native people. Too often in this hyperspatialization, we are left with little room for imagining connections to other people, alternative histories, places, or even futures.

While my story may be very different from that of other Native people (though I suspect it is not as rare as might be believed, and it is becoming much more common), the construction of the geographies at various scales and its impact on our family and cultural relationships have remained the cornerstone of my politics and who I am as a scholar, friend, mother, and family member. I speak of the place from which I come because it is the base of my memories and politics of location; it is also what forms the base of my academic work. Again, Bird's words best summarize why I am telling my story, which is much more complex than I could possibly delve into in this introduction:

> In and of itself my story is not important either. What makes it important are the other relevant issues that surround us as Native people and that are the context in which I am presenting my story. Without that discussion, telling my story would be parading my ethnicity. I need to believe that my story serves a useful purpose.

Often my memories correspond with places, movement, and my own gendered and racialized, or tribal, identity. My personal geographies or politics of location in reference to feminist Adrienne Rich intimately tie the spaces of body, Twelve Corners, the reservation, region, state, and nation together to map a place. When I speak to the spatial discourses (re)mapped by Native women, I also encourage us to move toward spatialities of belonging that do not bind, contain, or fix our relationship to land and each other in ways that limit our definitions of self and community. I rely on the creative strength my grandparents taught me as they tried to imagine a safe place for our family even if the ruptures at times were powerful. I also carry forth the responsibility they taught me about the politics of language, for instance, asserting sovereignty through language by choosing not to use "tribe" and only referring to Tonawanda as a nation. This reference to locating myself was an early lesson in the power dynamics of spatial metaphors.

Unsettling colonial maps is what drives this study of colonial spatial violence in twentieth-century Native American literature. The stories fill in the spaces between Native lives mapped onto reservations or urban centers or somewhere in between, or those lives relegated to a romanticized American past; the stories I am attuned to provide a window into the complexities of spatial subjectivities and geographic histories, giving us a richer understanding of how Native people imagine community and create relationships. My personal story ties the multiscalar spaces of body, Twelve Corners the reservation, region, state, and nation intimately together. By accounting for the various scales of geography in relation to Native peoples and a history of conquest, we can begin to understand the relationship between lands and bodies as more than just a surface upon which we travel or a descriptive geography. "Multiscalar discourses of ownership," contends Katherine McKittrick, who examines black women's geographies during the transatlantic slave trade, is "one of the many ways violence operates across gender, sexuality, and race . . . having 'things,' owning lands, invading territories, possessing someone, are, in part, narratives of displacement that reward and value particular forms of conquest." When I speak of the (re)mapping discourses created by the women in the pages of this book, I am speaking of the move toward geographies that do not limit, contain, or fix the various scales of space from the body to nation in ways that limit definitions of self and community staked out as property. My intervention into these various colonial scales and my interrogation of Native women's geographies should not be read as a longing to further construct or revamp that elusive "Indian" that is propped up through racial and gender codes, nor is it a putting of Indians in place or taking them out of it temporally and geographically. Instead, I am concerned with producing decolonized spatial knowledges and attendant geographies that acknowledge colonial spatial process as ongoing but imbued with power struggles. I ask a similar question to that of aboriginal scholar Irene Watson: "Are we free to roam?" and if so, "do I remain the unsettled native, left to unsettle the settled spaces of empire?" Rather than construct a healthy relationship to land and place, colonial spatial structures inhibit it by constricting Native mobilities and pathologizing mobile Native bodies.

Embodied geographies thus become pivotal to address in decolonization projects, and it is here that Native feminisms can play a major role in our thinking about the connections between land, individuals, and constructions of nations. Bodies that are differently marked through the corporeal or through a performance—whether through gender, race, sexuality, or nationality—articulate differently in different spaces. As Native bodies travel through various geographies, they are read differently and thus experience lived realities that are constantly shifting. For as Michel Foucault and ensuing scholars have argued, the body never exists outside of space and is connected to other indicators that are used to relegate power relations between the bourgeois and those deemed as degenerate subjects. For Indigenous people traveling through constructed colonial and imperial spaces, the body can be hypervisible as the abnormal body, and at times hyper-invisible as it becomes spatially disjointed from the map of the nation in both physical and mental imaginings. In "Fatal Couplings of Power and Difference," geographer Ruth Wilson Gilmore speaks about "the range of kinds of places—as intimate as the body and as abstract as a productive region or a nation-state," and it is in this range of connected places that I will discuss how Native women have mapped their lives.

In much Native American cultural production, place continues to hold these fragile, complex, and important relationships. But as Foucault's work with space and the body indicates, the state and citizen subjects' roles that come into being also had to perform a self-regulating mechanism in a field of surveillance. I contend that instead of ingesting the norm of immobile Native women, we open up the possibility of (re)mapping the Americas as Indigenous land, not only by rethinking dominant disciplining narratives but also critically examining how we have become a self-disciplining colonial subject. How might our own stories become the mechanism in which we can critically (re)map the relationships between Native peoples and communities? As Gilmore states, "if justice is embodied, it is then therefore always spatial, which is to say, part of the process of making place." In examining Native women's (re)mapping of the nation-state, my intention is not to focus on previously neglected texts, though I do believe the texts I include deserve more attention in the field of American literature and in race and ethnic studies as well as in culture geography. Neither do I aim to create or affirm an essential "female" or essential "Indian" category to address "common oppression." Rather, the focus on the gendered body in these texts provides sites in which we can examine gendered, sexualized, and racialized differentiations in relation to imagined geographies that buttress colonialism and enact violence in our daily lives.

Secondly, my focus on Native women's texts and the gendered scenarios they present takes into account Robert Warrior's foundational work in *Tribal Secrets*. In particular, I take seriously his call to examine the intellectual histories of Native writers and put forth a "generational view . . . [that] provides a new historical and critical site that invites us to see contemporary work as belonging to a process centuries long, rather than decades long, of engaging the future contours of Indian America." Warrior's work demonstrates the vitality of Native literatures to imagine a future for Native peoples who are not simple, exotic, insubstantial, or easily erased. Rather, Native stories, generations old and often labeled traditional or pure even when they are not, and new stories too often dismissed as tainted by Western literacy so therefore not Native enough, incite us to imagine literary possibilities that deconstruct tired colonial paradigms. My choice to put forth Native women's literary engagement with space and politics at various scales was very much influenced by Warrior's assertion that determining our future depends on "critically reading our own tradition[, which] allows us to see some of the mistakes of the past as we analyze the problems of the present." Though some critiques suggest there is an element of essentialism because of an emphasis on literary nationalism, they too often overlook Warrior's careful assertion that we must contextualize the writers as engaging with the world around them. A fruitful acknowledgment of the pain and chaos of colonization provides the fertile ground needed for decolonization. By "making ourselves vulnerable" and recognizing how "outside influences" have affected "our consciousness, and our imaginations," Warrior insists on an intellectual sovereignty as "a process of asserting the power we possess as communities and individuals to make decisions that affect our lives." The women whose texts I have chosen assert a spatial sovereignty literally grounded in their relationships among land, community, and writing. It is not a remythologizing of space that is occurring, such as that often performed by nationalist groups, but a (re) mapping that addresses the violent atrocities while defining Native futures.

My choice to concentrate on Native women's literature in relation to mapping new spaces is threefold. First, by examining Native women's engagements with twentieth-century spatial restructuring, I am able to delve critically into the construction of gender, heteropatriarchy, and race categories as instrumental to colonial logics. Rather than privilege writing as a hegemonic form of resistance, I contend that the Native women's writing I have included reflects the instability and mobility of the categories of race, gender, class, and sexuality at times when these intersections were most operable in colonial spatial restructuring. Kimberlé Crenshaw's feminist theory of intersectionality as a method to examine power relations influences much of my analysis. Although speaking to violence against women of color in general, Crenshaw's problematizing of the way identity has been conceived as a method of analysis is useful to my own thoughts on the spatial violence inflicted on Native communities:

> In the context of violence against women, this elision of difference in identity politics is problematic, fundamentally because the violence that many women experience is often shaped by other dimensions of their identities, such as race and class. Moreover, ignoring difference within groups contributes to tension among groups, another problem of identity politics that bears on efforts to politicize violence against women. Feminist efforts to politicize experiences of women and antiracist efforts to politicize experiences of people of color have frequently proceeded as though the issues and experiences they each detail occur on mutually exclusive terrains. Although racism and sexism readily intersect in the lives of real people, they seldom do in feminist and antiracist practices. And so, when the practices expound identity as woman or person of color as an either/or proposition, they relegate the identity of women of color to a location that resists telling.

By examining Native women writers through an intersectional approach, I am choosing a feminist method of analysis that presents us with a multiple grounded "telling" of violence and its impact on the structural, political, and representational lives of Native peoples and their communities.

Second, Native women's alternatives to heteropatriarchal representation of national space, referred to as traditional geography, are fundamental to understanding the ways in which nation-states in North America have built themselves through gendered spatial metaphors of dominance. For instance, civilization and frontier are metaphors that are engrained in Americans' imagining of their place in North America and on the global stage. Instead of presuming the naturalness of "Indians' relationship to the land" and Indians' victimization from land theft through masculinized Indian wars, I explore how E. Pauline Johnson (Mohawk), Esther Belin (Diné), Leslie Marmon Silko (Laguna Pueblo), and Joy Harjo (Muscogee Creek) attend to gender and land contesting U.S. nation-building *while they imagine a future for Native nations.* The patriarchal and racist nature of displacement becomes very clear in such policies as the Indian Act and relocation, which I discuss in the first and second chapters, respectively. Understanding these categories as stemming from the project of Enlightenment and tied to contested spaces enables a rethinking of settler nations by exposing the worldviews that rationalize the settler state and the project of liberal democracies, which rests on the individual.

Third, this approach to the relationship between gender and space demonstrates that Native people have had and continue to have their own discourses regarding the production of the world around them—discourses that produce a different set of economic, political, and social relations than the ones intended by implementation of various Indian policies in the twentieth century. My intent in mapping twentieth-century geographic imagining by Native women is to put forth sets of social relations that lead us in directions beyond a settler heteropatriarchal mapping of space. In thinking through the poetics involved in imaging new landscapes, I find Édouard Glissant's work important, though he is speaking to transatlantic blackness in the Caribbean and American South. For Glissant, who speaks to black alienation from the land, poetry and the narrative open up the production of space, providing alternative geographies. These alternative geographies contest dominant histories and geographies, even if they do not displace the regimes of power that assert spatial hierarchies. The Native women's texts with which I work are documents of the violence inflicted on their communities and a critique of the spatial restructuring of their lands, bodies, and nations; they are what Glissant refers to as a grammar of liberation that seriously engages alternative spatial practices to that of making land into property or treating land as purely a surface upon which we act. These women's stories and my Native feminist analysis are not testaments to geographies that are apart from the dominant constructions of space and time, but instead they are explorations of geographies that sit alongside them and engage with them at every scale. Even though these geographies may be marginalized, dismissed, concealed, or erased, they still constitute a part of our daily lives. These women's imaginative geographies are the stories that construct, contest, and compose a mapping of the Americas.

MAPPING EMPIRES

In these pages, I reiterate past concerns and link them to contemporary mappings of indigeneity, race, gender, and nation to unsettle the spatial ideologies at the foundation of nation-states. Maps, in their most traditional sense as a representation of authority, have incredible power and have been essential to colonial and imperial projects. The commission of surveying projects by both the Canadian and American nation-states was not a simple act of scientific research, but implicit involvement in creating empire. While many authors have examined this earlier period and mapping of the Americas as a colonial project, I argue that these mappings of Native land and bodies continue well into the contemporary time. I intend to interrogate the process of mapping, both as a metaphor and as the physical mapping of lands and bodies, as one that supports and naturalizes race, gender, heteronormativity, and colonial power relations. The mapping of settler nations is too often misunderstood as a "deceptively simple activity" while the power exerted through state structures is made normative through this deceptiveness. As human geographer Dennis Cosgrove tells us: "To map is in one way or another to take measure of a world, and more than merely take it, to figure the measure so taken in such a way that it might be communicated between people, places, or times. The measure of mapping is not restricted to the mathematical; it may equally be spiritual, political, or moral. By the same token, the mappings record is not confined to the archival; it includes the remembered, the imagined, the contemplated." As "a spatial embodiment of knowledge," maps can reveal much about the processes of producing settler colonial nations. As a "stimulus to further cognitive engagements," the mappings in Native women's literary texts challenge the organization of land and bodies into categories generated during the age of enlightenment, past surveying of Native land, and the continued use of these categories, albeit in different forms, sustains the settler nation-state. The literary mapping in the texts I work with in the following chapters represents and "communicates" a Native ethics and politics of their place in the world with potential to contest the ever-developing settler/imperial nations.

While the literary works I discuss begin in the twentieth century, I would like to step back a bit further into the eighteenth and nineteenth centuries, when European nations sought to solidify power, and newly forming nations, such as the United States, Mexico, and Canada, sought economic independence. It is no surprise that maps were instrumental to these projects, just as they were to early empires that sought domination of Native land in the Americas. Ricardo Padrón, in his book *The Spacious Word*, investigates the trajectory of cartography, specifically of the Spanish empire, as foundational to modern conceptions of space and the "invention of America" by the West. He traces not just the practical use of maps, such as planning of military operation, delineating control, or even those that laid out "the faithful or idolatrous" Indigenous peoples in order to proselytize them, but also the ideological uses of maps in early modern Spain. It is the residue of these ideologies that continues to influence contemporary understanding of space and authorize state force over Native land and bodies.

In speaking of the aesthetics used to "flatter" a monarch or contemporary uses of the "image of territory that inspires our affection, demands our loyalty, calls us home," Padrón discusses the ideological purposes of cartography at a time when European empires "were only beginning to learn how to imagine their world, relate to it, and transform it in ways that depended upon the unique conceptualization of space that lay at the heart of modern map." Padrón makes clear that in the Middle Ages the words "map" (*mapparmundi*) and "space" (*spatium*) were rarely found or used outside the context of traders and mariners, and, in fact, maps were limited to a few uses and not used by many people. The conception of space and "the cartographic revolution" ushered in new notions of space that would hold sway as America became invented in the European imagination. In this book, I aim to look at the ideological mapping that continued from these early formations. The development of the "scientific" modern map— one of geometric, abstract grids—is a development that coincides directly with Europe's war on Indigenous people. As Padrón, invoking Said's *Orientalism*, makes clear, however, and as I examine in my reading of Leslie Marmon Silko's novel *Almanac of the Dead*, the "invention of America" through the trajectory of cartographic development did not just reflect the Americas as "a purely natural object" but also defined Europe and its colonies. Padrón states, "America is indeed a slice of the natural world, but it is one that has been cut from the globe by a particular people, at a particular time, interested for particular reasons in carving the world up in the first place . . . this process of 'inventing America' can be understood as the process or 'remapping' the European imagination in ways that bring to light the connections between the early modern cartographic revolution, a larger process of cultural 'mapping,' and deep change in Europe's conception of itself and its world."

While maps were essential to earlier projects of exploration as well as the documentation of explorers and literate traders before the nineteenth century, it was in the 1800s that maps were understood by many to simultaneously represent the "real" as they symbolized the destiny of settler states. These early maps differed from their predecessors and were often naturalized and understood to project the real through the use of grids and mathematics. No longer were the maps laden with religious icons or pictorial symbols of the aristocracy that commissioned their making, yet the ideology behind the earlier forms of these maps remained. Hidden in the rhetoric and its visual presentation—in particular in the intent—was still the imagery of colonial empire. Exploring the discourses of mapping is necessary in understanding the way worldviews are represented. Maps exert political control by manipulating the representation of space into a language of normativity. For instance, the Louisiana Purchase as an inventive claiming of territory is still rarely questioned in the public imagination. Though we know that Sacagawea met with other Nations and translated languages, the relationship of Native people to place is absented and obscured. Without these stories, or in the suppression of them, the entire West is depicted as a blank slate, even though Native people were and are acknowledged as inhabiting the land. There remains a spatial imaginary of vast landscapes filled with flora and fauna. Native people in this unjust spatial imaginary become part of the flora and fauna open to settlement, while the state supports its fantasy through the law.

The development of modern nation-states depended on sending out official mapmaking expeditions as a state tool to find information that would enable the assertion of political force over territories and all contained within. For instance, it was President Thomas Jefferson who commissioned the famous mapmaking Corps of Discovery expedition led by Lewis and Clark. Interestingly, Jefferson was inspired by Enlightenment tales of the West and sagas of those who traveled to hostile lands, yet he was also prompted by the threat that the British were sending expeditions to Western lands. The famous expedition arose from the geographic imaginings of Jefferson, who often engaged in voyage and travel literature and for whom territorial accumulation was pivotal. His assignment to Meriwether Lewis reflects the goals of empire; the future of Jefferson's fledgling nation meant expanding the territory and exploring "for the purposes of commerce." In the instance of the Great Basin Indians, Ned Blackhawk contends that these early mappings were crucial to conquest: "Their maps, reports, and journals ultimately carried greater influence than the thousands of beaver pelts and horses ferried to market in St. Louis. By producing the knowledge from which conquest could flow, those who extended American claims in the region became agents for the most violent forms of imperialism. The settlement, law, policing, and governance—the mechanics of colonial rule—that followed within a generation overturned the worlds of Great Basin Indians forever." While Lewis and Clark's journey has perhaps been the most celebrated in United States history as an event that opened up the West to incorporation into the nation-state, there were many other cartographic projects that sought to survey and explore lands as the Indigenous world was carved up in settler imaginations and writings in a push to map and consolidate empire. In the imagination of Jefferson and his companions, these early expeditions into the West laid claim over the land and resources. While several studies have connected the geographical knowledge produced during colonization with that of the making of the modern nation-states and the advance of capitalism, I am also concerned with how these early events have set up gendered colonial structures that continue to dominate and enact violence at both the interpersonal and state level on Native peoples. The spatial violence asserted through the geographical imaginings and subsequent mappings would be tremendous throughout the West in what is now Canada, the United States, and Mexico securing an ongoing and violent spatial legacy.

Native nations, however, had and still have their own claims on the land, beginning with creation stories. Colin Calloway opens his book *One Vast Winter Count: The Native American West before Lewis and Clark* with a mapping of Native nations' place-based creation stories in the West. By centering these stories in relation to the Bering Strait theory's assumption of a land bridge in the context of a history of this region before Lewis and Clark's mapping expedition into those lands, Calloway adeptly tackles ongoing disputes over representations and relationships to time and space, or to history and place. He asserts: "Often in history what we think we know turns out to need revision and what we dismiss as nonsense proves to make a lot of sense. 'Other' stories of coming into America—whomever may be telling them—may not be any more or less 'accurate' than those we think may be true. Indian peoples had many stories to explain their presence in the West." He provocatively proposes a reconsideration of the archeological, historical, and anthropological narrations of understanding Native people as "first immigrants" by shifting the paradigm, suggesting that "perhaps the first pioneers did not come to the West: perhaps they were made in the West." Oral stories, often embedded in contemporary literature, predate the European maps made by Lewis and Clark and other early surveyors of the East and West who sought to claim land for their respective nations.

These colonial maps were instrumental in treaty making and creating national boundaries; they are still used to regulate and

determine spatial practices. Dispute of these maps was not uncommon, and tribal leaders would often draw on their own geographical interpretations to dispute the treaties. Native scholars,
researchers, and mapmakers who now have more access to the
archive are also using maps and documents as sources for land
reclamation. The exchange of knowledge that took place in the
early years was common, as Malcolm Lewis acknowledges in his
essay "First Nations Mapmaking in the Great Lakes Region,"
though, in fact, acknowledgment wasn't often given, and when it
was, "ambiguously so." In fact, it was the oral stories or words
that would convey distances, villages, landmarks, and so forth.
The additive oral component, according to Lewis, could be beneficial and at other times could lead to omissions or errors. At any
rate, what is made clear in cartographic historians' engagement
with colonial maps was the power that they would continue to
have after these early years. Cole Harris situates domination in
the early surveying of Native territory: "My conclusions are these:
the initial ability to dispossess rested primarily on physical power
and the supporting infrastructure of the state; the momentum to
dispossess derived from the interest of capital in profit and of settlers in forging new livelihoods: the legitimating of and moral justification for dispossession lay in a cultural discourse that located
civilization and savagery and identified the land uses associated
with each; and the management of dispossession rested with a set
of disciplinary technologies of which maps, numbers, law, and the
geography of resettlement itself were the most important." Harris
continues with his investigation by turning away from cultural
studies discourse, or what he frames as a concentration on the
word, and by concentrating on the "disciplinary technologies" of
mapping as the instruments of colonialism and later empire that
do the dispossessing.

  While I agree that to understand colonialism we must begin
with asking the question of how colonial power was deployed, it
is important to see mapping as a means of discourse that mapped
imperial imaginary. Later it would map discourses of spatial identities that would have the real effect on access to resources, such
as on-reserve/ation or off-reserve/ation. Native people did resist
the technologies of colonialism, as Harris reminds us: "Like oppressed people everywhere, they engaged in a virtually constant

micro-politics of resistance: moving fences, not cooperating with census enumerators, sometimes disrupting survey parties. There was a stream of letters and petitions, often written with missionary assistance, to officials in Victoria, Ottawa, and London, and meetings with cabinet ministers, prime ministers, and even, on one occasion, the king." Yet, in the end, it was the power of the word and marking of Native place passed on through stories that refuted settler power.

I start this book shortly after the signing of the 1870s Medicine Treaties and the corralling of Native people onto reservations as if they were wild animals needing containment. Not coincidentally, it was also in 1876 that Canada became a confederation, severing its ruling ties to the metropole of Britain. Academics have too often separated the Native policies of Canada and the United States and not explored junctures of power that support ongoing spatial violence. I contend that, while we must scrutinize the particularities around how each nation-state has incorporated and expunged Natives, and must do so at the local scale as well, it is also important to examine how inflicted violence supported suppression and colonization *throughout the Americas*. In this instance, the brutal physical violence inflicted by the U.S. Army led to signing of treaties and brutally forcing Native people onto reservations. Many of these Native nations' traditional homelands spread into what is now known as Canada and Mexico. The restrictions placed and enforced by the U.S. Army helped to settle the southern borderlands of Canada and the northern boundary lands of Mexico. Cities grew, white immigration flourished, and the colony no longer needed to rely on Britain for military protection. The settler nation-states of the Americas, in recognizing one another's boundaries and overlooking colonial violence, legitimate the settler state as an entity while overlooking the injustices toward Native people under its guise of the affairs of a sovereign nation. While mapping was indispensable to brute colonization of Native land in North America through genocide, it is at this point colonial logics took a spatial turn that changed the everyday practices of Native people. Colonial governmentality articulated and implemented structures that would regulate Native spaces and Native bodies through a variety of state practices. Family, clan, and intra- and intertribal relationships were reformulated in ways readable to the state. The authors with whom I work address the severing of these relationships by the pounding discipline of state force. Once territories and land were claimed by Western empires turned settler states, violent state practices were read as internal affairs. It is in this era I begin my project.

By drawing the connections between maps and what Andrea Smith refers to as the three pillars of heteropatriarchy in the forms of colonialism, slavery, and orientalism, we can think about Smith's call for us to combat heteropatriarchy by seeing beyond assertions of a "common property of all oppressed groups," which in many ways has become operating controlling spatialities such as the urban, ghetto, barrio, and reservation. Maps were instrumental in the navigation of the slave trade in the Black Atlantic that provided labor instrumental to conquest, maps erased Native land claims and sacred sites, and maps situate the borderlands that mark the immigrant as a foreign body to be policed and disciplined. So, while this project examines Native peoples in particular, it also is concerned with interlocking systems of oppression and other locations. The mapping and invention of America required the brute force of slavery and colonization and the ideological framework of orientalism—all of which were and are gendered forms of violence. Mapping as a tool of traditional geographies, then, becomes a site in which to explore the exchange of power and struggle over the ordering of cultural, physical, and embodied space and explore heteropatriarchy.

While I have spoken above of historical processes of mapping, and the book itself is arranged in chronological order, my aim is not to document a stable, historical, geographical discourse in the history of twentieth-century Native women's writing. Rather, I posit a study of spatial discourses that are always in movement and colonialisms always in contradiction in order to illuminate the fact that space is shifting, layered geographies with connecting and complex histories, histories that are too numerous to discuss in one book. My decision to strategically address historical elements that provide important context is meant to strengthen a social criticism of our approaches, which are too often spatially bounded. This book is not meant to be a decisive history of the spatial construction of our nations, but rather a social criticism that opens up and questions, through a study of the language and physicality of geography, normative nation-state maps that inform the present. Writers and artists work to free us from imposed rigid definitions set in place through Western interpretations and definitions of "Native," "Native land," "Native Sovereignty." The attempted interruption and displacement of Native spatial concepts by colonization has had a profound impact on our communities. By placing Native women's writing in a historical context, alternatives to the normative arguments arise. Ever present is the flexibility of tribal stories to hold communities together despite displacement from lands, the corroding of tribal ways of thinking, and a litany of Indian policies that produce self-surveillance and community inter- and intra-tensions.

DECOLONIZING SPATIAL RELATIONSHIPS

A spatial analysis of the social and geopolitical imagining of the colonial nations of Canada, Mexico, and the United States is pivotal in a critique of settler nation-states. The works of Native women writers address the intersections of economic, social, political, and cultural institutions that are mapping out their surroundings and constituting their lived realities. Native women, however, have engaged a changing geopolitical field by narrating geographies that unsettle the heteropatriarchal institutional structures that use race and gender as tools to support settler colonialism. Just as the colonizer never left the Americas, neither did the Native people who continue to engage with land, nation, and community in their own tribally specific and gendered ways.

As Native nations maneuver for power in the liberal nation-state, it is important not to be coerced by the power of abstracting land and bodies into territories and citizens. Henri Lefebvre's pivotal work warns about the roots of the abstract space of capitalism and the alienation of individuals from the everyday reality of living on, or with, the land: "As a product of violence and war, [abstract space] is political: instituted by a state, it is institutional. On first inspection it appears homogenous; and indeed it serves those forces which make a *tabula rasa* of whatever stand in their way, whatever threatens them—in short, of differences." Native people in North America have not only been made a tabula rasa, but also have been incorporated into national discourses in often unrecognizable forms. Liberal discourses that arose along with a budding nation-state have recently recognized past wrongs and past Native presences on the land, and, at times, current issues as well. Yet these discourses, rather than serve Native people, become incorporated into settler myths. Land remains the territory of the settler nation, and the stories of its birth are celebrated; this occurs simultaneously with the recognition of Native peoples' loss of land, political control, and many relatives—all of which are conceived of as an unfortunate *national* past even though colonization is ongoing. Bolstered by ideas of progress, both moral and in terms of the nations coming into adulthood, time and space are mapped, as are the material realities of Native people whose few small land holdings and lives remain threatened.

Native space is delegated to exist outside national settler terrains, even while it is controlled and manipulated by settler governance. As Native bodies are constructed as abnormal and criminal, they, too, become spatialized. Natives occupy certain spaces of the nation and are criminalized or erased if they step outside what are seen as degenerative spaces. Colonialism is not just about conquering Native lands through mapping new ownerships, but it is also about the conquest of bodies, particularly women's bodies through sexual violence, and about recreating gendered relationships. Thus, the making of Indian land into territory required a colonial restructuring of spaces at a variety of scales. Native bodies, as I speak to in relation to allotment in Joy Harjo's work, were conceived of as part of the flora and fauna. This animalization of Native bodies and subsequent codification of the doctrine of discovery during the 1830s that resulted in legalizing conquest and incorporating Native lands into the regimes of geographical knowledge produced by the state may not be apparent consciously, but they do order our reactions and relationships to those around us.

In *Human Territoriality*, Robert Sack, a foundational scholar in the field of human geography, denaturalizes territory by looking at its processes. It is not "biologically motivated . . . but rather . . . socially and geographically rooted." Humans do not ally themselves naturally along nation-state borders or contain themselves within those borders. The narrations of national myths normalize colonial closures, but the many creation and migration stories of Native people attest to their presence. This "deeply spatialized" story of the settler states "installs Europeans as entitled to the land, a claim that is codified in law." Sack uses the Anishinabeg band systems as an example of the social and geographic processes and sets out to discuss conceptions of the "modern" versus "premodern." Imposing European concepts of territory was a strategy of control and a method of creating empty space. While I appreciate this intervention, Sack detracts from his argument by not considering the storied relationships to the land that intricately tied together what Sack perceived of as "minimally territorial" bands. The power contained in stories of the Manitous, for instance, exert a control and regulation of human relationships to one another and the land beyond that of law and continue to do so. The Native literature I discuss does not portray land as blank, fixed, and linear in time, nor is it aligned mystically to Native people. Stories teach us how to care for and respect one another and the land. Responsibility, respect, and places created through tribal stories have endured longer than the Western fences that outlined settler territories and individual properties that continue to change hands.

Territory is not a simple artifact, impenetrable in the wave of economic and political power, but rather is constitutive of cultural, political, and economical practices. By recognizing the historic processes of enframing space and its corresponding cyclical turns and layering, the tangled threads produced in the claiming of Native lands and erasure of bodies begin to unravel. Walter Mignolo's definition of territoriality "as the site of interaction of languages and memories in constructing places and defining identities" speaks to the way Native stories create a literary map. Like Mignolo, I argue that territoriality develops not only through geographic place but also through time. The process of making territory extends beyond legal court systems that set in place political authority and borders, and relies on narrations and mythmaking. By proposing to examine the historical engagement among Native nations and the United States, Canada, and Mexico as it concerns the various overlapping, contested, and agreed upon concepts of geography, I am proposing that we need to see *through* the concept of territory and understand the processes and concept as a social product. Native literature provides a mechanism to see the limits of territory, as it is legally interpreted from original treaties, and give sustenance to Native people's relationship to the land. The scales of the interpersonal to the international in the texts I have chosen reflect a wide array of possibilities for political and social movements in Indian Country.

I am advocating that we take into account territories narrated through stories—both contemporary and those much, much older—that interrogate and complicate state bounded territory by examining the social orders expressed and denied in its representations. As one aboriginal scholar concludes about the possibilities of reconceiving territory for both Native and non-Native sums up: "Is aboriginal sovereignty to be feared by Australia in the same way as Aboriginal people fear white sovereignty and its patriarchal model of the state—one which is backed by power or force? Or is aboriginal sovereignty different . . . for there is not just one sovereign state body but hundreds of different sovereign aboriginal peoples. Aboriginal sovereignty is different from state sovereignty because it embraces diversity, and focuses on inclusivity rather than exclusivity." A spatial and literary analysis of settler colonial nations as examined in Native women's literary maps will put some teeth into Native political and social movements by exposing spatial practices that construct and maintain a white settler society.

Conceiving of land through narrative process, however, is not unique to Native people. Property law, European concepts of environment, and concepts of Nation all rely on tales to lend meaning to nature and ordered space. It is for this reason that James Scott opens with lines from the epic of Gilgamesh to talk of the "tunnel vision" of a "fiscal lens" by which the early modern state viewed its forest as revenue and created a "vocabulary used to organize nature . . . focusing on those aspects of nature that can be appropriated for human use." Colonial ideologies make truth claims and attempt to empty Native people's relationship to land and place through naturalizing of the relationship of people to land and naturalizing the conquest of both.

J. B. Harley and Denis Wood explore mapmaking cultures'

obsession with terra incognita, particularly as it is narrated and represented in Joseph Conrad's *Heart of Darkness*. Terra incognita, a concept of blank space in European thought, disavows Natives' socio-relationship with land and the communities that spring forth from this relationship. Blank spaces not only "stir the geographical imagination," but provide the means of "opening up" new territories: "But [a passage from Conrad] demonstrates the map's double function in colonialism of both opening and later closing a territory," Wood notes, and continues on to "argue that Conrad's thirst for blank spaces on the map—like that of other writers—is also a symptom of a deeply ingrained colonial mentality that was already entrenched in seventeenth-century New England. In this view the world is full of empty spaces ready for taken by Englishmen." Maps in this case also provide the narrative backbone of conquest. In this narrative of conquest, maps have affirmed "the truth" of territories. The "closure" of blank spaces or mapping of territories is a strategy to limit Native legal rights, ownership of land, and tribal imaginations. It is a means of transfiguring Native land into colonial territories in the socio-imaginary. As those imagined territories become liberal nation-states, the mythic narratives of exploration and heroic achievement remain part of the national terrain. Inclusiveness of a Native past becomes celebrated under multiculturalism, yet, as my work with the authors in this project demonstrates, the national space does not become imagined as Native space. If anything multicultural narratives serve to undermine the Native subject, and her land becomes abstracted and incorporated in the national polity. And, as Andrea Smith demonstrates by showing patterns of interpersonal and state violence in her important treatise *Conquest: Sexual Violence and American Indian Genocide*, gender violence functions as a tool for conquest. Conquest of land required a conquest of Native bodies both in its physical manifestation and in the mental maps produced.

By examining the writing of Native women, I unmoor settling narratives used to dislocate Native people and address concepts that extend from land that move us beyond simplistic and naturalized notions of "Indians" that began with contact. National mythmaking is key to the organization of space: it determines who belongs and does not belong. White settler societies' disavowal, erasure, and enslavement of labor are necessary to the project of the state and rely on the mapping of bodies into abstract national terrains. Bodies are organized, categorized, surveilled, and made readable to the state by mapping national and non-national spaces and appointing the appropriate bodies in those spaces. In the case of many Native people, this has supported genocide, containment on the reservation, or imprisonment in controlled spaces such as boarding schools or prisons. This colonial spatial construction is not unidirectional, and Native people have mediated these spatial constructions with the best tools at their disposal—storytelling, writing, and sense of place. When passing the Kmart that now stands on top of "storage pits," the poem is recalled, Native presence remembered, and experiences shared.

In simplifying the relationship to land as purely political or as evidence of governmental control, stories are understood in particular ways and bound into court cases and territorial claiming, tending to lose the sets of social relations regularly laid out in their structures. Stories keep us together—not court systems—and it is time we listen, as Schenandoah reasons, to answer our questions "why." Why do the dissolution, erasure, and denial of Native spaces continue even though there is recognition of a violent and torrid past? How are we caring for land and each other? What are the moral geographies we have come to in the twenty-first century? How do the stories that bear witness in many forms and map our intimate and social geographies guide us in the past, present, and toward a healthier future? These are questions that guide me throughout as I examine gendered patterns of twentieth-century spatial production in settler states.

My project attempts to move away from concepts of pure and unconnected Native spaces and acknowledges colonialism in its past, present, and even contradictory forms. The process of spatial restructuring is continual and substantiated through a variety of mechanisms such as force, laws, and ideology, and often these are not in agreement with one another, but nonetheless support domination and settlement. In (re)mapping Native lands and bodies in the twentieth century, my main goal is to ask the "why" so that Native nations will rethink spatializing and organizing our communities around the heteropatriarchal structure of the nation-state model. By replicating abstract space in Native nation-building, Native communities move away from imagining new possibilities beyond that mapped out for Native people in settler societies. Like Schenandoah, I want us to understand what is at stake, so that we can make the best decisions in our communities.

From a young age, many Native people are taught where revered points in the landscape are located, some are taught the stories that accompany the landscape, and many forge sets of relationship entwined in the responsibilities that come with this knowledge that belongs to past, present, and future generations. Unfortunately, the spatial violence inflicted on generations of Native peoples has also led to a disruption of this grounding knowledge, whether it occurs through environmental destruction, incorporation into capitalism, language eradication, displacement from lands, and a myriad of other disciplining geographic structures. Native stories speak to a storied land and storied peoples, connecting generations to particular locales and in a web of relationships. By exploring the narrative mapping of land, nation, community, and bodies in the works of twentieth-century Native women authors, I link the reconceptualization of Native land from the beginning of North American nation-building to current struggles with the settler state that continues to undermine the power of Native nations, Native women, and community relationships.

The pitfalls of simplifying Native peoples' relationship to land into romanticized and mystical or merely political categories are that these studies too often overlook the gendered and violent nature of colonizing Native lands, and in this book it is my intention to complicate the narrative maps constructed in the twentieth century and to intervene in the harsh realities of spatial violence that continue to produce colonial logics. These chapters bring into focus the importance of literature in enabling a (re)conceptualization of static assumptions of "Indian," borders, and gender. How do these women actively engage in the movement for representational, intellectual, and political sovereignty? "Sovereignty, community, and the vitality and power of a tradition that is constantly *evolving* are fundamental categories for the Laguna author," says Weaver, but I would also apply this statement to Belin, Harjo, and Johnson. In their fictional work, these women not only reflect at times their lived realities but they also conceptualize race and gender as evolving, and this is the key to understanding their power to disentangle Western geographical power/knowledge regimes.

As more Native people become mobile, reserve/ation land bases become overcrowded, and the state seeks to enforce means of containment, it is imperative to refocus Native nation-building efforts beyond settler models of territory, jurisdiction, borders, and race. Recent attempts at land acquisition by the Oneida, Narragansett, and Pequot are instances of the reversal of the colonial project of spatial dominance, but these have been met with much resistance by the state and its citizens who fear dispossession of "individual property." Other nations, such as the Cherokee and Menominee, hold elections in urban areas where large portions of their population reside off-reservation. Still, even others are creating maps in their own languages and with knowledge from the elders as a tool for land claims, environmental activism, fighting large corporations, and teaching the next generations. The Nunavut mapping project is exemplary of a decolonial project with immense potential. This reimagining of what constitutes Native space is important to antiviolence projects. As I document and explore Native women's writing and challenge Western forms of "narratives and maps [which] become violent when literalised, [and] mapped directly onto real people and places," I continually ask how rigid spatial categories, such as nations, borders, reservations, and urban areas, are formed by settler nation-states structuring of space.

While I study contemporary Native American literature and not stories from time immemorial (which is the case with many scholars who have looked in depth at the relationship of Native people and land), its tendency in a single breath or word to recall hundreds, even thousands of years back by employing community, personal, and historical stories in intertextual moments allows us to see these sets of relationships outside the mapping of the state. It allows us to see that the map is an open one and the ideological and material relationships it produces are still in process. The breadth of scale in terms of time, geography, and worldviews provokes a deep reflection on the landscape, and its meanings to Native people beyond the mere political or assumed corollary of Indian is to nature or land is to territory or resource. It comes down to power. In (re)mapping, we as Native people hold the power to rethink the way we engage with territory, with our relationships to one another, and with other Native nations and settler nations. And it is our stories that will lead the way as they have for generations. Native stories extend beyond a beautiful aesthetic and simple moral or fable. These connections are powerful in the struggle against colonialism and empire building—yet they are fragile and need tending. I venture that these stories in their contemporary forms are that tending and will continue to map our future. Mark my words, these imaginative geographies will open up new possibilities and inaugurate new and vital meanings.

Slow

BY SUSAN STINSON

Susan Stinson is a writer, teacher, activist, and the author of four novels, the most recent of which is *Spider in a Tree* (2013) about Northampton in the time of eighteenth-century preacher Jonathan Edwards. She received the Forbes Library Trustees' Award, the Outstanding Mid-Career Novelist Prize from the Lambda Literary Foundation, and the Benjamin Franklin Award in Fiction, as well as a number of fellowships. Stinson's "Slow" was originally published in 2018 in *The Kenyon Review*. This beautiful essay shares the struggles and joys of living in human bodies that are aging, fat, and sometimes disabled. "I want to speak plainly as a gift to the other fat, halt, and aging among us, and for the young who can't live within the stories the dominant culture tells on us," she writes, and her words are a gift.

One night at a play, I walked outside with a friend during intermission. I sat on a low concrete step because my knees hurt. My friend didn't sit. Some people he knew came over to us. I didn't know them. I've learned the hard way that if I am below eye level with someone I don't know well, my social presence is reduced or erased. I like to be fully present. I am a fat woman in my fifties with arthritis. Getting up from the low step would take some time.

As I shifted toward one knee, they all looked down at me with alarmed expressions as they murmured, "Don't get up."

I wanted to get up. It was already proving to be harder to do than I had expected. None of the others were fat. I listened to the murmurs, watching their faces and feeling as if I needed to calm their discomfort at the same time I was working to stand. I wasn't acrobatic enough that night to do both.

The first pressure I put on my knee made me wince, so I put my palms down on the step, turned my torso, and straightened my knees, slowly lifting my hips.

I was very aware of my belly. Shame was there, along with annoyance with all of them, and a wish to be generous, to make the moment easier. I also had a feeling of such difference, of finding myself out of the category of a casual interaction and into the category of—what?—a problem. I felt tension about my lack of ease with such a basic physical experience as getting up. I also thought that it was all a little funny, that it was no big deal. I really wanted to go take Motrin before I went back to sit in the tight theater seat. I felt sadness because something that had been easy for me was becoming hard. All of this was mixed with thoughts about the play and also a thought about how much of what I was experiencing wasn't ever going to find its way into words.

I began to walk myself up with my hands on concrete, butt in the air. There was more time than I wanted in which to think. The others were still murmuring. My friend half reached for me, then stopped.

I am slow. I move slowly. I walk slowly. I write slowly. I am not often slow enough to see a moment drop its allegiance to sequence and let wild layers of meaning rush out, geysers of the eternal transforming the insistent landscape of the daily. As I slid my palms across the gritty concrete, I was almost that slow.

The eternal is an old-fashioned idea. In *The Embers and the Stars: A Philosophical Inquiry into the Moral Sense of Nature*, Erazim Kohák wrote: "Eternity here does not refer to an endless prolongation of linear time, as it often does in common usage. It indicates, rather, the awareness of the absolute reality of being, intersecting with the temporal sequence of its unfolding at every moment."

Time shifted as my fingertips left the concrete.

I've been stubborn in offering up the gifts of long stories for those who can tolerate slowness. I am trying my best to say something with the tools I have. I love the life-changing pleasures of reading a novel, but am terrified of asking for such patience in a world in which minds go skipping through cyberspace.

Talking about the quality of slowness in my stories feels a little bit like talking about why I'm fat and whether or not my fatness caused my arthritis. One of the things being a lesbian has taught me is that only those qualities not widely perceived as normal are interrogated to discover what made them the way they are. I come back, then, to some of the things I know I am: Fat. Halt. Slow. Within these things, in writing, in walking, in pain, in discovery, in any given moment I am ringing like a bell, hollow, clappered, clamorous, musical, alarming, shivering with waves of all that I don't know but can sense. Time dissolves.

I moved my feet closer together on the concrete and raised my head.

I want to speak plainly as a gift to the other fat, halt, and aging among us, and for the young who can't live within the stories the dominant culture tells on us. I fear isolation. I fear poverty. I fear being punished for not spending more of my life regretting my physical shape.

Those fears, they have fuel. I live here, within my own limitations, within the limitations of an explicitly vindictive culture. But the story of everything that I am afraid of shifts with the most startling agility to the story, the stories, of skin brushing against concrete, which is rasping and warm; of the life between me and another slow person (also, amazingly, some who are fast); of the shaft of time that opens into the eternal, into all that can be known and experienced here, now, by me. We have all the stories, or, no, there is history, there are imbalances of power, there are inheritances of thought and culture. None of us has every story, but I have a body: slow, aching, and fat. It arches, I arch, out into time as if my body were a limb, something grown, something made, turning light into food, stories into smoothly bending joints, time into flesh that plants its palms on the concrete step and walks itself up on its hands like a baby righting itself, like a full-grown woman experiencing new degrees of slowness who rises, turns, and says, "Hello."

Feminism and Disability

BY JENNY MORRIS

Jenny Morris is a British disabled feminist, freelance writer/researcher, and former professor of housing policy and sociology. She is the author of *Pride against Prejudice: Transforming Attitudes to Disability,* and she edited the anthology *Able Lives: Women's Experience of Paralysis.* Before her retirement, she also worked in research consultancy for local authorities and has engaged in a variety of other work around social policy, housing equity, and disabled people. When Morris became disabled herself, she discovered that mainstream feminism too often treated disability as a tangential issue and that the disability movement did not account for gender differences in the disabled community. Morris's writing explores disability and its intersections with feminism, and her writing—such as this 1993 article published in *Feminist Review*—and activism bridge these communities to strengthen both. She notes that "there is a tendency when describing the 'double disadvantage' that disabled women experience to shift attention away from nondisabled people and social institutions as being the problem and onto disabled women as passive victims of oppression." In this piece Morris not only identifies that problem; she also suggests more effective ways of talking about disability and placing the culpability for discrimination against the disabled community where it belongs.

DISABILITY—A CHALLENGE FOR FEMINISM

Disability is an important issue for women but the subject of "disabled women" should not be tacked on as a "free-standing" research subject bearing no relationship to other research areas in which feminists are engaged. In my own research, I have recently come across three examples of oppression experienced by disabled women where gender issues intermesh with disability, although in different ways:

- the rape of a young disabled woman by an ambulance attendant while she was being taken home from a residential college with a broken arm;
- the recording, by a male social worker, in the case notes of a disabled client that he thought he had discovered her masturbating and the conclusions that he drew from this about her personality;
- a policeman and social worker waiting in a hospital corridor for a disabled woman to give birth at which point they removed her baby from her under a Place of Safety Order on the grounds that her physical disability prevented her from looking after the child.

These incidents are all concerned with violation of one kind or another and they all take place in the context of both unequal power relationships and oppressive ideologies. All three examples illustrate different ways in which the oppression experienced by women and by disabled people intermesh. What is more interesting to me, however, is whether the experience of the women described above appears on the main agenda of nondisabled feminist researchers—or is it, at best, tacked on as a supplementary issue, on the assumption that disabled women's experience is separate from that of nondisabled women? My challenge to feminists, therefore, is that they need to ask themselves whether these experiences of oppression are only of interest to disabled women.

I would also argue that it is not very helpful to talk about disabled women experiencing a "double disadvantage." Images of disadvantage are such an important part of the experience of oppression that research which seeks to further the interests of "the researched" must consistently challenge them. Therein lies one of the problems with examining the relationship between gender and disability, race and disability in terms of "double disadvantage." The research can itself be part of the images of disadvantage.

Feminist research and theorizing which is concerned with nondisabled women has often been driven by a sense of outrage at the consequences of women's powerlessness in relation to men. Whether it is domestic violence, rape, unequal pay or sex-role stereotyping in children's books, such research refuses to see women as passive victims and the motivating anger is an important part of the empowerment process. The focus has very much been on men and social institutions as the problem. In contrast, there is a tendency when describing the "double disadvantage" that disabled women experience to shift attention away from nondisabled people and social institutions as being the problem and onto disabled women as passive victims of oppression.

If disability research is to be unalienated research then it must be part of disabled people's struggle to take over ownership of the definition of oppression, of the translation of their subjective reality. As Alice Walker writes—"In my own work I write not only what I want to read. . . . I write all the things I should have been able to read." I don't think that I, or many other disabled women, want to read of nondisabled researchers analyzing how awful our lives are because we "suffer from" two modes of oppression.

If feminists are to concern themselves with disability research, such research must aim to empower disabled people. Nondisabled researchers have to start by questioning their own attitudes to disability. For example, why does Caroline Ramazanoglu dismiss disability and old age in the way that she does? Clearly, she cannot see either as a source of strength, celebration or liberation in the way that race, class and gender can become through a process of struggle. Nondisabled feminists need to examine why not.

Feminist research places women's subjective reality (i.e., experience defined in the subject's own terms) at its core. However, when researchers (feminist or not) approach disabled people as a research subject, they have few tools with which to understand our subjective reality because our own definitions of the experience of disability are missing from the general culture.

If nondisabled people are to carry on doing research on disability—as they undoubtedly will—they need to consider how they can develop an understanding of our subjective reality. It is also important that they do the kind of research which turns the spotlight on the oppressors. Nondisabled people's behavior toward disabled people is a social problem—it is a social problem because it is an expression of prejudice. Such expressions of prejudice take place within personal relationships as well as through social, economic and political institutions and, for example, a study of a caring relationship would therefore need to concern itself with prejudice (disablism), in the same way that studies of relationships between men and women concern themselves with sexism.

Disabled people's personal experience of prejudice must be made political—and space must be created for the "absent subject" in the way that feminist research has done for nondisabled women. An example of research which needs to be done is that concerning the experience of abuse within institutions. Such research should seek to do three things:

- name the experience as abuse;
- give expression to the anger, pain and hurt resulting from such experiences;
- focus on the perpetrators of such abuse, examining how and why it comes about.

The disability movement has started to identify the different forms of institutional abuse that disabled people experience. One example is what has been called "public stripping." This is experienced by many disabled people in a hospital setting. For example, Anne, a woman with spina bifida, described her experience throughout her childhood when she was required by an orthopedic consultant to be examined once a year. These examinations took place in a large room, with twenty or more doctors and physiotherapists looking on. After the hospital acquired videotaping equipment the examinations were videotaped. She described how, when she was twelve, she tried to keep on her bra which she had just started to wear. I quote from the article which described her experience: "The doctor, in order to explain something about her back, took it off without saying anything to her, but with noticeable irritation. A nurse quickly apologised—not to Anne but to the doctor." Anne knew that this kind of humiliation was inflicted on her because she was, as one doctor called her, "significantly deformed and handicapped."

The prejudice and the unequal power relationship which are an integral part of disabled people's experience of health services has led, in this type of situation, to both abuse and exploitation: abuse because privacy and personal autonomy have been violated, leading to long-lasting psychological consequences for many who have experienced this kind of public stripping; exploitation because, rather than being provided with a medical service (which is why people go to doctors and hospitals) people like Anne are actually providing a service to the medical profession.

All oppressed groups need allies and, by doing research which gives voice to our experience, feminist researchers can help to empower disabled women. However, nondisabled feminists must also ask themselves where are the disabled researchers? students? academics? If they are truly to be allies we need them to recognize and challenge both direct and indirect discrimination. Unfortunately, most nondisabled people don't even recognize the way that discrimination against disabled people operates within their workplace. Why do feminist academics put up with the way that most academic institutions fail to comply with the Disabled Persons (Employment) Act 1944 which requires them to employ a minimum of 3 percent registered disabled people. Getting disabled people into the positions where we play a full role in carrying out research and disseminating it is as important for disabled people as the same process was and is for women. As Audre Lorde says, "It is axiomatic that if we do not define ourselves for ourselves, we will be defined by others—and for their use and to our detriment."

THE RELEVANCE OF FEMINISM TO DISABILITY RESEARCH

My life as a feminist began with my recognition that women are excluded from the public sphere, ghettoized into the private world of the family, our standpoint excluded from cultural representations. When I became disabled I also realized that the public world does not take the individual, particular, physical needs of disabled people into account. Just as it assumes that children are reared, workers are serviced *somewhere else*—i.e., in the private world of the family—so people whose physical characteristics mean that they require help of some kind (whether this need is actually created by the physical environment or not) have no place in the public world.

As a feminist I recognized that men's standpoint is represented as universal and neutral. Simone de Beauvoir wrote, "the relation of the two sexes is not quite like that of two electrical poles for man represents both the positive and the neutral . . . whereas woman represents only the negative, defined by limiting criteria, without reciprocity." Women have thus been excluded from a full share in the making of what becomes treated as our culture. When I became disabled I realized that, although disability is part of human experience, it does not appear within the different forms that culture takes—except in terms defined by the nondisabled (just as the cultural representation of women was/is defined by men). A lack of disability is treated as both the positive and the universal experience; while the experience of disability "represents only the negative, defined by limiting criteria, without reciprocity."

Rereading such classic feminist texts as a disabled woman, I felt that I had rediscovered the validity of such ideas all over again—it was almost like becoming a "born again feminist." My feelings of elation, however, were churned up with a powerful sense of exclusion for—although feminist ideas seem so relevant to disability— none of the works which I was reading acknowledged this.

The way in which a feminist perspective so obviously helps to make sense of the experience of disability illustrates the exciting potential for bringing a feminist analysis to more traditional disability research. There are two points which I want to make in this respect.

THE ROLE OF RESEARCH
IN PERSONAL LIBERATION

For women like me, as Liz Stanley and Sue Wise write, feminism is a way of living our lives.

It occurs as and when women, individually and together, hesitantly and rampantly, joyously and with deep sorrow, come to see our lives differently and to reject externally imposed frames of reference for understanding these lives, instead beginning the slow process of constructing our own ways of seeing them, understanding them, and living them. For us, the insistence on the deeply political nature of everyday life and on seeing political change as personal change, is quite simply, "feminism."

In a similar fashion, a disability-rights perspective—which identifies that it is the nondisabled world which disables and oppresses me—enables me to understand my experience, and to reject the oppressive ideologies which are applied to me as a disabled woman.

I look to disability research to validate this perspective (in the same way that feminist research has validated a feminist consciousness). Susan Griffin identified the way in which, during the 1970s, women

asserted that our lives, as well as men's lives, were worthy of contemplation; that what we suffered in our lives was not always natural, but was instead the consequences of a political distribution of power. And finally, by these words, we said that the feelings we had of discomfort, dissatisfaction, grief, anger and rage were not madness, but sanity.

I look to disability research to confirm the relevance of these words to disabled people—our anger is not about having "a chip on your shoulder," our grief is not "a failure to come to terms with disability." Our dissatisfaction with our lives is not a personality defect but a sane response to the oppression which we experience.

Unfortunately very little disability research does anything other than confirm the oppressive images of disability.

THE PERSONAL EXPERIENCE
OF DISABILITY

Disabled researchers such as Vic Finkelstein and Mike Oliver have been arguing for years against the medical model of disability and in so doing they have been making the personal political in the sense that they have insisted that what appears to be an individual experience of disability is in fact socially constructed. However, we also need to hang on to the other sense of making the personal political and that is owning, taking control of, the representation of the personal experience of disability—including the negative parts to the experience.

Unfortunately, in our attempts to challenge the medical and the "personal tragedy" models of disability, we have sometimes tended to deny the personal experience of disability. (This is a tendency which Sally French discusses in the context of the experience of visual impairment, see French, forthcoming.) Disability is associated with illness, and with old age (two-thirds of disabled people are over the age of sixty), and with conditions which are inevitably painful. The Liberation Network of People with Disabilities, an organization which made an explicit attempt to incorporate the politics of the personal, recognized this in their policy statement. This statement included the point that, unlike other forms of oppression, being disabled is "often an additional drain on the resources of the individual, i.e., it is not inherently distressing to be black, whilst it may be to suffer from painful arthritis." To experience disability is to experience the frailty of the human body. If we deny this we will find that our personal experience of disability will remain an isolated one; we will experience our differences as something peculiar to us as individuals—and we will commonly feel a sense of personal blame and responsibility.

The experience of ageing, of being ill, of being in pain, of physical and intellectual limitations, are all part of the experience of living. Fear of all of these things, however, means that there is little cultural representation which creates an understanding of their subjective reality. The disability movement needs to take on the feminist principle of the personal is political and, in giving voice to such subjective experiences, assert the value of our lives. Disability research can play a key role in this.

INTO THE MAINSTREAM

The experience of disability is part of the wider and fundamental issues of prejudice and economic inequality. Black people's experience of racism cannot be compartmentalized and studied separately from the underlying social structure; women's experience of sexism cannot be separated from the society in which it takes place; and neither can disabled people's experience of disabilism and inequality be divorced from the society in which we all live. That society is characterized by fundamental inequalities and by ideologies which divide people against each other—the experience of disability is an integral part of this.

Just as feminists ask how and why the public world assumes that responsibilities and tasks which take place within the private world will not impinge on the responsibilities and tasks of the workplace, so disability research must ask how and why the public world assumes a lack of disability and illness. It is such a focus which takes both women and disabled people out of a research ghetto for these are fundamental questions about the very nature of social and economic organization.

Disabled feminists are also demanding that nondisabled feminists put our concerns and our experiences firmly on to their own agendas. Just as Black feminists have insisted that feminist research has to address the experiences and interests of Black women so we are insisting that our experience is no longer treated as invisible. Why are we missing from feminist research on women and employment/unemployment, women and sexuality, women and housing, women and social policy, women and health? Unless such research covers our experience it can only be incomplete and inadequate, in terms of both its empirical and theoretical significance. Feminism is the poorer for its failure to integrate disability into the mainstream of its concerns and it has much to gain by redressing this omission.

Toward a Feminist Theory
of Disability

BY SUSAN WENDELL

After working for years as a feminist scholar, Susan Wendell turned her attention to disability studies when she was diagnosed in 1985 with chronic fatigue syndrome. As Wendell points out in this 1989 article, 16 percent of women are disabled, and their personal experiences must be taken into account in any truly feminist movement. Disability, like gender, race, and sexuality, is not a biological given; instead, it is socially constructed from biological and cultural realities. Wendell's writing is important not just for expanding feminism to include disabled bodies, but to the disability movement, which historically privileged an individualistic and capitalist framing of disability that did not account for identity differences and their very real-world effects on disabled bodies. She also points out that when disabled bodies are oppressed, all bodies are oppressed, and so the fight for disability justice belongs to us all.

THE OPPRESSION OF DISABLED PEOPLE IS THE OPPRESSION OF EVERYONE'S REAL BODY.

Our real human bodies are exceedingly diverse—in size, shape, color, texture, structure, function, range and habits of movement, and development—and they are constantly changing. Yet we do not absorb or reflect this simple fact in our culture. Instead, we idealize the human body. Our physical ideals change from time to time, but we always have ideals. These ideals are not just about appearance; they are also ideals of strength and energy and proper control of the body. We are perpetually bombarded with images of these ideals, demands for them, and offers of consumer products and services to help us achieve them. Idealizing the body prevents everyone, able-bodied and disabled, from identifying with and loving her/his real body. Some people can have the illusion of acceptance that comes from believing that their bodies are "close enough" to the ideal, but this illusion only draws them deeper into identifying with the ideal and into the endless task of reconciling the reality with it. Sooner or later they must fail.

Before I became disabled, I was one of those people who felt "close enough" to cultural ideals to be reasonably accepting of my body. Like most feminists I know, I was aware of some alienation from it, and I worked at liking my body better. Nevertheless, I knew in my heart that too much of my liking still depended on being "close enough." When I was disabled by illness, I experienced a much more profound alienation from my body. After a year spent mostly in bed, I could barely identify my body as my own. I felt that "it" was torturing "me," trapping me in exhaustion, pain and inability to do many of the simplest things I did when I was healthy. The shock of this experience and the effort to identify with a new, disabled body, made me realize I had been living a luxury of the able-bodied. The able-bodied can postpone the task of identifying with their *real* bodies. The disabled don't have the luxury of demanding that their bodies fit the physical ideals of their culture. As Barbara Hillyer Davis says: "For all of us the difficult work of finding (one's) self includes the body, but people who live with disability in a society that glorifies fitness and physical conformity are forced to understand more fully what bodily integrity means."

In a society which idealizes the body, the physically disabled are marginalized. People learn to identify with their own strengths (by cultural standards) and to hate, fear and neglect their own weaknesses. The disabled are not only de-valued for their de-valued bodies, they are constant reminders to the able-bodied of the negative body—of what the able-bodied are trying to avoid, forget and ignore. For example, if someone tells me she is in pain, she reminds me of the existence of pain, the imperfection and fragility of the body, the possibility of my own pain, the *inevitability* of it. The less willing I am to accept all these, the less I want to know about her pain; if I cannot avoid it in her presence, I will avoid her. I may even blame her for it. I may tell myself that she *could have* avoided it, in order to go on believing that I *can* avoid it. I want to believe I am not like her; I cling to the differences. Gradually, I make her "other" because I don't want to confront my real body, which I fear and cannot accept.

Disabled people can participate in marginalizing ourselves. We can wish for bodies we do not have, with frustration, shame, self-hatred. We can feel trapped in the negative body; it is our internalized oppression to feel this. Every (visibly or invisibly) disabled person I have talked to or read has felt this; some never stop feeling it. In addition, disabled women suffer more than disabled men from the demand that people have "ideal" bodies, because in patriarchal culture people judge women more by their bodies than they do men. Disabled women often do not feel seen (because they are often not seen) by others as whole people, especially not as sexual people. Thus, part of their struggle against oppression is a much harder version of the struggle able-bodied women have for a realistic *and positive* self-image. On the other hand, disabled people who cannot hope to meet the physical ideals of a culture can help reveal that those ideals are not "natural" or "normal" but artificial social creations that oppress everyone.

Feminist theorists have probed the causes of our patriarchal culture's desire for control of the body—fear of death, fear of the strong impulses and feelings the body gives us, fear of nature, fear and resentment of the mother's power over the infant. Idealizing the body and wanting to control it go hand-in-hand; it is impossible to say whether one causes the other. A physical ideal gives us the goal of our efforts to control the body, and the myth that total control is possible deceives us into striving for the ideal. The consequences for women have been widely discussed in the literature of feminism. The consequences for disabled people are less often recognized. In a culture which loves the idea that the body can be controlled, those who cannot control their bodies are seen (and may see themselves) as failures.

When you listen to this culture in a disabled body, you hear how often health and physical vigor are talked about as if they were moral virtues. People constantly praise others for their "energy," their stamina, their ability to work long hours. Of course, acting on behalf of one's health can be a virtue, and undermining one's health can be a vice, but "success" at being healthy, like beauty, is always partly a matter of luck and therefore beyond our control. When health is spoken of as a virtue, people who lack it are made to feel inadequate. I am not suggesting that it is always wrong to praise people's physical strength or accomplishments, any more than it is always wrong to praise their physical beauty. But just as treating cultural standards of beauty as essential virtues for women harms most women, treating health and vigor as moral virtues for everyone harms people with disabilities and illnesses.

The myth that the body can be controlled is not easily dispelled, because it is not very vulnerable to evidence against it. When I became ill, several people wanted to discuss with me what I thought I had done to "make myself" ill or "allow myself" to become sick. At first I fell in with this, generating theories about what I had done wrong; even though I had always taken good care of my health, I was able to find some (rather far-fetched) accounts of my responsibility for my illness. When a few close friends offered hypotheses as to how they might be responsible for my being ill, I began to suspect that something was wrong. Gradually, I realized that we were all trying to believe that nothing this important is beyond our control.

Of course, there are sometimes controllable social and psychological forces at work in creating ill health and disability. Nevertheless, our cultural insistence on controlling the body blames the victims of disability for failing and burdens them with self-doubt and self-blame. The search for psychological, moral and spiritual causes of illness, accident and disability is often a harmful expression of this insistence on control.

Modern Western medicine plays into and conforms to our cultural myth that the body can be controlled. Collectively, doctors and medical researchers exhibit very little modesty about their knowledge. They focus their (and our) attention on cures and imminent cures, on successful medical interventions. Research, funding and medical care are more directed toward life-threatening conditions than toward chronic illnesses and disabilities. Even pain was relatively neglected as a medical problem until the second half of this century. Surgery and saving lives bolster the illusion of control much better than does the long, patient process of rehabilitation or the management of long-term illness. These latter, less visible functions of medicine tend to be performed by nurses, physiotherapists and other low-prestige members of the profession. Doctors are trained to do something to control the body, to "make it better"; they are the heroes of medicine. They may like being in the role of hero, but we also like them in that role and try to keep them there, because we want to believe that someone can always "make it better." As long as we cling to this belief, the patients who cannot be "repaired"—the chronically ill, the disabled and the dying—will symbolize the failure of medicine and more, the failure of the Western scientific project to control nature. They will carry this stigma in medicine and in the culture as a whole.

When philosophers of medical ethics confine themselves to discussing life-and-death issues of medicine, they help perpetuate the idea that the main purpose of medicine is to control the body. Life-and-death interventions are the ultimate exercise of control. If medical ethicists looked more closely at who needs and who receives medical help, they would discover a host of issues concerning how medicine and society understand, mediate, assist with and integrate experiences of illness, injury and disability.

Because of the heroic approach to medicine, and because disabled people's experience is not integrated into the culture, most people know little or nothing about how to live with long-term or life-threatening illness, how to communicate with doctors and nurses and medical bureaucrats about these matters, how to live with limitation, uncertainty, pain, nausea, and other symptoms when doctors cannot make them go away. Recently, patients' support groups have arisen to fill this gap for people with nearly every type of illness and disability. They are vitally important sources of knowledge and encouragement for many of us, but they do not fill the cultural gulf between the able-bodied and the disabled. The problems of living with a disability are not private problems, separable from the rest of life and the rest of society. They are problems which can and should be shared throughout the culture as much as we share the problems of love, work and family life.

Consider the example of pain. It is difficult for most people who have not lived with prolonged or recurring pain to understand the benefits of accepting it. Yet some people who live with chronic pain speak of "making friends" with it as the road to feeling better and enjoying life. How do they picture their pain and think about it; what kind of attention do they give it and when; how do they live around and through it, and what do they learn from it? We all need to know this as part of our education. Some of the fear of experiencing pain is a consequence of ignorance and lack of guidance. The effort to avoid pain contributes to such widespread problems as drug and alcohol addiction, eating disorders, and sedentary lives. People with painful disabilities can teach us about pain, because they *can't* avoid it and have had to learn how to face it and live with it. The pernicious myth that it is possible to avoid almost all pain by controlling the body gives the fear of pain greater power than it should have and blames the victims of unavoidable pain. The fear of pain is also expressed or displaced as a fear of people in pain, which often isolates those with painful disabilities. All this is unnecessary. People in pain and knowledge *of* pain could be fully integrated into our culture, to everyone's benefit.

If we knew more about pain, about physical limitation, about loss of abilities, about what it is like to be "too far" from the cultural ideal of the body, perhaps we would have less fear of the negative body, less fear of our own weaknesses and "imperfections," of our inevitable deterioration and death. Perhaps we could give up our idealizations and relax our desire for control of the body; until we do, we maintain them at the expense of disabled people and at the expense of our ability to accept and love our own real bodies.

Sick Woman Theory

BY JOHANNA HEDVA

Johanna Hedva is a genderqueer Korean American contemporary artist, writer, and musician working in Los Angeles. She is the author of the novel *On Hell* and as a musician, she released the album *The Sun and the Moon* in 2019. Hedva's work—such as this 2016 essay first published in *Mask* magazine—interrogates chronic illness and disability as social and cultural places of oppression and contests the meaning of "political space." Hedva's work also locates pain within embodied legacies of racism, colonialism, capitalism, and misogyny as well as the gendered, disabled body and expands cultural notions of activism to include spaces not historically considered to be public. Hedva demands an end to individualism and the myth of independence and calls for a future in which "we are all ill and confined to the bed," engaged in a collective dynamic of care, vulnerability, and dependence that might undo the productive motor of capitalism.

I.

In late 2014, I was sick with a chronic condition that, about every 12 to 18 months, gets bad enough to render me, for about five months each time, unable to walk, drive, do my job, sometimes speak or understand language, take a bath without assistance, and leave the bed. This particular flare coincided with the Black Lives Matter protests, which I would have attended unremittingly, had I been able to. I live one block away from MacArthur Park in Los Angeles, a predominantly Latino neighborhood and one colloquially understood to be the place where many immigrants begin their American lives. The park, then, is not surprisingly one of the most active places of protest in the city.

I listened to the sounds of the marches as they drifted up to my window. Attached to the bed, I rose up my sick woman fist, in solidarity.

I started to think about what modes of protest are afforded to sick people—it seemed to me that many for whom Black Lives Matter is especially in service, might not be able to be present for the marches because they were imprisoned by a job, the threat of being fired from their job if they marched, or literal incarceration, and of course the threat of violence and police brutality—but also because of illness or disability, or because they were caring for someone with an illness or disability.

I thought of all the other invisible bodies, with their fists up, tucked away and out of sight.

If we take Hannah Arendt's definition of the political—which is still one of the most dominant in mainstream discourse—as being any action that is performed in public, we must contend with the implications of what that excludes. If being present in public is what is required to be political, then whole swathes of the population can be deemed *a*-political—simply because they are not physically able to get their bodies into the street.

In my graduate program, Arendt was a kind of god, and so I was trained to think that her definition of the political was radically liberating. Of course, I can see that it was, in its own way, in its time (the late 1950s): in one fell swoop she got rid of the need for infrastructures of law, the democratic process of voting, the reliance on individuals who've accumulated the power to affect policy—she got rid of the need for policy at all. All of these had been required for an action to be considered political and visible as such. No, Arendt said, just get your body into the street, and *bam*: political.

There are two failures here, though. The first is her reliance on a "public"—which requires a private, a binary between visible and invisible space. This meant that whatever takes place in private is *not* political. So, you can beat your wife in private and it doesn't matter, for instance. You can send private emails containing racial slurs, but since they weren't "meant for the public," you are somehow not racist. Arendt was worried that if everything can be considered political, then nothing will be, which is why she divided the space into one that is political and one that is not. But for the sake of this anxiety, she chose to sacrifice whole groups of people, to continue to banish them to invisibility and political irrelevance. She chose to keep them out of the public sphere. I'm not the first to take Arendt to task for this. The failure of Arendt's politics was immediately exposed in the civil rights activism and feminism of the 1960s and 70s. "The personal is political" can also be read as saying "the private is political." Because of course, *everything* you do in private is political: who you have sex with, how long your showers are, if you have access to clean water for a shower at all, and so on.

There is another problem too. As Judith Butler put it in her 2015 lecture, "Vulnerability and Resistance," Arendt failed to account for who is allowed in to the public space, of *who's in charge* of the public. Or, more specifically, *who's in charge of who gets in*. Butler says that there is always one thing true about a public demonstration: the police are already there, or they are coming. This resonates with frightening force when considering the context of Black Lives Matter. The inevitability of violence at a demonstration—especially a demonstration that emerged to insist upon the importance of bodies who've been violently un-cared for—ensures that a certain amount of people won't, because they can't, show up. Couple this with physical and mental illnesses and disabilities that keep people in bed and at home, and we must contend with the fact that many whom these protests are for, are not able to participate in them—which means they are not able to be visible as political activists.

There was a Tumblr post that came across my dash during these weeks of protest, that said something to the effect of: "shout out to all the disabled people, sick people, people with PTSD, anxiety, etc., who can't protest in the streets with us tonight. Your voices are heard and valued, and with us." Heart. Reblog.

So, as I lay there, unable to march, hold up a sign, shout a slogan that would be heard, or be visible in any traditional capacity as a political being, the central question of Sick Woman Theory formed: How do you throw a brick through the window of a bank if you can't get out of bed?

2.

I have chronic illness. For those who don't know what chronic illness means, let me help: the word "chronic" comes from the Latin *chronos*, which means "of time" (think of "chronology"), and it specifically means "a lifetime." So, a chronic illness is an illness that lasts a lifetime. In other words, it does not get better. There is no cure.

And think about the weight of time: yes, that means you feel it every day. On very rare occasions, I get caught in a moment, as if something's plucked me out of the world, where I realize that I haven't thought about my illnesses for a few minutes, maybe a few precious hours. These blissful moments of oblivion are the closest thing to a miracle that I know. When you have chronic illness, life is reduced to a relentless rationing of energy. It costs you to do anything: to get out of bed, to cook for yourself, to get dressed, to answer an email. For those without chronic illness, you can spend and spend without consequence: the cost is not a problem. For those of us with limited funds, we have to ration, we have a limited supply: we often run out before lunch.

I've come to think about chronic illness in other ways.

Ann Cvetkovich writes: "What if depression, in the Americas, at least, could be traced to histories of colonialism, genocide, slavery, legal exclusion, and everyday segregation and isolation that haunt all of our lives, rather than to be biochemical imbalances?" I'd like to change the word "depression" here to be all mental illnesses. Cvetkovich continues: "Most medical literature tends to presume a white and middle-class subject for whom feeling bad is frequently a mystery because it doesn't fit a life in which privilege and comfort make things seem fine on the surface." In other words, wellness as it is talked about in America today, is a white and wealthy idea.

Let me quote Starhawk, in the preface to the new edition of her 1982 book *Dreaming the Dark*: "Psychologists have constructed a myth—that somewhere there exists some state of health which is the norm, meaning that most people presumably are in that state, and those who are anxious, depressed, neurotic, distressed, or generally unhappy are deviant." I'd here supplant the word "psychologists" with "white supremacy," "doctors," "your boss," "neoliberalism," "heteronormativity," and "America."

There has been a slew of writing in recent years about how "female" pain is treated—or rather, not treated as seriously as men's in emergency rooms and clinics, by doctors, specialists, insurance companies, families, husbands, friends, the culture at large. In a recent article in *The Atlantic*, called "How Doctors Take Women's Pain Less Seriously," a husband writes about the experience of his wife Rachel's long wait in the ER before receiving the medical attention her condition warranted (which was an ovarian torsion, where an ovarian cyst grows so large it falls, twisting the fallopian tube). "Nationwide, men wait an average of 49 minutes before receiving an analgesic for acute abdominal pain. Women wait an average of 65 minutes for the same thing. Rachel waited somewhere between 90 minutes and two hours," he writes. At the end of the ordeal, Rachel had waited nearly fifteen hours before going into the surgery she should have received upon arrival. The article concludes with her physical scars healing, but that "she's still grappling with the psychic toll—what she calls 'the trauma of not being seen.'"

What the article does not mention is race—which leads me to believe that the writer and his wife are white. Whiteness is what allows for such oblivious neutrality: it is the premise of blankness, the presumption of the universal. (Studies have shown that white people will listen to other white people when talking about race, far more openly than they will to a person of color. As someone who is white-passing, let me address white people directly: look at my white face and listen up.)

The *trauma of not being seen*. Again—*who is allowed* in to the public sphere? Who is allowed to be visible? I don't mean to diminish Rachel's horrible experience—I myself once had to wait ten hours in an ER to be diagnosed with a burst ovarian cyst—I only wish to point out the presumptions upon which her horror relies: that our vulnerability should be seen and honored, and that we should all receive care, quickly and in a way that "respects the autonomy of the patient," as the Four Principles of Biomedical Ethics puts it.

Of course, these presumptions are what we all should have. But we must ask the question of who is allowed to have them. In whom does society substantiate such beliefs? And in whom does society enforce the opposite?

Compare Rachel's experience at the hands of the medical establishment with that of Kam Brock's. In September 2014, Brock, a 32-year-old black woman, born in Jamaica and living in New York City, was driving a BMW when she was pulled over by the police. They accused her of driving under the influence of marijuana, and though her behavior and their search of her car yielded nothing to support this, they nevertheless impounded her car. According to a lawsuit brought against the City of New York and Harlem Hospital by Brock, when Brock appeared the next day to retrieve her car she was arrested by the police for behaving in a way that she calls "emotional," and involuntarily hospitalized in the Harlem Hospital psych ward. (As someone who has also been involuntarily hospitalized for behaving "too" emotionally, this story feels like a rip of recognition through my brain.) The doctors thought she was "delusional" and suffering from bipolar disorder, because she claimed that Obama followed her on twitter—*which was true*, but which the medical staff failed to confirm. She was then held for eight days, forcibly injected with sedatives, made to ingest psychiatric medication, attend group therapy, and stripped. The medical records of the hospital—obtained by her lawyers—bear this out: the "master treatment plan" for Brock's stay reads, "Objective: Patient will verbalize the importance of education for employment and will state that Obama is not following her on Twitter." It notes her "inability to test reality." Upon her release, she was given a bill for $13,637.10.

The question of why the hospital's doctors thought Brock "delusional" because of her Obama-follow claim is easily answered: Because, according to this society, a young black woman can't possibly be that important—and for her to insist that she is must mean she's "sick."

3.

Before I can speak of the "sick woman" in all of her many guises, I must first speak as an individual, and address you from my particular location.

I am antagonistic to the notion that the Western medical-insurance industrial complex understands me in my entirety, though they seem to think they do. They have attached many words to me over the years, and though some of these have provided articulation that was useful—after all, no matter how much we are working to change the world, we must still find ways of coping with the reality at hand—first I want to suggest some other ways of understanding my "illness."

Perhaps it can all be explained by the fact that my Moon's in Cancer in the 8th House, the House of Death, or that my Mars is in the 12th House, the House of Illness, Secrets, Sorrow, and Self-Undoing. Or, that my father's mother escaped from North Korea in her childhood and hid this fact from the family until a few years ago, when she accidentally let it slip out, and then swiftly, revealingly, denied it. Or, that my mother suffers from undiagnosed mental illness that was actively denied by her family, and was then exasperated by a 40-year-long drug addiction, sexual trauma, and hepatitis from a dirty needle, and to this day remains untreated, as she makes her way in and out of jails, squats, and homelessness. Or, that I was physically and emotionally abused as a child, raised in an environment of poverty, addiction, and violence, and have been estranged from my parents for 13 years. Perhaps it's because I'm poor—according to the IRS, in 2014, my adjusted gross income was $5,730 (a result of not being well enough to work full-time)—which means that my health insurance is provided by the state of California (Medi-Cal), that my "primary care doctor" is a group of physician's assistants and nurses in a clinic on the second floor of a strip mall, and that I rely on food stamps to eat. Perhaps it can be encapsulated in the word "trauma." Perhaps I've just got thin skin, and have had some bad luck.

It's important that I also share the Western medical terminology that's been attached to me—whether I like it or not, it can provide a common vocabulary: "This is the oppressor's language," Adrienne Rich wrote in 1971, "yet I need it to talk to you." But let me offer another language, too. In the Native American Cree language, the possessive noun and verb of a sentence are structured differently than in English. In Cree, one does not say, "I am sick." Instead, one says, "The sickness has come to me." I love that and want to honor it.

So, here is what has come to me:

Endometriosis, which is a disease of the uterus where the uterine lining grows where it shouldn't—in the pelvic area mostly, but also anywhere, the legs, abdomen, even the head. It causes chronic pain; gastrointestinal chaos; epic, monstrous bleeding; in some cases, cancer; and means that I have miscarried, can't have children, and have several surgeries to look forward to. When I explained the disease to a friend who didn't know about it, she exclaimed: "So your whole body is a uterus!" That's one way of looking at it, yes. (Imagine what the Ancient Greek doctors—the fathers of the theory of the "wandering womb"—would say about that.) It means that every month, those rogue uterine cells that have implanted themselves throughout my body, "obey their nature and bleed," to quote fellow endo warrior Hilary Mantel. This causes cysts, which eventually burst, leaving behind bundles of dead tissue like the debris of little bombs.

Bipolar disorder, panic disorder, and depersonalization disorder have also come to me. This means that I live between this world and another one, one created by my own brain that has ceased to be contained by a discrete concept of "self." Because of these "disorders," I have access to incredibly vivid emotions, flights of thought, and dreamscapes, to the feeling that my mind has been obliterated into stars, to the sensation that I have become nothingness, as well as to intense ecstasies, raptures, sorrows, and nightmarish hallucinations. I have been hospitalized, voluntarily and involuntarily, because of it, and one of the medications I was prescribed once nearly killed me—it produces a rare side effect where one's skin falls off. Another cost $800 a month—I only took it because my doctor slipped me free samples. If I want to be able to hold a job—which this world has decided I ought to be able to do—I must take an anti-psychotic medication daily that causes short-term memory loss and drooling, among other sexy side effects. These visitors have also brought their friends: nervous breakdowns, mental collapses, or whatever you want to call them, three times in my life. I'm certain they will be guests in my house again. They have motivated attempts at suicide (most of them while dissociated) more than a dozen times, the first one when I was nine years old. That first attempt didn't work, only because after taking a mouthful of sleeping pills, I somehow woke up the next day and went to school, like nothing had happened. I told no one about it, until my first psychiatric evaluation in my mid 20s.

Finally, an autoimmune disease that continues to baffle all the doctors I've seen, has come to me and refuses still to be named. As Carolyn Lazard has written about her experiences with autoimmune diseases: "Autoimmune disorders are difficult to diagnose. For ankylosing spondylitis, the average time between the onset of symptoms and diagnosis is eight to twelve years. I was lucky; I only had to wait one year." Names like "MS," "fibromyalgia," and others that I can't remember have fallen from the mouths of my doctors—but my insurance won't cover the tests, nor is there a specialist in my insurance plan within one hundred miles of my home. I don't have enough space here—will I ever?—to describe what living with an autoimmune disease is like. I can say it brings unimaginable fatigue, pain all over all the time, susceptibility to illnesses, a body that performs its "normal" functions monstrously abnormally. The worst symptom that mine brings is chronic shingles. For ten years I've gotten shingles in the same place on my back, so that I now have nerve damage there, which results in a ceaseless, searing pain on the skin and a dull, burning ache in the bones. Despite taking daily medication that is supposed to "suppress" the shingles virus, I still get them—they are my canaries in the coalmine, the harbingers of at least three weeks to be spent in bed.

My acupuncturist described it as a little demon steaming black smoke, frothing around, nestling into my bones.

4·

With all of these visitors, I started writing Sick Woman Theory as a way to survive in a reality that I find unbearable, and as a way to bear witness to a self that does not feel like it can possibly be "mine."

The early instigation for the project of "Sick Woman Theory," and how it inherited its name, came from a few sources. One was in response to Audrey Wollen's "Sad Girl Theory," which proposes a way of redefining historically feminized pathologies into modes of political protest for girls: I was mainly concerned with the question of what happens to the sad girl when, if, she grows up. Another was incited by reading Kate Zambreno's fantastic *Heroines*, and feeling an itch to fuck with the concept of "heroism" at all, and so I wanted to propose a figure with traditionally anti-heroic qualities—namely illness, idleness, and inaction—as capable of being the symbol of a grand Theory. Another was from the 1973 feminist book *Complaints and Disorders*, which differentiates between the "sick woman" of the white upper class, and the "sickening women" of the non-white working class.

Sick Woman Theory is for those who are faced with their vulnerability and unbearable fragility, every day, and so have to fight for their experience to be not only honored, but first made visible. For those who, in Audre Lorde's words, were never meant to survive: because this world was built against their survival. It's for my fellow spoonies. You know who you are, even if you've not been attached to a diagnosis: one of the aims of Sick Woman Theory is to resist the notion that one needs to be legitimated by an institution, so that they can try to fix you. You don't need to be fixed, my queens—it's the world that needs the fixing.

I offer this as a call to arms and a testimony of recognition. I hope that my thoughts can provide articulation and resonance, as well as tools of survival and resilience.

And for those of you who are not chronically ill or disabled, Sick Woman Theory asks you to stretch your empathy this way. To face us, to listen, to see.

5.

Sick Woman Theory is an insistence that most modes of political protest are internalized, lived, embodied, suffering, and no doubt invisible. Sick Woman Theory redefines existence in a body as something that is primarily and always vulnerable, following from Judith Butler's work on precarity and resistance. Because the premise insists that a body is defined by its vulnerability, not temporarily affected by it, the implication is that it is continuously reliant on infrastructures of support in order to endure, and so we need to reshape the world around this fact. Sick Woman Theory maintains that the body and mind are sensitive and reactive to regimes of oppression—particularly our current regime of neoliberal, white-supremacist, imperial-capitalist, cis-hetero-patriarchy. It is that all of our bodies and minds carry the historical trauma of this, that it is *the world itself* that is making and keeping us sick.

To take the term "woman" as the subject-position of this work is a strategic, all-encompassing embrace and dedication to the particular, rather than the universal. Though the identity of "woman" has erased and excluded many (especially women of color and trans and genderfluid people), I choose to use it because it still represents the un-cared for, the secondary, the oppressed, the non-, the un-, the less-than. The problematics of this term will always require critique, and I hope that Sick Woman Theory can help undo those in its own way. But more than anything, I'm inspired to use the word "woman" because I saw this year how it can still be radical to be a woman in the 21st century. I use it to honor a dear friend of mine who came out as genderfluid last year. For her, what mattered the most was to be able to call herself a "woman," to use the pronouns "she/her." She didn't want surgery or hormones; she loved her body and her big dick and didn't want to change it—she only wanted the word. That the word itself can be an empowerment is the spirit in which Sick Woman Theory is named.

The Sick Woman is an identity and body that can belong to anyone denied the privileged existence—or the cruelly optimistic *promise* of such an existence—of the white, straight, healthy, neurotypical, upper and middle-class, cis- and able-bodied man who makes his home in a wealthy country, has never not had health insurance, and whose importance to society is everywhere recognized and made explicit by that society; whose importance and care *dominates* that society, at the expense of everyone else.

The Sick Woman is anyone who does not have this guarantee of care.

The Sick Woman is told that, to this society, her care, even her survival, does not matter.

The Sick Woman is all of the "dysfunctional," "dangerous" and "in danger," "badly behaved," "crazy," "incurable," "traumatized," "disordered," "diseased," "chronic," "uninsurable," "wretched," "undesirable" and altogether "dysfunctional" bodies belonging to women, people of color, poor, ill, neuro-atypical, differently abled, queer, trans, and genderfluid people, who have been historically pathologized, hospitalized, institutionalized, brutalized, rendered "unmanageable," and therefore made culturally illegitimate and politically invisible.

The Sick Woman is a black trans woman having panic attacks while using a public restroom, in fear of the violence awaiting her.

The Sick Woman is the child of parents whose indigenous histories have been erased, who suffers from the trauma of generations of colonization and violence.

The Sick Woman is a homeless person, especially one with any kind of disease and no access to treatment, and whose only access to mental-health care is a 72-hour hold in the county hospital.

The Sick Woman is a mentally ill black woman whose family called the police for help because she was suffering an episode, and who was murdered in police custody, and whose story was denied by everyone operating under white supremacy. Her name is Tanisha Anderson.

The Sick Woman is a 50-year-old gay man who was raped as a teenager and has remained silent and shamed, believing that men can't be raped.

The Sick Woman is a disabled person who couldn't go to the lecture on disability rights because it was held in a venue without accessibility.

The Sick Woman is a white woman with chronic illness rooted in sexual trauma who must take painkillers in order to get out of bed.

The Sick Woman is a straight man with depression who's been medicated (managed) since early adolescence and now struggles to work the 60 hours per week that his job demands.

The Sick Woman is someone diagnosed with a chronic illness, whose family and friends continually tell them they should exercise more.

The Sick Woman is a queer woman of color whose activism, intellect, rage, and depression are seen by white society as unlikeable attributes of her personality.

The Sick Woman is a black man killed in police custody, and officially said to have severed his own spine. His name is Freddie Gray.

The Sick Woman is a veteran suffering from PTSD on the months-long waiting list to see a doctor at the VA.

The Sick Woman is a single mother, illegally emigrated to the "land of the free," shuffling between three jobs in order to feed her family, and finding it harder and harder to breathe.

The Sick Woman is the refugee.

The Sick Woman is the abused child.

The Sick Woman is the person with autism whom the world is trying to "cure."

The Sick Woman is the starving.

The Sick Woman is the dying.

And, crucially: The Sick Woman is who capitalism needs to perpetuate itself.

Why?

Because to stay alive, capitalism cannot be responsible for our care—its logic of exploitation requires that some of us die.

"Sickness" as we speak of it today is a capitalist construct, as is its perceived binary opposite, "wellness." The "well" person is the person well enough to go to work. The "sick" person is the one who can't. What is so destructive about conceiving of wellness as the default, as the standard mode of existence, is that it *invents illness as temporary*. When being sick is an abhorrence to the norm, it *allows us to conceive of care and support in the same way*.

Care, in this configuration, is only required sometimes. When sickness is temporary, care is not normal.

Here's an exercise: go to the mirror, look yourself in the face, and say out loud: "To take care of you is not normal. I can only do it temporarily."

Saying this to yourself will merely be an echo of what the world repeats all the time.

6.

I used to think that the most anti-capitalist gestures left had to do with love, particularly love poetry: to write a love poem and give it to the one you desired, seemed to me a radical resistance. But now I see I was wrong.

The most anti-capitalist protest is to care for another and to care for yourself. To take on the historically feminized and therefore invisible practice of nursing, nurturing, caring. To take seriously each other's vulnerability and fragility and precarity, and to support it, honor it, empower it. To protect each other, to enact and practice community. A radical kinship, an interdependent sociality, a politics of care.

Because, once we are all ill and confined to the bed, sharing our stories of therapies and comforts, forming support groups, bearing witness to each other's tales of trauma, prioritizing the care and love of our sick, pained, expensive, sensitive, fantastic bodies, and there is no one left to go to work, perhaps then, finally, capitalism will screech to its much-needed, long-overdue, and motherfucking glorious halt.

Making Space Accessible Is an Act of Love for Our Communities

BY LEAH LAKSHMI PIEPZNA-SAMARASINHA

Leah Lakshmi Piepzna-Samarasinha is a queer disabled nonbinary femme writer, educator, artist, and disability/transformative justice worker of Burgher/Tamil Sri Lankan and Irish and Roma ascent. Piepzna-Samarasinha is the co-founder of Toronto's Performance/Disability/Art collective and Asian Arts Freedom School. They are also a VONA fellow, and received the 2020 Lambda Foundation's Jeanne Córdova Prize for Lesbian/Queer Nonfiction. They wrote this 2010 essay, a call to action, for Creating Collective Access. Broadly, this piece reminds us of the necessity of making sure the spaces we share are spaces that can and will accommodate all people, in all bodies, as they come. Piepzna-Samarasinha also discusses going fragrance-free to make spaces accessible for those with chemical disabilities, with suggestions on how to best do that. When we are mindful of the spaces we share, and are accommodating to all people, we are demonstrating radical solidarity and love, she says.

When I think about access, I think about love. I think that crip solidarity, and solidarity between crips and non(yet) crips is a powerful act of love and I got your back. It's in big things, but it's also in the little things we do moment by moment to ensure that we all—in all our individual bodies—get to be present fiercely as we make change.

Embedded in this is a giant paradigm shift. Our crip bodies aren't seen as liabilities, something that limits us and brings pity or something to nobly transcend, cause I'm just like you. Our crip bodies are gifts, brilliant, fierce, skilled, valuable. Assets that teach us things that are relevant and vital to ourselves, our communities, our movements, the whole god damn planet.

If I'm having a pain day and need you to use accessible language cause I'm having a hard time language processing and you do, that's love. And that's solidarity. If I'm not a wheelchair user and I make sure I work with the non-disabled bottomliner for the workshop to ensure that the pathways through the workshop chairs are at least three feet wide, that is love and solidarity. This is how we build past and away from bitterness and disappointment at movements that have not cared about or valued us.

There is so much more I can say about this, but one small thing I will add, that is one small (and huge) thing you can do to ensure access: **Please be scent/fragrance free to the extent that you are able to.** Folks who have chemical disabilities need to be able to participate in the AMC! So it would be great if everyone could *avoid* using shampoo/cologne/deodorant/detergent/fabric softener that is scented/has lots of chemicals *all weekend*. (This includes essential oils.)

If you want more info about how to be fully scent/fragrance free, see http://www.peggymunson.com/mcs/fragrancefree.html, but the basics for the weekend will be great.

It's easy to get inexpensive scent/fragrance free products at Trader Joe's, Walgreens, Whole Foods (they suck, but they make $3 scent-free shampoo, conditioner and lotion), independent health food stores and co-ops, and you can also just get some cocoa butter, coconut oil or shea butter in the raw and make your own products, which is cheap and fun. Cutting out scents may seem like a pain in the ass, but it means that awesome, ass-kicking community members you love can attend the AMC without having seizures, throwing up or otherwise getting really sick, and/or spending the whole weekend in their rooms and not being able to be in workshops.

Partial list of products: http://takebacktheair.com/pdf/Fra granceFreeProducts.pdf

List of products, including people of color specific ones, from the East Bay Meditation Center:

http://eastbaymeditation.org/accessibility/scentfree.html\

More information, borrowed from the website of NOLOSE (http://www.nolose.org)

THE BASICS:

If you are not accustomed to reducing your use of scented products it is important to think carefully about all the products you use in your day. You can reduce your use of scented items like shampoo, soap, hair gel, hair spray, perfume/scented oils, skin lotion, shaving cream, makeup, etc., before the conference and while at the conference, and bring your own unscented products.

Many fragrance-free products can be bought in your local drugstore. For hard-to-find products (especially hair products), check out your local health food store or the NEEDS catalog: www.needs.com. If you are unable to find "fragrance-free" at a store, often the hypo-allergenic version of a product is scent-free. Simply read the ingredients on the label and see if the word "fragrance" appears. If not, you're OK. Suggestions for fragrance-free products are at the end of this page.

WHAT WILL IT DO FOR MY HEALTH, AND THE HEALTH OF OTHERS, TO LIMIT MY USE OF SCENT?

Reducing your use of scent or going scent free is an important step toward access for people with disabilities. Plus, you may be surprised to find that you feel better as well!

People with Multiple Chemical Sensitivities (also called Environmental Illness) experience serious and debilitating physical and neurological symptoms when exposed to the chemicals used in most scented products. Often, the damage caused by these chemicals causes an individual to react to other intensely volatile substances, such as essential oils, tobacco smoke, and "natural" fragrances. The process by which we "smell" something actually involves microscopic particles of that substance being absorbed through mucous membranes and entering the nervous system. The intense symptoms associated with chemical sensitivities have led most medical experts to theorize that the disorder is neurologically, not immunologically, based.

Because no government agency regulates the ingredients of household and personal care products, the last several decades have seen a huge increase in the number of harmful chemicals added to these products. Many of these chemicals are banned for use in industrial settings because of their known toxic effects. According to a 1986 U.S. House of Representative study: "Ninety-five percent of chemicals used in fragrances are synthetic compounds derived from petroleum. They include benzene derivatives, aldehydes, and many other known toxins and sensitizers— capable of causing cancer, birth defects, central nervous system disorders, and allergic reactions."

Symptoms of chemical exposure include dizziness, nausea, slurred speech, drowsiness, irritation to mouth, throat, skin, eyes, and lungs, headache, seizures, fatigue, confusion, and liver and kidney damage. As you can imagine, these symptoms constitute serious barriers for people with chemical sensitivities in work, life, and of course, conference attendance. Promoting low-scent and scent-free environments is very much like adding ramps and curb-cuts in terms of the profound difference in accessibility it can produce. We appreciate all participants in the NOLOSE Conference cooperating with the Low Scent Policy to make this an accessible conference.

IF YOU SMOKE:

Please smoke only in the designated smoking areas. Washing your hands after you smoke helps too! Please also keep in mind that many chemically-sensitive people will also get sick from the smoke clinging to your clothing and hair.

PART IX

LOOKING BACK, LOOKING AHEAD

Sisterhood Is Powerful

BY SUSAN BROWNMILLER

Susan Brownmiller—an activist, feminist, journalist, and author—is best known for her 1975 book *Against Our Will: Men, Women, and Rape*, which revolutionized the way our culture thinks about rape, and how it is adjudicated in the justice system. In her 1970 essay "Sisterhood Is Powerful," originally published in *The New York Times*, Brownmiller offered a sort of State of the Union of the feminist movement. She writes of the small groups women created where they could talk about their lives, the challenges of being a woman in the workplace, the constraints of marriage, and the burdens of motherhood and domestic responsibilities all too often shirked by husbands. And she also identifies the different factions within this sprawling sisterhood, and how each of the groups had different ambitions, some more radical than others. "Sisterhood Is Powerful" offers a snapshot of feminist consciousness-raising and a rising movement while articulating the ultimate project of feminism. She writes, "We want to be neither oppressor nor oppressed. The women's revolution is the final revolution of them all."

"Women are an oppressed class. Our oppression is total, affecting every facet of our lives. We are exploited as sex objects, breeders, domestic servants and cheap labor. We are considered inferior beings whose only purpose is to enhance men's lives. . . ."
—REDSTOCKINGS MANIFESTO.

"While we realize that the liberation of women will ultimately mean the liberation of men from the destructive role as

*oppressor, we have no illusion that men will welcome this lib-
eration without a struggle. . . ."*
    —MANIFESTO OF THE NEW YORK RADICAL FEMINISTS.

There is a small group of women that gathers at my house or at
the home of one or another of our 15 members each Sunday evening. Our ages range from the early twenties to the late forties. As
it happens, all of us work for a living, some at jobs we truly like.
Some of us are married, with families, and some are not. Some of
us knew each other before we joined the group and some did not.
Once we are settled on the sofa and the hard-backed chairs
brought in from the kitchen, and the late-comers have poured
their own coffee and arranged themselves as best they can on the
floor, we begin our meeting. Each week we explore another aspect
of what we consider to be our fundamental oppression in a male-
controlled society. Our conversation is always animated, often
emotional. We rarely adjourn before midnight.

Although we are pleased with ourselves and our insights, we
like to remind each other now and then that our small group is
not unique. It is merely one of many such groups that have sprung
up around the city in the last two years under the umbrella of that
collective term, the women's liberation movement. In fact, we had
been meeting as a group for exactly four Sundays when one of us
got a call from a representative of C.B.S. asking if we would care
to be filmed in our natural habitat for a segment on the evening
news with Walter Cronkite. We discussed the invitation thoroughly, and then said no.

Women's liberation is hot stuff this season, in media terms, and
no wonder. In the short space of two years, the new feminism has
taken hold and rooted in territory that at first glance appears an
unlikely breeding ground for revolutionary ideas: among urban,
white, college educated, middle-class women generally considered
to be a rather "privileged" lot by those who thought they knew
their politics, or knew their women. From the radical left to the
Establishment middle, the women's movement has become a fact
of life. The National Organization for Women (NOW), founded
by Betty Friedan in 1966, has 35 chapters across the country. Radical feminist groups—creators of the concept of women's libera-

tion, as opposed to women's *rights*—exist in all major cities side by side with their more conservative counterparts.

Without doubt, certain fringe aspects of the movement make "good copy," to use the kindest term available for how my brethren in the business approach the subject matter. ("Get the bra burning and the karate up front," an editor I know told a writer I know when preparing one news magazine's women's liberation story.)

But the irony of all this media attention is that while the minions of C.B.S. News can locate a genuine women's liberation group with relative ease (they ferreted out our little group before we had memorized each other's last names), hundreds of women in New York City have failed in their attempts to make contact with the movement. I have spoken to women who have spent as much as three months looking for a group that was open to new members. Unclaimed letters have piled up at certain post office box numbers hastily set up and thoughtlessly abandoned by here-today-and-gone-tomorrow "organizations" that disappeared as abruptly as they materialized. The elusive qualities of "women's lib" once prompted the writer Sally Kempton to remark, "It's not a movement, it's a state of mind." The surest way to affiliate with the movement these days is to form your own small group. That's the way it's happening.

Two years ago the 50 or so women in New York City who had taken to calling themselves the women's liberation movement met on Thursday evenings at a borrowed office on East 11th Street. The official title of the group was the New York Radical Women. There was some justification at the time for thinking grandly in national terms, for similar groups of women were beginning to form in Chicago, Boston, San Francisco and Washington. New York Radical Women came by its name quite simply: the women were young radicals, mostly under the age of 25, and they come out of the civil rights and/or peace movements, for which many of them had been full time workers. A few years earlier, many of them might have been found on the campuses of Vassar, Radcliffe, Wellesley and the larger coed universities, a past they worked hard to deny. What brought them together to a women-only discussion and action group was a sense of abuse suffered at the hands of the very protest movements that had spawned them. As "movement women," they were tired of doing the typing and fixing the food while "movement men" did the writing and leading. Most were living with or married to movement men who, they believed, were treating them as convenient sex objects or as somewhat lesser beings.

Widely repeated quotations, such as Stokely Carmichael's wise-crack dictum to S.N.C.C., "The position of women in our movement should be prone," and, three years later, a similar observation by Black Panther Eldridge Cleaver had reinforced their uncomfortable suspicion that the social vision of radical men did not include equality for women. Black power, as practiced by black male leaders, appeared to mean that black women would step back while black men stepped forward. The white male radical's eager embrace of *machismo* appeared to include those backward aspects of male supremacy in the Latin culture from which the word *machismo* is derived. Within their one-to-one relationships with their men, the women felt, the highly touted "alternate life-style" of the radical movement was working out no better than the "bourgeois" lifestyle they had rejected. If man and wife in a suburban split-level was a symbol of all that was wrong with plastic, bourgeois America, "man and chick" in a Lower East Side tenement flat was hardly the new order they had dreamed of.

In short, "the movement" was reinforcing, not eliminating, their deepest insecurities and feelings of worthlessness as women—feelings which quite possibly had brought them into radical protest politics to begin with. So, in a small way, they had begun to rebel. They had decided to meet regularly—without their men—to talk about their common experience. "Our feminism was very underdeveloped in those days," says Anne Koedt, an early member of the group. "We didn't have any idea of what kind of action we could take. We couldn't stop talking about the blacks and Vietnam."

In Marxist canons, "the woman question" is one of many manifestations of a sick, capitalist society which "the revolution" is supposed to finish off smartly. Some of the women who devoted their Thursday evening meeting time to New York Radical Women believed they were merely dusting off and streamlining an orthodox, ideological issue. Feminism was bad politics and a dirty word since it excluded the larger picture.

But others in the group, like Anne Koedt and Shuli Firestone, an intense and talkative young activist, had begun to see things from different, heretical perspective. Woman's oppressor was Man, they argued, and not a specific economic system. After all, they pointed out, male supremacy was still flourishing in the Soviet Union, Cuba and China, where power was still lodged in a male bureaucracy. Even the beloved Che wrote a guidebook for revolutionaries in which he waxed ecstatic over the advantages to a guerrilla movement of having women along in the mountains—to prepare and cook the food. The heretics tentatively put forward the idea that feminism must be a separate movement of its own.

New York Radical Women's split in perspective—was the ultimate oppressor Man or Capitalism?—occupied endless hours of debate at the Thursday evening meetings. Two warring factions emerged, dubbing each other "the feminists" and "the politicos." But other things were happening as well. For one thing, new women were coming in droves to the Thursday evening talk fest, and a growing feeling of sisterhood was permeating the room. Meetings began awkwardly and shyly, with no recognized chairman and no discernible agenda. Often the suggestion, "Let's sit closer together, sisters," helped break the ice. But once the evening's initial awkwardness had passed, volubility was never a problem. "We had so much to say," an early member relates, "and most of us had never said it to another woman before."

Soon *how* to say it became an important question. Young women like Carol Hanisch, a titian-haired recruit to the civil rights movement from a farm in Iowa, and her friend Kathie Amatniek, a Radcliffe graduate and a working film editor, had spent over a year in Mississippi working with S.N.C.C. There they had been impressed with the Southern revival-style mass meeting at which blacks got up and "testified" about their own experience with "the Man." Might the technique also work for women? And wasn't it the same sort of thing that Mao Tse-tung had advocated to raise political consciousness in Chinese villages? As Carol Hanisch reminded the group, Mao's slogan had been "Speak pain to recall pain"—precisely what New York Radical Women was doing!

The personal-testimony method encouraged all women who came to the meeting to speak their thoughts. The technique of "going around the room" in turn brought responses from many who had never opened their mouths at male-dominated meetings and were experiencing the same difficulty in a room full of articulate members of their own sex. Specific questions such as, "If you've thought of having a baby, do you want a girl or a boy?" touched off accounts of what it meant to be a girl-child—the second choice in a society that prizes boys. An examination of "What happens to your relationship when your man earns more money than you, and what happens when you earn more money than him?" brought a flood of anecdotes about the male ego and money. "We all told similar stories," relates a member of the group. "We discovered that, to a man, they all felt challenged if we were the breadwinners. It meant that we were no longer dependent. We had somehow robbed them of their 'rightful' role."

"We began to see our 'feminization' as a two-level process," says Anne Koedt. "On one level, a woman is brought up to believe that she is a girl and that is her biological destiny. She isn't supposed to want to achieve anything. If, by some chance, she manages to escape the psychological damage, she finds that the structure is prohibitive. Even though she wants to achieve, she finds she is discouraged at every turn and she still can't become President."

Few topics, the women found, were unfruitful. Humiliations that each of them had suffered privately—from being turned down for a job with the comment, "We were looking for a man," to catcalls and wolf whistles on the street—turned out to be universal agonies. "I had always felt degraded, actually turned into an object," said one woman. "I was no longer a human being when a guy on the street would start to make those incredible animal noises at me. I never was flattered by it, I always understood that behind that whistle a masked hostility. When we started to talk about it in the group, discovered that every woman in the room had similar feelings. None of us knew how to cope with this street hostility. We had always had to grin and bear it. We had always been told to dress as women, to be very sexy and alluring to men, and what did it get us? Comments like "Look at the legs on that babe" and "would I like to—her."*

---

* My small group has discussed holding a street action of our own on the first warm day of spring. We intend to take up stations on the corner of Broadway and 45th Street and whistle at the male passersby. The confrontation, we feel, will be educational for all concerned.

"Consciousness-raising," in which a woman's personal experience at the hands of men was analyzed as a *political* phenomenon, soon became a keystone of the women's liberation movement.

In 1963, *before* there was a women's movement, Betty Friedan published what eventually became an American classic, "The Feminine Mystique." The book was a brilliant, factual examination of the post-World War II "back to the home" movement that tore apart the myth of the fulfilled and happy American housewife. Though "The Feminine Mystique" held an unquestioned place as the intellectual mind-opener for most of the young feminists—de Beauvoir's "The Second Sex," a broad, philosophical analysis of the cultural restraints on women, was runner-up in popularity—few members of New York Radical Women had ever felt motivated to attend a meeting of Friedan's National Organization for Women, the parliamentary-style organization of professional women and housewives that she founded in 1966. Friedan, the mother of the movement, and the organization that recruited in her image were considered hopelessly bourgeois. NOW's emphasis on legislative change left the radicals cold. The generation gap created real barriers to communication.

"Actually, we had a lot in common with the NOW women," reflects Anne Koedt. "The women who started NOW were achievement oriented in their professions. They began with the employment issue because that's what they were up against. The ones who started New York Radical Women were achievement-oriented in the radical movement. From both ends we were fighting a male structure that prevented us from achieving."

Friedan's book had not envisioned a movement of young feminists emerging from the college campus and radical politics. "If I had it to do all over again," she says, "I would rewrite my last chapter." She came to an early meeting of New York Radical Women to listen, ask questions and take notes, and went away convinced that her approach—and NOW's—was more valid. "As far as I'm concerned, we're *still* the radicals," she says emphatically. "We raised our consciousness a long time ago. I get along with the women's lib people because they're the way the troops we need come up. But the name of the game is confrontation and action, and equal employment *is* the gut issue. The legal fight is enormously important. Desegregating The New York Times

help-wanted ads was an important step, don't you think? And
NOW did it. The women's movement needs its Browns versus
Boards of Education."

Other older women, writers and lifetime feminists, also came
around to observe, and stayed to develop a kinship with girls
young enough to be their daughters. "I almost wept after my first
meeting. I went home and filled my diary," says Ruth Hersch-
berger, poet and author of "Adam's Rib," a witty and unheeded
expostulation of women's rights published in 1948. "When I
wrote 'Adam's Rib,' I was writing for readers who wouldn't accept
the first premise. Now there was a whole roomful of people and a
whole new vocabulary. I could go a whole month on the ammuni-
tion I'd get at one meeting."

In June of 1968, New York Radical Women produced a mimeographed booklet of some 20 pages entitled "Notes from the First
Year." It sold for 50 cents to women and $1.00 to men. "Notes"
was a compendium of speeches, essays and transcriptions of tape-
recorded "rap sessions" of the Thursday evening group on such
subjects as sex, abortion and orgasm. Several mimeographed edi-
tions later, it remains the most widely circulated source material
on the New York women's liberation movement.

The contribution to "Notes" that attracted the most attention
from both male and female readers was a one-page essay by Anne
Koedt entitled, "The Myth of Vaginal Orgasm." In it she wrote:

"Frigidity has generally been defined by men as the failure of
women to have vaginal orgasms. Actually, the vagina is not a
highly sensitive area and is not physiologically constructed to
achieve orgasm. The clitoris is the sensitive area and is the female
equivalent of the penis. All orgasms [in women] are extensions of
sensations from this area. This leads to some interesting questions
about conventional sex and our role in it. Men have orgasms essentially by friction with the vagina, not with the clitoris. Women
have thus been defined sexually in terms of what pleases men; our
own biology has not been properly analyzed. Instead we have
been fed a myth of the liberated woman and her vaginal orgasm,
an orgasm which in fact does not exist. What we must do is redefine our sexuality. We must discard the 'normal' concepts of sex
and create new guidelines which take into account mutual sexual
enjoyment. We must begin to demand that if a certain sexual

position or technique now defined as 'standard' is not mutually conducive to orgasm, then it should no longer be defined as standard."

Anne Koedt's essay went further than many other women in the movement would have preferred to go, but she was dealing with a subject that every woman understood. "For years I suffered under a male-imposed definition of my sexual responses," one woman says. "From Freud on down, it was men who set the standard of my sexual enjoyment. Their way was the way I should achieve nirvana, because their way was the way it worked for them. Me? Oh, I was simply an 'inadequate woman.'"

By September, 1968, New York Radical Women felt strong enough to attempt a major action. Sixty women went to Atlantic City in chartered buses to picket the Miss America pageant. The beauty contest was chosen as a target because of the ideal of American womanhood it extolled—vacuous, coiffed, cosmeticized and with a smidgin of talent.

But New York Radical Women did not survive its second year. For one thing, the number of new women who flocked to the Thursday evening meetings made consciousness-raising and "going around the room" an impossibility. The politico-feminist split and other internal conflicts—charges of "domination" by one or another of the stronger women were thrown back and forth—put a damper on the sisterly euphoria. An attempt to break up the one large group into three smaller ones—by lot—proved disastrous.

Several women felt the need for a new group. They had become intrigued with the role of the witch in world history as representing society's persecution of women who dared to be different. From Joan of Arc, who dared to wear men's clothes and lead a men's army, to the women of Salem who dared to defy accepted political, religious mores, the "witch" was punished for deviations. Out of this thinking grew WITCH, a handy acronym that the organizers announced, half tongue-in-cheek, stood for Women's International Terrorist Conspiracy from Hell.

Much of WITCH was always tongue-in-cheek, and from its inception its members were at great pains to deny that they were feminists. The Yippie movement had made outrageous disruption a respectable political tactic of the left, and the women of WITCH decided it was more compatible with their thinking to be labeled "kooks" by outsiders than to be labeled man-haters by movement men.

In the WITCH philosophy, the patriarchy of the nuclear family was synonymous with the patriarchy of the American business corporation. Thus, four women took jobs at a branch of the Travelers Insurance Company, where a fifth member was working, and attempted to establish a secret coven of clerical workers on the premises. (For the Travelers' project, WITCH became "Women Incensed at Travelers' Corporate Hell.") In short order, the infiltrators were fired for such infractions of office rules as wearing slacks to work. Undaunted, a new quintet of operatives gained employment in the vast typing pools at A.T. & T. "Women Into Telephone Company Harassment" gained three sympathizers to the cause before Ma Bell got wise and exorcised the coven from her midst. Two WITCHes were fired for insubordination; the rest were smoked out and dismissed for being "overqualified" for the typing pool.

WITCH's spell over the women's movement did not hold. "At this point," says Judith Duffett, an original member, "you could say that WITCH is just another small group in women's liberation. We're concerned with consciousness-raising and developing an ideology through collective thinking. We don't do the freaky, hippie stuff anymore."

While WITCH was brewing its unusual recipe for liberation, another offshoot of New York Radical Women emerged. The new group was called Redstockings, a play on *bluestockings*, with the blue replaced by the color of revolution. Organized by Shuli Firestone and Ellen Willis, an articulate rock-music columnist for the New Yorker and a serious student of Engels's "Origins of the Family," Redstockings made no bones about where it stood. It was firmly committed to feminism and action.

Redstockings made its first public appearance at a New York legislative hearing on abortion law reform in February, 1969, when several women sought to gain the microphone to testify about their own abortions. The hearing, set up to take testimony from 15 medical and psychiatric "experts"—14 were men—was hastily adjourned. The following month, Redstockings held its own abortion hearing at the Washington Square Methodist Church. Using the consciousness-raising technique, 12 women "testified" about abortion, from their own personal experience, before an audience of 300 men and women. The political message of the emotion-charged evening was that women were the only true experts on unwanted pregnancy and abortion, and that every woman has an inalienable right to decide whether or not she wishes to bear a child.

Redstockings' membership counts are a closely held secret, but I would estimate that the number does not exceed 100. Within the movement, Redstockings push what they call "the pro-woman line." "What it means," says a member, "is that we take the woman's side in *everything*. A woman is never to blame for her own submission. None of us need to change ourselves, we need to change men." Redstockings are also devout about consciousness-raising. "Whatever else we may do, consciousness-raising is the ongoing political work," says Kathie Amatniek. For the last few months, the various Redstocking groups have been raising their consciousness on what they call "the divisions between women that keep us apart"—married women *vs.* single, black women *vs.* white, middle class *vs.* working class, etc.

While Redstockings organized its abortion speak-out, the New York chapter of NOW formed a committee to lobby for repeal of restrictive abortion legislation. These dissimilar approaches to the same problem illustrate the difference in style between the two wings of the women's movement.

But within New York NOW itself, a newer, wilder brand of feminism made an appearance. Ti-Grace Atkinson, a Friedan protegée and the president of New York NOW, found herself in increasing conflict with her own local chapter and Friedan over NOW's hierarchical structure, a typical organization plan with an executive board on top. Ti-Grace, a tall blonde who has been described in print as "aristocratic looking," had come to view the power relationship between NOW's executive board and the general membership as a copycat extension of the standard forms of male domination over women in the society at large. She proposed to NOW that all executive offices be abolished in favor of rotating chairmen chosen by lot from the general membership. When Atkinson's proposal came up for a vote by the general membership of the New York chapter in October, 1968, and was defeated, Ti-Grace resigned her presidency on the spot and went out and formed her own organization. Named the October 17th Movement—the date of Ti-Grace's walkout from NOW—it made a second debut this summer as The Feminists, and took its place as the most radical of the women's liberation groups. (New York NOW suffered no apparent effects from its first organizational split. Over the last year it has *gained* in membership as feminism has gained acceptability among wider circles of women.)

The Feminists made anti-élitism and rigorous discipline cardinal principles of their organization. As the only radical feminist group to take a stand against the institution of marriage they held a sit in at the city marriage license bureau last year, raising the slogan that "Marriage Is Slavery." Married women or women living with men may not exceed one-third of the total membership.

Differences over such matters as internal democracy, and the usual personality conflicts that plague all political movements, caused yet another feminist group and another manifesto to make their appearance this fall. In November, Shuli Firestone and Anne Koedt set up a plan for organizing small groups—or "brigades," as they prefer to call them—on a neighborhood basis, and named their over-all structure the New York Radical Feminists. Eleven decentralized neighborhood units (three are in the West Village) meet jointly once a month.

The Radical Feminists coexist with the Feminists and the Redstockings without much rivalry, although when pressed, partisans of the various groups will tell you, for instance, that Redstockings do too much consciousness-raising and not enough action, or that the Feminists are "fascistic," or that the Radical Feminists are publicity hungry. But in general, since interest in the women's liberation movement has always exceeded organizational capacity, the various groups take the attitude of "the more the merrier."

Despite the existence of three formal "pure radical feminist" organizations, hundreds of women who consider themselves women's liberationists have not yet felt the need to affiliate with anybody larger than their own small group. The small group, averaging 8 to 15 members and organized spontaneously by friends calling friends has become *the* organizational form of the amorphous movement. Its intimacy seems to suit women. Fear of expressing new or half-formed thoughts vanishes in a friendly living-room atmosphere. "After years of psychoanalysis in which my doctor kept telling me my problem was that I wouldn't accept quote—*my female role*," says a married woman with two children who holds a master's degree in philosophy, "the small group was a revelation to me. Suddenly, for the first time in my life, it was O.K. to express feelings of hostility to men." Says another woman: "In the small group I have the courage to think things and feel feelings, that I would never have dared to think and feel as an individual."

The meetings have often been compared to group therapy, a description that most of the women find irritating. "Group therapy isn't political and what we're doing is highly political," is the general response. In an early paper on the nature and function of the small group, Carol Hanisch once wrote, "Group therapy implies that we are sick and messed up, but the first function of the small group is to get rid of self-blame. We start with the assumption that women are really 'neat' people. Therapy means adjusting. We desire to change the objective conditions."

The groups are usually leaderless and structureless, and the subjects discussed at the weekly meetings run the gamut of female experience. The Radical Feminists offer to new groups they organize a list of consciousness-raising topics that includes:

- Discuss your relationships with men. Have you noticed any recurring patterns?
- Have you ever felt that men have pressured you into sexual relationships? Have you ever lied about orgasm?
- Discuss your relationships with other women. Do you compete with women for men?
- Growing up as a girl, were you treated differently from your brother?
- What would you most like to do in life? What has stopped you?

"Three months of this sort of thing," says Shuli Firestone, "is enough to make a feminist out of any woman."

The kind of collective thinking that has come out of the women's liberation movement is qualitatively different from the kinds of theorems and analyses that other political movements have generated. "Women are different from all other oppressed classes," says Anne Koedt. "We live in isolation, not in ghettos, and we are in the totally unique position of having a master in our own houses." It is not surprising, therefore, that marriage and child care are two subjects that receive intensive scrutiny in the small group.

If few in the women's movement are willing to go as far as the Feminists and say that marriage is slavery, it is hard to find a women's liberationist who is not in some way disaffected by the sound of wedding bells. Loss of personal identity and the division of labor within the standard marriage (the husband's role as provider, the wife's role as home maintenance and child care) are the basic points at issue. "I have come to view marriage as a built-in self-destruct for women," says one divorcée after 12 years of marriage. "I married early, right after college, because it was expected of me. I never had a chance to discover who I was. I was programed into the housewife pattern." Many married women's liberationists will no longer use their husbands' last names; some have gone back to their maiden names, and some even to their mothers' maiden names.

One paper that has been widely circulated within the movement is entitled "The Politics of Housework," by Pat Mainardi, a Redstocking who is a teacher and painter. "Men recognize the essential fact of housework right from the beginning," she wrote. "Which is that it stinks. You both work, you both have careers, but *you* are expected to do the housework. Your husband tells you, 'Don't talk to me about housework. It's too trivial to discuss' MEANING: *His* purpose is to deal with matters of significance. *Your* purpose is to deal with matters of insignificance. So *you* do the housework. Housework trivial? Just try getting him to share the burden. The measure of his resistance is the measure of your oppression."

Not only the oppression of housework, but the oppression of child care has become a focus of the women's movement. Much of the energy of young mothers in the movement has gone into setting up day-care collectives that are staffed on an equal basis by mothers and fathers. (Thus far they have proved difficult to sustain.) "Some of the men have actually come to understand that sharing equally in child care is a political responsibility," says Rosalyn Baxandall, a social worker and an early women's liberationist. Rosalyn and her husband, Lee, a playwright, put in a morning a week at an informal cooperative day nursery on the Lower East Side where their 2-year-old, Finn, is charter member.

In November, at the Congress to Unite Women, a conference that drew over 500 women's liberationists of various persuasions from the New York area, a resolution demanding 24-hour-a-day child care centers was overwhelmingly endorsed. Women in the movement have also suggested plans for a new kind of lifestyle in which a husband and wife would each work half-day and devote the other half of the day to caring for their children. Another possibility would be for the man to work for six months of the year while the woman takes care of the child-rearing responsibilities—with the roles reversed for the next six months.

The "movement women" who did not endorse the separatism of an independent radical feminist movement last year and chose to remain in what the feminists now call "the male left" have this year made women's liberation a major issue in their own political groups. Even the weatherwomen of Weatherman meet separately to discuss how to combat male chauvinism among their fellow revolutionaries. The women of Rat, the farthest out of the underground radical newspapers, formed a collective and took over editorial management of their paper last month, charging that their men had put out a product filled with sexist, women as-degraded-object pornography. Twenty-two-year-old Jane Alpert, free on bail and facing conspiracy charges for a series of terrorist bombings, was spokesman for the Rat women's *putsch*. A black women's liberation committee functions within S.N.C.C., and its leader, Frances M. Beal, has said publicly, "To be black and female is double jeopardy, the slave of a slave."

The new feminism has moved into some surprisingly Establishment quarters. A spirited women's caucus at New York University Law School forced the university to open its select national scholarship program to women students. Women's caucuses exist among the editorial employees at McGraw Hill and Newsweek. Last month, 59 women in city government, sent a petition to Mayor Lindsay demanding that he actively seek qualified women for policy-making posts.

The movement is a story without an end, because it has just begun. The goals of liberation go beyond a simple concept of equality. Looking through my notebook, I see them expressed simply and directly. *Betty Friedan: "We're going to redefine the sex roles." Anne Koedt: "We're going to be redefining politics."* Brave words for a new movement, and braver still for a movement that has been met with laughter and hostility. Each time a man sloughs off the women's movement with the comment, "They're nothing but a bunch of lesbians and frustrated bitches," we quiver with collective rage. How can such a charge be answered in rational terms? It cannot be. (The supersensitivity of the movement to the lesbian issue, and the existence of a few militant lesbians within the movement once prompted Friedan herself to grouse about "the lavender menace" that was threatening to warp the image of women's rights. A lavender *herring*, perhaps, but surely no clear and present danger.)

The small skirmishes and tugs of war that used to be called "the battle of the sexes" have now assumed ideological proportions. It is the aim of the movement to *turn men around*, and the implications in that aim are staggering. "Men have used us all their lives as ego fodder," says Anne Koedt. "They not only control economics and the government, they control us. There are the women's pages and the rest of the world." It is that rest of the world, of course, that we are concerned with. There is a women's rights button that I sometimes wear and the slogan on it reads, "Sisterhood is Powerful." If sisterhood were powerful, what a different world it would be.

Women as a class have never subjugated another group; we have never marched off to wars of conquest in the name of the fatherland. We have never been involved in a decision to annex the territory of a neighboring country, or to fight for foreign markets on distant shores. Those are the games men play, not us. We see it differently. We want to be neither oppressor nor oppressed. The women's revolution is the final revolution of them all.

How does a sympathetic man relate to a feminist woman? Thus far, it has not been easy for those who are trying. The existence of a couple of *men's* consciousness-raising groups—the participants are mostly husbands of activist women—is too new to be labeled a trend. "When our movement gets strong, when men are forced to see us as a conscious issue, *what are they going to do?*" asks Anne Koedt. And then she answers: "I don't know, but I think there's a part of men that really wants a human relationship, and that's going to be the saving grace for all of us."

Killing Joy

Feminism and the History of Happiness

BY SARA AHMED

Sara Ahmed is a British Australian scholar whose writing examines the intersection of feminist theory, lesbian feminism, queer theory, critical race theory, and postcolonialism. She was appointed to the Department of Media and Communications at Goldsmiths in 2004 and was the inaugural director of its Centre for Feminist Research. In 2016, Ahmed resigned from her post, protesting the sexual harassment of students, and began working as an independent scholar. This essay—published in her 2010 book *The Promise of Happiness* and in the collection *Living a Feminist Life*—began on Ahmed's blog, *feministkilljoys*. In the essay, Ahmed interrogates our cultural understanding of happiness, the ways in which happiness acts as a "social pressure" to push us toward or away from certain experiences, objects, and behaviors, and methods of resistance based in intersectional feminism. In the excerpt shared here, Ahmed dissects the idea of the feminist killjoy and how all too often feminists are labeled as killjoys for daring to articulate their concerns about the world we live in. She asks, "Does the feminist kill other people's joy by pointing out moments of sexism? Or does she expose the bad feelings that get hidden, displaced, or negated under public signs of joy?" These important questions seemed like an ideal place to bring to a close an anthology of feminist scholarship.

My experience of being the feminist daughter in a conventional family taught me much about rolling eyes. I recall feeling at odds with the performance of good feeling. Say we are seated at the dinner table. Around this table, the family gathers, having polite conversations, where only certain things can be brought up. Someone says something you consider problematic. You respond, carefully perhaps. You might be speaking quietly, or you might be getting "wound up," recognizing with frustration that you are being wound up by someone who is winding you up. The violence of what was said, the violence of provocation, goes unnoticed.

Let us take this figure of the feminist killjoy seriously. Does the feminist kill other people's joy by pointing out moments of sexism? Or does she expose the bad feelings that get hidden, displaced, or negated under public signs of joy? Does bad feeling enter the room when somebody expresses anger about things? Or does the entry of anger simply mean that the bad feelings that circulate through objects get brought to the surface in a certain way? The feminist subject in the room hence brings others down, not only by talking about unhappy topics such as sexism but by exposing how happiness is sustained, by erasing the signs of not getting along. Feminists do kill joy in a certain sense: they disturb the very fantasy that happiness can be found in certain places. To kill a fantasy can still kill a feeling. It is not just that feminists might not be happily affected by the objects that are supposed to cause happiness but that the failure to be happy is read as sabotaging the happiness of others. Feminists might be strangers at the table of happiness.

We can consider the relationship between the negativity of the figure of the feminist killjoy and how certain bodies are encountered as being negative. Marilyn Frye argues that oppression involves the requirement that you show signs of being happy with the situation in which you find yourself: "It is often a requirement upon oppressed people that we smile and be cheerful. If we comply, we signify our docility and our acquiescence in our situation." To be oppressed requires that you show signs of happiness, signs of being or having been adjusted. As a result, for Frye, "anything but the sunniest countenance exposes us to being perceived as mean, bitter, angry or dangerous." To be recognized as a feminist is to be assigned to a difficult category and a category of difficulty. You are already read as not easy to get along with when you name yourself a feminist. You have to show that you are not difficult through displaying signs of good will and happiness. Frye alludes to such experiences when she describes how "this means, at the very least, that we may be found to be 'difficult' or unpleasant to work with, which is enough to cost one's livelihood." We can also witness an investment in feminist unhappiness (the myth that feminists kill joy because they are joyless). There is a desire to believe that women become feminists because they are unhappy, perhaps as a displacement of their envy for those who have achieved the happiness they have failed to achieve. This desire functions as a defense of happiness against feminist critique. This is not to say that feminists are not unhappy (they might be or they might not be). My point here would be that feminists are read as being unhappy, such that situations of conflict, violence, and power are read as about the unhappiness of feminists rather than about what feminists are unhappy about.

Of course, within feminism, some bodies more than others can be attributed as the cause of unhappiness. We can place the figure of the feminist killjoy alongside the figure of the angry black woman, explored so well by writers such as Audre Lorde and bell hooks. The angry black woman can be described as a killjoy; she may even kill feminist joy, for example, by pointing out forms of racism within feminist politics. She might not even have to make any such point to kill joy. You can be affectively alien because you are affected in the wrong way by the right things. Listen to the following description from bell hooks: "A group of white feminist activists who do not know one another may be present at a meeting to discuss feminist theory. They may feel bonded on the basis of shared womanhood, but the atmosphere will noticeably change when a woman of color enters the room. The white women will become tense, no longer relaxed, no longer celebratory."

It is not just that feelings are in tension but that the tension is located somewhere: in being felt by some bodies, it is attributed as caused by another body, who thus comes to be felt as apart from the group, as getting in the way of its organic enjoyment and solidarity. The black body is attributed as the cause of becoming tense, which is also the loss of a shared atmosphere. Atmospheres might become shared if there is an agreement as to where we locate the points of tension. As a feminist of color, you do not even have to say anything to cause tension. The mere proximity of some bodies involves an affective conversion. We learn from this example how histories are condensed in the very intangibility of an atmosphere, or in the tangibility of the bodies that seem to get in the way. You can be affectively alien because you affect others in the wrong way: your proximity gets in the way of other people's enjoyment of the right things, functioning as unwanted reminder of histories that are disturbing, that disturb an atmosphere.

To speak out of anger as woman of color is to confirm your position as the cause of tension. Lorde points out: "When women of Color speak out of the anger that laces so many of our contacts with white women, we are often told that we are 'creating a mood of helplessness,' 'preventing white women from getting past guilt,' or 'standing in the way of trusting communication and action.'" The woman of color must let go of her anger in order for the white woman to move on. Some bodies become blockage points, points where smooth communication stops; they disturb the promise of happiness, which I would redescribe as the social pressure to maintain signs of getting along. When the exposure of violence becomes the origin of violence, then the violence that is exposed is not revealed.

Acknowledgments

I owe a debt of gratitude to all the writers and estate representatives who generously granted permission for me to include their work in this reader.

This book would not have been possible without the invaluable assistance of Megan Pillow, my project manager and a remarkable, lyrical writer in her own right. Thank you to Mel Moorer, who helped with the research for this volume. Thank you to my executive assistant, Kaitlyn Adams, for whom no job title would adequately encompass the support and counsel she offers. Elda Rotor, this book's editor, has the patience of a saint and persisted in making this book happen. Thank you, also, to my longtime agent Maria Massie.

Suggestions for Further Reading/ Watching/Seeing/Listening

ANTHOLOGIES

The Black Woman: An Anthology, edited by Toni Cade Bambara

Black Sexual Politics: African Americans, Gender, and the New Racism by Patricia Hill Collins

Burn It Down: Women Writing about Anger, edited by Lilly Dancyger

But Some of Us Are Brave: Black Women's Studies, edited by Akasha (Gloria T.) Hull, Patricia Bell-Scott, and Barbara Smith

The Chicana Motherwork Anthology, edited by Cecilia Caballero, Yvette Martínez-Vu, Judith Pérez-Torres, Michelle Téllez, and Christine Vega

Feckless Cunt: A Feminist Anthology, edited by Susan Rukeyser

The Feminist Porn Book: The Politics of Producing Pleasure, edited by Tristan Taormino, Celine Parreñas Shimizu, Constance Penley, and Mireille Miller-Young

The Feminist Utopia Project: Fifty-Seven Versions of a Wildly Better Future, edited by Alexandra Brodsky and Rachel Kauder Nalebuff

Gendered Lives, Sexual Beings: A Feminist Anthology, edited by Joya Misra, Mahala Dyer Stewart, and Marni Alyson Brown

Home Girls: A Black Feminist Anthology, edited by Barbara Smith

Indigenous Women and Feminism: Politics, Activism, Culture, edited by Cheryl Suzack, Shari M. Huhndorf, Jeanne Perreault, and Jean Barman

It's Not about the Burqa, edited by Mariam Khan

Killing the Black Body: Race, Reproduction, and the Meaning of Liberty by Dorothy Roberts

Sex and the Single Woman: 24 Writers Reimagine Helen Gurley Brown's Cult Classic, edited by Eliza Smith and Haley Swanson

This Bridge Called My Back: Writings by Radical Women of Color, edited by Cherríe Moraga and Gloria Anzaldúa

Whiter: Asian American Women on Skin Color and Colorism, edited by Nikki Khanna

Women of Resistance: Poem for a New Feminism, edited by Danielle Barnhart and Iris Mahan

Words of Fire: An Anthology of African-American Feminist Thought, edited by Beverly Guy-Sheftall

NONFICTION

Against Memoir: Complaints, Confessions & Criticisms by Michelle Tea

Asking for It: The Alarming Rise of Rape Culture—and What We Can Do about It by Kate Harding

The Beauty Myth: How Images of Beauty Are Used Against Women by Naomi Wolf

Belabored: A Vindication of the Rights of Pregnant Women by Lyz Lenz

Big Friendship: How We Found One, Almost Lost It, and Kept It Together by Aminatou Sow and Ann Friedman

A Bigger Picture: My Fight to Bring a New African Voice to the Climate Crisis by Vanessa Nakate

Black Feminism Reimagined: After Intersectionality by Jennifer C. Nash

A Black Women's History of the United States by Daina Ramey Berry and Kali Nicole Gross

Delusions of Gender by Cordelia Fine

The Empathy Exams by Leslie Jamison

Entitled: How Male Privilege Hurts Women by Kate Manne

Feminism Is for Everybody by bell hooks

Feminism for the 99%: A Manifesto by Cinzia Arruzza, Tithi Bhattacharya, and Nancy Fraser

The Feminism of Uncertainty: A Gender Diary by Ann Snitow

Gender Trouble: Feminism and the Subversion of Identity by Judith Butler

Good and Mad: The Revolutionary Power of Women's Anger by Rebecca Traister

Guerrilla Girls: The Art of Behaving Badly by the Guerrilla Girls

How We Get Free: Black Feminism and the Combahee River Collective by Keeanga-Yamahtta Taylor

Hood Feminism: Notes from Women That a Movement Forgot by Mikki Kendall

In Our Prime: How Older Women Are Reinventing the Road Ahead by Susan J. Douglas

Invisible Women: Exposing Data Bias in a World Designed for Men by Caroline Criado Perez

Living a Feminist Life by Sara Ahmed

Mediocre: The Dangerous Legacy of White Male America by Ijeoma Oluo

The New Woman of Color: The Collected Writings of Fannie Barrier Williams, 1893–1918 by Fannie Barrier Williams, edited by Mary Jo Deegan

A Room of One's Own by Virginia Woolf

Sister Citizen: Shame, Stereotypes, and Black Women in America by Melissa V. Harris-Perry

Sister Outsider: Essays and Speeches by Audre Lorde

Stop Telling Women to Smile: Stories of Street Harassment And How We're Taking Back Our Power by Tatyana Fazlalizadeh

Talkin' Up to the White Woman: Indigenous Women and Feminism by Aileen Moreton-Robinson

They Didn't See Us Coming: The Hidden History of Feminism in the Nineties by Lisa Levenstein

Unapologetic: A Black, Queer, and Feminist Mandate for Radical Movements by Charlene A. Carruthers

We Should All Be Feminists by Chimamanda Ngozi Adichie

The Witches Are Coming by Lindy West

Women & Power: A Manifesto by Mary Beard

Women Who Run with the Wolves: Myths and Stories of the Wild Woman Archetypes by Clarissa Pinkola Estés

You Play the Girl: On Playboy Bunnies, Stepford Wives, Train Wrecks & Other Mixed Messages by Carina Chocano

FICTION

The Awakening by Kate Chopin

Beloved by Toni Morrison

The Blazing World by Siri Hustvedt

The Book of Longings by Sue Monk Kidd

The Country of the Pointed Firs by Sarah Orne Jewett

Fates and Furies by Lauren Groff

Girl, Woman, Other by Bernardine Evaristo

The Golden Notebook by Doris Lessing

Green Girl by Kate Zambreno

The Handmaid's Tale by Margaret Atwood

Homegoing by Yaa Gyasi

The Joy Luck Club by Amy Tan

Libertie by Kaitlyn Greenidge

The Night Watchman by Louise Erdrich

Of One Blood by Pauline Hopkins

Of Women and Salt by Gabriela Garcia
Passing by Nella Larsen
Possessing the Secret of Joy by Alice Walker
Remembrance by Rita Woods
A River of Stars by Vanessa Hua
The Round House by Louise Erdrich
Salvage the Bones by Jesmyn Ward
Song of Solomon by Toni Morrison
Sorrowland by Rivers Solomon
Stone Butch Blues by Leslie Feinberg
Thin Girls by Diana Clarke
The Vegetarian by Han King
Their Eyes Were Watching God by Zora Neale Hurston
Written on the Body by Jeanette Winterson
A Woman Is No Man by Etaf Rum
The Woman Upstairs by Claire Messud

MEMOIR/AUTOBIOGRAPHY

The Argonauts by Maggie Nelson
An Autobiography by Angela Davis
The Bell Jar by Sylvia Plath
Brown Girl Dreaming by Jacqueline Woodson
Bury My Heart at Chuck E. Cheese's by Tiffany Midge
The Chronology of Water by Lidia Yuknavitch
The Collected Schizophrenias by Esme Weijun Wang
Crazy Brave by Joy Harjo
A Cup of Water under My Bed by Daisy Hernández
Don't Call Me Inspirational: A Disabled Feminist Talks Back by Harilyn Rousso
Fairest by Meredith Talusan
Girl Decoded: A Scientist's Quest to Reclaim Our Humanity by Bringing Emotional Intelligence to Technology by Rana el Kaliouby
Girlhood by Melissa Febos
Heart Berries by Terese Mailhot
A History of Scars by Laura Lee
How to Be a Woman by Caitlin Moran
I Am Malala: The Girl Who Stood Up for Education and Was Shot by the Taliban by Malala Yousafzai
In Open Country by Rahawa Haile
Love Is an Ex-Country by Randa Jarrar
Maid: Hard Work, Low Pay, and a Mother's Will to Survive by Stephanie Land

M Train by Patti Smith
Men Explain Things to Me by Rebecca Solnit
Minor Feelings: An Asian American Reckoning by Cathy Park Hong
Redefining Realness by Janet Mock
See No Stranger: A Memoir and Manifesto of Revolutionary Love by Valarie Kaur
Somebody's Daughter by Ashley Ford
This Is One Way to Dance by Sejal Shah
Trick Mirror: Reflections on Self-Delusion by Jia Tolentino
Unbought and Unbossed by Shirley Chisholm
Wandering in Strange Lands: A Daughter of the Great Migration Reclaims Her Roots by Morgan Jenkins
Waiting in the Wings: Portrait of a Queer Motherhood by Cherrié Moraga
Whipping Girl: A Transsexual Woman on Sexism and the Scapegoating of Femininity by Julia Serano
The Woman Warrior: Memoirs of a Girlhood among Ghosts by Maxine Hong Kingston
Wow, No Thank You by Samantha Irby

SHORT STORIES

"The Brutal Language of Love" by Alicia Erian
"Drinking Coffee Elsewhere" by ZZ Packer
"Everyday Use" by Alice Walker
"Fits" by Alice Munro
"A Good Man Is Hard to Find" by Flannery O'Connor
"Girl" by Jamaica Kincaid
"The Great Awake" by Julia Armfield
"The Husband Stitch" by Carmen Maria Machado
"I Stand Here Ironing" by Tillie Olsen
"Is Your Blood as Red as This?" by Helen Oyeyemi
"Like a Winding Sheet" by Ann Petry
"Neighbors" by Diane Oliver
"A Romantic Weekend" by Mary Gaitskill
"Sweat" by Zora Neale Hurston
"A Temporary Matter" by Jhumpa Lahiri
"Virgins" by Danielle Evans

POETRY

"All the Good Women Are Gone" by Susan Nguyen
"Cannibal" by Safiya Sinclair

"Citizen" by Claudia Rankine
"Dancing with Strom" by Nikky Finney
"The Dream of a Common Language" by Adrienne Rich
"Feminist or Womanist" by Staceyann Chin
"Final Performance" by Cynthia Cruz
"Gate A-4" by Naomi Shihab Nye
"Her Kind" by Anne Sexton
"Lady Lazarus" by Sylvia Plath
"Motherland Fatherland Homelandsexuals" by Patricia Lockwood
"My Mother Was a Freedom Fighter" by Aja Monet
"The Period Poem" by Dominique Christina
"Pocket-Sized Feminism" by Blythe Baird
"Poet as Housewife" by Elisabeth Eybers
"Postcolonial Love Poem" by Natalie Diaz
"Raised by Women" by Kelly Norman Ellis
"Respect" by Melissa Studdard
"Sadie and Maud" by Gwendolyn Brooks
"Still I Rise" by Maya Angelou
"Teaching My Mother How to Give Birth" by Warsan Shire
"They Shut Me Up in Prose" by Emily Dickinson
"To the Woman Crying Uncontrollably in the Next Stall" by Kim Addonizio
"Wade in the Water" by Tracy K. Smith
"What They Don't Want You to Know" by Amanda Lovelace
"A Woman Speaks" by Audre Lorde

ESSAYS

"Being Lovingly, Knowingly Ignorant: White Feminism and Women of Color" by Mariana Ortega
"The Bitch Is Back" by Sandra Tsing Loh
"Cash/Consent" by Lorelei Lee
"Choose Your Words with *Cuidado*" by Daisy Hernández
"The Contra-sexual Manifesto" by Beatriz Preciado
"Coventry" by Rachel Cusk
"The Grand Coolie Damn" by Marge Piercy
"Heroin/e" by Cheryl Strayed
"Heterogeneity, Hybridity, Multiplicity: Marking Asian American Differences" by Lisa Lowe
"Joy" by Zadie Smith
"Lift and Separate" by Ariel Levy
"My Misspent Youth" by Meghan Daum
"No Name Woman" by Maxine Hong Kingston

"Notes from a Difficult Case" by Ruthann Robson
"Notes Toward a Politics of Location" by Adrienne Rich
"Pause" by Mary Ruefle
"The Sexual Politics of Meat" by Carol J. Adams
"Shunned" by Meredith Hall
"Something About Me" by Emilie Pine
"Thanksgiving in Mongolia" by Ariel Levy
"The Trash Heap Has Spoken" by Carmen Maria Machado
"Trashing: The Dark Side of Sisterhood" by Jo Freeman
"Toward a Trans* Feminism" by Jack Halberstam
"What Is Socialist Feminism?" by Barbara Ehrenreich
"The Women's Movement" by Joan Didion

FILMS

4 Months, 3 Weeks and 2 Days (2007)
9 to 5 (1980)
The 40-Year-Old Version (2020)
The Accused (1988)
Alien (1979)
All about My Mother (1979)
Audition (1999)
The Babadook (2014)
Baby Boom (1987)
Beaches (1988)
Black Panther (2018)
Born in Flames (1983)
Bound (1996)
Carmen Jones (1954)
Carrie (1976)
The Circle (2000)
Cleo from 5 to 7 (1962)
Cleopatra Jones and the Casino of Gold (1975)
Clueless (1995)
Coffy (1973)
The Color Purple (1985)
Cuties (2020)
Daisies (1966)
Dark Girls (2011)
Daughters of the Dust (1991)
Desperately Seeking Susan (1985)
Diary of a Lost Girl (1929)
Erin Brockovich (2000)

The Fear Street Trilogy (2021)
Female Trouble (1974)
Foxy Brown (1974)
Frida (2002)
Fried Green Tomatoes (1991)
A Girl Walks Home Alone at Night (2014)
Hairspray (1988)
Hidden Figures (2016)
His Girl Friday (1940)
How Stella Got Her Groove Back (1998)
Hustlers (2019)
It Follows (2014)
Jennifer's Body (2009)
The Joy Luck Club (1993)
Jumpin' Jack Flash (1986)
Ladies and Gentlemen, the Fabulous Stains (1982)
Legally Blonde (2001)
A League of Their Own (1992)
Love & Basketball (2000)
Kill Bill (2003/2004)
Mad Max: Fury Road (2015)
Meshes of the Afternoon (1943)
Midsommar (2019)
Miss Juneteenth (2020)
Miss Sloane (2016)
Monster (2003)
Mustang (2015)
My Brilliant Career (1979)
Norma Rae (1979)
On the Basis of Sex (2018)
One Sings, the Other Doesn't (1977)
Orlando (1992)
Pariah (2011)
The Passion of Joan of Arc (1928)
The Perfection (2018)
Persona (1966)
The Piano (1993)
Promising Young Woman (2020)
Pussy Riot: A Punk Prayer (2013)
Queen of Katwe (2016)
Revenge (2017)
Rosetta (1999)
Scream (1996)

Set It Off (1996)
The Kids Are All Right (2010)
The Silence of the Lambs (1991)
Silkwood (1983)
Teeth (2007)
Thelma & Louise (1991)
The Watermelon Woman (1996)
Waiting to Exhale (1995)
What's Love Got to Do with It (1993)
Wild (2014)
Winter's Bone (2010)
The Wiz (1978)
A Woman Under the Influence (1974)
Working Girl (1988)
Zero Dark Thirty (2012)

TELEVISION

The networks given here are for US release only.
Alias (ABC)
Ally McBeal (Fox)
Big Little Lies (HBO)
Broad City (Comedy Central)
Claws (TNT)
Doctor Who 2018 (BBC)
Fleabag (Amazon)
Girls (HBO)
Girlfriends (UPN/the CW)
GLOW (Netflix)
Grace & Frankie (Netflix)
I May Destroy You (HBO)
Jessica Jones (Netflix)
Killing Eve (BBC)
Living Single (Fox)
Mad Men (AMC)
Orange Is the New Black (Netflix)
Parks and Recreation (NBC)
P-Valley (Starz)
Scandal (ABC)
Sex and the City (HBO)
Sex Education (Netflix)
Shrill (Hulu)
South Side (Comedy Central/HBO Max)

The Golden Girls (NBC)
The L Word (Showtime)
The L Word: Generation Q (Showtime)
The Mindy Project (Fox)
Unorthodox (Netflix)

THEATER

Beauty's Daughter (1995) by Dael Orlandersmith
Dusa, Fish, Stas, and Vi (1976) by Pam Gems
Fefu and Her Friends (1977) by María Irene Fornés
For Colored Girls Who Have Considered Suicide / When the Rainbow Is Enuf by Ntozake Shange (1975)
The How and the Why (2011) by Sarah Treem
In the Next Room (or the Vibrator Play) (2009) by Sarah Ruhl
Mary Jane (2017) by Amy Herzog
A Raisin in the Sun (1959) by Lorraine Hansberry
Rapture, Blister, Burn (2013) by Gina Gionfriddo
The Scene (2006) by Theresa Rebeck
Top Girls (1982) by Caryl Churchill
Trifles (1916) by Susan Glaspell
Uncommon Women and Others (1977) by Wendy Wasserstein
The Vagina Monologues (1996) by Eve Ensler

MUSIC

21 (2011) by Adele
Aaliyah (2001) by Aaliyah
All Over the Place (1984) by the Bangles
Amor Prohibido (1994) by Selena
. . . Baby One More Time (1999) by Britney Spears
Back to Black (2006) by Amy Winehouse
Bad Girls (1979) by Donna Summer
Baduizm (1997) by Erykah Badu
Be Altitude: Respect Yourself (1972) by the Staple Singers
Bella Donna (1981) by Stevie Nicks
Beauty and the Beat (1981) by the Go-Go's
Big Science (1982) by Laurie Anderson
Blacks' Magic (1990) by Salt-N-Pepa
Black Reign (1993) by Queen Latifah
Blue (1971) by Joni Mitchell
Blue Light 'til Dawn (1993) by Cassandra Wilson
Broken English (1979) by Marianne Faithfull

Car Wheels on a Gravel Road (1998) by Lucinda Williams
Coal Miner's Daughter (1971) by Loretta Lynn
Coat of Many Colors (1971) by Dolly Parton
Control (1986) by Janet Jackson
Cowboy Carter (2024) by Beyoncé
CrazySexyCool (1994) by TLC
Cut (1979) by the Slits
Daydream (1995) by Mariah Carey
Diamonds & Rust (1975) by Joan Baez
Diamond Life (1984) by Sade
Dig Me Out (1997) by Sleater-Kinney
Dirty Computer (2018) by Janelle Monáe
¿Dónde Están los Ladrones? (1998) by Shakira
Enta Omri (You Are My Life) (1964) by Umm Kulthum
Exile in Guyville (1993) by Liz Phair
Fanny Hill (1972) by Fanny
Fearless (2008) by Taylor Swift
Fifty Gates of Wisdom (1987) by Ofra Haza
First Take (1969) by Roberta Flack
Flaming Red (1998) by Patty Griffin
The Glamorous Life (1984) by Sheila E.
Hard Core (1996) by Lil' Kim
Heart Like a Wheel (1974) by Linda Ronstadt
Horses (1975) by Patti Smith
Hounds of Love (1985) by Kate Bush
I Do Not Want What I Haven't Got (1990) by Sinéad O'Connor
I Feel for You (1984) by Chaka Khan
I Love Rock 'n' Roll (1981) by Joan Jett and the Blackhearts
I Thought about You: Live at Vine St. (1987) by Shirley Horn
Imagination (1973) by Gladys Knight and the Pips
Indigo Girls (1989) by the Indigo Girls
Ingénue (1992) by k.d. lang
It's a Mighty World (1964) by Odetta
Jagged Little Pill (1995) by Alanis Morrissette
Journey in Satchidananda (1971) by Alice Coltrane
Kala (2007) by M.I.A.
King's Record Shop (1987) by Roseanne Cash
La Pareja (1978) by Tito Puente and La Lupe
Last Splash (1993) by the Breeders
Leader of the Pack (1965) by the Shangri-Las
Lemonade (2016) by Beyoncé
Little Plastic Castle (1998) by Ani DiFranco
Like a Virgin (1984) by Madonna

The Litanies of Satan (1982) by Diamanda Galás
Little Earthquakes (1992) by Tori Amos
Live through This (1994) by Hole
Mercedes Sosa en Argentina (1982) by Mercedes Sosa
The Miseducation of Lauryn Hill (1998) by Ms. Lauryn Hill
Moussolou (Women) (1989) by Oumou Sangaré
My Life (1993) by Iris DeMent
New York Tendaberry (1969) by Laura Nyro
Nick of Time (1989) by Bonnie Raitt
Nightbirds (1974) by Labelle
Nightclubbing (1981) by Grace Jones
Nina Simone Sings the Blues (1967) by Nina Simone
Ode to Billie Joe (1967) by Bobbie Gentry
On How Life Is (1999) by Macy Gray
Parallel Lines (1978) by Blondie
Pata Pata (1967) by Miriam Makeba
Pearl (1971) by Janis Joplin & the Full Tilt Boogie Band
Peace beyond Passion (1996) by Meshell Ndegeocello
Post (1995) by Björk
Pretenders (1980) by the Pretenders
Private Dancer (1984) by Tina Turner
Rapture (1986) by Anita Baker
Rid of Me (1993) by PJ Harvey
The Roches (1979) by the Roches
Rocks the House (1964) by Etta James
Rumor Has It (1990) by Reba McEntire
Rumours (1977) by Fleetwood Mac
The Runaways (1976) by the Runaways
Sassy Swings Again (1967) by Sarah Vaughan
The Scream (1978) by Siouxsie and the Banshees
A Seat at the Table (2016) by Solange
She's So Unusual (1983) by Cyndi Lauper
Sister (1987) by Sonic Youth
Son con Guaguanco (1966) by Celia Cruz
Songs in A Minor (2001) by Alicia Keys
Spice (1996) by the Spice Girls
Supa Dupa Fly (1997) by Missy Elliott
Tapestry (1971) by Carole King
Tidal (1996) by Fiona Apple
Touch (1983) by Eurythmics
Tracy Chapman (1988) by Tracy Chapman
Tragic Kingdom (1995) by No Doubt

Transgender Dysphoria Blues (2014) by Against Me!
Tuesday Night Music Club (1993) by Sheryl Crow
WAP (2020) by Cardi B and Megan Thee Stallion
What's the 411? (1992) by Mary J. Blige
Where Did Our Love Go (1964) by Diana Ross and the Supremes
Whitney Houston (1985) by Whitney Houston
Wide Open Spaces (1998) by the Dixie Chicks
Wild and Peaceful (1979) by Teena Marie
Wrecking Ball (1995) by Emmylou Harris
The Writing's on the Wall (1999) by Destiny's Child
Yeah Yeah Yeah Yeah (1993) by Bikini Kill
Young, Gifted and Black (1972) by Aretha Franklin
Ys (2006) by Joanna Newsom

VISUAL ART

American People Series #20: Die by Faith Ringgold
"Anatomy of a Kimono" by Miriam Schapiro
"The Benglis ad" by Lynda Benglis
Black Woman University by Genesis Tramaine
The Broken Column by Frida Kahlo
Cut Piece by Yoko Ono
A Fantastic Sunset by Alma Thomas
Le Dejeuner sur l'Herbe: Les Trois Femmes Noires by Mickalene Thomas
The Dinner Party by Judy Chicago
Do Women Have to Be Naked to Get into the Met. Museum? by the
    Guerrilla Girls
Early Color Interiors by Laurie Simmons
El Tendedero: The Clothesline Project by Mónica Mayer
Femme Maison by Louise Bourgeois
In Mourning and in Rage by Suzanne Lacy, and Bia Lowe
Interior Scroll by Carolee Schneemann
Miss Hybrid series by Shirin Aliabadi
Paper Women by Sanja Iveković
Rainbow Series by Candice Breitz
Rape Scene by Ana Mendieta
Self-Portrait with Fried Eggs by Sarah Lucas
Semiotics of the Kitchen by Martha Rosler
Some Living American Women Artists/ Last Supper by Mary Beth Edelson
S.O.S.—Starification Object Series by Hannah Wilke
Torture of Women by Nancy Spero
Untitled Film Stills by Cindy Sherman

"Untitled (It's a Small World but Not If You Have to Clean It)" by Bar-
    bara Kruger
We Can Do It! by J. Howard Miller
Untitled (We Don't Need Another Hero) by Barbara Kruger

MISCELLANEOUS

Anita Hill's Opening Statement
African American Women in Defense of Ourselves
Chanel Miller's Victim Impact Statement
What Is Feminist Art? by Judy Chicago

Credits

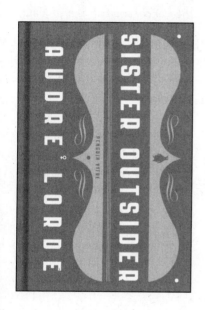

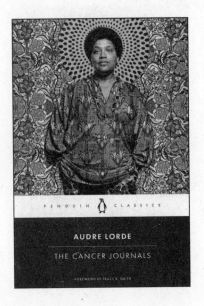